The Companion to
Gaelic Scotland

The Companion to
Gaelic Scotland

EDITED BY

Derick S. Thomson

Blackwell Reference

Copyright © Basil Blackwell Ltd 1983
© Derick S. Thomson editorial matter and organization 1983

First published 1983
Reprinted and first published in paperback 1987
First published in USA 1987

Basil Blackwell Ltd
108 Cowley Road, Oxford, OX4 1JF, UK

Basil Blackwell Inc,
432 Park Avenue South, Suite 1503
New York, NY 10016, USA

British Library Cataloguing in Publication Data
The Companion to Gaelic Scotland.
   1. Civilization, Gaelic
  I. Thomson, Derick
  941.1   D772
   ISBN 0–631–12502–7
   ISBN 0–631–15578–3   Pbk

Library of Congress Cataloging in Publication Data
The Companion to Gaelic Scotland.

  (Blackwell reference)
  Bibliography: p.
  Includes index.
   1. Scotland—Civilization—Dictionaries
  2. Scotland—Antiquities, Celtic—Dictionaries.
  3. Celts—Scotland—History—Dictionaries.
  4. Civilization, Celtic—Dictionaries. 5. Gaelic
philology—Dictionaries. I. Thomson, Derick S.
DA772.C62 1987   941.1   87.10331
ISBN 0–631–15578–3 (pbk.)

Publication subsidized by
The Scottish Arts Council

Typeset in 10 on 11½ pt Monophoto Ehrhardt
by Santype International Ltd., Lansbury Wilts.
Printed in Great Britain by Bell & Bain Ltd., Glasgow.

Contents

Preface

It was in late 1978 that John Davey of Basil Blackwell Publisher first raised the question of a Gaelic Companion and asked me to devise and edit it. I was immediately attracted to the idea. There is great curiosity about Gaelic Scotland, and no readily available way of satisfying it, and even for professional students of Gaelic matters there has been no set of tools that will produce quick results for a variety of enquiries. This Companion is intended to be a mine of information in itself, and a key to further sources of information, opinion and assessment, as detailed in the extensive Bibliography.

I was fortunate, once the plan of the work was completed, to have available a large team of willing helpers. Many of these were colleagues and/or former students at the University of Glasgow, but many friends and colleagues from the other Scottish Universities, from the Highlands, and from other countries, have willingly helped in the enterprise. Two of these, David Green and Cedric Thorpe Davie, have not lived to see the final result. All the contributors are due the warmest thanks for their cooperation.

A word may be said about the perils of planning such a book. It can be neither comprehensive nor perfect. It will always be possible to say 'If this is included, why not that?', and there will be errors and omissions. There has been, for example, no previous Dictionary of Gaelic Bibliography, nor a Dictionary of Gaelic Writers, and new names might be added (and perhaps some omitted). Sir Walter Scott is featured, but not every writer who showed interest in the Highlands. There is not much about industry in Gaelic Scotland. But it may fairly be claimed that this is by far the most comprehensive compendium in existence, of information and assessment on matters of Gaelic interest, and it can be used with profit by scholar and layman, Gaelic writer and French tourist, in fact by anyone who is interested in any aspect, past or present, of Gaelic Scotland.

My thanks are due to a number of people other than the contributors. Christine Macinnes typed a great part of the book, and several members of the Blackwell team did a great deal of work to translate the typescript into the book.

Derick S. Thomson
August 1983

Acknowledgements

The Editor and Publishers are grateful to the following persons and institutions for permission to reproduce photographs and other illustrations on the pages specified below.

Aberdeen City Library   31
Professor Leslie Alcock   85 (left)
The Argyll and Sutherland Highlanders   249
Ashmolean Museum Oxford   167
The Duke of Atholl's Collection at Blair Castle   140
Janet and Colin Bord   19 (left and right), 52 (left and right), 83, 85 (right), 275
British Broadcasting Corporation   55
British Library   134, 150, 202
The Syndics of the Cambridge University Library   61, 195
College of Piping, Glasgow   20, 163
Distillers' Company   307
Trustees of the Conference of Scottish Medievalists   232
The Master and Fellows of Corpus Christi College Cambridge   303
Andrea Cringean   276
The Revd Donald MacDonald of St Columba's Church, Glasgow   164
Edinburgh City Library   142
Michael Edwards   88
The Trustees of the late Mrs Magdalen Sharpe Erskine   207
Robert Fleming Holdings Ltd   69
Free Church of Scotland   87
'Gairm' Publications   67, 206, 224
Glasgow University, Hunterian Art Gallery   178
Glasgow University Library   71
Harris Tweed Association   288
Illustrated London News   3
Imperial War Museum   25
Inverness Museum and Art Gallery   15
Dr Joan MacKinnon — endpapers
Sir William Macpherson of Cluny and Blairgowrie   247
Mansell Collection   57
Jessie Ann Matthew   172, 268
Mitchell Library, Glasgow   46
National Gallery of Scotland   12, 146, 192, 212
National Library of Scotland   33, 173
National Museum of Antiquities of Scotland   9, 10, 11, 18, 26, 28 (right), 29, 118, 198, 199 (left and right), 254, 255, 256
Norwegian Universities Press   234

A*

Oxford University Press 125, 126, 127
Jane Routh 28 (left) 278 (top and bottom)
Royal Commission on the Ancient and Historical Monuments of Scotland 2, 6, 7, 8, 50, 53, 203, 221, 264, 271, 289
Royal Irish Academy 185
Glyn Satterley jacket, 45, 51, 77, 133, 200
School of Scottish Studies 165, 174, 187, 267
Scotch Whisky Association 306
Scottish Development Department, Ancient Monuments 16
Scottish Fisheries Museum Trust, Anstruther, Fife 76
Scottish National Gallery of Modern Art 14
Scottish National Portrait Gallery 74, 143, 144, 189
Scottish Record Office 64
Scottish Tourist Board 120, 197
Edwin Smith 149
Stiftsbibliothek, St Gallen 48
Sudley Art Gallery, Liverpool 13
Thames and Hudson 43
D. R. Thomson — photograph of Derick Thomson on jacket flap
Board of Trinity College Dublin — 38
Victoria and Albert Museum 304
West Highland Museum, Fort William 84

Contributors

Leslie Alcock **LA**
University of Glasgow

John W. M. Bannerman **JWMB**
University of Edinburgh

Colm Ó. Baoill **CÓB**
University of Aberdeen

G. W. S. Barrow **GWSB**
University of Edinburgh

Ronald Black **RB**
University of Edinburgh

Alan Bruford **AB**
School of Scottish Studies,
University of Edinburgh

John M. Bryden **JMB**
Nethy Bridge, Inverness-shire

J. B. Caird **JBC**
University of Dundee

David H. Caldwell **DHC**
National Museum of Antiquities,
Edinburgh

J. L. Campbell **JLC**
Isle of Canna

Roderick Cannon **RC**
University of East Anglia

R. D. Clement **RDC**
Linguistic Survey of Scotland,
University of Edinburgh

Cedric Thorpe Davie **CTD**
deceased, formerly
Emeritus Professor of Music,
University of St Andrews

A. A. M. Duncan **AAMD**
University of Glasgow

Ian Fisher **IF**
Royal Commission on Ancient and
Historical Monuments of Scotland,
Edinburgh

Carol Galbraith **CMG**
Aberfeldy

Farquhar Gillanders **FG**
University of Glasgow

William Gillies **WG**
University of Edinburgh

J. W. Gleasure **JWG**
University of Glasgow

Malcolm Gray **MG**
University of Aberdeen

David Greene **DG**
deceased, formerly
Senior Professor, Dublin Institute for
Advanced Studies

Ian Grimble **IG**
London

Frank Harrison **FH**
Canterbury

D. M. Henderson **DMH**
HIBD, Inverness

Isabel Henderson **IH**
Cambridge

James Hunter **JH**
Aberdeen

K. H. Jackson **KHJ**
Edinburgh

James G. Kellas **JGK**
University of Glasgow

Donald A. Low **DAL**
Department of English, University of Stirling

Donald MacAulay **DMcA**
University of Aberdeen

Fred Macaulay **FM**
Inverness

Donald A. MacDonald **DAMcD**
University of Edinburgh

F. A. Macdonald **FM**
c/o *Army School of Piping, Edinburgh*

Ian MacDonald **IMcD**
Gaelic Books Council, Glasgow

Kenneth D. Macdonald **KDMcD**
University of Glasgow

Roderick Macdonald **RM**
Dunoon

Malcolm MacDonell **MMcD**
St Francis Xavier University, Nova Scotia

Margaret MacDonell **Sister MMcD**
St Francis Xavier University, Nova Scotia

John MacInnes **JMcI**
School of Scottish Studies, University of Edinburgh

Paul Macinnes **PM**
Edinburgh

Kenneth MacKinnon **KMMcK**
Hatfield Polytechnic

Hugh D. MacLennan **HDMcL**
Inverness

A. M. MacLeod **AMMcL**
Lews Castle Technical College

Donald Macleod **DM**
Edinburgh

Ian MacLeod **IMcL**
Dingwall

Roderick MacLeod **RMcL**
Bernera, N Uist

Duncan Macmillan **JDM**
University of Edinburgh

Seumas MacNeill **SMcN**
University of Glasgow

John MacQueen **JMcQ**
School of Scottish Studies, University of Edinburgh

William Matheson **WM**
Edinburgh

Stuart Maxwell **SM**
National Museum of Antiquities, Edinburgh

Donald Meek **DEM**
Department of Celtic, University of Edinburgh

R. J. Morgan **RJM**
Beaton Institute, Sydney, Nova Scotia

Donald Morrison **DM**
Oban

T. M. Murchison **TMM**
Glasgow

W. F. H. Nicolaisen **WHFN**
State University of New York, Binghamton

Magne Oftedal **MO**
University of Oslo

R. A. Rankin **RAR**
University of Glasgow

Ann Ross **AR**
University of Southampton

David Sellar **WDHS**
University of Edinburgh

John Shaw **JS**
St Francis Xavier University, Nova Scotia

John A. Smith **JAS**
Glasgow

David Stevenson **DS**
University of Aberdeen

R. B. K. Stevenson **RBKS**
Edinburgh

Hugh Sutherland **HBS**
University of Glasgow

Elmar Ternes **ET**
University of Hamburg

Derick S. Thomson **DST**
University of Glasgow

R. L. Thomson **RLT**
University of Leeds

M. Bruce Watson **MBW**
Isle of Skye

Charles W. J. Withers **CWJW**
College of St Paul and St Mary,
Cheltenham

Guide to Contents by Subject

The main topics dealt with in the *Companion* are classified below to give readers a quicker access to particular subjects in which they are interested. The listing within classes is alphabetical, but in addition the section on Literature has a classification of writers according to the century in which they mainly worked. Only a selection of non-literary biographical entries is included here, and the full alphabetical listing in the body of the work, and also the index, should be consulted in any search for biographical information.

Archaeology
Breccbennach
brochs
Dumbarton
forts and fortified sites
sanctuaries, temples, shrines
souterrains
St Ninian's Isle Treasure
stone circles
Towers, round
Traprain Law

Art and architecture
architecture, medieval Highland
art, Gaelic in modern times
art, Pictish
brooches, early Celtic
crosses, sculptured
manuscripts, illuminated
metalwork
sculpture, monumental

History
1. ECCLESIASTICAL
Céli Dé
Celtic Church
Church of Scotland
Disruption
Episcopal Church
Free Church of Scotland
Ladies' Highland Association
monastic orders
Nova Scotia Roman Catholic Church in
    Roman Catholic Church
Saints of Gaelic Scotland

Biographical
Adamnán
Baxter, Richard
Colum Cille
Finlayson, Robert
Kirkwood, James
MacDonald, John (Apostle of the
    North)
MacDonald, Norman (Tormod
    Sona)
Macinnes, John
Mackay, John (Lairg)
Mackenzie, Neil
Maclean, Donald
MacLeod, Malcolm
MacLeod, Roderick (Bracadal)
MacRae, John (MacRath Mór)
MacRae, Kenneth
Maol Rubha
Monro, Archdeacon Donald
Munro, Donald

2. POLITICAL, MILITARY AND SOCIAL
Bàthadh Mór Nis
Bede
Bernera Riot
Campbells and Macleans, rise and
    conflict
Celtic law, survival of
clan tartans
clans, origin of
Dalriada
Druim Cett, Convention of
Duan Albanach
Dùthaich Mhic Aoidh
emigration

abbeys, *see* architecture, medieval Highland; monastic orders.

Adamnán (*c*.624–704) Ninth abbot of Iona. Prominent as writer, legislator and ecclesiastical politician. He used the reports of the Gaulish bishop Arculf, shipwrecked at Iona on his return from the Holy Land, as the basis for his *De Locis Sanctis* (Meehan 1958), but his most celebrated work is his life of Colum Cille (q.v.), written *c*.690 (A. O. and M. O. Anderson 1961; Kenney 1929; Reeves 1857). At the Synod of Birr in 697 he promulgated a law for the protection of women, children and clerics (Meyer 1905). Contacts with Northumbria made him a vigorous champion of the Roman Easter among the northern Irish Churches.   KDMCD

Aed Find (d. 778) Leader of the Cenél nGabráin (q.v.) and king of Dalriada (q.v.). Fought a battle in 768 in the Pictish province of Fortriu. This seems to mark at once the elimination of the Cenél Loairn as contenders for the kingship of Dalriada and the resurgence of Scottish military and political power at the expense of the Picts, which led directly to the union of the two peoples under Kenneth mac Alpín (q.v.), king of Dalriada, *c*.843. (See Bannerman 1971, 76.)   JWMB

Aedán mac Gabráin (d. *c*.608) Consecrated king of Dalriada (q.v.) by Colum Cille (q.v.) on Iona in 574. He increased the military power and prestige of the Scots, fighting successful battles as far apart as the Orkneys and the Isle of Man. The constant support that he received from Colum Cille until the latter's death in 597 initiated a partnership between Church and State which goes far towards explaining the ultimate success of the Scots in making the country of Scotland their own. Aedán and the battle of Degsastan is discussed under **Bede**. (See Bannerman 1971, 68; 1974, 80–90.)   JWMB

agriculture About 18,000 people in the Highlands and Islands obtain at least part of their livelihood from agricultural production, and in many areas of the west one in every two households is based on an agricultural holding. On a full-time equivalent basis, agriculture provides about 11,000 jobs, employing about 10 per cent of the labour force (Bryden and Houston 1976). In 1979 the gross output of Highland agriculture was some £90 million, or roughly 10 per cent of Scottish agricultural output. Agriculture is thus the most important primary land use in terms of output, employment, and income created, and it plays a vital part in the economic and social structure of the Highlands and Islands.

Agrarian structure in the region owes much to the clearances of the eighteenth and nineteenth centuries, the resettlement of population both then and in the period of land settlement after the First World War, and the security of tenure granted to crofters after the Napier Commission (Royal Commission on the Condition of Crofters and Cottars in the Highlands and Islands of Scotland 1884). These factors largely explain the existence of at least two distinct 'sectors' in Highland agriculture, represented on the one hand by the large number of part- and spare-time units (just under 20,000 in 1971) occupying about a quarter of the land area and, on the other, by a relatively small number of full-time holdings (3,117 in 1971) occupying a proportionately large area of land. In general, moreover, the harsher the environment and the poorer the soil, the greater the relative preponderance of part- and spare-time farms, most of which are crofts (see **crofting system**). In terms of output, roughly three-quarters comes from full-time farms and one-quarter from part- and spare-time units. The family base of Highland agriculture is significant compared with that in other parts of Britain, and some two-thirds of labour input on Highland farms and crofts comes from family labour (Bryden and Houston 1976, 76).

Livestock and livestock products dominate the region's agriculture, particularly beef cattle (36 per cent of output in 1971) and sheep (30 per cent of output in 1971) (see **stock-rearing**). Farm crops accounted for only 7·6 per cent of output in 1971, compared with 15·8 per cent for Scotland. This reflects the predominance of rough grazings (3·07 million hectares), the paucity of arable ground and permanent pasture (0·24 million hectares) and the associated geographical and environmental limitations facing producers (Darling 1955; Tivy 1973; Bryden and Houston 1976).

The relative economic and social decline of the Highlands and Islands has been reflected in agricul-

An upland farm near Fort William, c. 1880.

tural trends, and agricultural production and employment have declined in absolute and relative terms over the past century. Income per head in Highland agriculture was about three-quarters of the Scottish average in 1971, and average income per holding less than one-third of the Scottish average. A major limiting factor to improvement is the restricted area of arable land that can produce sufficient animal feed to winter-stock, and the high costs of transport all but prohibit supplementary purchases. Calving and lambing are thus concentrated in the spring of the year, and surplus stock must often be sold in the autumn. The store livestock, particularly from the north and west, are therefore younger, smaller and less marketable when in competition with stock from better areas. Market structures also tend to be at their least efficient in such circumstances.

The distinctively regional characteristics and problems of Highland agriculture explain why the Highlands and Islands Development Board (q.v.) has, in conjunction with the Colleges of Agriculture, the Crofters Commission, the Department of Agriculture, the Scottish National Farmers' Union and other bodies, developed a characteristically regional approach to development and change in the agricultural sector. This approach places emphasis on land and livestock improvement, higher feed production, co-operation among small producers, the improvement of market structures and the diversification of the income and employment base of rural areas. (See Bryden 1979; Bryden and Houston 1976, ch. 5; HIDB 1976.)   JMB

Aignish Riot (1888) A late Lewis incident in the Land Troubles (see **politics, Highland, nineteenth century**).   DST

Ailean an Ridge, *see* MacDonald, Allan.

Ailean Dall, *see* MacDougall, Allan.

Ailean mac Ruaidhri Named as author of the ballad 'Gleann Sìdh an gleann so rem thaoibh' (N. Ross 1939, 70) and of 'Bàs Oscair' (ibid., 152) in the Book of the Dean of Lismore (q.v.).   DST

Ailean nan Sop (d. *c.*1552) Son of Lachlann Catanach of Duart and half-brother of Eachann Mór of Duart. Brought up in Carnaburg Castle in the Treshnish Isles. Noted pirate on Scottish and Irish seas; his last plundering expedition was known as Creach na h-Aisne. Buried in Iona. The song 'Caismeachd Ailean nan Sop' is attributed to An Cléireach Beag (q.v.). (See Bannerman 1977b, 147–8; W. J. Watson 1929, 115ff.) DST

Aithbhreac inghean Coirceadail (fl. 1470) Author of a lyrical lament for her husband Niall Óg Mac-Néill, Constable of Castle Sween, Knapdale. (See W. J. Watson 1937, 60, 27.) DST

Alasdair Mac Aonghuis (*c.*1665–1745) Author of poem on 1745 Rising and of 'Tòrradh Iain Luim'. (See K. N. MacDonald 1900, 18.) DST

Alasdair Mac Mhurchaidh, *see* MacKenzie of Achilty, Alasdair.

Alasdair Mac Uisdein According to Fernaig Manuscript (q.v.), author of religious poem 'Mo chomraich ort, a Rìgh'. DST

Alasdair Mór Under this pseudonym Iain N. MacLeòid contributed a column, 'Litir a Beàrnaraigh', to the *Stornoway Gazette* from 1917 to 1954. A native of Skye, he was schoolmaster in Bernera for a period and used well-known local personages as the 'characters' in his 'letters', which dealt with local and general Gaelic topics. The column was read avidly, and a collection entitled *Litrichean Alasdair Mhóir* was published in 1932. MacLeòid was an important contributor to Gaelic periodicals and edited a collection of Lewis verse, *Bàrdachd Leódhais* (1916). DMCA

Anderson, Alexander (1802–66) Born Elgin. Gaelic schoolteacher, Barvas, Lewis, 1825–31; Inspector, 1831–42; Free Church minister, Rothesay. (See Harding 1980.) DST

Anderson, Christopher (1782–1852) Baptist minister, Edinburgh. A founder of the Edinburgh Gaelic Schools Society (see **school societies, Gaelic**), its first Secretary, etc. (See Harding 1980.) DST

Angus Óg, Lord of the Isles (d. *c.*1314) A supporter of Robert Bruce who played a prominent part in the Battle of Bannockburn in 1314. He married

The sheriff of Stornoway reading the Riot Act at Aignish Farm (from the Illustrated London News *21 January 1888).*

Áine Ní Cathán of Keenaght, whose marriage retinue (*Tochradh Nighean a' Chathanaich*), according to tradition, was notable for its size and for the number of Scottish families whose progenitors formed part of it. (See Steer and Bannerman 1977, 203.)　　　JWMB

Angus Óg MacDonald (d. 1490) The natural son of John II, Lord of the Isles, who, having become dissatisfied with his father's management of affairs, defeated him in the sea battle of Bloody Bay (*c.*1481). He was murdered by his Irish harpist at Inverness in 1490 (Steer and Bannerman 1977, 110–11). Two elegies by MacMhuirich poets are to be found in the Book of the Dean of Lismore (q.v.) (See W. J. Watson 1937, 82–8, 96–8.)　　　JWMB

Anndra mac an Easbuig (?*c.*1635–?*c.*1720) Of Knock in Morvern. The eldest son of Hector Maclean (1605–87), minister of Morven and Bishop of Argyll (Sinclair, A. Maclean 1899, 304). Five of his poems are extant, from the period 1680–1718. (See C. Ó Baoill 1979, 60.)　　　CÓB

Antrim, 2nd Marquis of, *see* MacDonnell, Randal.

Aonghas Barrach, *see* Macmillan, Angus.

Aonghas Mac Alasdair Ruaidh, *see* MacDonald, Angus (*c.*1665–1745).

Aonghus nan Aoir (Angus of the Satires) (sixteenth century) A native of Harris; surname unknown. He discovered in himself a facility for versifying and became a wandering bard, demanding hospitality from the Gaelic aristocracy. His forte was the squib or petty lampoon (*aoir*), and his demands were usually met by his hosts, who were fearful of becoming the butt of his scathing rhymes; nevertheless, few escaped the lash of his tongue. He died while a guest of Chisholm of Strathglass. (See Bannatyne MS.; G. Henderson 1910a; W. Matheson 1977, 105–8.)　　　WM

Aos-dàna (Men of Art) A collective noun which in medieval times denoted the learned orders of Gaelic society. In Ranald MacDonald's Eigg Collection of 1776 four or five poets are given this appellative: am Bàrd Mac Shithich, Eachann Bacach Mac Gilleathain, Iain Mac Ailein, am Bàrd Mac Mhathain and perhaps Iain Dubh mac Iain mhic Ailein.

This apparently eccentric semantic development has not been explained entirely satisfactorily. Ranald MacDonald alone cannot be held responsible for the change. As early as 1707 we find the Revd John Maclean, in his congratulatory ode to Edward Lhuyd (q.v.), using *aoisdán* (*sic*) in the same sense. It may be that as an honorific the word had only a limited circulation in the eighteenth century in learned Gaelic society. The accepted view is that the precise meaning of *Aos-dàna* had been lost, leaving the term free to be applied to poets who held a position of some importance in a chief's household at about the end of the seventeenth century and the beginning of the eighteenth. This accords well enough with the circumstances of the age, in which a cultural vacuum was being created by the decay of the schools of poetry and rhetoric. There would then have been a natural tendency for certain vernacular bards to rise in society. The surviving work of the men who bear the title of *Aos-dàna* indicates that while they were poets who composed in vernacular, not classical, Gaelic (and two of them also bear the title of *Bàrd*), their status was that of a superior grade of demotic poet. There is no evidence that they were classed with the literate order of *Filidh*. Indeed, it may be significant that Niall MacMhuirich (q.v.), who composed in classical and vernacular Gaelic alike, is never given the appellative *Aos-dàna*.

Am Bàrd Mac Shithich is the author of an elegy for Archibald, Earl of Argyll, who was beheaded in 1685 for his leadership of an attempted rebellion. Beyond this, nothing is known about him. The elegy is a vernacular composition of great dignity and gravity, which blends the tones of political and religious homily within an essentially panegyric framework that preserves many bardic themes. It is obviously the work of a highly cultured man who might well have had some instruction in classical Gaelic, but more than that we cannot say. (Text in Watson 1918.)

Eachann Bacach, a Mull poet of the seventeenth century (fl. *c.*1630–51 +) was, according to his own testimony, attached from infancy to the household of Maclean of Duart, who is said to have paid him 'a small annuity'. According to tradition he was the last poet in Mull to enjoy this privilege. (See further Eachann Bacach.)

Iain mac Ailein, also from Mull, was a great-grandson of the sixth chief of the Macleans of Ardgour. Dr Samuel Johnson and James Boswell, who visited Mull in the course of their tour of 1773, both give short accounts of the poet. According to Boswell he had died a few years earlier; in fact he appears to have been born some time after 1650 and to have died after 1738 but perhaps before 1745. Both writers were informed that he was illiterate. Yet Iain mac Ailein too shows that he was so well acquainted with the high learning of Gaelic tradition that his alleged inability to read or write has been called in question. It is possible that his knowledge was acquired from learned contemporaries – the Ó Muirgheasáin poets (q.v.), for instance, or the Revd John Beaton, member of a family which had produced distinguished physicians all over the Highlands and Islands for centuries. At all events, Iain mac Ailein displays considerable originality in his humorous adaptations of Gaelic legendary history – for instance, in his prose and verse accounts of the coming of the Milesians (the ancestors of the Gaels) and their encounter with the Tuatha Dé Danann who had shape-shifted themselves to become the whisky of Ross-shire, Glasgow and Tiree; or in his 'Battle of Alphort', in which he makes the Campbell sheriff-depute of Argyll send his sheriff-substitute, another Campbell, to fight against the Tuatha Dé Danann in Mull. This kind of satirical composition may have some tenuous connection with the tradition of satire that appears in the Irish 'Parliament of Clan Thomas', for example, and in related writings.

Murdoch Matheson, am Bàrd Mac Mhathain (c.1670–c.1757), was bard to William, 5th Earl of Seaforth and until 1719 held lands from him in the Kirkton of Lochalsh. He was a direct descendant of Alasdair mac Mhurchaidh, chief of the Mathesons, who is on record in 1427.

There is a story that he was in Glencoe on the night of the Massacre, in February 1692, on his way home from Inveraray Castle, which he had been visiting on an embassage from his master, the Earl of Seaforth. In 1715 he helped to defend Seaforth's estate against the Government Commissioners and fought in the band who recaptured Brahan Castle from the Munros. Such traditions give some indication of his status both as poet and warrior. In his old age he is said to have become a great penitent and to have composed religious poetry, but the staple of his surviving verse is the panegyric which enshrines the customary expectations of Gaelic society.

Iain Dubh mac Iain mhic Ailein, roughly contemporary with Iain mac Ailein of Mull, was one of the MacDonalds of Morar, an aristocrat of Clan Ranald. He lived on the island of Eigg. Ranald MacDonald does not couple his name with the title *Aos-dàna*; rather, two songs in the Eigg Collection, which are generally accepted as Iain Dubh's compositions, are ascribed to 'the *Aos-dàna*'. Most of his extant poems were composed in the years around 1715 and are of considerable importance from a historical point of view. (See A. MacMhathain 1954; D. S. Thomson 1974a.) JMCI

architecture, medieval Highland

architecture, medieval Highland The earliest surviving buildings in the Highland area, the forts, duns and brochs of Iron Age date (G. and A. Ritchie 1981), were constructed of unmortared stone. As in Ireland, however, the churches and other buildings of the early Christian monasteries were at first of timber, known at Iona (founded c.563) from the description of Adamnán (A. O. and M. O. Anderson 1961) and from excavations (*RCAHMS* 1982, no. 3), although in a few remote and treeless islands, such as Eileach an Naoimh and North Rona (Nisbet and Gailey 1960), drystone beehive cells or chapels are found. In the Pictish area of eastern Scotland the use of dressed and mortared stone was introduced early in the eighth century by Northumbrian masons, and work of that period may survive at Restenneth (W. D. Simpson 1963). The finest monument in this area is the 100-foot high round tower of Irish type (?early eleventh century) at Brechin.

The Romanesque style of architecture was probably brought to western Scotland in the twelfth century by Irish masons, as in the west doorway of St Oran's Chapel, Iona, and in carved fragments from Saddell Abbey, Kintyre, itself founded from Mellifont, Co. Louth, c.1160–70 (*RCAHMS* 1971, no. 296). The Benedictine abbey and Augustinian nunnery on Iona, both begun c.1200, have a similar Irish background (*RCAHMS* 1982, nos. 4, 5), best seen at the nunnery in features such as continuous moulded frames around windows (one of which has a triangular head) and circular or octagonal shafts at external angles. The nunnery church, 60 feet in length, had a rib-vaulted chancel and a nave separated by three arches from a north aisle with vaulted eastern chapel. Parts of the original east range, containing the chapter-house and dormitory, are preserved, but the cloister was enlarged c.1500, when the existing refectory was built. As a typical small nunnery, that on Iona is one of the most complete in the British Isles.

The earliest surviving work at Iona Abbey, in the north transept, is an austere version of the same Irish style. This church of c.1200 had a short chancel which, perhaps even before completion, was extended to its present length, with aisles and an undercroft, in

Iona. The restored Abbey and early Christian crosses, with St Oran's chapel in the foreground.

a Gothic style marked by profuse use of 'dog-tooth' ornament, probably derived from lowland Britain. Work of the thirteenth century is also preserved in the cloister, with pointed arches carried on elegant paired shafts, and in the chapter-house and dormitory; while the refectory, with its impressive buttressed north wall, dates from the end of the century, when a large transept, apparently modelled on that of St Andrew's Cathedral, was begun south of the choir but never completed. The fourteenth century saw the development at Iona of a distinctive 'West Highland' school of monumental carving, producing crosses, effigies of churchmen and warriors, and graveslabs (Steer and Bannerman 1977), so that when the abbey church was rebuilt *c*.1450–90 there existed a local group of decorative carvers, some of whom were familiar with Irish buildings but also copied earlier work at Iona itself. The present church, with its elaborate traceried windows and noble central tower, dates largely from this period. It contains notable carved capitals in the choir arcade and crossing

(which bore the signature of the mason Donald Ó Brolchán); these combine animal and foliage ornament with religious scenes (Adam and Eve; the Virgin and Child; the Crucifixion; St Michael weighing souls) and everyday scenes containing interesting examples of secular costume. Much of the ornament is of archaic character, perhaps reflecting the use as models of earlier manuscripts or metalwork.

The buildings of the other monasteries in the Highlands were much less ambitious. Saddell Abbey (Cistercian) and Ardchattan Priory (Valliscaulian, founded *c*.1230: see *RCAHMS* 1975, no. 217) both had small cruciform churches, now fragmentary; while the church of Oronsay Priory (Augustinian, *c*.1330: see *RCAHMS*, (forthcoming)) was an elongated rectangle with little carved detail, although a massive west tower was begun in the early sixteenth century. At the same period the small cloister was partly remodelled with triangular-headed arches carried on upright slabs, two of which bear inscriptions naming the mason (*saer*), Mael-Sechlainn Ó

Cuinn, and the supervisor, Canon Celestinus (Steer and Bannerman 1977, 120). Late medieval work at Ardchattan included the refectory, with its fine reader's pulpit and timber roof, and the enlargement of the choir, which contains some decorative carving including 'vine-leaf' ornament of Irish type.

The Cathedral of Argyll on Lismore was a rectangle some 120 feet long, probably of early fourteenth-century date, with a small (?post-medieval) west tower and a sacristy or chapter-house attached north of the choir. The building at Skeabost, Skye, used from about 1390 to 1500 as the Cathedral of the Isles but now reduced to foundations, may have been a parish church of the early thirteenth century.

The earliest stone buildings for the worship of the laity were small chapels, whose remains are particularly numerous in Islay. They closely resemble the 'keills' of the Isle of Man, often measuring less than 18 feet in length; and although some may be of pre-Norse date, most are probably no earlier than the tenth century. The creation of parishes in the twelfth and thirteenth centuries led to the erection of numerous churches. Typical (?)twelfth-century examples in Knapdale (Keills, Kilmory, Craignish) measure about 35 feet by 15 feet and have simple round-headed doors and windows. The early thirteenth-century chancel added to Killean church, Kintyre (*RCAHMS* 1971, no. 287) shows influences from Iona Nunnery and has a fine pair of east windows, while the chapel close to Dunstaffnage Castle, 65 feet in length, is in a developed version of the same style, with rich dog-tooth ornament in the windows (*RCAHMS* 1975, no. 243). Other churches of the thirteenth century, such as Inch Kenneth, Mull, and Howmore, South Uist, show pairs of narrow, pointed windows within plain, wide-splayed recesses.

The churches of the late medieval period often resemble earlier ones in plan, and their surviving details are so simple that, as at Teampull na Trionaid, Carinish, North Uist, close dating is impossible. That at Rodel, Harris (*RCAHMS* 1928, no. 111), built by the MacLeods of Harris and Dunvegan early in the sixteenth century, is unique in having proper transepts and a west tower, and a wealth of carved details obviously copied from the slightly earlier work at Iona Abbey. Panels built into the tower include a female exhibitionist figure or *sheela na gig*, found also at Iona Nunnery (Andersen 1977, 102–3, 142–3), and its male equivalent, while the tomb of Alexander MacLeod (1528), decorated with a galley, castle and hunting scene as well as religious images, is the mas-

terpiece of medieval west Highland sculpture (Steer and Bannerman 1977, 78–80, pls 31–4).

The west Highlands preserve an unusual number of early stone castles, many of them 'castles of enclosure', having a curtain wall enclosing a courtyard with buildings on at least two sides (Cruden 1960; Dunbar 1981; *RCAHMS* 1971, 1975, 1980). One of the earliest (?late twelfth century) is Castle Sween, Knapdale, a rectangle 52 feet by 68 feet, and thirteenth-century examples of the same plan are Tarbert (Loch Fyne) and, with the addition of small square angle-towers, Achadun (Lismore), Duart (Mull) and Innis Chonnell (Loch Awe). Simple round-angled enclosures, following the outlines of their rocky sites, are found at Mingary (Ardnamurchan) and Castle Tioram (Moidart), and

The tomb of Alexander MacLeod (erected 1528), St Clement's church, Rodel, Harris. Around the canopy are the Trinity and the twelve apostles. Above the effigy the upper tier of carvings represents Alexander's castle (on the left) and his ship (on the right), between them the Virgin and child flanked by St Clement and another bishop. The lower tier contains a fine hunting scene, and a representative of St Michael weighing souls on the Day of Judgement.

Duart castle (restored c. 1910), Mull, from the north east, showing the massive late fourteenth-century tower at right.

Kisimul castle, Barra, Inverness-shire, from the east.

both preserve parts of their original battlements, fossilized by later heightenings of the walls. A more elaborate castle of this type is Dunstaffnage, which has two substantial towers containing private chambers, and a range of arrow-slits. In the 'hall-houses' the hall, built above an undercroft, became predominant. They include Fraoch Eilean (Loch Awe), Castle Coeffin (Lismore), Ardtornish (Morvern) and the imposing example, 82 feet in length, at Aros (Mull). In the late thirteenth century strong southern influence is seen in the Comyn strongholds of Lochindorb and Inverlochy, the latter of 'Edwardian' plan with an enclosure almost 100 feet square with massive round angle-towers, and in the conversion of Skipness (Kintyre) from a simple 'hall-house' with adjacent chapel into a powerful rectangular fortress.

Simple dwellings, often on crannogs (artificial islands), remained in use throughout the late medieval period, and the principal residence of the Mac-Donald Lords of the Isles was a group of buildings on an unfortified island in Loch Finlaggan, Islay (*RCAHMS* forthcoming); while in the strongholds of Dùn Chonnuil in the Garvellachs (ibid.) and Cairn na Burgh in the Treshnish Isles (*RCAHMS* 1980, no. 335) defence was effected by filling gaps in the circuit of precipitous cliffs. The characteristic castle of this period, however, was the 'tower-house', and about twenty towers of fourteenth- and fifteenth-century date have been identified in the Highlands (Dunbar 1978b). The mighty tower added to Duart by one of the first MacLean chiefs is one of the largest in Scotland, and with Dunvegan, Urquhart and Eilean Donan it is among the earliest in the area, while typical fifteenth-century towers are Kilchurn and Dunollie and the smaller ones at Moy (Mull), Breackacha (Coll) and Kisimul (Barra), which, with its later courtyard buildings, entirely covers a small island. Towers of the following century display ingenious planning and considerable ornamental detail, as at Carnassarie, erected by Bishop John Carswell *c.*1570 and preserving a Gaelic inscribed panel (Bannerman 1974); at Gylen (Kerrera), 1582 (*RCAHMS* 1975, no. 291); and at Dunderave, (? *c.*1580 and 1596). Towers such as Barcaldine continued to be built in the early seventeenth century, and many castles were adapted for firearm-defence by the addition of musket loops and corbelled angle-turrets, while the range of barracks added to Kilchurn by the 1st Earl of Breadalbane in the 1690s is an interesting transition to the Hanoverian forts and garrisons preserved at Fort Augustus, Bernera and Ruthven (Stell 1973). (See also Dunbar 1978a, 1981; MacGibbon and Ross 1887–92, 1896–7; numerous articles by W. D. Simpson on individual buildings.)

See also **Celtic Church; towers, round.**   IF

Argyll, Earl of (Colin) (d. 1492) Author of poem entitled 'A bhean da dtugussa grádh' in the Book of the Dean of Lismore (q.v.). (See Quiggin 1937, 81; 'Ge ta, a bhean', MS of Dean's Book, p. 271.)   DST

Argyll, 9th Earl of (Archibald Campbell) (1629–85) Gained possession of Mull and other MacLean lands but was executed after rebelling against James VII. (See Willcock 1907.)   DS

Argyll, 1st Marquis of (Archibald Campbell) (1607–61) The most powerful of the Covenanters in the 1640s but humiliated by the defeats inflicted on his clan by Montrose and Alasdair MacColla in 1644–7. (See Willcock 1903.)   DS

Argyll/An Calbhach Treaty A unique survival (like the 1408 Gaelic charter: see **documents, Gaelic**) is the Gaelic deed that records the terms of a treaty between Archibald, Earl of Argyll, and An Calbhach O Donnell, of Tirconnell in Ireland. In this treaty, made in 1555 and confirmed in 1560, Argyll agrees to provide a piece of artillery for breaking castle walls and a force of men when needed (presumably in Irish campaigns). In return Argyll receives a tribute of 100 English or 400 Scots marks. The apparent ease of the document's style suggests that such deeds were not uncommon. (The document, which is in the Argyll archives at Inverarary, with several partial copies in the Argyll Transcripts, is edited in J. Mackechnie 1951, where the contraction for *Anno domini* is misunderstood.)   DST

Argyll and Sutherland Highlanders, *see* regiments, Highland.

Argyll's Highlanders, *see* regiments, Highland.

arms and armour From the Middle Ages to the '45 a man's ability to survive often depended on his skill with weapons, in the Highlands as elsewhere in Europe.

While it may be assumed that knights wore the armour appropriate to their rank as Europeans, there is evidence, on their grave-slab carvings, that west Highland chivalry wore distinctive forms of mail and plate armour (see Steer and Bannerman 1977). The earliest figures (second half of the fourteenth century) wear a high, pointed helmet (bascinet) and knee-length, long-sleeved, quilted garments (aketons); mail covers their neck and shoulders; and they carry a spear and a sword with a lobed pommel and depressed quillons, probably derived from that of their Norse ancestors, which in turn affected the design of the later two-handled sword which we call a claymore (from Gaelic *claidheamh mór*). Plate armour

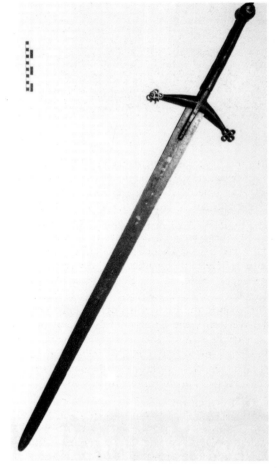

Two-handled claymore, sixteenth century. National Museum of Antiquities of Scotland.

appears on the slabs from the end of the fifteenth century. 'Gallowglasses' (mercenaries in Ireland) dressed in a fashion much like that of the earlier warriors as late as the sixteenth century. Their jackets were reinforced with metal plates, and they wore similar helmets; they also had spears and axes, though some 'Irish-Scots' were musketeers before 1600. Lochaber axes, probably axe blades on long shafts, seem to have been in general use in the Highlands. Highlanders were foot soldiers, but mounted warriors appear on the slabs and crosses, along with the galleys which also represent fast transport.

The Highland foot soldiers levied for service in the Scots army from the fifteenth to the seventeenth centuries carried pikes or spears or were archers; some were armed with two-handed swords and had bucklers, the earlier form of the targe, for protection. The two-hander, which had been introduced from Europe, may have been used by the massed infantry as a cross between a pike and a bill, presenting a hedgehog-like defence to the enemy's charge but turning quickly into a deadly offensive weapon. Several Highland and Lowland claymores have survived, the former having depressed quillons which end in quatrefoil terminals. Musketeers had begun to take the place of archers before 1600, but their weapons were not the graceful guns with fluted, curving butts that have survived; these were hunting weapons, and many of the carved, flat powderhorns bearing late seventeenth century dates were also associated with the 'huntings', which were major social occasions.

The importance of their weapons to Highlanders is often shown in their poetry. A Maclean poet (C. Ó Baoill, 1979, 34–7) writes:

> You placed the steel helmet on the head of flowing locks; a slim polished blade, perfectly straight from hilt to tip; the strong shield, with the hard bosses and the devices of high spirited trout, and a fine pair of pistols on the silver embossed belt.

Scots favoured all-metal pistols (brass, then steel) throughout the seventeenth century, and, characteristically, the conservative Highlanders (those who could afford them) remained faithful to the engraved and silver inlaid pistols with ramshorn butts which were the finest products of the Campbells and Caddells of Doune (Stirlingshire) in the eighteenth century. Some makers may have had Highland names, but, like the swordsmiths of Glasgow and Stirling, they worked south of the Highland line. An

exception was Hector McNeill, pistol maker in Mull in the 1730s and 1740s, whose one extant pistol (in the National Museum of Antiquities) is in the Doune style. The scrolling patterns of the pistols are European Renaissance in origin and do not carry on the Hiberno-Scotic tradition (see **metalwork**). The splendid eighteenth-century sword hilts were the culmination of a century's evolution; the makers of the early to mid-eighteenth century (Walter Allan of Stirling was the supreme artist) could take the greatest liberties with the metal yet produce a functional handguard. The best blades were of European origin.

There remain the targes and dirks, the indigenous Highland weapons, decorated with traditional motifs – the leather surface of the targes with animals, birds and fish in some cases and always with the interlace found on the West Highland tombstones, the grips of the dirks also carved with interlace. The dirk, true to form, evolved from European daggers; by the seventeenth century it had a wedge-shaped blade, curving haunches, a slender wooden grip and a broad, flat, brass-shod pommel. It was probably the earliest personal weapon, and it has survived longest, as a glass-studded, silver-mounted travesty of itself. The targe, as the poet described it, had brass bosses and plates

Targe, probably late seventeenth century, with the two-eagled emblem of the MacDonalds. National Museum of Antiquities of Scotland.

Dirk, seventeenth century. National Museum of Antiquities of Scotland.

as decoration and sometimes a central spike; made from two plies of wood, and leather-covered, it was some 20 inches in diameter and often had a sheath in its hide-covered back for its companion, the dirk. The other weapons were for the Highlander at war — targe and dirk were his 'peace-time' companions. (See Caldwell 1979 and 1981.)   SM

See also **soldiers, Highland.**

Armstrong, Robert Archibald (1788–1867) Son of Robert Armstrong, schoolmaster in Dull and Kenmore. Author of dictionary (1825). (See *An Gaidheal* Dec. 1924, Feb. 1942.)   DST

art, Gaelic, in modern times The old visual traditions of Celtic Scotland gradually declined through the late Middle Ages to suffer final eclipse some time in the sixteenth century. Their decline coincided with the decisive shift of power in Scotland to the bourgeois urban centres of the Lowlands. Visual art in northern Europe during the centuries after the Reformation depended almost entirely on such centres, and as a consequence it played little direct part in the later development of Gaelic culture. Such painting as was carried out for the leaders of Highland society was usually done by outsiders, who were not necessarily even Scots. (There is very little Scottish painting at Inveraray Castle, for example.) Although some patrons were more patriotic, it seems that no significant artist of the time came from a Highland background.

In spite of this negative picture of the place of the visual arts in Highland culture, Gaelic culture itself nevertheless played a significant, though indirect, part in the development of the visual arts in Scotland as a whole during the eighteenth and early nineteenth centuries. Indirect because this was the product of ideas about Gaelic culture and society rather than of any direct experience of them. It is well known that among the followers of Thomas Blackwell of Aberdeen the analysis of literary ideas led to some quite startling conclusions about the nature of poetry and poetic inspiration in the origins of society. These led in turn to the first formulation of the ideal of non-classical or primitive art.

Gavin Hamilton was the first European artist to attempt to translate these ideas into the visual arts in a series of paintings illustrating Homer begun in 1759 in which he tried to give expression to the new literary idea of him as a primitive poet. Hamilton in the end found it impossible to separate Homer from the accretions of classical culture, but his younger follower Alexander Runciman (q.v.) solved this problem by turning from Homer to the primitive ideal of Gaelic culture as it was available to him in MacPherson's *Ossian*. Runciman chose Ossian as the subject of a major series of paintings that he carried out in Penicuik House during the summer of 1772. The paintings were destroyed by fire in 1899, and their loss was a sad one, for they were not conceived in a spirit of drawing-room romanticism, but, as David Laing put it, were truly national designs. The discrediting of MacPherson should not blind us to the impact that the poems had at the time of their publication, both in Scotland and throughout Europe. It was through them that the two halves of Scots culture began again to be seen as one, however imperfectly. Runciman had been an associate of Hamilton in Rome, but in Edinburgh he was also a member of a circle which included such people as David Herd and Robert Fergusson, who were very consciously involved in Scottish culture and history. He approached Ossian, therefore, firmly committed to Blackwellian primitivism and to the idea of the special validity of Scots culture, freed from the influences of ancient and of modern Rome alike. In interpreting Ossian he gave full reign to the idea of the intensity and naturalness of ancient Gaelic poetry and created a style of rapid immediacy that was wholly original.

Runciman was responding to the idea of Gaelic poetry, as transmitted very imperfectly by MacPherson, rather than to any authentic manifestation of Gaelic culture, but he also located his inspiration in a way that had far-reaching effects. In the Hall of Ossian, as the drawing-room at Penicuik House came to be called, he did not attempt to set up a narrative sequence based on the poems. Instead he used the space as a model of the poet's imagination. The centrepiece, which was an oval painting 24 feet across, showed Ossian singing, surrounded by listeners and against a background of shoreline and hills (a sketch for the painting survives in the National Gallery of Scotland). The four other panels in the main part of the ceiling showed figures representing the Spey, the Tay, the Clyde and the Tweed, each river in its characteristic landscape. The twelve remaining scenes, which were in the cove of the

ceiling, were on the whole more nearly illustrative of the poetry, but in them too landscape was of unprecedented importance in compositions of this kind. Although none of this painting represents actual places, what Runciman had done was to establish for the first time, and specifically in the context of Highland scenery, the idea of the poetic landscape of Scotland. In germ at least he had extracted from Ossian more Gaelic poetry than Ossian itself contained.

The tradition of Scottish landscape painting was handed down by Runciman through his pupils, such as Alexander Nasmyth (q.v.) and George Walker, and by the early nineteenth century – in the paintings of John Thomson of Duddingston, for example – the modern iconography of Highland scenery was more or less mature. With the work of Horatio MacCulloch that iconography was fixed in a form that endures to this day. MacCulloch was a painter of real stature. He should not be confused with the 'Highland Cow' and 'Stag at Bay' school that flourished as a result of the Victorian fashion for the Highlands. His pictures reflect a real and sensitive involvement with the landscape that he painted, but it is notably a landscape without people.

It is perhaps a comment on the gap that persisted between true Gaelic culture and its reflection in the

Horatio MacCulloch 'Inverlochy Castle' 1857. National Gallery of Scotland.

William Dyce 'Gethsemane' c. 1855. Sudley Art Gallery, Liverpool. In this and a number of related paintings, Dyce brings his biblical subject closer to common reality by setting it in a recognisably Scottish landscape.

visual arts that up to the mid-nineteenth century, during an age in which documentary painting is relatively common, representations of the people of the Highlands and their environment are rare. In his much vaunted paintings of Highland chiefs, Raeburn, with the subtlety of Goya, reveals them for the charade that they were. By contrast, half a century later Landseer's *Rent Day in the Wilderness*, takes the charade for the truth, though it is no worse than many of the genre. Other painters in the mid-century achieved a more sympathetic view of the Highlands, as in some of the inhabited landscapes of Alexander Fraser and William Dyce, and even at times reflected, though remotely, the contemporary crisis of Gaelic society, for example, in Tom Faed's *The Last of the Clan* and other pictures of the 1860s dealing with the tragedy of emigration, if not with its causes.

In the 1860s also, however, a painter emerged who for the first time gave an active rather than passive role to Gaelic culture in the evolution of Scottish painting. William MacTaggart (q.v.) was the outstanding artist of the later nineteenth century in Scotland. He was born and brought up at Machrihanish in Kintyre, though he was not a Gaelic speaker. Many of his finest paintings are of his native countryside. Like it, they are dominated by the sea, and in them there is a directness of involvement in the physical nature of the landscape that could only spring from his deep identification with it. They are the landscapes of a native, not a tourist; and, like the best Gaelic poetry, they eschew the theatrical to achieve drama by concentrating on the specific character of an experience. Significantly, too, MacTaggart's pictures are almost always inhabited, and by people who are entirely at home in their environment – so much so, indeed, that they are sometimes almost indecipherable as separate entities within it.

MacTaggart has not been seen as a Celtic painter, though that is undoubtedly what he was. Others in his time, however, were very consciously Celtic, though their efforts have far less authenticity even than those of Runciman in the century before. The international success of Wagner gave a fresh impetus to the old pursuit of national roots in national myths, bringing back to Scotland, in an international form, something that had begun there and had almost been forgotten. Both in Edinburgh and Glasgow in the 1890s painters returned to Celtic myth and image for inspiration in Art Nouveau decoration and in search of themes for mural decorations. One of the most notable of the latter is the series of paintings done in Ramsay Lodge, Edinburgh, by John Duncan under the inspiration of Patrick Geddes, though only the first two of these are strictly Celtic, *The Awakening of Cuchulin* and the *Combat of Fionn and Swaran*; thereafter the logic of the series is difficult to follow, as it proceeds by way of King Arthur to the Admirable Crichton.

Formally, the inspiration of Celtic art in the late nineteenth century was more vital in its effect as it provided inspiration for designers ranging from Phoebe Traquhair to Charles Rennie Mackintosh. An important result of this formal interest was the encouragement of the study and preservation of Picto-Celtic monuments and the spread of their appreciation to a new and wider public. It was this new and essentially academic interest in Celtic art that led to one of the most interesting and unexpected manifestations of its inspiration. The painter William Johnstone returned from California to Scotland in 1929, inspired by the imaginative recognition

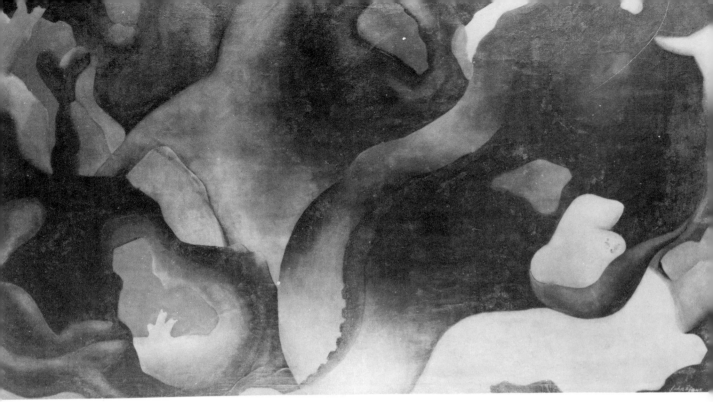

William Johnstone 'A Point in Time' c. 1936. Scottish National Gallery of Modern Art.

of an affinity between the Picto-Celtic art that he had learned about from Professor Baldwin Brown at the University of Edinburgh and Navajo sand paintings that he had seen in America. It was an intuitive recognition of his own primitive cultural roots in ancient Scotland, and his journey from California was a symbolic return to those roots. At this time Johnstone was already a close friend of Hugh MacDiarmid, as he was also of Francis George Scott, who was his cousin, so the problem of an authentic Scottish root for his painting had clearly already been posed for him by the example of MacDiarmid's poetry. The result of the new inspiration in Johnstone's work was a remarkable series of paintings leading up to one major painting of about 1936, *Point in Time*, now in the Scottish National Gallery of Modern Art. In this painting the conjunction of history and place is located in the experience of the individual. Johnstone achieves this by using the running line of historical Celtic art to create an image evocative of the Border landscape of his youth. Some of Johnstone's ideas have an affinity with the contemporary poetry of Eliot, but their real analogy is with the poetry of MacDiarmid and with the ideal of the ultimate unity of Scots culture.

In the post-war generation Johnstone's inspiration lay behind the earlier paintings of Alan Davie, in whose work Celtic imagery is clearly identifiable. In his Abstract Expressionist pictures Celtic wheels and crosses, though they are elusive and in constant transformation, appear as the only ultimately irreducible elements in a shifting field of dissolving imagery. Whether or not it is merely fanciful to see old Celtic art in this way as a remote but still vital presence, it is clear that over the last two centuries it and the landscape with which it is identified have provided a constant resource for Scottish artists in their search for a form of expression that they can see as entirely their own.   JDM

art, Pictish consists of a large corpus of stone sculpture (Allen 1903) and a small quantity of metalwork (Small, Thomas and Wilson 1973; R. B. K. Stevenson 1976). The sculpture falls into three categories: erratic boulders set up so that symbolic designs can be incised on a flat surface; quarried and dressed slabs decorated in relief with symbols, a full-length cross and other figurative and ornamental motifs; slabs, decorated recumbent grave-markers and fragments of stone box shrines, also decorated but without symbols. The Picts, unlike their Irish and English neighbours, did not turn their cross-slabs into free-standing crosses, although in the ninth century they narrowed and heightened their slabs, presumably in imitation of that style of monument (I. Henderson 1978).

The discovery in 1958, on St Ninian's Isle, Shetland (q.v.), of a hoard of twenty-eight pieces of ornamented silver greatly increased knowledge of the range of Pictish metalwork. It led to the recognition of a distinctively Pictish type of brooch, and a clear relationship was established between decorative motifs used by the metalworkers and the sculptors. The more recent find of a mould for a hanging-bowl escutcheon on a site near Inverness brings the Picts into the controversy concerning the place of manufacture of these bowls (Small and Cottam 1972). Symbols are engraved on the terminal rings of a small series of silver neck chains and on a few other silver pieces, but so far they have not been found on Pictish brooches.

The Pictish symbols are uniform designs found all over the Pictish area (that is, modern Scotland north of the Forth–Clyde line). They consist of animals, birds, and fish, geometric shapes with curvilinear decoration, and diagrammatic pictures of objects such as mirrors and combs. The Picts are best known for their animal art. The profile bull, wolf and stag symbols are powerful, accurate evocations of the nature of these animals. An enigmatic but frequently occurring symbol is an imaginary animal known as the 'elephant' or 'Pictish beast'. Its origin, which has an important bearing on the dating of the symbols, remains a major problem in Pictish art-historical studies (I. Henderson, 1957–8, 57, and 1967, 118; R. B. K. Stevenson 1955, 108–10; Thomas 1961, 49–53).

The Picts were expert at laying out interlace, key and spiral patterns and were competent portrayers of the human figure. Narrative art is represented most frequently in an effective, if stereotype, hunting scene, in which horsemen and hounds pursue deer in a slanting composition that runs from right to left over the slab. On the slab in the churchyard of Aberlemno, Angus, there is a unique extended narrative of a battle set out on three registers (see illustration on p. 52).

The handful of Ogam inscriptions (see **Ogam stones**) on the symbol stones and slabs is in an eighth-century script but provides no clue to more

Pictish symbol stone, wolf. Inverness Museum and Art Gallery.

Pictish interlace. Nigg stone, Nigg, Ross-shire.

exact dating (K. H. Jackson 1955b, 139–42; Wainwright 1959). There are no closely datable archaeological or architectural contexts for boulders or slabs. Dating by stylistic analysis has produced a number of different dating schemes (R. B. K. Stevenson 1958–9, 54–5). It is broadly agreed that the animal symbols relate in some way to the designs for the animal Evangelist symbols in the Book of Durrow (Dublin, Trinity College MS A.4.5 (57)), dated to *c*.680, and that the zoomorphic ornament on the early cross-slabs comes from manuscripts of the time of the Lindisfarne Gospels (London, British Library Cotton MS Nero D. IV), dated 698–721 (I. Henderson 1967, 104–60; R. B. K. Stevenson 1971). Later sculpture, particularly that in Easter Ross, has many parallels in the Book of Kells (Dublin, Trinity College MS A.1.6 (58)), dated 750–800, and on the high crosses of Iona (I. Henderson 1982; R. B. K. Stevenson 1956–7). The tomb shrine at St Andrews, Fife, with its complex iconography of David and the grandeur of its execution, shares the classicizing style and developing intellectual role of psalter illustration in England and on the Continent in the eighth and ninth centuries.

The most serious dating discrepancy concerns the beginning of the series. Symbols are found all over Pictland and are consistent in style. Either they were invented, the designs being taken in part from the seventh- and eighth-century art of their neighbours and promulgated by a central authority, or they were evolved over a long period and incised on stones at the point at which their style and form were fixed. The style in the latter reasoning is seen as preserving aspects of the early Celtic La Tène style, which was itself revived in the art of the seventh century. The weak point of the latter argument is the lack of evidence for the evolutionary phase; of the former, that there seems no obvious reason why the Picts should have created a new and pervasive social system of this sort as late as the seventh and eighth centuries. Knowledge of the meaning of the symbols would, of course, greatly assist judgement in this matter. The most conservative view is that the symbols are the tattoo designs mentioned in late classical texts as being used by the tribes of North Britain. The individual symbols would then refer to the role and status of the Pict buried beneath or memorialized by the stone, and the mirror and comb placed at the bottom of groups of symbols would be a reference to the Pictish law of succession, which passed through the female (Thomas 1963). A more recent suggestion is that the symbol stones commemorate political alliances between different lineages. If this is the case, the stones with the mirrors and combs commemorate marriage alliances, these symbols being taken as referring to the giving of bridewealth (A. Jackson 1971). Another interpretation sees the stones as notice boards marking land boundaries, the individual symbols defining aspects of land tenure (I. Henderson 1971). Yet another theory is that they were placed by deer forests and salmon rivers in order to promote successful hunting (C. A. Gordon 1964–6). On balance, the probabilities favour the ancient origin of the symbols on some other medium – skin, wood or metal.

Pictish art takes its place as a distinguished school of Christian art in early medieval Europe, but the fact that it resolutely maintains on its monuments a symbolic affirmation of an aspect of the native culture alongside the universal visual language of Christianity suggests that the system was deeply entrenched in Pictish society.   IH

Arthur, King The belief that Arthur – if he was an historical figure (Bromwich 1975–6; Jackson 1959; Jones 1964) – was active in northern Britain has had two main supports. The first, the former claim that the Arthurian battles listed in *Historia Brittonum* can be located in Scotland, has been effectively demolished by Jackson (1945, 1958). The second is that our knowledge of early British, or Welsh, history and literature derives entirely from north British sources, and therefore if we know Arthur as an historical figure it is because he was a northerner (Bromwich 1963). This is to exaggerate, or at least to oversimplify, the dependence of the Welsh Annals and the *Historia Brittonum* on exclusively northern sources (Alcock 1971, 81–5). The balance of evidence places Arthur in southern Britain. Arthurian placenames and associations in Scotland probably reflect the spread of Arthurian romances, and of chivalrous ideals, in the twelfth and later centuries (Loomis 1955–6).

LA

Artúr Dall Mac Gurcaigh Author of poem probably about John MacSween's expedition against John of Menteith, usurper of his Knapdale lands (1310). Some lines appear to describe Norse-type weapons and ornamentation. (See W. J. Watson 1937; D. S. Thomson 1974a.)

DST

Athole Highlanders, *see* regiments, Highland.

Auldearn, Battle of (9 May 1645) The Covenanters surprised the army of Montrose (q.v.) but were routed after Alasdair MacColla (q.v.) held up their advance to give Montrose time to gather his men and counter-attack. (See D. Stevenson 1980, 172–92.)

DS

B

bagpipe, Highland The Highland bagpipe consists of a chanter and three drones attached to a bag which is filled with air by the mouth through a blowpipe fitted with a non-return valve. The chanter is a conical pipe with a double reed, so it belongs to the shawm or oboe family of instruments. The drones are made up of cylindrical sections, with sliding joints for tuning and with special reeds having a single vibrating tongue. The melody is played on the chanter, which has a scale of nine notes from g' to a'', while the drones give the fixed notes A (the bass drone) and a (the two tenor drones). (These are the pitches as conventionally noted; the actual sound is about one semitone higher.) The air pressure is kept constant to produce an even tone, and for this reason, and because the reeds are not taken into the mouth, there can be no loud or soft emphasis in the music and no pauses between notes. Rhythm and expression are achieved by means of very precise timing and the use of grace notes. These range from very short single notes, interposed between two melody notes, to complicated strings of notes, some of them reminiscent of ornaments of baroque music but most of them peculiar to the bagpipe. Fine tuning of the pipes is essential, and a good player spends a great deal of time and trouble selecting and adjusting reeds to achieve this. Before playing any piece he plays informal preludes and short tunes until the whole instrument has settled into a steady state.

In Western Europe generally bagpipes were popular through the Middle Ages and into the sixteenth century, since when they have disappeared gradually and now survive mostly as folk instruments in isolated regions (Baines 1960). Traditionally they have belonged to shepherds and to village musicians of the humblest sort. In the Gaidhealtachd, by contrast, historical references to bagpipes do not begin until the mid-sixteenth century, and they reveal a rather different picture. Irish (Donnelly 1981) and Scottish (Dalyell 1849, 20) sources tell of pipers playing in battle and at funerals. If piping was then an integral part of the Gaelic way of life, it was presumably not new, but beyond that it is impossible to guess when the bagpipe reached either Scotland or Ireland. Perhaps *c.*1400 is the latest reasonable date.

Sources of the seventeenth and early eighteenth century give a fairly full picture of the status and functions of the piper. There were village pipers in the Highlands, as elsewhere, but the ones we hear most about enjoyed much higher positions. Houses like Dunvegan and Duntuilm were centres of patronage for poets, harpers and pipers. The laird's personal piper played to wake the household in the morning (W. Matheson 1970, l–liii), and to honour guests on their arrival and departure (Dalyell 1849, 35); and later traditions (e.g. titles of tunes) indicate that he

Piper to the Laird of Grant. Painted in 1714 by Richard Waitt. National Museum of Antiquities of Scotland.

composed special pieces to salute his patrons and to lament their deaths. A piper would be dressed at the chief's expense (A. Morrison 1967, 335) and would carry the chief's banner on his pipes (Dalyell 1849, 35). In battle he may well have played specific tunes that were recognized as calling signals; there was at any rate a tradition that at Falkirk in 1746, the Jacobites failed to consolidate their victory because the pipers who should have sounded the clan rallies had given their pipes to their servants and gone in with the sword (Kermack 1957, 131). The military character of the pipes is evident in many passing references in poetry of the time. The line 'Pìob agus bratach air faich Inbhir Lòchaidh' epitomizes the tradition (Collinson 1975, 139). There are also references to the pipes as accompaniment to general merrymaking in the castle, though it seems clear that for more intimate and expressive music the harp was preferred (W. Matheson 1970, l–liii). However, professional harp playing died out during the first half of the

eighteenth century, and to some extent piping took its place. When Johnson and Boswell travelled through the Hebrides in 1771 pipers played to them indoors at mealtimes (Johnson 1924, 152; cf. also 71, 187).

About 1700 we first hear of piping 'colleges', in the sense that some chiefs would send their pipers for a course of training under a master player (J. L. Campbell 1975, 49). Later accounts give the names of some of these teachers, or rather families, for it appears that successive generations kept up the traditions: the Rankins of Mull, MacArthurs of Skye, MacKays of Gairloch and others ('Account of the Hereditary Pipers', prefixed to A. MacKay 1838, 7–14) but above all the MacCrimmons, pipers to the MacLeods of Dunvegan (R. H. MacLeod 1977a, b and c). Documentary agreements, in which a chief undertakes to send his piper to a MacCrimmon for tuition for a specified period, are extant, dated 1698 (R. H. MacLeod 1977a) and 1743 (Dixon 1981). Again there is no reason to doubt that these traditions had been established for some time before they were first recorded.

Pipe music today falls into two sharply distinct classes, *ceòl beag* and *ceòl mór*, terms first recorded in the late nineteenth century but by implication in regular use by then (Keltie 1877, vol. 2, 107; J. F. Campbell 1880). *Ceòl beag* is the Scottish counterpart of the type of bagpipe music found in other countries: dance tunes, especially reels, strathspeys and jigs; marches, which have multiplied enormously in the past 150 years as the bagpipe has been taken up by the Army; and slow airs similar to the airs of Gaelic songs. Over a hundred collections of this music have been published since 1784 (Cannon 1980), and the total repertoire must now be one of the richest 'folk music' traditions in the world. Indeed, 'folk music' is hardly the appropriate term to describe this culture which has spread far beyond its original confines and flourishes through modern methods of communication. There are detailed instruction books (e.g. *The College of Piping Tutor for the Highland Bagpipe*, Glasgow, 3 vols., 1953–69; *The Scottish Pipe Band Tutor and Textbook*, Glasgow, 2 vols., 1962–71) and a steady supply of recordings, both of solo performances and of pipe bands (advertised regularly in e.g. the *Piping Times*, and the *Pipe Band*). Lack of space precludes further discussion, however, and the remainder of this article is concerned with the other branch of piping, *ceòl mór*, best known today as *pìobaireachd* (MacNeill 1968).

Although the Gaelic meaning of *pìobaireachd* is

simply 'piping', the word (often spelled 'pibroch') has passed into English as the name for a particular class of pipe tune, composed on an altogether grander scale than that of the airs and marches mentioned so far. A pibroch consists of a slow theme, called *ùrlar* in Gaelic, 'ground' in English, followed by variations and ending with a repetition of the ground. The ground may be much longer than an ordinary tune, and it may have a formal structure of phrases arranged in one of a number of set patterns, which were presumably once taught as part of the 'theory' of composition (Haddow 1982, 149–77; R. L. C. Lorimer 1962, 1964). The variations follow the melody of the ground in a simplified form, and the final ones, culminating in the *crùnluath*, contain only the principal notes of the melody, played in a steady rhythm and embellished with conventional figures of grace notes. The full performance takes usually some ten to fifteen minutes.

The names of pibrochs reflect the old Highland way of life. The commonest are laments (e.g. 'Cumha Mhic an Tòisich'), salutes ('Fàilte Mhic Ghille Chaluim') or 'gatherings' ('Cruinneachadh Chloinn Chatain'). Some are named after famous battles, and others have titles which are simply the opening words of songs which are or which were once associated with the same tune, such as '‘S fhada mar so tha sinn' ('Too long in this condition'). (The English translations of these names are often rather stilted, but they are now much better known to pipers than the original Gaelic.) The musical character of a piece often seems appropriate to the title, at least to the trained listener. Gatherings tend to emphasize short, memorable phrases, which could indeed be imagined as rallying calls. Laments are often longer and more free-flowing, though still always metrically constructed. The tunes are generally pentatonic, which means that they use even fewer notes than the restricted scale of the chanter will allow. Because of this, however, keys and modes can be selected which have entirely different flavours when played against the constant background of the drones. Themes in A major and G major seem to be preferred for salutes and gatherings, while modes approximating to A minor and D major can make particularly effective laments. But there are no hard and fast rules in these matters, and it is not true to say that laments, salutes, etc., form distinctive musical genres in the way that marches, reels, etc., are distinguished in the lighter pipe music.

As far as we know, pibrochs were originally composed and taught entirely by ear, or rather by mouth, since the practice was to sing the tune in a syllabic 'language' called *canntaireachd*. A specimen of Mac-Crimmon *canntaireachd* illustrates the principle. (The tune, 'The Union of Scotland with England', is from N. MacLeod 1828, 13; the vocables have been edited and matched to the staff notation by the writer of this entry.) When this is sung to the appropriate melody, the vowel sounds give out the principal notes and the consonants approximate the effect of the grace notes.

Collections of pibrochs in ordinary music notation began to be made at the end of the eighteenth century, mainly at the instigation of the Highland Society of London (Archibald Campbell 1948, 2nd edn, 11; *Pìobaireachd* 1925, bk 1, ii–iii), as a step towards preserving the music when it was evidently dying out. Printed collections began in 1822 (D. MacDonald 1822), though manuscripts continued to circulate among the small coterie of pibroch players throughout the nineteenth century. The total number of pibrochs now extant is about 300, but it was once larger, as indicated by various short fragments quoted in early manuscripts and by songs which apparently preserve the melodies of pibrochs no longer known (James Ross 1957c, 131ff.). A fully trained player would once have been able to play 100 or 200 pieces entirely from memory (Dalyell 1849, 17; Collinson 1975, 199). Today printed texts are the basis of the repertoire (Cannon 1980), but the oral tradition still continues to some extent, since it is felt that proper expression can be learned only from a teacher who has himself been traditionally taught, and so on back to the old masters. A piper today will learn a new piece from the published books of the Piobaireachd Society (*Pìobaireachd*, bks 1–13, 1925–80), which he

I hin-dro   dilì-ù hie chin hin-do   hì-udrie   hi - à   chin

Angus MacKay, Piper to Queen Victoria. A noted collector of pibrochs as well as a player. His work became a definitive source for later generations of players. He was appointed piper to the Queen in 1843, but later succumbed to mental illness and died in 1859.

will regard as definitive, and will then learn the nuances of timing from a more experienced player who will help him to 'put the song in it' (Cooke 1972, 41–59) by going over various phrases in his personal form of *canntaireachd*. The advent of tape recording has of course made oral communication much easier than before. The written notation is generally admitted to be quite misleading in some ways (Archibald Campbell 1948, 2nd edn, 17; S. MacNeill 1968). Whether this is because the writing system has been faulty from the beginning or because playing style has altered in spite of all efforts to keep it constant is a controversial point (Cooke 1978).

Live public performances of pibroch today consist almost exclusively of competitions, held throughout the summer at the traditional Highland Games and at other times of the year as organized by a number of piping societies in Glasgow, Edinburgh, London and elsewhere. These contests dominate the professional piping world, and the technical standards are extraordinarily high. The gold medals offered at the Northern Meeting, Inverness, in succession to the competitions started by the Highland Society in 1781 (Archibald Campbell 1948, 2nd edn, 7), and the Argyllshire Gathering, Oban, are the most coveted prizes for the rising player; but beyond these there are competitions at which the general standards are even higher, since entrants are confined to former winners in these and a few other specified events. A recent development has been the competition for invited entrants, such as the annual competition at Blair Castle sponsored by William Grant & Sons' Whisky Distilleries (*Piping Times*, vol. 34, no. 3, 1981, 11). What has not yet been found viable is the non-competitive piping recital, apart from semi-private occasions organized by piping societies. By the same token, it is noteworthy that the audience at a pibroch competition will consist almost entirely of other pipers. This is not to say that the 'pibroch culture' is dying: on the contrary, the numbers both of competitors and of non-competing amateurs are growing rapidly, but this increase is taking place within the numerous ranks of pipers in general. Pibroch is still relatively little known outside the piping world. Whether and how this situation can be changed it is not easy to see.

Today pibroch is looked on as 'classical' pipe music. The term is apt in so far as pibroch is a minority pursuit within piping, and it is certainly the most subtle and demanding form of pipe music both to play and to listen to. It is also classical in the sense that the repertoire is fixed and has scarcely been added to in the past 150 years. There have been attempts at composing new pieces, and there is currently something of a resurgence of composition (see *New Pibrochs . . . Adjudged the Best among the Entries in a BBC Competition*, Edinburgh 1966; *Comunn na Pìobaireachd . . . Collection of Ceòl Mór Composed during the Twentieth Century*, the Piobaireachd Society 1980), but so far there is no sign of any new piece competing in popularity with the established ones. One reason suggested for this is that the principles of composition – which have not been handed down traditionally – have still to be rediscovered (R. L. C. Lorimer 1962, 1964; Haddow 1982). Another view is that, rather than attempting to revive old forms, composers should seek new ones. Whether or not there is a new and still more excellent form of pipe music still to be invented, a truly modern *ceòl mór*, only time will tell. RC

Bannerman, John M. (Lord Bannerman of Kildonan) (1902–69) Born Glasgow. Prominent Gaelic propagandist, Liberal politician and rugby football internationalist. DST

Bannerman, John W. M. (1932–) Born Balmaha. Son of John M. Bannerman (q.v.). Lecturer in Scottish History, University of Edinburgh; authority on early Dalriada (q.v.), Beatons (q.v.) (See bibliography.) DST

Bannerman, Lord, of Kildonan, *see* Bannerman, John M.

Bantock, Granville (1868–1946) Professor of Music, Birmingham University. Composed 'Hebridean' symphony and opera, 'The Seal-Woman', using Hebridean tunes. DST

Bàrd Baile, *see* verse, village.

Bàrd Bhaile Mhàrtainn, *see* Maclean, John (1827–95).

Bàrd Bharbhais, *see* MacDonald, Donald (1861–1916).

Bàrd Bochd, *see* MacLeod, Norman (d. 1970).

Bàrd Conanach (Donald MacDonald) (*c.*1780–1832) From Strathconnon, Ross-shire. Author of a song to Napoleon, etc. (See K. N. Macdonald 1900, 48.) DST

Bàrd Eadarra-Mhucaidh, *see* Caimbeul, Aonghas (*c.*1740–1814).

Bàrd Loch Fìne, *see* MacColla, Eóghan.

Bàrd Mac an t-Saoir (fl. ?1515) Author of two poems in the Book of the Dean of Lismore (q.v.), both describing fantastical ships (made of rushes, reeds, bracken, etc.), each with a complement of lascivious women, one on Loch Insh (?Badenoch) the other on Loch Rannoch and connected with Duncan of Argyll. The poet is presumably the 'Bardu[s]

Makintier' mentioned in *MacFarlan's Geographical Collections* (Mitchell and Toshach 1906–8, vol. I, 212) as having been brought to Badenoch from Rannoch by William Mackintosh before 1515. (See W. J. Watson 1937, 218, 224.) DST

Bàrd Mac Mhathain, *see* Aos-dàna.

Bàrd Mac Shithich, *see* Aos-dàna.

Bàrd Mucanach (fl. ?1700) From Argyll. A MacDonald poet who lived in Muck and composed a poem on the Massacre of Glencoe. (See K. N. MacDonald 1900, 20.) DST

Bàrd Mùgach, *see* Macintosh, Duncan (fl. 1831).

Bàrd Sgallach (Angus Campbell) (fl. 1900) From Benbecula. A traditional poet. DST

Bàrd Thighearna Cholla, *see* MacLean, John (1787–1848).

Bàrd Thùrnaig, *see* Cameron, Alasdair.

bardic schools, *see* schools, bardic.

Barron, Evan MacLeod (1879–1964) Editor and proprietor of the *Inverness Courier*. Author of *The Scottish War of Independence* (2nd edn 1934) and books on medieval Inverness. DST

Barún Eóghan MacCombaigh (dates unknown) Author of poem in the Book of the Dean of Lismore (q.v.). Probably a descendant of Wolf of Badenoch. (See W. J. Watson 1937, 194). DST

Bàthadh Mór Nis (Great Ness Drowning) Half the tenants of Sgigersta, Lewis, were drowned on a fishing trip in January 1840. DST

Baxter, Richard (1614–91) An English Puritan divine, some of whose works (for instance, *Call to the Unconverted*) were translated into Gaelic (1750). DST

Bealach na Bròige A victory in Ross-shire, in 1369, for the western clans of Ross over the Earl of Ross and his allies, the Munros and the Dingwalls. (See W. Matheson 1963, 204–5.) JWMB

Bean Torra-Dhamh (Mary Clark) (*c*.1740–*c*.1815) Daughter of Ewan MacPherson, schoolmaster of Laggan, Badenoch. Of her Gaelic hymns, seven theologically and linguistically robust specimens survive. Two of these were published by Rose (1851) and republished, with an additional hymn and English translations, by John Kennedy (J. Kennedy n.d.). A further four were published by Sinton (Sinton 1906), and all seven were later edited by Alexander MacRae (MacRae n.d.).   KDMCD

Beathag Mhór (Big Beathag) Author of a group of songs in praise of Màrtainn a' Bhealaich (Martin of Bealach) in Skye (e.g. 'An cùl bachalach', 'Gur h-e mo ghaol am fireannach'). Budge (1976) suggests that this was Martin Martin, author of the *Description*, but the songs are probably late eighteenth-century ones.   DST

Beaton, Revd Donald (b. 1872) Author of Caithness and Sutherland *Bibliography* (1923).   DST

Beaton, Revd John (*c*.1640–1715) Born in Pennycross, Isle of Mull. The last learned member of the famous Beaton medical family. Episcopalian (later, presumably, non-jurant) minister of Kilninian in Mull, *c*.1670–1701. Informant of Edward Lhuyd (q.v.), who listed the Gaelic manuscripts in his possession in 1700. (The statement in Scott's *Fasti* that Beaton was 'outed' from his parish in 1701 for immoral conduct requires confirmation, considering the political and sectarian tensions of the time.) (See Bruford 1965; J. L. Campbell 1975, 1976; Campbell and Thomson 1963; W. R. MacKay 1980; Ó Concheannáin 1975.)   JLC

Beaton Institute of Cape Breton Studies Founded in 1957 as the Cape-Bretoniana Collection at the College of Cape Breton by Sister St Margaret of Scotland (Margaret Beaton), the Institute changed its name in her honour after her death in 1975.

The Institute serves as an archive and centre for the fostering and preservation of Cape Breton culture, and its holdings include manuscripts, tapes, maps, photographs and books. Of special interest is an extensive Gaelic manuscript and tape collection of Cape Breton material, which includes *sgeulachdan* (traditional stories), music, poetry and reminiscences of Scottish settlement and immigration. The Institute also maintains a large collection of books in Gaelic on Scottish and Canadian topics.   RJM

Beaton, Sister St Margaret Isabel (1894–1975) Born Broad Cove Banks, Cape Breton. Daughter of Eoin Beaton and Ann MacDonald. She entered religious life as a Sister of the Congregation of Notre Dame in 1913 and for the next sixty years served as high-school teacher, principal, Dean of Women at Mount St Bernard College, Antigonish, Nova Scotia, and librarian, archivist and Gaelic instructor at the College of Cape Breton. At the latter institution she founded the Beaton Institute.   RJM

Beatons, the Generally surnamed MacBeatha or MacBeth until the end of the sixteenth century, they practised medicine on an hereditary basis in the classical tradition of the Gaelic learned orders. Traditionally they came to Scotland in about 1300, from Achadowey, Co. Derry, and settled initially at Ballenabe in Islay. The first on record was Patrick, chief physician to King Robert I (*d*.1329). Thereafter two distinct divisions can be discerned, one based mainly in the islands, the other on the mainland; by the sixteenth century the most important families in the former group were those of Ballenabe (Islay) and of Pennycross (Mull) and, in the latter, those of Culnaskea (Ross-shire), and of Husabost (Skye).

More medieval Gaelic manuscripts known to have been in the possession of Beatons have survived than for any other professional kindred. Their commitment to classical Gaelic scholarship came to an end in the person of Christopher, who was the compiler of the so-called Black Book of Clanranald (q.v.) (National Museum of Antiquities of Scotland, MCR 40), completed not earlier than 1715 (Bannerman, forthcoming).   JWMB

Bede Bede's *Ecclesiastical History of the English People*, completed in 731, contains much relating to Lothian, including a short account of the see of Abercorn, a bishopric for the Picts, abandoned by the Angles in 685. His main Scottish value, however, has been taken to be his version of the mission of Colum Cille (q.v.) to the 'northern Picts', the 'southern Picts' having been converted by Ninian. A recent view argues that Bede has misunderstood his source, a letter from Nectan, king of Picts, and that Ninian worked south of Forth. This letter was composed by Egbert, an Anglo-Irish monk anxious to bring about the conversion of the Picts and Iona to the Roman Easter. Egbert used Iona annals, and therefore Bede's account of Colum Cille and later events is not independent of the Irish annals, which are a better source. The 'defeat' of Aedán of Dal Riada by the Angles at Degsastan in 602 is a hybrid created by Bede from a victory by Aedan over the Angles in about 600 and a victory by the Angles over the Welsh at Degsastan. (See Bede 1969 edn; Duncan, 1981.)

AAMD

Beith, Alexander (1799–1891) Born Campbeltown. Leading Free Church clergyman. Minister in Oban, Glasgow, Kilbrandon, Glenelg, Stirling. Published a number of books on Highland church affairs between 1823 and 1869, including two Gaelic works on baptism, *Dearbhaidhean an Aghaidh Teagaisg nan Anabaisteach* (1823) and *Leabhar Cheistean mu Nadur a Bhaistidh* (1827).

RMCL

beliefs, pagan, *see* paganism, survivals of.

Bernera Riot In 1874 Donald Munro (q.v.), Sir James Matheson's factor, moved to convert into deer forest the hill grazing on the mainland of Lewis that was held by Bernera crofters. A sheriff's officer sent to serve summonses of removal on them was intercepted and severely warned about his threat to shoot youngsters who had pelted him with sods. Three of the ringleaders of the Bernera men were summonsed. One was apprehended in Stornoway after a fierce struggle, and the Bernera men marched on the town demanding an audience with Sir James Matheson. At their trial the Bernera men were found not guilty, and Munro's tyranny was exposed, a breakthrough in the crofters' struggle for security. (See *Report of the Trial of the So-Called Bernera Rioters,* 1874; D. MacAmhlaigh 1981.)

DMCA

Bethune, John (MacBethac) (fl. 1770) Tutor to the Duke of Argyll and author of the scurrilous satire 'Baran Supair' on James Maxwell, Argyll's factor in Kintyre and Mull. (See *Feuds and Conflicts,* 101–6.)

DST

Bhaile Mhàrtainn, Bàrd, *see* MacLean, John (1827–95).

'Bhruidhean Chaorthuinn, 'A' ('The Rowan Hostel') Alias 'Fionn ann an Taigh a' Bhlàir Bhuidhe' (?'Fionn in the House of the Yellow Field'). Romance and derived folktale: Fenians are enticed into an enchanted *bruidhean* (hostel), where they stick to their seats until released by Diarmaid with the aid of the blood of three kings. (See Bruford 1969, 115.)

AB

Bible, Gaelic translations of Although religious translation in Gaelic Scotland began in 1567 (see **Carswell, John**), two centuries passed before any part of the Bible was translated for Scottish Gaelic speakers. The translation of the entire Bible was not completed until 1801, almost two centuries after the Authorized Version. Before the publication of the Gaelic New Testament in 1767 the people's knowledge of the Scriptures depended largely on their ministers and their own memories. Ministers normally made extempore translations based on the Authorized Version or on Kirk's Bible, a modification by the Revd Robert Kirk of the Irish translations of William O'Donnell (New Testament, pub. 1603) and Bishop Bedell (Old Testament, pub. 1686).

The Gaelic translation of the Bible was sustained by the Society in Scotland for Propagating Christian Knowledge (SSPCK), as part of its attempt to civilize the Highlands after the '45. Public figures such as Dr Samuel Johnson supported the project, and three Gaelic scholars – the Revd James Stuart (q.v.) (Killin), the Revd James Fraser (Alness) and Dugald Buchanan (q.v.) – undertook the translation of the New Testament. Yet, as Johnson himself discovered when he visited the minister of Coll in 1773, the new translation was not immediately acceptable: 'Mr MacLean said he did not use it, because he could make the text more intelligible to his auditors by an extemporary version. From this I inferred that the language of the translation was not the language of the Isle of Coll.'

Johnson's inference was not unfounded. The translators had used a vocabulary and style that was significantly different from that of contemporary Gaelic. They tended to follow Kirk's Bible, modifying it where it diverged greatly from vernacular Gaelic (for example, in the verb system). Thus the new translation was really an adaptation of an existing version in a related language, the overall style being closer to the older Classical language once shared by Ireland and Gaelic Scotland.

A similar technique was used in the translation of the Old Testament, divided into four volumes. The first three were translated by the Revd John Stuart (q.v.) (Luss), son of the Revd James Stuart, and the fourth by the Revd John Smith (q.v.) (Campbeltown). Stuart's first volume appeared in 1783, but the third was not published until 1801. Smith's volume, the Prophets, was published in 1786. Smith was the more audacious translator, since he consulted the most recent textual and critical works by Lowth, Blaney, Newcome, Houbigant and Kennicot. Initially, his efforts were applauded by the SSPCK, which planned to print a commentary by him on the Prophets.

A second edition of the New Testament (revised by the Revd John Stuart) was published in 1796 and a second edition of the Old Testament begun in 1802. But the SSPCK was now critical of Smith's volume. Its Minutes refer to complaints 'of the fourth volume . . . being too free, corresponding much more with Dr Lowth's translation than with the English one, which had a bad effect upon the Minds of those who understand both languages'. The volume was revised by the Revd Alexander Stewart (Dingwall), who brought it into line with the Authorized Version. In several instances (for example, Isaiah 9:1), Smith's 'deviations' were later upheld by the English Revised Version of the Old Testament (pub. 1885). Ironically, the rejected translation was included in the British and Foreign Bible Society's edition, published at Chelsea in 1807, simultaneously with the SSPCK's second edition. The printing of the latter was supervised by the Revd Thomas Ross, who later criticized the SSPCK's translation and tried, unsuccessfully, to have his own rival translation accepted by the 1820 General Assembly.

Ross's rebuff assured the success of the SSPCK's translation of the Bible. In spite of initial hostility, its effect was profound, stimulating prose writers – for example, the Revd Dr Norman Macleod (q.v.) – and prompting people to become literate in Gaelic. Several important revisions were made subsequently in order to remove Irishisms, to correct typographical errors and to modify the text in view of more recent scholarship. These revisions resulted in the circulation of editions that diverged slightly from one another. From 1861 the National Bible Society of Scotland assumed responsibility for the translation.

In 1875 Father Ewen MacEachen published a translation of the New Testament that was based on the Vulgate and used vocabulary marginally closer to contemporary speech than that of the earlier Gaelic version. In 1980 the National Bible Society of Scotland completed a pilot translation of Mark's Gospel into Gaelic, for use mainly among young people less familiar with the language of the older Gaelic Bible. (See D. MacKinnon 1930; SSPCK Committee Minutes, Scottish Record Office GD.95.)   DEM

Black Book of Clanranald, *see* Clanranald, the Books of.

Black Watch, *see* regiments, Highland.

Blackwell, Thomas, *see* art, Gaelic, in modern times.

Blair, Duncan, *see* Blàr, Donnchadh B.

Blàr, Donnchadh B. (Revd Duncan Blair) (1815–93) Born Badenoch. Emigrated to Canada. Author of descriptive poem on Niagara Falls. His manuscripts, now in the Public Archives of Nova Scotia, include his translation of the Psalms and of the *Iliad*, Bk. 3, as well as original poems such as the lengthy 'Tòimhseachan a' Chreidmhich' (1839) and 'Am Breitheanas Deireannach' (1883).   DST

Blàr na Léine (*Battle of the Tunics*) (Loch Lochy, 1544) A victory for John of Moidart over the Frasers of Lovat in defence of Clan Ranald territories. The day being warm, they fought in their tunics, hence the name. (See Gregory 1881, 157–63.)   JWMB

Blàr na Pàirc (*Battle of the Park*) (Strathconon, 1491) A defeat inflicted on Alexander MacDonald of Lochalsh and the forces of the Lordship of the Isles by the MacKenzies. (See Gregory 1881, 55–7.)   JWMB

Bloody Bay, *see* Angus Óg MacDonald.

Boban Saor (Goban Saor) Legendary craftsman. The name is perhaps derived from the Old Irish smith-god Goibniu: hero of folktales generally about cunning escapes undertaken with the help of his son and daughter-in-law. (See J. Ross 1958, 133.)   AB

Bochanan, Dùghall (Dugald Buchanan) (1716–68) Born in Strathyre, Perthshire. Became a teacher and catechist at Kinloch Rannoch and the outstanding Gaelic poet of the eighteenth century evangelical movement. A turbulent religious conversion, chronicled in his *Diary* (Macbean 1919), led him to the works of English writers such as Isaac Watts and Edward Young, and these influences fused with native stimuli in the eight 'spiritual songs' that he published in 1767 (D. Maclean 1913).

The poems are extensions of his role as religious instructor and evangelist. 'Mòrachd Dhè', heavily indebted to Watts is a meditation on the nature of God, 'Fulangas Chrìosd' a smooth-flowing summary

The 9th Black Watch celebrating Hogmanay on the Somme, January 1917. Imperial War Museum.

of the Gospel story and 'Là a' Bhreitheanais' a dramatic presentation of the cosmic and moral upheaval of the Day of Judgement. 'Am Bruadar' is a reflection on the 'vanity of human wishes' theme, while 'An Gaisgeach' debunks the conventional hero of Gaelic literature in favour of the moral and spiritual champion. 'An Claigeann' views through the prism of their mortality a cross-section of social types, with some biting criticism of the contemporary rack-renting landowner. 'An Geamhradh' exploits the vogue for seasonal poetry to present a Highland winter as a parable of death. 'Urnaigh' is a penitent's prayer.

Few of his evangelical successors can match the artistry of Buchanan's carefully sculptured verses, shot through as they are with images culled from his own and his hearers' environment. (See J. MacInnes 1951; Sutherland 1875; D. S. Thomson 1958d, 1974a.) KDMCD

Bocsair, am *see* Caimbeul, Aonghas (1908–49).

Book of the Dean of Lismore, *see* Dean of Lismore, Book of the.

Book of Deer, *see* Deer, Book of; manuscripts, illuminated.

Book of Durrow, *see* manuscripts, illuminated.

Book of Kells, *see* manuscripts, illuminated.

Books of Clanranald, *see* Clanranald, the Books of.

Bounty Mutiny The author of a diary account of this event, James Morrison, was a Lewisman and may have been a great-grandson of An Clàrsair Dall (q.v.). (See J. S. Grant 1981.) DST

Breadalbane, 1st Earl of (John Campbell) (*c.*1635–1717) Employed by William of Orange in 1690–1 to bribe Jacobite chiefs into submission. DS

The Breccbennach. A reliquary in the shape of an early Celtic oratory. Tradition maintains that it was once used to house the relics of St Columba. National Museum of Antiquities of Scotland.

Breccbennach, the (the 'Speckled, Peaked One') Also known as the Monymusk Reliquary. A typical Celtic Church house-shrine, of eighth-century date, made of wood decorated with metalwork. One of its later functions was to bestow victory in battle on the Scots. (See Eeles 1933–4, 433–8.) JWMB

Breve, the *see* Morrison, George.

Brian, am Bàrd Asainteach (fl. 1675) Possibly a MacMhuirich. Author of eulogy on Iain Mollach Mackenzie (*c*.1650) and of elegy on Mackenzie of Suddie (d. 1688). A flyting between him and Iain Lom survives. (See R. I. Black 1979a, 358; A. and A. MacDonald 1911, xxix; A. M. Mackenzie 1964, 261.) DST

broadcasting, Gaelic The BBC is the only source of Gaelic radio programmes in Scotland.

Gaelic was broadcast by the BBC in Scotland as early as 1923, but programmes were transmitted only very occasionally until 1935, when a Gaelic producer was appointed for the first time. Output from then on became regular, although limited to a couple of prog-rammes per week; but the operation ceased with the outbreak of the Second World War and was not resumed until towards its end. It could be said, therefore, that Gaelic broadcasting did not really get under way until 1945, when a second producer was appointed and the output gradually increased to one and a half hours per week.

In 1965 a third producer was recruited and a weekly topical magazine was added on VHF (North and West only). This to some extent foreshadowed events in 1974, when the BBC transferred all Gaelic output to VHF, except for the religious service on Sundays, which for a time remained available on MF also. The weekly output at this time was roughly three hours of fairly wide-ranging programmes; a balance of content was achieved over the year rather than in the week or month.

A Schools producer was appointed in 1975, and during the following year local broadcasting began from Radio Highland in Inverness, when three prod-ucers and three station assistants were recruited for Gaelic broadcasting. In 1979 Radio nan Eilean began broadcasting from Stornoway, with two producers and one station assistant.

The BBC currently provides the following Schools radio broadcasts to Gaelic-speaking areas: a ten-minute programme (*Culaidh Mhìogais*) for five to seven year-olds; a twenty-minute programme (*Cò Iad?*) for eight to eleven year-olds; a ten-minute programme (*Say it in Gaelic*) mainly for five to seven year-olds but deemed of use to any learner in primary school; a twenty-minute programme (*Toiseach Tòiseachaidh*) funded by Highland Regional Council, which caters for learners in upper primary and early secondary stages. The first two assume 'native-speaker' fluency on the part of pupils; the last two are scripted in English and introduce Gaelic conver-sation and constructions to learners.

A Gaelic version of *Clann Og ri Ceilear* (*Singing Together*), designed and introduced by Arthur Brock-lebank, has proved very popular over the past ten years.

This combination of developments has resulted in output increasing to over twelve hours per week, but it would seem that in spite of the varied nature of the operation there is still room for expansion, given the necessary budget and the opportunity to opt out of Radio Scotland without restriction.

The BBC's commitment to Gaelic on television has been less enthusiastic and has not progressed much from spasmodic programmes in the early

1960s. Certainly, a pattern of output in light entertainment and current affairs was established from 1965 onwards, but not until 1972 was a producer appointed expressly for television. This was followed by the appointment of a production assistant in 1979, since which time output has stabilized at about thirty programmes a year. Of these twelve are children's programmes (financed directly from London and for that reason not necessarily permanent). The remainder are of a current affairs nature with a high film content, programmes from the National Mod and the occasional film documentary, budget permitting.

To be effective, Gaelic television programmes would have to be transmitted on a regular daily or weekly basis; the BBC's output at present is a long way from achieving this.

Over the years Scottish Television has transmitted occasional series in Gaelic, but so far it has not committed itself to any regular output. Grampian TV, on the other hand, has played a significant part in Gaelic

The entrance passage of Carn Liath broch, near Golspie, Sutherland.

Mousa broch, Dunrossness, Mousa. One of two brochs which overlooked the sound between Mousa and the mainland of Shetland, this broch is unusually high, rising to over 13m. Within the thickness of the wall are three cells at ground level, with a stairway leading up through six mural galleries to the top of the surviving wall (Piggott 1982).

television broadcasting, particularly with *Cuir Car*, a very successful series for younger viewers. Grampian also provides a weekly news round-up, an important innovation which may indicate further developments. If these take place, the two commercial companies may eventually overtake the BBC in Gaelic coverage on television. Unlike the BBC, however, neither of these companies yet has posts for Gaelic producers.

FM/PM

brochs These uniquely Scottish structures appear to have been the defended homesteads of wealthy farmers and represent a high point of human achievement in building in dry-stone masonry (R. W. Feachem 1963, 1977, 162–74; Graham 1946–7; MacKie 1975). The standard ground plan is an immensely thick circular wall, enclosing a court or suite of rooms about 40 feet in diameter. Entry is by a narrow passage, defended by one or two guard chambers and closed by a stout door. There are other chambers and a staircase in the thickness of the wall. Above the ground floor the broch is carried up as a

Dun Carloway broch, Lewis. The wall still stands to a height of over 9m. The broch measures about 7.6m in diameter inside a wall up to 3.6m thick. Within the thickness of the wall is a guard cell and three other chambers. Steps from one of these give access to the interior of the wall at a higher level (Piggott 1982).

cavity wall, with inner and outer faces tied together by horizontal slabs. Some brochs rose to a height of between 33 and 40 feet, but it is likely that most were no more than two storeys (about 15–20 feet) high.

Brochs are concentrated in the Western (MacKie 1965) and Northern Isles (Hamilton 1962, 1966) and on the northern mainland, but they occur sporadically even south of the Forth. The earliest were built in the last centuries BC, with a main *floruit* in the first two centuries AD. Thereafter they rapidly became obsolete, and most were derelict before the historical Pictish period.   LA

brooches, early Celtic To fasten their cloaks the Pictish, Scottish and British nobility used penannular brooches, that is, brooches consisting of a long pin which was passed through the folds of the garment and was then secured by a hoop which locked behind the pin. To facilitate this the hoop normally had a gap: hence the term penannular. The brooches were of bronze or silver and might be gilded or ornamented with filigree, amber or glass inlays, or enamelling. The decorative motifs included both zoomorphic elements (Kilbride-Jones 1980), ultimately of Germanic origin, and Insular curvilinear patterns. Outstanding examples are the Hunterston (Ayrshire) brooch (R. B. K. Stevenson 1974) and those in the St Ninian's Isle treasure (q.v.), but most excavated sites yield evidence of brooch manufacture.   LA

Brown, Dorothy, *see* Nic a' Bhriuthainn, Diorbhail.

Brown, Revd John (1722–87) Minister of Haddington and author of two Catechisms, translated into Gaelic by MacDonald (an SSPCK teacher), of which 3,000 copies were published in 1764 and distributed by the author's sons, the Revd Ebenezer and the Revd John Brown. (See *DNB*; Harding 1980, 35.)
                                                                DST

Bruce, George James (1869–19?) From Helmsdale. Active official of Highland Land League *c.*1913. Contested Inverness-shire, 1918. (See Macbean 1921.)
                                                                DST

The Hunterston brooch. A richly decorated ring brooch of the eighth century. National Museum of Antiquities of Scotland.

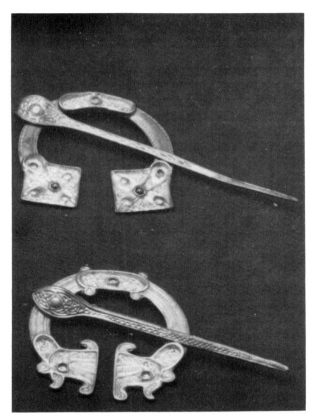

Two silver-gilt pennanular brooches from the St Ninian's Isle treasure (much reduced). National Museum of Antiquities of Scotland.

fication with Craig Phàdraig is now rejected), where his court included a 'magician' – druid and a sub-king of Orkney. He entertained Colum Cille (q.v.); Adamnán does not say that he was converted, but later Pictish sources do, and certainly the conversion of Pictland began in his time. The extent of his kingdom, particularly to the south, is uncertain. He may have died in a battle in 'Circinn'. (See A. O. and M. O. Anderson 1961; M. O. Anderson 1973; I. Henderson 1967.)   AAMD

Buchan, Revd Alexander (d. 1730) A long-serving soldier from the Gaelic area of Aberdeenshire. From 1705 catechist, schoolmaster and minister in St Kilda, of which he wrote an account. (See *Fasti*, VII, 193; A. Buchan 1818.)   TMM

Buchanan, Dugald, *see* Bochanan, Dùghall.

Buchanan, George (1506–82) Born at Killearn, Stirlingshire. Became one of the outstanding Latinists of Europe. He enjoyed the patronage of Queen Mary until her downfall, when he composed vile libels about her. Nevertheless, his few comments about Gaelic society are valuable. (See Aikman 1827–9.)   IG

Brudei mac Bili King of Fortriu, ?672–93 and probably over-king of the Picts. Son of Bili, king of Dumbarton (a good example of Pictish exogamy). He took over a Pictish kingdom partly dominated by Anglian Northumbria. He may have been responsible for the sieges of Dunottar, Dunadd and Dundurn (681–3) and certainly devastated Orkney in 682. In 685 King Egfrith of Northumbria invaded and was crushingly defeated at Dunnichen (Nectansmere), near Forfar, by Brudei, who claimed that he was fighting 'for the inheritance of his grandfather' – a puzzling reference, since his grandfather can scarcely have been a Pictish king. The Angles were expelled from Pictland. (See A. O. and M. O. Anderson 1961; M. O. Anderson 1973; I. Henderson 1967.)   AAMD

Brudei mac Maelchon King of Picts, ?555–?584. Vividly described in Adamnán's life of Colum Cille (q.v.) as having a hall near the river Ness (the identi-

C

Caimbeul, Alasdair (d. *c.*1810) From Atholl. Bard. Author of poem about eighteen people who were drowned while being ferried across the river at Invergarry in 1767. (See P. Cameron 1892.)   DST

Caimbeul, Aonghas (Bàrd Eadarra-Mhucaidh) (*c.*1740–1814) From Perthshire. Collection, 1785. (See P. Cameron 1892.)   DST

Caimbeul, Aonghas (am Bocsair) (1908–49) Born Ness, Lewis. Versatile poet in the traditional mould, distinguished by tunefulness and lyrical sweetness.

Poems on nature and on philosophical themes (some over 100 lines long), love lyrics and genuinely amusing comic poems are among sixty-four of his poems collected in *Bàrdachd a' Bhocsair* (1978).

IMCD

Caimbeul, Aonghas (1903–82), *see* Puilean, am.

Caimbeul, Daibhidh (1797–1830) From Loch Rannochside. Bard and author of fine lovesong 'Oran Seasaidh Chois-a-Bhileadh'. (See P. Cameron 1892.)

DST

Caimbeul, Dòmhnall, *see* Dòmhnall Phàil.

Caimbeul, Gilleasbuig (1804– post-1881) From Bun-Raineach but lived later in Lochearnhead. Bard. Collection, 1851. (See also P. Cameron 1892.) DST

Caimbeul, Iain (fl. 1760) From Perthshire. Bard. (See P. Cameron 1892.) DST

Caimbeul, Iain (1823–97) Born in Oban but always associated with Ledaig in Benderloch, where he grew up and spent most of his life. Pieces such as 'Is Toigh Leam a' Ghaidhealtachd' and 'Taobh Mo Theine Féin' were collected in *Poems* (1884). IMCD

Caimbeul, Maoilios M. (1944–   ) Born Staffin, Skye. Author of collection of poems, *Eileanan* (1980).

DST

Caimbeul, Pàdraig (1789–1867) From Glen Lyon. Bard and schoolmaster. (See P. Cameron 1892.) DST

Caimbeul, Seonaidh mac Dhòmhnaill 'ic Iain Bhàin (1859–1944) Born in South Lochboisdale, South Uist. Bard and storyteller. Made first recording of traditional Gaelic anecdote for BBC in 1935. Manuscript of songs in George Henderson papers (Glasgow University Library) and in Canna papers. (See S. Caimbeul 1936; J. L. Campbell 1939, 1955–77.)

JLC

Calbhach O Donnell, an, *see* Argyll/An Calbhach Treaty.

Calder, Revd Dr George (1859–1941) Born in Kincardineshire. Minister at Strathfillan and lecturer in Celtic at the University of Glasgow, 1912–35. Edited Irish texts and Gaelic poems of Duncan Bàn MacIntyre (q.v.) and William Ross (q.v.). Published a Gaelic grammar (1923). (See J. Cameron 1941; A. Mackay 1912.)

TMM

Caledonian Canal A report presented by Thomas Telford (q.v.) in 1803 endorsed earlier recommendations by James Watt (1774) and John Rennie (1793) for the construction of a waterway from Fort William to Inverness, the main reason advanced being the need for a more rapid and safer passage to either coast of Scotland, particularly in times of war.

The Caledonian Canal was built between 1803 and 1824. Delays arose as a result of land-acquisition problems, and construction difficulties were posed by the poor foundation conditions and the escalation of costs from the original estimate of £474,000 to over £900,000.

The Canal was virtually obsolete by the time it was completed as a consequence of the development of steam propulsion. HBS

Calgacus In his *Agricola* Tacitus depicts the inhabitants of the region north of the Forth (whom he calls *Caledonii*) as having many leaders, of whom the chief was Calgacus. In AD 83 and 84 the Romans marched north of the Forth; on the second occasion Agricola appears to have penetrated to the Moray Firth where he was engaged by Calgacus whom he heavily defeated. The site of the battle, Mons Graupius, is still unidentified. Tacitus attributes to Calgacus a fine speech ('They make a desert and call it peace'), which represents his own criticism of Roman policy. The name Calgacus may be cognate with Gaelic *calg* (point, or sword). (See Ogilvie and Richmond 1967; Richmond 1958.)

AAMD

Call Ghàdhaig (the Loss of Gaick) Refers to the death of five huntsmen in a snowstorm in Badenoch in January 1800. (See Sinton 1906, 273–86.) DST

Callanish, *see* stone circles.

calquing, *see* Gaelic: calquing.

Calum Dubh nam Protaigean (Malcolm Macintyre) (fl. 1800) Author of poem on Call Ghàdhaig (q.v.). DST

Calum Sgàire (Calum MacAulay) (nineteenth century) From Bernera, Lewis. Bard and author of 'Och hi-rì gur trom m'osna'. (See I. N. MacLeòid 1916, 188.)

DST

The Caledonian canal at Fort Augustus, in the background the flight of locks. c. 1880s.

Cameron, Alasdair (Bàrd Thùrnaig) (1848– post-1928) His poems, some essays and letters are to be found in Moffatt-Pender (1926). DST

Cameron, Alexander (d. 1788) From Lochaber. Jacobite poet. (See J. L. Campbell 1933.) DST

Cameron, Revd Dr Alexander (1827–88) From Badenoch. Free Church minister at Renton and Brodick. Pioneer Celtic philologist, transcriber of ancient manuscripts and translator of hymns. Conducted Gaelic class in Glasgow for divinity students. (See J. Kennedy 1892.) TMM

Cameron, Dugald Roy (fl. 1745) From Lochaber. Jacobite poet. (See J. L. Campbell 1933.) DST

Cameron, Ewen (d. 1660) Minister of Dunoon from 1626. Son of John, minister there from 1610, who was himself probably son of Ewen, minister there from 1590. Helped Dugald Campbell (q.v.) in translating into Gaelic psalms, Shorter Catechism and *Brief Sum of Christian Doctrine*. (See *Fasti*; MacTavish 1934.) IG

Cameron, Sir Ewen, of Lochiel (1629–1719) The most famous of the Royalist and Jacobite chiefs of the seventeenth century. (See Drummond 1842.) DS

Cameron, John (fl. 1745) From Lochaber. Poet and author of praise song for Dr Archibald Cameron, who was later hanged at Tyburn (1753) for participating in the '45. (See J. L. Campbell 1933.) DST

Cameron, Dr John (1882–1950) From Mull. Practised as a lawyer in Glasgow. President of An Comunn Gaidhealach (q.v.), 1946–9. (See Murchison 1950, 115.) TMM

Cameron, Margaret (fl. ?1760) From Badenoch. Poet. (See Sinton 1906.) DST

Campbell, Alexander (1764–1824) Editor of *Albyn's Anthology* (1816–18), a collection of Gaelic songs with melodies, Gaelic texts and English translations, some by Walter Scott, who took music lessons from Campbell. (See C. Lamont 1975.) DST

Campbell, Angus, *see* Bàrd Sgallach.

Campbell, Archibald (1607–61), *see* Argyll, 1st Marquis of.

Campbell, Archibald (1629–85), *see* Argyll, 9th Earl of.

Campbell, Lord Archibald (1846–1913) Second son of 8th Duke of Argyll; father of 10th Duke. First president of An Comunn Gaidhealach (q.v.). Wrote on Highland dress, etc., and edited two notable collections of folktales and historical traditions (See Lord A. Campbell 1885, 1889–95.)   AB

Campbell, Colin (1644–1726) Minister of the parish of Ardchattan and Muckairn and younger son of Patrick (Dubh Beag) Campbell of Innergeldies. Had the reputation of being one of the most profound mathematicians and scholars of his day. It is claimed that Sir Isaac Newton, in a letter to Professor James Gregory that appears no longer to be extant, wrote of him: 'I see that were he among us he would make children of us all.' (See *DNB*, 1886, 348.)   RAR

Campbell, Donald (1690–1783) From Scalpay, Harris. Forester in Harris. Gave shelter to Prince Charles in 1746. Emigrated to North Carolina. (See MacChoinnich 1906, 144–5; M. M. McKay 1980.)   DST

Campbell, Archbishop Donald (1894–1963) Born Lochaber. Roman Catholic Archbishop of Glasgow, 1945–63.   DST

Campbell, Donnchadh Dubh (1550–1631) Laird of Glenorchy, who was knighted in 1590. He greatly increased his landed possessions, partly at the expense of the persecuted Clan Gregor. His remarkable range of interests included afforestation and a considerable building programme (Innes 1855, 23–72). He is the subject of a fine elegy in the classical Gaelic tradition, now preserved in Register House in an elaborate presentation copy. (See W. J. Watson 1917, 6–10.)   JWMB

Campbell, Dugald (1599–1673) Son of Patrick of Stuck, son of Donald, first of Kilmory. Minister of Knapdale from 1620 and of Kilmallie from 1658. Father of Patrick, minister of Glenaray, and of Duncan (c.1630–1711), minister of Knapdale. Helped by Duncan, he was partly responsible for Gaelic translations of fifty psalms (*Caogad*) published in 1658–9 and of the Shorter Catechism and *Brief Sum of Christian Doctrine*. (See *Fasti*; MacTavish 1934.)   IG

Campbell, Sir Duncan (?1443–1513) of Glenorchy. Eldest son of Colin, first of Glenorchy, and Margaret Stewart. Laird of Glenorchy from 1480 until his death at Flodden in 1513 (J. R. N. MacPhail 1914–34, 1.142, 2.95–8; W. J. Watson 1937, 260). He

played an important part in the expansion of Campbell influence into Breadalbane. One side of this imperialism was the preferment of men who gave their allegiance to Campbell chiefs – for example, the Fortingall MacGregors, who compiled the Book of the Dean of Lismore (q.v.), by whom Sir Duncan was termed *an Ridire Math* ('the Good Knight').

The Dean's Book commemorates another side of Duncan's activity in nine mostly humorous and bawdy poems by him (W. Gillies 1978–83). It also contains literary efforts by several Argyll and Perthshire men whose names appear to be linked with the Glenorchy family in documentary sources, and it may be permissible to infer, on these and other grounds, the existence of a literary coterie of which Duncan was a leading member.   WG

Campbell, Duncan (1827–1916) Editor of the *Northern Chronicle*, 1881–1907, and author of *Reminiscences of an Octogenarian Highlander* (Glen Lyon background: 1910).   DST

Campbell, Revd Dr Duncan MacGregor (1854–1938) Born Benderloch. Minister of Cumlodden, 1889–1901; teacher and collector of Gaelic folktales (Lord A. Campbell 1889, 46), words (Dwelly 1920, iii), proverbs (D. M. Campbell 1978), songs and other lore.   AB

Campbell, James C. M. (d. 1980) Born Dornie. Banker in London, where he also studied singing. Mod Gold Medallist, 1928. Outstanding singer of the òran mór (see **song, Gaelic**).   CG

Campbell, John (1635–1717), *see* Breadalbane, 1st Earl of.

Campbell, John Francis (Iain Òg Ìle) (1822–85) From Islay. Aristocrat, courtier, lawyer, public servant, world traveller and man of many talents. Today best remembered for his work on Gaelic oral tradition. In 1859, inspired by the example of the Grimm brothers in Germany and by Scandinavian scholars, he 'set to work in earnest to gather the popular tales of the West Highlands'. He enlisted the help of competent writers of Gaelic such as Hector MacLean (q.v.), Hector Urquhart, John Dewar, Alexander Carmichael (q.v.) and numerous friends and correspondents. His declared aim was to capture, as nearly as possible, the exact words of the storytellers and to translate them literally. Some of the

"and the hen said.
"Leig mo eoin leam
" mo cuid do'n eorna
Leave me my birds My share of the corn
and the cock pecked her. and she started out from
him and said.
Geog Geog Geōa
a cuimhne leat an latha 's
chuir mi bathiach falamh
air do shon.
I an cuimhne leat an latha
a thuibh mi n sabhal
air do shon. -
I an cuimhne leat an latha
glac mi n' fhailain
air do shon. -
I an cuimhne leat an latha
bhath mi m'athair
air do shon. —

Some lines from John Francis Campbell's manuscript 'The Battle of the Birds', National Library of Scotland Adv. MS 50.1.1. f. 78, published in Popular Tales of the West Highlands *(1890). In translation the verse reads: . . . dost thou remember the day/that I emptied the byre for thee/dost thou remember the day/that I thatched the barn for thee/dost thou remember the day that I caught the filly for thee/dost thou remember the day/that I drowned my father for thee.*

results can be seen in the splendid collection of manuscripts in the National Library of Scotland and in the Dewar Manuscripts at Inveraray. Published works include *Popular Tales of the West Highlands*, 4 vols. (1860–2); *Leabhar na Féinne* (1872) and, posthumously, *More West Highland Tales*, 2 vols. (1940, 1960), edited by the late J. G. McKay, *et al.*

DAMCD

Campbell, Revd John Gregorson (1836–91) Born Kingairloch. Minister of Tiree (Kirkapol) from 1860. Collected folktales, historical traditions and belief legends, which he published (often in English paraphrases with significant words of Gaelic noted) in journals. His work is represented in *The Fians* (Lord A. Campbell 1891b) and in three posthumous selections (J. G. Campbell 1895, 1900, 1902).

AB

Campbell, John Macmaster (1859–1938) Born Inverness. One of the founders of the Glasgow Gaelic Society (q.v.) and of An Comunn Gaidhealach (q.v.). Sheriff-Substitute of Argyllshire.   DST

Campbell of Canna (John Lorne) (b. 1906). Author and editor of numerous works on Gaelic language and literature, local and natural history; particularly noted for his work on Gaelic oral tradition and song and for his outstanding achievements as a collector. Using various types of recording machinery, since 1937 he has built up a magnificent sound archive of songs, tales and traditions from informants in both Canada and Scotland, but particularly from sources in South Uist and Barra. (See bibliography.)   DAMCD

Campbell's Highlanders, *see* regiments, Highland.

Campbells and Macleans, rise and conflict The Campbells first attained prominence as supporters of the Bruces during the Wars of Independence. Before the mid-fifteenth century Donnchadh, grandfather of the 1st Earl, was accounted one of the wealthiest barons in Scotland. The family early developed ambitions in the national context, but they also operated within the traditional framework of clan politics, retaining a healthy respect for the Lordship of the Isles and enjoying the latter's goodwill (Gregory 1836, 84–5, 126–7; Steer and Bannerman 1977, 210–11).

Maclean traditions likewise claim support for the Bruces. The brothers Lachlann and Eachann, founders of the Duart and Lochbuie houses, were apparently *protégés* of John, Lord of the Isles, who preferred them to lands formerly possessed by the MacDougalls (from whose decline the Campbells also profited) and the Mackinnons (A. M. Sinclair 1899, 44–53; Steer and Bannerman 1977, 105).

After the break-up of the Lordship, the principal powers in the southern Highlands were the MacDonalds of Islay, the Macleans (whose several branches collectively held most of Mull, Tiree and Coll and also lands in Morvern, Lochaber, Islay, Jura and Knapdale) and the Campbells (now masters of much of mainland Argyll and of a corridor extending from Lochawe eastwards into Perthshire). Whereas the MacDonalds and Macleans did not transcend the old system of loyalties based on kinship, the Campbells evolved a more positive response to the Crown's increasing concern with Highland affairs, proffering

themselves as intermediaries between the state and their more backward-looking neighbours. As early as 1514 the Earl of Argyll was commissioned to suppress insurrection by Macleans and others; similar lieutenancies followed in 1529 and on many subsequent occasions.

The sixteenth century saw the Macleans at the height of their power. This involved them in serious conflict with the Camerons and with the MacDonalds of Islay, not to mention internecine strife. The Earls of Argyll were often concerned in these quarrels, either through marriage and other ties or as mediators, and they not infrequently intervened in the Maclean interest – provided such action would help to enhance their own standing and influence in the southern Highlands as a whole. Before the end of the century, however, the Campbells were pursuing territorial ambitions beyond the mere extension of their influence and using all available means to gain new territories. The Macleans were obvious targets for their imperial designs (Campbell and Thomson 1963, 17–22; Gregory 1836, 426–7; Steer and Bannerman 1977, 211–13).

The Campbell assault on the Macleans hinged on the financial enslavement of their chiefs. In 1642 Argyll, having bought over certain rents outstanding from the Macleans, presented Lachlan of Duart with a bill for £30,000. This tactic was repeated several times (the alleged debt eventually totalling £200,000) until in the 1670s the Campbells used these debts as the pretext for laying claim to the Maclean lands and rentals. In 1679 the last Maclean strongholds were surrendered to Argyll, who received a general commission to proceed against any Macleans who resisted him at any time. He soon stimulated resistance, crushed it and, in 1681, was granted the coveted Duart lands; although Argyll himself was soon forced to flee the country, they remained Crown property and were confirmed to the Campbells after the Revolution. Macleans figured prominently in the risings of 1715 and 1745, but their legal superiors were Campbells from that time on. (See C. Ó Baoill 1979, xxxvii–xliii and *passim*; A. M. Sinclair 1899, 178–246.)   WG

Camshron, Pàra (d. *c*.1836) From Atholl. Bard. (See P. Cameron 1892.)   DST

Camshron, Somhairle (d. *c*.1792) From Rannoch. Bard. Author of 'Mi 'm shuidhe 'm ònar'. (See P. Cameron 1892.)   DST

canntaireachd, *see* bagpipe, Highland.

Caogad, *see* Campbell, Dugald; psalms, metrical.

Caraid nan Gaidheal (Friend of The Gaels) (Revd Dr Norman MacLeod, 1783–1862) The sobriquet was bestowed on Dr MacLeod in recognition of his work in the Highlands on education and for organizing relief during the distress of the 1830s and 1840s. He was instrumental in promoting the Church of Scotland's educational scheme for the Highlands and Islands and in securing publication of a quarto edition of the Gaelic Bible. With the assistance of Thaddeus Connellan, he produced an Irish Gaelic version of the metrical psalms for the Church of Ireland.

In addition to sermons and dialogues on ecclesiastical issues, MacLeod's major works are *A Gaelic Collection for the Use of Schools* (1828–34), two periodicals, *An Teachdaire Gaelach* (1829–31) and *Cuairtear nan Gleann* (1840–43), with Dr Daniel Dewar *A Dictionary of the Gaelic Language* (1831, many editions), and *Leabhar nan Cnoc* (1834). A selection of his prose writings was published in 1867 under the title of *Caraid nan Gaidheal*, with subsequent editions.

MacLeod is one of the leading figures in the history of Gaelic prose. His declared aim for the periodicals which he founded and edited, and to which he contributed much original material, was to provide his readers with 'every kind of useful information' which had hitherto been 'locked up in English books'. In these and other works there are articles on history, geography, the natural sciences, current affairs, religious topics, as well as descriptive essays and book reviews. Stylistically the intention was to develop from the pre-existing traditions, written and oral, a formal standard Gaelic prose which could handle a wide range of subject-matter. MacLeod's success lay in exposition, where his Gaelic at its best has a classical strength and clarity, rather than in creative writing, the style of which too often tends to be dull and unwieldy. In spite of this, and because almost everywhere he was breaking new ground, he created a genuinely popular readership, and the standards that he set influenced Gaelic writers for over a century. JMcI

Carmichael, Alexander (1832–1912) Born Lismore. Reputedly of the same family as An t-Easbuig Bàn

Alexander Carmichael, as he appears in the frontispiece to Carmina Gadelica, *1900.*

(the Fair Bishop). Worked as an exciseman, serving in Islay, Skye, Uist and Oban, among other places. Contributed papers on antiquarian topics to the *Transactions of the Society of Antiquaries of Scotland*, to J. F. Campbell's (q.v.) *Popular Tales of the West Highlands* and *Leabhar na Féinne*, Dr Alexander Nicolson's (q.v.) *Proverbs*, *Transactions of the Gaelic Society of Inverness*, *Celtic Review*, etc. Contributed chapter on land customs to Skene's *Celtic Scotland* and to Napier Commission Report. His daughter Ella was married to W. J. Watson (q.v.). His greatest monument is the material he collected, and in part edited, for *Carmina Gadelica* (q.v.). (See obituary and tribute in *Celtic Review*, October 1912.) DST

Carmichael, Elizabeth (Ella) (d.1929) Daughter of Alexander Carmichael (q.v.), mother of J. C. Watson (q.v.). Editor of the *Celtic Review*, 1904–16. Instituted, with her brothers, The Celtic Union, The Edinburgh Gaelic Choir and other bodies.   DST

Carmina Gadelica A large and fascinating collection of Gaelic lore, mostly in the form of verse, made by Alexander Carmichael (q.v.) between 1855 and 1899 (*see* Carmichael 1900, Introduction). Five volumes of texts and translations have been published (vols. 1 and 2, 1900 and reprinted 1928; vol. 3, 1940; vol. 4, 1941; vol. 5, 1954) and a volume of indexes (1971). The original two volumes of 1900 were edited by Carmichael, the reprint by his daughter Elizabeth Carmichael (q.v.), volume 3 and 4 by his grandson, J. C. Watson (q.v.), and volume 5 and 6 by Angus Matheson (q.v.).

The material includes the following as main categories: invocations (e.g. prayers for protection, justice, before sleep, house blessing, baptism and death blessings); seasonal hymns or prayers; addresses to saints (especially Bride and Michael); blessings for common or everyday tasks (e.g. smooring or banking up the fire, reaping, grinding with the quern, milking, weaving, herding, hunting); incantations or charms (e.g. for the skin condition known as 'rose', toothache, jaundice, sprain, evil eye, stye, indigestion), many of these using herbal specifics such as yarrow, St John's Wort, catkin wool; prayers for baptism, morning prayers, prayers for protection, supplication of the saints, invocations of the Graces, journey prayers, prayers to moon and sun; rhymes about animals and birds; blessings on cattle and stock; milking songs; waulking songs; fairy songs; auguries; miscellaneous songs, including songs of love and praise songs. There is classification within volumes, but certain classes recur within two or three volumes, since different methods of editorial selection were involved.

The material is rich and varied; it clearly represents a lengthy time-span in terms of composition, as it contains many archaic forms and obsolete words (e.g. *cumhal mhuinntir*, 'serving maid'), many of which were interpreted, or had their meaning guessed at, by Carmichael, who supplied translations that are often ornate and stately. Many of the items are marked by simplicity and piety and reflect an intense spiritual and communal life. Some are clearly of pagan origin, although sometimes adapted to Christian needs.

The names and provenance of reciters are given in most cases, and it is clear, as Carmichael says in his Introduction, that 'The greater portion of the collection has been made in the Western Isles,' usually from people in humble circumstances. It is apparent from internal evidence that a significant proportion of the material is of literary as opposed to 'folk' origin, however, and probably much was composed in places other than the Western Isles. This is sometimes evident in the language – as, for instance, in the frequent instances of undiphthongized *io* attested in rhyming position (e.g. *mìn: dìon: lìon; ìsleach: Crìosda; Chrìosd: mì; Iosa: sìthe*), or in the rhyming of *oidhche* with *fìor, tìr, dhìon*, or in the use of *teine* as a feminine noun, or of specific lexical items. There are few specific ascriptions ('Altach Shomhairle Mhic Calmain' in vol. 3, 54, may contain one such, 'an clèireach stucanach', vol. 2, 168, another). The literary affiliations of much of this matter with Gaelic and Latin hymns has not yet been closely investigated. It may be that some of the material was popularized in the Western Isles and elsewhere by the Franciscan Mission (q.v.) in the early seventeenth century, but probably a pre-Reformation origin can be postulated for many items.

The collection, especially Carmichael's notes on lore heard from reciters, contains a wealth of curious information – for example, the survival of bears to the mid-sixteenth century (vol. 2, 327) and of religious fairs in relatively recent times (vol. 3, 141), traditions about Allan of Clanranald, d. 1715 (vol. 2, 26). Some recent work (H. Robertson 1976) has examined critically some of Carmichael's editorial methods, and has provoked a spirited rejoinder (J. L. Campbell 1978), but much analysis and assessment of this body of material, including dating, remains to be done.
    DST

Carswell, John (?1520/5–72) A native of the parish of Kilmartin in Argyll. Translator of the Book of Common Order into Gaelic in 1567. He graduated MA from The University of St Andrews in 1544. By 1551 he had taken orders and was treasurer of the Cathedral of Lismore. He became rector of Kilmartin in 1553 and of Southwick and Kingarth in Bute in 1558. Most significant, he was chaplain to the Earl of Argyll. After the Reformation in 1560 Carswell was appointed one of the five superintendents, his district being the old dioceses of Argyll and the Isles, and in 1567 he was presented to the bishopric of the Isles. He was buried in the priory of Ardchattan.

Carswell's translation of the Book of Common Order, entitled *Foirm na n-Urrnuidheadh*, was the first book to be printed in Gaelic. The language is generally the standard literary Irish of the time rather than vernacular Scottish Gaelic, but in the catechism (q.v.), which he added, the language is simpler, and Scottish syntax and vocabulary are in evidence throughout. (See R. L. Thomson 1970.)   RLT

Cassillis, Earl of (Archibald Kennedy) (1872–*c*.1943) Wrote on the Gael in Carrick and Galloway. Presented Cassillis Cup for literary competitions, National Mod.   DST

castles, *see* architecture, medieval Highland.

catechisms, early Gaelic The earliest reformed catechism in Scottish Gaelic is that of Carswell (q.v.) in his Book of Common Order (1567). It was based on Calvin's little Catechism but considerably expanded. Calvin's larger Catechism appeared in Scottish Gaelic *c*.1630 (the unique copy lacks the title page). The translator is thus not directly known but was probably the poet Neil MacEwen (see *MacEwen poets*), to judge by the literary Irish character of the language. The Shorter Catechism of the Westminster Assembly (1648) was translated by ministerial members of the Synod of Argyll in 1653 (second edition, 1659). It is the first printed text to exhibit unmistakably Scottish Gaelic characteristics. (See R. L. Thomson 1962, 1970, 1971.)   RLT

Cathach, *see* manuscripts, illuminated.

Catholic Church, *see* Roman Catholic Church.

Catholic Church in Nova Scotia, *see* Nova Scotia, Roman Catholic Church in.

'Ceatharnach Caol Riabhach, An' ('The Lean, Grizzled Kern') Sixteenth-century tale satirizing contemporary Irish chiefs made ridiculous by the supernatural Kern. Remembered as folktale in Scotland probably because of its elaborate wording, which makes it a showpiece. (See MacDonald and Bruford 1970.)   AB

Céli Dé (Clients of God) A reform movement within the late eighth-century monastic Church in Ireland and Scotland, which borrowed *céle* in its technical sense from the contemporary kin-based society. Emphasizing again the asceticism of the early anchorites, they founded new monasteries or became a distinct element in existing monasteries (Hughes 1966, 173–93). They were particularly strong in Scotland, with communities at Iona, at Dunkeld less certainly, and at St Andrews, the three successive administrative centres of the Dark Age Church. The twelfth-century reorganization of the Church saw their conversion into canons, regular and secular. (See Cowan and Easson 1976, 46–51.)   JWMB

Celtic Church, the (sixth to twelfth centuries). The sixth century AD saw the rapid expansion in Ireland of a monastic Church which had its roots in the third-century religious communities of the Egyptian desert (Hughes 1966, 10–16). From Ireland it spread to Scotland, particularly in the person of Colum Cille (q.v.), who was to become the paramount saint of the Scots. He arrived in 563 and founded his monastery on Iona *c*.565. In the interval he may have made his famous journey to the stronghold of Brudei mac-Maelchon (q.v.), king of the Picts, near Inverness. His lasting friendship with, and apparent conversion of, Brudei facilitated the extension of the Church into Pictland, so that Iona, Bede tells us, 'held for a long time pre-eminence over the monasteries of all the Picts'. Oswald, king of Northumbria, educated at Iona, sent there for help in converting his people to Christianity, and in response Bishop Aedán (q.v.) founded a monastery in 635 on the island of Lindisfarne, which became the centre of the Celtic Church in Northumbria and played a considerable part in the conversion of the southern Anglo-Saxon kingdoms. Finally, many important monasteries in northern Ireland, such as Derry and Durrow, both founded by Colum Cille himself, looked to Iona as their superior. Iona was thus at the apex of the most extensive *paruchia* of monasteries in the Celtic Church (Colgrave and Mynors 1969, 218–20; Bannerman 1971, 67).

The typical monastery, often sited on an island, was a complex of separate establishments enclosed within a *vallum*, or wall, delimiting an area of sanctity which should not be violated. The wall surrounding the monastery of Iona is still visible in part. But the main feature was the church. The monks had separate sleeping huts or cells. There was a *domus*, or common house, in Colum Cille's time, probably a refectory and kitchen combined. There was too an *hospitium*, or hospice, where guests were received, and doubtless a school, *scriptorium* and workshops for metalworkers and stonemasons (A. O. and M. O. Anderson 1961, 105–18).

The emphasis on learning in all its aspects was a notable characteristic of the Celtic Church, which accorded well with a society which placed its learned class on something of a pedestal. In turn this class was a fertile recruiting ground for a missionary Church, and the result was a fusion of Christian and Mediterranean cultural influences with pagan and vernacular learning. Perhaps the pre-eminent intellectual centre of the early Celtic Church was Iona. Colum Cille set the trend; portrayed by Adamnán, abbot of Iona (q.v.), as an accomplished Latin scribe and scholar, he was also a poet in the vernacular, according to early tradition. The surviving eighth-century ringed crosses (q.v.) at Iona are sufficient evidence for stone carving of the highest quality. Recently excavated on Iona were two moulds for producing inlaid glass beads for metalwork, which bear a motif present in the Book of Kells, as indeed do the ringed crosses. The Book of Kells, almost certainly begun at Iona towards the end of the eighth century and perhaps completed there, is surely the supreme example of the school of manuscript illumination (q.v.) that has been described as 'the finest flower of

Manuscript illumination from the Book of Kells. Trinity College Dublin MS 58, f.129v.

Celtic art' (Dillon and Chadwick 1967, 287–321; Bannerman 1971, 72–4).

The Celtic and Roman or continental versions of the universal Church clashed in England, where their spheres of influence met, though the dispute was not over the fundamental difference, which was one of organization (monasticism versus episcopalianism), but over points of observance, like the date of Easter and the shape of the tonsure. The Synod of Whitby was convened c.664 by Oswiu, king of Northumbria. Although trained in the Celtic Church, Oswiu favoured the arguments of the Roman party, and its date for Easter was preferred. Those of the Columban clergy who refused to conform retired to Iona, and a rapid penetration of Roman Church organization followed in Northumbria. Iona itself finally accepted the new date of Easter in 716, but it is important to realize that the monastic organization of the Church in Dalriada remained unaltered, and there is evidence to show that, if anything, Iona's influence in Ireland increased as the century progressed. The Church in Pictland seems to have accepted the Roman date of Easter in 717. Since this move was accompanied by the expulsion of the Columban clergy – although probably only those unwilling to accept the change and perhaps unaware of Iona's decision of the previous year – Roman Church organization may have made some headway there. However, the evidence is slight, and it was doubtless checked and probably reversed on the takeover of Pictland by the Scots c.843. (See Bannerman 1962, 116; Dickinson 1961, 46–9.)

At the beginning of the eighth century the *rapprochement* between the Pictish king Nechtan, son of Derile (706–c.?729), and the Church of Northumbria, brought decisively within the Roman fold by the Synod of Whitby, seemed to herald a new era for Scottish Christianity. The monks of Iona had been banished to the west; the up-to-date Catholic tonsure and Easter dating had been imposed upon the Church of Pictland; and Nechtan had even imported masons to build for him a newfangled stone church to be dedicated to St Peter (probably represented by Restenneth, near Forfar, with which the telltale name Egglespether, Peter's Church, was associated in a twelfth-century charter). But although there is evidence of a Petrine cult that ran up the eastern seaboard of Scotland as far as the Moray Firth and of minor cults of Northumbrian saints (for instance, Cuthbert, Oswald and the obscure Alhmund of Kennethmont, Aberdeenshire), the outcome of Nechtan's dealings with Bede's monastery of Jarrow-Monkwearmouth was probably quite different from what Nechtan and the English Church had intended. Northumbria became irreversibly weakened during the eighth century, at the close of which it fell easy prey to full-scale Scandinavian invasion, leading to the conversion of Christian Deira into a heathen Danish kingdom of York, which endured until 954.

Pictland had no contacts with southern England, still less with Rome, and the seventh-century romanizing impetus was lost. Moreover, the Pictish kingdom, after the apparently triumphant reign of Onuist, son of Urguist (Oengus MacFerguso), underwent an internal collapse similar to that of Northumberland, and by 843 Kenneth, son of Alpín (q.v.), king of the Scots of Dalriada (who had never become absorbed by the Pictish-speaking peoples occupying the main part of Scotland north of Clyde and Forth), made himself ruler of the Picts as well and inaugurated a truly Scoto-Pictish dynasty and realm.

Little is known of the Church in northern Scotland between the time of Nechtan, son of Derile, and the reign of Giric, son of Dungal, towards the end of the ninth century. Such scanty evidence as exists suggests that Irish influences were reasserted, especially after the union of the Scots and Picts. Norse attacks and settlement would have made the survival of Christianity problematical for a time in the far north and in the Western Isles. An early tradition credits King Giric with giving liberty to the Scottish Church, 'hitherto in servitude, as it normally was under Pictish rule'.

It may be assumed that by the tenth century Gaelic had become the *lingua franca* of Scotland north of Clyde and Forth, and in this area there is evidence of some thirty monastic or quasi-monastic communities. Their distribution is very uneven, few being recorded for the west Highland seaboard and none at all for the Western Isles or (excepting Rosemarkie) for the mainland north of Strath Tay and west of upper Banffshire and Aberdeenshire. The largest churches, Cennrigmonaid (St Andrews), Abernethy on the Tay, Brechin and possibly Dunkeld, acquired strongly marked Irish characteristics and were provided with communities following the 8th-century Irish monastic reforming movement whose adherents called themselves Céli Dé (q.v.) ('Culdees' in later popular usage). Besides their association with the most important churches, Céli Dé were established at some dozen sites, all (except for Iona) in eastern Scotland.

The degree to which the still obviously 'Celtic' Church in northern Scotland before the later 11th century was episcopally ruled or organized is still debatable. Of the existence of bishops at certain chief churches (e.g. St Andrews, Dunkeld) there is no doubt, and it would hardly be rash to posit a true episcopal succession at least at St Andrews. But there seems little evidence of any system of territorial dioceses or episcopal hierarchy, the titles *ardescop* and *primescop* accorded to St Andrews bishops certainly not implying metropolitan authority. Place names preserve many traces of features familiar in contemporary Ireland: *cill* for a small stone church or shrine (Kil-); *díseart* for a monastic retreat (Dysart); *apdaine*, abbot's jurisdiction and hence territory (Appin, Abdie, Abden); *scrín*, shrine (Scryne); *termon*, boundary of monastic sanctuary (Tillytarmont), etc. The probability seems to be that instead of territorial dioceses composed of territorial parishes each with its 'mother Church', the Christian faith in Scotland between the eighth and the twelfth centuries was sustained by a clerical caste divided into fully monastic and quasi-monastic communities (who, with a handful of bishops, would constitute the élite), schools nourishing the Old Irish literary and scriptural tradition, priests attached to the very numerous smaller churches or shrines scattered widely across the country, small congregations of hermits and clerics of an indeterminate status and solitary hermits. The cult of saints (mostly of insular origin) was strongly entrenched. It is noteworthy that although the Anglo-continental reformers and the papacy found much to be deplored in the late eleventh-century Scottish Church in terms of organization, observance and discipline, they apparently did not find heresy or false doctrine. (See Ashley 1958; Barrow 1973; Duncan 1975; Hughes 1966; McNeill and Nicholson 1975; Reeves 1864.)

JWMB/GWSB

Celtic law *see* law, Celtic survivals.

Cenél Loairn (Kindred of Loarn) One of the three chief peoples of Dalriada (q.v.) in the seventh century. They inhabited the present district of that name, the island of Colonsay and all the islands and mainland districts to the north of these that were not inhabited by the Picts, which included Mull, Coll and Tiree and, on the mainland, Ardnamurchan and Morvern. By the eighth century their main strongholds were Dunollie and Dunadd.

Ferchar Fota (q.v.) was the first *rí*, or king, of the Cenél Loairn to attain the position of overlord of Dalriada. JWMB

Cenél nGabráin (Kindred of Gabrán) One of the three chief peoples of Dalriada (q.v.) in the seventh century. They occupied Kintyre, Gigha, possibly Jura and certainly Cowal with its islands, Bute and probably also Arran. By the eighth century their strongholds were Dunaverty and Tairpert Boitter, presumably near Tarbert, Loch Fyne.

The *rí*, or king, of the Cenél nGabráin was undisputed overlord of Dalriada until the death of Domnall Brecc (q.v.) at the battle of Strathcarron *c*.642 marked the end of his people's dominance. JWMB

ceòl beag, *see* bagpipe, Highland; music of Gaelic Scotland.

ceòl mór, *see* bagpipe, Highland; music of Gaelic Scotland.

Chamshron, Mòr (d. *c*.1815) From Rannoch. *Bana-bhàrd* (female poet). (See P. Cameron, 1892.) DST

Church, *see* Celtic Church; Church of Scotland; Episcopal Church; Free Church of Scotland; Nova Scotia, Roman Catholic Church in; Roman Catholic Church.

Church of Scotland The Church of Scotland claims to be part of the Catholic or Universal Church and to be Trinitarian, reformed, free from state control, national (with territorial responsibilities) and ecumenically minded in its inter-Church relations. (For its constitution, see Cox 1964.) Each of these descriptive terms has behind it a long and often controversial history. The Church is not only *reformata* but also *reformanda*, committed to a continuing process of reformation, as in each generation it faces new challenges, convinced that the Gospel is infinitely greater than the best interpretations and formulations of it so far.

Claiming continuity with the Church of the early centuries, including the early Celtic Church (q.v.), the Church of Scotland Reformed was recognized by the Scots Parliament in 1560, but not until 1690 was it, in its Presbyterian pattern, established by law as the national Church. It was well into the eighteenth century before the Church could effectively assert itself in the Gaelic areas of Scotland. It established only a presence in areas in which Roman Catholicism still predominates, with a few pockets of Episcopalians, who for long had disputed with the Presbyterians the hegemony of the Reformed Church. The 150 or so years from 1560 were a period of political and ecclesiastical strife, during which now one party was in power, now another. Throughout the same period the Highland area suffered the turmoil of *Linn nan Creach* (the Age of Feuds and Forays), was difficult of access, and almost all the population were monoglot Gaelic speakers. Of the over 900 parishes in Scotland in the eighteenth century, some 300 were Gaelic-speaking. Highlands and Islands parishes were very extensive, and the power of chiefs and lairds was such that the inhabitants changed from one creed to another at the behest of local potentates. (For these earlier periods, see W. Mackay 1896; MacTavish 1943, 1944.)

Because of the centuries-old differences – geographical, historical, sociological, and linguistic – between the Gaelic areas and the rest of Scotland, there developed in the former distinctive cultural features, social attitudes and religious practices that to some extent still persist. The Church of Scotland, however, as the national Church, has room within it for a variety of opinions, attitudes and practices, subject to the fundamental truths set forth in its standards. Reference should be made to the many books available on the history of the Church in the Highlands and Islands, the development of 'militant Presbyterian Evangelicalism', the conflict between Moderatism and Evangelicalism, the Disruption of 1843 (q.v.) and the formation of the Free Church (q.v.), the theological and other tensions within the Free Church, the formation of the Free Presbyterian Church in 1893 and of the United Free Church in 1900, and on to the Union of 1929. There are features of special interest, like the activities of 'The Men'; the revivals; the great open-air Communions; the Free Church yacht the *Breadalbane*, celebrated by John Morrison, poet-blacksmith of Harris; the West Coast Mission ship *Friend of the Isles*; the 'floating church' of Ardnamurchan; the 'Question Day'; and the peculiar rhythmic chant once used in preaching and prayer. There is also the work of such bodies as the Royal Bounty Committee, the Society in Scotland for Propagating Christian Knowledge (see **schools, SSPCK**), the story of the Gaelic Bible (q.v.) and Gaelic versions of the Confession of Faith and the

Catechisms (q.v.), and the wealth of Gaelic hymnody. (See Burleigh 1960; Collins 1974; Drummond and Bulloch 1973, 1975, 1978; MacCalmain 1927; J. MacInnes 1951; J. Mackay 1914; D. Maclean 1927; N. Maclean 1911; Murchison 1962, 1967, 1972; P. C. Simpson 1909; N. L. Walker 1896. Many of these give guidance on further reading in the obscurer byways of Highland Church history.)

A primary principle of the Reformation was intellectual, as well as spiritual, development, and from the first it was planned to have schools in every parish for all who wished to use them. The Church can justly claim to have played a large part in the educating of Scotland, especially in the Gaelic areas. In addition to the parish schools, there were General Assembly Schools, Free Church schools, SSPCK schools (q.v.) and schools provided by the various Gaelic school societies (q.v.) and by the Ladies' Highland Association (q.v.). When, from 1872 onwards, the state took control of education, the Church still continued to be involved in education, as many ministers were members of parish school boards and on the succeeding educational administrative bodies.

From the very first the Church in the Highlands, serving a largely monoglot Gaelic population, laboured to provide qualified Gaelic ministers, to recruit and train students, to provide bursaries and to ensure that only Gaelic ministers were inducted to Gaelic charges; the present system operates a classification of 'Gaelic essential' and 'Gaelic desirable' charges. It has been alleged that Presbyterian ministers in the Highlands, through their hostility to Gaelic culture, have wrought much damage. Of course, like the Christian Church facing Greek and Roman paganism and pagan systems in other lands, Presbyterian ministers, out of loyalty to their Christian convictions, have felt obliged to root out superstitious beliefs and practices, which, though of great interest to anthropologists and folklorists, are an enslavement to those who believe and practise them. On another level it is true that some Presbyterian ministers regard as frivolous or harmful certain activities which other Christians consider legitimate. Nevertheless, the fact is that since the Reformation ministers, members and adherents of the Church of Scotland and its branches have done more than any other body for the maintenance and promotion of Gaelic language, literature and culture.

The charge is often made that when the notorious Highland Clearances (q.v.) were taking place during the nineteenth century, the Church of Scotland stood aloof. Certainly, there was no formal denunciation of the Clearances by the General Assembly – but how could there be when the majority of the Assembly were non-Highland, and the majority of the Highland members, ministers and elders, belonged to the tacksman class (q.v.)? The parish accounts in the Old (1790s) and New (1840s) Statistical Accounts give evidence of much disquiet among ministers about the developing situation, and long before the Disruption (q.v.) ministers such as Lachlan Mackenzie of Lochcarron (q.v.) denounced the iniquities of landlordism. The Free Church, which in its early days included many men who had been parish ministers before the Disruption, strongly championed the movement for land-law reform, in which movement the leaders were mostly men who had learned their politics from the Gaelic Bible and their speaking prowess from sharing in Church activities (see Hunter 1976). Among those supporters of the crofter movement (see **crofting system**) who were imprisoned there was one minister, Donald MacCallum (q.v.), parish minister of Waternish (J. Cameron 1912, 109). In the last fifty years the Church of Scotland, through its courts, committees and agencies has demonstrated an active concern for social and economic, as well as for moral and spiritual, conditions in the Highlands and Islands.

The Church has ministered to Gaelic exiles in Canada and Australia, Gaels in HM Forces (from the Highland regiments of the eighteenth century to the soldiers, sailors and airmen of the present day), the Highland reapers in the Lowlands in the nineteenth century and the fisherfolk around the coasts, and especially the Gaels in the cities, where Gaelic congregations have been active since the eighteenth century. Two ecumenical adjuncts to the Church's work have been the West Coast Mission, founded in 1855 and taken over by the Church in the 1950s (Murchison 1955), and the Glasgow Highland Mission (Comunn Soisgeulach Gaidhealach Ghlaschu), founded in 1898 (Stirling 1932). The latter issued a Gaelic Hymn Book, *Laoidhean Soisgeulach*, in 1899, of which there have been several editions since.

Much has been said and written about Highland religion, alleging it to be gloomy, narrow and life-denying. Such types of religion have existed, but they are not exclusive to the Highlands. Highland religion shows as much variety of experience as that of other places: a sense of the divine concern for all human activities, as seen in *Carmina Gadelica* (q.v.); the soul-searching and heart-warming influence of the evangelical tradition; a sense of awe and mystery fostered by the great mountains and the vast ocean, which makes men brave and keeps them humble, and a great reverence for God – his Word, his Day, his House, his Holy Table. At times, of course, good qualities swerve to extremes, as in the case of rigid Sabbatarianism and the reluctance to become Communicants. There may also be a certain conservatism, which takes longer to tire of a good thing and is slow to recognize the excellence of other good things that happen to be new. The 'acids of modernity', however, are affecting religion in the Highlands as elsewhere.   TMM

Ciaran Mabach, an/Gilleasbaig Ruadh Mac-Dhòmhnaill (Archibald MacDonald) (fl. 1650) Brother of Sir James MacDonald of Sleat. Helped to bring the Keppoch murderers to justice and celebrated by Iain Lom (q.v.) in a poem (Mackenzie 1964, 128). Author of 'B'annsa cadal air fraoch', which anticipates the mood of Donnchadh Bàn's (q.v.) poetry of the deer, and of two laments for Sir James (d. 1678). (See J. Mackenzie 1877.)   DST

clan tartans The word 'tartan' derives from the French *tartaine* (which defined a type of cloth – not its design or colour) and became the English term for the Gaelic *breacan*, meaining 'parti-coloured cloth'. This was generally worn in the form of a plaid, as Martin Martin of Skye (q.v.) described in *c*.1700:

> The plaid worn only by the men . . . consists of diverse colours . . . . Every isle differs from each other in their fancy of making plaids, as to the stripes in breadths and colours. This humour is as different through the mainland of the Highlands.

But tartans had not become the emblems of particular clans before Highland dress was proscribed by statute (1746–82). Thereafter the restored costume was gradually adopted as the national dress of every Scotsman. Particular tartans were identified with each clan and were even bestowed on Lowland families whose forbears had neither constituted a tribe nor worn Highland dress. The convention was adopted that a clan tartan was that which the chief of a name ordained. The Campbell, Gordon, Sutherland and Mackenzie clan tartans were adapted from those of Highland regiments, in which alone the Gael could wear his national dress during the period of the proscription. Others were chosen from the patterns found to have been favoured in districts in which particular clans lived. James Logan, son of an Aberdeen merchant, published fifty-five of them after a careful search throughout the Highlands. He was followed by the brothers who called themselves Sobieski Stolberg Stuarts and who published seventy-five, which they claimed to have recovered from a sixteenth-century manuscript. Despite the fraud, their profound knowledge of the craft earned respect for their setts (patterns), many of which form the originals of clan tartans.   IG

Clanranald, the Books of The Red and Black Books of Clanranald (RB, BB) formed part of the Clanranald bequest to the National Museum of Antiquities in 1944, where they are numbered MCR 39–40. Paper manuscripts of the late seventeenth and early eighteenth centuries, they are best known for their account of MacDonald history and of the Montrose wars. They were edited by A. Cameron (1892–4, 2.138–309); a new edition is presently being prepared for the Scottish Gaelic Texts Society (W. Gillies, forthcoming).

RB was largely written by Niall MacMhuirich (q.v.) (see D. S. Thomson 1970, 283), who compiled the contemporary history from personal experience and inquiry. The earlier history incorporates bardic doctrine on early Irish history and genealogy, official poems to Clanranald chiefs and an earlier compilation or compilations relating to the Lordship of the Isles. RB also contains further bardic poems, both formal and occasional, by MacMhuirichs and others.

BB is more miscellaneous, preserving historical, geographical and calendrical material in English, in addition to Gaelic prose and verse. Its MacDonald history derives from RB, the scribe concerned being identifiable as one Christopher Beaton (R. I. Black, forthcoming). Taken as a whole, BB's MacDonald associations point to Antrim rather than Clanranald.

BB was presented to MacDonald of Clanranald in 1892 by W. F. Skene (q.v.), who had earlier discovered it in Dublin. RB's Clanranald association is stronger: it was obtained for James ('Ossian') MacPherson in South Uist from a grandson of Niall MacMhuirich (A. Cameron 1892–4, 2.138–41). Yet the title 'Red Book of Clanranald' should probably be reserved for another, more venerable manuscript, now lost (see R. I. Black 1979b).   WG

clans, origins of Of the various terms used in Gaelic to describe a kindred (such as *cinél*, *sìol*, and *sliochd*) *clann* is the best-known and has had the widest currency. The literal meaning of *clann* is 'children'; in medieval Highland society the term was used to describe a patrilineal kindred, the members of which descended by known steps from a named ancestor. In a looser sense a clan might also be taken to include the clients and dependants of the leading kindred.

The traditional pedigrees of many Highland clans have survived, traced back to their eponym (or name-father) and beyond, but it is difficult to know what reliance to place on them. Record evidence confirming the earlier stages of the pedigrees is scanty, and the genealogical forger has always been active (Macbain 1902, 175; Skene 1886–90, III, 326).

Nevertheless, it is possible to identify many of the eponyms as historical characters, and, with one

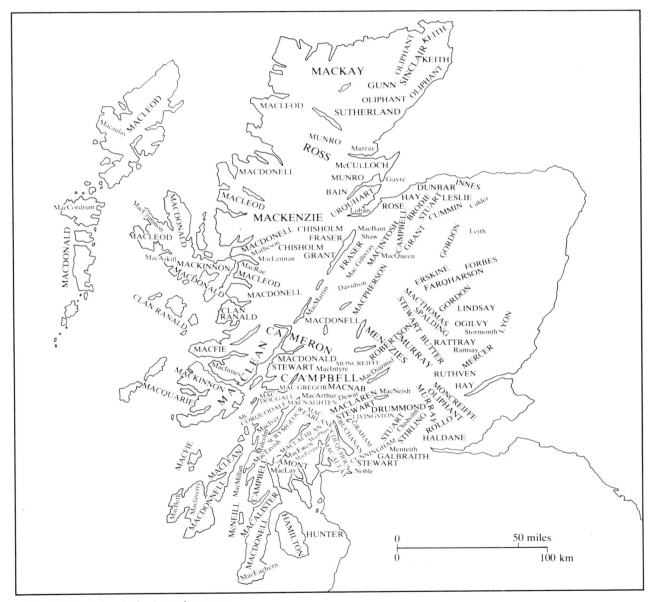

The Highland clans in the sixteenth century.

exception, it has not been shown that any of them are mythical figures or were not, indeed, the ancestors of the kindred in question. The exception is the mythical hero Diarmaid O'Duibne, claimed latterly as a name-father by the Campbells; the original eponym was an earth-bound Duibne, and the claim to descend from Diarmaid emerged through an association of names (Sellar 1973). Two clans, each under its *toisech* (leader or thane), are mentioned in the Book of Deer (see *manuscripts, illuminated*): the Clann Chanann and the Clann Morgainn. They must antedate AD 1100, but nothing further is known about them. The eponyms of the later Highland clans can be dated for the most part to the period 1150–1350. Thus Dugald, from whom the Macdougalls, can be assigned to the later twelfth century; Fingon (Mackinnon) likewise to the twelfth century; Donald (MacDonald) to the early thirteenth century; Lagman (Lamont) and Gilleoin (Maclean) also to the thirteenth century; and Gregor (MacGregor) to the fourteenth century. Sometimes a kindred segmented and a new name-father was taken: the descendants of Somerled (q.v.), for example, were known for a time as Clann Somhairle but later segmented into the Clan Donald, the Clan Dugall and the Clan Ruari.

Why the Highland clans should have emerged in the period 1150–1350 is a question which has not yet been answered – indeed, it has rarely been asked. It is interesting to note, by way of comparison, that in Gaelic Ireland the eponymous ancestor often belongs to an earlier period than in Scotland; thus the O'Neills descend from Niall Glundubh (d. 919), the O'Connors from Conchobar (d. 973) and the O'Briens from Brian Boroimhe (d. 1014).

In genealogical terms, the origins of the clans are surprisingly varied. Some clans, such as the Macfarlanes, descend from the rulers of provinces; others, such as the Macnabs, are of ecclesiastical descent. Not all, by any means, are of Gaelic stock: the Macleods and the Gunns are of Scandinavian origin and the Frasers and Chisholms Scoto-Norman, while the Galbraiths and the Campbells may descend from the Britons of Strathclyde. (See I. F. Grant 1935; Kermack 1957; W. Matheson 1963; Moncreiffe 1967; Sellar 1966, 1971.)   WDHS

Clark, John (b. *c*.1745) From Badenoch. A pupil of James Macpherson (q.v.), literally and metaphorically. Author of *Works of the Caledonian Bards* (1778), in which the spurious poems 'Morduth' and 'The Chief of Scarlaw' and some authentic pieces (for example, MacMhaighstir Alasdair's 'Oran an t-Samhraidh') are translated. (See D. S. Thomson 1958a, 178ff.)   DST

Clark, Mary, *see* Bean Torra-Dhamh.

clàrsach (harp), *see* Clarsach Society; harpers; harps; music of Gaelic Scotland.

Clarsach Society (Comunn na Clàrsaich) founded in 1931 to promote the use and development of the Scottish harp or *clàrsach*. The Society co-operates with An Comunn Gaidhealach (q.v.) in running musical competitions at the National Mod, has recently been promoting an Edinburgh Harp Festival and has stimulated growing interest in the instrument. It has helped to encourage the production of clarsachs by Henry Briggs (d. 1962), for example, and others.   CG

Clàrsair Dall, an (the Blind Harper: Roderick Morison) (*c*.1656–1713/14) The sobriquet was that of the son of John Morison of Bragar, Lewis (q.v.). He completed his musical training in Ireland and was a member of a band of travelling entertainers until 1681, when John MacLeod of Dunvegan became his patron after meeting him in Edinburgh. He received the farm of Claggan, near Dunvegan, on the understanding that he would act as MacLeod's harper in an unofficial capacity, but by 1688 the two had become estranged, partly because of differing reactions to the Revolution of that year. The Harper was retired to the remote farm of Totamor in Glenelg and lived there until *c*.1700, when once more he took to a life of travel and engaged in a round of visits to the houses of the Highland gentry. Towards the end of his life he appears to have returned to Dunvegan and was buried there. He composed a number of songs to the MacLeods, including one in which he castigated his patron's son Roderick (*c*.1674–99) for his spendthrift habits, neglect of his estate and lack of the virtues expected of a chief. With no successor who combined the skills of poet, musician and performer, he may be regarded as Gaelic Scotland's last minstrel. (See W. Matheson 1970.)   WM

Clearances A term used in a Highlands and Islands context to signify the forcible removal of native people from their ancestral lands. Such shifting of rural populations occurred throughout Europe as a result of changes in land use; what distinguished the

The Duke of Sutherland's estate, Loch Brorag Sutherland.

Highland experience was that it occurred relatively late, and was both sweeping and brutal because the Highland landlord possessed powers more unrestricted than those of any other in Europe.

The eighteenth century witnessed a rapid rise in population, pressing on the means of subsistence. This led to the subdivision of agricultural holdings in an archaic 'run-rig' system of farming and in a rigid, stratified social framework. Titles to the clan lands were for the most part the exclusive property of tribal chiefs, who carved tacks, or tenancies, from them to distribute to their relatives. The tacksmen granted sub-tenancies in return for rent and often burdensome services. Many did not even enjoy this degree of security; they existed on sufferance upon the estate, but, as the Napier Commission reported in 1884, all believed that they had an 'inherited inalienable title to security of tenure in their possessions while rent and service [were] duly rendered'. It was their painful discovery during the Clearances that this had 'never been sanctioned by legal recognition' and had 'long been repudiated by the action of the proprietors'.

Economic crises in the eighteenth century led to periodic famine, although they were alleviated in various ways. There was massive voluntary emigration, especially up to the outbreak of the American War of Independence in 1775. Military recruitment gave many young men employment abroad for pay that they remitted home – until the peace of 1815 undermined this source of emolument. The introduction of the potato provided a new source of food, on which the Gaels came to depend to such an extent that they were exposed fatally to the consequences of the Potato Blight (q.v.). The sale of cattle could pay for the import of grain and help to pay the rent of all who enjoyed access to the pasture lands, and a boom in the kelp industry benefited the landlords of the Hebrides in particular until a substitute for seaware was found; but all too often the meagre surplus of the Highland economy was dissipated outside the region by the proprietor.

There was a Draconian solution to the problems of overpopulation, recurrent famine and unprofitable estates. It involved the wholesale removal of native populations so that their lands could be handed over to foreign farmers who were able to offer a high rent and to stock them with black-face and Cheviot sheep. This had already occurred further south, but it had done so gradually and where the rural peasantry had access to an alternative livelihood in the new industrial towns among people who spoke their own language. As the process spread through the southern Highlands it caused increasing hardship and social dislocation. By the time it passed the Great Glen it amounted to genocide and caused the violence of 1792, remembered as the Year of the Sheep. Hundreds of the natives of Ross-shire, joined by others from Sutherland, attempted to drive out the sheep from the pastures on which they had formerly kept their cattle. Troops were called in; the ringleaders were brought to trial; resistance was crushed.

The most notorious of the Clearances that followed took place on the estates of the Countess of Sutherland, whose husband was the wealthy Marquis of Stafford and able to subsidise a grandiose plan to transform the economy of Sutherland. Its people were to be retained on the estate, but removed to its coasts and encouraged to take up fishing. However well-intentioned, the scheme occasioned terrible hardship to the inhabitants as well as loss to the proprietor. The chief beneficiary was the estate agent Patrick Sellar, who, after being brought to trial and acquitted on charges of cruelty in 1816, left the service of the Countess to become a large-scale sheep farmer in Strathnaver and subsequently in Morvern.

It has been estimated that over 8,000 people were uprooted in Sutherland, victims of a plan for resettlement that proved for the most part a fiasco. The Hebridean properties of John Gordon of Cluny provide an example of the alternative policy of forcible deportation. An Aberdonian, Gordon purchased Barra, Benbecula and South Uist. The first he planned to turn into a convict settlement after removing its inhabitants. In 1850 the appearance of Barra people in Edinburgh, 'in a state of absolute starvation', caused a national outburst of indignation. There was a similar instance in Canada in 1851, when islanders from Barra and South Uist arrived after being seized and carried aboard their ship, some handcuffed, some felled with truncheons, others hunted by press gangs after they had swum back to shore.

The 1850s marked a watershed in the Clearances.

Eviction of tenant farmers. Engraving from Donald Ross, Real Scottish Grievances, *Glasgow 1854.*

When the evicted islanders of North Uist resorted to violence in 1849 Lord Cockburn gave lenient sentences to the ringleaders. He observed:

> They had nothing but the bare ground, or rather, the hard, wet beach, to lie down upon. It was said, or rather insinuated, that 'arrangements' had been made for them, and in particular that a ship *was to have been* soon on the coast. But, in the meantime, the people's hereditary roofs were to be pulled down, and the mother and her children had only the shore to sleep on, fireless, foodless, hopeless.

When the people of Coigach, and particularly the women, resisted similar attempts to evict them in 1853, these were abandoned. Public opinion, expressed both in the national press and in Parliament by this time, had become a restraining influence. It was fortified by the Free Church ministry, to which the Highlanders had seceded *en masse* at the Disruption (q.v.) of 1843.

After 1855 there were no more large-scale Clearances, but they continued by attrition and stealth during decades in which sheep became less profitable and the land became more valuable in the form of sporting estates. In 1857 a property in Ross-shire which had netted £400 a year as a sheep farm was let for five times that amount as deer forest, and this proved a portent for the future, as did the growing capacity of Highlanders for presenting their case in the English-speaking world and organizing resistance in the Gaelic one. Instead of continuing to plead deferentially for pity from landlords or to claim non-existent rights in their homeland they began to agitate for the reform of the land laws.

Their increasingly aggressive tactics culminated in the events of 1882 that heralded the Crofters' War. Alexander Mackenzie, historian of the Clearances, was present when the proprietor of Lochcarron attempted to evict two families because of the conduct of their sons. He wrote:

> The whole case is a lamentable abuse of the existing law, and such as will do more to secure its abolition, when the facts are fully known than all the other cases of eviction which have taken place in the Highlands during the present generation.

A few days later the Battle of the Braes broke out in Skye, witnessed by press reporters, including those of the *Illustrated London News*. By the following year Commissioners of Inquiry into the condition of the crofters and cottars of the Highlands and Islands of Scotland were touring the region by order of Parliament. In 1884 they presented a report which contains the most comprehensive and eloquent body of comment on the Clearances by Highlanders apart from their own Gaelic literature. It led directly to the passing of the Crofters' Acts, which terminated the landlord's right to evict. (See Richards 1982.)   IG

Cléireach Beag, an (Hector Maclean) (*c.*1490–*c.*1560) Chief of Macleans of Coll. According to Dr Hector Maclean (MS of 1768), in 1537 he composed a poem on Ailean nan Sop (q.v.), the 'Caismeachd' (Sinclair, A. Maclean, 1898, 25), winning his freedom from imprisonment by Ailean thereby, and he also composed Latin verse.   DST

Clerk, Revd Dr Archibald (1813–87) From Lorn. Minister at Kilmallie. Edited *Fear-tathaich nam Beann* and Gaelic Supplement of *Life and Work*.   TMM

Cluny of the '45 (Ewen MacPherson) (1706–64) Remained concealed in Badenoch (in a cave on Ben Alder) for nine years after the '45; died in France. Elegy by Lachlan Macpherson of Strathmashie (q.v.).   DST

Coats, James Jnr (1841–1912). From Ferguslie. Established many school and village libraries in both north and south. (See Holmes 1909.)   TMM

Coddy, the (John MacPherson) (1876–1955) From Barra. A great character, whose stories were collected and edited by J. L. Campbell. (See J. L. Campbell 1960.)   DST

Coinneach Odhar (Sallow Kenneth) (fl. mid-sixteenth century) A native of Easter Ross. Surname unknown. On record in 1577–8 as a practitioner of the occult arts, but it is as a *fiosaiche* (seer) that he is remembered – although his alleged prophecies were not recorded until after the events they purported to foretell. Convicted of witchcraft, he suffered death by burning at Chanonry. (See A. Mackenzie 1877, etc.; W. Matheson 1971, 66–88.)   WM

colleges, Gaelic teaching in, *see* universities and colleges.

Colum Cille (St Columba) (521–97) Missionary abbot and ecclesiastical statesman, whose foundation of the monastery of Iona (*c.*563) gave to the Irish

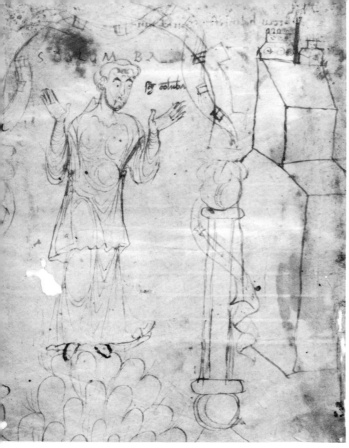

Pen drawing of St Colum Cille from Adamnán's Vita.
Stiftsbibliothek St Gallen, Codex 555, page 166.

colony of Dál Riada in western Scotland a prestige
and influence which contributed to its eventual
ascendancy over the kingdom of the Picts. Born a
prince of the royal Uí Néill line, in youth he became
a devotee of the burgeoning monasticism of the sixth-
century Irish Church and personally founded the
monasteries of Durrow and Derry. His declared
motive for his move to Scotland was to become an
'exile for Christ'. The principal source for his career
is the late seventh-century *Vita* by Adamnán (q.v.),
which, despite its character as a spiritual panegyric
and its preoccupation with the supernatural, is a
document of immense historical value (A. O. and M.
O. Anderson 1961; Hughes 1972; Reeves 1857).
Colum Cille moved among the contemporary kings of
Dál Riada and Pictland and was a participant in the
Convention of Druim Cett (575) when relations
between the Irish Dál Riata and Scottish Dál Riada
were discussed (Bannerman 1966). The *Vita* indicates
that he made frequent journeys in Scotland and
Ireland. It also provides much information about the

life of a sixth-century monastery – its devotions,
scholarship, crafts, economy and the steady traffic of
visitors. Colum Cille himself emerges as a man of
imperious energy mingled with spiritual sensitivity
and gentleness. He founded several daughter monasteries of Iona in Scotland, and his later *paruchia*
included some forty Irish and over fifty Scottish
churches. An early eulogy, the *Amra Choluim Chilli*,
may be an eighth-century reworking of a late sixth-
century original. The elaboration of his cult in later
medieval times led to the attribution of many Gaelic
poems to him as author (Kenney 1929).   KDMcD

Comhairle nan Eilean (Western Isles Regional
Council) Has an official bilingual policy which is
reflected in the encouragement of bilingual education,
support for a local bilingual publishing venture, the
establishment of a Bilingual Development Officer's
post and some use of Gaelic in the conduct of its
business.   DST

Commun Beul-aithris na h-Albann, *see* Folklore
Institute of Scotland.

Comunn Gaidhealach, An (The Highland
Association) Founded in Oban in 1891, its aims, as
currently stated, are to encourage and support the
teaching, learning and use of Gaelic; the study and
cultivation of Highland literature, history, music, art
and traditions; the social and economic welfare (until
recently 'the native industries') of the Highlands and
Islands; and the wearing of Highland dress. These,
with slight verbal variations, have been the aims from
the beginning.

A major undertaking from the start has been the
Mod (modelled on the Welsh Eisteddfod), an annual
competitive festival of speech, literature and music
(vocal and instrumental), with senior and junior Sections. The first Mod was held in Oban in 1892, and
since then, ever growing in size and variety, it has
been located in many places. Since 1905 it has been
supplemented by an annual programme of local or
provincial Mods, itinerant music teachers being at
times employed in rural areas to train choirs and
individuals for the Mods.

An Comunn has had the support of many branches
and many affiliated societies over the years and has
recently encouraged a larger measure of grass-roots
participation by creating four regional councils

(North, South, Argyll, Western Isles). The Association has also become much more closely involved with statutory and voluntary bodies, while also receiving more financial aid from public funds and private sponsors. In earlier years its ordinary income was boosted by special fund-raising and publicity efforts – the 1907 *Fèill* (bazaar), the Highland *Clachan* (traditional small Highland village) in the Scottish Exhibition of 1911, the 1927 *Fèill*, the *Clachan* in the Empire Exhibition of 1938 and the 1950 *Fèill* for the War Memorial and Thanksgiving Fund (*Cuimhnich na laoich, Cuidich an òigridh*).

A primary concern has always been the position of Gaelic in schools. In 1891 Gaelic was permitted as a 'specific subject', but after arduous campaigning the Education Act of 1918 made it mandatory in Gaelic-speaking areas. By means of conferences, training classes, summer schools, deputations and the publishing of textbooks and other material, An Comunn has striven to improve the availability and quality of Gaelic teaching. The year 1950 saw the launching, in conjunction with Highland education committees, of a Gaelic informal education project, employing three full-time regional organizers. Among An Comunn's many publications has been its official magazine, begun in 1905 as *An Deò-Grèine*, later called *An Gaidheal* and latterly *Sruth* (in recent years produced as an inset in a Highland newspaper). An Comunn pioneered Gaelic drama and has published many Gaelic plays.

In 1929 an inner all-Gaelic circle, Clann an Fhraoich, was formed, under whose aegis in 1933 Comunn na h-Oigridh was founded, with its many local branches (*feachdan*) and summer camps, latterly becoming the concern of Highland education committees. In earlier years An Comunn found markets for those engaged in native arts and crafts and was the major influence in founding the Highland Home Industries Association. (See J. M. Campbell 1927; J. Macdonald 1927; M. Macfarlane 1905; M. Macleod 1921; M. N. Munro 1907; Murchison 1953, 1955; D. S. Thomson 1979b.) TMM

Comunn Leabhraichean, An, *see* Gaelic Books Council.

Comunn na Clàrsaich, *see* Clarsach Society.

Comunn na Gàidhlig an Lunnainn, *see* Gaelic Society of London.

Conall Gulbann Ancestor of rulers of Tyrconnel, hero of sixteenth-century romance and derived folktale, in which he pursues Eithne, abducted by Macaomh Mór while Conall slept, through several kingdoms and defeats the Turks, who are invading Europe. A notable run describes Conall's sword. (See Bruford 1965; 1969, 72–9.) AB

Conanach, Bàrd, *see* Bàrd Conanach.

Constantine II (d. 952) The success of Constantine as king of Scots from 900 to 943 is implicit in the length of his reign. In 917 he and his allies invaded England but were defeated by Athelstan at the famous Battle of Brunanburh. Constantine abdicated in 943, 'in his old age, being decrepit', to become abbot of the Céli Dé (q.v.) monastery at St Andrews. This is at once an illustration of the peaceful operation of tanistry (q.v.) and an indication that the administrative centre of the Church had already removed from Dunkeld to St Andrews, where it remained until the Reformation. (See Bannerman 1971, 78; Duncan 1975, 91–4.) JWMB

Creach na h-Aisne, *see* Ailean nan Sop.

Creideamh a' bhata bhuidhe ('Yellow-Stick Belief') Protestantism enforced by strong-arm methods. The phrase is usually associated with Alexander MacDonald of Boisdale, South Uist, but John Walker's (q.v.) reports on the Hebrides (1761–71) apply the phrase *credivk chall vuy* ('the religion of the yellow hazel stick') to conversions in Rum in the 1720s. (See M. M. McKay 1980, 197, 243.) DST

criticism, literary, *see* literary history and criticism.

crofting system The system of small-unit 'family farming' long characteristic of the north-west Highlands and the Hebrides. A croft was not a house but a piece of land (usually small), the tenant (crofter) paying rent to the landowner and sharing grazings in common with other crofters in a 'crofting township' (A. Carmichael 1884). Usually a crofter owned his house but was only the tenant of his land. In 1979 there were 17,997 crofts on the Register of Crofts; of these 1,290 were owner-occupied. (For a description of the crofting system and related legislation, see J. S. Grant 1967; Guide 1976; MacCuish 1966, 1979.)

The crofting system grew out of the land system of the eighteenth century – in which the chief elements were the chief (or laird), the principal tenants (leaseholders, tacksmen) and the sub-tenants (tenants-at-will), with many landless labourers, cottars or scallags – which itself evolved from early Celtic tribalism, influenced by feudalism. With the abolition of hereditary jurisdictions after 1746, the relationship between chiefs (or lairds) and tenants became commercial rather than military, personal and pseudo-patriarchal. A Highland estate's real value was no longer its fighting men but the rental it provided. The advent of large-scale sheep farming raised the rents and cleared the glens of the old tenantry; at first many substantial tenants (tacksmen) with their dependants and later, increasingly, masses of the common people came under pressure to emigrate. Initially lairds, needing manpower to work their farms, to toil at kelp and to provide recruits for the Highland regiments, and fearing depopulation, changed the old run-rig joint-occupancy system into individual holdings and also created new small crofts ('lots'), usually on inferior soil requiring reclamation. The crofters literally 'created' the crofts, usually by the *feannagan* ('lazy-bed') system. These 'lots', mostly in coastal and insular areas, were deliberately kept small to compel the tenants to work part-time at kelp, fishing or farming, and were made smaller still by subdivision to accommodate the maximum number of people on the smallest unit of land. This 'lotting' system was the basis of the crofting system as we know it. There was no security of tenure. At the will or whim of laird or factor, a crofter could be evicted, left with only his scanty household goods and the roof beams (*cabair*) to make a dwelling elsewhere. Many cottars and squatters had not even a small 'lot', which resulted in serious congestion in communities of crofter-fishermen. (See **Clearances**; A. Mackenzie 1883a; Prebble 1963; Richards 1982.)

The vagaries of the fishing, bad harvests and the Potato Blight (q.v.) (the potato being the staple food) raised widespread destitution in the 'Hungry Forties', only partially alleviated by Relief Boards in Glasgow and Edinburgh. Despite unceasing emigration, the population reached its peak in the mid-nineteenth century, coincident with widespread poverty. There ensued two decades of apathy and despair. In the 1870s signs emerged of a growing determination to redress grievances, to champion crofters' rights and to campaign for 'land and language' (see **Land League movement**).

In 1883 the Government appointed a Royal Commission of Inquiry into Crofting Conditions (chairman, Lord Napier), following which came the Crofters Holdings Act of 1886, the 'Magna Carta' of Gaeldom, giving crofters security of tenure, fair rents and compensation for improvements – basic rights on which all later crofting legislation was to build. Its first effect was a rapid improvement in housing. A permanent Crofters Commission was set up to adjudicate on rent arrears, to fix fair rents, to assess compensation, to enlarge crofts, etc. Another Royal Commission (1892) showed that 1·7 million acres of Highland land were suitable for land settlement. In 1897 the Congested Districts Board was created to enlarge holdings and to establish settlements to relieve overpopulated areas.

In 1911 the Small Landholders (Scotland) Act extended the crofting legislation to all Scotland and replaced the Crofters Commission by the Land Court and by the Board (later Department) of Agriculture, with a special remit for land settlement. The 1919 Land Settlement Act gave further powers and finance to the Board of Agriculture to acquire land, create new smallholdings and provide loans for stock and equipment. Many of the new settlements were 'club farms', with co-operative ownership of sheep stock. For many of these inflated sheep-stock valuations at

Croft at Dalmally, Argyll.

Stacking peats for drying, near Achavanish, Caithness.

entry, followed by depressed markets in the 1930s, caused serious difficulties (Murchison 1935).

Between the 1930s and the 1960s there was a plethora of reports, inquiries and ventures concerned with aspects of the 'Highland Problem' – including the Highland Development League (1936), the Hilleary Report (1938), the Hydro-Electric Board (1945), the Highland Advisory Panel (1946), the Highland Fund Limited (1953) and the Highlands and Islands Development Board (1965) – but from the crofters' point of view the most important was the appointment in 1951 of a Commission of Inquiry into Crofting Conditions (chaired by Sir Thomas Taylor). The Commission's Report (1954) issued in an Act (1955) setting up a permanent Crofters Commission (chairmen, successively, Sir Robert Urquhart, Dr James Shaw Grant, Mr J. F. M. Macleod) to organize, control and develop crofting and to administer grants and loans. The Commission began by trying to reorganize 'decaying townships', to use abandoned crofts and to reallocate existing crofting land. Having encountered various difficulties, it con-

cluded that the old crofting system – under which, between 1886 and 1943, 2,776 new holdings and 5,162 enlargements (totalling 805,523 acres) had been created – was 'obsolete' and that traditional crofting tenure (a great boon when instituted in 1886) had become, in view of the new non-agricultural uses for crofts, a 'barrier to progress'. The Crofting Reform Act of 1976 introduced a revolutionary development. Crofters have long been able to acquire ownership of their crofts (and some have done so), but this Act makes croft ownership more practicable, while still retaining the benefits of crofting tenure. (See Collier 1953; Day 1918; Dickie 1961; Fenton 1976; Gillanders 1968; I. F. Grant 1961; Grassie 1983; Gray 1957; Hunter 1976; Leigh 1929; MacCuish 1971, 1976; C. Macdonald 1955; D. G. F. Macdonald 1878; Macphail 1976.)   TMM

crosses, sculptured The sculptured crosses of the British Isles were a unique achievement in Christian Europe. Distinctive forms, developed during the seventh to ninth centuries AD in three of the separate kingdoms of what is now Scotland, attained master-pieces of design and execution. Ideas and examples from the Christian art of the Near East and from Germanic and Celtic traditions were adapted in brilliantly original interrelated manuscripts, sculpture and metalwork, at first perhaps principally in the monasteries of Anglo-Saxon Northumbria. In the art of the early Church the Cross was the symbol not of the sacrifice of the Crucifixion, as generally it was later, but of Victory over Death and was thus to be assimilated, with the vine, to the Tree of Life.

Large wooden crosses, probably plain, were set up at open-air preachings and, in 633, before a battle. But the sculpting of monumental crosses in stone may have begun in the mid-eighth century rather

Pictish cross-slab at Glamis, Angus.

Pictish cross-slab in Aberlemno churchyard, Angus.

than, as formerly thought, in the late seventh, when figure sculpture was introduced by stonemasons from the Continent. Of the earliest (and finest) Northumbrian crosses, that at Ruthwell in Dumfriesshire has, on a tall narrow shaft with small head, figures of Christ in panels as well as biblical scenes, reminiscent of earlier Armenian sculptured pillars, and up the sides continuous vine trees 'inhabited' by birds and beasts. As if influenced by contemporary iconoclasm, another cross at Hexham carries only vines, in part stylized into roundels of interlace. Later Northumbrian crosses in Scotland are variants on these basic ideas, and such sculpture spread north.

Among the largely Celtic Picts the main monument, instead of a free-standing cross, was a 'cross-slab', like a simplified page of the Lindisfarne Gospels 7 or more feet high. Around the massive cross and on the back is a profusion of creatures as those in Gospels and in the Bestiaries, figures from the life of David, scenes not necessarily biblical incorporating figures of warriors and hunters – and the still enigmatic Pictish symbols, prominent until the Scots took over *c*.850. On the cross itself elaborate roundels of interlace may represent the vine, rarely naturalistic in Pictland. After beginning in Strathmore (Glamis, Meigle, Aberlemno), a second generation (Aberlemno, and Nigg in Ross-shire) with high relief and bosses on the front, and more snaky creatures and spirals taking the place of interlace, seems to indicate a two-way relationship with Iona.

Important features of the Irish High Crosses may also have been derived *c*.800 from and through the Iona group of free-standing crosses rather than vice versa. For the Iona cross-heads are of Northumbrian shape, and the earliest were not monolithic but put together with a carpentry technique and without the 'Celtic halo'; this could have been invented there to provide structural support, though signifying the ancient encircling victor's wreath. Figure sculpture was subordinate, but elaborate patterning and spirals, as in the Book of Kells (probably penned at Iona), testify to local originality.

A few free-standing crosses were erected in the East, ringless even when the Scots ruled, but covered with rows of figures. Some late ambitious Pictish cross-slabs flaunted symbols (that at Shandwick in Ross-shire and the Maiden Stone in Aberdeenshire), but afterwards small often crude slabs, frequently ringed, were long popular; the great monument at Forres is exceptional. Cross-slabs appeared at last in Strathclyde, with free crosses, in the tenth century and were revived in Argyll (Ardchattan) and, *c*.950, in half-Norse Man (reached somehow also in the 9th century), with a few in the Hebrides.

After nearly four centuries tall crosses reappeared in the West Highlands, along with many elaborate tombstones, in the context of the Lordship of the Isles (q.v.). The spirit and some of the forms of the surviving ancient sculpture were renewed in interlacing roundels of Romanesque plant scrolls, in plain and cruciform interlace panels and in the cross-heads which bear a crucifix surrounded by a disc. Generally there were some other figures, pairs of animals or a galley. Most in Islay and Kintyre can be assigned to Iona sculptors. Latin inscriptions (late fourteenth – early sixteenth century) show that they were votive, not funerary; donors include Reginald, eponym of Clanranald, and Mariota before she was Countess of Ross.

(See Close-Brooks and Stevenson 1982; Cruden 1964; Steer and Bannerman 1977.) RBKS

Early Christian cross from Kildalton, Islay. East face.

Cuimeanach, Donncha (b. *c*.1778) From Rannoch. Bard. Emigrated to America *c*.1822. Author of fine love song 'Eala nan cuantan'. (See P. Cameron 1892.)
DST

'Culdees', *see* Céli Dé.

Cunningham, William, *see* Glencairn, 9th Earl of.

current affairs, coverage in Gaelic The volume and scale of writing on current affairs in Gaelic has always been limited because of the relatively depressed role of Gaelic in print. In earlier periods we find Gaelic used occasionally, as in Robert MacDougall's guide to prospective emigrants to America (R. MacDougall 1841), a bilingual tract on herring curing (1846) the bilingual Harris Estate Regulations

C*

(1891), a pamphlet addressed to Scottish fishermen (1896), or Lord Leverhulme's address of 1919 (Leverhulme 1919). It could be argued that the need for bilingual or Gaelic-only pamphlets and tracts has become greatly reduced with the disappearance of an adult population that spoke only Gaelic, but need and desirability are not to be equated.

There are occasional modern instances of informational pamphlets being produced bilingually or in Gaelic only – for example, a Nature Conservancy pamphlet or the Commission of the European Communities' *Alba anns an Roinn-Eòrpa* (1978). An Comunn Gaidhealach (q.v.) has published many such: the account of its aims and constitution (1938), Mod programmes, its earlier manual of First Aid, *Ceud-fhuasgladh do na daoine leòinte* and so on.

Another instance is the Gaelic publication of the Scottish National Party's Gaelic Policy document (*Gairm*, 104, 1978), which remains the chief exposition of the policy in print. The book *Gàidhlig ann an Albainn/Gaelic in Scotland* (D. S. Thomson 1976) is a bilingual symposium, in which the main expositions are in one language and, in each case, a shorter summary is in the other. Iain Aonghas MacLeòid's *Criomagan Ioma-dhathte* (1973) is a collection of essays on technological and other themes of current interest, including atomic power and space travel, and *Cuairt an Teaghlaich Rìoghail gu Uibhist-a-tuath* (1977) was a somewhat belated celebration of a royal visit to North Uist in 1956.

Naturally enough, the main media for the discussion of current affairs are the periodical press, radio and television (see **broadcasting, Gaelic**). Since 1952 *Gairm* has always devoted space to articles on economic, political, social, practical, musical, literary and other topics of current interest. The bilingual *Sruth* (1967), first appearing separately, then in the Stornoway Gazette, also dealt with current affairs. *Crùisgean* (1977–9; restarted 1980) has reported on industrial, cultural and other developments and runs features on sport, gardening, etc. *North 7* (1972–81), having begun rather laboriously as a bilingual bimonthly (1972) and having for a time provided Gaelic translations/summaries of all its English articles, settled down to featuring a few Gaelic articles in their own right, which concentrated on economic topics and book reviews; its economic reporting was informed and sprightly.

The flavour of periodical writing on current affairs may be suggested by a short list of some items that have appeared over the last thirty years: 'Na Ceistean a dh'fheuch ri Catto' (*Gairm* 1952), 'An Coimisean Ur' and 'Ball Coise' (*Gairm* 1954), 'Na Rocaidean' (*Gairm* 1955), 'An t-Oireachtas' (*Gairm* 1956), 'Profile of Calum Kennedy' and 'Ski-eadh ann an Albainn' (*Gairm* 1959), 'Rubair' and 'Cumhachd an Smùirnein' (*Gairm* 1961), 'Maise Gnùis' (*Gairm* 1963), 'Còcaireachd le Càise' (*Gairm* 1965), 'Fasanan Ura, Am Bòrd Ur' (HIBD) and 'Beachd air Obair a' Bhùird' (*Gairm* 1967), 'Ceòl air Clàr' and 'Ulster '71' (*Gairm* 1971), 'Factoraidhean-fighe' and 'Lagh Ur nan Croitean – Beachd' (*Gairm* 1972), 'Ola' (*Gairm* 1973), 'Craobh-sgaoileadh agus a' Ghàidhlig', 'UFO's is Eile' and 'Jorge Luis Borges' (*Gairm* 1975), 'Gàrnaileireachd' (*Crùisgean* 1977), 'Aite Chroiteireachd' (*North 7* 1977), 'Obraichean nan Eilean' and 'Cinema Sgire' (*Crùisgean* 1978), 'Riaghladh Ionadail' (*North 7* 1978), 'Cealla-deug san Ruis' (*Gairm* 1978), 'A' bruidheann air ball-coise' (*Crùisgean*, 1979), 'Còig ceud dachaidh ri lorg' (*North 7* 1979), 'Na Ceiltich còmhla mu chion craobh-sgaoilidh' (*North 7* 1980), 'Bliadhna san Iràin' (*Gairm* 1980). This list indicates the range of the topics covered, but the scope of other media, including books on current affairs in Gaelic, is still restricted.   DST

customs, pagan, *see* paganism, survivals of.

D

Dalriada The embryonic kingdom of the Scots, which came into being when the royal dynasty of Dalriada in Ireland, in the person of Fergus Mór mac Eirc (q.v.), took up permanent residence in Scotland *c*. AD500. This was the culmination of a movement of population from the coastal area of present Co. Antrim across the North Channel to modern Argyll that may have begun as early as the third century. In their own language, Gaelic, the inhabitants of Ireland called themselves *Gaidheil*, or Gaels, and their expansion into Scotland is commemorated in the place name Argyll, or *Earraghàidheal* ('coastland of the Gaels'). It was from their contemporary Latin designation, *Scotti*, or Scots, that Scotland itself was ultimately named.

The military power and prestige of Dalriada never stood higher than during the reign of Aedán (q.v.), grandson of Fergus Mór, from 574 to *c*.608. He was fortunate in that he received the support of Colum Cille (q.v.), one of the most celebrated churchmen of his time, who came over from Ireland in 563.

By the seventh century there were three chief peoples in Dalriada: the Cenél nOengusa ('kindred of Angus'), who were in Islay; the Cenél Loairn ('kindred of Loarn'), who inhabited the present district of that name, the island of Colonsay and all the islands and mainland districts to the north of these not inhabited by the Picts, which certainly included

Dalriada in the seventh century AD

Mull, Coll and Tiree and, on the mainland, Ardnamurchan and Morvern. Gabrán, Aedán's father, gave his name to the third kindred, the Cenél nGabráin, who occupied Kintyre with Gigha, possibly Jura and certainly Cowal with its islands, Bute and probably also Arran. By the eighth century the main strongholds of the Cenél Loairn were Dunollie and Dunadd, and those of the Cenél nGabráin were Dunaverty and Tairpert Boitter, presumably near Tarbert, Loch Fyne.

As the names of these peoples suggest, society was kin-based. The ultimate kin-group was the *derbfhine*, or 'certain kin', which consisted of four generations of male descendants, including the common ancestor. All were heirs in respect of property, personal and landed, and all were responsible for liabilities incurred by each individual member. Society was also hierarchical. Each kindred was ruled by a *rí*, or 'king'; the king of the Cenél nGabráin was overlord of Dalriada. Tanistry (q.v.) was the system that decided succession to the kingship. The other grades of free-born in society were the nobles and the commoners. Most of the former were related to the king of their respective kindreds and ranked according to the amount of property and the number of clients that they possessed. The commoners were the clients of the nobles. This relationship was expressed in terms of houses, so the Cenél nGabráin possessed 560 houses or clients, while the Cenél Loairn and the Cenél nOengusa had 420 and 430 respectively. The system of naval recruitment was based on house numbers, every twenty houses producing two seven-benched boats or twenty-eight oarsmen. Each kindred also mustered a fixed number of men for a *slógad*, or 'hosting'.

Domnall Brecc (q.v.), grandson of Aedán and king of Dalriada, was killed by the Britons at the battle of Strathcarron *c*.642. His reign represented a considerable setback for the political aspirations of the Scots of Dalriada. One result of the weakening of his own kindred, the Cenél nGabráin, was the emergence of the Cenél Comgaill, who assumed their place alongside the other three chief peoples of Dalriada. The Cenél Comgaill, named after Comgall, brother and predecessor of Gabrán as king of Dalriada, were that section of the Cenél nGabráin who inhabited Cowal and its islands. Soon too the Cenél Loairn began to compete for the overlordship of Dalriada, and Ferchar Fota (q.v.) was the first of their leaders to attain that position. For the next half-century they were to be the dominant people, although the Cenél nGabráin defeated them in a *bellum maritimum* in 719, the first sea battle on record in the British Isles.

The Cenél Loairn had to bear the brunt of a period of Pictish aggression that resulted in the capture of Dunadd in 736 and culminated in the 'smiting of Dalriada' by Angus, son of Fergus, king of the Picts, in 741. It was not until 768, seven years after Angus's death, that we hear again of the Scots of Dalriada in a political context, but this was a record of a battle fought by Aed Find (q.v.), king of Dalriada, in the Pictish province of Fortriu. Aed Find was of the Cenél nGabráin, and the Pictish interlude seems to have ensured that the Cenél Loairn were eliminated as contenders for the leadership of Dalriada.

Clearly, also, Scottish expansionist policies at the expense of the Picts were renewed, and from now on we hear of kings of Dalriada who were also kings of Fortriu. The culmination of these policies came in the reign of Kenneth mac Alpín (q.v.), king of Dalriada, who united Scots and Picts *c*.843. Kenneth may have had a claim, through his mother, to the kingship of the Picts, but he seems also to have conquered them in battle, probably with the aid of reinforcements from Ireland and perhaps also after the Picts had been heavily defeated by a marauding Danish army. But the most likely explanation for the rapid disappearance of the Picts from history thereafter is that they had long been undergoing a process of Scoticization, the main impetus of which came from their acceptance of Christianity from the Scots.

The administrative centre of the Church moved from Iona to Dunkeld in 849, following the shift in political power, and Scone became the *caput* or legal centre of the new kingdom of the Scots whose southern boundary was now the Forth–Clyde line. In Gaelic it was known as *Alba* and in Latin *Scotia*, names which are current today. (See Bannerman 1971, 66–79; 1974, 73–154; 1975, 13–15.)   JWMB

dance in Gaelic society As dance is a fundamental human activity and one of the primary forms of art, we might expect to find evidence of its practice in Gaelic literature and tradition. The record is, in fact, disappointingly meagre. For 'dance' Gaelic uses the common western European term, no doubt introduced from English but borrowed ultimately from French. The standard form is *dannsa*. A Gaelic origin has been suggested for *ruidhle*, *ruithle*, etc. ('reel'); a Scots or northern English origin is at least as likely. Such words may have displaced a native terminology, just as the introduction of new modes and fashions of dancing appear to have displaced the old dances, ritual or dramatic. In some instances dances associated with seasonal festivities have been relegated to the status of dance-games or children's entertainment. This survey deals only with those dances that are rooted in the older Gaelic social order or seem to have been assimilated into Gaelic culture, at least to the extent that they were called by Gaelic names.

Of the standard surviving solo dances 'Dannsa a' Chlaidhimh' (Sword Dance) is probably the oldest. The alternative name 'Gille Caluim' is taken from the tune to which it is danced, the words of which begin: 'Gille Caluim dà pheighinn' ('Gille Caluim, two pence'). Before 1850 it is said to have been danced clockwise around the swords, not anti-clockwise as now. There are several fragmentary references to other sword dances: one of these was 'Mac an Fhorsair' (Son of the Forester, Keeper of the Deer Forest). In this dance, and probably in other 'war dances', the dancer flourished a naked sword or, by the mid-eighteenth century, a staff of oak. In 'Gille Caluim' the swords are laid flat on the ground: originally they seem to have been placed edge uppermost, which would have required a different means of support. A solo resembling a sword dance, performed over crossed sticks with a bonnet placed at their intersection, was known as 'A' Bhonaid Ghorm' (The Blue Bonnet). 'Dannsa na Biodaig' (Dirk Dance) could be danced over a dirk fixed with its point upwards; in another version it was sometimes flourished, sometimes danced over on the ground. Still another dirk dance was performed by two men, each armed with dirk and targe. In this connection it is to be noted that 'Gille Caluim' is also recorded as a dance for two, three or four men. According to a popular tradition, the solo dance 'Seann Triubhas' (Old Trews) was the only dance that the Gaels would condescend to perform in the dress imposed by the Disclothing Act. Another tradition claims that, on the contrary, it recalls the celebrations that attended the repeal of the Act: neither of these traditions, however, seems to have a firm historical basis.

Nor is Gaelic nomenclature in itself a sure indication of native origin. For instance, 'Ruidhle nam Pòg' (Reel of Kisses), almost invariably performed as the last dance of the evening, is in all its essentials simply the popular and widely distributed kissing dance known elsewhere in Scotland under a variety of names: 'Babbity Bowster', 'Blue Bonnets', 'The White Cockade', etc. (The last is the name of its tune.) In Gaelic Scotland, however, where it was also known as 'Dannsa nam Pòg' ('Dance of Kisses') and 'An Ruidhle Mór' (The Great Reel), it incorporated a unique prelude. The 'leader' (who selected the first lady – the belle of the ball – who in turn selected a man, and so on) danced some steps of 'Gille Caluim' or a very similar solo. This was executed in a clockwise direction over the handkerchief which featured in the selecting ceremony. (A bonnet was sometimes substituted for a handkerchief.)

While this is not, in fact, recorded for those versions that were preceded by a sword dance, the references, taken together, probably link 'A' Bhonaid Ghorm' with 'Ruidhle nam Pòg' and may also throw some incidental light on an allusion to 'slow Highland dances, emblematical of war or courtship'. It has been observed that the words of 'Gille Caluim' fit the actions of the kissing reel much better than those of a solo sword dance (for example, 'Gheibhinn leannan . . . rogha is taghadh . . . gheibhinn bean' – 'I'd get a sweetheart . . . the pick and choice . . . I'd get a wife'). The tune of 'Ruidhle nam Pòg' may thus originally have been 'Gille Caluim' and may only latterly have been displaced by 'The White Cockade', perhaps when the white handkerchief was substituted for a sword. In Barra and South Uist the piper would always play a musical phrase known as *pòg an toiseach* ('kiss first') several times as partners were selected.

The term 'Ruidhle Mór' was used for at least three other dances: the 'Old West Highland Circular Reel' for two couples, a variant of this in which as many dancers as pleased took part, and the eight-handed reel of Cape Breton. The first of these is also known as 'Ruidhle man Cuairt nan Cailleachan' (The Old Women's Roundabout Reel), alternatively 'Seann Ruidhle' (Old Reel) and so on. It is described as the 'Old Scotch Reel' or the 'old-fashioned way' of dancing the Scotch reel. Although 'Scotch reel' first denoted a threesome, this description takes it to be a circular foursome reel, the dance which is also known as 'An Ruidhle Gàidhealach' or in some places by its English equivalent, the 'Highland Reel'. That it was always circular in pattern, and did not describe a figure of eight, is corroborated by evidence from Cape Breton. 'Ruidhle na Bainnse' (Wedding Reel) has the same basic form.

'Ruidhle Thulachain' (Reel of Tulloch) seems not to have been composed before about 1800, although the tune, 'The Reel of Tulloch', is older. Perthshire tradition claims that Iain Dubh Gearr, a MacGregor, and Isabel his wife, created the dance-steps in Strathspey *c.*1600. They are also said to have improvised the port-a-beul: *O Thulaichean gu Bealaichean*. It was also a foursome reel and was combined, with variants recorded from district to district, with the 'Highland Reel'. Names such as 'Scotch Reel' were then given either to the original foursome reel or to the combined dance. In Cape Breton the four-handed reel was known as 'Ruidhle Cheathrar' (Reel of Four) or 'Ruidhle Beag' (Small Reel), the latter to distinguish it from the reel of eight, known there as 'An Ruidhle Mór', which was a form of the 'Reel of Tulloch'

The Reel of Tulloch.

known in Scotland as 'The Roundabout Hullachan' or 'Reel of Tulloch in a Circle'. Versions of this and of the 'Double Reel of Tulloch' (two sets in the form of a cross) were quite well-known in Lochaber and parts of Argyll. It is interesting to note that the distinctive swinging and setting of 'Ruidhle Thulachain' seem to have been known in Gaelic society before the first recorded appearance of the 'Reel of Tulloch'. It is also worth noting that Frances Peacock (1723–1807), an Aberdeen dancing master who knew, and was prepared to learn from, students from the Highlands and Islands, records a number of reel steps with their Gaelic names – for instance, the promenade is *Ceum-siubhail*, from *ceum* ('step') and *siubhail* ('to glide', 'to move', 'to proceed with rapidity'). This suggests that within Gaelic society there were developments that were independent of those in the rest of Scotland. In certain instances old forms may have blended with new and incoming fashions.

The survival in the Hebrides of a number of curious dances points in this direction. 'Cath nan Coileach' (The Cockfight) is danced by two couples and is divided into two distinct parts. This appears to be a native dance (it is said to represent the circling of fighting cocks), but it is danced with reel steps, the first part at slightly less than reel tempo, the second much faster. It is danced to the tune 'Boc Liath nan Gobhar' (The Shaggy Grey Buck), a well-known pipe tune which Barra pipers also know under the name of this dance. 'Ruidhle nan Coileach Dubha' (The Blackcocks' Reel) involves a mime of 'blackcocks' and 'ducks'. As an adult dance, it is a reel for two couples. The first couple kneel on one knee while the second couple set to them; the positions are reversed; then all four join hands in a ring. (Both of these dances have affinities with the old circular reel.) A variant existed as a children's game in which 'blackcocks' (two boys) danced as 'ducks' (two girls) knelt or squatted, waddling around with hands held in front of their mouths, palms together, to represent ducks' beaks. 'Dannsa nan Tunnag' (Ducks' Dance) possibly existed in variant forms on the mainland and in the Hebrides; it also appears to have gone under slightly different names – 'Turraban' (Waddling), 'Ruidhle', and so on. It is described as a foursome reel with a setting step which consisted of dancing on the hunkers and shooting out a leg to the side. Where it is recorded as a solo the dancer moved around the room on his hunkers, using the kibby step. As a dance-game, one child or many hopped around in a circle with hands clasped under the thighs.

There are three dances with Gaelic names that exclude *dannsa*: 'Marbhadh na Béiste Duibhe' (Killing the Otter), 'A' Choille Bharrach' (The Barra Wood') and 'An Long Bharrach' (The Barra Ship). The first is a mime or 'folk play' about stalking and killing the otter; it may once have had musical accompaniment. The second, danced to a reel tune, involved six dancers who formed the outline of a ship while the seventh represented the mast in the centre and danced with each of the six in turn. The third is a variant of the foursome reel with any number of dancers and one man in the centre.

In some of these dances at least there may be vestiges of what were originally fertility rites. There are one or two clues still to be found in oral tradition that suggest a connection with rituals performed long ago at wakes. A dance which is obviously of great antiquity and which was once known throughout the Gàidhealtachd is '(Dannsa) Cailleach an Dùdain' (The Carlin of the Mill Dust). Alternative names have *dùrdan* or *dòrdan* (humming). It was performed by two people, in male and female roles, to a tune of the same name played on the pipes or fiddle or sung as a *port-a-beul*, either by a third person or by the performers themselves. The words begin: 'Carlin of the *dùdan/dùrdan*, keep your rear to me . . . .' The two characters enact a primitive drama in which the man kills the woman, becomes overcome with grief and then resuscitates her, limb by limb, until finally he touches her hair and restores her to life. In some versions both characters are armed with sticks; in others the man holds a 'magic wand' (*slachdan draoìdheachd/geasachd*). This death-and-resurrection drama was latterly played by children on May Day. Adults are recorded as dancing it on St Michael's Day, 29 September.

A unique dance is 'An Dannsa Mór' (The Great Dance), a ring dance of Skye origin performed by twelve men or more, two of whom move with a formalized 'walk' inside the ring, singing alternate lines of song, then taking their places in the ring as all the dancers join in the chorus. During the chorus the dancers hop around on the left foot, with their legs straight and their feet about 18 inches from the floor. There are two songs, the second of which refers to mill dust (*sadach na muilne*); both of these exist in variants, one of which mentions 'Ruidhle nam Pòg'. It is at least possible that more than one dance of this type existed and that these songs reflect a diversity of which we now have no record.

The so-called Hebridean Dances are quite different from these and are said to have been introduced by one Ewen Maclachlan, a dancing master-cum-catechist in South Uist who had studied for the priesthood at the Scots College of Douai, in France, around the middle of the nineteenth century. One of the dances has a Gaelic name, 'Mac Iain Ghasda' (Son of Fine/Excellent/Ingenious Iain). The associated song is simply a variant of the well-known 'Hieland Laddie':

> Where have you been a' the day
> Bonnie laddie, Hieland laddie?

but the connection is otherwise obscure.

All these dances, with the partial exception perhaps of some dance-games and dances which may have been associated with seasonal festivals, were generally danced indoors. Outdoor dancing, however, was also very popular, particularly on moonlit nights. Each district had its favourite spot, usually on a level roadway and often at a crossroads or on a bridge. The common term for such dances was *dannsa an rathaid/rothaid* (road dance). As an institution 'road dancing' survived until fairly recently.

Finally, there is a dance which is supposed to have been created out-of-doors on 23 July 1745. Tradition claims that seven Moidart fishermen were digging for lug-worm bait when Prince Charles Edward Stuart landed. Their joy was such that, having thrust a spade into the sand to make up the eighth member of a dance, they composed 'The Eight Men of Moidart' to an improvised song, which ran:

> Thàinig mo Righ air tìr am Mùideart!
> Thàine tu Thearlaich! Thàine tu Thearlaich. . . .
>
> My King has landed in Moidart!
> You have come, Charles! You have come, Charles. . . .

There are, in fact, two dances of this name, the older one being composed of two of the old west Highland circular reels and hence known by the alternative name of 'An Ruidhle Dùbailte' (The Double Reel). The name at any rate is referred to in an eighteenth-century song attibuted to John MacCodrum (1693–1779). On formal grounds it could easily date back to 1745 or even earlier. (See Emmerson 1967; Flett and Flett 1964, which has an excellent bibliography.)

JMCI

Darling, Sir Frank Fraser (1903–79) Born Derbyshire. Graduated in agriculture at the University of Edinburgh. Director of West Highland Survey 1944–50, and published *West Highland Survey* 1955. Had an international reputation as a conservationist. (See obit., *Royal Society of Edinburgh Year Book* 1980, 53–4.)

DST

Davie, Alan, *see* art, Gaelic, in modern times.

Dean of Lismore, Book of Undoubtedly the most precious and significant Gaelic literary manuscript to survive, for it helps us to reconstruct, in a large measure, important parts of Gaelic history which would otherwise remain conjectural. A page is reproduced on p. 173. It shows us the bardic order and its patrons interacting in Perthshire and Argyllshire, especially in the fifteenth and early sixteenth centuries, and preserves a unique record of some less formal by-products of that system: the bawdy and burlesques of such poets as Duncan Campbell of Glenorchy (q.v.) and the Bàrd Mac an t-Saoir (q.v.), and the *dànta grádha* (literary, sometimes courtly, love poetry) of professionals and amateurs such as Eòin MacMhuirich (q.v.) and Iseabail Ní Mheic Cailéin (q.v.). It demonstrates that Irish–Scottish literary contacts were being maintained and that the work of Irish poets such as Muireadhach Albanach and Gearóid Iarla was circulating and was appreciated. There are only hints of similar activity outwith Perthshire and Argyllshire, and these survive through some connection with the 'heartland' (the Bàrd Mac an-t-Saoir's Rannoch connections beside his Badenoch ones; MacEachaig's patron's wife being a Maclean of Lochbuie). The fact that the manuscript was written in a non-traditional orthography based on that of current Scots provides a valuable linguistic 'fix' (to use a navigational metaphor), once the system is fully understood and its evidence analysed.

The anthology would seem to have originated with Finlay, chief of the Macnabs (see **Fionnlagh Mac an Aba**), who urges Dugald MacGregor of Fortingall to continue the work Finlay has started. He has collected material from packmen and recommends that the *lorgánaigh*, or strolling bards, should be approached among other sources, including clerical ones. James MacGregor (q.v.), son of Dugald, was a notary public and an ecclesiastic, and he and his brother Duncan, a practising poet, seem to have taken over the work which was mainly compiled between 1512 and 1526.

The Dean's manuscript includes a chronicle of

obits and miscellaneous matter such as Latin lines on Scottish kings, English memoranda, verses in Scots, a letter in Scots, etc. (see Quiggin 1937, for Catalogue). It is mainly composed of poetry, however, including a good deal of religious verse, a large section of heroic verse and poetry by Scottish family poets, together with the miscellaneous verse mentioned above (see also **verse**). The anthologists' taste is catholic, in moral and political as well as in literary senses. The manuscript includes the work of highly trained bards, loosely trained ones and amateurs; work by Campbell and MacDonald and MacGregor bards (as though the growing feuds of the Campbells with their neighbours did not impinge on the anthologist); religious verse and outright bawdy. It also includes a large representation of verse by Ó Dálaigh poets (Aonghus Fionn, Aonghus mac Cearbhaill Bhuidhe, Cúchonnacht mac Cearbhaill Bhuidhe, Donnchadh Mór, Gofraidh Fionn, Tadhg Camchosach and Muireadhach Albanach – some eighteen poems) but relatively little by their Scottish cousins, the MacMhuirichs. It looks as though in this matter the Dean was drawing on some manuscript anthology which had come into his possession, possibly through ecclesiastical channels. He includes Fionnlagh Ruadh's satire on Clanranald but not the official praise (see **MacMhuirich, Eòin**). All in all, we get the impression that the Dean's stance was not dogmatic.

His choice of orthography must have shocked any bardic professional who saw his book, for the bardic metrics are founded on traditional spelling. It is clear that the Dean had manuscript sources, sometimes variant ones, for some of his items, while others seem to have come to him from oral sources. It is clear also that the oral versions at least have often taken on the colouring of Perthshire Gaelic and so have become an invaluable source of evidence for that dialect and for the history of Gaelic phonology, morphology and syntax (see **Gaelic**), since the Dean's method and spelling allow vernacular forms to appear (W. J. Watson 1937, introduction; O'Rahilly 1932, etc.).

For the earlier history of Book of the Dean scholarship, see W. J. Watson (1937). Quiggin's work appeared posthumously in the same year. O'Rahilly had published his *Indexes to the Book of the Dean of Lismore* in 1934. Neil Ross subsequently published the heroic verse (q.v.) (N. Ross 1939). Single poems were edited by Bergin, O'Rahilly, Murphy, McKenna and Greene. William Gillies has published analyses and texts of material in the Book of the Dean

(W. A. Gillies 1977, 1978), and Donald Meek is re-editing the heroic verse.

It is thought that the Dean's manuscript came to light in the course of James MacPherson's (q.v.) collecting tours of 1760–1, and that MacPherson had it from Alexander MacPherson, blacksmith in Portree, who in turn had acquired it in Lochcarron. Donald T. Mackintosh speculates that it may once have belonged to Duncan Macrae of Inverinate, compiler of the Fernaig Manuscript (q.v.), and may have influenced his choice of orthography (Mackintosh 1947, 20). The manuscript was among those handed over in 1803 by the Highland Society of London to the Highland Society of Scotland; it later passed to the Advocates' Library and finally to the National Library of Scotland.   DST

Deer, Book of The earliest example we have of continuous Gaelic written in a manuscript in Scotland is in the Book of Deer. Deer was a sixth-century Celtic monastic foundation in Buchan, close to the site of the thirteenth-century Cistercian abbey. The main text of the Book is in Latin, and it is ascribed to the ninth century. It contains, in somewhat corrupt or careless versions, the complete Gospel of St John, portions of the other three Gospels, the Apostles' Creed, a fragment of a prayer for the visitation of the sick and the charter granted by David I (1124–53) to the clerics of Deer. The manuscript is illuminated in a style related to that of the Books of Dimma and Durrow and other gospel books. It has an Old Irish colophon, probably of ninth-century date, and an Old Irish rubric.

The Gaelic notitiae are written later by five hands on blank spaces and margins in the Book. The notes include the legend of the foundation of the monastery, an account which ends in a piece of *Dindshenchas*, or place-name legend, connecting Deer with *dér* ('a tear'). The foundation is ascribed to Colum Cille (q.v.) and his disciple Drostan, son of Coscrach (the son having a Pictish, the father a Gaelic name), and references to grants of land were written in, probably between 1131 and 1153 and perhaps in the context of litigation which took place c.1150. The notitiae provide valuable evidence as to the forms of Gaelic used at the time (the literary dialect, but influenced by the vernacular) and also evidence of place and personal names (Gaelic titles such as *brithem* and *fer léginn* and titles deriving from an area of Gaelic/-Pictish overlap, e.g. *mormaer*). The manuscript was once in the possession of John Aubrey, and perhaps

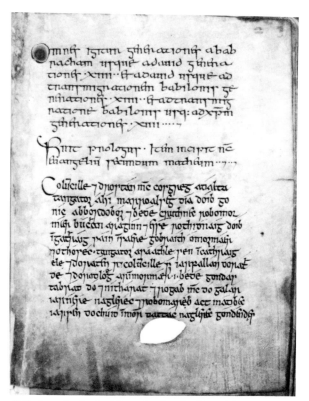

Folio from the Book of Deer showing Gaelic notitiae.
Cambridge University Library MS Ii.6.32, f.3r.

came to him in the late seventeenth century, when we know he was in correspondence with Professor Garden of King's College, Aberdeen. It is now in Cambridge University Library. (For texts, translation and discussion, see K. H. Jackson 1972.)   DST

Deò-Gréine, An The official magazine of An Comunn Gaidhealach (q.v.), which was first published in 1905. Its name was later changed to *An Gaidheal* (q.v.) and, latterly, to *Sruth* (in recent years produced as an inset in a Highland newspaper).   DST

Dewar, Donald (1739–92) From Fortingall, Perthshire. Poet. (See P. Cameron 1892; D. Maclean 1915.)   DST

dialect(s), *see* Gaelic: dialects, principal divisions; subdivisions.

Dick, Cairistìona (born 1935) Born in Glasgow, of North Uist and Islay parents. Author of *Raonaid* (1981), etc.   DST

dictionaries, Scottish Gaelic The earliest surviving Scottish Gaelic vocabularies were by-products of literary and research activity in the late seventeenth century. First to appear in print, as an appendix to W. Nicolson's *The Scottish Historical Library* (1702), was a list from the Revd Robert Kirk (q.v.) of Gaelic equivalents for some sections of John Ray's *Dictionariolum Trilingue* (J. L. Campbell 1938a, 76–93, 1961a, 89–90). Among the research notes of Edward Lhuyd (q.v.) are lists of equivalents for some parts of Ray's work from an Argyll and an Inverness-shire dialect (Campbell and Thomson 1963, 91–218).

In 1741 the Society in Scotland for Propagating Christian Knowledge published *Leabhar a Theagasc Ainminnin*, compiled by Alasdair Mac Mhaighstir Alasdair (q.v.) on the basis of *A New Vocabulary for the Use of Schools* (1720) (J. L. Campbell 1937, 1971). The first attempt at a full-scale dictionary was made by William Shaw (q.v.), whose *Galic and English Dictionary*, an indiscriminate collection of Irish and Scottish Gaelic words, appeared in 1780 (K. D. MacDonald 1979). In 1795 Robert Mac Farlan, the first and only Gaelic 'Professor' to the Highland Society of Scotland published a work of modest compass, *Nuadh Fhoclair Gaidhlig agus Beurla*. Peter MacFarlane, translator of English religious works into Gaelic, issued in 1815 *A New English and Gaelic Vocabulary*, in which an English–Gaelic section is followed by *Focalair Gaelig agus Beurla*.

The third and fourth decades of the nineteenth century were a high point in the making of Gaelic dictionaries. Following the labours of its Ossian committee, the Highland Society of Scotland (q.v.), founded in 1784, set up in 1806 a committee to organize the production of a large-scale dictionary. Its first editor was the Revd Dr John MacLeod, but the mainspring of the enterprise, until his death in 1822, was Ewen MacLachlan (q.v.). In 1826 Dr MacKintosh MacKay was appointed to steer this troubled project to its eventual publication in 1828 (R. I. Black unpublished paper), by which time there had already appeared, in 1825, the substantial *Gaelic Dictionary* by Robert Armstrong (q.v.). In 1831 came the *Dictionary of the Gaelic Language* by Dr Norman MacLeod (Caraid nan Gàidheal: q.v.) and Dr Daniel Dewar, a work which went through many impressions in the nineteenth century. Neil MacAlpine, a divinity student from Islay, published his *Pronouncing Gaelic Dictionary* in 1832, and in 1845 there appeared a second edition with an English–Gaelic section, of limited usefulness, by John MacKenzie (q.v.) of Gairloch. The MacAlpine–MacKenzie combination was in print until recently.

In 1842 Father Ewen MacEachen (q.v.) published his Gaelic–English dictionary, based on MacLeod and Dewar with words added from his native Arisaig dialect. A revised and enlarged edition of MacEachen, prepared by Alexander MacBain and John Whyte, was published in 1902 and has become the standard school dictionary of the twentieth century. In 1896 Alexander MacBain (q.v.) produced his own *Etymological Dictionary of the Gaelic Language* (reprinted 1982), a useful, scholarly work not yet superseded.

The opening years of the twentieth century saw the first appearance of the remarkable *Illustrated Gaelic to English Dictionary* by Edward Dwelly (q.v.), a work based on MacLeod and Dewar, with a large accession of additional words from printed sources and over twenty correspondents in different parts of the country. In 1912 Malcolm MacFarlane (q.v.) published a school dictionary *Am Briathrachan Beag*. The Revd Dr Malcolm MacLennan, a native of Uig, Lewis, published in 1925 *A Pronouncing and Etymological Dictionary of the Gaelic Language*, based on MacAlpine, with words added from current literature and common speech, especially the speech of west Lewis. In 1932 Henry Cyril Dieckhoff, a Russian monk at Fort Augustus Abbey, produced *A Pronouncing Dictionary of Scottish Gaelic, based on the Glengarry Dialect. Abair Facail*, a small, pocket-size dictionary, aimed primarily at learners of Gaelic and compiled by John A. MacDonald and Ronald Renton, was published in 1979. A new English–Gaelic Dictionary, by Derick Thomson, was published in 1981.

Publications of specialist vocabulary are John Cameron's *Gaelic Names of Plants* (1883), H. Cameron Gillies's *Gaelic Names of Diseases and Diseased States* (1890) and Alexander R. Forbes's *Gaelic Names of Beasts, Birds, Fishes, Insects, Reptiles, etc.* (1905). There have also been published collections of unusual words from different areas, notably those of Father Allan MacDonald (q.v.) (J. L. Campbell 1958a), Alexander MacDonald (A. MacDonald 1922), Duncan MacDonald (D. MacDonald 1946), Norman MacDonald (N. MacDonald 1966) and Derick Thomson (D. S. Thomson 1979c).

Unpublished Gaelic dictionary materials include a short manuscript biblical concordance, compiled in the early eighteenth century by William Gordon and now in the Countess of Sutherland's library; the 'Highland Gentlemen's Dictionary', a collaborative venture begun c.1776 by a number of clergymen (NLS MSS. Adv. 73.3.5, 7–12, 22–3); the dictionary of Sir James Foulis of Colinton (NLS MS. Adv. 72.2.16), part of a late eighteenth-century dictionary by Archibald Fletcher (NLS MS. Adv. 72.2.17; Ingliston MS. A. vi.17); and the dictionary of Alexander Robertson, c.1800, partially printed (NLS MS. Adv. 72.2.18) and the remainder surviving in manuscript copy (NLS MSS. Adv. 72.2.19–21). An English–Gaelic dictionary by Alexander MacLaurin survives as NLS MSS. Adv. 72.2.22–5, and another English–Gaelic vocabulary, compiled in 1812 by Malcolm MacPherson, is NLS MS. Adv. 73.2.6. A two-volume musical glossary, compiled by Angus Fraser, is now NLS MSS. Adv. 73.1.5–6. The unpublished supplement to Dwelly's dictionary is NLS MSS. 14957–8. Materials for an English–Gaelic dictionary, assembled 1939–51 by Henry C. Maitland, are now NLS MSS. 14959–64.

Work on an Historical Dictionary of Scottish Gaelic was begun at the University of Glasgow in 1966 on the initiative of Professor Derick S. Thomson and with the appointment of the writer of this entry as dictionary editor. The aim of the project is to produce a dictionary of Scottish Gaelic which will illustrate the history of all the recoverable words in the language by means of citations selected from all available sources. This involves the scrutiny of manuscripts and printed sources ranging in date from the sixteenth century to the present, as well as the collection of hitherto undocumented oral vocabulary.

The excerpting of printed sources has to a considerable extent been carried out by a constantly changing band of volunteer readers. A wide range of texts has also been processed for computer sorting, using a program called Nalolan, first written for the project by Nickolas Papasimacopoulos in 1972 and extensively revised and improved by Dr William Sharp of Glasgow University Computing Service. In the specialist area of manuscript excerption, a valuable contribution has been made by Mr Ronald Black, who between 1973 and 1977 excerpted bardic and other classical sources of Scottish origin in libraries in Dublin and Edinburgh.

In view of the recession of Gaelic over many parts of Scotland it was thought a matter of some urgency to try to collect as much as possible of the hitherto unrecorded vocabulary of Gaelic speakers. Funded by a grant from the Carnegie Trust Mr Angus J. Smith served as fieldworker for the dictionary between 1967 and 1972, visiting all Gaelic-speaking areas of Scotland and spending some months in Nova Scotia. A recent, smaller grant from the Carnegie Trust is being devoted to further field collection. Vocabulary has also been gathered by the distribution to individuals and schools of questionnaires on different aspects of the culture.

In 1973 Glasgow University gave further support to the project with the appointment of an assistant editor, an editorial assistant and a part-time flexowriter operator. Mr Donald Meek served as assistant editor from 1973 to 1979 and was succeeded in that capacity by Mr Ian Quick. The pace of progress towards publication will largely depend on the available levels of finance and manpower in the years ahead.   KDMcD

Dieckhoff, Rev. Henry C. (1869–1950) Author of *A Pronouncing Dictionary of Scottish Gaelic* (1932), based on the Glengarry dialect. Contributor to *Revue Celtique, Scottish Gaelic Studies*, etc.   DST

Disruption, the The name given to the secession in 1843 of a large number of ministers and people from the Church of Scotland to form the Free Church of Scotland. The primary cause was the Patronage Act of 1712, whereby, through the machinations of English Jacobites, lay patronage was reintroduced into the Church of Scotland against the wishes of the Church. In the settling of ministers in vacant charges, the choice of the patron (who might be ill-disposed to the Church's interests) increasingly prevailed over the will of the parishioners and Church courts. By the 1830s there was much strife within the Church and between the Church and the civil courts about patronage (which had already caused secessions in the eighteenth century). After the 'Ten Years' Conflict' matters came to a head in 1843, when, claiming spiritual independence for the Church, as set forth in its Claim of Rights and its Protest at the encroachment of the civil courts on the Church's spiritual domain, the great secession took place. In the Highlands and Islands the Protestant population adhered almost unanimously to the Free Church.

This mass movement had several ancillary causes: the effect of religious revivals; the increasing alienation between people and clergy, who too often seemed indifferent to the agrarian injustices of the time; an upsurge of enthusiasm for a cause after the century of repression (since 1746); rack-renting, evictions, clearances, emigration and abject poverty; a resurgence of the old spirit of loyalty to a leader (formerly a chief, now a popular preacher). There were those of course who understood the issues at stake, some who sympathized generally with the Evangelical Party and probably many who 'simply went where they saw good men going'. There may also have been a measure of blind adherence.

The Free Church faced a huge task, especially in the Highlands, providing churches, manses, schools, ministers, catechists and opportunities for education on a scale hitherto unknown. From the 1860s onwards tensions developed, causing much controversy and proposals for church union, disestablishment, innovations in modes of worship, Moody's revivalism, biblical criticism and new trends in theology. In 1893 a secession from the Free Church formed the Free Presbyterian Church. In 1900 the union of the Free Church with the United Presbyterian Church to form the United Free Church left a minority to continue as the 'legal' Free Church. In 1929 the Church of Scotland joined with the United Free Church to form the reunited Church of Scotland, national and spiritually independent. (See bibliography for **Church of Scotland**; Beith 1874; 'Disruption Worthies of the Highlands' (1877); W. M. Macgregor 1907; N. Maclean 1911; P. C. Simpson 1909.)   TMM

documents, Gaelic The Islay Charter appears to be the only surviving Gaelic charter. It was granted in 1408 by Donald, second Lord of the Isles, to 'Brian Bhicaire Magaodh' (Brian Vicar Mackay), probably an ancestor of the Mackays who were *maors* (crowners) of the South Ward (roughly Kilarrow and Kilmeny) on Islay. The charter was first published by Dr W. Reeves 1850–3); it was then held by John Magee of Antrim, whose ancestor was probably related to Somhairle Buidhe (Sorley Boy) and who came to Ireland in about 1560. The charter, written on a strip of goatskin, is now in the General Register House, Edinburgh. The witnesses seem to include both a *brehon* (judge) (Pat McAbriuin), and one of the MacBeth family (Fercos MacBetha); the latter is the only witness who signs his name, and it is likely that he was the author of the document. (See W. J. Watson 1915 etc., for text, W. D. Lamont 1960, and D. Mackinnon 1912, for discussion.)

The grant is of 11·5 marklands (about 400 acres), and the reddendo is given at 4 cows or 42 marks annually (perhaps we should understand 4 cows per markland).

This survival suggests that Gaelic continued to be written for legal purposes, a hypothesis that appears to be borne out by the one known surviving Gaelic contract of fosterage, that made in 1614 between Ruairi Mór MacLeod (q.v.) of Harris and Dunvegan and 'Eoin mac mic Cainnigh', for the fosterage of Rory's son Norman. The witnesses are two ministers, Ewen MacQueen of Diurinis and John MacColgan of Bracadale, a Donald MacQueen and Toirdealbhach Omurgeasa, one of the Ó Muirgheasáin family (q.v.) who were bards to MacLeod. The document is in National MSS of Scotland, Part III, No. LXXXIV. (See D. Mackinnon 1912, 296.)

A rare surviving Gaelic letter (of sixty-eight words) from the late sixteenth century (1593–6) is the one written by Lachlann Mór (q.v.), chief of the Macleans, to the physician Malcolm Beaton (q.v.). This survived because it was used in the binding of a

Gaelic contract of fosterage, 1614. Scottish Record Office, Edinburgh, RH.9/17/35.

Beaton manuscript. It is edited in Bannerman and Black (1978). (See also Bannerman 1983, and **law, Celtic survivals,** for a discussion of the Macdougall lease, *c.*1600.) DST

Dòmhnall Donn (MacDonald) (d. 1691) From Bohuntin. Cattle lifter and poet. Said to have killed son of Iain Lom (q.v.) in a duel *c.*1690. Caught while preparing to elope with daughter of Grant chief (Glenurquhart) and executed. Author of ' 'S truagh a Rìgh, mo nighean donn', etc. (See K. N. Macdonald 1900, 12–13, 95–6; A. M. Mackenzie 1963, 31–5.) DST

Dòmhnall Mac Fhionnlaigh nan Dàn (fl. *c.*1585) Of Loch Tréig in Lochaber. The author of the long valedictory and topographical poem 'Oran na Comhachaig'. The poem, which survives in various manuscript, printed and oral versions (Rankin 1958, 122), is clearly a conflation of several poems on different subjects. The five main themes are a dialogue with an owl, praise of hunting, praise of Keppoch chiefs, farewell to well loved places and old age. RAR

Dòmhnall nan Cleas, *see* MacPherson, Donald (1905–81).

Dòmhnall nan Oran (Donald of the Songs: Donald MacLeod) (1787–1873) From Skye. Composed personal poetry and songs on topics of local interest but saw himself also in the role of bard to Clan MacLeod. In this capacity he takes up a convention used by MacCodrum and others and employs it in 'Smeòrach nan Leòdach'. His anthology of 1811 contains some of his poems; others were printed in 1871, including his satire on the church elders of Lonmore. JMCI

Dòmhnall Phàil (1798–1875) Born Dalnaspidal. Author of 'Duanag a' Chìobair' and 'Guma slàn do na fearaibh', composed *c.*1838, when many Kingussie people emigrated to Australia; the poet changed his mind and stayed. (See Sinton 1906, 36, 69.) DST

Dòmhnall Ruadh Chorùna (Donald MacDonald of Corùna) (1887–1967) Born North Uist. His early poems reflect his First World War experiences and include one of this century's best-known songs, 'An Eala Bhàn'. Together with his last poems, they are probably his best; but all of the poems in *Dòmhnall Ruadh Chorùna* (1969) are the work of a good traditional craftsman. IMCD

Dòmhnullach, Murchadh (Murdo Sheumais) (fl. 1920) Born Melbost, Borve, Lewis. Author of 'Cailin òg an fhuilt bhàin', etc. (See D. I. MacLeòid 1972; T. MacLeòid 1969, 1–4.)   DST

Domnall Brecc (d. *c*.642) Became king of Dalriada (q.v.) in 629. As ambitious as his grandfather Aedán (q.v.), he was infinitely less successful, all four recorded battles of his reign being defeats. His ill-judged participation in 637 in the fabled battle of Magh Rath in Meath probably cost him his Irish territories. He was killed by the Britons of Strathclyde at the battle of Strathcarron *c*.642, the earliest certain record of hostility between Scot and Briton in Scotland. It was a famous victory, for included in the British poem 'y Gododdin' is a commemorative stanza, which ends 'and the head of Domnall Brecc, ravens gnawed it'. (See Bannerman 1971, 75; 1974, 99–103.)   JWMB

Donald, Lord of the Isles (d. *c*.1422) Donald, son of John I, became Lord of the Isles on his father's death in 1387. He fought the battle of Harlaw in 1411 to make good his wife's claim to the earldom of Ross. He is said to have died a monk in the monastery of Iona. (See Steer and Bannerman 1977, 148–50, 205.)   JWMB

Donncha Gobha, *see* Macintosh, Duncan (*c*.1806–*c*.1846).

Donncha Loudainn/Loudaidh, *see* Lothian, Duncan.

Donnchadh Bàn, *see* Mac-an-t-Saoir, Donnchadh Bàn.

Donnchadh Clachair, *see* MacDonald, Duncan (d. 1954).

Donnchadh Dubh, *see* Campbell, Donnchadh Dubh.

Donnchadh Gobha (Duncan Mackay) (fl. 1790) Author of lengthy elegy for James ('Ossian') MacPherson. (See Sinton 1906, 262.)   DST

Donnchadh mac an Phearsúin (dates unknown) Author of verse fragments in the Book of the Dean of Lismore (q.v.).   DST

Donnchadh Mór (dates unknown) Author, according to the Fernaig Manuscript (q.v.), of 'Breisleach Dhonnchaidh Mhóir', elsewhere ascribed to Baothghalach MacAodhagáin. (See MacPhàrlain 1923, 77, 328.)   DST

Donnchadh Mór ó Leamhnacht (d. ?1425) Possibly Duncan, 8th Earl of Lennox. Author of poem in the Book of the Dean of Lismore (q.v.). (See W. J. Watson 1937, 248.)   DST

Donnchadh nam Pìos (Duncan MacRae of Inverinate) (*c*.1640–*c*.1700) Chief of his house and member of a cultured family which produced a number of prominent ecclesiastics. He was educated at the University of Edinburgh, where he is said to have demonstrated outstanding mechanical and engineering skills. His literary talents and tastes, together with his Episcopalian piety and Jacobite politics, are evidenced in the Fernaig Manuscript (q.v.), which he began to compile in 1688. (See D. MacKinnon 1885.)   KDMCD

Donnchadh Óg (dates unknown) Author of poem on the Seven Deadly Sins in the Book of the Dean of Lismore (q.v.) and in the Fernaig Manuscript (q.v.). (See M. MacFarlane 1923, 22; J. W. Watson 1937, 252.)   DST

Donnchadh Óg Albanach Author of poem 'Dá ghabhladh dhéag insan dán' in the Book of the Dean of Lismore (q.v.). (See Quiggin 1937, 69.)   DST

drama, Gaelic As part of the general output of Gaelic programmes on radio and television drama has not featured particularly prominently – a situation that has arisen as much because of budgetary constraints on producers as because of a dearth of material or lack of appetite for drama among listeners. Unless one moves around frequently in the right areas or scans the local papers for festival details, the impression could be gained that Gaelic drama scarcely exists. But, against considerable odds, it does; and in many rural areas, for brief but glorious moments, it is seen to thrive. As yet no central library of Gaelic plays exists and no training in stagecraft or production is available to the Gaelic actor or producer, which, together with the lack of impact made centrally through radio and television, ensures that a considerable amount of energy and experience at the grass roots remains unco-ordinated and unrecognized.

Since 1945 Gaelic drama has not been without its false dawns, its fits and starts, but a steady development is, nevertheless, discernible. In the late 1940s a radio series by Finlay J. Macdonald dealt, in dramatized terms, with the early history of Oban, Inverary, Campbeltown, Fort William, Dingwall and Inverness. In 1951 Mr Macdonald produced Gaelic adaptations on radio of *The Wild Duck*, *William Tell* and *Don Quixote*. By the late 1950s fairly ambitious drama festivals were being organized at the Glasgow Lyric and the Highlanders' Institute. During this era Iain Crichton Smith (q.v.) wrote highly entertaining plays, such as *A' Chùirt* and *An Coileach*. At the 1957 festival a translation of a Eugene O'Neil one-act play (*An Dul*) by Paul Macinnes was the most successful and later in the year *Maith dhuinn ar Peacaidhean*, by the same author, was broadcast. By the early 1960s a new and highly original voice emerged – that of Finlay MacLeod (q.v.), whose skill in developing Pinteresque dialogue and atmosphere was seen in such plays as *Ceann Gropaig* and *Shoni*. There were radio versions of both, and in March 1967 *Ceann Gropaig* was televised, as was *Chan fhàs iad sean* by Iain Crichton Smith (q.v.). To date these are the only two instances of televised Gaelic drama.

In 1975 drama productions began to feature for the first time on the syllabus of the National Mod, and in 1976 a decision was taken to hold district festivals rather than oblige teams to travel expensively to Glasgow each year. These two developments certainly helped to encourage Gaelic drama in the heartland, if not in the larger cities.

Again in the heartland – in Tarbert, Harris – the first ever professional Gaelic drama company was established in 1978. This company, Fir Chlis, provided mime, music, song and pantomime, as well as conventional dramas. John Murray, Norman Macdonald and Paul Macinnes wrote original work for it, and although unfortunately it has now dispersed, the team's bold and experimental approach to production should encourage many others. There was recently a fairly successful run of half-hour Gaelic plays on radio by a variety of authors, among whom was a welcome newcomer, Donald Smith, with his play *Cadal is Còmhstri*. PM

Druim Cett, Convention of The Convention, a *rígdál* or 'meeting of kings' between Aed, king of the northern Uí Néill, and Aedán (q.v.), king of Dalriada (q.v.) in Scotland and Ireland, was held in 575 near Limavady in Co. Derry. The main topic of discussion was the future status of the Irish Dalriada, and it was decided that the armed forces thereof should go to

Aed, as overlord of northern Ireland, while taxes and tribute should continue to be levied by Aedán, confirming that effective government of the territory was to remain in his hands and that of his successors. (See Bannerman 1974, 157–70.) JWMB

Duan Albanach A poem of twenty-seven verses, most probably composed around 1093 by an Irish poet, purporting to give the names of the kings of Scotland from legendary times to the time of Malcolm III. The poet uses the Irish Nennius and the Book of Invasions (*Lebor Gabála Erenn*) for the earlier period, and for the later probably a lost Scottish king-list which existed in Ireland. (For the text, see K. H. Jackson 1956, and for translation and further discussion, K. H. Jackson 1957.) DST

Dubhghall mac an Ghiolla Ghlais (fl. 1500) Author of poem in the Book of the Dean of Lismore (q.v.) in praise of MacGregor chief (d. 1519). (See W. J. Watson 1937, 204.) DST

Dumbarton The town first comes to reliable historical notice in Bede's *Ecclesiastical History* (I.i; I.xii). He describes it as 'a strongly defended political centre of the Britons', with the British name Alcluith (Clyde Rock). Archaeological evidence demonstrates occupation in the seventh to eighth centuries AD (and perhaps as early as the sixth), when a rampart controlled access to Clyde Rock from the landward side (Alcock 1975–6). This defence was destroyed by Irish Vikings in AD 870, and thereafter the site lay derelict for centuries. The Gaelic name, Dùn Breatann (fort of the Britons), does not appear in records before the thirteenth century, when a royal burgh was founded, and a castle was built upon the Rock. (See MacPhail 1979a.) LA

Dunaverty, Massacre of (June 1647) About 300 Highlanders in Dunaverty Castle surrendered unconditionally to the Covenanters and were massacred a few days later. (See D. Stevenson 1975, 27–37.) DS

Dunadd, *see* forts and fortified sites.

Duncan I (d. 1040) Before becoming king of Scots, Duncan was already king of Strathclyde, which had enjoyed a client relationship with Scotia since the early tenth century. His succession to the kingship of the Scots on the death of his grandfather, Malcolm I (q.v.), in 1034 fixed the southern boundary of Scotland more or less as it is today. (See Duncan 1975, 98.) JWMB

Duncan, John (fl. 1920) Born Dundee. Associated with Sir Patrick Geddes (q.v.) in the Celtic renaissance movement of the 1890s in Edinburgh. Two of his paintings on Ossianic themes survive. His portrait of Marjory Kennedy-Fraser is reproduced on p. 143. (See also **art, Gaelic, in modern times**.) DST

Duncan, Margrat (d. 1948) Native of Islay. Mod Gold Medallist, 1909. CG

Dundee, Viscount (John Grahame of Claverhouse) (1648–89) Mortally wounded while leading the Jacobites to victory over the forces of William of Orange at Killiecrankie. (See A. N. and H. Tayler 1939.) DS

Durrow, Book of, *see* manuscripts, illuminated.

Dùthaich Mhic Aoidh (Mackay country) The Mackay country, now part of Sutherland county, was named Strathnaver after the Naver river, which flows through its centre. It extended from Cape Wrath to the Caithness border and was protected to the south by a chain of hills extending east from Assynt. Clan Aodh are believed to descend from the royal house of Moray and to have moved into Strathnaver during the twelfth century. When a Mackay chief married the sister of the Lord of the Isles in 1415, he was stated to be the leader of 4,000 clansmen capable of bearing arms. In 1628 the chief raised a regiment to fight in the Thirty Years' War and was created Lord Reay. But the Gordon Earls of Sutherland had already obtained the feudal superiority of Strathnaver, and from this chief they purchased the Naver valley. Here the notorious Sutherland Clearances (q.v.) were begun in 1806 and extended to the limits of the Mackay country after the 7th Lord Reay sold the remainder of his clan patrimony to the house of Sutherland in 1829. (See Grimble 1965, 1979a; A. Mackay 1906; R. Mackay 1829.) IG

Dwelly, Edward (1864–1939) An Englishman who, while serving as an Army piper and later in employment with the Ordnance Survey, developed a consuming interest in Gaelic and produced, singlehandedly, his comprehensive *Illustrated Gaelic to English Dictionary*, first published pseudonymously

Cover design by Alasdair Gray for Edward Dwelly's Gaelic to English Dictionary. *Eighteen trees represent the letters of the Gaelic alphabet.*

by 'Ewen MacDonald' in thirty-three parts at Lyminge and Herne Bay, 1902–11, and now published in one volume by Gairm Publications. An unpublished Appendix is MS. 14957 in the National Library of Scotland. (See obit. in *An Gaidheal*, vol. 34, 93.)

KDMcD

Dyce, William, *see* art, Gaelic, in modern times.

Eachann Bacach (Lame Hector: Hector Maclean) (*c*. ?1600–post-1651) One of the group of seventeenth- and eighteenth-century poets referred to as Aos-dàna (q.v.), he seems to have been a semi-official poet of the court of that Sir Lachlan Maclean of Duart (Mull), whose death in 1649 was marked by his finest extant poem, 'A' Chnò Shamhna'. Six other poems are ascribed to him (one doubtfully), the earliest probably from the mid-1630s. The earlier poems are somewhat unconfident or perfunctory, 'Iorram do Shir Lachann' being a good example of the transfer of classical bardic themes to the vernacular bard (description of weapons, indication of allies, mention of hospitality, courtly reference to wife) but with minimal poetic excitement. 'A' Chnò Shamhna' is altogether more supple and densely textured (D. S. Thomson 1974a, 128ff). The two latest poems are a semi-elegy and a lament for Sir Hector Maclean, Sir Lachlan's successor, who was killed at Inverkeithing in 1651. The 'Oran do Shir Eachann' was composed before the chief's death was confirmed but seems to anticipate it; this is fluent, rhythmical panegyric. 'Gur bochd naidheachd do dhùthcha' is more popular, less formal. (See C. Ó Baoill 1979.) DST

Eachann Dròbhair (the Drover: Eachann Mackenzie) (fl. ?early eighteenth century.) From Lochbroom area. Reputed to be author of original version of 'Bruthaichean Ghlinn Braoin'. (Information from Mr Archie Mackenzie, Halifax, Nova Scotia.) DST

Eairdsidh Sheumais, *see* MacKenzie, Archibald, J.

early Christian Latin inscriptions, *see* Ogam stones and early Christian Latin inscriptions.

education, Gaelic, *see* broadcasting, Gaelic; school societies, Gaelic; schools, Gaelic; schools, Gaelic teaching in; universities and colleges, Gaelic studies in.

emigration In the British Isles the countries that have suffered most from emigration in recent times have been Ireland, Wales and Scotland, and in Scotland especially the Border counties and the Highlands and Islands. (For statistics of Highland emigration, which has been going on continuously and at varying rates since the mid-eighteenth century, see the Decennial Census Reports; also Darling 1955; Hilleary 1938; Struthers n.d.)

The break-up of the clan system during the eighteenth century caused large-scale emigration from the Highlands, from the 1760s onwards, to the cities and Lowlands and to America – first to the Carolinas, and Albany (New York) and, after the American War of Independence, to Canada (Prince Edward Island, Cape Breton, the eastern provinces and central Canada). From the 1840s emigrants began to favour Australia and New Zealand. One group from Assynt, led by the Revd Norman Macleod, moved first to Canada in about 1820 and thence in 1850 to Waipu in New Zealand (Macdonald 1928). (For successive waves of emigration and their connection with the Clearances for sheep farming, and periods of destitution, see Day 1918; Hunter 1976; Leigh 1929.) There were Government inquiries, but not until later in the century was emigration officially controlled, and usually by the new self-governing colonies. Emigration has continued at a high rate well into the twentieth century. Between 1850 and 1950 the Highland population declined by at least 100,000.

Wherever they went, the Highland emigrants carried their language, culture and traditions and eased their homesickness by transporting to their new lands the place names of their homeland – Glengarry, Glenelg, etc. In the Gaelic periodicals of the nineteenth century there is much about the emigrants and their new countries. One thinks too of Norman Macleod's work in Gaelic, *The Emigrant Ship*, and John Maclean's Gaelic poem, 'The Gael in Canada' (See Dunn 1953; S. Maclean 1962; Bumsted 1982.)

TMM

'Lochaber no more' by John Watson Nicol, 1883. ▶

Eóghan (?Athairne) mac Eóin mheic Eichthighearna (fl. *c.*1475) Author of lament for Eoin Ciar (of Dunolly) (W. J. Watson 1937, 166). One of the MacEwen poets (q.v.). DST

Eòin Mac Briain, *see* MacMhuirich, Eòin.

Episcopal Church The Scottish Episcopal Church, a province of the Anglican Communion, is an indigenous Scottish denomination. In the Gaelic north-west its members are comparatively few, mostly to be found among the gentry, but it has remained strong among the common people in north Argyll, especially in Appin and Glencoe.

The Church of Scotland Reformed dates from 1560, but there ensued 130 years of political and religious conflict, presbytery and episcopacy being dominant in turns (with presbyterian elements persisting under episcopacy). A potent factor in the conflict was the insistence of the Stewart kings on their 'divine right' of royal supremacy in Church and State, their preference for episcopacy best suiting their interests and their desire for Church conformity in all their realms.

With the deposition of King James VII(II) and his royal house, the Church of Scotland, episcopal since 1662, was in its presbyterian form established by law as the national Church in 1690. The bishops refused allegiance to the new regime, and throughout the eighteenth century the Episcopal Church, being actively pro-Jacobite, was harassed by 'penal laws' until after the death of Prince Charles Edward in 1788. After 1690, however, many Episcopalian clergy, favoured by lairds and people, continued as parish ministers until they died, while the first Presbyterian ministers in the north-west met with strong local opposition.

There are Gaelic versions of the Book of Common Prayer and of the Scottish Communion Office. In the early 1970s the Episcopal Church Gaelic Society was formed. This body organizes occasional Gaelic services and has published *An Aifrionn*, Norman Burns's Gaelic version of the 'alternative' Eucharist Service (1970). (See Goldie 1976; Highet 1950; J. Mackay 1914; also general Church histories and yearbooks and Directory of the Scottish Episcopal Church.) TMM

Erskine of Mar, the Hon. Stuart Ruaraidh (1869–1960) Born in Sussex of old Scottish family. First learned Gaelic from his nurse from Harris. Became a pioneer and perfervid Scottish nationalist, his aim being a 'self-governing Celtic Scotland', and strove both to achieve this and to raise standards of Gaelic literature through various publications that he founded, sponsored, edited and wrote for, in Gaelic and English – *Am Bard, Guth na Bliadhna, Alba* (the first weekly Gaelic newspaper), *An Sgeulaiche, An Rosarnach*, etc. (See D. J. Macleod 1977, 210ff.; *Gairm*, vol. 4, 367; S. Mac a' Ghobhainn 1972; L. Macbean 1921, 38.) TMM

Faed, Tom, *see* art, Gaelic, in modern times.

Farquharson, Fr John (1699–1782) Born Braemar. Priest in Strathglass. Reputedly made large collection of Gaelic verse, deposited in Douay and later lost. Probable author of 'Rabhadh Mhic Shimidh'. (See G. Henderson 1898, 140.) DST

Fear Ghlinn Nodha, *see* Macintyre, James.

'Fear na h-Eabaide' ('The Habited Man') Alias 'Sgeulachd an Dìthreabhaich' ('The Tale of the Hermit'). Romance in which mysterious 'hermit' tells Murchadh mac Briain how he won and kept his wife. The only early manuscript (National Library of Scotland 72.1.36) lacks an end, supplied by fine folk versions. (See Bruford 1968, 301–26; 1969, 136–40; 1978, 27–35; Matheson and Thomson 1953.) AB

Fear na Pàirce (MacCulloch of Park, Strathpeffer) (fl. late sixteenth–early seventeenth century) Great-grandfather of Donnchadh nam Pìos (q.v.) (MacRae, 1899, 67). The Fernaig Manuscript (q.v.) contains six of his religious poems. Their principal theme is reliance on Christ in the struggle against the world, the flesh and the Devil. KDMCD

Fearchar mac Phàdraig Grannd (dates unknown) Author of fragment in the Book of the Dean of Lismore (q.v.). (See Quiggin 1937.) DST

Ferchar Fota King of the Cenél Loairn (q.v.) when they were defeated by the Britons in 678. He died in 697 as the first recorded ruler of his kindred to be overlord of Dalriada (q.v.). The eleventh-century ruling family of the province of Moray (see **MacBeth**), descendants of the Cenél Loairn, may have based their claim to the kingship of the Scots, in part at least, on the fact that the Cenél Loairn once provided kings of Dalriada. (See Bannerman 1971, 75, 77.) JWMB

Fergus Mór mac Eirc King of Dalriada in Ireland in the second half of the fifth century. His removal *c.*500 to Scotland is generally taken to mark the foundation of the kingdom of Dalriada in Scotland, and it certainly indicated that the colony was overtaking the mother country in importance. He died *c.*501 and was succeeded by his son, Domangart. From Fergus Mór, with a few early exceptions, descended all subsequent kings and queens of Scots, and pride in the antiquity of the dynasty was to be a unifying factor at periods of crisis in the later history of the Scots. (See Bannerman 1974, 73–5.) JWMB

Ferguson, Professor Adam (1723–1816) Born Logierait. Chaplain to 42nd Regiment. Fought at Fontenoy. Professor of Moral Philosophy at the University of Edinburgh; author of *Principles of Moral and Political Science* (1792). DST

Fernaig Manuscript So called from its having come to light, early in the nineteenth century, in the possession of Mr Matheson of Fernaig, Wester Ross. The manuscript consists of two notebooks, approximately 7 inches by 3 inches, written in a neat, late seventeenth century hand. Later in the nineteenth century it came into the hands of Dr Mackintosh MacKay (q.v.), whose trustees passed it on to Dr W. F. Skene (q.v.), who, in turn, presented it to the Revd John Kennedy of Arran. Kennedy bequeathed it to the University of Glasgow, where it is now lodged in the University Library.

A page from the Fernaig Manuscript, Glasgow University Library MS Gen. 85, f.25r, showing the beginning of Murchadh Mac Mhic Mhurchaidh's poem on King Charles I. ▶

The first notebook is headed 'Doirligh Loijn Di/Skrijwig Lea Donochig/Mackrah 1688'. 'Donnchadh MacRath', the compiler, has been conclusively identified by Donald Mackinnon, (D. Mackinnon 1885) as Duncan MacRae of Inverinate, better known as Donnchadh nam Pìos (q.v.). The latest date to appear in the manuscript is 1693.

The manuscript is a verse anthology with both a thematic and a territorial emphasis. Of the fifty-nine pieces it contains, ten are anonymous; twelve are ascribed to the compiler himself and the remainder to seventeen different authors, the most strongly represented being Fear na Pàirce (q.v.) with six pieces, Alasdair Mac Mhurchaidh (q.v.) with four, Murchadh Mór mac Mhic Mhurchaidh (Mackenzie of Achilty: q.v.) with six, and Donnchadh Mac Raoiridh (q.v.) with four. Most of the authors were seventeenth century gentlemen, drawn into the collection by their northern ambience and, in some cases, their family links with the compiler. Among the few chronological and regional outliers are John Carswell, to whom two pieces are attributed (one of them wrongly), Sir John Stewart of Appin, who flourished in the late sixteenth century, and the early seventeenth century Irish poet Gille-Bríghde Ó hEoghusa.

More than half the compositions are in syllabic metre. The dominant thematic note is disillusionment with the changes and vanities of the world, coupled with religious aspiration. Towards the end of the manuscript there are some songs expressing a Jacobite view of the dynastic revolution of 1688–9, including translations of two English broadsheet ballads.

Scholarly interest in the manuscript has focused chiefly on MacRae's eccentric Scots-influenced orthography and the linguistic provincialisms which it betrays, though Fraser's remark that the poems are 'of next to no value as literature' (J. Fraser 1926) is somewhat extreme. The earliest published transcription was that of Cameron and MacBain in *Reliquiae Celticae*, vol. 2 (A. Cameron 1894), including also a transliteration of some pieces. George Henderson included in *Leabhar nan Gleann* (1898) a transliteration of twenty-eight pieces from the manuscript, with some historical and biographical notes. In 1899 Ludwig Stern published a paper on 'Crosanachd Illebhrighde', with a breakdown of MacRae's system of vowel representation (Stern 1899). The most thorough exploration of the language of the manuscript to date was undertaken by John Fraser, both in his introductory paper to the Gaelic Society of Inverness

(1914) and in his later more detailed study (1926). W. J. Watson published transliterations of a few pieces in *An Deò-Gréine* (1918a) and in his anthology *Bàrdachd Ghàidhlig* (1918b). An accurate transcription, and a less reliable transliteration, of the complete manuscript was published in 1923 by Calum MacPhàrlain (1923; J. Fraser 1924). Samuel Maclean has published an interesting profile of one of the Fernaig poets, Alasdair Mac Mhurchaidh (1953). KDMcD

feudal system and its antecedents In the absence of land charters before 1094 and of reliable early statements of land law, historians of pre-feudal Scotland have been tempted to rely on analogies drawn from Irish and Welsh law tracts and comparisons with Scandinavian custom taken from Norwegian and Icelandic sources. Such analogies may mislead, and it seems safer to start with the evidence for modes and patterns of landholding in the feudal age and search for traces of native systems older than the twelfth century. This evidence points both to a kin-based system and to strong royal lordship. Land seems to have been inherited by all the freeborn males within a particular lineage and held, perhaps jointly, by the sons of a single owner as his equal heirs – hence place names such as Balcanquhal, Fife (Balemacanecol, farm of Anecol's sons), and Petmacdufgille, Perthshire (farm of Dougal's sons). References to clans or lineages between the twelfth and the fourteenth centuries concern either lesser free men below the rank of tenant-in-chief (e.g. the Kennedys of Carrick or the Clan Morgan in Buchan) or else men of even lower status, unfree or semi-free (e.g. the men of Tweeddale transferred by David I from dependence on the Crown to the service of Dunfermline Abbey). Lordship of a territorial type was nevertheless present well before 1100, involving the king, the provincial *mormaer* (governor) and the *toisech* (local officer: Scots *toshach*, or thane) who exercised the king's or *mormaer*'s authority yet was also related to a local kindred group. Thus notices of twelfth century (and earlier) grants in the Book of Deer (q.v.) mention such a person as Donnchad, *toisech* of Clann Morgainn, while many documents of this and later date show thanes and *toshachs* associated with territorial units usually called 'shires' or 'thanages'.

With the advent of military feudalism under Norman impact and royal initiative in the twelfth century, important modifications took place in the landholding pattern at the upper levels of Scottish society, though to a notably lesser extent in the Highlands than in the Lowlands. Monarchy and provincial rulers (now usually called earls) retained their dominant role, and the nature of their lordship proved slow to change, but a new aristocratic class, based on the knight's fief, the barony and the castle, was brought into existence and spread from south to north between *c*.1120 and 1250. Feudalism made little headway in the west Highlands and none at all in the islands, yet the nobility of these areas was strongly influenced by feudalism. Some accepted specific military or naval service as the condition on which they held their estates; even more strikingly, from the early thirteenth century some began to build formidable stone fortresses, often on rocky islets or promontories (for example, Kisimul in Barra, Castle Tioram in Moidart, Dunstaffnage near Oban and Castle Sween in Knapdale).

Only a minority of these Gaelic-speaking lords were tenants-in-chief of the Crown, on a par with the greater baronial magnates of eastern and southern Scotland. Most of the Highland nobility were tenants of the greater lords, enjoying hereditary pre-eminence, by virtue of their lineage and holding (often without any charter of infeftment), by an essentially kin-based tenure which was echoed by the 'kindly (i.e. kin-based) tenure' characteristic of their own lesser dependants. It was thus possible for a relatively fluid and vigorous clan organization to survive within the Highland area alongside a formally universal and Crown-imposed feudalism and for it to remain after feudalism had been reduced to little more than a set of legal rules governing the ownership of land. (See Bannerman 1974; Barrow 1973, 1980; Duncan 1975; K. H. Jackson 1972; Skene 1886–90.) GWSB

fiddle music, Highland Gaelic *fidheall* (violin, or fiddle), unlike Irish *fidil*, seems to derive from English 'viol' rather than from 'fiddle' – the *-dh-* merely shows that the two vowel sounds are distinct. 'Violers', such as the James Glass mentioned in the Dunvegan accounts between 1693 and 1706, played the four-stringed fretless violin as well as its six-stringed predecessor; the name was simply taken over for the more common instrument (D. Johnson 1972, 24–5). Glass bore a surname common in Perthshire but was not a Gaelic-speaker if he was the 'Gall Glas' mentioned by An Clàrsair Dall (the Blind Harper: q.v.) The Harper, whose own father was evidently a violinist, mentions fiddling for dancing with approval, but he is said, understandably, to have con-

demned the playing of harp music on the violin (W. Matheson 1970, l–li, 206, 62, 164–5). Earlier evidence for the rebec or other bowed string instruments in the Highlands is scanty, though both the instruments mentioned, along with the harp, as typical of Scotland by Giraldus Cambrensis in the twelfth century (O'Meara 1951, 88), *tympanum* and *chorus*, have been interpreted as bowed instruments, the first a bowed psaltery, the second sounding like the Welsh *crwth*. Four centuries later, however, George Buchanan mentions only the harp as a Highland instrument.

Whatever its predecessors, towards 1700 the violin became a popular instrument throughout Scotland. By 1703 Martin Martin (D. J. Macleod 1934, 95) had heard of eighteen men in Lewis alone who could 'play on the violin pretty well without being taught'. As in the Lowlands, the repertoire of such Highland fiddlers at this time no doubt consisted largely of song tunes, with or without variations, a form seen at its best in Simon Fraser's *Airs and Melodies Peculiar to the Highlands of Scotland and the Isles* (1816). But dance music – reels, Scots measures and the like – also suited the fiddle: Stewart of Garth (D. Stewart 1822, App. M) claimed that indoor dancing was always accompanied by the fiddle if possible and that the pipes were only used out of doors, though the rule may not have been as strict north of Perthshire. The well-known 'Mrs MacLeod' is a traditional reel tune collected in Skye by Malcolm MacLeod of Raasay and dedicated to his wife. He may have heard it on the pipes, but he played it on the fiddle himself, and in his house Boswell and Johnson watched Highland dancing to the fiddle in 1773. Song and dance tunes with Gaelic titles appear in most of the early manuscript and printed collections of Scottish fiddle music, and the sets of variations played by the more advanced fiddlers owe much to Italian and French models but something too to pibroch or the harp-variation form on which pibroch was modelled (D. Johnson 1983). Indeed, our knowledge of early Highland harp music derives largely from violinists such as Daniel Dow (Dow 1775) and Simon Fraser's son Angus (Collinson 1966, 45). The bagpipes, apart from tunes and forms including the 6/8 march, contributed the 'pipe-style' structure of tunes, imitative phrases built alternately on major chords a tone apart, like A and G. This is the basis of many dance tunes, such as the famous 'Reel of Tullochgorum'.

Tullochgorum is probably named after a place on Speyside, and the tune is a strathspey, the most distinctive type of Scottish dance tune. From the first strathspeys have been fiddle tunes, needing the contrast between Scotch snap (short–long) figures, with an audible change of bow direction in the middle, and other pairs of notes played in one bow, to get the full effect of the spiky dotted rhythms. The extract from 'The Braes of Tullymet', as published by Alexander McGlashan (1778, 29), shows the irregular bow lengths of a typical opening figure, a short forceful down-bow followed by a lingering up-bow, and the tendency to link anacrusis and stressed note in one bow across the bar-line.

careers mainly in Edinburgh as players and composers. They too helped to establish the classical Scots style continued by Skinner and more recent players in the area between Perth and Peterhead.

Of the traditions of the north and west Highlands and Hebrides at this period we know much less, apart from the dance tunes (mostly for pipes rather than fiddle) published by Patrick McDonald (1781) and those that were not compositions by Simon Fraser (1816). The association with dancing may have inspired the mass destruction of fiddles by nineteenth

The Braes of Tullymet.

Strathspey is short for 'strathspey reel', a slower and more ornamental treatment of the tune of Scotland's most widely known dance form. Its Speyside originators, according to tradition, were the Brown family of Kincardine; the Cummings, of whom Angus Cumming of Grantown published *Strathspeys or Old Highland Reels* in 1780, and the legendary outlaw James MacPherson, who played and then broke his fiddle 'below the gallows tree' at Banff in 1700, were other fiddlers in the region before the style spread throughout Scotland in the later eighteenth century. In Burns's time 'the first composer of strathspeys of the age', William Marshall from Fochabers, knocked some of the rough edges off the style and may have been the originator of the graceful slow strathspey for listening, not dancing, to. Some of his techniques were handed down to James Scott Skinner, the Aberdeenshire 'strathspey King' of the turn of this century.

Even more admired at this time than Marshall were the Gow family, 'famous Niel' and his sons, of whom the most successful was the composer and publisher Nathaniel Gow. Central Perthshire was the birthplace of many of the leading fiddlers of the time: hence perhaps the term 'Athole reels' used by publishers to distinguish the faster tunes in even notes from strathspeys. Niel Gow and Malcolm McDonald came from Inver, near Dunkeld, 'Red Rob' Mackintosh from Tullymet, Daniel Dow and 'King' McGlashan from the same district; all of them but Niel Gow himself had, as did Gow's sons, successful

Niel Gow (1727–1807). By Sir Henry Raeburn. Scottish National Portrait Gallery. (Gow also appears, in identical tartan breeches and hose, in the painting 'A Highland Wedding' by David Allan reproduced on p. 207).

century evangelists in many Protestant areas, eloquently described by A. Carmichael (1900–71 , vol. 1, xxix–xxx, xxxii), and too few players remained in other parts until the coming of the tape-recorder for it to be possible now to say whether a distinct local style existed. The modern 'West Highland' style taught by Angus Grant, with one bow per beat, frequent ornaments and open lower strings sounded as drones, clearly imitates the pipes: the bowing at least has nothing in common with older fiddle traditions, and the style seems to have been developed recently by players mostly of east Highland origin. Some older tunes, however, have been preserved by modern fiddlers; some fiddle tunes have been arranged for the pipes; and others, sometimes with remarkably complex cross-rhythms, have survived as *puirt-a-beul* (mouth-music).

Traces of an older fiddling style may also be found among players of Highland ancestry in Cape Breton Island. The most notable feature is the playing of reels more slowly than in most of Scotland today, little faster than strathspeys, as in Shetland and Ireland, whose reels were also imported from Scotland about 200 or 150 years ago. Cape Breton players also use many mordents, 'birls' (a bowed figure with the same note repeated three times quickly) and other ornaments, and open strings both above and below the melody. The distinctive bowing of strathspeys is emphasized. These features suggest a style that has changed little since Cumming, McGlashan and other early Highland fiddlers published their collections and was probably much the same from Strathspey to the Outer Hebrides. AB

Finlayson, Robert (Fionnlaghstan nan Loch) (1793–1861) Born Caithness. Minister at Knock, 1829–31; Lochs, 1831–56; Helmsdale, 1856–61. Joined Free Church (q.v.), 1843. He was a dramatic preacher, his effective use of allegory earning him the title of 'John Bunyan of the Highlands'. (See J. MacPherson 1870.) RMCL

'Fiona Macleod', *see* Sharp, William.

'Fionn', *see* Whyte, Henry.

Fionnlagh an Bàrd Ruadh (fl. 1490) Bard to John, Chief of Clan Gregor (d. 1519). Five of his poems are included in the Book of the Dean of Lismore (q.v.) He shows a good knowledge of poetic *sgeula*

(legendary lore) and had been at the court of the Irish Chief Aodh MacDiarmada *c*.1478. He composed a virulent poem in dispraise of Allan of Clanranald (d. 1509). (See W. J. Watson 1937.) DST

Fionnlaghstan nan Loch, *see* Finlayson, Robert.

fisheries, Highland Traditionally, in the eighteenth century and earlier, fishing by the coastal dwellers of the north-west Highlands and Islands was for subsistence, to eke out the food grown on the smallholdings which provided the basic occupation. Tiny boats, owned in shares by the mass of the population, were used to catch a variety of fish, such as cod, ling, skate and saithe, by hand line and herring by drift net. While the appearance of herring shoals within the narrow waters of the lochs (the main areas for fishing) was uncertain, most families had the security of a barrel of salt herring kept for consumption through the year. Exceptionally, the great-line fishing for cod and ling, pursued offshore, also provided a saleable product and the assurance of a small income for a few communities from which there was access to the main cod banks. Herring, sometimes caught much in excess of local food needs, might on occasion be sold to curers arriving from the south with the needed stores or to the greater vessels which were fitted out in the Clyde region for long sojourns at sea and had facilities for curing on shipboard (Gray 1978, 101–6; Youngson 1973, 101–9).

The nineteenth century saw the advance of commercial fishing and the involvement of the people of the north-west in the struggle to earn money by fishing, both because of increased need and because of widening opportunity. In Caithness profitable and fairly dependable herring fishing, of which the output was cured and largely exported, was growing decade by decade, and soon many of the east-coast ports were turned over to this fishing in the summer. This essentially east-coast fishing had great effects on the west. Hundreds, ultimately thousands, of men moved seasonally to the east-coast ports to engage as hired hands, an important form of employment that was to last until 1914. Further, a handful of crews round the north-west corner were able to acquire the larger boats that allowed them to participate directly in the east-coast fishing and to bring home unprecedentedly high incomes.

The most influential development, however, was the establishment in the 1840s of a deep-water herring fishing in the Minch, starting annually in

May. This fishing was based on the stations established by curers at several points along the east coast of Lewis and latterly in Barra. About a hundred boats of local origin found employment in this (Gray 1978, 106–17). The home locations of these necessarily large boats and crews now shifted from the mainland coasts to Lewis and Barra, and there, by 1900, were to be found communities of farmer-fishermen able to make increasing incomes from a herring fishing that extended from May to September. Between 1900 and 1914 they reached the height of their prosperity, but the men never lost their hold on the land.

The higher incomes being earned along the eastern side of the Long Island were not matched in the widespread loch fishings of the mainland. Here the fishings continued to be utterly unreliable; while a few crews were able to improve their prospects after 1900 by fitting paraffin engines to their boats to give them greater mobility, and while marketing was made somewhat easier by the use of steam vessels for transport, fishing became increasingly an activity pursued by a minority clustered around the main marketing centres of Lochalsh and Mallaig. They made higher incomes than in the past, but there were many fewer of them (Gray 1978, 181–209).

The inter-war years brought all-round decline.

Herring fishing generally was perplexed by the loss of the main markets in the Baltic, and the Long Island fishermen, equipped mainly with sailing boats dating from before 1910, remained herring fishermen only because of the low running costs of such boats as compared with those of the more efficient steam drifters, of which very few were owned by west-coast crews. Even this precarious activity ran down in the 1930s, when the boats reached the end of their useful lives; without funds for replacement, the fleet and the number of men with any true dependence on fishing shrank markedly. So it was, too, on the mainland, where the best yield of the sea was found to be lobsters, caught with tiny boats and on a part-time basis (Darling 1955, 347–52).

In recent times fishing, which was once the almost universal mainstay of the coastal communities of the west coast, has become restricted to the few communities which have been able to equip themselves with the boats and gear needed fully to exploit the still great resources of the Minch. As in the past, it is still boats from elsewhere, and particularly from the east coast, that skim the cream of this fishing, operating out of west-coast stations such as those of Sutherland and using the complicated and expensive apparatus of modern inshore fishing vessels. MG

Scottish sailing drifters on their way to the herring grounds off the east coast. A photograph from before 1914, when it was still quite common for fleets of hundreds of boats to fish together. Scottish Fisheries Museum, Anstruther, Fife.

Salmon netting, Berriedale beach, Caithness.

Fletcher, Archibald (b. *c.*1735) Collector of heroic ballads in Perthshire. (See J. F. Campbell 1872.)

DST

Folklore Institute of Scotland (Comunn Beul-aithris na h-Albann) Founded 1947. Within a few years (thanks mainly to J. L. Campbell) it had recorded much material and had published *Gaelic Folksongs from Barra* (gramophone records and a booklet). Superseded in 1951 by the School of Scottish Studies (q.v.). TMM

folksong, early (to *c.*1645) For the purposes of this article 'folksong' is a convenient term with which to describe verse that was composed for singing and used styles popular with the non-learned; these styles are sometimes referred to as sub-literate, but the use of such tags must not be held to exclude possible literary origins for some of the styles, nor their use by literate or even learned members of society. In the flux of fifteenth to seventeenth century Gaelic society class demarcations are often obscured or diminished, and this is probably another element in the 'melting-pot' we find at the time of the early emergence of Scottish Gaelic vernacular verse styles.

Another way of defining such folksong, a severely practical one, would be to say that it is what we have left once we have abstracted the professional classical

D

Gaelic or bardic verse (q.v.) and the semi-bardic verse (q.v.). Such a residue must suffer from the tendency of the professionals to limit their manuscript anthologies to their own type of poetry. Thus we do not find this folksong in the Book of the Dean of Lismore (q.v.), nor in the MacMhuirich Manuscripts, nor even in the Fernaig Manuscript (q.v.). When we eventually come to the collectors who display an interest in it we are already far removed in time from its source, and this explains the relative paucity of examples, at least from the sixteenth century and earlier. It is mainly from the mid-eighteenth century that such collections as we have date, but very old songs may continue in the tradition until the nineteenth or twentieth centuries, and in areas remote from their original locales. So, for example, the 'Iorram Dharaich', a pre-1585 song about a mainland character, was first noted in Lewis about the middle of the nineteenth century (A. Matheson 1954, 16).

Some of the earlier folksong collectors (see **folksongs, collections of**) were the Revd James McLagan, the Revd Donald MacNicol, the Revd Eoghan MacDhiarmaid, all of Perthshire or Argyllshire, and McLagan's presence is to be found also in the Gillies Collection of 1786, the earliest printed anthology to include a significant number of folksongs, according to our definition – for example, 'An Crònan Muileach' (The Mull Croon), 'Bràighe Loch Iall (Braes of Loch Eil),' 'Is daor a cheannaich mi 'n t-iasgach' (Dearly I paid for the fishing).

There are only a few snatches of song that can be ascribed with much precision to a date earlier than 1570. We do not know whether the stanzas said to have been composed by the Earl of Mar at the time of the first battle of Inverlochy (1431) were sung, but they survived as folk verse (W. J. Watson 1915, 100, 102). The song 'Pìobaireachd Dhòmhnaill Duibh' (Black Donald's Pibroch), however, presumably from the first half of the sixteenth century, is still sung traditionally, to a magnificent air. No doubt many of the charms and prayers in *Carmina Gadelica* (q.v.) are as old, and older, but this has not been demonstrated as yet.

The song known by the short title of 'Griogal Cridhe' (Beloved Gregor) seems to date without much dubiety to 1570, when Gregor MacGregor of Glenstrae was executed at Kenmore (D. S. Thomson 1955, 11–13). This instance may illustrate the elasticity of the term 'folksong'; its metre, though irregular, is based on the classical metre *séadna*, and its

author was a laird's daughter, but it is a folksong theme that is imposed on this literary metrical pattern, and it has the folksong's passion and direct statement, as well as the use of incremental repetition. It also includes a reference to the ancient practice of drinking the blood of a dead sweetheart:

Chuir iad a cheann air ploc daraich
'S dhòirt iad fhuil gu làr;
Nam biodh agam an sin cupan
Dh'òlainn dith mo shàth . . . .

They placed his head on a block of oak
And spilt his blood on the ground;
Had I but had a cup then
I'd have drunk of it my fill . . . .

Other MacGregor songs are to be dated to about 1600 and to the two following decades – for example, a song on the Battle of Glenfruin, 1603 (ibid., 14, 17), 'Saighdean Ghlinn Lìobhann' (The Arrows of Glen Lyon), 'Mi 'm shuidhe seo 'm ònar' (As I sit here alone) and 'MacGriogair a Ruadhshruth' (MacGregor of Roro) (ibid. 14–16). The stirring praise song 'A Mhic Iain 'ic Sheumais' (O Son of John, son of James), addressed to Donald MacDonald, hero of the Battle of Cairinish in North Uist (1601), and a few other associated songs (see A. and A. MacDonald 1911) belong to this period also, as do, probably, 'Chaidh mis' a dh'Eubhal imprig' (I went to Euval on a flitting) (J. L. Campbell and F. Collinson 1977, 94; *Carmina Gadelica*, vol. 5, 10) 'B'fheàrr gun cluinninn sud a màireach' (*Gairm*, vol. 2, 125), 'Iomair thusa Choinnich chridhe' (Row, beloved Kenneth) (*Eilean Fraoich*, no. 30), etc., 'Tàladh Dhòmhnaill Ghuirm' (Lullaby of Donald Gorm; i.e. the MacDonald chief of Sleat) (D. S. Thomson 1974a, 59) and perhaps 'Mhic Iarla nam bratach bàna' (Son of the Earl of White Banners) (J. L. Campbell n.d. 24), both these last waxing eloquent about the splendour of the chief's galley:

She had a gold rudder and two silver masts,
ropes made of the silk of Galway,
the thick red silk of Spain.

The song 'Là Mille-gàrraidh' ('The Battle of Milleg') (Tolmie, 1911, 200) on the MacLeod–MacDonald feud of *c.*1570 is probably contemporary also.

One of the most intense and passionate of early folksongs is 'Cumha Sheathain' ('Lament for Seathan', son of the King of Ireland). Alexander Carmichael presented it in a conflated edition in which its grandeur may be enhanced, but there is no doubting both the essential integrity of the song and its considerable age (see D. S. Thomson 1974a, 75ff.). It is a song composed in irregular paragraphs that are marked by the same end-rhyme; this has all the appearance of being a mellow literary form by the second half of the sixteenth century (it was also the structure used in 'An Iorram Dharaich', The Oak-Vessel Boat Song, pre–1585). The lullaby 'B'fheàrr leam gun sgrìobhteadh dhuit fearann' (Would that land were given you by charter) (*TGSI*, vol. 12, 212), a series of rhyming lines punctuated by a refrain, probably dates from before 1550.

Another common song structure is the one that we find in 'A' Bhean Eudach' (The Jealous Woman) (McLagan MS 119; M. F. Shaw 1977, 254, etc.), which is perhaps older than any of the songs referred to above. This song has a theme like that of the story of Binnorie; a jealous woman persuades her sister to gather dulse, not noticing the incoming tide; the sister is drowned, and the jealous woman marries her widower. Here the line is split into two short half-lines, punctuated by refrain vocables:

O, 'se 'n t-àilgheas   hùg ò
   chuir dhan tràigh mi   hùg ò
A bhuain duilisg   hu ri a bhò,
   no bhuain bhàirneach,   hùg ò

The second line of the first couplet becomes the first line of the second couplet, but with the vocables appropriate to line 1.

It is probable that metres and structures of this kind have a long previous history when we first find them recorded, and that the earliest datable examples are late in their series. It has been suggested (D. S. Thomson 1974a, 63) that the 'syntactic cacophony' which often results from the breaking up of the line in such songs may have 'attained the status of a stylistic device', and that the vocables and the manner of using them are a legacy from imported song styles.

Such evidence as we have of authorship and internal evidence as to class and milieu suggest that the styles of the early folksongs are not the prerogative of any one section of society but perhaps the alternative range of styles open to persons not of, or not thirled to, the professional literary castes. (For general description and discussion, see e.g. D. S. Thomson 1974a, 57–98; D. S. Thomson 1955. For discussion in particular of the waulking-song element, see J. L. Campbell and F. Collinson 1969. For some detailed discussion of early song datings, see A. Whyte 1972.)

DST

folksong, later (1645–1800) This century and a half almost coincides with what we think of as the high age of vernacular poetry. The collectors and editors who compiled the repertoire of the age were concerned with establishing that 'compositions of great merit . . . majesty, simplicity, and elegance' (Ranald MacDonald 1776, vi–vii) existed in Gaelic rather than with the preservation of what was later to be known as 'folksong'. That record has largely to be constructed from the collections of later periods and from modern oral tradition. As we can date such songs only occasionally by internal or other evidence, an exact inventory cannot be compiled. Some songs have undergone constant reshaping, of course, and may be said to belong to several centuries.

There is, however, a more fundamental problem. The term 'folk', in itself a word of uncertain connotation, is particularly difficult to fit into the context of Gaelic cultural history. This does not mean that there was no social stratification; nor does it mean that there is no disjunction between written and oral poetry. The problem is rather that authors from different strata share the same (essentially aristocratic) values. Thus it is often very difficult, if not impossible, to make any distinction between the work of an aristocrat and a peasant on grounds of content, style or social attitudes. Second, the difference between written and oral is not a simple contrast between art song and folksong: orally composed and transmitted song is not confined to any social grade. Third, the test of anonymity, sometimes taken to be a mark of folksong, has a limited application: Gaelic oral tradition often transmits authors' names and accounts of the circumstances of composition.

Starting from modern tradition and its variants we can at least make certain qualified judgements as to what we ought to include in an inventory of folksongs for the period. For instance, we have in Gaelic, as in other cultures, songs of indubitably aristocratic provenance (composed to or by members of the upper classes) which in one sense or another have become popular. In Gaelic, however, the lines of transmission are of crucial importance. Thus we can recover from contemporary oral tradition songs by Iain Lom (q.v.), John MacCodrum (q.v.), Mairearad Nighean Lachlainn (q.v.) and other oral poets of comparable stature. If these are to be classed as folksongs (for instance, because they have a certain quality that enables them to survive into the modern folk repertoire), we must note that they are nevertheless textually no different from the canonical versions of the great collections of the past. In certain instances the written word may have helped to stabilize a singer's versions: Gaelic oral tradition is not unique in being influenced at several points by writing. We could set these aside as 'non-folk' were it not for the proven fact that in some cases conservative oral tradition alone is responsible, as when no published version has been available. The truth is that this kind of 'folk' transmission simply continued the processes of primary transmission which preserved such songs in an upper-class milieu when Gaelic society was still stratified.

On the other hand, we have a less conservative, secondary transmission which produces a much greater range of textual variation. We may be justified in assuming, then, that folk versions of aristocratic songs were being created in the period under review. At any rate, secondary transmission can produce a variant such as the text of Mairi nighean Alasdair Ruaidh's 'Cumha do Shir Tormod' (Lament for Sir Norman, 1705), taken down in 1861 in Skye, which stands apart from all the variants used in establishing the standard text (J. C. Watson 1934, 141–2). It is also responsible for the interesting conflation of Iain Lom's 'A bhean leasaich an stòp dhuinn' (Woman, fill the stoup [goblet] for us), composed shortly after 1663, and Niall Mac Mhuirich's elegy to Clanranald, who was killed at Sheriffmuir in 1715, 'Och a Mhuire mo dhunaidh' (Alas, O Mary, my misfortune). This conflated version circulates among the Gaelic travelling folk, who are themselves one of the most distinctive communities in the preservation of folksong within Gaelic society. Since they were undoubtedly associated in the past with the Cliar Sheanchain, the travelling bards, it is possible that these folk versions have a partial origin in the lower castes of bards and craftsmen.

A different and important corpus of song consists of folk versions of heroic ballads, a great number of the pioneer collections of which were made in the eighteenth century. The majority of these ballads are Ossianic (that is, they celebrate the feats and adventures of Fionn and his band of warriors); others deal with heroes such as Fraoch and Cu Chulainn. As a genre they are traceable to literary origins in the common Scoto-Irish inheritance of classical Gaelic, but some ballads are specifically Scottish, either ascribed to Scottish authors or composed in the stream of popular tradition. At all events, those of literary origin became demotic, and the Ossianic ballads were accorded the highest status of any genre

in a singer's repertoire. A few still survive traditionally in the Hebrides, particularly in Uist.

The classes of song hitherto mentioned are all in some sense (and not only from the viewpoint of modern Gaelic society) of minority interest or specialist function. Those that have survived best and enjoy the widest distribution, however, are songs of a lyrical nature, and it is fair to assume that they were equally popular within the period 1645–1800. One such song is 'Luinneag Chaluim a' Ghlinne' (Calum of the Glen's Ditty) (Ranald MacDonald 1776), composed by Malcolm Maclean of Kinlochewe (c.1690–1764) and addressed to his daughter. In spite of her beauty and virtue, the poet explains, she remains unwed because his love of the tavern has left him unable to provide her dowry. Another is 'Tha tighinn fodham éirigh' (I have a desire to rise up) (Ranald MacDonald 1776), composed in 1715 by Iain mac Dhùghaill mhic Lachlainn (q.v.) to Alan of Clanranald. This lyrical panegyric was sung as a rowing song by Malcolm, brother of MacLeod of Raasay, when Boswell and Johnson were being ferried across from Skye during their tour of 1773. The presence of one or more of the lyric constants ensures a comparable degree of popularity to the present day for both of these songs, dissimilar as they are in theme. Qualities of passion, tenderness, vividness of imagery, a personal tone and so on are, in fact, the criteria which have determined whether a song is favoured or rejected in the general folk tradition of the Gaels. In the eighteenth century, for instance, this applies as much to the songs of the literate Alexander MacDonald as it does to those of the non-literate Duncan Bàn Macintyre (q.v.), despised as a mere folk poet by MacDonald. The folksingers are impartial in that respect and draw selectively on the compositions of these and similar poets.

The two songs cited above have refrains, which implies audience participation. In Scots Gaelic tradition the existence of a choral refrain is at least an indication that the song is lyrical in quality. Another indicator is female authorship. In spite of the fact that Màiri Nighean Alasdair Ruaidh and other women composed high-grade panegyrics, there is a distinctive female culture in Gaelic poetry which always tends towards lyricism. Probably within our period fall such songs as 'Tha sgrìob dighe orm nas leòir' (Drink has left its mark on me indeed), 'An Gille Dubh Ciar-dhubh' (The Dark, Swarthy Lad) and 'Is e mo leannan th'ann' (It is my sweetheart), 'A Dhomhnaill mhic Neill mhic Iain Bhuidhe' (Donald, son of Neil, son of Yellow John) (Ranald MacDonald 1776). From just after the Battle of Culloden we have the great lament 'Mo rùn geal òg' (My fair young love). The first is a strophic metre, therefore without refrain; the second and fourth have rudimentary refrains; the third has a three-lined verbal refrain. There is a class of song, closely associated with women – a MacGregor song, 'Mi am shuidhe seo m'ònar' (Sitting here alone) – of the earlier seventeenth century, apparently composed by a man, is in mainland tradition attributed to a woman – in which couplets are repeated to form quatrains, (that is, lines 2 and 3 become lines 1 and 2 of each successive stanza). To this category belong the three surviving laments for Iain Garbh of Raasay, drowned on Easter Friday 1671, composed by his sister Sìleas. 'Is daor a cheannaich mi an t-iasgach' (Dearly I paid for the fishing), which may be an Islay song, 'A Mhic Dhubhghaill mhic Ruairi (Son of Dugald, son of Roderick) and 'Gura muladach sgìth mi' (I am sad and weary) are further examples. 'Bràighe Loch Iall' (Braes of Loch Eil), structurally of the same type, is of male authorship. Some of these have full refrains of meaningless vocables of the kind common in songs of communal labour, with which they share a common stock of imagery. Sometimes the connection is even closer: variants of the one song may be found in both classes.

The choral songs (J. MacInnes 1971a) of diverse origins which we now know as waulking songs are lyrical, mostly anonymous (one of the few songs attributed to an author is said to have been composed by Màiri Nighean Alasdair Ruaidh, q.v.) and can be traced back to the end of the sixteenth century, although as a class they are much more ancient. By the second half of the eighteenth century they were concentrated in the north-west, 'from Lorne and in all the Hebrides'; the form had apparently died out among the people of 'Breadalbane, Rannoch, Atholl, and the southern parts of Argyleshire . . . though, little past memory of man, their forefathers practised it as constantly as the north-west Highlanders do at present' (A. Allardyce 1888, vol. 2, 415–16). Most of these songs were composed by women; there are a few of male authorship, some of them originally rowing songs. The latter probably exemplify traditions of the lower grades of society. Women authors of higher classes are represented, but references to herding cattle, sheiling (summer pasture) life, reaping with the sickle, etc., give the impression that the settings at any rate are plebeian. In addition, we have songs of complaint by girls made pregnant or jilted by higher-born men. This is the mainstream of Gaelic folksong. Among the datable examples 'Tha mo rùn-sa air Clann Dòmhnaill' (I love Clan Donald), composed while the memory of the battle of Auldearn (1645) was still fresh, is a panegyric to Clan Donald:

> You swore on the Bible
> On the low strath of Auldearn
> That no sword would be sheathed
> Until King Charles was crowned . . . .

Alasdair MacColla (q.v.), in Gaelic tradition the foremost hero of this campaign, is celebrated in 'Alasdair mhic [son] ó hó': 'I heard yesterday a tale that gave me no joy; that little Glasgow was in flames and Aberdeen plundered.' Both of these are anonymous. Diorbhail Nic a' Bhriuthainn's great song to Alasdair is structurally more akin to 'A Dhòmhnaill mhic Nèill mhic Iain Bhuidhe' (above), but the imagery is drawn from a common stock. The '45 dates 'Có sheinneas an fhìdeag airgid?' (Who will play the silver chanter?):

> My king's son is coming to Scotland
> On a great ship with three masts of silver
> Golden pulleys on each rope
> And rigging of French silk . . . .

Another song of the '45 with the same theme, 'Hì rì rì tha e tighinn' (Hurrah, he is coming), ascribed to Mac Mhaighstir Alasdair (q.v.), is in the quatrain-and-refrain form familiar in modern *ceilidh* songs. From the eighteenth century also, and in waulking-song (q.v.) form, comes 'Ailein Duinn ó hì shiubhlainn leat' (Brown-haired Allan, I'd go with you), composed by Anna Campbell of Scalpay to her lover, Alan Morrison of Lewis, who was drowned while on his way to visit her. This, one of the greatest of Gaelic poems, contains an allusion, found very rarely elsewhere but known in some Irish keens, which functions here as an image of distraught grief: 'I would drink a drink in spite of my kinsfolk; not the red wine of Spain but the blood of your body, to me a better drink.'

There are many other compositions from the categories briefly noted: only constraints of space prevent us from listing more than a few representative types. In addition to those that can be securely dated, there are numerous songs which can be assigned on stylistic grounds more or less confidently to the 1645–1800 period. Together these indicate that there is a range that encompasses many of the types and common themes of folksong in other cultures: love, satire, complaints by girls married to old men, verse debates, match-making songs, lullabies, etc. Characteristically Gaelic are mouth music (*puirt-a-beul*) and pibroch songs (*puirt-mhóra*). Throughout all of them can be traced the capillaries of Gaelic panegyric tradition. (See J. MacInnes 1968; J. Ross 1957a; D. S. Thomson 1974.)   JMCI

folksongs, collections of Folksong does not appear to have been clearly differentiated from song and poetry in general in the minds of collectors until relatively recently. This may be due as much to the equation of poetry with song in Gaelic tradition as to the rise of folk cults and folk studies in modern times. The early collectors included anonymous verse, occasional songs by named individuals and ballads with spurious ascriptions (for example, to Ossianic heroes) alongside concentrations of the work of well-known poets such as Iain Lom (q.v.).

The geographical location of collectors to a large extent matches the threat and advance of English and Scots speech at different times. Perhaps we may except from this the two earliest collections, that of the Book of the Dean of Lismore (q.v.) and that of the Fernaig Manuscript (q.v.), although both the Dean and Macrae of Inverinate were themselves bilingual; but the pattern shows clearly enough if we take the eighteenth-century collectors: James McLagan, born in the parish of Logierait; Jerome Stone, a Fifer settled in Dunkeld; Alexander Pope of Reay, Sutherland; and Irvine and MacDiarmid who both operated in Perthshire also. In the nineteenth century the location moved westward and northward with John MacDonald of Ferintosh, Alexander Carmichael of Lismore, J. F. Campbell, Thomas Sinton in Badenoch and Hector Maclean with Argyllshire connections, and Frances Tolmie in Skye. In the present century the chief location is the Western Isles, with Mrs Kennedy-Fraser, Kenneth MacLeod, A. and A. MacDonald, J. L. Campbell, K. C. Craig, Calum Maclean, Seumas Ros and others.

A summary analysis of the McLagan Collection of manuscripts (in Glasgow University Library) may serve to give the flavour of the eighteenth-century collections more generally. Consisting of approximately 250 paper manuscripts, some being single sheets, a few booklets, this collection contains approximately 100 Ossianic or heroic items, running to some 9,670 lines; approximately 270 items the poets of which are named or which do not have a strong folk flavour; about 160 items which have a folk flavour; and some 45 miscellaneous items (English, Scots, Latin verses, prayers, prose items). Thus although the bias is towards non-folk items, there is a very good representation of folksong in the collection, and it includes a version of 'A' Bhean-eudach' and a good number of seventeenth-century songs (e.g. MacGregor songs).

Similar collections were made by Donald MacNicol (National Library, but unfortunately missing), Dr Alexander Irvine of Little Dunkeld and Ewen MacDiarmid (being prepared for publication), all of which were compiled in the second half of the eighteenth century. By 1776 the Eigg Collection was published by Ranald MacDonald (q.v.), and this began the stream of published collections which include at least some folksong. The selected list which follows draws attention, where appropriate, to details of location, bias and so on.

An Sùgradh 1777; Margaret Cameron's Collection 1785 (she came from Glenorchy); Gillies (q.v.) 1786 (with a strong representation of folksong); Patrick MacDonald's *Highland Vocal Airs* 1784; A. and D. Stewart, 1804; Inverness Collection 1806; Simon Fraser's *Airs and Melodies Peculiar to the Highlands of Scotland and the Isles* 1816; Albyn's Anthology 1816–18 (including melodies); Duncan MacCallum's Collection 1821; John Mackenzie's *Sàr Obair* 1841; Finlay Dun's Collection 1860; D. C. Macpherson's *An Duanaire* 1868; Archibald Sinclair's *An t-Oranaiche* 1876–9 (a wide selection, mainly of the eighteenth and nineteenth centuries); C. Stewart's *The Killin Collection* 1884; K. N. MacDonald's *Gesto Collection* 1895 (words and airs); Alexander Carmichael's *Carmina Gadelica* 1900–71 (collections made in the second half of the nineteenth century, vol. V (1954) containing most of the folksong); Thomas Sinton, *The Poetry of Badenoch* 1906; A. and A. MacDonald, *The MacDonald Collection of Gaelic Poetry* 1911 (poems and songs of MacDonald authorship or relevance); Frances Tolmie's Collection in the *Journal of the Folk Song Society* 1911 (with valuable discussion of modes, etc.); An Comunn Gaidhealach's *Coisir a' Mhòid* 1896–1925, and *Orain a' Mhòid* 1924–38; *Eilean Fraoich* 1938 (mainly Lewis songs, texts and melodies); K. C. Craig's *Orain Luaidh* 1949 (waulking songs noted from one South Uist singer); Margaret Fay Shaw's *Folksongs and Folklore of South Uist* 1955, 1977 (texts and melodies, with discussion); H. Creighton and C. I. N.

MacLeod's *Gaelic Songs in Nova Scotia* 1964; J. L. Campbell and F. Collinson's *Hebridean Folksongs* 1969, 1977, 1981 (vol. 1 consisting of Donald Mac-Cormick's South Uist collection made in 1893, vols. 2 and 3 of Campbell's collections from the 1930s onwards, incorporating earlier collections – for example, that of Annie Johnston, with texts, translations, airs, notes, etc.); D. A. Fergusson's *From the Farthest Hebrides* 1978, and *Beyond the Hebrides* 1977 (texts, translations, airs, notes, etc.; both to be used with caution – see reviews in *Gairm* 103 1978, and the *Scottish Review* 16 1979). There were also many shorter collections, including periodical and newspaper publications of song: for example, Otto Andersson's 'On Gaelic Folk Music from the Isle of Lewis', in *Budkavlen*, Åbo, Finland 1952; Lucy Broadwood's collections in the *Journal of the Folk Song Society* 1931, 1932, etc.; songs and collections of songs published in *An Gaidheal, Gairm, Tocher, Stornoway Gazette*, etc. Only one or two of the island or district collections, usually of texts only, have been listed above. Many others (Cameron's *The Tiree Bards* or MacLeod's *Bàrdachd Leòdhais*, for instance) might be added. The bibliographies in Shaw (1977) and Campbell and Collinson (1969), are recommended.

The most intensive collection has been made in the present century, by collectors such as J. L. Campbell, Callum Maclean, Seumas Ros, K. C. Craig and collectors currently working with the School of Scottish Studies, but most of this work, apart from Campbell's, is as yet unpublished.   DST

Forbes, Alasdair R. (d. 1924) Son of John Forbes (q.v.). Author of *Gaelic Names of Beasts, Birds, Fishes, Insects and Reptiles* (1905) and *Place Names of Skye . . .* (1923).   DST

Forbes, Revd John (1818–63) Minister of Sleat. Author of *Gràmar Dùbailte* (1843) and various religious works.   DST

forestry After agriculture, forestry is the second most important land use in the Highlands and Islands, in terms both of the value of output and of the employment, direct and indirect, which is associated with it. Forestry is also an important feature in the Highland landscape and is significant both ecologically and environmentally.

The history of Highland forestry can be divided into two stages. The first consisted of the removal of the once extensive natural forest (mainly pine, birch,

Forest on Craig Phadrig, near Inverness.

oak and alder), through burning, to clear land for agriculture and to remove predators, and felling for fuel, charcoal (for the once important iron-smelting industry) and construction, including ship building (O'Dell and Walton 1962; M. L. Anderson 1967). The second stage has involved reafforestation, mainly by non-native, largely softwood species, including Sitka spruce, Norway spruce, Lodgepole pine and Japanese larch. The first period lasted until the early nineteenth century, intensifying with the expansion of the iron industry in the eighteenth century, the increasing demand for ships, particularly during the Napoleonic Wars, and the clearance of land and people for extensive sheep farming. Attempts were made to plant trees during the eighteenth century, and these were continued by a few far-sighted lairds in the nineteenth century, but the process of large-scale reafforestation in the Highlands owes much to the establishment of the Forestry Commission in 1919. Thus the area of land under trees in the Highlands and Islands increased from some 261,000 acres in 1880 to some 961,000 acres by 1980, despite further large-scale felling during the two world wars, and at least three-quarters of this forest is in the hands of the Forestry Commission (Bryden and Houston 1976; Bryden 1979).

The output of the Highland forest in 1979, valued at 'forest gate' prices, may be reckoned at some £30 million, including the value of the annual increment to immature trees, which, because of the immaturity of most of the forest, currently accounts for more than four-fifths of the output.

Direct employment in planting, maintaining, felling and managing forestry in the Highlands accounts for some 2,000 jobs. The wood-processing industries in the Highlands represent an important source of income and employment, accounting, with associated employment in the transport industry, for a further 1,250 employees.

Apart from the pulp and paper mill at Fort William, the future of which has given rise to much concern, there are several modern sawmills in the region, some of which are capable of producing building-grade timber. As forests increasingly reach maturity towards the end of the century, these and other wood-processing and wood-using industries are likely to be of increasing significance.

Forestry is the subject of much debate in the Highlands, largely as a result of the way it is carried out and financed. Many people accept that there is still great scope for further afforestation in the region, and such expansion could provide important regional benefits in the future. However, many farmers – and other rural dwellers – fear that the continued expansion of forestry will inevitably lead to a decline in hill sheep farming and a radical shift in social structure and settlement patterns. This need not be so, given appropriate imaginative and sensitive policies (including far greater attempts, backed by appropriate incentive schemes, actively to involve farmers and crofters in further planting schemes), allied with deliberate policies to select land for large block planting in under-used areas of deer forest and grouse moor, particularly in the north and west. Such policies would, however, involve a radical departure from established practice in Britain. (See HIDB 1976; Centre for Agricultural Strategy 1980.)   JMB

Fort Augustus (Cille Chuimein) Built 1726 as complement to Fort William.   DST

Fort George Built 1747–63 to garrison the northeast Highlands after the 1745 Rising.   DST

Fort William (An Gearasdan) Built in the early 1690s, to garrison Lochaber.   DST

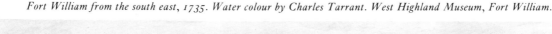

Fort William from the south east, 1735. Water colour by Charles Tarrant. West Highland Museum, Fort William.

forts and fortified sites During the seventh and eighth centuries the Annals of Iona (later incorporated in the Ulster Annals) record a number of military or paramilitary events at fortified sites in Scotland (J. W. M. Bannerman 1974, 9–26). Examples are the sieges of Edinburgh in 638, of Dunottar (near Stonehaven) in 681, of Dunadd (on the Crinan isthmus) and Dundurn (in Strathearn) in 683; the burning of Dunollie (near Oban) in 686 and of Tarbert Loch Fyne in 712 and 731; and the devastation of Dalriada and capture of Dunadd by Oengus mac Fergus, King of Picts, in 736. Some of these events, especially the burnings, can have been no more than incidents in inter-kindred (or even intra-kindred) feuding, but others were of deeper significance. The siege and capture of Edinburgh led to three centuries of Anglian dominance in Lothian. The sieges of Dunadd and Dundurn mark the swinging fortunes of war in the struggles of invading Scots and native Picts, while Oengus's capture of Dunadd was a major threat, albeit a temporary one, to the Scottic hold on mainland Dalriada.

Archaeological research has identified most of the forts mentioned in the Annals, and several have been excavated (Alcock 1981). Characteristically they occupy very craggy hilltops, often in areas of demonstrable strategic significance, especially by the coast or on tidal estuaries. The defences are mostly built of dry stone, and the use of mortar is totally unknown. At Dundurn the original citadel had its wall reinforced with wickerwork and oak beams fastened together with iron nails, a feature otherwise known only at the Pictish stronghold of Burghead on the Moray Firth (Alcock 1980, 75–7). A common but not invariable plan has the summit of the hill defended by a citadel, with lesser fortified enclosures on terraces at lower levels. At Dundurn the original terrace defences were massive timber stockades, but these were later rebuilt in stone.

Nothing is known of the buildings within the

The human footprint at Dunadd fort, near Kilmartin, Argyll.

defences, which implies that they were of perishable timber, not stone. A royal hall, and its ancillary buildings, may reasonably be inferred. Activities revealed by archaeology include the making of high-class jewellery, no doubt under royal patronage which also inspired the importation of wine from Gaul. Weapons are rare except at Dunadd. An economic basis of mixed farming is demonstrated by the occurrence of abundant bones of cattle, pig and sheep as kitchen refuse, by hand mills and even, very rarely, by cereal grains.

Dunadd is unique, in that it has carvings on a slab of rock just below the citadel: the outline of a boar, a human foot, a rock-cut basin and an unintelligible Ogam inscription (see **Ogam stones**). The boar may be a token of the Pictish victory in 736, and the Ogam inscription is also considered Pictish (K. H. Jackson 1965). It is generally agreed, however, that the footprint and the basin played some role in the ritual inauguration of the kings of Dalriada (q.v.).

Pictish fort at Dundurn, near Comrie, Perthshire.

By comparison with the hillforts of earlier centuries, these Early Historic forts have nothing like the size range. Above all, there is nothing comparable with *oppida* such as Traprain Law (q.v.). This implies that a quite different social unit is involved: the king and his war band, not the tribe. Moreover, the historic forts are generally at a lower altitude, and on more rugged hills, than the earlier ones. By contrast they are frequently overlaid by medieval castles, implying that they anticipated the medieval pattern of military and administrative arrangements. In this Dunadd and Dundurn are exceptional because they have no medieval overlay. Evidently they were created specifically in response to the Scotto-Pictish struggles of the seventh and eighth centuries.

Finally, it should be emphasized that seats of power among the Picts and Scots were not confined to fortified hilltops. Among the ancestor legends of the united kingdom are traditions that the last Pictish king was slain at Scone or Forteviot and that Kenneth mac Alpín (q.v.) died 'in the palace of Forteviot'. These are both low-lying sites, with no trace of fortifications. Indeed, there is no topographic or archaeological evidence at all at Scone. At Forteviot a fragmentary carved arch from the chapel royal has long been known, and aerial photography has begun to reveal a palace complex, much of it lost under the modern village. The site is adjacent to a group of ritual and ceremonial monuments in use from the second millennium BC up to the Christian era. This association recalls the comparable succession of ritual monuments at Tara and Cruachain, and perhaps at Dunadd as well. Long-lived ritual and ceremonial traditions may lie behind the power centres of the early kings of both Picts and Scots (Alcock 1980, 84–5).   LA

Franciscan Mission From 1619 to 1637 several Irish Franciscan priests laboured, with considerable success, in the western Highlands and Isles. Their work consisted mainly in reviving the Catholicism of areas which had been without priests for many years rather than in converting Protestants. After being driven out of Scotland the priests continued their work from Bonamargy Friary, Co. Antrim, to which many Highlanders came to receive the sacraments. In 1641 the Scottish army in Ireland captured the head of the Mission, Father Patrick Hegarty. He was released in 1646 but died before he could revive the Mission. (See Giblin 1964; D. Stevenson 1979, 54–61; D. Stevenson 1980, 53–5.)   DS

Fraser, Alexander (1827–99), *see* art, Gaelic, in modern times.

Fraser, Alexander (d. 1936) Born Inverness-shire. Provincial Archivist, Ontario. Author of *Leabhar nan Sonn*, etc. (See Macbean 1921.)   DST

Fraser, Allan Henry Hector (1900–79) From Strathpeffer. Doctor, agricultural scientist and novelist. Author of Gaelic biography of Sir Hector MacDonald, the popular Army hero of the Sudan and Boer War campaigns.   DST

Fraser, Revd James (1634–1709) Minister of Wardlaw. Author of the Polichronicon or Wardlaw Manuscript composed between 1666 and *c.*1699 (for which see W. Mackay 1905.)   DST

Fraser, Professor John (1882–1945) From Glen Urquhart. First Lecturer in Celtic, University of Aberdeen. Professor of Celtic, University of Oxford, 1921–45. Grammarian, philologist and editor of Quiggin's *Poems from BDL*. (See *Gairm*, vol. 20, 42ff.)   DST

Fraser-Mackintosh, Charles (1828–1907) Liberal politician, with strong pro-crofter sympathies in Land Agitation (see **Politics, Highland (nineteenth century)**). MP for Inverness Burghs, 1874–85, and for Inverness-shire, 1885–92. Member of Napier Commission (q.v.). Lawyer and antiquarian. (See Hunter 1976, 137, *passim;* I. M. M. MacPhail 1976a.)   DEM

Fraser's Highlanders, *see* regiments, Highland.

Free Church of Scotland The roots of the Free Church lie in two separate events involving quite distinct principles: the Disruption of 1843 and the Union of 1900.

The issue in 1843 was the spiritual independence of the Church. For more than a century a system of patronage had prevailed, allowing local dignitaries to 'intrude' ministers into congregations against the wishes of the people and the judgement of presbyteries. In 1834 the General Assembly passed an Act which gave to the majority of the 'male heads of families' the power to veto the induction of any minister whom they did not want. There followed the 'Ten Years' Conflict' between the Church and the Court of Session, which, in a succession of cases,

'First General Assembly of the Free Church of Scotland, signing the Act of Separation and Deed of Demission at Tanfield, Edinburgh, May, 1843. By D. O. Hill. Free Church of Scotland Presbytery Hall, Edinburgh. (The picture was painted on the basis of Hill's sketches and Adamson's calotype photographs of all those present. It was finished in 1866. Hill appears with his sketch book and Adamson with his camera.)

found that in applying the Veto Act presbyteries were violating the legal rights of patrons. In 1842 the Church presented to the government *The Claim of Rights*, setting forth its grievances and stating its claims. This brought no response and at the opening of the General Assembly in 1843, 475 ministers demitted their charges in the Established Church and formed the Church of Scotland Free. Support in the Highlands was almost total. But the problems were enormous. First, landlords refused to grant sites for churches and manses. In 1845 Dr James Begg, visiting Wester Ross, remarked:

> Every new spectacle I witnessed deepened my impression of astonishment. These poor Highlanders must face all the storms of winter on the bare sea-beach, denied a single inch of land on which to erect a place of worship. Such a state of matters in Ireland would shake the empire and it is Christian principle alone which has borne it so meekly. (T. Brown 1890, 661)

Second, there was the difficulty of providing preachers. Of the ministers who had 'come out', 101 regularly used Gaelic in their services. But this still left 150 vacant Gaelic congregations, and there were only thirty-one unattached ministers to supply them.

To meet the need twelve of the most eminent Highland ministers were freed from their congregations for six months to itinerate. Another eighty agreed to give similar service for a month. A schooner, the *Breadalbane*, was built for the special purpose of transporting these ministers from island to island and along the western shores of the mainland.

The new Church had a deep interest in education, and by 1869 it had built 596 schools and two training colleges. The Highlands benefited from these in fair measure, but the standard approach was ill-adapted to the more remote districts. A scheme was devised to supply these with aid-schools staffed by students who taught during the summer and pursued their studies during the winter. Financial support came from the Edinburgh Free Church Ladies' Association, which eventually sponsored 133 schools, the first being opened in Harris in 1851. The Glasgow ladies had similar schools, mainly in the Roman Catholic islands.

The Free Church published two Gaelic periodicals: *An Fhianuis* (monthly; first issue January 1845, last issue May 1850) and *Eaglais Shaor na h-Alba*, subtitled *Lomradh air Craobhsgaoileadh an t-Soisgeil leis an Eaglais Shaoir* (quarterly; first issue February 1875).

The Free Church was interested from the beginning in forging closer links with other presbyterian denominations. In 1852 union was effected with the United Original Secession Church and, in 1876, with a majority of the Reformed Presbyterians. In 1863 there began the fateful negotiations with the United Presbyterian Church. These were officially broken off in 1872, resumed in 1894 and finalized with the formation of the United Free Church in 1900. Twenty-six ministers refused to enter the new denomination and resolved instead to continue the name and the testimony of the Free Church. They did so for two main reasons.

The first was fear of voluntaryism. Despite its separateness, the Free Church was deeply committed to the establishment principle (i.e. that it is the duty of government to recognize and support the Christian faith). The United Presbyterians, by contrast, were voluntaries, holding that it is wrong for the Church to accept any support from the state. The anti-Union party in the Free Church dreaded the 'atheistic state' to which the consistent application of this principle would lead.

Second, the Union involved acceptance of the Declaratory Act. The voluntarism *v.* establishment controversy raised issues far larger than itself. No person holding the United Presbyterian view could conscientiously subscribe to the Westminister Confession, which explicitly endorsed the establishment principle. There arose, therefore, an insistent demand for a conscience clause, and in 1879 the United Presbyterian Church passed a Declaratory Act which granted liberty of opinion on such points *in the Standards* as did not enter into the substance of the faith. The Free Church, to facilitate union, passed a similar Act in 1892, sanctioning the existence of 'diversity of opinions on such points *in the Confession* as do not enter into the substance of the Reformed Faith therein set forth'. This introduced a fatal distinction between what was confessional and what was fundamental, and history would show that the plea 'It does not enter into the substance' could be used to justify even the most radical departures from historic Christianity.

The Free Church believes in the spiritual independence of the Church, in the right of congregations to

Free church, parish of Fort William and Kilmonivaig.

choose their own ministers and in the duty of government to recognize and obey the Christian faith. In public services the use of 'uninspired materials of praise' is disallowed, and there is no instrumental accompaniment. No theological commitment is required of ordinary members. The only condition of admission is a credible profession of faith in Christ. Ministers, elders and deacons profess their allegiance to every doctrine contained in the Westminster Confession. (See R. Buchanan 1852; Stewart and Cameron n.d.) DMCL

Freer, Ada (Adela Monica) Goodrich (1857–1931) Born Uppingham, Leicestershire. Commissioned by the Society for Psychical Research to investigate Highland second sight, 1894–7. Published *Outer Isles* (1902). (See J. L. Campbell and T. H. Hall 1968.) JLC

Freiceadan Dubh, am, *see* regiments, Highland.

G

Gaelic (general survey) Although Gaelic is the Celtic language most closely associated with Scotland, its coming was relatively late. The oldest Celtic languages associated with the country belonged to the Brythonic rather than the Goidelic group, and these were widely spoken not only in the British (i.e. Brittonic-speaking) kingdoms in central and southern Scotland (Strathclyde, Gododdin, including the district of Manaw about the head of the Firth of Forth, and Rheged) but also in large areas of Pictland (as, for example, from the Firth of Forth to the Moray Firth). The fact that all these areas (which comprise a very large part of Scotland) were long inhabited by people using Brittonic and associated dialects is proved mainly by the place names but is often corroborated by early Latin and Greek accounts (see, for

detail, **place-names, British and Pictish; place-names, pre-Gaelic**; and, e.g., K. H. Jackson 1953, 1969). It is thought that one or more of these Brittonic dialects may have survived until the eleventh century.

Gaelic probably began to make some impact on Scottish speech habits as early as the third century AD. (Eumenius in AD 297 refers to Picti and Hiberni as enemies of the south Scottish Britons, and Ammianus Marcellinus says that in AD 360 and 365 Scotti and Picti/Pecti were operating as allies against the Romans in the neighbourhood of the Roman Walls.) There was perhaps a growing Gaelic settlement in western Scotland by the late fifth century and the coming of Fergus Mór mac Eirc (q.v.) (see DALRIADA; and, e.g., Bannerman 1974, 122ff.). Ecclesiastical colonization came during the sixth century with Columba and his followers, and there ensued a lengthy period of conflict and adjustment, especially between the Scots of Dalriada and the Picts but also between Scots and Britons, in which religious conversion, military conquest, cultural influence and dynastic alliance all played important parts (see **art, Pictish; Brudei mac Maelchon; Celtic Church; Colum Cille; Dalriada; Dunadd; Maol Rubha; Ogam stones; Picts, pre-Union contact with the Scots; Picts, union with the Scots; place names, ecclesiastical; place names, Gaelic, in Galloway and Ayrshire; place names, Gaelic, in Pictland**). It is not claimed that the detailed pattern of Gaelic colonization can be discerned as yet, and it is doubtful whether much of this can ever be recovered, but the evidence of place names (see especially **place-names, Gaelic, in Scotland**, *baile* and *achadh* maps, p. 232) shows clearly that Gaelic settlement, *at one time or another*, has included practically the whole of Scotland (the thinnest representation being at the extremities, East Lothian and the Northern Isles). It is worth emphasizing this point, as propaganda to the contrary has for long been part of the stock in trade of popular, and sometimes of academic, writers.

There are few Gaelic documents from the premedieval period; the evidence for Gaelic use rests largely on historical references to the Gaelic people (Scotti, etc.) and to named people and places, and on the Irish Annals, some of which were based on Scottish records (see **Iona Chronicle**). The Gaelic account of the settling of Dalriada (q.v.) probably goes back to a *c.* seventh century (?) original. Gaelic in this period is synonymous with Old Irish/Old Gaelic, and the earliest continuous Gaelic writings of

Scottish provenance are of this nature, for example, the twelfth century notitiae in the Book of Deer (q.v.). Latin supersedes Gaelic as the language of inscriptions on West Highland grave slabs and monuments *c*.AD 1250–1300 (see SCULPTURE, MONUMENTAL), though it returns in the sixteenth century for a time.

There are a few Brittonic loanwords in Gaelic (e.g. *monadh*) and fewer Pictish, but probably these dialects influenced Gaelic syntax (see **loanwords, British and Pictish**; **Gaelic: syntax**). The Anglian linguistic invasion began to gain ground significantly from the twelfth century, encouraged by the setting up, in the east, of the burghs, important centres of commerce, and Gaelic was in due course supplanted at the king's court in the twelfth and thirteenth centuries. Inglis, moving towards Scots, became the language of landowning classes in Strathclyde, central Scotland and the east coast to Buchan. From the thirteenth century onwards the area dominated by Gaelic speech has been contracting, fairly slowly in this long perspective, but in such a way as to leave the centres and organs of power predominantly in the hands of people of non-Gaelic speech (though often of predominantly Gaelic or Celtic ancestry).

In the north and west, and especially on the islands off the west coast of Scotland, Norse settlement from the late eighth century built up significantly, and the Norse language was widely used, though perhaps not to the exclusion of Gaelic. (Norse may have coexisted with Pictish in some places for a short time.) Again, our main evidence comes from place names but Norse loans in Gaelic and Norse influence on Gaelic phonology and intonation (see under GAELIC), together with some references in Norse sources, supplement this evidence. The Norse loans are generally of a technical nature, indicating probably some technological superiority at the time in matters of boat building, sailing and fishing – cf. such loans as *sgoth*, *birlinn*, *sgòd*, *stiùir*, *nòs*, 'harbourage', *dorgh*, *trosg*, *rùm* in the phrase *fo rùm* 'below decks' (from Old Norse *rùm*, 'rowingbench'). Christian names and surnames of Norse origin (Tormod, Torcall, Raoghnailt, MacLeoid, MacAsgaill, MacAmhlaigh) are still common in the Western Isles. It is worth noting that there are not many Norse loanwords of a 'central' character. Just as such 'central' Latin loans are scarce (*uair*, *nuair* being a good example), so with Norse loans (*nàbaidh*, *lagh* and *cus* being perhaps suitable examples).

Latin loan words (q.v.) are also of a technical nature, many of them associated with the Church, learning and abstract thought. To begin with, this may have been truer of English loans (q.v.), and of course technological innovation still acounts for some such, but in the past three centuries at least English has become the main source of loanwords in Gaelic. We see Iain Lom (q.v.) using technical military loans in the seventeenth century and Mac Mhaighstir Alasdair (q.v.) borrowing freely and unself-consciously in the eighteenth. Their borrowings wear the air of an exuberant acceptance of extra riches; many later borrowings, especially in twentieth century speech, betray poverty of native resources. Such slack and unnecessary borrowing is common in unsophisticated speech contexts and has been bred by contacts made in industry, the armed forces, at the fishing, on oil rigs and around the radio or television 'hearth'. Sometimes, through inverted snobbery, such loans come to be preferred in writing also. On a different level there has been a good deal of conscious and planned borrowing, as of vocabulary for advertising, literary criticism or the exposition of biological topics (see PERIODICALS, GAELIC; R. MacLeòid 1976).

There is no evidence of the significant divergence of Scottish from Irish Gaelic before the tenth century and little before the thirteenth (see K. H. Jackson 1951; *hiatus*, etc.), but it is likely that had we fuller evidence, we would find dialect differences arising well before the earlier of these dates. Now there are significant dialect differences within Scottish Gaelic (see DIALECTS, PRINCIPAL DIVISIONS; DIALECTS, SUBDIVISIONS); some of these dialects are closer to northern and western Irish dialects than others, and it is possible to argue about whether the Gaelic of Rathlin was more Irish or Scottish. Some dialects (e.g. that of Lewis) show marked conservative features alongside strongly innovative ones. All the Scottish dialects are mutually comprehensible, although a modicum of concentration is sometimes needed initially.

For phonology, syntax, orthography, etc., see appropriate entries under **Gaelic**.

As the total number of Gaelic speakers has decreased (see **Gaelic speaking in Scotland, demographic history of**) to the 1981 figure of 79,000 or so and the perhaps realistic figure of approximately 65,000 fluent speakers, some of the characteristics of a siege economy appear, and it is difficult to achieve an acceptable balance of Gaelic-area particularism and Scottish (i.e. national) generalism. In the long term it is probably necessary to have a national framework and a local 'reserve', but the rivalries engendered are serious (and perhaps suicidal). A very strong national political dynamic might resolve the problem, but this is still unavailable. In this uneasy situation, now long-continuing, particular initiatives have increased Gaelic prestige, while the figures of speakers tell their own story (see **broadcasting, Gaelic; Comunn Gaidhealach, An; current affairs, coverage in Gaelic; press, Gaelic; schools, Gaelic teaching in; societies, learned; universities and colleges, Gaelic studies in**). We are still left, however, with a diglossic situation which is full of practical, and sometimes psychological, problems. Bilingualism in the Gaelic context is no less complex than elsewhere: there is the usual range of language mixes (see **Gaelic: calquing, switching**), whether these are correlated with location, age, class or educational sophistication. There are domains in which Gaelic is more widely used (domestic, religious, occupational) and registers which are more systematically developed (literary prose and verse, pulpit Gaelic), and there are attempts to develop other registers. But a workable, wide-ranging solution of the diglossic problem has not yet been formulated, let alone effected. On the national stage Gaelic remains attractive, romantic, moving, as well as being the occasional object of vituperation, but the powerful political, social and economic logic of our society involves the Gael with the national as well as the parochial stage and forces consequent choices on him. He does not have the option of existing in an enclave, with his own literature, Church, media, educational system, commercial and economic systems and communications. He has, indeed, strong defences in his language, culture and history, as long as his will to use them survives. (See K. Mackinnon 1978; R. MacThòmais 1976; D. S. Thomson 1979b, 1981.)

DST

Gaelic: calquing Structural remodelling based on English is not a new phenomenon in Gaelic (see, for example, W. J. Watson 1927), but nowadays calques occur in spoken and at all levels of written discourse, though the more formal the discourse, the fewer the neologisms. Typical examples are *Tha e a' cur dealbh math tarsainn* (he is putting a good image across), *a' faighinn a' chuid as miosa a mach as a' bheatha* (getting the worst out of life), *ciamar a rachadh iad mu dheidhinn a dhèanamh* (how they would set about doing it); *'na ghàirdeanan* (in his arms) and *a-steach dhan an loch* (into the loch), both from a recent translation of

St Mark's Gospel; and, finally, the prophetic *Ciamar a tha sin mar char-a-mhuiltean?* (How is that for a somersault?).

DMCA

Gaelic: dialects, principal divisions The history of Scottish Gaelic dialectology goes back to the turn of the century. C. M. Robertson's articles in the *Transactions of the Gaelic Society of Inverness* and in the *Celtic Review*, followed by those of John Fraser in *Scottish Gaelic Studies* and the *Revue celtique*, were the pioneering works which set the scene for the more scientific approach brought to bear at a later date by scholars such as Dieckhoff, Borgstrøm, Holmer, Oftedal and others. Robertson was remarkable in that he ranged over much of the Gaelic-speaking area, especially the mainland, and his articles are still a source of useful information and interest. However, the 'pre-scientific' approach lays them open to the posssibility of different interpretation; one looks forward, therefore, to the findings of the Linguistic Survey of Scotland (q.v.) for an up-to-date and accurate picture of the various dialects.

Writings on Irish dialects by scholars such as Finck, Quiggin and Sommerfelt pointed to the gap so far as Scotland was concerned. It is an interesting fact that, here too, it was foreigners who embarked on the task of describing the dialects which, in certain aspects of their phonology, were more 'archaic' than the Irish. Published in 1932, Dieckhoff's *A Pronouncing Dictionary of Scottish Gaelic Based on the Glengarry dialect* was the first serious scientific study. Despite the title it is really a phonology first and foremost. It was followed in 1937 by the epoch-making description of the Barra dialect by Borgstrøm (1937) in the *Norsk Tidsskrift for Sprogvidenskap*, the first comprehensive study of the phonology and morphology of a Scottish Gaelic dialect, which shows the influence of Trubetzkoy's linguistic theory (the Prague School). The following year saw the appearance of Holmer's *Studies on Argyllshire Gaelic* (Islay and Gigha, but also part of Skye). This rather idiosyncratic work was later followed by studies of Arran (Holmer 1957) and Kintyre (Holmer 1962). These are more conventional, though the data is sometimes ambiguous so far as the phonology is concerned. Borgstrøm continued his promising beginning with his *Dialects of the Outer Hebrides* (1940), in which all the Outer Isles were covered and some of his comments on Barra were revised. A year later his *Dialects of Skye and Ross-shire* appeared. This is somewhat more sketchy than either of the earlier works, and the

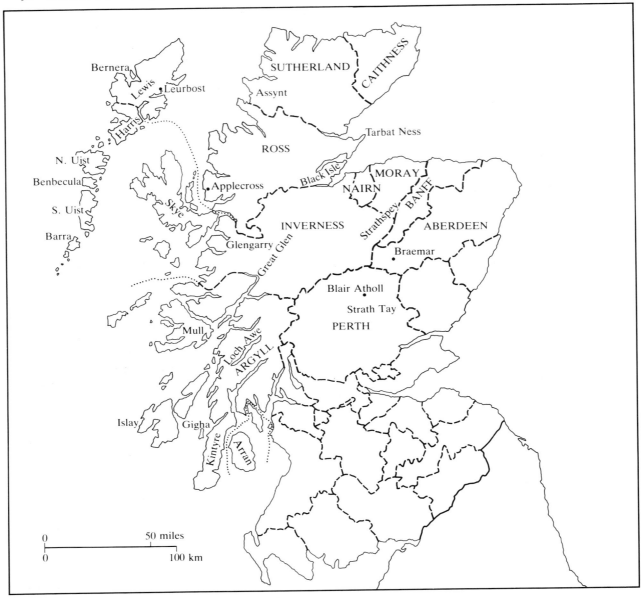

Gaelic dialects : principal divisions.

Ross-shire material was collected from points on the western coast only. Oftedal's *The Gaelic of Leurbost Isle of Lewis* (1956) represents a significant advance in approach and was the first comprehensive treatment of a dialect in phonemic terms. It includes a fairly full morphology. This book is probably the most important milestone in Gaelic dialectology of recent times.

Apart from some articles the next publication of note was Ternes's *Phonemic Analysis of Scottish Gaelic* (1973). This work, based on the dialect of Applecross, Ross-shire, provides us with an extremely interesting and worthwhile discussion of various problems of Gaelic phonetics/phonology. Watson's paper on part of the phonology of a north-eastern Ross-shire dialect (J. Watson 1974, 9ff.) gave us the first systematic account of an eastern dialect. This has been augmented by Dorian's very com-

petent phonology and morphology of the east Sutherland dialect (1978). It is now possible to obtain an
overall impression of most of the area in which Gaelic
has been the main language until comparatively
recent times. However, an accurate statement of the
dialect boundaries throughout the whole Gaelic area
is not yet possible. This will be feasible only when
the results of the Linguistic Survey are published.
(For a useful bibliography of dialect studies up to
1954, see Woolley 1954, 24–7.)

The term 'dialect' has been used above several
times without qualification. Some discussion of it is
appropriate in order that the situation regarding the
Gaelic language may be better understood. All languages vary both geographically or spatially as well as
on the social and related scales. Traditionally, dialectology has to do with the geographical aspect of such
variation. (A fascinating article by MacAulay (1978)
draws attention to other, and possibly equally important, avenues of research in dialect study.) It must be
remembered that the inherent diversity among individual speakers has to be allowed for – the term
'idiolect' is used for the total speech characteristics of
a single individual – but in order to approach the
subject in a practical way it is usual to think of dialects as including rather more substantial numbers of
people over a given area. But differences of pronunciation, grammar and vocabulary tend to shade continuously into each other, and isoglosses commonly
cross each other at all angles. Hence, dialect boundaries are notoriously difficult to define, and it is only
when a concentration or 'bundle' of isoglosses coin-
cide that a significant boundary may be recognized.
These 'bundles' of isoglosses are usually found in
conjunction with geographical features such as mountain ranges, rivers, etc., and also former political lines
of demarcation. The different linguistic status of isoglosses of different types must be borne in mind.
Variation in vocabulary may make communication a
problem; the use of the same form to indicate
separate referents will confuse even more. Grammatical variation is also of significance; here we include
morphological and syntactical phenomena. It is in the
realm of phonology and phonetics that much energy
has been spent on drawing attention to features
which may or may not be of great significance (other
than to the ear) unless they play a systematic role in
the phonological sense.

For some time now it has been customary to view
Gaelic dialects as falling into two major groups, the
'central' and the 'peripheral'. According to the
leading authority (K. H. Jackson 1968, 67):

the central dialect covers the Hebrides as far
south as Mull and sometimes further, Ross
exclusive of the north-east corner, Assynt,
Inverness-shire, western Perthshire, and mainland Argyll roughly north of Loch Awe; while
the peripheral dialects comprise Caithness and
Sutherland exclusive of Assynt, the north-east
corner of Ross, Braemar, eastern Perthshire, the
rest of mainland Argyll with Kintyre, and
Arran. Moray and the adjacent lower region of
the Spey, the wide valley of Strathspey from
Rothiemurchus to the Moray border, may go
with the peripheral dialects, linking up with
Braemar and east Perth.

On the other hand, Jackson has pointed out (ibid.,
67) that certain isoglosses divide Gaelic Scotland
roughly north and south, while others indicate a
roughly east and west division. This indicates very
clearly the dangers inherent in the loose use of the
term 'dialect' to which we have become accustomed.
It also needs to be stressed that the plotting of isoglosses (essentially statistical abstractions) is an
extremely tenuous exercise from the structural point
of view, in that isolated features may be taken out of
context without due consideration of the possibly different status of those features within the various
systems.

The centre/periphery approach illustrates well the
focal area/relic area theory, which assumes a centre of
diffusion in which a change has its beginning,
working its way out in all directions, spreading tenta-
cles along river valleys and even railway lines. The
areas not yet touched, or bypassed, are relic areas and
are mostly to be found on the periphery of the language in question. A readily recognized phonetic/
phonological phenomenon may be cited here.
Preaspiration of -c, -p, -t is a feature of all the major
dialects. It is only in the peripheral areas such as east
Sutherland, Strathtay in east Perthshire (but not
Blair Atholl: see C. M. Robertson 1900, 15; Ó
Murchú 1976, 188), Arran and Kintyre that it is not
found. There are some instances in Kintyre, particularly in the north (Holmer 1962) where forms with
and without it exist side by side. This shows the
southerly direction that preaspiration is taking. The
interesting, if rather strange, pronunciations of
Nollaig and *rud-eiginn*, with *ch* before *g*, quoted by
Holmer (ibid., 52) exist alongside the expected forms.
This is analogy at work. The outward spread of preaspiration is also illustrated by the fact that it reached

the eastern seaboard in the Black Isle and northwards into the Tarbat Ness peninsula, which seems to be a transitional area (J. Watson 1974, 52–3). Quite clearly, the importance of the Great Glen cannot be overestimated as a geographical feature which facilitated the eastward spread of a number of innovations. The Perthshire position is remarkable in that preaspiration is absent in Strathtay, though a strong type, associated with the central Highlands, is found at Blair Atholl (C. M. Robertson 1900). Within the 'central' dialect area isoglosses may be drawn between (a) the Lewis type (Lewis, north and west Sutherland and the greater part of mainland Ross-shire; (b) the *ht, hp, chc* type in the Outer Hebrides (except Lewis), Skye and most of the Inner Hebrides and some areas of the adjacent mainland; (c) part of the central Highlands as mentioned above, where *ch* is found before *p* and *t*, as well as *c*. If the theory of a Lewis origin (Borgstrøm 1974, 91ff.) is correct, it is difficult to explain adequately the fact that the area of greatest intensity is on the mainland (Jackson, quoted in Oftedal 1962, 117).

Another feature which parallels the above is the svarabhakti phenomenon (q.v.). In the central area the svarabhakti vowel is a clear one, and it often echoes the previous vowel, usually also bearing a degree of stress. (In addition to the standard monographs, see also Dilworth 1958.) In east Sutherland, north-east Ross-shire, east Perthshire, Arran and Kintyre the situation is different. Here Islay and Gigha have also to be included, though a clear vowel may surface under certain conditions (Holmer 1938, 34). In these areas the vowel takes the form *ə/i*, for the most part making it similar to vowels in unstressed syllables. In this respect it resembles the Irish type. Borgstrøm's theory (Borgstrøm 1938, 35ff.) that, from the historical point of view, the clear vowel type is older and that the other type developed from it in Ireland and in the peripheral areas in Scotland, though attractive in many ways, has not gained general acceptance (K. H. Jackson 1951b, 84).

An example of another phonological feature, common also to southern Irish, is the diphthongization of certain stressed vowels (e.g. (*e*)*a* and *o*) before *ll, nn, m* in monosyllables (or in polysyllables when these consonants are not followed by a vowel). In this case the central area is again the innovating one and extends to the whole of Sutherland, while east Perthshire, Kintyre, Arran, Islay and Gigha have forms such as [gaN:] (*gann*), [ToN:] (*tonn*) (Holmer, 1962, 22) and *mbót:* (*am poll*), *ndó:ɬ* (*an toll*)

(Ó Murchú, 1976, 188–90). We can see here that the periphery includes Islay in the case of svarabhakti and non-diphthongization but not in the case of preaspiration, and that east Sutherland is excluded in the case of diphthongization. It is necessary, therefore, to keep in mind that fact that though the peripheral dialects may have important features in common, they may also in some instances belong with the central area. However, it may be correct to assume that, by and large, these dialects have preserved more archaic features, in the realm of phonology at any rate. The view that there is a north *v.* south dialect division, or indeed an east *v.* west one, may very well be a mere modification of the well founded theory that the centre of innovation is in the mid-west, if one accepts that some features spread more rapidly than others. The possibilities are then quite numerous.

Within the central dialect area one of the most striking 'sub-dialects' is that of Lewis. Borgstrøm (1940, 9) distinguishes between northern (Lewis) and southern Hebridean dialects (from Harris to Barra). The isoglosses which enabled him to draw this distinction are listed by him (ibid., 222ff.). The reasons for this 'border' are physical and historical, the boundary coinciding with Loch Resort on the west and Loch Seaforth on the east, the intervening terrain being extremely hilly. A purely phonetic difference which has little significance in the phonological sense is the realization of the phoneme /u/ on either side of the border. The most common Lewis allophone is considerably more advanced than in Harris, so that words like *bùth* and *dùil* sound rather different in Lewis from the usual southern type. Though striking to the ear, this feature is not very important. A rather more important isogloss is that which marks off the different types of preaspiration found on either side of this border. In Lewis the feature may be regarded phonologically as part of the following stopped consonant and need not therefore be shown in a phonemic transcription; [ka^ht] (*cat*), for example, will be phonemically /kat/. The southern dialects, on the other hand, have 'stronger' preaspiration, giving the clusters [ht], [xk], etc. These have to be interpreted as phonemic clusters; thus, Harris /kaht/ (*cat*), /muxk/ (*muc*) contrast with Lewis /kat/ and /muk/. Indeed, a more precise phonemic approach will have Harris /kahd/ and /muxg/ (Gleasure 1968, 260–1). A purely phonemic transcription indicates a very important difference in the systems of the two dialects, but it can mislead the unwary if the conventions underlying such transcriptions are not fully understood.

A morphological isogloss of note here is the -(e)amaid/sinn phenomenon in the first person plural of the imperfect/conditional. The southern dialects appear to have an ending -(e)amaid, paralleling the -(a)inn ending of the first person singular, whereas this has been replaced by a system in Lewis in which all persons save the first singular have independent pronouns. In a large class of feminine nouns the genitive singular is formed (in the southern dialects in part) by the addition of an ending -(e)adh (e.g. cas → coiseadh, fuil → faladh) except when an adjective with initial consonant follows. In Lewis the older genitive remains, though here, in many cases, the final vowel is present only when a following adjective has an initial consonant. The fact is, of course, that it is largely only when these nouns are *in pausa* that the distinction is made, so that this isogloss represents quite a complex feature. Another isogloss which Borgstrøm lists is the non-inflexion in the singular of masculine nouns with the suffix -an. He maintained that final -n here could not be palatalized for the genitive singular (or for the plural), the Bernera form for the genitive singular being no different from the non-genitive, and that the plural was formed by the addition of the ending -an. In fact, Oftedal showed that this is not so for the whole of Lewis, as in Leurbost (Oftedal 1956, 184) the suffix -an may be palatalized in the normal way.   JWG

Gaelic: dialects, subdivisions Gaelic dialectology has generally been based on a consensus concerning the most important heteroglosses. We have general 'dialectal' areas such as Lewis, Uist, Sutherland, etc., which are divided into 'proper' dialect areas such as Bernera, Ness, South Uist, Embo, etc. (Borgstrøm 1940; Oftedal 1956; MacGill-Fhinnein 1966; Dorian 1978). These dialects may in turn be divided into areal sub-dialects. A typical basis for subdivision is the village, which, for historical reasons has developed a significant identity reflected in language usage. There are divisions that transcend the village to include a group of villages, and there are also sub-village divisions, such as neighbourhoods, that have their own linguistic distinctiveness – not to mention the differentiation that derives from networks such as kin groups and coteries (D. MacAulay 1978).

The most extensive area of sub-dialectal difference is the sound system, often at the sub-phonemic level, involving differences in phonation or in the degree of aspiration and voicing, for example, or showing a velarized alveolar [l] instead of a velarized dental lateral [L]; less usually at the phonemic level we find, for example, conflation of the /d'/ and /g'/ phonemes or of the phonemes /L'/ and /l'/. Vocabulary differences range from differences in terms of address (*a bhalaich* v. *'ille*) to different names for common utensils (*peile* v. *keada*). Differences in morphology and syntax are less common, except where one sub-dialect has generalized recent innovations, confined in another to the language of the younger age group (D. MacAulay 1978).   DMCA

Gaelic dictionaries, *see* dictionaries, Scottish Gaelic.

Gaelic: divergence from Irish and Manx The extent to which Scottish Gaelic had become a distinct language is largely concealed in the sixteenth and early seventeenth centuries by the adherence of written and printed material to the Irish literary standard. The Book of the Dean of Lismore (q.v.) through its unconventional spelling, Carswell's (q.v.) translation of the Book of Common Order and the translator of Calvin's larger Catechism through their lapses from that standard, and the translators of the Shorter Catechism and to a lesser extent those of the metrical psalms, by their indifference to that standard, all sporadically reveal the changes that had occurred. These changes can often be confirmed by the evidence of early Manx (c.1610), which was entirely uninfluenced by standard Irish. The developments outlined below are true of Manx as well as of Scottish Gaelic unless otherwise stated.

The preaspiration (q.v.) of *c*, first externally attested by Lhuyd (q.v.) c.1700, is found in Metrical Psalms (1659), as well as [xk] for *chd* (not Manx); *bh-* is prefixed to forms of the preposition *ó* from the Book of the Dean onwards; final -n of the article begins to disappear in some positions. Already present in the Book of the Dean is a decline in the frequency of the nasal mutation, particularly after the first and second person plural possessives and (*i*)*ar* (after) (neither in Manx), after numerals and in the genitive plural of adjectives; there are also signs of nasalization becoming a permanent consonant -n in *an* (in) and *an* (their). From the Book of the Dean onwards lenition gains ground after preposition plus singular article, in the present/future and preterite of irregular verbs with *t-* (e.g. *tha, thig, thug*) and in the preterite passive/impersonal (no Manx evidence); and in the genitive plural of indefinite nouns (not Manx) perhaps only from the seventeenth century.

Verbal innovations include the use of the old present as future, the loss of the old *f-* future and related conditional, and the creation of the new periphrastic present, i.e. *tha mi (ag)* plus verbnoun, already very common in Carswell and the Catechisms. Analytic verb forms (i.e. third person singular plus pronoun) gradually become more frequent in the second and third persons, but the first person singular and plural are more resistant (and in Manx never disappear). The second person plural imperative is generally *-idh*, but the Book of the Dean has examples of *-ibh* (from the pronoun; not Manx). The particle *do*, reduced to *a*, is reinterpreted as a relative. The participle of verbs in *-ughadh/-achadh* is frequently *-aighte*, not *-aighthe*, in the Shorter Catechism. The personal pronouns *mi, mise, thu, é, í, iad* replace *mé, meise, tú, sé, sí, siad* as early as the Book of the Dean, and the demonstrative *so* is often written there when metre requires enclitic *-sa*. The negative particle *cha* runs in parallel with *ní* throughout these two centuries but gradually wins the exclusive position it always has in Manx. Examples of the peculiarly Scottish Gaelic doubling of the prepositions *i n-* and *do* to *ann an* and *do dh'* are found first in the metrical psalms.   RLT

Gaelic: ē broken

Classical Old Irish/Gaelic had *é/ia* < **ei* (also < Lat. *ē, oe*), which were for the most part in complementary distribution, *é* occurring before palatal (slender) consonants and *ia* before non-palatal (broad) consonants. But Old Irish/Gaelic also had *é* from a compensatorily lengthened *ĕ* (sometimes also *ă*), which did not break to *ia*, though it was affected in other ways under certain conditions – for example, *én* 'bird', ds. *éun*, gs. *éuin/éoin/éiuin*, acc. pl. *éonu*, (Thurneysen, 1946, 37–8). It is this *é* which later develops into a diphthong in certain areas of Gaelic and Irish, but only before a non-palatal consonant.

The Linguistic Survey of Scotland (q.v.) has shown (K. H. Jackson 1968, 65ff.) that (excepting traditional wrong spellings in words with final *-m*, such as *beum, feum, leum* etc., where the earlier *béim*, etc., would be more appropriate) modern written *eu < éa < é* has diphthongized in most cases (as [iə] or [ia], thereby overlapping with written *ia < é < *ei*) in the 'central' area, which includes the Hebrides as far south as Mull and roughly west of a line

through the mainland taking in the part of Argyll north of Loch Awe, western Perthshire, Assynt and Ross (excluding the north-east corner). Outside this area the periphery has varying degrees of less breaking, the area least affected being the remainder of Argyll. The central northern mainland is the area of greatest concentration.   JWG

Gaelic: hiatus

Traditionally, a distinction is made between diphthongs (two adjacent vowels in one syllable) and hiatus, which occurs when the two vowels belong to different syllables.

In Old Irish hiatus occurred where a consonant had been lost between vowels in the period before the first manuscripts. This affected Celtic **/w/,* /j/* and **/s/*: *biid* ('of food', cf. Welsh *bywyd*), *móa* ('bigger', cf. Latin *major*) and (mo) *fiur* ('(my) sister', cf. Sanscrit *svasar*; G. *bithidh, motha* and *mo phiuthar*). Gaelic (but not Irish or Manx) inherited many of these instances.

In addition, the number of words with hiatus has been greatly increased in modern times by the loss of medial voiced fricatives /v/, /γ/ and /j/ (*domhainn, dubhachd, odhar, foghainn, slighe*). In some dialects – for example, those of Argyll – medial /h/ was also lost (/a ʔir'/*athair*, cf. Inverness/*ahir'*/).

Most dialects still distinguish between historical hiatus forms and diphthongs (or long vowels): *fitheach* (raven) *fiach* (debt), but the phonetic manifestation varies widely. In Argyll and parts of the Hebrides the syllabic break is marked with a glottal stop; in Lewis and Sutherland there is a tonal opposition (see **Gaelic: word tones and svarabhakti**); and in Wester Ross (see Ternes, 1973) we find length distinctions.   RDC

Gaelic: language organizations

Scotland has not proved, as yet, fertile ground for militant language groups. The Celtic League has flourished better in Wales than in the other Celtic countries; it plays a very minor role in Scotland, although it has an organization here. It publishes a periodical, *Carn*, with news snippets and comment (often inaccurate in various ways) about Gaelic Scotland and has published yearbooks also. The Gaelic League of Scotland had done much more effective work in its time, especially in running language classes and publishing learners' manuals. Its most productive period was during the regime of John M. Paterson, author of *Gaelic Made Easy*, with cassettes for each booklet (1952, etc.), *The Gaels Have a Word for It*

(1964), etc. Its main activities are centred in Glasgow, where classes are still run. Comunn na Cànain Albannaich, founded in 1971, was a militant language society modelled on the Welsh Language Society which mounted various campaigns designed to inform and change public opinion on matters of Gaelic usage (e.g. on the right to use Gaelic addresses on letters; on the need for more Gaelic broadcasting; on road signs). Though the Post Office has succeeded in diverting a letter addressed in Gaelic (to Peairt, i.e. Perth) to Perth, Australia, it may be that such campaigns have some effect that is not immediately apparent; it seems likely that demonstrations against the BBC in 1974, though not producing recantations from that body, helped to change its policy ultimately. But Comunn na Cànain Albannaich has not been prominent in recent years. The student Celtic Societies (Celtic Society, Aberdeen; Ossianic Society, Glasgow; Highland Society, Edinburgh) from time to time make militant declarations or take a lead in demonstrations; all three have published magazines which sometimes promote such militancy. But again there is no history of follow-up in such matters, as there is in Wales, although the Ossianic Club at Glasgow (the graduate association) was very active in the founding of a Celtic Chair at the University, and new organizations, Strì and Ceartas, hit the headlines in 1981. (See K. MacKinnon 1974.)   DST

Gaelic: morphology, verbal Even today there is a chain of dialects from northern Scotland to southern Ireland which forms a speech continuum. Southern Irish preserves the greatest complexity in verbal morphology, Scottish Gaelic the least. I exclude the extreme case of Manx, which has long been isolated but which in the seventeenth or eighteenth century was perhaps at much the same stage as Arran (W. Shaw 1972).

All the Scottish dialects distinguish future, past and conditional, though only the last has any personal endings. *Bith* alone has a present as well as a future. The copula has only the forms *is* and *bu*. Some dialects preserve a full paradigm of the imperative (Oftedal 1956, 237). Curiously, Arran lacks the first person singular in Shaw's account but has a first person singular present (= future), as does Manx; others do not even have the second person plural (usually *-ibh*). The impersonal endings may be replaced by the periphrastic *chaidh a mharbhadh*. The commonest survivors are *rugadh* and *thogadh*.

The Scottish dialects can be divided morphologi-cally into western and eastern, the latter forming a crescent from eastern Perthshire to Sutherland. Lewis in the north-west and west Perthshire can be characterized as frontier zones.

Characteristic of this crescent is the future paradigm with (*a*)*s* endings: Lewis has *bios i* (Oftedal 1956, 244), but *bios e* and *bios aid* (*aid* < the old present tense ending) are common in the Eastern dialects. Historically, the forms *bios tu/thu*, which also occur, seem to be later (O'Rahilly 1932, 132). The origin of this ending may be the identical relative ending. There is no *-s* in the responsive *bithidh* (yes), which is the form for all persons in the western dialects. Whether or not we need to evoke in the previous case *sé*, *si* and *siad*, which are assumed to be the late Common Gaelic personal pronouns, we need them to explain the conditional ending /əx/ which develops in Perthshire. The past impersonal and verbal noun ending *-adh* regularly became zero in these dialects, but the identical conditional ending was apparently devoiced in contact with pronouns beginning with *s* and was thus preserved. The same development occurs in Munster Irish and Manx (O'Rahilly 1932, 71–5). Western dialects have *-adh* except in the first person singular (*-inn*) and the first person plural (*-amaid*); the last form is not found in Lewis.

In the dialects that do have synthetic forms for the impersonal, we find *-ar* (future), *-adh* (past) and *-te* (conditional; also *-ichte* and *-iste*), with *-ar* spreading to the past (cf. Manx *ruggyr*) and even the conditional (J. MacInnes 1977, 452–4). This morphological element even occurs in structures such as *agusar* (ibid., 454) by analogy with *agus iad*. The impersonal endings are added, of course, not only to transitive verbs but also to auxiliaries (*feumar, dh'fheumte, theabadh*) and to some intransitives (*dh'fhalbhadh leis*). The *-ar* morpheme also combines in parts of Wester Ross with the *-as* found in many irregular verbs – for example, *chualas* to form *bhasar*.   RDC

Gaelic: mutations (lenition and nasalization) The Celtic languages are notorious for initial mutations, or changes at the beginning of words. These are phonetic in origin but have become grammaticalized, thus: *cù, a cù, a chù, an cù* (a dog, her dog, his dog, their dog).

The most important mutation is lenition, the weakening of articulation of certain consonants, especially between vowels. This is not confined to Celtic (cf. Martinet 1952, for Western Romance and

Hebrew parallels), but Celtic goes further: Latin *māter*, but Gaelic *màthair* and *mo mhàthair* with word initial mutation (i.e. in position – vowel + consonant + vowel).

The development of phonemic status and hence the grammatical status of mutations came about in the Dark Ages, when the Celtic languages lost most of their morphological endings (Lewis and Pedersen 1937, 64). Developments in Primitive Irish and Late British were similar but not identical.

For the modern Goidelic languages we have a series of non-lenited and lenited consonants, in pairs (see the tables in Oftedal 1956, 166–7). Over the centuries certain sound changes have taken place, some common to all dialects, others more limited (e.g. t:θ > t:h is general; the falling together of some liquid and nasal oppositions is dialectal). Rules for lenition have changed with widespread minor variation (Oftedal 1956; Borgstrøm 1940).

Lenition occurs after a number of particles (Oftedal 1956, 258–9), in the noun phrase (ibid., 208) and independently in the past tense, in the conditional (unless a nasalizing particle precedes), in masculine proper nouns in the genitive and the genitive plural without the article.

Nasalization (or eclipsis) has a parallel history in the Goedelic languages. Where vowel + nasal + consonant occurred originally in the word, certain consonants coalesced with the nasal – for example, Old Irish *cét*, Gaelic *ceud* (hundred) (cf. Latin *centum*) and similarly within the phrase – for example, after *secht* (seven) or *ar* (our).

In Scotland there was radical restructuring, all particles that ended in a consonant ceasing to nasalize. The surviving nasalizing particles are now spelled with *-n* or *-m* (eg *gun/gum*), perhaps because the nasal is pronounced in some dialects. The article *an/am* also nasalizes, apparently a relic of the defunct neuter or accusative.

The liquids and nasals are not subject to nasalization. In a dialect area that extends from Loch Fyne (Wagner and Ó Baoill 1969, 227) through Perthshire (C. M. Robertson 1897–8, 26) to Aberdeenshire, we find eclipsis of *f* and *s*; *f* is universally eclipsed in Ireland, but the eclipsis of *s* is very unusual there. Broad *s* is [z] when eclipsed; slender *s* is [dʒ] and hence the same as the lenited form after the article: *an seann* (*bhodach*) and *an t-seann* (*chailleach*) are homophonous. Outside this area *s* is untouched by nasalization, but /f/ is eclipsed to /b/ in Strathspey (MacBain 1891–2, 88) and in Ross-shire.

Nowhere is the phonetic manifestation of nasalization of stops quite like the Irish eclipsis, yet there seems to be no dialect that is completely unaffected by it. We find the following types: (a) the neutralization of the two sets of stops *p*, *b*, etc. after nasals – for example, in Sutherland (Dorian 1978, 71); (b) the voicing of both sets without merger because *p*, *t*, etc. retain their aspiration – for example, in Wester Ross (Ternes 1973, 13); (c) the Lewis type of mutation, which is also found in Assynt and in parts of Skye. This is like the nasal mutation in Welsh; /b, d/, etc. are replaced by the corresponding nasal, /m/, etc., whereas /p, t/, etc. are replaced by nasal + /h/. (See Oftedal 1956, 100–2, for details.)   RDC

Gaelic: Norse influence The Scandinavian colonization that followed in the wake of the Viking raids affected the different parts of Great Britain and Ireland in different ways. In Ireland there was no Norse settlement of an agricultural type; the Vikings founded towns and settled in them as merchants. Their language influenced Irish only to a very limited extent, and there are hardly more than a couple of dozen Scandinavian place names in Ireland. On the Isle of Man and in Scotland the Vikings and their descendants became agricultural landowners; in both areas they left a rich heritage of place-names, but Man differs from Scotland in that the former has received far fewer linguistic impulses from Norse than the latter apart from toponymy. In some parts of Scotland (Shetland, Orkney, Caithness) the Norse language prevailed completely and did not disappear until it was superseded by Anglo-Scots. In other parts (the Outer and Inner Hebrides, many parts of the mainland coast, including an area facing the North Sea) it must have lived side by side with Gaelic for several centuries and has, consequently, influenced the Gaelic dialects in various degrees, according to the relative density of the respective two populations, the social superiority of one or the other language and – presumably – the duration of Norse economical supremacy in the various districts.

Some linguistic data seem to indicate that only Norse was spoken on the Isle of Lewis during one significant period, although we do not know the dates of this period. Nor do we know when the Norse influence on Gaelic began to work and how long it lasted, but as all linguistic interference presupposes at least an incipient bilingualism, the year AD 800 is the earliest date at which it can have begun. It probably reached its peak about the twelfth century and declined after the Treaty of Perth (1266), until Norse lost the last traces of social prestige before becoming extinct, perhaps during the fifteenth century or a little earlier.

Linguistic interference can take place on three different levels of language: phonology, grammar (morphology and syntax) and lexicon (including the names of places and persons).

In phonology Scottish Gaelic differs from Irish and Manx in having been influenced considerably by the Norse sound system. There is not complete agreement between scholars on this point, but it is my opinion that the Scottish Gaelic preaspiration of the consonants *p*, *t* and *c* is a Norse feature. Preaspiration – the breath, here symbolized by a superscript *h*, which precedes these consonants after vowels, as in *lea*ʰ*pa* (of a bed), *ba*ʰ*ta* (stick), *ma*ʰ*c* (son) – is also found in Icelandic, in certain dialects of Norwegian, and to a certain extent in Faroese, although it is nowhere rendered in orthography. Among the Scottish Gaelic dialects, those of Lewis have the most 'Scandinavian-like' system, while the central Highlands and the Inner Hebrides often 'exaggerate' the preaspiration, making it a full consonant – causing *muc* (pig) to rhyme with *uchd* (breast), for instance – and some marginal dialects (the North Sea coast, the Isle of Arran) seem not to have developed preaspiration at all and, in this respect, are like Irish and Manx.

Tonality is another part of the phonological system where Norse seems to have influenced Gaelic, but only in one group of dialects, on the Isle of Lewis and on the mainland coast opposite Lewis. The general interplay between pitch and stress in this area is surprisingly similar to corresponding features in the dialects of the extreme south-west of Norway and very different accentually from all other dialects of Gaelic. Methodical investigation of these phenomena is still only at an initial stage.

Norse influence on the grammar of Gaelic has been negligible; one possible instance may be the relative particle *far*, sometimes spelt *bharr* (where), which may be Old Norse *huar*, with the same meaning.

The most tangible evidence of Norse interference is the corpus of loanwords from Norse found in Gaelic (see **loanwords: Norse; place-names: Norse**).   MO

Gaelic: orthography The historical development of Scottish Gaelic orthography has not been researched

as yet. The archive of the Historical Dictionary of Scottish Gaelic, Celtic Department, Glasgow University (see **dictionaries, Scottish Gaelic**), already provides most of the material for this research. What is offered here, however, does not claim to be more than a sketch of the topic.

There is a strong thread of continuity in the history of Gaelic orthography. It is primarily an etymologically based system, and in its essentials is the same for the old and modern stages of the language, deriving from the system most familiar in Middle and Old Irish. Our earliest Scottish sources are in the literary language we describe as Classical Common Gaelic, but at all times this language is open to modification in the direction of spoken Scottish Gaelic, just as in Ireland there is modification in the direction of spoken Irish Gaelic. This often results in 'pronunciation spellings' (K. H. Jackson 1972, 126), as the Book of Deer *ienasi* for *fiadnaise*, and can explain some of the variation in orthographical forms even within the one text (e.g. Book of Deer *tosech, taesec, o thesseach*); often, however, such variation is arbitrary (cf. Deer forms *mormaer, mormair, mormoir, mormar*), and on the Irish side there is a notorious lack of consistency in the writing of the language in medieval times. A particular area of inconsistency is in the indication of the vowels of unstressed syllables (e.g. Deer forms *dorodloeg/dorodlaig, brether/brethir, cannech/cainnich*).

There are few early Gaelic inscriptions, Latin having supplanted Gaelic as the language of inscriptions between 1200 and 1350; an Iona inscription of *c.* 1203, no longer extant, is reported to have run *Bethag niin Shorle vic Ilvrid Priorissa* (Bannerman 1977b, 90) and shows some contraction (*Shorle*) and a shorthand use of *v* for *mh* and *bh*. Personal names, of course, are often in Gaelic form, and follow standard medieval spelling, e.g. *du(n)began* for later *Dun-Bheagan* (1528), *Maelseachl(ai)nd saer* (late fifteenth century), *[M]auricius macaeda* (1500–60) with the Christian name Latinized, *margeta filia rodorici meic leoyd de leodhuis* (1503), with a more thorough mixture of Latin and Gaelic and using the Scots *y* for Gaelic *i*. Sometimes the spelling is rough and ready, as in two fifteenth-century references – *Doncani mecinnirlegin* and *Macinnirlegyn*, referring to a surname 'Mac ind fhir léginn' (Son of the scholar/teacher) (Bannerman 1977b, 124). The 1408 Charter (see *documents, Gaelic*) follows the Classical Common Gaelic standard.

Carswell (q.v.) in 1567 follows basically the Classical Common Gaelic norm, but with a good deal of alternation in forms, e.g. *b* alternating with *p*, *-bh-* with *-mh-*, *-dh-* with *-gh-* (e.g. *uibhir* as well as etymological *uimhir*, *i ndiaidh* as well as *i ndiaigh*) and *sh* alongside *sp*, *sd* with *st*, *sg* with *sc*; also *-as* with *-us*, *-aidh* with *-uidh*, *-aibh* with *-uibh*, etc. Carswell uses diacritics, the acute accent most commonly (R. L. Thomson 1970, xiff.).

Calvin's Catechism (*c.*1630) also uses Classical Common Gaelic; it has forms with *j* instead of *i* – e.g. *jondaind* (in us) and *jondas* (*ionnas*) – alternates the forms *a nois* and *anois*, writes *amach*, *arson* and *amhain* (*a-mhàin*) as one word, and uses *-ugh-* in such forms as *breathnughadh* and *dhaingniughadh*.

By contrast, the Shorter Catechism (of ?1651 and 1659) is written in the spoken form of Gaelic, 'with some rather half-hearted attempt at keeping up the fiction of a standard literary language different from the spoken one' (R. L. Thomson 1962, xxxix). This is the case also with the 1659 Psalms, and with subsequent religious literature (with the exception of the ?1690 edition of the Irish Bible). It was therefore in the second half of the seventeenth century that the traditional orthography of Classical Common Gaelic was adapted to vernacular Scottish Gaelic on a significant scale.

There had, of course, been one large-scale employment of a different system of orthography, the Dean of Lismore's use of a Scots-type orthography for his early sixteenth-century anthology of verse (see **Dean of Lismore, Book of**). This was by no means an isolated instance, for there were similarities between his system and that often used to record Gaelic names in Scots (and sometimes Latin) documents such as the Register of the Privy Council. And in the late seventeenth century Duncan Macrae in the Fernaig Manuscript (q.v.) had also turned his back on the traditional Gaelic system. Fortunately, neither of these aberrations led to a new norm. Both the Dean and Macrae, by using unorthodox systems, give some valuable insights into contemporary pronunciations, which a standard system might well have obscured, and in the 1659 Psalms we see, for example, evidence of preaspiration in the spellings *slochd* (for *sloc*) and *achd* (for *ac'*) (R. L. Thomson 1977, 130).

The Confession of Faith, translated into Gaelic by the Synod of Argyle and published in 1725, is in Scottish Gaelic laced with Classical forms, and so retains orthographical characteristics of the older system – for example, *reitigh*, *air ttus*, *edir*, *ge go*

bhfuil, *oibrighe*, *foillsiughadh*, *na dhiaigh*, *anois*, *Naomhtha*, *ni gcoir*, *achd* (pp. 1–5 of text). In the translation of Baxter's (q.v.) *Call to the Unconverted* (1750) such forms are not in evidence, although *roibh* occurs regularly; two peculiarities of this publication are its use of doubled consonants (*chreiddeimh*, *obbann*, *obbair*, *staidd*, *chuidd*) and of forms such as *ag-am* and *or-m*, and palatal *s* written *sh*. By contrast, the Revd. John Mackay's manuscript sermons (SGS, vol. 9, 176ff.) are half-illiterate in their spelling, though providing valuable evidence of Sutherland forms, e.g. *cha do chaomhin Dia na hainlu a pheacich*, *ach hilg e iad difrin* (ibid., 179).

The main stabilizing influence on Gaelic spelling in the eighteenth century was of course the 1767 Gaelic New Testament. The presence of a carefully considered system in this publication is underlined by the prefatory 'Rules for Reading the Galic Language' which are given. The remarks there on the basic Gaelic spelling rule may be quoted:

> In a word of two or more syllables, if the last ends with a broad or small vowel, the next syllable must begin with a vowel of the same kind. Accordingly it would be improper to write *canibh* (sing ye) and not *canuibh*; *sinadh* (stretching) and not *sineadh*. But, in words derived from other languages, and frequently in compounds, this rule may be properly dispensed with. (p. 3)

This and other conventions are applied with a commendable degree of consistency. Only the grave accent is used to indicate vowel length, and it is used sometimes but not regularly on *eu* (e.g. *fèuch* but *dh'fheudadh*); it is not used on *fein*. There is some fluctuation in usage (e.g. *gu bhuil*, *nach bhuil*, *am bhuil*, *ni 'm bheil*, *d'am bheil*). Expressions such as *amach*, *amuigh*, *amhàin* are usually written as one word, but *air son* as two. Unstressed vowels are often written as *u* rather than *a* (e.g. *ceaduicht'*, *gabhuidh*). There are numerous vestigia of classical Gaelic (e.g. *cuirfidh*, *nochdfuidh*, *do chuaidh*, *gu'n raibh*, *taireis*), and going with these are spellings such as *fia'nais*, *ocras*, *neimh-chiontach*, *breitheamhnus*, *àdhbhar* and *comhartha*. Despite these, it is the modernity of the spelling that seems most striking in the 1767 New Testament.

There is a strong tendency in the second half of the eighteenth century to write *amach* as one word, while *ar son* and *a(i)rson* both occur; we get *eisean*, *eisan*, *easan* and *esan* for the emphatic third person singular masculine pronoun; *fuidh* is common, rather than *fo; cha'n'eil* becomes common, though other forms occur, (e.g. *Channeil* in the first edition of Donnchadh Bàn, q.v.); *am bheil* and *a' bheil* alternate; *sa* and *san* are common. The 1767 system was broadly reinforced by the 1796 revision of the New Testament and by the publication of various parts of the Old Testament. By the end of the century, in most essential respects, the modern orthographical system of Gaelic was settled (not to say fixed by divine example).

Most of the exemplars referred to have been works of religious translation. There were a few secular exemplars also e.g. Robert Kirk's *Vocabulary* (published 1702); Kirk's spelling was fairly regular though there were aberrations – *bóo, groshaid, ness* (i.e. *neas*), *sbor, sec* (i.e. *seic(e)*). His use of diacritics is minimal and not very logical (J. L. Campbell 1938a). Alasdair Mac Mhaighstir Alasdair's (q.v.) *Vocabulary* (1741) was more erratically spelled – *rinnag, amhainn* (river), *ault, sceir, aisag, lenabh, caillach, banis* – somewhat in contrast to his *Ais-eiridh* (1751), which has less extreme aberrations. The eighteenth century manuscript anthologies of Gaelic verse vary widely in the orthodoxy of their spelling systems.

The present century has seen a gradual tidying up of minor features of the spelling system, the restoration of some historical forms (*adhbhar, dachaigh,* etc.), the standardizing of *a* and *ea* rather than *u* and *io* to represent the obscure vowel (*cionnas, doras, boireann, timcheall,* etc.) the decimation of apostrophes (*chan eil, san, gad, don, den* etc.), the joining of bound forms by a hyphen when stress is on the second element (*a-mach, an-dè, a-null, a-measg,* etc.), the more universal indication of consonant quality by use of the appropriate type of vowel (*seo, siud, taigh, dèante,* etc.), the prescription of forms for borrowed words (*làraidh, naidhlean, sutha, deàs* (jazz), etc.), and the use of only the grave accent to indicate vowel length. Some of these reforms had been introduced, or reintroduced into Gaelic writing, especially by the periodical *Gairm* over the period from 1952 onwards, and those listed above were formally adopted as a package by a special Committee on Gaelic Orthography set up by the Scottish Certificate of Education Examination Board (1978; with minor modifications 1980). DST

Gaelic: palatalization The palatal/palatalized series of consonants contrast with a non-palatalized series denoting minimal distinctions between words – e.g.

/g'aul/ (bet) and /gaul/ (foreigner); serving to distinguish morphologically between the nominative and genitive cases of certain noun declensions (e.g. /baLəx/ and /baLəx'/) and typically marking the future endings of verbs.

It has been suggested that the phonological palatal/non-palatal distinction does not operate in the case of labials b, p, m, f, v. Phonetically the facts appear to be that labials are palatalized when in contact with front vowels: there are also palatalized labials in contact with back vowels – e.g. [b'irəɣ], [b'ʲaRəɣ], [baRəɣ] (pricking, shearing and riveting respectively). Part of the problem would appear to arise from the fact that labials cannot by definition be palatal and that we do not get neutral or velarized labials before front vowels. This combination makes the labials different from the other consonant classes in their realization, but despite contrary suggestions (Oftedal 1956, 1963; see K. H. Jackson 1967, for comparative study) there seems to be a good case for regarding the same *phonological* distinctions to hold for them as for the other consonants. This case rests on intrinsic evidence and on the extrinsic demands for elegance in the phonological system.

In the first place, as we have seen, we do find palatalization before front vowels. Second, in the case of *f*-initial words when lenited after the article, for example, we get the reduction of the *f* to *ø* and the assumption by the -*n* of the article of the quality of the originally following segment. For example, the two verbal nouns *feannadh* (skinning) and *fannadh* (moving slowly), in their oblique cases after the preposition *le* with the article, give us [les'ən'anəɣ] and [les'ənanəɣ] respectively, in exactly the same way as we find with *n*-initial nouns. It is clear, therefore, that if we wish to be able to retrieve the derivational connection between the oblique [ən'anəɣ] and the nominative [əf'anəɣ], we must regard the palatal quality as distinctive. If this case holds for *f*, then it would be most inelegant (as well as unnecessary) to treat the other labials differently. (See D. MacAulay 1966b; Ternes 1973). DMCA

Gaelic: phonemic structure The number of descriptions of Scottish Gaelic dialects comprising a comprehensive phonemic analysis is rather limited: Oftedal (1956), Ternes (1973) and Dorian (1978). The approach of other descriptions is not strictly phonemic, but phonetic. Some of the latter, however, thanks to the clear arrangement of their phonetic data, may consistently be reinterpreted in phonemic terms. Among these are Dieckhoff (1932), Borgstrøm (1937, 1940, 1941) and Mac Gill-Fhinnein (1966).

In the absence of a standard pronunciation, no standard phonemic system can be established for Scottish Gaelic. Any choice for a specific dialect would be more or less arbitrary. The phoneme system presented below may be regarded as 'typical' and may, without taking into account the specific features of a particular locality, roughly be localized on the Outer Hebrides. For every subsection of the system thus defined the most important dialectal variations of the Scottish Gaelic speaking area as a whole will be indicated.

VOWELS

The Scottish Gaelic vowel phonemes represent a tri-angular system with three classes (front-unrounded, back-rounded, back-unrounded) and four degrees of opening. Length is distinctive for all vowel qualities:

$$
\left.
\begin{array}{ccccc}
\text{i} & & & \text{ɯ} & \text{u} \\
& \text{e} & & \text{ɤ} & \text{o} \\
& & \text{ɛ} & & \text{ɔ} \\
& & \text{a} & &
\end{array}
\right\} \pm /\!:\!/
$$

The precise phonetic values of the front-unrounded and back-rounded vowels are near to cardinal vowels nos. 1–4 [i, e, ɛ, a] and 6–8 [ɔ, o, u]. The back-unrounded vowels correspond to secondary cardinal vowels [ɯ, ɤ] or may have a slightly advanced tongue position. /ɤ/ in unstressed position approaches central [ə]. For the back-unrounded vowels, the symbols /ɯ, ɤ/ or /ɨ, ə/ may be used. The former set has the advantage of being closer to their actual phonetic values, the latter of using more familiar symbols.

The allophonic variation of Scottish Gaelic vowels is rather slight as compared with Irish, although front vowels are somewhat retracted when adjacent to the velarized consonants /N, L, R/ and back vowels somewhat advanced when adjacent to palatalized consonants. For /a/, the retracted variety is cardinal vowel no. 5 [ɑ].

The system of oral vowels as described above is quite stable throughout the entire Scottish Gaelic-speaking area. The only deviation is the reduction of the two back-unrounded vowels to one phoneme /ɤ/ or /ə/ in some progressive dialects, as described in Dorian (1978).

Unlike Irish, in which nasalization of vowels is gradually disappearing, nasalization is one of the most prominent features of Scottish Gaelic phonetics.

Nasalization is phonemically distinctive in all Scottish Gaelic dialects. The number of vowels affected varies from one dialect to another. In some dialects (e.g. Oftedal 1956; Dorian 1978), each oral vowel has a nasalized counterpart (i.e. /ĩ, ẽ, ɛ̃, ã, ɔ̃, õ, ũ, ũ, ɤ̃/), both long and short. In most dialects, however, the set of nasalized vowels is somewhat reduced. The most common pattern shows exemption from nasalization for all half-close vowels (e.g. Borgstrøm 1940, 1941; Ternes 1973); thus one finds /ĩ, ɛ̃, ã, ɔ̃, ũ, ũ/ both long and short, but long and short /e, o, ɤ/ are without nasalized counterparts. Nasalization is distinctive both adjacent and non-adjacent to nasal consonants. The phonetic quality of nasalized vowels, including allophonic variation, is the same as for oral vowels.

This description of nasalization conforms with traditional analyses of languages with phonemically nasalized vowels such as French. The true nature of nasalization in Scottish Gaelic is more complex, however. The vowels enumerated above function as the *centres of nasalization*. Every word with distinctive nasalization contains one such centre, always located in the stressed syllable. From this centre nasalization usually spreads over several segments to the left and right, but not beyond word boundaries. The precise extension of these nasalized stretches is strictly rule-governed. The only description so far of these rules for a specific dialect is in Ternes (1973, 134–6). Examples from that source are:

màthair	/maː·har/	['maː·h̃ãr]	(mother)
soitheamh	/sɔ̃hi/	['sɔ̃h̃ĩ]	(tame)
dèanamh	/tʲianu/	['tʲĩãnũ]	(to do)
samhradh	/sãurɤk/	['sãũr̃ãk]	(summer)
connspeach	/kʰɔ̃ispaxk/	['kʰɔ̃ĩspaxk]	(wasp)

Thus nasalization is not simply an inherent feature of the vowel segment; rather, the word as a whole is either nasalized or non-nasalized. This is most economically shown in phonemic transcription by placing the mark for nasalization on the centre of nasalization (i.e. the vowel nucleus of the stressed syllable). A phenomenon of this kind is called a *long nasal component*. A detailed analysis of nasalization in Scottish Gaelic is to be found in Ternes (1973, 123–42).

CONSONANTS

The typical Scottish Gaelic consonant system is shown in the table below.

	1	2	3	4	5	6
voiceless stops	p	t	t′	k′	k	
voiceless aspirated stops	pʰ	tʰ	t′ʰ	k′ʰ	kʰ	
nasals		m	n	n′		N
laterals			l	l′		L
vibrants			r	r′		R
voiceless fricatives	f	s	ʃ	ç	x	h
voiced fricatives	v			j	ɣ	

(1 = labial, 2 = dental, 3 = dental palatalized, 4 = velar palatalized, 5 = velar, 6 = glottal.)

In addition, in many dialects (e.g. Oftedal 1956; Ternes 1973) the voiced fricative /j/ is to be distinguished from the voiced approximant /i̯/.

/N, L, R/ are a velarized dental nasal, lateral and vibrant respectively. Thus nasals, laterals and vibrants form three-way contrasts: plain – palatalized – velarized. The phonetic realization of all other symbols corresponds to their respective IPA values.

Allophonic variation is negligible except for the voiceless aspirated stops. These are postaspirated [pʰ, tʰ . . .] in word initial position, and preaspirated [ʰp, ʰt . . .] in medial and final position. Examples are:

| *cat* | /kʰatʰ/ | [kʰaht̩] | (cat) |
| *peacadh* | /pʰɛkʰɤɣ/ | [ˈpʰɛʰkəɣ] | (sin) |

In addition to the typical two-way contrast aspirated v. non-aspirated for stops, some progressive dialects (e.g. Dorian, 1978; Ternes, 1973) have developed a third series of voiced stops, /b, d, d′, g′, g/. A few dialects have a fourth series of voiced aspirated stops, /bʰ, dʰ, d′ʰ, g′ʰ, gʰ/ (Ternes, 1973). The latter appears to be a transitory stage, whereas the two-way and three-way contrasts are more stable. The historical development is from /p – pʰ/ over /p – pʰ – b – bʰ/ to /p – pʰ – b/. (For details, see Ternes 1973, 10–22.)

In some dialects, especially in the east, the three-way contrast of nasals, laterals and vibrants /n – n′ – N/ etc. is reduced to a two-way contrast /n – n′/, etc., but rarely to one single phoneme. In this process vibrants seem to be affected first, nasals second and laterals last (cf. Dorian 1978, 40).

On the other hand, some isolated dialects, usually in the west, have four or even more lateral phonemes.

A description of four *l* phonemes is given by Oftedal (1975, 138–40). Hamp (1970) reports five laterals and five nasals (not counting /m/) for Islay (Inner Hebrides).

Some very progressive dialects, especially in the east, may merge the palatalized dental and the palatalized velar series into one, as in Dorian (1978).

In various dialects there seems to be a tendency for a series of voiceless aspirated sonorants [m̥ʰ, n̥ʰ, l̥ʰ, r̥ʰ . . .] to develop, the precise phonemic status of which is open to discussion. Although I favour (Ternes 1973, 66–79) a biphonemic solution /hn, hl . . ./ for Applecross (Ross-shire), I would at the same time support the monophonemic solution /m̥, n̥ . . ./ advocated by MacAulay (1962) for Bernera (Lewis). The two series of voiceless sonorants have a different morphophonemic status in their respective dialect and are of a different historical origin. Borgstrøm (1940, 73f.; 1941, 100) also reports voiceless aspirated sonorants, some of them different again in nature from the ones described in MacAulay (1962) and Ternes (1973).

SUPRASEGMENTALS

Except for a small number of English loans, stress is always on the first syllable of the word stem and is thus not phonemically distinctive.

Quantity (short v. long) is phonemically distinctive for all vowel qualities, oral and nasalized (see above). Consonant quantity, on the other hand, is typically non-distinctive, although it may play a marginal role in some dialects, as in Dorian (1978, 54).

A special problem of Scottish Gaelic phonemics lies in the interpretation of diphthongs, hiatus and svarabhakti groups.

The number of diphthongs in descriptions of Scottish Gaelic dialects is usually very high. Numbers range from about twenty to eighty diphthongs. Long and short, oral and nasalized diphthongs occur.

Scottish Gaelic distinguishes historically between short vowels, long vowels, and dissyllabic sequences of two identical vowels (e.g. /a/ v. /a:/ v. /a-a/). Similarly, there is phonemic contrast between two vowels forming a diphthong and the same sequence forming a dissyllabic cluster (e.g. /i̯a/ v. /i-a/). Of these, /a-a/ and /i-a/ are instances of hiatus. These distinctions are preserved in most dialects.

Scottish Gaelic distinguishes historically between original consonant + vowel + consonant sequences and similar sequences in which the vowel originates from an epenthetic vowel inserted into certain consonant clusters. The latter sequences are traditionally called svarabhakti groups. The distinction is preserved in most dialects.

These three phenomena are closely interrelated. For a discussion of the whole complex, see Ternes (1973, 96–123). All of the distinctions listed above may be reduced to one fundamental phonemic distinction, which on the synchronic level has to be described in terms of suprasegmental features. The precise phonetic expression varies from one dialect to another. Three different manifestations, corresponding to three distinct dialect areas, have been observed so far: in the northern Hebrides Oftedal (1956, 1978) describes the distinction as one of phonetic pitch comparable with the accent 1–accent 2 distinction in Swedish and Norwegian; in the southern Hebrides and Argyll Borgstrøm (1937, 1940) and Holmer (1938) describe the distinction as one of plain *v.* glottalized syllables; in Ross-shire Ternes (1973) describes the distinction as one of three vowel quantities – short *v.* half-long *v.* long (or short *v.* long *v.* overlong). A synopsis of these three suprasegmental features is given in Ternes 1980.   ET

Gaelic: phonetics, experimental and instrumental Compared with the relatively large number of accounts of Gaelic dialects based on articulatory and auditory analyses from MacFarlane (1889) to Dorian (1978) – and further studies on Islay and Skye are in progress – instrumental and experimental phonetics is a much neglected branch of Gaelic linguistics. At the time of writing only Cynthia Shuken (1977, 1979) has published anything on the subject.

Apart from Shuken's thesis (1980), there is virtually nothing in manuscript either. Macaulay (1953) and Ó Dochartaigh (Doherty 1966) wrote class essays for the Phonetics Department of the University of Edinburgh. They used kymography to study preaspiration in a North Uist and a Lewis speaker respectively.

Shuken's thesis deals with the stops and sonorants of two Lewis and two Harris speakers. Palatography was used to investigate articulation; kymography for airflow, duration and larynx vibration; and spectography to investigate acoustic output. Some topics covered in detail are preaspiration, eclipsis, secondary articulation and sonority. (See also Doherty 1966; Dorian 1978; F. E. G. Macaulay 1953; MacFarlane 1889; Shuken 1977, 1979, 1980, forthcoming.)   RDC

Gaelic: preaspiration Aspiration in phonetic terms is an h-like sequence preceding or following the production of a consonant (For aspiration, as in the older Gaelic grammars, see lenition, *sub* **mutations.**) Occurring *after* certain consonants (postaspiration), it is a feature of most Germanic languages (including English) and of Gaelic. Occurrences *before* consonant (preaspiration) are limited to some Scandinavian languages and to Scottish (but not Irish or Manx) Gaelic.

As in Norse, Gaelic preaspiration originated in the voiceless geminates (/tt/, /kk/, etc.) and is used today to describe a variety of realizations. Before non-palatals we find: (a) true preaspiration (a period of voicelessness or breathy voice between vowel and consonant: /^{h}p/, /^{h}t/; (b) an /h/ between vowel and consonant – see Ternes 1973, 53–66 for discussion of the difference between types (a) and (b); (c) /x/ before /k/, but /h/ before /p/ and /t/; (d) /x/ before all stops; (e) /x/ before /k/, otherwise no preaspiration.

The distribution after short vowels is most significant, as it was here that the merger took place between /xk/ from Common Gaelic /xt/ as in *bocht* (poor) and /xk/ in types (c), (d) and (e), before which preaspiration is not shown in the spelling. It is significant that there was no merger with /xt/ of type (d), which shows that (d) is a development of (b) or (c).

Some peripheral dialects have no preaspiration: Caithness, Sutherland, south Kintyre (Holmer 1962), Arran (Holmer 1975) and east Perthshire (C. M. Robertson 1897–8). Most of south Argyll has it only before *c* (type (e)): *mac* and *mic*) but not in *cat* or *tapaidh.*

The dialect distribution of the other types can be roughly summarized as follows: (a) only Lewis; (b) parts of Ross-shire; (c) western Inverness and all Inner and Outer Hebrides except Lewis; (d) Argyll north of Loch Etive, Lorne, western Perth and eastern Highlands.

The position before palatal consonants is similar, but after long vowels preaspiration is much less widespread.

Preaspiration is not shown in Standard Gaelic spelling, except in error in case of /xk/ ambiguity: *slochd/sloc.* It first occurs sporadically in the Book of the Dean of Lismore (q.v.), (early sixteenth century) *socht* written for *sok(ke)* as a spelling of *soc* (snout). Until the merger, preaspiration may have existed for several centuries unrecorded. It probably developed under Norse influence (Borgstrøm 1974; Clement, forthcoming; for opposing views, see K. H. Jackson 1962, 9–10; D. P. Ó Baoill 1980.) RDC

Gaelic: switching Switching from Gaelic to English (and back) happens so regularly that its absence marks the discourse as being quite unusually formal. Switching may indicate areas in which the speaker (for socio-cultural reasons) feels that a Gaelic expression would be inadequate (for example, *Tha e as well as can be expected*, of a hospital patient, or *Tha gale force ten aca*, referring to the weather forecast). It often has affective force, as when an item is recast in English translation: *Cha chreid mi facal dheth – not a word*. It may serve a useful function in conversation by marking a change of topic. For example, in buying and selling transactions it indicates the move from phatic preambles to the transaction proper, with phrases such as *What can I do for you today, ma-thà?*, or the end of the transaction: *That's all, an diugh*. (See D. MacAulay 1982a, b.) A good if rather extreme text for studying the phenomenon is J. L. Campbell (1972). DMCA

Gaelic: syncope Syncope, the loss of medial vowels, is a relatively common phenomenon in language. In Gaelic it usually refers to the development (Thurneysen 1946, 27, 67), dated to the sixth century AD (K. H. Jackson 1953, 141–3) that took place after the loss of final syllables (the Ogam inscriptions show both; *see* **Ogam stones**). Except for a few Irish dialects, Gaelic has always had a strong stress on the first syllable of the word. In words of more than two syllables the vowel of the second (and fourth) was liable to disappear, the resulting cluster, if incompatible, being subject to modification. The effects of syncope are clear in the second word of each of the following pairs: *caraid/càirdean; abhainn/aibhnichean; bràthair/bràithrean; leabhar/leabhraichean; samhail/cosmhail; fosgail/fosgladh*. JWG

Gaelic: syntax The primary elements of basic Gaelic sentence structure we may take as verb, subject, complement and adjunct. Imperative sentences may consist only of a verb, as (1) *Seas!* (Stand up!) or (2) *Seasamaid* (Let us stand up); particularizing imperatives contain the pronoun, as (3) *Seas thusa!* (You stand up!) and third person imperatives must contain the subject, as (4) *Seasadh Iain* (Let Iain stand up). Intransitive sentences consist of verb and subject, as (5) *Sheas Iain* (Iain stood up).

Transitive sentences have complements, (6) *Cheannaich Iain leabhar* (Iain bought a book). 'Transactional' sentences, (7) *Thug Iain leabhar do Anna* (Iain gave Anna a book) and (8) *Fhuair Iain leabhar bho Anna* (Iain got a book from Anna), have an additional complement (an indirect as well as a direct object) expressing the 'source' or 'goal' of the transaction. There are other types of complement: adjectival, (9) *Tha Iain òg* (Iain is young); locative, (10) *Tha Iain aig an taigh* (Iain is at the house); sentential, e.g. noun clauses in reporting sentences, (11) *Thubhairt Iain gun cheannaich e leabhar* (Iain said that he had bought a book), or in causative sentences, (12) *Thug Iain air Anna leabhar a cheannach* (Iain made Anna buy a book).

Complements are obligatory (transitive) elements; adjuncts are optional. They may be adverbs, (13) *Sheas Iain gu h-aithghearr* (Iain stood up quickly); locative or temporal phrases, (14) *Sheas Iain aig an taigh* (Iain stood up at the house), (15) *Sheas Iain aig sia uairean* (Iain stood up at six o'clock), or adverbial clauses, e.g. of time, (16) *Sheas Iain nuair a cheannaich Anna leabhar* (Iain stood up when Anna bought a book).

The above statements apply to 'complete' sentences. Elliptical sentences are those from which elements that must be retrievable from context if communication is to be viable have been omitted. They occur as responses, often (not always) in question-and-answer sequences. The following responses could all 'stand for' *Thug Iain leabhar do Anna*, as replies to their related questions: (17) *An tug Iain leabhar do Anna?* (Did Iain give Anna a book?) – (18 '*Thug*' (lit. Gave = Yes); (19) *Có thug leabhar do Anna?* (Who gave Anna a book?) – (20) *(Thug) Iain* (Iain [did]); (21) *Dé thug Iain do Anna?* (What did Iain give Anna?) – (22) *(Thug) leabhar* ([Gave] a book); (23) *Có dha thug Iain leabhar?* (To whom did Iain give a book?) – (24) *Do Anna* (To Anna).

Sentences (except imperatives) are either affirmative or interrogative and positive or negative. Negative sentences are marked by the negative element *cha*, e.g. (25) *Cha tug Iain leabhar do Anna* (Iain did not give a book to Anna) (cf.(7)). In subordinate finite clauses the element is *nach*, (26) *Thubhairt Iain nach do cheannaich e leabhar* (Iain said he did not buy a book) (cf.(11)); in non-finite clauses it is *gun*, (27) *Thug Iain air Anna gun leabhar a cheannach* (Iain made Anna not buy a book). When the sentence proposition is questioned the interrogative element is *an*, and there are pronominal and pro-adverbial forms for questioning subjects and direct objects and indirect objects, adjuncts, etc.; see (17), (19), (21) and (23). Positive affirmative sentences are not overtly marked (cf.(7)), except when subordinate, when *gun* has this function (cf.(11)). Negative interrogative sentences are marked by *nach*, (28) *Nach do cheannaich Iain leabhar?* (Did Iain not buy a book? (cf.(26)). These elements come in initial position. Topicalized elements are questioned by prefixing *An e* and *An ann* and negated by prefixing *Chan e/Nach e* and *Chan ann/Nach ann* instead of *'S e* and *'S ann*.

Basic element order is verb + subject + object. As we have just seen, elements defining sentence function (question denial, etc.) come even before the verb. Also the *lexical* verb does not always precede the subject in periphrastic structures – for example (29) *Tha Iain a' ceannach leabhar* (Iain is buying a book). The same holds in the stylistically marked (30) *Rinn Iain seasamh* (lit. Iain made a standing = Iain stood up), generally equivalent to (5). It would be more accurate to say that the predicator (or sentence classifier – as between 'stative' and 'processive', for example) always precedes the subject and that the lexical verb precedes when it is combined with the predicator, as is normally the case in simple sentences.

The noun phrase is basically a structure with a nominal 'head' to which modifying elements are added, both before and after, in class sequence. Before the head come the definite article (there is no indefinite), and the set of pre-possessives (mutually exclusive with it); enumerators, both ordinal and cardinal, and 'each' 'all' 'same'; a restricted set of adjectives, 'good' 'bad' 'real'/'true', etc. – for example, *a'/mo cheud dà dhroch latha* (the/my first two bad days) *gach aon fhìor Ghaidheal* (every single real Gael).

After the head come adjectives, normally size, then quality, then colour, e.g. *cù mór briagha dubh* (a fine big black dog); genitive-case nouns denoting 'function' and/or 'substance'; prepositional phrases with *le* (with) or *gun* (without); demonstratives/referentials; post-possessives; qualifying clauses – for example, *a' chiste aodaich fhiodha gun cheann ud le Iain a thog sinn a steach* (that wooden clothes chest without a lid belonging to Iain that we carried in).

Combined with this fixed order there is a set of devices for highlighting or topicalizing sentence elements. This entails the prefixing of *'S e* or *'S ann* (see below) to the element, placing it in clause initial position and relativizing the verb. Taking (7) *Thug*

Iain leabhar do Anna as an example, subject topicalization gives (31) *'S e Iain a thug leabhar do Anna* (It is Iain who gave Anna a book); direct object topicalization gives (32) *'S e leabhar a thug Iain do Anna* (It is a book that Iain gave to Anna); indirect object topicalization gives (33) *'S ann do Anna a thug Iain leabhar* (It is to Anna that Iain gave a book). *'S e* topicalizes subjects, direct objects and 'noun clauses' and *'S ann* topicalizes indirect objects, adverbial and adjectival complements and all adjuncts. The verb and its objects may be topicalized as a unit, e.g. (34) *'S e leabhar a thoirt do Anna a rinn Iain* (lit. It is give a book to Anna that Iain did = What Iain did was give a book to Anna). Here the 'process' predicator *rinn* (which takes a direct object) is used (cf. (30)).

There are two verbs 'to be' in Gaelic, *is* and *tha* (traditionally copula and substantive verbs respectively, terms no longer very helpful). Generally *tha* functions as the stative verb. It denotes a state, (35) *Tha an oidhche ann* (It is night), or a condition (non-inherent), (9) *Tha Iain òg* (Iain is young), or class membership, (36) *Tha Iain 'na oileanach* (lit. Iain is in his student = Iain is a student). When combined with *ann* (in it) it is the existential verb, (37) *Tha Dia ann* (God exists) (cf.(35)). It is the stative periphrastic auxiliary (cf.(44) and (45)).

The main function of *is* is in topicalization, combined with the third person singular masculine (and unmarked) pronoun *e*, and *ann* (this pronoun in combination with the preposition 'in') (cf. (31)–(35) above). It operates unsupported to topicalize adjectives, especially in sentences with noun-clause subjects, (38) *Is math gun cheannaich Iain leabhar* (It is good that Iain bought a book); and adverbs, (39) *Is tric a cheannaich Iain leabhar* (Often has Iain bought a book). It does not topicalize phrases when unsupported. It functions in equative sentences when the subject is a pronoun, (40) *Is mise Iain* (I am Iain). When the subject is a noun *'S e* is used, (41) *'S e Iain a t-oileanach* (Iain is the student). It appears in classificatory sentences (where class membership is permanent), (42) *Is duine Iain* (Iain is a man). The structure of these is verb + complement + subject (cf. also (38)).

Having no verb 'to have', Gaelic denotes possession by means of a locative structure with the 'possessed' noun in the subject phrase and the 'possessor' noun in the locative phrase: (43) *Tha an càr aig Iain* (lit. The car is at Iain = Iain has the car), cf. (44) *Tha Iain aig a' chàr* (Iain is at the car). *Aig* (at) denotes 'in the possession/control of'. 'Belonging to' is denoted by *le*: (45) *Tha an càr le Iain* (The car belongs to Iain).

Aspect, progressive, perfective and prospective, is expressed in periphrastic sentences with auxiliary *tha* having as complement a prepositional phrase in which the preposition governs a verbal noun (i.e. a non-finite verbal lexeme), together with complements, if any. With progressive aspect we get (46) *Tha Iain a' seasamh* (Iain is standing up), and when there is a direct object it is in genitive relation with the verb (marked when the object is definite), (47) *Tha Iain a' ceannach an leabhair* (lit. Iain is at buying of the book = Iain is buying the book). In perfective and prospective aspect the structure governed by the preposition is not a clustering one (as in (48) and in noun phrases) but is structurally identical with a non-finite noun clause (as in (12)): (49) *Tha Iain air leabhar a cheannach* (lit. Iain is after a book to buy = Iain has bought a book). Pronominal direct objects in both types are realized as 'possessive' pronouns coming before the verb: (50) *Tha Iain ga cheannach* (lit. Iain is at its buying = Iain is buying it); (51) *Tha Iain air a cheannach* (Iain has bought it). Many modals operate on similar principles also, (52) *Feumaidh/Faodaidh Iain leabhar a cheannach* (Iain must/-may buy a book), as do requests and commands.

DMCA

Gaelic: syntax, similarities with British syntax

The Old Irish verb normally shows five inflected tenses in the indicative: present, imperfect (or past habitual), preterite, future and secondary future (or conditional). The substantive verb *a-tá* and the copula *is* have a sixth tense, the present habituals *biid* and *bid* respectively. Most verbs form a perfect from the preterite by means of the prefix *ro*; a few have a suppletive perfect. Leaving aside the pluperfect, which is clearly calqued on that of Latin, the original British verbal system shows only three tenses in the indicative: present/future, imperfect/past habitual/conditional and preterite, formally corresponding to the Irish present, imperfect and preterite respectively. The verb 'to be', however, has both a present and a present habitual/future, corresponding to the Irish present and habitual present respectively. A particle identical with Irish *ro* is used to mark perfectivity.

Both Irish and British lost their distinction between preterite and perfect. Apart from this, modern Irish shows precisely the same indicative verbal system as that of Old Irish. With the same

reservation, modern spoken Welsh shows precisely the indicative verbal system postulated for common British, while Breton and Cornish show a great deal of innovation. Scottish Gaelic and Manx also show massive innovation, since they have brought the verbal system inherited from Old Irish into complete conformity with that of modern spoken Welsh, including an identity of function between Sc.G. *bithidh* and W. *bydd* in the category of future/present habitual. Since we know that Scottish Gaelic displaced British, and since it is probable that Manx Gaelic also did so, the argument for the influence of the substratum seems very stong. Fraser's (1912) view that the revision of the system can be explained by the loss of contrast between present and future as the result of phonetic developments is too mechanical to be convincing and ignores the fact that similar phonetic developments in Irish evoked morphological innovations designed to preserve the contrast.

In the Scottish Gaelic and Welsh verbal systems the only unambiguous present tense is the periphrastic formation of the substantive verb + particle + verbal noun seen in Sc.G. *tha mi a' dol*, W. *ydw i'n mynd* (I go, I am going), contrasted with *théid mi, mi â i* (I will go). This periphrastic formation is found in all the Insular Celtic languages and had originally the function of a present continuous similar to that of English, which is still preserved in Irish, where *tá mé ag dul* (I am going) contrasts with *téann mé* (I go). Welsh, alone of the neo-British languages, shows another periphrastic tense, attested since the thirteenth century, where the particle is *wedi* (after), and the function is that of a perfect: *ydw i wedi mynd* (I have gone), *ydw i wedi torri'r ffenest* (I have broken the window). It can also be used to form a passive: *mae'r ffenest wedi (i) thorri* (the window has been broken). These constructions took a long time to penetrate into the literary language, but in modern spoken Welsh they have almost complete correspondence with English perfects; thus the equivalent of the AV *No man hath seen God at any time* (John 1:18) is *Ni welodd neb Dduw erioed* in the sixteenth century Welsh Bible but *Nid oes neb wedi gweld Duw erioed* in *Y Beibl Cymraeg Newydd* of 1975.

Scottish Gaelic shows similar constructions with the particle *air*, ultimately deriving from Old Irish *iar N* (after) and the prepositional phrase *an déidh* (after) *tha mi air dol* (I have gone), *tha mi an déidh an uinneag a bhristeadh* (I have broken the window), *tha an uinneag air a bristeadh* (the window is broken). In Scottish Gaelic their yield is notably less than that of the parallel constructions in Welsh, while Manx is very like Welsh; thus the Manx Bible of 1819 has *Cha vel unnane ar vakin Jee ec traa erbee* at John 1 : 18, while the equivalent construction **Chan eil neach air faicinn Dé uair air bith* would not be acceptable in Scottish Gaelic, which uses the simple past here. What we seem to have here is a common development in Scottish Gaelic, Manx and Welsh, which has proceeded at a faster rate in the latter two than in the first. There are traces of similar constructions in Early Modern Irish, but they have not been continued into the modern language and are probably to be interpreted as penetrations of Scottish usage into the Irish literary norm. Recent modern Irish has a construction which is identical in surface form but has a highly restricted semantic range, and therefore a very low yield. This is the 'I'm after breaking the window' pattern (so much exploited in comic representations of the English of Ireland), which derives from *tá mé tar éis/i ndéidh an fhuinneog a bhriseadh*. Its function is that of a recent perfect, and the English equivalent is 'I have just broken the window', while that of Welsh is *ydw i newydd dorri'r ffenest*. The Irish construction is entirely unattested in the earlier literature and must be seen as a development completely independent from those which took place in Eastern Gaelic and in Welsh. (See J. Fraser 1912; D. Greene 1966, and forthcoming; H. Wagner 1959.) DG

Gaelic: word tones and svarabhakti As a linguistic device for distinguishing otherwise identical-sounding words, tone is not uncommon in the world's languages. Apart from the well-known cases of Chinese and Vietnamese, many languages of south Asia, Africa and the Americas have word tones. In Europe it has limited distribution, being confined (with the exception of Slovenian and Serbo-Croat) to northern Europe. Of all the Celtic languages, only the dialects of Lewis (Ternes 1980) and Sutherland (Dorian 1978, 60–1) in the extreme north of the Gaelic-speaking area have tones. Phonetically and historically, these resemble the tones of Norway, Sweden and western Denmark. In view of the documented connections between Norway and northern Scotland during the Viking colonization, we may assume influence. (Sentence intonation, type of pre-aspiration and centralization of /u/ all link Lewis phonetically to western Norway.)

There are also notable differences; several hundred pairs can be found in the Scandinavian languages differentiated by having Tone 1 or Tone 2, while in Lewis Gaelic it is difficult to find minimal pairs at all: *bodha* (underwater rock) *bó* (cow) or *fitheach* (raven) *fiach* (debt) work for most Lewis speakers. But this is a typological feature of Gaelic; for some segmental phonemes also minimal pairs hardly exist. On the other hand, in both Scandinavia and Scotland, pitch differences became phonologically distinctive through a re-evaluation of syllabic signals: original monosyllables became disyllabic and vice versa.

If we look at svarabhakti, where an epenthetic vowel develops between certain consonant combinations, we have *ainm* (name) with Tone 2 (because once monosyllabic) and *anam* (soul) which has the tonal contour appropriate to a disyllable. In Ireland, Sutherland (Dorian 1978, 57) and the southern dialects (Arran and parts of Argyll) this vowel is treated no differently from other unstressed vowels. In the other northern dialects a new distinction arises. In Lewis this is based on tone, elsewhere on factors such as stress or overlength. (See Ternes 1973, 1980.) RDC

Gaelic Books Council (An Comann Leabhraichean) Set up in 1968 in the Celtic Department of the University of Glasgow to administer the Gaelic Books Grant (initially £5,000 a year; £22,000 a year for 1980–3), which was awarded by the Scottish Education Department to the University to subsidize the publication of new and original works in Gaelic. The University provides accommodation and services, and it receives an additional yearly grant (£16,500 in 1982–3) from the Scottish Arts Council.

The twelve members of the Books Council, which meets four times a year, include representatives of the two funding bodies, of An Comunn Gaidhealach (q.v.) and of the Universities of Aberdeen and Edinburgh. The full-time staff are an editorial officer, a field officer and a secretary.

Gaelic publishing still labours under a handicap that is the product of the language's history, and this is compounded by the small size of the potential readership. In the face of this, the Council's role is to support and stimulate, and its most important financial contribution is the payment of direct grants, particularly publication grants. A book is submitted in typescript before publication, with details of printing costs, and if it is approved, a grant is allocated; the grant is paid out immediately after publication. The total allocation since 1968 stands at £100,000 for 220 books; of these, 200 have been published, and publishers have been paid £90,000.

Some categories of book are needed particularly acutely, and since the beginning the Council has been offering cash prizes in literary competitions in order to encourage the writing of them. In 1975 it began to supplement this incentive with commission grants for writers who would produce books on agreed subjects. Like books resulting from competitions, these have then been placed with publishers, and they have attracted publication grants in the normal way.

In 1976, after a series of tours by temporary staff in the summer months, the Council began to provide a full-time mobile bookselling service, employing a field officer to drive a van capable of carrying all Gaelic books in print; since then most of the Gaelic-speaking areas have been visited at least once. Occasional literary events and book exhibitions have also been organized in the Highlands and Lowlands.

A catalogue of Gaelic books in print was published by the Council in 1975, and a revised third edition appeared in 1983. IMCD

Gaelic Society of London (Comunn na Gàidhlig an Lunnainn) Founded in 1777 to promote Gaelic language, literature, traditions, etc., and the well-being of Highlanders. After a period of fluctuating fortunes, since 1830 it has had a praiseworthy record of vigorous devotion to its aims, helping to establish a university Celtic Chair, encouraging the teaching of Gaelic in schools, supporting Highland charities, etc. (See *Celtic Magazine*, vol. 2, 353; J. Logan 1840; N. Stewart 1966.) TMM

Gaelic speaking in Scotland, demographic history Early statements about the extent of Gaelic speaking note only the presence of Gaelic in Scotland as a whole, or its existence in certain places, and do not readily lend themselves to a definition of the Gaidhealtachd's actual extent or of the numbers speaking Gaelic (e.g. Aeneas Sylvius; Tucker, in Hume Brown 1891, 27, 74). The earliest known spatial extent of the Gaidhealtachd is for 1698 (Withers 1980); the population of the Gaelic-speaking areas cannot be assessed earlier than 1755 (Flinn 1977, 4; Webster 1755, in Kyd 1952).

The area covered for 1698 includes the recognized 'Highland counties', the greater part of Caithness, Nairn and Perth, and parts of Moray, Banff, Aberd-een, Stirling and Dumbarton. The boundary of this area is shown in Fig. 1. J. Walker (1808), using material he collected in the 1760s and 1770s, provides the next outline of the areal extent of the Gaidhealtachd. Through his work we may estimate the likely numbers of Gaelic speakers for about 1769. Walker's criterion was whether Gaelic was 'preached or spoken by the natives' in the parish (J. Walker 1808, 29). He enumerated 130 mainland and thirty-two island parishes, the boundary of whose total area appears in Fig. 1. Using Webster's population figures for Scotland (1755), Walker's Gaidhealtachd had an estimated population of 289,798 persons, 22·9 per cent of Scotland's total population of 1,265,380.

The statements on language in the *Old* and *New Statistical Accounts* have comparative value for the social aspects of Gaelic usage (Price, 1977). The fact that they do not provide complete coverage of the Highland parishes precludes their incorporation here.

Selkirk's second edition allows an evaluation of the numbers of Gaelic speakers for about 1806 (Selkirk 1806, App. V, lvi–lxi). Selkirk's criterion was those areas in which the language was 'in common use' and in which 'that language is so prevalent that the clergy are required to perform divine service in it' (1806, App. V, lvi). Selkirk's Gaidhealtachd included the counties of Argyll, Ross, Cromarty, Inverness and Sutherland and the islands of Bute and Arran. It also embraced the Caithness parishes of Reay, Thurso, Halkirk, and Latheron; the Nairn parishes of Ardclach, Calder and Nairn; Duthil parish in Morayshire; Kirkmichael in Banffshire; the Perthshire parishes of Balquhidder, Blair Atholl, Callander, Comrie, Dull, Fortingall, Kenmore, Killin, Kirkmichael, Logierait, Moulin and Weem; and the Dunbartonshire parishes of Arrochar and Luss. The boundary of the 1806 Gaidhealtachd thus defined is included in Figure 1.

Selkirk stated that his definition should also include about 4,500 persons in parishes in which some inhabitants used Gaelic but not the majority. The addition of this figure to the 1801 Census populations of the above areas gives an estimate of 297,823 persons speaking Gaelic in Scotland for 1806 (18·51 per cent of Scotland's 1801 population of 1,608,420). The estimated Gaelic-speaking populations of Walker and Selkirk must be treated with caution, since they do not allow for social differences in Gaelic usage, or for Gaelic speaking outwith this Gaidhealtachd, or for bilinguals within it. Nevertheless, both totals are useful to the study of the past demography of Gaelic.

E

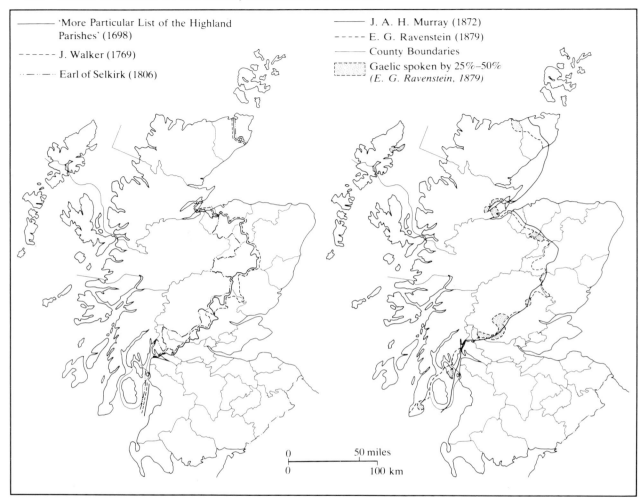

——————— 'More Particular List of the Highland
            Parishes' (1698)

- - - - - J. Walker (1769)

·—·—·— Earl of Selkirk (1806)

——————— J. A. H. Murray (1872)

- - - - - E. G. Ravenstein (1879)

——————— County Boundaries

⬚⬚⬚⬚⬚ Gaelic spoken by 25%–50%
        (E. G. Ravenstein, 1879)

0   50 miles

0   100 km

*1. Varying definitions of the spatial extent of the
Gaidhealtachd: the language border as defined for 1698 by
Walker (c. 1769) and Selkirk (1806).*

*2. The spatial extent of the Gaidhealtachd as defined by
Murray (1872) and Ravenstein (1879).*

J. A. H. Murray delimited those areas where 'Gaelic is still *spoken by any natives*, regardless of the fact that English may be spoken by the majority of the people' (Murray 1872, 232). Ravenstein included only those districts 'in which Gaelic continues the language of the majority' (Ravenstein 1879, 592). He also distinguished between a majority line and those areas where Gaelic was spoken by between 25 and 50 per cent of the people. The language borders of both authors are shown in Figure 2.

The first official recording of Gaelic began in 1881. That Census enumerated only those who spoke

Gaelic 'habitually' (1881 Census, I(1), xi). Of Scotland's 1881 population of 3,735,573, 6.2 per cent (231,594 persons) were so recorded. The 1891 Census distinguished between speakers of 'Gaelic only' and speakers of 'Gaelic and English' (1891 Census, Table XII, xxi); not surprisingly, the number of Gaelic speakers rose dramatically. The questions on Gaelic have varied little since, except that from 1901 enumeration was only of persons aged three years and over. The Gaelic-speaking population of Scotland from Walker to the 1981 Census is presented in the table on p. 111.

The Gaelic-speaking population of Scotland, c.1769–1981

Source	Population of Scotland	Gaelic-only speakers	Gaelic-only speakers as % of population	Gaelic-and-English speakers	Gaelic-and-English speakers as % of population
J. Walker (1808)	1,265,380[a]	289,798	22·9		
Selkirk (1806)	1,608,420[b]	297,823	18·5		
Censuses					
1881	3,735,573	231,594	6·2		
1891	4,025,647	43,738	1·1	210,677	5·2
1901[c]	4,472,103	28,106	0·6	202,700	4·5
1911	4,760,904	18,400	0·4	183,998	3·9
1921	4,573,471	9,829	0·2	148,950	3·3
1931	4,588,909	6,716	0·1	129,419	2·8
1951	5,096,415	2,178	0·04	93,269	1·8
1961	5,179,344	974	0·01	80,004	1·5
1971	5,228,965	477	0·009	88,415	1·7
1981	5,035,315	no data	—	82,620[d]	1·6

[a] Using Webster (1755).
[b] Using the 1801 Census.
[c] Persons aged three years and over.
[d] Speaks, reads or writes Gaelic (1981 Census).

Throughout the past century substantial migration from the north-west and the Hebrides has produced a numerical and proportional decline of Gaelic in its heartland and a corresponding percentage increase in Lowland Gaelic speakers (25·24 per cent of all Gaelic speakers in 1881, 25·27 per cent in 1931, 26·90 per cent in 1951, 29·34 per cent in 1961 and 43·42 per cent in 1971.) Whether because of migration or increases among learners, the overall 9·77 per cent increase in Gaelic speakers 1961–71 was attributable to an increase in the Lowlands from 23,756 to 38,594 (while Highland Gaelic speakers declined from 57,222 to 50,303). The 1971 Gaelic population divided roughly into thirds: between the Western Isles 23,511 (26·45 per cent), the Highland Region 26,680 (30·01 per cent) and Strathclyde 30,805 (34·65 per cent). Figures 3, 4 and 5 show the percentages of Gaelic speakers (both Gaelic-only and English-and-Gaelic) in relation to population density for 1891, 1931 and 1971.

In 1891 the area of indigenous Gaelic was particularly extensive. In the whole Highland massif (as far east and south as Nairnshire and upland areas of Moray, Banff, Aberdeen, Perth, Stirling and Dunbarton counties) there was an above-average (6·84 per cent) incidence of Gaelic. Buteshire was quite strongly Gaelic (20·7 per cent), and only a short distance separated the great Lowland cities from a Gaelic-speaking countryside. Gaelic predominated in the central Highlands, north-west Perthshire, Badenoch, Strathspey, Lochaber, Loch Ness-side, mainland Argyllshire (except the tip of Kintyre and eastern Cowal), most of Easter Ross (except eastern Black Isle) and throughout Sutherland. Over three-quarters of the population spoke Gaelic throughout the Hebrides, the mainland coasts from Lorne to Strath Hall-adale and the inland parishes of Fortingall, Laggan, Daviot, Moy, Urquhart and Glenmoriston, Kiltarlity, Kincardine (Ross-shire) and Rogart.

By 1931 Gaelic speakers in much of the eastern Highlands had slipped below 25 per cent, although in central areas such as Lochaber and Loch Ness-side Gaelic speakers still represented between 25 and 50 per cent of the population. The coastland north-west of Lorne still remained over 75 per cent Gaelic (especially Ardnamurchan, Arisaig, Moidart, Glenshiel, Kintail, Applecross, Gairloch, Lochbroom, Assynt, Eddrachillis, Durness and Tongue), as did the Hebrides (except Lismore and eastern Mull.)

The 1971 Census showed further weakening –

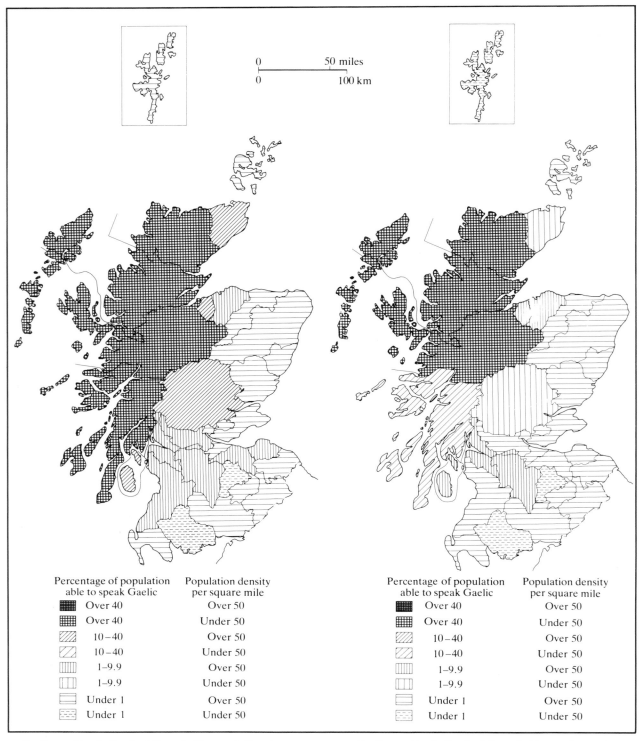

Percentage of population able to speak Gaelic	Population density per square mile
Over 40	Over 50
Over 40	Under 50
10–40	Over 50
10–40	Under 50
1–9.9	Over 50
1–9.9	Under 50
Under 1	Over 50
Under 1	Under 50

3. Gaelic-speaking in Scotland from the Census of 1891, by county

Percentage of population able to speak Gaelic	Population density per square mile
Over 40	Over 50
Over 40	Under 50
10–40	Over 50
10–40	Under 50
1–9.9	Over 50
1–9.9	Under 50
Under 1	Over 50
Under 1	Under 50

4. Gaelic-speaking in Scotland from the Census of 1931, by county

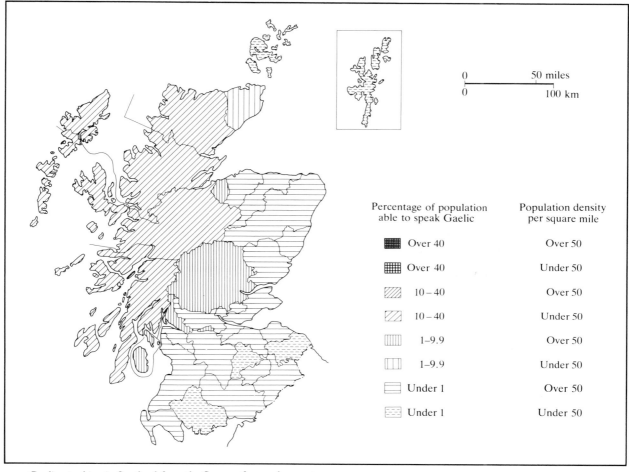

Percentage of population able to speak Gaelic	Population density per square mile
▓ Over 40	Over 50
▦ Over 40	Under 50
▨ 10 – 40	Over 50
▨ 10 – 40	Under 50
▥ 1–9.9	Over 50
▥ 1–9.9	Under 50
▤ Under 1	Over 50
▦ Under 1	Under 50

5. Gaelic-speaking in Scotland from the Census of 1971, by county

although there were some surprising strengths. On the mainland only Applecross and Stoer remained over 50 per cent Gaelic and within the southerly Hebrides only western Islay, Tiree, Colonsay and the Small Isles. Skye fared little better at 66·8 per cent (although Raasay, Braes, Kilmuir and Duirinish West remained above 75 per cent). The Western Isles contained two areas of weakness: Benbecula (61·1 per cent) and Stornoway (53·6 per cent). Percentages conceal the fact that incomers depress the incidence of local Gaelic speakers, who may indeed maintain the language reasonably well. Analysis of the 1971 Census revealed areas where the proportion of Gaelic speakers was higher among the under-25s (Sleat, Kilmuir, Duirinish West, Lewis – excepting Stornoway and Park – Harris, North Uist, South Uist and Barra). It was remarkable that even in 1971 an above-average incidence of Gaelic persisted throughout the traditional Highland area. Percentages also concealed large Gaelic minorities in Lowland cities. Clydeside contained a 'Gaelic archipelago' of significance similar to that of the Western Isles.

The Census illuminates certain social characteristics of the Gaelic speech community. Today Gaelic monolingualism is vestigial, prevalent only among pre-school infants and the oldest women. Significantly more women read and write Gaelic than do men. Females predominate among Gaelic-speakers significantly more than among the non-Gaelic population – except within the most strongly Gaelic areas of the Western Isles, where there are significantly fewer women than men in younger age groups (perhaps because of greater migration among younger women.) Religion affects Gaelic literacy. Comparisons of Catholic and Protestant areas in the outer islands and or the west coast indicate considerable differences in the ability to read and write Gaelic even among schoolchildren. Gaelic literacy rates of 75 per cent and over occur only in areas combining a high incidence of Gaelic, community adherence to Presbyterianism and a supportive bilingual educational policy. The former education authority areas of Sutherland, Perthshire and Argyll evidence particularly low Gaelic literacy among young Gaelic speakers. In terms of incidence of Gaelic by age, children aged 3–9 in 1971 comprised only 5 per cent of the Gaelic-speaking population, compared with 13·1 per cent of Scotland's English-only population. Young adults comprised a much higher proportion of the Lowland Gaelic population than within the Gaidhealtachd, where the over-65s formed a conspicuously higher proportion than did those among Lowland Gaels or English monoglots in either part of the country.   CWJW/KMMcK

Gaelic-speaking in Scotland, sociology The census gives useful information on age, sex and geographical distribution of abilities to speak, read and write Gaelic but no data on class, occupation, religion, degree of ability, attitudes or patterns of usage and acquisition of Gaelic. Few specifically sociological studies of Gaelic communities have examined such matters. However studies by Caird and Moisley, Hunter, Mewett, Owen, Parman, Vallee, and my own recent surveys of Harris. Barra and Cape Breton communities, have explored these relationships (*see* bibliography, under these authors).

Gaelic–English bilingualism is diglossic. Most speakers use Gaelic exclusively with family, friends and neighbours and for worship. English predominates in public places and entertainments, in school matters and among children. It is in religious, social and educational contexts that the inter-generational shift towards English is most evident.

Gaelic communities are biased towards the elderly and are further distorted by migration among the young and middle-aged. The Gaelic speech community is more significantly female than the general population in Scotland. (The reverse is true in Canada.) Of all age and sex groupings, young women in the most Gaelic areas are the most supportive of Gaelic, the most literate in Gaelic and the most likely to migrate – a serious implication for the future of the speech community. Islanders identify most

strongly with such descriptions as 'Islander', 'Barrach', 'Hearach' rather than 'Scot', 'Gael' or 'Highlander' (and similarly in Nova Scotia). Surveys have revealed that most respondents are moderately supportive of, and favourably disposed to the Gaelic language and culture. In Cape Breton Catholics are more inclined to regard themselves as 'Gaels' and Protestants as 'Scots'. Traditional cultural skills are claimed by some two-thirds of Catholics and over three-quarters of Protestants, compared with 27 per cent and 15 per cent respectively in Barra and Harris (11 per cent among Free Presbyterians). In both countries Protestants are far less committed to the value of Scottish traditions and Gaelic musical skills. As in Scotland, the use of Gaelic is stronger among the Cape Breton Catholics – especially with family, neighbours, shopkeepers and other community figures and at social and religious gatherings.

In Barra 60 per cent of respondents have been assessed at the highest Gaelic fluency level, 52 per cent in Harris (49 per cent and 32 per cent among eighteen to forty-four-year-olds). Cape Breton has manifested a similar pattern. Gaelic usage patterns in everyday situations are higher in Barra than in Harris (except when consulting a doctor or reading a Gaelic book). Gaelic literacy is stronger among Protestants in both countries. Traditional cultural skills are transmitted exclusively through the family in both countries, although in Cape Breton transmission of Gaelic to the under-forty-fives has ceased (except in the most strongly Gaelic Catholic communities). Literacy rates are much influenced by family tradition, fluency and language loyalty. The use of Gaelic at work is significantly stronger in Harris than Barra, despite a more general shift to English in Harris. This seems also to have reduced age differences in usage and promoted a greater awareness of language in everyday life.

Indices of Gaelic loyalty based upon answers to questions about support for language and culture and a belief in language maintenance, the value of traditions and the viability of the current lifestyle have produced higher incidences of greater loyalty in Barra than in Harris. The most supportive are the older and more fluent. Loyalty to Gaelic is also strongly associated with regular church attendance (but not denomination), self-taught literacy, possession of cultural skills and education to junior secondary level only (the more highly educated, who have left the community, having been replaced by incomers). Those with more favourable attitude scores and higher usage levels are those most imbued with cultural traditions and older behaviour patterns.

Voting preferences, occupational class and mobility have also been studied, but no marked associations with Gaelic fluency, literacy, or cultural transmission have resulted. Labour and SNP voters evidenced the highest language and cultural loyalty and intergenerational maintenance of Gaelic. Socio-economic class is not a relevant determinant of social structure in Gaelic communities. The crofter core is strongly Gaelic, and any weaknesses may lie in the other occupational groups. The highest loyalties lie among native Gaelic speakers of skilled and semi-skilled manual parentage, present-day semi- and unskilled manual occupations, and the downwardly mobile in occupational and marital terms. Possibly the most marked differences are those between Gaelic speakers who remain in the home community and those who leave to work and live elsewhere.　　KMMCK

Gaidheal, An The official magazine of An Comunn Gaidhealach (q.v.), which was first published under the title of *An Deò-Gréine* in 1905. Later the magazine changed its name again, this time to *Sruth*, which in recent years has been published as an inset in a Highland newspaper. The editors of *An Deò-Gréine/An Gaidheal* were the following: Malcolm Macfarlane, 1905–6; the Revd Malcolm Maclennan, 1906–8; Duncan Reid, 1908–12; Donald Macphie, 1912–22; the Revd Neil Ross, 1923–36; the Revd Malcolm MacLeod, 1936–46; the Revd T. M. Murchison, 1946–58; James Thomson, 1958–62; Donald Grant, 1962–4; Roderick Mackinnon, 1964–7.　　DST

Gàidhealtachd, *see* Gaelic speaking in Scotland, demographic history of.

Galbraith, William Campbell (b. 1870) From Campbeltown. Author of *Airson Tir agus Teanga* (1904). (See Macbean 1921.)　　DST

Galloway, *see* place names: Gaelic in Galloway and Ayrshire.

Geddes, Sir Patrick (1854–1932) Sociologist and town planner. Having studied biology under T. H. Huxley, he became professor of botany at the University of Dundee, during which period he studied civic design and town and regional planning. From 1919 he spent his time largely in India and was appointed Professor of Sociology at the University of

Bombay, 1920–3. On his death an Outlook Tower Association – the name was a reference to the Tower on Castlehill, Edinburgh, which he had purchased in 1892 and which had become an international centre of research and propaganda for planning – was formed to disseminate his theories. (See also **art, Gaelic, in modern times**.)　　DST

Geinidh, *see* Moireasdan, Dòmhnall.

geography, *see* Highlands and Islands, geography of.

Ghobha, Anna (fl. early nineteenth century) Perthshire bana-bhàrd. Author of song about working at Lowland harvest in 1827. (See P. Cameron 1892.)　　DST

Ghobha, Mairearad, *see* Macintosh, Duncan.

Gibson, W. J. (1865–1944) Born Greenock. First headmaster of the Nicolson Institute, Stornoway, 1894–1925. A man of creative ability, great industry and clear vision, who dedicated himself to the development of education in Lewis.　　JAS

Gille Caluim Garbh Mac Ghille Chaluim (MacLeod of Raasay) (d. *c.*1616) Author of 'Na trì làmha bu phailte' in the Fernaig Manuscript (q.v.).　　DST

Gille na Ciotaig, *see* MacDonald, Archibald (*c.*1750–1815).

'Gille nan Cochull Chraiceann' ('The Skin-Clad Servant') Alias 'Ceudach'. Folktale perhaps based on lost romance. Ceudach takes service with the Fenians; after victory he is killed by an old enemy but is resurrected by his wife (or mother). (See Bruford 1969, 123–7.)　　AB

Gilleasbaig Ruadh MacDhòmhnaill, *see* Ciaran Mabach, an.

Gilleasbuig na Ceapaich, *see* MacDonald, Archibald (d. 1682).

Gillies, John (fl. 1780) Bookseller in Perth. Publisher of *Sean Dàin agus Orain Ghaidhealach*, usually called the Gillies Collection, in 1786 (see also **James McLagan**).　　DST

Gillies, William (b. 1942) From near Oban. Professor of Celtic, University of Edinburgh, 1979–
Has published editions of poems from the Book of the Dean of Lismore (q.v.) and is editing the Books of Clanranald (q.v.). DST

Giolla Coluim Mac an Ollaimh, *see* MacMhuirich, Giolla Coluim.

Giolla Crìost Brúilingeach (fl. 1440) Described in the Book of the Dean of Lismore (q.v.) as 'bard in leymm', which probably refers to Leim in Gigha and identifies Giolla Crìost as a MacBhreatnaigh or Galbraith and probably a member of a hereditary line of poet-harpers (see D. S. Thomson 1968, 69). He has an interesting poem in the Book of the Dean of Lismore (q.v.) (32) addressed to a Connacht chief, in which he asks for a harp as fee; there is a vernacularized version in Rel. Celt. I, 326 (from Turner MS 14), also another poem with Irish subject-matter (Book of the Dean, 46). DST

Giolla Crìost Táilliúir (fl. ?1460) Author of four poems in the Book of the Dean of Lismore (q.v.), one urging John Stewart of Garth (?) to burn out the wolf dens in Schiehallion. (See W. J. Watson 1937, 176.) DST

Giolla Glas mac an Táilliúir (fl. ?1490) Elegy in the Book of the Dean of Lismore (q.v.) on Duncan MacGregor, Keeper of Castle of Glenorchy, (d. 1518). Probably father of Dubhghall mac an Ghiolla Ghlais (q.v.). (See W. J. Watson 1937, 196.) DST

Giolla Naoimh mac Mharcais (dates unknown) A member of the Mac Mharcais bardic family (q.v.). Two quatrains of his are in the Book of the Dean of Lismore (q.v.). (See Quiggin 1937, 99.) DST

Gleannach, *see* MacDonald, Alexander (1860–1928).

Glencairn, 9th Earl of (William Cunningham) (c.1610–64) Commander of the Highland Royalist rising of 1653–4 against Cromwellian rule. DS

Glencoe, Massacre of (13 February 1692) The killing by Government forces of about thirty-eight MacIans (or MacDonalds) of Glencoe, including their chief, as he had failed to take an oath of allegiance to William of Orange before a time limit expired. (See D. J. MacDonald 1965; Prebble 1966.) DS

Glendale Martyr, *see* MacPherson, John (?1845–1924).

Goban Saor, *see* Boban Saor.

Gobha na Hearadh, *see* Morison, John (c.1796–1852).

Gordon, George, *see* Huntly, 2nd Marquis of.

Gordon, George Ross (fl. 1800) Born Creich, Sutherland. His songs were published c.1804, when he served in the 42nd Regiment in Ireland. (See Beaton 1923, 26.) DST

Gordon, William (1770–1820) Born Creich, Sutherland. Brother of George Ross Gordon (q.v.). He wrote spiritual songs, which were published in Galway in 1802. DST

Gordon Highlanders, *see* regiments, Highland.

Gormshuil Mhór na Maighe (dates unknown) A celebrated Lochaber witch. (See A. Camshron 1957.) DST

Gow, William, *see* Uilleam Ruighe 'n Uidhe.

Grahame, John, of Claverhouse, *see* Dundee, Viscount.

Grannd, Pàdraig (Revd Peter Grant) (1783–1867) Native of Strathspey. Became a Baptist minister at Grantown and writer of some of the most singable and sung of Gaelic hymns. Since the early nineteenth century his hymns have gone through many editions, the latest of which contains some forty extant compositions (H. MacDougall 1926).

His two main preoccupations, expressed in verses with a strong emotional pulse, are a warm devotion to Christ and a fervent appeal to the impenitent. Among his best-known pieces are 'Oran mu Leanabh Og', which mingles theology with pathos in the words of a dead child, and 'A' Chulaidh Sgiamhach', satisfyingly unified by the central image of the robe of righteousness. KDMcD

Grannda, Gilleasbuig (1785–p.1863) Born in Glenmoriston. Related to Alexander Grant (q.v.), laird of Glenmoriston, and to Sìleas na Ceapaich (q.v.). His collection *Dain agus Orain* (1863) includes poems (to Grants and others) which skilfully deploy panegyric formulae and references to the Fian (some using an unusually long strophic paragraph of between ten and thirteen lines), as well as poems to Victoria and Albert and occasional verses. DST

Grant, Alexander (b. *c.*1772) Born in Glenmoriston. His songs were collected by William Mackay (q.v.) and published in 1884. DST

Grant, Donald (1903–70) Native of Skye. Headmaster of a Glasgow school. Crowned Bard at the National Mod, 1935. Editor of *An Gaidheal*, 1962–4. President of An Comunn Gaidhealach, 1965–8. Wrote short stories, plays and poetry, mainly humorous. (See D. Grannd 1971.) IMCL

Grant, James (1847–1918) Born Glen Urquhart. The James Grant Memorial Prize, for a solo singing competition at the National Mod, is awarded each year in his memory. DST

Grant, Katherine Whyte (1845–1928) Translator and author of children's playlets; translated 'God save the King'. (See K. W. Grant 1911, Macbean 1921, 52; *TGSI*, vol. 17, 302.) TMM

Grant, Revd Peter, *see* Grannd, Pàdraig.

Gunn, Revd Adam (b. 1859) Born Strathy. Joint editor of an 1899 edition of the works of Rob Donn (q.v.). DST

H

Hamilton, Gavin, *see* art, Gaelic, in modern times.

harp, *see* Clarsach Society; harpers; harps; music of Gaelic Scotland.

harpers There are many references to harpers, in various parts of Scotland and over a long period. Some of these were Irish (*see* Ó Baoill 1972); some of

them were not Gaelic-speaking at all; of those who were Gaels, some may have belonged to harpist dynasties that have not been recognized or cannot be reconstructed, while others seem to have not belonged to such dynasties, such as an Clàrsair Dall (q.v.) (*see* W. Matheson 1970). The topic has not as yet been investigated in depth.

Among famous Irish harpers there was Ruaidhrí Dall Ó Catháin, who spent some time in Perthshire and is associated with the seventeenth-century Robertson of Lude. An earlier harpist visitor, Diarmaid Ó Cairbre, had murdered Angus Óg MacDonald (q.v.) in 1490 and met his death as a result. We meet with a Eugenius Klerscharch in 1434 (Highland Papers, II, 175, 177) and with Giolla Críost Brúilingeach (q.v.), bard and harper, also in the mid-fifteenth century. It is likely that the latter belonged to a family of harpers with the surname Mac an Bhreatnaigh or Galbraith, in Gigha and Kintyre, and that their line may have included a Lachlann in the early fifteenth century, while descendants were still in Gigha in 1685 (D. S. Thomson 1968, 69). But we have much fuller information about another Kintyre family of harpers who served the Lords of the Isles, the people whose surname was Ó Senóg, variously written in records – for example, Muriach McMaschenach (*leg.* Macshenach) in 1505, Gallicallum McCosenach in 1506, Moreach McSchinnocht in 1525–8, McIlschanoch in 1541, Gilleis McCochennan in 1596, etc. – as tenants of lands held as *citherista*. Their descendants are MacShannons (colloquially Shenogs) at the present time.

Although the harp was soon to be ousted by the pipes, we have a late instance of its use in connection with war in 1627, when 'Harie m'gra, harper fra Larg' and two pipers joined a company of bowmen 'shipped' at Campbeltown for service in France (Collinson 1975, 164), and the harpists continued to be patronized. Among those who patronized harp music after 1600 are the Macleans. The Duart chiefs still maintained a harper in 1674 (J. R. N. Macphail 1914–34, vol. 1, 280) and perhaps in 1685 (*Account*, 1816, 70), possibly members of a family called Mac-Néill na Caillich (Logan 1831b, II, 268). Iain Garbh, 8th Maclean of Coll (d. *c.*1678), was a composer for the harp (Collinson 1966, 237–8). Eachann, 13th of Coll, was maintaining a harper in 1734, a MacDonald known as Murchadh Clàrsair (Sanger 1979, 16).

We have very little information about harping in the eighteenth century, in the course of which it disappeared. We know of one Lachlann Dall, a harper (perhaps a Mackinnon) who brought news from the MacDonald lands to the north-east and probably died in the 1720s; one of the tunes he is said to have played may have survived only as a pipe tune (C. Ó Baoill 1972, 175–9), as did other harp tunes (Collinson, 1966, 247). Alexander Grant, 4th of Sheugly in Glenurquhart, a performer on harp, pipe and fiddle (S. Fraser 1816, 106, n. 3), died in prison after Culloden. But the MacLeods of Dunvegan still had a harper, the last on record, in 1755 (I. F. Grant 1959, 489).

Other harpers whose names we know include Donald Mackean, who died in 1602 (R. Gordon 1813, 246), Thomas Potts, 1649 (Dalyell 1849, 243n.), Jago McFlahertie 1682 (Marshall 1973, 73) and one Melvin, c.1700 (W. Matheson 1970, lxxvi). (See also Fergusson 1978, 73–110.) DST/CÓB

harps There is evidence of harpers and of their harps in many parts of Scotland until their disappearance in the eighteenth century. The historian George Buchanan refers in 1582 to the harps used, 'some of which are strung with brass, and some with catgut':

In playing [the harpers] strike the wires with a quill, or with their nails, suffered to grow long for the purpose; but their grand ambition is to adorn their harps with great quantities of Silver and gems . . . . (R. W. Munro 1961, 43–4)

The two surviving old harps are the Lamont Harp (? fifteenth century) and the Queen Mary Harp (sixteenth century), both of which were in the possession of the Robertsons of Lude. There are, however, much more ancient representations of harps on stone. (See Collinson 1966, ch. 8.) DST

The Queen Mary Harp (sixteenth century). Said to have been given to a member of the Lude family by Queen Mary in 1563, this harp is about 31 inches high and artistically decorated. National Museum of Antiquities of Scotland.

Hay, George Campbell (Mac Iain Deòrsa) (Born 1915) Son of John MacDougall Hay, author of *Gillespie*. Has identified himself with Kintyre, especially Tarbert, and learned Gaelic in his teens but lived mainly in Edinburgh. Not only is he the only modern poet to write in Gaelic, Scots and English, but he included French and Norwegian verse in his *Wind on Loch Fyne* (1948) and subsequently published translations from modern Greek, Croatian, Arabic, Italian, Finnish, Icelandic and Welsh. He has been deeply influenced in his metrics especially by medieval and early modern Irish verse.

His first Gaelic collection, *Fuaran Sléibh* (Upland Spring) (1947), includes poems of sharp, delicate natural description (such as 'Do Bheithe Bòidheach' and 'Na Baidealan'); his evocative 'Cinntìre'; poems of the *dánta grádha* type (a Gaelic modification of courtly love poetry), using Irish models; some humorous verse; 'Tilleadh Uiliseis', a most effective dramatic reconstruction; and poems of a philosophical and political nature which anticipate the later thrust of his poetry. *O na Ceithir Airdean* (From the Four Airts) (1952) develops his philosophical and political verse greatly in such poems as 'Atman', 'Truaighe na h-Eòrpa', 'Feachd a' Phrionnsa', 'Meftah Babkum es-Sabar?' and 'Ar Blàr Catha', the latter three expressing his deeply felt Scottish nationalism. This volume also included the brilliantly vivid 'Bisearta', from his North African war experience, and his many translations. Hay continues to write and publish now almost exclusively in Gaelic.

He contributed to the *Akros* anthology of contemporary Gaelic verse (1976) and publishes regularly in *Gairm* (q.v.). In 1982 a long poem, *Mochtàr is Dùghall*, written mainly in the mid-1940s came to light and was published. This includes powerful descriptive and narrative writing, especially in the Arab (Mochtàr) section.

His salient contributions to Gaelic verse have been his skilled and varied metrical craftsmanship, his passionate nationalist verse and his reflective philosophical poems. (See also D. MacAulay 1976, 1981; D. S. Thomson 1974a, 1974b, 1976a.)   DST

Hay, Revd John MacDougall (1881–1919) From Tarbert, Loch Fyne. Author of *Gillespie* (1914). Father of George Campbell Hay (q.v.).   DST

Henderson, Angus (1866–1937) From Ardnamurchan. Gaelic journalist concerned mainly with Gaelic culture and politics. Edited Gaelic weekly newspaper *Alba*, 1908–9. (See Macbean 1921, 59; D. J. Macleod 1977, 311.)   TMM

Henderson, Dr George (1866–1912) Born Kiltarlity. Pupil at Raining's School, Inverness, at the time of Alexander MacBain (q.v.). Student at Edinburgh, Oxford, Berlin, Leipzig, Vienna. Lecturer in Celtic, University of Glasgow, 1906–12. Author of *Dàin Iain Ghobha* (1893–6), *Leabhar nan Gleann* (1898) *The Norse Influence on Celtic Scotland* (1910) and other works.   DST

hiatus, *see* Gaelic: hiatus.

Highland Association, *see* Comunn Gaidhealach, An.

Highland charge In firing one volley before dropping their muskets and charging to engage in hand-to-hand fighting with sword and targe, Highland armies employed a tactic (evidently first used in Ulster in 1642) which made them formidable in the century 1644 to 1745. (See D. Stevenson 1980, 82–4.)   DS

Highland Games The first Highland Society Gathering at the Falkirk Tryst of 1781 was really a piping competition – and the pipers are still the true aristocrats of the games. By the 1820s, however, full-scale games were being held throughout the country. The programme for the St Fillans games of 1826 makes interesting reading; for example, the second prize for *pìobaireachd* consisted of Ossian's poems in three volumes in the original Gaelic, with a literal translation into Latin (Webster 1973, 13).

By attending the Braemar gathering in 1848, Queen Victoria conferred on Highland Games a degree of respectability which has guaranteed their popularity ever since. They have had their ups and downs over the years, but now, thanks to sponsorship and the growth of tourism, they are second only to football as a spectator sport in Scotland.

The dancing competitions, once for men only, are nowadays often won by women, many of them still wearing male attire (i.e. the kilt) despite the creation of the Aboyne dress. Purists watching one of these lassies doing the Sword Dance and visualizing Malcolm Canmore dancing over the body of his newly slain adversary may be forgiven for considering the performance somewhat incongruous, but the rest of us can sit back and enjoy it, worrying only about the fact that if she touches a sword, she loses marks, and if she displaces one, she is disqualified.

For athletic events the professional rules are in some respects less strict than those of the amateurs (no take-off board for the long jump, no circle for the weight-putting, etc.), and conditions on the field are sometimes very different. Landing conditions for the high jump are often Spartan and for the pole-vault truly frightening – a relic of the 'grass-to-grass' tradition in these events. In the interest of self-preservation the athletes must cultivate a cat-like ability to land on their feet, and in these circumstances high jumpers cannot take advantage of modern techniques – indeed, neither diving nor somersaulting over the bar is permitted. Nevertheless, Jay Scott has cleared 6ft 3½in using the old scissors style.

The pole-vaulter needs the courage of his soldier ancestors, who vaulted over moats and ramparts in the Middle Ages. The sharpened piece of pine (later of bamboo) has now been superseded by a steel pole with a spiked plate on the end; but the heights cleared cannot be compared with those recorded in amateur athletics, for which conditions are entirely different, with fibre-glass poles, boxes and soft landing facilities.

In a programme which may range from ancient Greek pastimes like wrestling and the tug-of-war to sky diving and haggis hurling, one of the most spectacular events is throwing the hammer. In the old days an ordinary heavy hammer was used, but now

School children competing at the Durness Highland Games, Sutherland.

the head must be spherical, the handle of wood or cane and the overall length 4ft 2in. Turning with the hammer was practised at one time but was stopped because of the danger to onlookers. Throwers must keep both feet on the ground, and for the last thirty years they have been anchoring themselves to the earth by means of pointed plates protruding forward from the soles of their boots.

The crowd's favourite event, however, is undoubtedly the cabar (Gaelic for 'tree trunk'). The secret of tossing the cabar (given the necessary skill and strength) is to run forward with it at elbow-level, stop dead and, as it topples over, take its feet from it at exactly the right moment – not too soon and not too late – so that the heavy end hits the ground and the light end falls away in a direct line. If it falls to either side, it is not a perfect toss, and the angle of deviation proclaims the degree of success. Distance, of course, is not involved in proper cabar tossing. If the stick is too heavy to start with, pieces are cut off from the thick end.

Cabar lengths and weights vary. The cabar used at Braemar for sixty years (untossed until George Clark turned it in 1951) was 19ft 3in long and weighed 120lb. Its successor is 6in longer and 12lb heavier – a tribute to today's strong men. The cabar used at the Scottish championships at Crieff is 15ft 2in long and weighs 154lb, being weighted with plugs of lead.

Standards in the heavy events have risen dramatically in recent times. The record performances of such legendary figures as Donald Dinnie, A. A. Cameron and George Clark have all been surpassed by those of Bill Anderson, MBE. He had been the undisputed Scottish heavyweight champion for four years when, in 1962, he met his match in Arthur Rowe, an Olympic athlete who had just turned professional. The contests between these two, the Aberdeenshire farmer and the Yorkshire blacksmith, were the highlights of the Games throughout the 1960s and 1970s.

Arthur Rowe has putted the 16lb stone 61ft 2in (3ft 1in short of his European record with the 16lb ball) and has won the heavyweight championship many times; but Bill Anderson's achievements make him the greatest Scottish heavyweight athlete of all time. He has thrown the 16lb hammer 151ft 2in (gaining him a place in the *Guinness Book of Records*), the 22lb hammer 123ft 5in, the 28lb weight 87ft 2in and the 56lb weight 41ft 11in. In 1977 he equalled the British record of 16ft for the 56lb weight over the bar (set by Grant Anderson earlier in the season), and he carried all before him in the heavyweight division that year.

The most successful heavyweight athlete of 1979 was Hamish Davidson, who topped the Tamnavulin trophy league table with his performances at nine gatherings. At Oban he broke Arthur Rowe's ground records by putting the heavy stone 46ft 9in and the light stone 56ft 8$\frac{1}{2}$in; and his 28lb weight throw of 89ft 1in not only broke Bill Anderson's ground record but would have been a national record if the ground had not been off-level.

Highland Games are now held in Canada, the United States, Australia, New Zealand and South Africa. Competitors from these countries are coming to Scotland in increasing numbers and are carrying off major prizes, particularly for piping and dancing. (See Webster 1973.)   DMO

Highland Host (1678) A force of about 8,000 men (about one-third of whom were Lowlanders) raised by the Government of Charles II and quartered in Ayrshire and Renfrewshire to force the Conventiclers (Presbyterian religious dissidents) into submission. (See Elder 1914.)   DS

Highland Land Law Reform Association, *see* politics, Highland (nineteenth century).

Highland Land League, *see* politics, Highland (nineteenth century).

Highland Society of Glasgow Founded in 1727 to educate children of Highland parentage, providing schools initially but latterly bursaries. Owned the Black Bull Inn. Had links with the founding of the first Gaelic Chapel in Glasgow (now St Columba's) in 1770 and of the Gaelic Club in 1780. (See GHS 1902; Strang 1864, 106.)   TMM

Highland Society of London Founded in 1778 to maintain the Highland 'martial spirit, dress, music . . .' and still flourishing. The Society founded

the Royal Caledonian Schools in 1815 and a Gaelic Chapel in 1812. It presented prizes for piping and poetry at the Falkirk Tryst in 1781 and still offers gold medals for piping at the Inverness and Oban Highland Gatherings. It possesses old Gaelic manuscripts, including the Book of the Dean of Lismore (q.v.), which is on loan to the National Library of Scotland, plate, medals and ancient tartans. (See *Celtic Magazine*, 2, 353; A. MacLeod 1952, 238, 512ff.)   TMM

Highland Society of Scotland This body (now the Royal Highland and Agricultural Society of Scotland) had a cultural remit between 1784 and 1844. At the height of this period (1797–1825) it functioned dynamically as a Gaelic academy of letters, gathering a legacy of manuscripts, papers and printed work without which Gaelic studies would today be incomparably the poorer.

It was founded in Edinburgh in 1784 by a group of Improvers, who defined their aim as an inquiry into 'the present state of the Highlands and Islands of Scotland, and the condition of their inhabitants' and 'the means of the improvement of the Highlands'. They added: 'The Society shall also pay a proper attention to the preservation of the language, poetry, and music of the Highlands.' Two years later, however, by obtaining a Royal Charter, they became the sole established body for promoting agriculture in Scotland.

The driving forces behind the Society's cultural work were Sir John Sinclair (1754–1835), Henry Mackenzie (1745–1831), Sir William MacLeod, (Lord Bannatyne) (1743–1833) and Sir John MacGregor Murray (d. 1822). In its early days the Society supported a bard, a piper and a 'Professor of Gaelic', sponsored Gaelic classes, declined to publish the poems of Rob Donn (q.v.), encouraged the writing and publication of *piobaireachd* and ran piping competitions: these last survived to 1844.

The next phase was triggered by the death of James Macpherson in 1796. At Mackenzie's suggestion, a committee was set up to inquire into the authenticity of Ossian. With Mackenzie as convener, it set about contacting informants and collecting manuscripts, and it co-opted two of the few men in Scotland who could read Gaelic script, Dr Donald Smith (1756–1805) and the Revd Donald Mackintosh (1743–1808). Mackintosh secured part of the Kilbride Collection in 1801, and Mackenzie obtained Macpherson's manuscripts (the Highland Society of

London Collection) in 1803. Mackenzie's invaluable *Report* was published in 1805.

In 1806 Sinclair set the Society the task of preparing a Gaelic dictionary. No editor was appointed, as during 1806–12 he and Murray were seeking the establishment of a Chair of Celtic at the University of Edinburgh and felt that the task should fall to the first professor. By 1811 the Society's candidate was Ewen MacLachlan, but the plan failed. MacLachlan worked on the Society's manuscripts from 1811 to his death in 1822, in 1814 becoming joint compiler of the dictionary with the Revd John MacLeod (1757–1841). Progress on the dictionary was marked by such vicissitudes that the Society grew disillusioned with the commitment long before its publication in 1828. In 1859 the manuscripts were transferred to the Advocates' Library. (See Ramsay 1879; Society's archives, Ingliston.) RB

Highlands and Islands Development Board The Highland Development (Scotland) Bill (No. 86), presented to Parliament on 23 February 1965, had eighteen clauses and provided for the creation of a Highland Development Board, consisting of a chairman and up to six members. In addition, there was to be a Highland Development Consultative Council, drawn from local authorities and other Highland interests, to advise the Board, whose general function would be preparing, concerting, promoting, assisting and undertaking measures for the economic and social development of the Highlands and Islands. It would keep under general review all matters relating to the economic and social well-being and development of the area, consult with local authorities and other bodies and submit development proposals to the Secretary of State for Scotland. Where there was no authority to carry out any proposal that had been approved, the Board itself would be empowered to do the job. It would have the power also to request the furnishing of information about any business or undertaking, subject only to specific restrictions on the disclosure of such information. The Labour Party formed HM Government when the Bill was presented to Parliament.

The new Board was to be empowered to: erect buildings or other structures and carry out works on land; provide equipment and services on or in connection with land; and hold, manage, maintain, hire, let or otherwise dispose of such works, equipment or services. These proposals, on the publication of the Bill, provoked immediately a hostile reaction from the Conservative Party and from the former Secretary of State for Scotland, who suggested that they amounted virtually to the nationalization of almost the whole of the North of Scotland. Consequently, he gave notice that his Party could not support the Bill as presented.

It seemed to many observers, at this stage, however, that the crux of the matter was no longer political but financial, and it was here that the Bill was most disappointing, providing only for a sum of £150,000 in the financial year 1965–6 to meet the cost of the Board's administration of operations carried out by it. But by 1968–9 the expenditure was estimated to have risen to about £1 million. This sum was, of course, over and above what was already paid to the crofting counties by Government Departments and official agencies, but the modesty of the amount was quite startling in the imaginative context of the Bill itself, and it was said, unkindly perhaps, that the amount of money to be made available explained why even the Scottish Landowners' Federation was not really unenthusiastic about the Bill as a whole. Without adequate money, the Board could not succeed in its task.

Since then the Highlands and Islands Development Board has had four chairmen, each appointment reflecting the politics of the Party in power at Westminster when the appointment was made. Annual reports are published, and in the 1979 report it is recorded that since its creation the Board has spent £250 million (£800 per person) in loans and grants to projects in the Highlands and Islands. In 1978 an important document was published in which proposals were made by the Board for changes in the Highlands and Islands Development (Scotland) Act 1965 to give it more effective powers over rural land use. Until then the Board had not made use of the land-acquisition powers available to it, and this document maintained that these powers were so limited by the Act as to be hardly worth using. Certainly, the powers available to the Board were not strong, but they had not been put to the test at any time by initiating compulsory purchase procedures. In the summer of 1980 the Conservative Secretary of State for Scotland turned down the Highlands and Islands Development Board's application, maintaining that if the Board had not used the powers it already possessed, why should it be given new ones? Logic was on his side.

The British economy is now oil-based, a development which has had consequent positive and negative

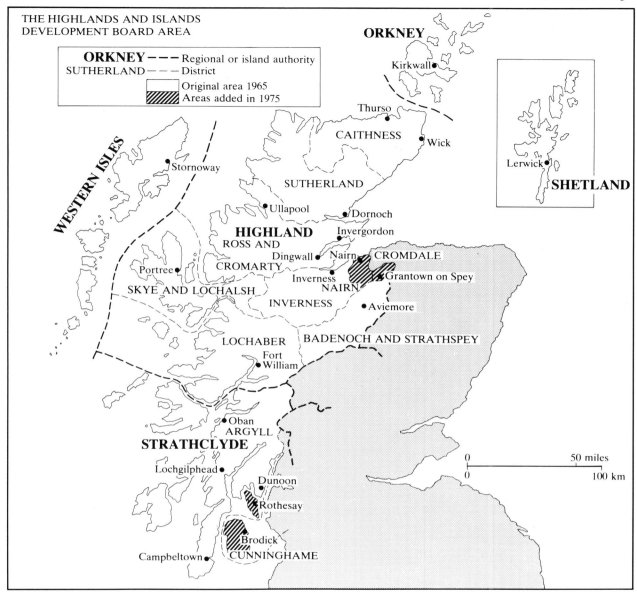

THE HIGHLANDS AND ISLANDS
DEVELOPMENT BOARD AREA

ORKNEY — — — Regional or island authority
SUTHERLAND — — — District
Original area 1965
Areas added in 1975

ORKNEY

Kirkwall●

SHETLAND

Lerwick●

WESTERN ISLES

Stornoway●

Thurso●
CAITHNESS
Wick●

SUTHERLAND

Ullapool●
Dornoch●

HIGHLAND
ROSS AND
Invergordon●
Dingwall● Nairn● CROMDALE
CROMARTY
Inverness● Grantown on Spey●
SKYE AND LOCHALSH NAIRN
Portree● INVERNESS
Aviemore●

LOCHABER BADENOCH AND STRATHSPEY
Fort●
William

Oban●
ARGYLL
STRATHCLYDE

Lochgilphead●

Dunoon●
Rothesay●

Brodick●
Campbeltown● CUNNINGHAME

0   50 miles
0   100 km

repercussions, and this is reflected in the Highlands and Islands, where workers move in large numbers to areas of considerable economic activity, such as Easter Ross, Kishorn and Stornoway. It can be argued that the Highlands and Islands Development Board has accepted this easy solution to the Highlands' economic problem and has not fulfilled its primary function. Land is the basic resource of the Highlands and Islands, and its private ownership overall by absentee landlords is an affront to eco-

nomic development. Until such time as the present sterilization of the land is tackled effectively, neither economic nor social progress can come to the area. A survey of land use was undertaken in 1969–70 but on the condition that the findings would be confidential. This is surely absurd in any democracy.

The four chairmen so far appointed have been Scotsmen: none has been a Highlander. All four have been interested in, and sympathetic to, Gaelic culture but none could speak to a Gael in his mother tongue.

I suspect that all, on occasion, have had difficulty in understanding the mentality of the men and women with whose lives, economically, socially and culturally, they were professionally involved.

Land must be taken from those who cannot, or will not, use it and given to the young, the enterprising and the far-seeing. Such people do exist, and they are Highland, not Scottish or English. And it is vital to Highland development that the Board should persuade the people of the area to support it. This is not the case now. As a matter of urgency, the Board must seek its inspiration not from the politician nor the academic but from the people of the area which it serves.   FG

Highlands and Islands, geography By convention, the Highlands and Islands are defined as the northern area of Scotland, bounded to the south by the populous Lowlands. Yet in the context of the present or recent distribution of Gaelic speakers, much of the eastern Highlands, Buchan and Moray Firth Lowlands have to be excluded, and this bibliographical note concentrates on the geographical literature on the counties of Argyll, Inverness, Ross and Cromarty and on Sutherland, Caithness and the Highland District of Perthshire.

In the one comprehensive and substantive geographical text on the Highlands and Islands the authors state that 'generalisations have been attempted to give the broad view without too much glossing of critical differences' (O'Dell and Walton 1962, v.). Despite changes over the last two decades, it still provides a sound overview and has a good bibliography up to 1962 and has not been fully replaced by *Patterns of Highland Development* (Turnock 1970) which draws most of the detailed examples from Lochaber. The late Sir Frank Fraser Darling's *West Highland Survey, An Essay in Human Ecology* (1955) is a detailed study of the west coast parishes and the Outer and Inner Hebrides – the Gaelic-speaking heartland. There are two short, up-to-date introductions (Turnock 1974; Highlands and Islands Development Board 1977).

MAPS AND PLACE NAMES
Apart from a good reference atlas, for example, the *Atlas of Great Britain and Northern Ireland* (Bickmore and Shaw 1963), the Ordnance Survey 1 : 625,000 series provides a range of topical maps on diverse topics. Glasgow University Geography Department's Population Distribution Map of Scotland based on the 1961 Census which plotted burghal, village (over 200 inhabitants) and dispersed rural population (one dot representing 25 persons) (Caird and Diamond 1962), can be updated using the *Index of Scottish Place Names* (General Register Office Scotland, 1975) which locates most settlements in Scotland by a grid reference, and records the population of those with over one hundred inhabitants. For general study, the 1 : 50,000 Ordnance Survey maps are invaluable: for more detailed study, the six-inch to the mile and 1 : 10,000 maps should be consulted: copies of all editions are held in the National Library of Scotland Map Room and in the British Library Map Room. For maps before 1850, *Early Maps of Scotland* (Royal Scottish Geographical Society, 1936 and 1973) provide comprehensive lists and information on availability. The *Historical Atlas of Scotland* also provides some information on earlier distributions in the Highlands and Islands (P. McNeill and R. Nicholson 1975). See also **place-names (bibliographical note)**.

TOPICAL ASPECTS
There are few books giving a comprehensive cover of specialised aspects of the Geography of the Highlands and Islands; much of the key information is published in journals.

THE ENVIRONMENT OF THE HIGHLANDS AND ISLANDS
The late Sir Frank Fraser Darling's volume in Collins' New Naturalist series (Darling and Morton Boyd 1969) gives the most comprehensive general account of environment and ecology; for land forms and scenery, *Highland Landforms* is a good introduction (R. J. Price 1976) and there are detailed studies of beaches and coasts (Ritchie 1973; Mather and Ritchie 1976); for Geology, the British Regional Geology Handbooks provide detailed material (Phemister 1960).

THE EVOLUTION OF THE MAN-MADE LANDSCAPE
No one has yet attempted to write a single volume on the Highlands and Islands on this complex topic and the literature available is widely scattered. The *"Old"* and *"New" Statistical Accounts of Scotland*, (Sir J. Sinclair 1791–99 and New Statistical Account of Scotland, 1834–45), provide what were meant to be but not always were comprehensive accounts of the parishes of Scotland, written by the ministers, and

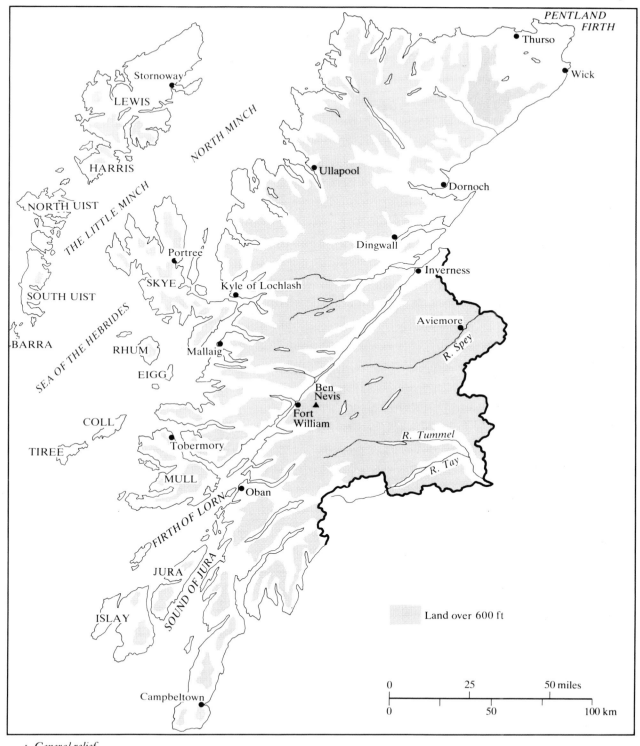

1. General relief

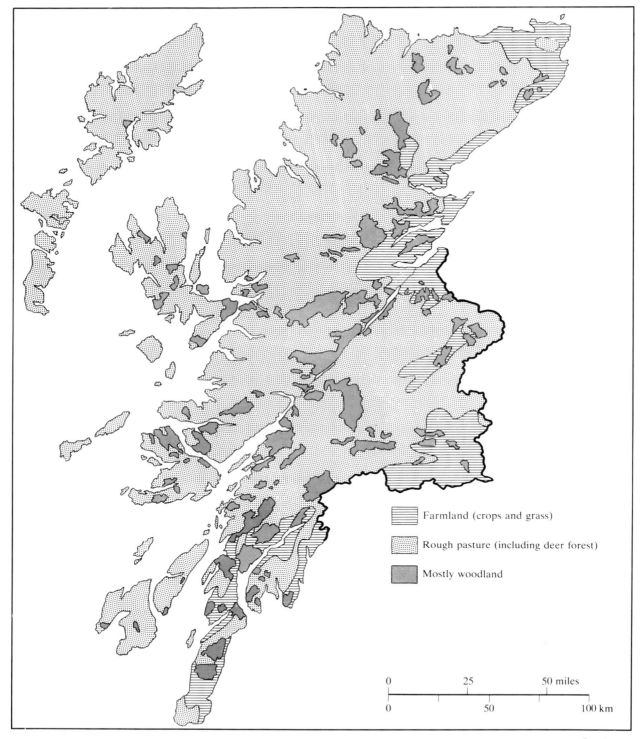

Farmland (crops and grass)

Rough pasture (including deer forest)

Mostly woodland

0   25   50 miles

0   50   100 km

2. Land use

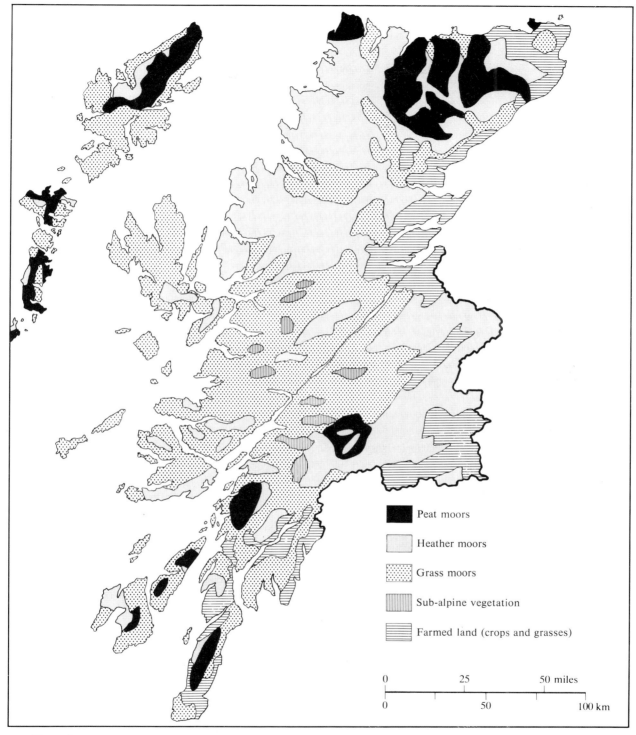

Peat moors

Heather moors

Grass moors

Sub-alpine vegetation

Farmed land (crops and grasses)

0   25   50 miles

0   50   100 km

3. Vegetation

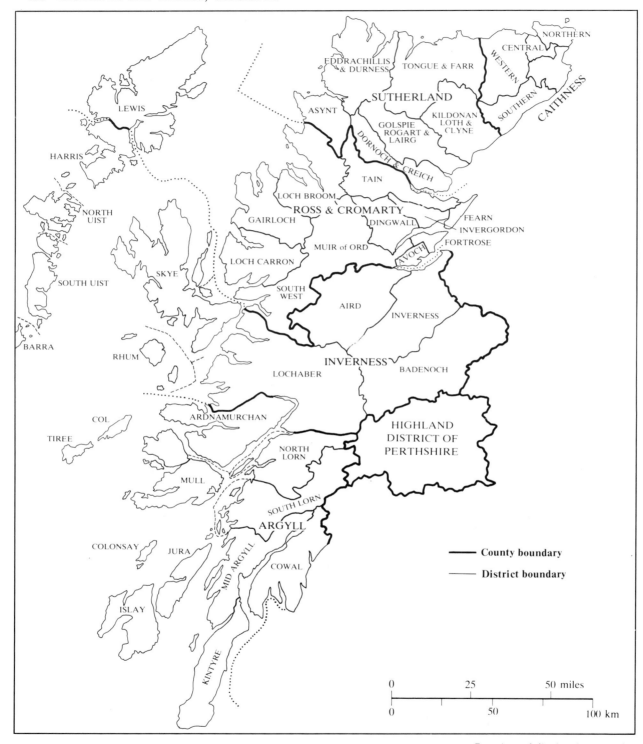

4. Counties and districts (pre-1975)

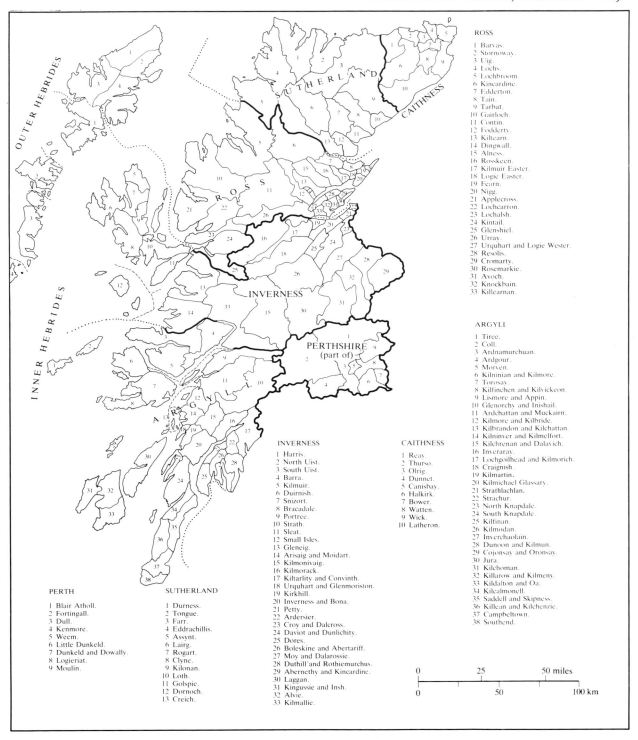

ROSS

1 Barvas.
2 Stornoway.
3 Uig.
4 Lochs.
5 Lochbroom.
6 Kincardine.
7 Edderton.
8 Tain.
9 Tarbat.
10 Gairloch.
11 Contin.
12 Fodderty.
13 Kiltearn.
14 Dingwall.
15 Alness.
16 Rosskeen.
17 Kilmuir Easter.
18 Logie Easter.
19 Fearn.
20 Nigg.
21 Applecross.
22 Lochcarron.
23 Lochalsh.
24 Kintail.
25 Glenshiel.
26 Urray.
27 Urquhart and Logie Wester.
28 Resolis.
29 Cromarty.
30 Rosemarkie.
31 Avoch.
32 Knockbain.
33 Killearnan.

ARGYLL

1 Tiree.
2 Coll.
3 Ardnamurchan.
4 Ardgour.
5 Morven.
6 Kilninian and Kilmore.
7 Torosay.
8 Kilfinchen and Kilvickeon.
9 Lismore and Appin.
10 Glenorchy and Inishail.
11 Ardchattan and Muckairn.
12 Kilmore and Kilbride.
13 Kilbrandon and Kilchattan.
14 Kilninver and Kilmelfort.
15 Kilchrenan and Dalavich.
16 Inveraray.
17 Lochgoilhead and Kilmorich.
18 Craignish.
19 Kilmartin.
20 Kilmichael Glassary.
21 Strathlachlan.
22 Strachur.
23 North Knapdale.
24 South Knapdale.
25 Kilfinan.
26 Kilmodan.
27 Inverchaolain.
28 Dunoon and Kilmun.
29 Cojonsay and Oronsay.
30 Jura.
31 Kilchoman.
32 Killarow and Kilmeny.
33 Kildalton and Oa.
34 Kilcalmonell.
35 Saddell and Skipness.
36 Killean and Kilchenzie.
37 Campbeltown.
38 Southend.

INVERNESS

1 Harris.
2 North Uist.
3 South Uist.
4 Barra.
5 Kilmuir.
6 Duirinish.
7 Snizort.
8 Bracadale.
9 Portree.
10 Strath.
11 Sleat.
12 Small Isles.
13 Gleneig.
14 Arisaig and Moidart.
15 Kilmonivaig.
16 Kilmorack.
17 Kiltarlity and Convinth.
18 Urquhart and Glenmoriston.
19 Kirkhill.
20 Inverness and Bona.
21 Petty.
22 Ardersier.
23 Croy and Dalcross.
24 Daviot and Dunlichity.
25 Dores.
26 Boleskine and Abertariff.
27 Moy and Dalarossie.
28 Duthill'and Rothiemurchus.
29 Abernethy and Kincardine.
30 Laggan.
31 Kingussie and Insh.
32 Alvie.
33 Kilmallie.

CAITHNESS

1 Reay.
2 Thurso.
3 Olrig.
4 Dunnet.
5 Canisbay.
6 Halkirk.
7 Bower.
8 Watten.
9 Wick.
10 Latheron.

PERTH

1 Blair Atholl.
2 Fortingall.
3 Dull.
4 Kenmore.
5 Weem.
6 Little Dunkeld.
7 Dunkeld and Dowally.
8 Logieriat.
9 Moulin.

SUTHERLAND

1 Durness.
2 Tongue.
3 Farr.
4 Eddrachillis.
5 Assynt.
6 Lairg.
7 Rogart.
8 Clyne.
9 Kilonan.
10 Loth.
11 Golspie.
12 Dornoch.
13 Creich.

0   25   50 miles
0   50   100 km

5. Parishes

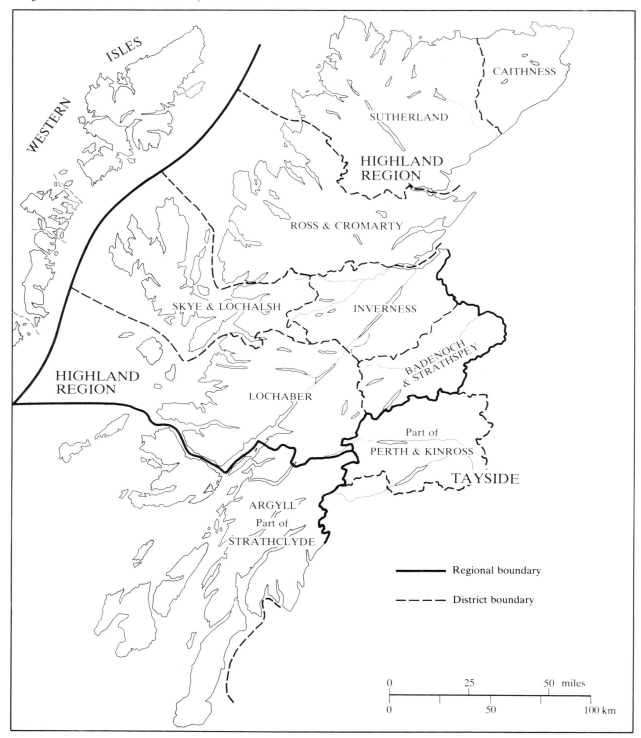

WESTERN ISLES

CAITHNESS

SUTHERLAND

HIGHLAND REGION

ROSS & CROMARTY

SKYE & LOCHALSH

INVERNESS

HIGHLAND REGION

BADENOCH & STRATHSPEY

LOCHABER

Part of PERTH & KINROSS

TAYSIDE

ARGYLL
Part of STRATHCLYDE

—————— Regional boundary

- - - - - - District boundary

| 0 | 25 | 50 miles |
| 0 | 50 | 100 km |

6. *Local government regions and districts*

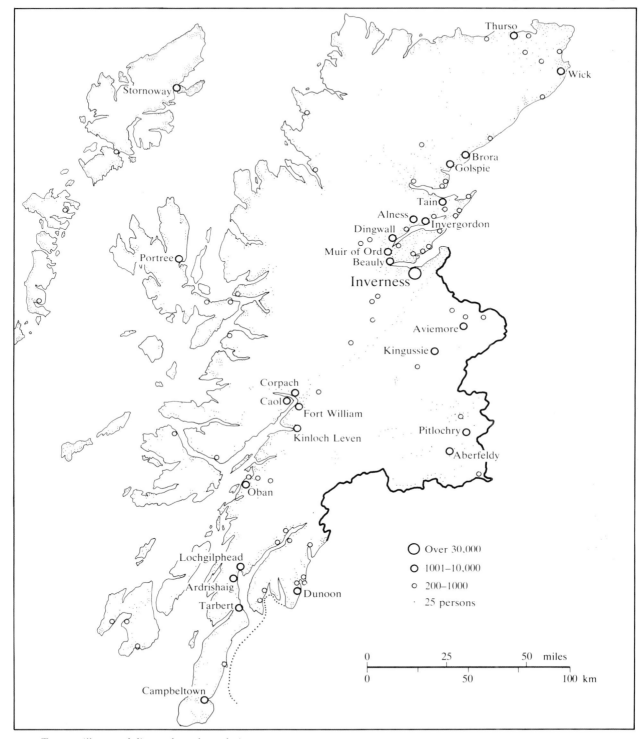

7. Towns, villages and dispersed rural population

there are two series of *General Views of the Agriculture of the Counties of Scotland*, written in the 1790s and the first two decades of the nineteenth century (J. Macdonald 1811). For the many eighteenth and nineteenth century tours *see* **Highlands and Islands: Travellers' accounts of the Highlands.** There are superb coloured plates for the early nineteenth century by William Daniell (Ayton 1814–25) which give an artist's impression of the appearance of the early nineteenth century Highland landscape. Detailed studies of certain estates are published with valuable introductions in the Scottish History Society series, (McArthur, 1936; R. J. Adams 1960; Cregeen 1964; R. J. Adams 1972); there is also one outstanding study of the evolution of a Highland estate (Gaskell 1968). Shorter works record the changing landscape of smaller areas (Gailey 1960; Storrie 1961; Fairhurst 1964; Caird 1979) and there is one substantial work on agricultural techniques, tools and buildings (Fenton 1976). Malcolm Gray's seminal account of the economic history of the Highlands from 1750–1850 (Gray, 1957) provides the essential background to economic change.

LAND OWNERSHIP, LAND USE, AND FISHERIES

If detailed maps of contemporary estate boundaries in the Highlands have become available recently (Millman 1969 and 1970), a national Land Utilisation Survey at a scale of 1 : 63,360 was compiled in the 1930s and 40s (Stamp 1948, 460–463) and commentaries published (F. T. Smith 1939; Vince 1944). The Highland Panel overview and a British Association symposium on land use (Department of Agriculture and Fisheries for Scotland 1964; Stamp 1964) have been updated (Bryden and Houston 1976; Mather 1979). Detailed studies exist only for a few areas (Highlands and Islands Development Board 1970, 1973; Turnock 1977) but more are available on crofting (Collier 1953; Darling 1955; Caird 1958, 1972 and 1979; Moisley 1962(b); Caird and Moisley 1964; Tivy 1966; Coull 1968; Turnock 1970 and 1977). Sources for the evolution of crofting include the Minutes of Evidence of the Napier Commission (Evidence taken . . . . 1884; Storrie 1962; Hunter, 1976; Caird 1979). Data and discussion on Forestry (Forestry Commission, 1919; Mather 1971, 1972), and Marketing (Carlyle 1978) are also available, and on fisheries (Highlands and Islands Development Board 1972; Dunlop 1978). There is also a growing literature on recreational land use (Millman 1971; TRRU 1978; Duffield and Coppock 1979).

ECONOMIC DEVELOPMENT AND TRANSPORT

Broad issues and discussions of general and regional development are available (Highlands and Islands Development Board 1965; O'Dell 1966; Grieve 1972; Caird 1973; Prattis 1978; Turnock 1979). Specialised studies of economic topics include hydro-electricity (Lea 1969) and transport (Vamplew 1970; Turnock 1979; Nutley 1979). Basic to economic development are population trends and, in addition to the decennial Census reports since 1801 (except for 1941) and the additional sample census of 1966, most of the general works included some discussion of population, and there are specialised articles (Moisley 1966(b); Caird, 1973).

AREA STUDIES AT VARIOUS SCALES

Broad regional studies (Mitchell 1962), county accounts (Omand, 1973; McLean 1975) are supplemented by the David and Charles Islands series (McNab 1971; Thompson 1974; Banks 1976). Studies of individual Ordnance Survey sheets (Small and Smith 1971; Cruickshank and Jowett 1972) and parish or small area accounts (Gillies 1936; Tivy 1959) are now being added to by numerous booklets and leaflets on local aspects and matters of interest throughout the Highlands and Islands. *North 7*, published four times a year by the Highlands and Islands Development Board provides articles on contemporary developments, social and economic in the Highlands and Islands. (Publication ceased in 1982.) Finally, the Highlands and Islands Development Board library has a very comprehensive collection of modern literature on the area.   JBC

Highlands and Islands, travellers' accounts Of the travellers' tales of the many invaders and passers-by who in ancient times knew something about the Highlands and Islands, mostly by hearsay, all that survives is a number of cryptic allusions and faint echoes in classical authors, in Irish lore and in Norse sagas. Adamnán tells of Columba and his times. There are glimpses of the 'wild' Scots, speaking Gaelic, in Hume Brown's books, *Early Travellers in in Scotland* and *Scotland Before 1707*. Some early accounts, derived from administrative inquiry, are given in Skene (1886) and Macfarlane (1906).

The first really detailed account of the Western Isles, dating from the late seventeenth century, is that of Martin Martin (D. J. Macleod 1934), who also visited and described St Kilda. At about this time a Welshman from Oxford, Edward Lhuyd (q.v.), pioneered Celtic research in the Highlands (J. L. Campbell and D. S. Thomson 1963). *Letters from a Gentleman in the North of Scotland to His Friend in London*, (*c.*1720–30), believed to be by a Captain Edward Burt (Youngson 1974), must have intrigued Londoners, for at that time (according to Lord Macaulay) the English knew little about the Highlands and the little they knew caused loathing and contempt.

Only after Culloden, when the new military roads facilitated travel, did southerners begin to venture north to see the habitat of so warlike a race, who were now winning fame in the Highland regiments of the British army and who, when Macpherson's 'Ossian' burst upon the European literary scene, pretended to so ancient a culture. First to come were the scientists and antiquarians – Bishop Pococke (between 1747 and 1760), then Thomas Pennant (1769, 1772) and Sir Joseph Banks ('discoverer' of Staffa). In 1773 came the most famous of Highland tourists, Samuel Johnson and James Boswell. Johnson, old and near-blind, was induced to come by his reading of Martin

Martin (q.v.), his interest in second sight and his scepticism about 'Ossian'. Boswell's account, more about Johnson than about the Highlands, is best read in the 1936 edition of the unabridged original manuscript (Pottle and Bennett 1936). Although Johnson thought Gaelic 'the rude speech of a barbarous people', he advocated the publication of the Gaelic New Testament, testified to the high level of learning in Highland manses and of culture in Highland mansions and publicized the economic and social plight of ordinary Highlanders. We are also obliged to him for provoking the Revd Donald Macnicol of Lismore to issue his erudite *Remarks* on Johnson's book. Gaelic bards felt moved to versify, praising Macnicol and censuring Johnson, and the great Englishman passed into Gaelic folklore alongside Ossian.

John Knox (1786) was one of the first to reach the Outer Hebrides and to report on them. Later the Revd John Lane Buchanan, a missionary of the Society in Scotland for Propagating Christian Knowledge with an axe to grind, gave a grim picture of lay and ecclesiastical tyranny (1793).

The old coast road at Latheronwheel, Caithness.

DUNVEGAN CASTLE.

Dunvegan Castle. From Thomas Pennant's *Tour in Scotland*, 1776 edn.

Before the nineteenth century was much advanced the trickle of tourists became an ever-increasing annual invasion, thanks mainly to Sir Walter Scott's *Lady of the Lake* and *Lord of the Isles*, to Thomas Telford's (q.v.) splendid new roads and to the coming of the age of steam, which powered the West Highland steamboats and, later, the railway lines north and west. In the 1880s Oban became the 'Charing Cross of the West'. To St Kilda, Iona and Staffa, as places of interest, were added Glencoe and, on Skye, Loch Coruisk, the Spar Cave and the Quiraing. The visitors came to shoot and fish, to climb and ramble, to sketch and paint, to sail, to inspect old ruins and hear old tales (some invented for their benefit), to observe an unfamiliar way of life, odd superstitions and 'Highland religion', to study the flora and fauna, the rocks, and social and economic conditions, to hear 'plaintive' music and generally to enjoy themselves in this great natural playground of the Highlands and Islands. Many of them wrote accounts of what they saw and heard – some superficially and superciliously, some ignorantly and maliciously, but some with knowledge and understanding. The number of these accounts, in both books and articles, runs into hundreds. Full details can be found in Mitchell (1902) and in Cooper (1979). The twentieth century has brought a further spate of accounts, some reporting on their writers' own lives in the Highlands, their adventures and their ploys, usually enhanced by splendid photographs. Among these twentieth-century writers may be mentioned Miss M. E. M. Donaldson, T. Ratcliffe Barnett, Alasdair Alpin Macgregor, Frank Fraser Darling, Colin Macdonald and Seton Gordon (doyen of them all), while

John Prebble has retold Highland history and Otta F. Swire old legends, both with impressive flair. Not all the travellers' accounts have pleased the Gaels. As Johnson roused Macnicol to protest, so John Mac-Culloch's 'libellous trash' was exposed in James Browne's *Critical Examination* (1825), and A. A. Macgregor's calumnies in his *The Western Isles* (1949) evoked a 'critical analysis' from the Lewis Association.

The following is a select list of the most significant visits up to 1904: Monro's *Western Isles* (1549), Sacheverell's *Voyage to Iona* (1688), Martin's *Western Isles* (1703), Edward Burt's *Letters from the North* (1720–30), Pococke's *Tours* (1747–60), Kenneth Macaulay's *History and Description of St Kilda* (1764), Pennant's *Tours* (1769, 1772), Mrs Grant's *Letters from the Mountains* (1773–1807), Johnson's *Journey* and Boswell's *Tour with Johnson* (1773), Macnicol's *Remarks on Johnson's Journey* (1779), John Lane Buchanan's *Travels in the Hebrides* (1782–90), Faujas de Saint Fond's *Travels in Scotland* (1784), John Knox's *Tour* (1786), John Leyden's *Journal of a Tour in the Highlands and Western Islands of Scotland in 1800* (1903), James Hogg's (1802–3), Necker de Saussure's (1806–8), John MacCulloch's *The Highlands and Western Isles of Scotland* (1811–21), James Wilson's *Voyage Round the Coasts* (1842), Robert Somers, *Letters from the Highlands* (1848), A. Smith's *A Summer in Skye* (1865), Joseph Mitchell's *Reminiscences* (1883–4), A. Goodrich Freer's *Outer Isles* (1902).   TMM

history of Gaelic literature, *see* literary history and criticism.

humour (post-1600) It is likely that certain features of Gaelic society have a strong bearing on the incidence and nature of humour, and especially satire, in the literature. Satire normally flourishes in a sophisticated and settled society and receives a special impetus from a metropolitan milieu. The courts of the chiefs, when they were powerful, provided some of these conditions, and there is some satirical verse associated with these courts (*see* **verse, courtly and satiric (to 1600)**. Probably we can regard eighteenth-century verse satire as having been influenced, to some extent, by extraneous (English) models, though more often what is referred to as satire is better described as flyting (a mode popular in Lowland Scots also). Also, the lengthy hiatus in the history of

prose-writing – from, say, the fifteenth century to the late eighteenth or early nineteenth century, with only occasional exceptions such as the MacMhuirich history – seriously delayed various developments, including humorous and satirical writings, and diverted such literary initiatives into the oral literature. This was especially the case with humorous creation, and there is much in this genre to be found in the folktales, especially the novella-type tales. The late Aonghas Barrach (q.v.) had many good examples of such humorous creation, sometimes tending to ribaldry, in his repertoire. (There was of course much humour, as well as satire, in the medieval and ancient sagas also.) Possibly another consequence of the excessive oralizing of the literary tradition was the status accorded to anecdotage. Anecdotes, funny stories, instances of repartee are deeply entrenched in the social tradition and are more readily acceptable than literary wit, for example. This tradition is very evident in Aonghas Caimbeul's autobiography *A' Suathadh ri iomadh Rubha* (1973) and is reflected in social interchange in the Gaelic area and in the tradition of compèring musical entertainments.

In the field of village poetry (q.v.) a sufficiently close and stable society allows some development of satire, but again humour is more likely to be favoured and developed here. It may sometimes be difficult to decide questions of demarcation between village and other poetry.

The trained (classical) poets used satire, as, for example, Cathal MacMhuirich's satire of a fellow poet An Calbhach or Niall MacMhuirich's of the poet Giolla-easbuig (D. S. Thomson 1977c, 237, 235), and Niall Mòr MacMhuirich has a satire on the bagpipes (D. S. Thomson 1977a, 18ff.), which probably owes a little to earlier harp satires and seems to have started a line of satires on pipes and pipers (ibid., 19–21).

An Clàrsair Dall (q.v.) has a humorous poem 'Fèill nan Crann' (Harp Key Fair), in which he uses sexual *double entendre* (W. Matheson 1970, 12). His younger contemporary Sìleas na Ceapaich (q.v.) composed 'An aghaidh na h-Obair Nodha', a moralistic reply (with some freedom of language) to George Mackenzie's (q.v.) original song in satirical praise of sexual licence (C. Ó Baoill 1972, 166, suggests possible influence from bawdy Restoration verse in English).

A slightly larger body of humorous and satiric verse is to be found in the work of Iain Mac Ailein (q.v.), especially his songs on Fear nan Druimnean. This poet used the form *crosdhanachd*, alternating verse and prose, in one of the Fear nan Druimnean poems and also wrote a humorous prose description to go with his verses 'Fògradh Thuatha De Danann' (The exiling of T. de D.) (*see* A. MacLean Sinclair 1898, 133ff.).

Mac Mhaighstir Alasdair (q.v.) composed a good deal of verse which has a ribald and sometimes a bitter humour and satire which often becomes flyting or outright vituperation. His themes are political, inter-clan (as in 'Aoir nan Caimbeulach') and sexual, as in his writings on an outbreak of sexual disease in Ardnamurchan (for the latter, and similar poems, see J. L. Campbell 1971, 64ff.). Donnchadh Bàn (q.v.) has a satire of John Wilkes which first appeared as a pamphlet in 1768, but this mostly degenerates into unamusing abuse. Rob Donn (q.v.), on the other hand, has a much more delicate and subtle touch and produced what is the only sizeable body of true Gaelic satire (of morals, fashions, individuals both high and low) in the eighteenth century (*see* Grimble 1979 *passim*). Uilleam Ros (q.v.) mingles humour and satire in such poems as 'Oran do Dhuine Araidh' and 'Oran eadar am Bàrd agus Cailleach-mhilleadh-nan-dàn' (Calder 1937, 156, 126).

There is a good deal of rollicking humour in both prose and verse writings from the late nineteenth century and the early years of the twentieth, as in Niall MacLeòid's (q.v.) poems 'Turas Dhòmhnaill do Ghlascho' and 'Oran na Seana-mhaighdinn' (N. MacLeòid latest edn 1975); Iain MacPhaidein (q.v.) celebrating Halloween in Pollokshaws or New Year in the Gallowgate (Glasgow) (MacPhaidein, 1921, 11, 28), or a fracas in the Saltmarket (ibid., 91); Fr Allan MacDonald's fragmentary 'Pàrlamaid nan Cailleach' (J. L. Campbell 1965, 49ff.). Dòmhnall MacEacharna's (q.v.) prose is less boisterous, more gently humorous; Donald Lamont's (q.v.) includes much gentle but effective satire, especially of pretentious leaders of local society in Cille Sgumain (D. Lamont 1960, especially 88ff.); John N. MacLeod (q.v.) uses an authentic local style of humour in his 'Letters from Bernera', printed for many years in the 1920s and 1930s in the *Stornoway Gazette;* Donald Macintyre (q.v.) of Paisley is an effective humorist and satirist in his poetry (*Sporan Dhòmhnaill*).

Gairm has been the vehicle for humour and satire also, as in the stories by members of the Cabairneach school of writers (John Steele, Finlay J. MacDonald), by Donald Morrison (Oban), Norman MacLeod (am Bàrd Bochd) and Tormod Caimbeul (who wrote for a time under the pseudonym 'MacOnghail'). There is

some hilariously funny writing in Iain Mac a' Ghobhainn's short novel *Murchadh* (*Gairm*, 106–9, 1979). But it is true to say that we still lack a truly sustained work in Gaelic either of humour or of satire.   DST

Huntly, 2nd Marquis of (George Gordon) (*c.*1592–1649) Montrose's consistently unsuccessful rival in organizing Royalist resistance to the Convenanters in the 1640s.   DS

hydro-electricity, *see* North of Scotland Hydro-Electric Board.

I

Iain Chaluim Ruaidh, *see* Mac a' Ghobhainn, Iain (late nineteenth century).

Iain Dòmhnallach an Dall, *see* MacDonald, John (*c.*1812–84).

Iain Dubh mac Iain mhic Ailein (John MacDonald), *see* Aos-dàna.

Iain Lom (*c.*1625–post-1707) Belonged to the MacDonalds of Keppoch, descended from the first Lord of the Isles. One of his earliest dated poems is on the Battle of Inverlochy, fought in February 1645; as he was present at the battle and the poem shows highly developed poetic skills, we may assume that he was born some time around 1625. He was still alive in 1707, as an invective against the Union of the Parliaments in that year bears the marks of his authorship. Of his personal life we know little beyond what we can extrapolate from his verse.

Iain Lom was keenly involved in the politics of his time, and his comments on events such as the Montrose wars, the Restoration, the Hanoverian succession and especially the Keppoch murders (see below) and the Massacre of Glencoe are of considerable historical interest. He was a Royalist and a hater of the Protestant Succession, as his song to William and Mary illustrates:

> Even drowning is not the death I would wish you, but thousands looking on as you are torn between horses and tossed up in the air in bits, like coloured ash being riddled.

He strongly objected to the Union of 1707, and its perpetrators suffered his scathing invective.

National politics, however, were for Iain Lom always secondary to the affairs of his own people. Alasdair MacColla (q.v.) is the focus of praise in the Montrose campaigns, and personages (Huntly, for example) are valued according to their allegiance at the time. The Campbells are the constant focus of hatred. The poem on the Battle of Inverlochy illustrates this well:

> Alasdair of the sharp, wounding blades, if you had the heroes of Mull with you, you would have stopped those that got away, the retreating, dulse-eating rabble.

> Damn you, if I am sorry for your plight, as I listen to your children's distress, lamenting the crew left on the battlefield, the howling of the women of Argyll.

Some of his most powerful verse is to be found in poems that constituted a campaign to avenge the murder of the young chief of Keppoch and his brother in 1663. They reveal his gifts of emotional intensity and intellectual power and show his ability to express powerful personal feelings in commanding public language:

> What has cancelled my merriment and makes my eyes unable to hold their tears is that you are placed in the vault while the scum remain in this country immune.

(See A. M. Mackenzie 1964.) DMCA

Iain mac Ailein (John Maclean), *see* Aos-dàna.

Iain Mac Dhòmhnaill 'ic Iain, *see* MacDonald, John (1795–1853).

Iain mac Dhùghaill mhic Lachlainn, *see* MacDonald, John (fl. 1715).

Iain mac Mhurch' 'c Ailein, *see* Morison, John (*c.*1630–1708).

Iain mac Mhurchaidh (John MacRae) (fl. mid-eighteenth century) Emigrated from Kintail to North Carolina in 1774, joined the Royalists in the American War of Independence and was captured in February 1776 at Moore's Creek. (See C. W. Dunn 1959; MacRae 1899.) IG

Iain Óg Ile, *see* Campbell, John Francis.

Iain Phàdraig, *see* Mac a' Ghobhainn, Iain (1848–81).

Iain Sealgair, *see* MacDonald, John (1795–1853).

Indulf King of Scots from 954 until his death at the hands of Scandinavians in 962. It was in his reign that the stronghold of Dun Eideann or Edinburgh, the present capital of Scotland, was captured by the Scots. (See Duncan 1975, 95.) JWMB

institutions and orders, learned and professional Contrary to much late medieval and modern propaganda, emanating from Lowland and English sources, the Gaelic area had its own elaborate civilization, which had an ancient history. It had once extended more widely over Scotland, and the king's court had been Gaelic, but from the twelfth century it gradually contracted, being supplanted (and sometimes resolutely attacked) by French, Scots and English influences. Gradually the Gaelic institutions, or their remnants, come to appear as eccentric and old-fashioned survivals in a general Scottish context, but they may have, even at a late date, a much more central and contemporary character in certain parts of the country, as, for example, the Lordship of the Isles.

Gaelic legal orders and institutions are discussed elsewhere (see **law, Celtic survivals**); next to these in ancient importance, and achieving primacy later, are the orders that are based on the use of the written word, those of historians, genealogists, archivists, propagandists, secretaries, scribes. Many of the personnel in these offices would seem to have been trained in schools run by hereditary bardic families, but the close connections between these learned orders and the Church would have led to mutual exchanges between bardic and Church schools. The power of patronage which rested with landowners, including clan chiefs, led to a further concentration of both lay and ecclesiastical office in the same hands, or at least within a well defined network. There was a tendency to bring into this network other offices and functions – for example, those connected with music, architecture, sculpture and, very important, medicine.

A few examples will help to illustrate the general processes referred to above. *Matadin brithem* (M. the judge) is a witness to a grant of land recorded in the Book of Deer in 1131–2, and a long line of people with Gaelic names who also bear the title *judex* has been distinguished in the twelfth and thirteen centuries (Barrow 1966); the office of breve (*brithem*) survived in Lewis into the seventeenth century. Hereditary medical families have a long history also; for example, the Beatons (q.v.), the MacLachlans (q.v.) and the O'Conachers or MacConachers (the fluctuation in their name indicating a relatively late arrival from Ireland). The MacDuffies or MacPhies of Colonsay are reputed to have kept the records of the Lordship of the Isles and continued to be influential in lay and ecclesiastical matters long after the end of the Lordship. One-time harpers of the name of O'Senog or MacSenach (now MacShannon) have been prominent in Kintyre from at least 1505 to the present day. Families of poets/genealogists/historians have even longer spans (see, for example, **MacMhuirichs**, **MacEwen poets**, **Ó Muirgheasáin family**). There are many hereditary ecclesiastical dynasties – those of the Obrolchans (Ua Brolcháin), MacDuffies, MacEacherns (formerly armourers), Martins or MacMartins, MacArthurs, etc. And we find the MacMhuirichs appearing quite early in ecclesiastical as well as literary office, as also the MacLachlans; while the Dean of Lismore had one foot in the law and another in literature. (See Bannerman 1977a; Bannerman forthcoming; D. S. Thomson 1968.) DST

institutions and orders, legal, *see* law, Celtic survivals.

Inverlochy, Battle of (2 February 1645) A major defeat of the Campbells and their Highland and Covenanter allies by the Irish and Highland forces commanded by Montrose and Alasdair MacColla. (See E. J. Cowan 1977, 181–7; D. Stevenson 1980, 155–8.) DS

Iolaire A naval yacht used to transport returning servicemen to Lewis and Harris after the 1914–18 war. She sank near the mouth of Stornoway harbour on New Year's morning 1919, with the loss of 181 lives. This is the theme of various poems, etc., and an account which incorporates eye-witness reports was published by Tormod Dòmhnallach (1978). DST

Iona Chronicle Compiled on Iona *c*.686–*c*.740. The fullest versions are preserved in the Annals of Ulster and the Annals of Tigernach. An important source for the history of the Scots of Dalriada and their neighbours, particularly the Picts, it also includes a comparatively full record of events associated with the monastery of Iona (Bannerman 1974, 19–26). It is possibly the sole basis of all existing sets of Irish annals which contain contemporary material (Smyth 1972, 1–48). JWMB

Iona Club Founded in Edinburgh in 1833 to 'investigate and illustrate' Highland history, antiquities and early literature and to 'substitute authentic history for too long prevalent fables'. Its first Secretary was Donald Gregory, who was succeeded by W. F. Skene (q.v.). Its transactions, including much valuable material from various sources, were published in *Collectanea de Rebus Albanicis* (1847). TMM

Iona, Statutes of The forfeiture of the Lordship of the Isles in 1493 realigned the political power field within the Highlands. Government attempts to provide basic administration, engineered by such loyal agents as the Campbells and Gordons, were sparse and ineffective. Acts in 1597 instigated a concerted campaign of feudalization, requiring production of deeds, failure in which entailed forfeiture and settlement by Government colonists (Kermack 1957, 79–86). The main opposition stemmed from endeavours to inhibit the Clan Ian Mór, especially post-1603, when this became more readily identifiable with troubles in north-eastern Ireland (Donaldson 1965, 228).

A military expedition to Kintyre in 1605 exacted the chief's promises of loyalty to the Crown, while another in 1608 arranged for all southern chiefs to meet on Mull. Invited to board a ship on the pretext of hearing a sermon, they were transported to imprisonment in Edinburgh. Released in 1609, they subsequently swore to observe nine enactments for amendment, known as the Statutes of Iona (Icolmkil). Each signed a general bond of obedience to the Crown and the Established Church, while the statutes themselves limited the chiefs' retinues, curtailed certain localized problems such as sorning (the forceable exaction of hospitality), heavy drinking and the use of fire arms. The enforcement of Lowland education on heirs of gentlemen possessing sixty cattle and the banishment of vagrant bards practising their incitatory art aimed at further political assimilation (Register of the Privy Council, vol. 9, 26–30).

However, after Government subjugation of the Clan Ian Mór (D. Stevenson 1980, 35–47), the 1609 enactments were more auspiciously reinforced in 1616. Chiefs were, additionally, limited to one galley; they were to live in designated residences and to lease land at fixed rents; and no heirs were to be recognized unless schooled in English (Register of the Privy Council, vol. 10, 773–81). The main significance of these enactments was perhaps that James succeeded, to a degree, in his aim of reducing the military class in the Highlands as outlined in 1609 (I. F. Grant 1959, 209).   FMCD

Irish, divergence from Gaelic, *see* Gaelic: divergence from Irish.

Iseabail Ní Mheic Cailéin (fifteenth century) A poetic member (or members) of the household of the Earl of Argyll (the form indicates a daughter, but one poem is ascribed to 'Contissa Ergadien Issobell'). There are three poems by this poet/these poets in the Book of the Dean of Lismore (q.v.), 'Is mairg dá ngalar an grádh', 'Éistidh a lucht an tighe-se' and the sexually frank 'Atá fleasgach ar mo thí'. (See W. Gillies 1977a; Quiggin 1937, 78; W. J. Watson 1937, 234, 307.)   DST

Islay Charter, *see* documents, Gaelic.

J

Jackson, Kenneth Hurlstone (b. 1909) Londoner. Professor of Celtic at University of Edinburgh, 1950–79. Formerly lecturer at the University of Cambridge and professor at Harvard. Philologist, historian. Author of *Language and History in Early Britain* (1953), *Historical Phonology of Breton* (1967), *The Gaelic Notes in the Book of Deer* (1972), etc., and of books, lectures, arts, reviews on Common Gaelic, Manx, Pictish, sagas, early Nature poetry, Gododdin. Translator of *A Celtic Miscellany* (1951).   DST

Jacobitism Following the flight of James VII and II in 1688 Jacobitism pursued its primary aim of returning the main line of the Stuarts to the united throne on home and international fronts. Foreign aid was essential but, despite the authenticity of the claim, never impressive or extensive.

The first Jacobite rebellion, led by Dundee in 1689, had the purpose of restoring the rightful heir, and since the Glorious Revolution, with its associated Presbyterian and Whig ideologies, had effectively been fashioned in England, there was optimism that Scotland could accomplish this with Irish aid (Petrie 1959, 100–33). Although the small Jacobite army defeated the Williamites at Killiecrankie by means of intelligent tactical judgement, the absence of major nobles is an indication of prevailing political opinion with respect to James. Highland support for this and other rebellions is explained partly by traditional clanship esteem for the hereditary claimant; hence Dundee's death, eliminating the charismatic leadership necessary to maintain factional Highland unity at the heart of this rebellion, hindered the cause (Lenman 1980, 28–50).

The next two decades, however, with their intermittent famine, extended wars and deteriorating Anglo-Scottish relations, particularly post-Union, sufficiently fuelled social discontent to formulate Jacobitism into a recognizable political alternative, although its religious affiliation to episcopacy worked largely as a deterrent in urban areas. Conversely, this contributed to the appeal of Jacobitism in the Highlands and the north-east, though Jacobitism can never be equated simplistically with episcopacy. France always showed sufficient interest in Jacobitism to create confusion, as exemplified by the abortive '08, which heralded the introduction of the more severe English treason law.

But it was largely the abolition of the Privy Council, the only effective executive in Scotland, and the ensuing conflict between the introduction of the patronage-dependent English JP system and the existing heritable jurisdictions (resulting in increased brigand activity and a general arms augmentation) that encouraged further rebellion (Mitchison 1970, 26).

The '15, led by Mar, the major Jacobite spokesman, began at Braemar, under the pretext of a deer hunt. The manipulability of such clan musterings and their relative inaccessibility, which enabled unhindered mobilization, always favoured Highland beginnings. It was followed by a rising in Northumberland, ending in defeat at Preston, while a 5,000-strong Scottish force fought the inconclusive battle of Sheriffmuir. But a highly optimistic situation, encompassing Highland, north-eastern and English support and fired by strong social discontent, was thwarted by general incompetence (Lenman 1980, 126–54). Reprisals were leniently extended (Mitchison 1970, 30–2), and little was done to advance Government control in the Highlands. The independent companies were disbanded in 1717, encouraging outlaws; the 1716 Disarming Act was heeded basically by Whig clans; while plans for four permanent garrisons were achieved only with financial obstructions.

After the Spanish-backed fiasco of 1719 (Dickson 1895, Intro.), Jacobitism declined for a while. By 1724, however, renewed Jacobite intrigue, coupled with urban economic unrest, led to the formation of six independent Highland companies, a new Disarming Act, the implementation of Wade's programme of road building and Rob Roy's informer network. In 1739 the Scottish Jacobite Association was formed, reopening negotiations with France, whence a major expedition left in 1744 but was dispersed by storms (Blaikie 1916, xxv–xlviii). But it was largely government complacency of the 1730s, which saw the drafting of the independent companies into a regiment, the commercialist policies of the clan Campbell, which placed finance before political loyalty, and marked government unpopularity that brought about the phenomenon of the '45.

The Young Pretender did little more than march, unopposed, from Glenfinnan to Edinburgh, gathering forces. Each side had only 2,500 men at Prestonpans, but Cope's disorganized band panicked. Disillusioned by lack of interest after reaching Derby, the Jacobites retreated, winning a fortunate victory at Falkirk and eventually occupying Inverness. The stronger Hanoverian army triumphed at Culloden, and the succeeding punitive measures soon extinguished the Jacobite cause (Lenman 1980, 231–82). Besides Cumberland's well-known atrocities there were mass transportations and about 120 executions. The '45 failed to attract much influential support, though some Highland chiefs attempted to safeguard all

Lord George Murray. The Young Pretender's lieutenant-general and the ablest general in his army. By an unknown artist.

eventualities by sending out younger sons with the Jacobites; the economic programme for those estates which failed to escape forfeiture through legal concurrence did little to improve the Highland situation. A further Disarming Act of 1746 and the banning of Highland dress were relatively ineffective, while the abolition of the heritable jurisdictions affected only those few with regalian courts. The abolition of archaic military tenures further served to underline the precipitated tendency to estate commercialism.

What remains at the end of the day is the irony of the final devastation of traditional clanship, a core which since 1707 had increasingly marched under the banner of a poetic Jacobite nationalism for pretenders whose main aspiration was ever the throne of England. (See Baynes 1970; Bell 1916; Blaikie 1916; John Cameron 1949; J. L. Campbell 1933; Cregeen 1970; Cunningham 1932; Ferguson 1968, 1977; Imrie 1969; Insh 1952; G. H. Jones 1954; Lenman 1977; Mason 1947; A. H. Millar 1909; Paton

1895–6; Prebble 1961; Seton and Arnot 1928; Smout 1963; A. N. and H. Tayler 1936, 1938, 1980; Tomasson 1958; Whiteford 1966–8; Youngson 1973.)

FMCD

John I, Lord of the Isles (d. 1387) John became chief of the Clan Donald in 1325 and Lord of the Isles by 1335. Until his death some fifty years later he pursued a consistent policy of consolidation which ensured that the Lordship of the Isles would remain with the Clan Donald to the exclusion of all other descendants of Somerled. He married Amy Mac-Ruairi in 1337 and acquired the territories of the Clan Ruairi on the death of her brother Ranald in 1346. In 1350 he had his marriage to Amy annulled and took as his second wife Margaret, daughter of Robert Stewart, Regent of Scotland and heir presumptive. The latter's accession to the kingship of the ʻScots in 1371 doubtless explains the decision, taken before John died and in accordance with the system of tanistry (q.v.), that Donald, eldest son of Margaret, should succeed to the Lordship of the Isles rather than Reginald, eponym of the Clan Ranald, or Gofraid, John's sons by Amy MacRuairi. (See Steer and Bannerman 1977, 203–5.)

JWMB

John II, Lord of the Isles (d. 1503) John succeeded to the Lordship of the Isles and the earldom of Ross in 1449. In 1462 he entered into the Treaty of Westminster-Ardtornish with the exiled Earl of Douglas and Edward IV of England. This resulted in his eventual forfeiture by Parliament in 1475, and although it was rescinded in the following year, Kintyre, Knapdale and the earldom of Ross were not restored. Dissatisfaction with John's conduct of affairs led to the naval battle of Bloody Bay, fought in the Sound of Mull (c.1481) by John, supported by the vassal clans of the Lordship, against his son, Angus Óg, and the Clan Donald. Thereafter Angus Óg played a major part in the affairs of the Lordship until his murder in 1490. John was again forfeited by Parliament in 1493 and deposed as *Rí Innse Gall* (King of the Foreigners' Isles) in 1494. He died in 1503, a pensioner of the Crown. (See Steer and Bannerman 1977, 207.)

JWMB

Johnston, Annie (1886–1963) Born on Barra. Known, with her brother Calum Johnston (q.v.), as Clann Aonghais Chaluim. Had an extensive knowledge of Barra oral tradition, including many fine songs learned from her mother, Catriana MacNeil.

Taught in Castlebay school. An important informant of Mrs Marjory Kennedy-Fraser (q.v.), the Folklore Institute of Scotland and the School of Scottish Studies, University of Edinburgh (q.v.). (See *Tocher*, 13, 1971.)

JLC

Johnston, Calum (1891–1972) Born on Barra. Brother of Annie Johnston (q.v.). Spent many years in Edinburgh, where he was Secretary of the Highland Pipers' Society. Like his sister, an important source of information about Barra oral tradition for Mrs Marjory Kennedy-Fraser (q.v.), the Folklore Institute of Scotland and the School of Scottish Studies, University of Edinburgh. He died on 4 December 1972, after piping the remains of Sir Compton MacKenzie to his grave at Eoligary.

JLC

Johnston, Duncan (b. 1881) From Islay. Attendant in Natural Philosophy Department, University of Glasgow. Author of *Crònan nan Tonn* (1938), including 'Sìne Bhàn', 'Birlinn Ghoraidh Chròbhain', etc.

DST

Johnstone, William (b. 1897–), *see* art, Gaelic, in modern times.

Johnstone's Highlanders, *see* regiments, Highland.

Keith's Highlanders, *see* regiments, Highland.

Kells, Book of, *see* manuscripts, illuminated.

kelp-making The burning of seaweed until it is reduced to an alkaline essence. At the beginning of the nineteenth century kelp-making became a main source of income for the populations of many parts of the Hebrides; in mainland districts it remained a minor activity. The steep rise in the price of the

Kelp-burners on Orkney at the turn of the century.

product after 1790 put great profits into the hands of the landlords, who both owned the raw material on the kelp shores and had almost complete control over their tenantry. Landlords marshalled their small-holding tenants during the summer and paid relatively low rates for each ton produced in order to reserve for themselves a large margin of profit. Holdings were subdivided as landlords sought to increase the available labour force, and tenants had to use much of their income to meet the food bill and the increased rent. Prices collapsed in 1814, and profits declined, but some production was sustained till the 1830s, when a further price fall virtually destroyed the industry (Gray 1951, 197–209; Youngson 1973, 134–9; Hunter 1976, 12–24, 32–48). In more recent times a small industry has grown up, producing sodium alginate by drying of seaweed (Darling 1955, 345–6.)   MG

Kennedy, Archibald, *see* Cassillis, Earl of.

Kennedy, Mrs Archie (b. 1904–) From Inverness County, Nova Scotia. Gaelic-language teacher and folklore informant.   JS

Kennedy, Duncan (fl. 1780) Schoolmaster in Kilmelford, Argyll. Made collections of Ossianic poems in Argyll and Lochaber, 1774–83 (*Report*, 273) and of hymns, published in 1786.   DST

Kennedy, James (fl. 1890) Schoolmaster of Logierait and author of *Folklore and Reminiscences of Strathtay and Grandtully* (1927), which quotes many Gaelic names and sayings.   DST

Kennedy-Fraser, Marjory (1857–1930) Born in Perth. One of large musical family. Used to accompany her father on his singing tours and was first attracted to the study of Gaelic music in 1882. She had Gaelic lessons from the poet Mary Mackellar. In 1908 she met Kenneth MacLeod, who collaborated with her in compiling her collection *Songs of the Hebrides* (1909); her aim was to try 'to blend traditional melody with appropriate harmonic setting'. (See Kennedy-Fraser 1929.)   CG

Marjory Kennedy-Fraser. Painted by John Duncan (q.v.). Scottish National Portrait Gallery.   ►

John Duncan

Kenneth mac Alpin (d. 858) Kenneth of the Cenél nGabráin became king of Dalriada (q.v.) *c.*841. Having brought the neighbouring Picts under his sway *c.*843, he died in 858 as king of Alba, or Scotia, the southern boundary of which was the Forth–Clyde line. To take account of his vastly increased territories, he moved his political centre eastward to Scone, and in 849 the administrative centre of the Church followed suit when some of Colum Cille's (q.v.) relics were transferred from Iona to Dunkeld. Kenneth's achievement finally ensured that the Scots would shape and give their name to the country that we now know as Scotland. (See Bannerman 1971, 76–84.)   JWMB

Keppoch murders, *see* Iain Lom.

kilt A foreign word, apparently introduced in the eighteenth century, derived from 'quilt', a padded material. The padding in this case consists of the folds in the cloth, in the form of pleating. The Gaelic term is *féileadh*. The Celtic peoples of Ireland seem to have adopted their male fashion of dress, a skirt worn to the knee, from the Romans, by whom they had not been conquered. The *tunica* evolved into a long linen shirt called a *léine*. Over this might be worn a *brat*, or mantle. The earliest Gaelic description of Scots wearing such a costume occurs in Lughaidh O'Cleirigh's Life of Aodh Ruadh Ó Domhnaill (Irish Text Society, vol. 42, pt. 1, 73), describing Hebrideans in 1594: 'Their exterior dress was mottled cloaks of many colours with a fringe to their shins and calves; their belts were over their loins outside their cloaks.' Although he used *brat* in the term *breacbhrait ioldathacha*, O'Cleirigh was contrasting a costume that differed by this time from the dress of the Irish and appears to have been describing the *féileadh mór*. Unlike the *brat*, this was not tailored but consisted of a single piece of cloth about 5 feet wide and up to 18 feet in length. The wearer folded it into pleats on the ground before belting it round his waist. Its ends crossed one another over his stomach and hung as an apron that did not reach to his knees. The remainder of the material would certainly have reached his shins unless it was gathered in folds to his shoulders and secured there by a pin. In the rain he could pull it over his head. At night he might sleep in it, soaked in water to provide greater warmth. Bishop Lesley described it in Latin as a mantle, long and flowing, gathered into folds (*De origine, moribus et rebus gestis Scotorum*, Rome 1578).

Charles Campbell of Lochlane (d. 1751). By an unknown artist. Scottish National Portrait Gallery. The painting shows the 'little kilt', separate from the plaid over the shoulder and extending from waist to knee.

An illustration of ways in which it was worn long after the *léine* had gone out of fashion in Scotland was published in Edward Burt's *Letters from a Gentleman in the North of Scotland* (1725–6). Six engravings made in 1743 of soldiers of the Black Watch by Van der Gucht show in more explicit detail how this dress was adopted by the army (see *McClintock* and *Dunbar*). The proscription of Highland dress in 1747–82 resulted in its continuing use exclusively as a military costume during that period (Prebble, 1975). The evolution of the *féileadh beag* had taken place before then, in circumstances that have aroused controversy. It was found convenient to separate the *féileadh mór* into two garments, enabling the part worn between waist and knee to retain its folds permanently by stitching. This became known as *féileadh beag* in Gaelic and as the 'kilt' in English. The remainder of the material could be worn as a plaid in various ways and discarded when it was wet without undressing entirely. (See Dunbar 1962; McClintock 1950.)   IG

king-lists, Pictish These lists of Pictish kings fall into two groups of manuscripts (none of which is earlier than the fourteenth century), conventionally designated P and Q. It is possible to reconstruct P and Q with fair certainty; each was a list of names, usually with a patronymic and a reign length. P has a mythical section of early kings; P and Q then share some thirty kings (third to sixth centuries), who may be partly historical. From Brudei mac Maelchon (c.550) to c.730 the lists agree on names but not on reign lengths; the Irish Annals seem to confirm the names and agree somewhat with P's reign lengths. After 730 the lists diverge, both as to names and to reign lengths; the annals have almost no Pictish content. It seems possible that lost Pictish annals were the source for the lists from c.550 to at least 730 and also of the annals now included in the Irish Annals. The lists therefore give an impression of Pictish unity which may be wholly misleading. (See M. O. Anderson 1973; M. Miller 1979a.)　　AAMD

Kirk, Revd Robert (1644–92) From Aberfoyle. Minister of Balquhidder and Aberfoyle. Published the first complete edition of the Gaelic Metrical Psalms (1684) and saw through press the Irish Bible in roman type (1690). Author of Gaelic vocabulary, printed in 1702, and of *The Secret Commonwealth of Elves, Faunes and Fairies* (1691). (See J. L. Campbell 1938; D. Maclean 1927.)　　DST

Kirkwood, Revd James (1650–1709) Born Dunbar. An influential figure in the controversies surrounding the position of Gaelic in Church and education in the late seventeenth and early eighteenth centuries, Kirkwood had been introduced to Gaelic probably during his chaplaincy to the Earl of Breadalbane. He helped to distribute the Irish Old Testament to Highland parishes in 1688, was involved in the printing and distribution of Bedell's Bible in roman type (1690) and later urged the importance of Gaelic literacy on the founders of the Society for the Propagation of Christian Knowledge (Durkacz 1978, 28–39). Kirkwood also had copied for him the 'Collection of Highland Rites and Customes' compiled by Edward Lhuyd c.1699 (J. L. Campbell 1975).　　DST

Knoydart, Men of The group of seven men who staged the last 'land raid', in 1948, on the farms of Scottas and Kilchoan, by Inverie, Knoydart, on the estates of Lord Brocket; the outcome was unsuccessful. (See Starmore 1980.)　　DST

L

Lachann nam Mogan, *see* Maclean, Lachlan.

Lachlann Mór MacLean (d. 1598) A notable political and military leader – he had taken over direction of the MacLeans of Duart by 1576 – and a man of culture; we possess a Gaelic letter written by him in the current literary dialect and script (Bannerman and Black 1978, 56–65). He was a supporter of the Campbells of Argyll and of James VI. Latterly in close touch with the English authorities in Ireland, he was probably responsible for blowing up a Spanish galleon in Tobermory Bay in 1588. He certainly employed Spanish soldiers from it as mercenaries in the continuing feud between his kindred and the Clan Donald of Islay, which led to his death there in 1598 at the Battle of Tràigh Ghruineart (Sinclair 1899, 108–58).　　JWMB

Lachlann mac Theàrlaich Oig (Lachlan MacKinnon) (c.1665–1734) Skye poet. Author of 'Latha siubhal slèibhe', in praise of famous chiefs, some village verse and a lament for MacLeod of Talisker. (See D. Lamont 1913; J. Mackenzie 1877; A. and D. Stewart 1804.)　　DST

Ladies' Highland Association Established in Edinburgh in 1850 'for the religious improvement of the remote Highlands and Islands'. For just over a century – it was disbanded in 1966 – it was connected successively with the Free Church, from 1900 with the United Free Church and, from 1929, with the Church of Scotland. It supported some 160 schools, helped to provide nursing services and employed women (latterly deaconesses) for youth work. The Association also operated children's libraries and distribution schemes for literature, clothing and comforts. (See J. T. S. Watson and Murchison 1954.)　　TMM

Laing, Uisdean (d. c.1977) Born on South Uist. Inspector of Schools in Australia. Author of a collection of poems entitled *Gu Tìr mo Luaidh* (1964), among other works.　　DST

Lamont, Donald (1874–1958) Native of Tiree. Minister at Glenurquhart, 1902–8 and at Blair Atholl, 1908–46. Arguably the greatest Gaelic prose writer of all time. He edited the Gaelic supplement of the Church of Scotland monthly magazine *Life and Work*, 1907–51, and it was in this that the majority of his articles, over 2 million words in all, originally appeared. He wrote in a flowing, natural, idiomatic style. He created an imaginary parish called Cille-Sgumain and described, in a humorous and entertaining way, the life of its inhabitants. Published in Gaelic supplement articles on world affairs, nature, Highland Church life, sermons and book reviews. Selected prose in Murchison (1960). RMCL

Land Agitation, *see* politics, Highland (nineteenth century.)

Land League movement Decades of inequity and deprivation reduced the mass of Highland people, in about 1850, to apparent apathy and despair. Religion was their only solace. But from 1870 onwards there was an upsurge of widespread concern for 'land and language', basic rights and the redress of grievances. There were land raids, rent strikes, confrontations with law officers, police and military, petitions, propaganda tours, rallies and conferences. Societies were established, notably the Highland Land Law Reform Association (1882), which became (1886) the Highland Land League, and in 1885–6 'crofter representatives' were elected to Parliament. The Napier Commission (q.v.) and resulting Crofters Act (1886) were epoch-making. (See Blackie 1885; James Cameron 1912; Crowley 1956; Grigor 1979; Hunter 1976; D. MacCallum 1909; A. Mackenzie 1883a; S. Maclean 1962; Joseph Macleod 1917; I. M. M. MacPhail 1976a, 1977, 1979b; Meek 1977a,b; J. Smith 1973.) TMM

Land Troubles, *see* politics, Highland (nineteenth century).

landholding, pre-feudal, *see* feudal system and its antecedents.

Landseer, Edwin (1802–73) Popular painter of Highland scenes and animals from the 1820s onwards. His *Monarch of the Glen* dates from 1851. DST

Edwin Landseer 'Rent Day in the Wilderness', 1868. National Gallery of Scotland. Painted in commemoration of Donald Murchison, who after the Jacobite defeat of 1715 defended the confiscated Ross-shire estates of the attainted Earl of Seaforth, regularly transmitting rent to the exiled earl and forcibly resisting government attempts to regain control of the Seaforth estates. Landseer shows him calmly conducting business affairs with tenants, the Seaforth rent book open in front of him, while beside and behind him Highlanders watch the approach of Redcoats disembarking from a boat in the background.

Latin inscriptions, early Christian, *see* Ogam stones.

Law, Celtic survivals Unlike Ireland, where Celtic law and Anglo-Norman law were sharply opposed to each other, Scotland witnessed no outright rejection of Celtic law and custom. Instead Celtic law was gradually absorbed into the main body of Scots law, merging with later influences such as Anglo-Norman, Canon and Roman law. Documentation in the early medieval period is disappointingly sparse, but Celtic law survivals can be traced for many centuries, sometimes in unexpected places.

The most obvious survivals were at institutional level. The Crown itself remained (and remains) in the line of Kenneth mac Alpín (q.v.) and Malcolm III (Cennmor) (q.v.). Alexander III was inaugurated in Celtic fashion in 1249, his *sloinneadh* (pedigree) recited by a *seanchaidh* (oral historian). The successor of the *seanchaidh*, Lyon King of Arms, retained a prominent place in the later Scottish coronation service. The title of *mormaor* gave way to that of earl, but to this day one Scottish earldom can be traced back to a Celtic *mormaor*. The *maor* too had a long history, surviving, for example, in medieval sheriff-doms as hereditary mair-of-fee, while the Captain of Dunstaffnage still glories in the title of *marnichty*. The *tòiseach*, in some cases, became a thane – the thane of Cawdor retains the title – and later a feudal baron. The mysterious *toiseachdeora* was often equated with the coroner (Dickinson 1941, 85). Custodians of sacred relics continued to function: an inquest of 1428 sets out the duties and privileges of the keeper of the *coigreach* (crozier, staff) of St Fillan. (Some keepers have their relics still.) The *breitheamh* (brieve, brehon), in his Latin guise of *iudex*, is mentioned in the legislation of William the Lion, and appears in the witness list of early charters (Barrow 1966, 16). Later the office merged with that of doom-ster, the speaker of the sentence or doom of the court. The doomster survived in the High Court of Justiciary until the eighteenth century, by then doubling as executioner (Dickinson 1928, lxvi). Even in the twentieth century a tenuous link with the past remained when the judge pronouncing sentence of death in Scotland concluded with the words, 'which is pronounced for doom'.

Traces of Celtic law can also be seen in the procedure of the Courts of Regality that were such a distinctive feature of the Scottish legal scene until their abolition in 1747. The privilege of 'repledging' or reclaiming a man from the Sheriff Court or the Justiciar's Court to the Court of the Regality in return for a pledge that justice would be done was a much cherished and frequently exercised right (Dickinson 1928, 344). The technical term for the caution lodged was Gaelic – *culrath* (literally, 'back surety'). The element *rath* also appears in the term *fuilrath*, given as the equivalent of 'bloodwite'.

Other technical terms too have had a long history. The ancient exaction of *càin* (tax) survived into modern times in the guise of 'cane-fowl', 'kain-wedder' and the like. Various medieval compilations of Scots law contain Celtic terms. Thus the *Leges inter Brettos et Scotos*, perhaps originally compiled in the eleventh century but included in later legal manuscripts, contain the Gaelic terms *cro* and *enach* as well as the Cumbric *galnes* and *kelchyn*, all terms relevant to notions of honour, compensation and the blood feud (K. H. Jackson 1955a, 88; D. S. Thomson 1968, 57).

Scotland indeed remained for long a kin-based society and this is reflected in the law. In Bruce's time the royal chancery had a set style for recognizing the head of a kindred in Galloway. Later whole clans were prosecuted by name. The Abbot of Dunfermline had the right to repledge 'men of the progeny of Makcaroun', while the privilege of the 'law of Clan Macduff' was claimed in Fife as late as the sixteenth century. Bonds of manrent and maintenance, involving heads of kindreds and not infrequently seeking to resolve a blood feud, were common in the later Middle Ages. Actions for assythment, with their attendant 'letters of slains' granted by the kin of the victim, were regularly pursued and were only finally abolished by statute in 1976, after a belated attempt at revival.

Vestiges of Celtic law, then, survived for many centuries in the mainstream of Scots law. In the Highlands and Islands, however, particularly in areas under the influence of the Lordship of the Isles, Celtic law survived – or was revived – in more pristine form. The Lords of the Isles continued to be inaugurated in the ancient manner, with Macvurich reciting the roll of their ancestors. The hereditary learned classes, poets, doctors, musicians and lawmen, continued to flourish, holding their lands in return for professional services rendered (D. S. Thomson 1968). In 1485 *Hullialmus Archiiudex* witnesses an island charter. A seventeenth-century account states:

There was a judge in every Isle for the discussion of all controversies, who had lands from
Macdonald for their trouble, and likewise the
eleventh part of every action decided. But there
might be still an appeal to the Council of the
Isles. (J. R. N. Macphail 1914, 24)

The best-known of these island judges are the Morrison brieves in Lewis. Dean Monro wrote in 1549 of
the Council of the Isles:

Thir fourteen persons sat down into the
Counsell-Isle, & decernit, decreitit & gave suits
furth upon all debaitable matters according to
the Laws made be Renald McSomharkle callit in
his time King of the Occident Iles. . . . In their
time thair was great peace & welth in the Iles
throw the ministration of justice. (R. W. Munro
1961, 57)

Of the 'Laws of Renald McSomharkle' (Ranald,
son of Somerled) not a trace has survived. There are
indications, however, that Celtic secular marriage
continued in the Isles until the seventeenth century
and that the law of succession was influenced by
tanistry (q.v.). Fosterage remained a popular institution, and a Gaelic contract of fosterage, dated 1614,
for Norman Macleod, son of Ruari Mór (q.v.), still
exists. Other surviving legal documents in Gaelic are
a Macdougall lease, *c.*1600, and a charter of land in
Islay granted in 1408 by Donald, Lord of the Isles
(see **documents, Gaelic**). (See John Cameron 1937;
K. H. Jackson 1972.)   WDHS

legends, historical Among Gaelic folktales the clan
legends occupy a unique place: there is nothing quite
like them this side of Africa, even in Ireland, because
the clan society which produced them was unique in
modern Europe. There are other historical legends –
tales of saints or Vikings from longer ago (the latter
mostly fictions accounting for place names), post-
Macphersonian romantic inventions about princesses
of Lochlann and, from the last century or two, tales
such as may be found almost anywhere of shipwrecks
and plagues, robbers and murderers, strong men and
holy men. The later tales are most often exaggerated
truth ('memorate') but may include migratory motifs,
most noticeably in stories about illicit liquor saved
from the excisemen, which may be the same in Uist,
Islay or Orkney; but similar parallels within and
outside the Gaelic area can be found even in traditions of the Clearances.

Clan legends, however, are largely about events of
the sixteenth and early seventeenth centuries, when

there was little to restrict the fierce feuding between
and within clans. The larger-scale campaigning of the
Lords of the Isles, the Jacobites or even Montrose
were remembered only when they impinged violently
on the storyteller's own district. Clan legends are the
product of a heroic age (Chadwick and Chadwick
1932, 10–18), and local hero figures generally play a
central role: not only chiefs themselves but also their
gifted followers, physicians such as the Beatons (q.v.),
pipers such as the MacCrimmons (q.v.), prophets,
enchanters – who might be poets like the MacMhuirichs (q.v.), heirs of the druid order, or even chiefs
themselves like Domhnall Duaibheal – unerring
archers and mighty swordsmen. A sometimes tenuous
basis of historical fact is assimilated to known patterns of heroic legend, borrowing details from native
Gaelic hero tales, international folktale and supernatural legend. Witches delay a hero's birth or sink
his ship; seers and fairy lovers warn or advise him.
Episodes such as the hero's death following inevitably
from the breaking of one *geis* (taboo) after another, or
his posthumous birth and return from exile to avenge
his father and claim his heritage, appear in the
legends of the death of Lachlann Mór MacLean
(q.v.), and the return of Murchadh Geàrr of Lochbuie (MacCoinnich 1923, 92–102) little changed since
their use in Old Irish saga. If, as often happens, the
same event is celebrated by a song or pipe tune, it
amounts to an impressive body of tradition.

Not all clan tales are eulogistic: sensational events
– treacherous murders, fearful punishments, churches burned with their congregations inside – which
reflect no credit at all on the chiefs responsible, also
play their part and may well have been emphasized
more in the post-Clearance Highlands. But even
nineteenth-century landowners could be credited in
their own locality with fantastic feats – like the
Captain Campbell who founded Portnahaven in Islay
and is said there to have stolen the Golden Calf from
a Chinese temple (during the Opium Wars?) while
his piper distracted the priests by playing outside in
full Highland dress.   AB

legends, supernatural Gaelic tradition is rich in
legends, especially legends of the supernatural. *Sagen*,
or local legends, have been defined as stories believed
by their tellers to be true (at least until recent times)
and generally linked with persons or places from the
storyteller's own locality. A further distinction may
be made between 'memorates', 'true' experiences of
the narrator or of a named person from a recent

generation, with no discernible strong narrative pattern (most tales of second sight, for instance, are memorates), and migratory legends, pre-existing stories which can be recognized as attached to different names in different places. It is possible to generalize about the latter only as tale types. Migratory motifs play an important part in historical legends (q.v.), and migratory legends are used to account for the origin of a local place name or natural feature – though such legends were seldom entirely believed. Some recurrent types of tale are told about second sight or ghosts (for example, a man who misuses a gravestone is haunted by its owner every night until he replaces it). The largest classes, however, are those concerning witches and other human beings with extraordinary powers (enchanters, physicians, prophets, saints), and fairies and other supernatural beings such as the *each uisge* (water horse), the *glaistig* (supernatural female) and *ùruisg* (water-brownie) and such spirits of the wild, or tutelary beings. Some migratory types are known to exist in other countries – tales of the Black Book and Black School, the witch selling fair winds, the midwife at a fairy confinement, the fairy complaining about a drain or tether pin through the roof of his house, even the changeling surprised into speaking by the pretence of brewing in an eggshell. Others – the piper who vanishes in a fairy cave, the man carried off by a magic cap when he imitates witches crying (in English) 'Off to London!' – are shared with, and in the second case evidently borrowed from, Lowland Scots or English tradition. Purely Gaelic legends are difficult to pinpoint unless they involve beings unknown elsewhere, such as the *each uisge* who becomes a young man to seduce girls or the prophetic *bean-nighe*, but the sheer wealth and variety of supernatural legend types known in Gaelic can hardly be equalled in neighbouring countries, even Ireland. AB

'Leigheas Coise Céin' (The Healing of Cian's Leg) Early romance and derived folktale, famous for length of its 'in-tale', told by mysterious visitor to Cian, who tried to ravish his host's fairy wife and got his leg broken. Folk versions are more complete than surviving manuscripts, but one (G. Henderson 1903, 175) was deliberately lengthened by the addition of other hero tales (Bruford 1969, 134–6, 240; Craig 1950). AB

lenition, *see* Gaelic: mutations.

A group of the Lewis chessmen.

Lewis chessmen Set made of walrus ivory, discovered in Uig, Lewis, in 1831 and now in the British Museum and the National Museum of Antiquities, Edinburgh. DST

Lhuyd, Edward (1660–1709) Born near Oswestry. Entered Jesus College Oxford, 1682. Assistant Keeper, Ashmolean Museum, 1683; Keeper, 1691. Made grand tour of Celtic countries 1697–1701, backed by subscribers, in search of archaeological, botanical, historical and linguistic material, in the course of which he visited Kintyre, Knapdale, Lorne, Mull and Iona, making the first sketches known of ancient monuments in the area and recording information relating to its botany and Gaelic dialects. In Ireland in early 1700 he met the Revd John Beaton (q.v.), last learned member of the famous Mull medical family, the contents of whose manuscript library he recorded. Lhuyd collected many Gaelic manuscripts in Ireland and the Scottish Highlands, which are now in the Library of Trinity College, Dublin. Published *Archaeologia Britannica* in 1707. Gaelic studies are deeply indebted to the pioneer

Sketches from Edward Lhuyd's Archaeologia Britannica, *1707. British Library, Stowe MS 1024.*

efforts of this famous Welsh polymath. (See Bruford 1965; J. L. Campbell 1975; J. L. Campbell and D. S. Thomson 1963; W. R. MacKay 1980; Ó Concheannáin 1975.)   JLC

Linguistic Survey of Scotland The Gaelic survey was initiated under the late Professor M. Dillon of the University of Edinburgh during the session 1949–50. Professor K. Jackson of the University of Edinburgh took over in 1950 and began collecting material, with the help of a questionnaire, to elicit phonological and morphological data (K. H. Jackson 1958a). Conversation and stories were also recorded.

By 1958 areas other than the Outer Hebrides had been covered, and by 1963 192 points had been researched (Oftedal 1968). The Survey had a series of assistants, one at a time, over the years.

In 1960 Professor Magne Oftedal (Oslo) was appointed co-editor of publications, the intention being to prepare the corpus for publication in dialect atlas form, Professor Jackson undertaking to write a history of the dialects. Oftedal resigned in 1968 owing to pressure of work, and he was succeeded by Mr Máirtín Ó Murchú, who in turn resigned in 1970. Mr D. Clement then took over and began a programme of fresh field collection, finding many hitherto undiscovered informants in areas where the language was either dead or dying. Much new material has been collected, both in phonetic transcription and on tape, and this has amplified many areas that were formerly sketchily covered.

Analysis of the material in the archives has begun, but its nature is such that it will be some time yet before an atlas can be published. It is also intended to publish studies of individual dialects, and the Survey has both given advice about suitable regions and informants and put its equipment at the disposal of scholars (J. Watson 1974, 9; Dorian 1978, xix).

Professor Jackson retired from the Chair of Celtic at Edinburgh in 1979. His contribution to the work of the Survey has been enormous. Professor W. Gillies succeeded him in the Survey as well as in the Chair.   JWG

Lismore, Dean of, *see* MacGregor, James (*c.* 1480–1551).

literary history and criticism There are jottings on literary history in the manuscript collections of James McLagan and Donald MacNicol (second half of the eighteenth century), and the Ossianic controversy continued to stimulate such interest well into the nineteenth century. Dr Donald Smith contributed a short account of some literary manuscripts in the possession of the Highland Society of Scotland, in their *Report* of 1805, App. XIX. The *Report* is also the location of Lachlan MacVuirich's 'declaration' regarding the MacMhuirich bardic family (App. XVII), the 'testimony' of Hugh McDonald of Killephedar (App. II) and the 'declaration' of Ewan MacPherson (App. VI, no. 2), all set down in 1800. The Revd Alexander Irvine's *Prospectus of a work to be intitled The Lives of the Caledonian Bards* (1801) was all that appeared in print. Early in the nineteenth century Ewen MacLachlan wrote his *Analysis* of fourteen manuscripts held by the Highland Society (Nat. Lib. 72.3.4); this deals with eighteenth century as well as older manuscripts. John Reid's *Bibliotheca Scoto-Celtica* (1832) includes biographical as well as bibliographical information about Gaelic authors and also ventures critical judgements; Reid draws on tradition and on published accounts, using, for example, the *Scots Magazine* obituary notice on Donnchadh Bàn (q.v.) (October 1812; Reid, pp. 91–3).

Lectures 3 and 4 in Thomas McLauchlan's *Celtic Gleanings* (1857) deal with Gaelic literature, though they scarcely ever get to grips with any author's work. Donald Campbell's *Treatise on the Language, Poetry, and Music of the Highland Clans* (1862) is the earliest published book which has an extensive section (pp. 53–146) devoted to Gaelic poetry, though he reaches page 123 before extricating himself from druids and Ossianica; the section on music, however (pp. 147–279), is largely concerned with seventeenth- and eighteenth-century poetry.

Thereafter there is a series of literary histories, many of them drawing partly on the introduction to individual poets in John Mackenzie's *Sàr Obair nam Bard Gaelach* (1841), introductions which combine some literary history with background information, traditions and many round phrases of praise. Thomas Pattison, *The Gaelic Bards* (1866, 1890), gives extensive translation and brief critical comments; the most detailed treatment is of Alasdair Mac Mhaighstir Alasdair (q.v.) and Donnchadh Bàn. John Stuart Blackie's *The Language and Literature of the Scottish Highlands* (1876) is a very summary history of the literature, intended to introduce non-Gaels to the subject; it contains little criticism. Nigel MacNeill's *The Literature of the Highlanders* (1892; 1929, with an additional chapter by John MacMaster Campbell), attempts to delineate a wider background, with chapters on Patrick, Brigit, Columba, Latin hymns of the Celtic Church, etc. In the chapter on ancient ballads MacNeill distinguishes clearly between genuine and spurious. The chapters on Gaelic literature of the seventeenth to nineteenth centuries have long and short notes on many poets. Translations are quoted throughout, but there is more exposition than translation. Keith Norman Macdonald's *Macdonald Bards from Mediaeval Times* (1900, 1929), gives short accounts of over sixty bards, providing principally biographical and background information; it shows some reliance on Maclean Sinclair's editions. Magnus Maclean's *The Literature of the Celts* (1903, 1926) is

devoted mainly to Old Gaelic (Irish and Scottish) literature, with some reference to Welsh, but is discursive and underinformed (Maclean says, for example, that only two of Niall MacMhuirich's poems are extant). The same author's *The Literature of the Highlands* (1904) is inadequate on early poetry, whether classical or folk. It highlights the work of Mac Mhaighstir Alasdair (this being perhaps the best chapter) and of Donnchadh Bàn. Donald Maclean's *The Literature of the Scottish Gael* (1912) had previously appeared as three articles in the *Celtic Review*. His treatment is very compressed, with much bibliographical information and little critical comment, but it makes a sound, brief introduction. D. J. MacLeod compared the poetry of Mac Mhaighstir Alasdair and Donnchadh Bàn in an essay in *An Solaraiche* (1918). Aodh de Blácam has a short chapter on Scottish Gaelic literature in his *Gaelic Literature Surveyed* (1929, etc.).

Literary criticism in the modern sense appears in occasional papers and reviews in *Transactions of the Gaelic Society of Inverness*, *Scottish Gaelic Studies*, *Gairm*, *Lines* and anthologies such as those of *Akros*, no. 31 (1970) and *Poetry Australia*, no. 63 (1977) and in chapters on literature by D. S. Thomson in I. Grimble and D. S. Thomson, *The Future of the Highlands* (1968) and in J. E. C. Williams, *Literature in Celtic Countries* (1971), and by John Macinnes in *Scottish Literature in the Secondary School* (1976). D. S. Thomson's *An Introduction to Gaelic Poetry* (1974) is the most comprehensive treatment in print so far; the same author's *The New Verse in Scottish Gaelic: A Structural Analysis* (1974) is concerned with mid-twentieth-century verse. Donald MacAulay provides a valuable introduction to this same body of verse in *Nua-bhàrdachd Ghàidhlig* (1976). DST

Livingstone, Duncan, *see* MacDhun-léibhe, Donnchadh.

Livingstone, William, *see* MacDhun-léibhe, Uilleam.

loanwords, British and Pictish Words not explicable from Gaelic, which are either wholly absent in Irish or were first borrowed there from Wales and subsequently brought to Dalriada and were not therefore adopted in Scotland directly from the Britons or Picts. The category also excludes words existing in Gaelic in place names only (see **Pictish languages**). Various examples have been suggested, such as *bad* (cluster), but there are only four which seem certain. *Dail* (field, meadow), probably earlier *dol*, *doil*, must be Welsh or Pictish *dol* (meadow). *Monadh* (mountain, moor) is early Welsh or Pictish *monid* (mountain). This occurs in many place names also: hence Mounth (the Grampians), extended in poetry to mean all northern Scotland, and *Rí Monaid* (King of Monad), synonymous early with *Rí Alban* and used of, for example, Malcolm II in the Duan Albanach, late eleventh century. It was borrowed at least as early as 728, when the Irish Annals record the Battle of Monad Craoibh (Moncreiffe). *Pòr* (grain, crops) is from Pictish *por*, cognate with Welsh *pawr* (pasture) and occurs in the name Púréne, a diminutive, in the mid-twelfth-century Book of Deer (q.v.). *Preas* (bush, thicket) is Pictish *pres* or Welsh *pres*, *prys* (brushwood). (See K. H. Jackson 1955, 149; 1972, 44, 72; W. J. Watson 1926, 376, 391, 414, 419.)

KHJ

loanwords, English and Scots English loanwords in Scottish Gaelic may come from several sources: they may be genuinely English (as *staidhir*), or of French or other Romance origin, or of Latin origin, directly or through French; it is not easy without detailed information about dates and early forms, such as the *Historical Dictionary of Scottish Gaelic* (q.v.) will eventually provide, to determine the most probable source. Risk (1974) has studied the French loanwords in Irish, most of which are Norman French in character. These may reasonably be supposed to have circulated throughout the Gaelic world, and indeed a good many of them are found also in Manx, but in Scotland one of their principal characteristics, the presence of long and perhaps stressed vowels in syllables other than initial ones, disappears. As the words are generally also found in English and are for the most part of classical or medieval Latin origin, these alternative sources are often equally possible, and authorities therefore disagree. 'English' is taken here to include the Romance element without limiting it strictly to words introduced directly from English. Borrowing from English includes borrowing from Scots, as shown by the form, meaning, or pronunciation of the word, as *trang* (busy), *polas* (police).

A second problem at all periods is the question of when a loanword becomes fully naturalized. Useful indications are the thorough Gaelicization of the spelling (minor modifications or none probably point in the opposite direction – for example, Calvin's Catechism has *argument*, *definition*, *experiens*, *per-*

suasion, *providens*, *reverens*, *symbol*); any modification of the nature and order of the sounds by dissimilation, assimilation or transposition; and full incorporation into the inflectional and derivational systems.

Borrowing takes place chiefly when new things and ideas are introduced and bring with them the names used by the introducers, less frequently when some gap is perceived in the vocabulary of the borrowing language. (The overwhelming number of English loanwords in Scottish Gaelic are nouns; verbs and adjectives fall very far behind.)

A little over a hundred of Risk's Anglo-Norman loans also occur in Scotland: among those with original long vowels in non-initial syllables are (with *á*) *ofrail* (Carswell, Calvin's Catechism); *sòlas* (Cars.), *tu(bh)ailt*, (*é*) *buideal*, *dìnnear*, *painntear* (snare), *peileir* (bullet), *seipeal*, *similear* (chimney), *spideal*, *stuidear*, *suipear* (Cars., CC), *tàillear*, (*i*) *martair*, *seirbhis* (CC), (*ú*) *fortan*, *galan*, *miosar*, *prìosan* (Cars.), *sgriobtuir* (Cars., CC), *siosar*, *statuid* (Cars., CC), later *statuin* (Metr. Pss.), *uinnean*. The transposition of [tš, dž] into *st* is found in *broiste* (brooch), *bunndaist* (profit), *cuiste* (couch), *lòisdean* (lodging), *pàisde* (child) (against Manx *paitchey*), *parraist* (parish); later loans imitate the English sound, *puidse* (pouch), *coitse* (chariot) (Metr. Pss.) against Irish *cóiste*. In the following the treatment of the final syllable as *-all*, *-ar*, against Irish *-la*, *-ra*, suggests borrowing from English, not French: *bucall*, *càball*, *cupall*, *sampull*, *seòmar*, *siùcar*, *stàball*. *Paidhir* also suggests an English origin against Irish *péire* from French.

Many, however, lack any particular marks: *àirneis* (equipment), *amhantuir* (CC) later *amhartan*, *bàilidh*, *bangaid* (feast), *barantas* (protection) (Cars), *bàrd* (ward), *batail(t)*, *béist* (worm) (cf. *piasd*, Cars., and *biast*, CC), *cailis* (cup), *caiptein*, *cairt* (perhaps Scots against Irish *cárta*), *caisteal*, *clòca*, *coileir*, *còrd*, *còta*, *cùirt*, *cunntas* (account) (Cars., CC), *cùrsa* (course) (CC), *dìg* (ditch), *diùc*, *dusan*, *fabhd* (fault, or Scots), *feusd*, *fòirneis*, *giùisdis* (a justice) (Cars.), *gùn*, *liuetenanda* (deputy) (Cars.), *lìobhair(t)* (deliver), *màille* (mail, armour), *màla* (bag), *marasgal* (marshal), *meirneal* (merlin, hawk), *oighre* (heir), *òsd* (host, hospitality), *plùr* (flour), *pòca* (pocket), *sabhs*, *searbhont* (Cars., CC), *spéis* (regard) (CC), *spìd* (spite) (Metr. Pss.), *spoll* (joint of meat), *spòrs* (sport) (Metr. Pss.), *stàt(a)* (state, dignity) (Cars.), *stòr*, *-as* (wealth), *taiplis* (board game), *trùp*, *tùr*.

Others found in Carswell are *aibél* (able), *blaisbhéime* (blasphemy), *builpíd* (pulpit), *coinsias* (conscience), *cosdus* (cost), *fallsa*, *fàbhor*, *minisdir*, *pátrún*, *puindsiun* (poison), *résún*, *sdoc*, *sbeclair* (mirror), *tálenta*, *teagsa*, *uindemint* (ointment), *úsuruidhe* (usurer). Calvin's Catechism has a rather long list of apparently unassimilated loanwords, but among those better established are *biotaile* (victuals), *compánach*, *dúpalta*, *geata*, *guibhearnoir*, *priondsa*, while the Shorter Catechism exhibits few of either: *catachiosma* (beside native *foirceadul*), *créd* (creed), *cumhnant* (covenant), *eifeachdach* (effectual) and *translaision*.

For the present day a recent issue of the magazine *Gairm* contained some 120 loanwords, some early but many belonging to the present century, and these illustrate the areas in which borrowing has been found necessary. In connection with food and drink we find *lof, tioclaid, trèiceil, branndaidh, dram, làgair, tea; bracaist, dinnear; and tombaca*. In contrast to the simplicity of buildings native to the Gàidhealtachd, there are *clòsaid, lobaidh, garaids, gaileiridh, musaem, staidhir, stioball* and, among furnishings, *cleoc, fòn, dasc, sòfa, stòbh, porsalain*. It is only chance that this number did not include such familiar items as *citsean, cucair*. To clothing and fashion belong *aparan, ceap, cleòca, cufaichean* (a widespread plural type in loanwords), *dreasachan, gabardain, lìnigeadh* (lining), *neapaigear, poilieastair, pàtaran, paidhir, seacaid*, and, of course, *fasan* itself and *stoidhle*. Other amenities and forms of entertainment are *dràma, dibhearsain, magasain, nobhail, prógram, pàrtaidh, rèidio, telebhisean, teip*.

Outside the home new occupations are *clàrc, doctair, draibhear, gàidsear* (excise man), *peantair* and *strainnsear*. Novel forms of transport are *bus, càr, làraidh, tractair, tram, trèan*, with its associated *stèisean, ticeid;* among vessels only *tugaichean* are mentioned here but *stiomair* is common elsewhere. Unfamiliar containers include *baga, bocsa, botal, canastair, ceus, dradhair, pacaid, tanca, tumblair*, and the tools *gunna, peansail, ràsar, ròpaichean* and *spaid*. From commerce and industry come *banca, cidhe, cunntar, companaidh, docaichean, gas* (but native *dealan* for electricity), *oifis, pàidheadh, peinsean, punnd* and *seic*. Government and administration appear in *coimisean, coimitidh, poileasaidh, seisean* (a much older word in a kirk context). Educational terms are *atlas, clas, map, matamataic* and *teicneolachd* (technology, a hybrid).

All the above are nouns. Only four verbs occurred, all with the same suffix – *dèiligeadh, planaigeadh, smocaigeadh* and *trèinigeadh* – and only eight adjectives, all with Gaelic suffixes – *clèireachail* (secretarial), *cul-*

turach, eaconamach, fàbharach, fortanach, primideach, sòisealta and *teicneolach*.

In addition to the visible and essentially superficial borrowing of words, there is a less obvious and more insidious borrowing of idiomatic phrases, such as 'look after', and the conversion of partial into total synonyms, such as *banca na h-aibhne*, which indicates a deeper penetration of one language by another. (See MacBain 1896; M. MacLennan 1925; Risk 1974.)

RLT

loanwords, Gaelic, in English The earliest Gaelic loanwords in English are found in Northumbria in the tenth century and probably originate in the mission of men such as Aedán (q.v.), who moved from Iona to Lindisfarne to evangelize the Northumbrians in the seventh century (Bede, *Ecclesiastical History*, III, 3). The loans include *brat* (mantle), *cursung* (punishment, with English suffix), *gabolrind* (pair of compasses), *mind* (diadem) and, more widely known in Old English, *clugge* (bell), *dry* (magician), *cine* (quire, collation of a manuscript) and perhaps *stær* (history).

The next stratum of loanwords and those immediately following are found in Lowland Scots documentary sources having reference to Gaelic institutions, law and topography. Such are *Culdee* (1144), *cain* and *cuneveth* (c.1190, the latter also known as *coynye* or *coigny*, 1449, in an Irish context, two legal terms for dues payable by tenants, perhaps *caple* (c.1290) for some kind of horse, but the relationships of this word are complicated, and three other law terms all c.1300, *cro* (composition for manslaughter), *sorn* (free quartering, or payment in lieu), a synonym of *cuneveth* above, and *toscal* ([reward for] giving information [leading to the recovery of stolen cattle]).

In the fourteenth and fifteenth centuries the largest single group is topographical: *loch* and *mull* (1375), *clachan* and *inch* (c.1425), *glen* (1489). From a more warlike context come *cateran* (c.1371, from a Latinized form of the word) but also vernacular *ketherin, kernaugh* (Gaelic *ceithearn, -ach*), also acquired in the Irish form *kern, clan* and *spreath* (cattle-raid, c.1425), and its object *mart* (beef, 1307). *Beltane* (1424), *bard* (1449, originally applied to a lowly kind of entertainer), *airt* (1470), *tocher* (dowry, 1496), *coronach* (lament) and *messan* (lap-dog, 1500) might loosely be described as cultural.

The sixteenth century continues the geographical series with *bog* (1505), *cairn* (1535), *strath* (1540), and *kyle* (1549, singular from the supposed plural *kyles* = Gaelic *caolas*) and also provides three animal names, *capercailzie* (1536), *garron* (1540) and *ptarmigan* (1599), with its pseudo-learned spelling. The remainder fall into no obvious categories: *pillion* (1503), *ingle* (fire as in *ingleneuk*, 1508), perhaps *plaid* (1512), *caber* and *slogan* (battle-cry, in the more nearly correct form *slogorn*, 1513), *sonsy* (1533, but the simplex *sonse*, 1300, and the antonym *donsy*, 1717, help to show how far the date of record may be from the real date of first currency), *gob* (1550), *dunniwassal* (1565), *usquebaugh* (1583, also from Ireland and in a great variety of spellings) and finally *Gaelic* itself (1596), the language being usually called Irish in English and Erse or *Ersche* in Scots. The oldest spelling is *Gathelik*, which, despite the late date of record, is shown by the *-th-* to have been borrowed at a period when Gaelic *-dh-* and *-th-* (cf. *ketherin* above) were still pronounced as dental spirants, that is, not later than the thirteenth century.

The seventeenth century has only a small and late harvest, perhaps reflecting a decline in Scots literature and the fact that it was still too early for any English interest in the Highlands: *caird* (tinker, 1663), *quaich* (1673), *gillie* (1681), *dulse* (an edible seaweed, 1684). The eighteenth century is a little richer: *whisky* (1715) is a second borrowing of the first element in *usquebaugh*, *pibroch* (1719), *filibeg* (1746) (in the Disclothing Acts), *kelpie* (1747), *claymore* (1772), *spleuchan* (1785), *ben* (1788), *corrie* (1795) and *cran* (1797). The nineteenth century supplies few more: *caschrom* (1806), *sporran* (1818; though it is difficult to believe this must not have been known earlier), *gralloch* (1882) and *mod* (1893).

Some of the novels of Sir Walter Scott helped to give currency to some Gaelic words for the first time in an English context and to revive or reinforce others: such are *bodach* and *cailleach*, *brochan* (1700), *brogues* (1586, with reference to Ireland then), *creach*, *deoch an doruis*, *dorlach* (quiver, 1574 baggage, 1660) *galloglass* (1703, but *c.*1515 from Ireland), *kyloes*, *Sassenach* (1771), *sprechery* (apparently a crossing of *spreath* above and *creach*, with English suffix), *taish* (1775, Gaelic *taibhse*), *tinchel* (a ring of beaters, 1549) 1549) *trews* (1568). A very few proper names of Gaelic origin have become common nouns: *strathspey* (1653), *cairngorm* (1794), *mackintosh* (1836), *glengarry* (1858).

It is noticeable that almost all the Gaelic loanwords entering English during the past few centuries remain firmly associated with the land of their origin, its terrain and the life of its people. Official record or literary art has introduced those mentioned here; the extent of penetration into Scots at the popular level remains to be explored. (See Serjeantson 1935.) RLT

loanwords, Latin These are, in the main, a legacy of the influence of British Latin on the early Christianization of Ireland, and they became embedded in the language during its Primitive Irish and Archaic Irish stages. The patterns of phonological adaptation which the borrowed words underwent have led to the conclusion that there were two distinct groups of early borrowings, now customarily labelled as the Cothriche and Pádraig groups, from the different forms which Latin *Patricius* assumes in Irish. This was first demonstrated by Sarauw (1900, 3–20), and his arguments were further developed and modified by E. MacNeill (1931) and K. H. Jackson (1953, 122–48). T. F. O'Rahilly (1942) proposed a chronology which would place both groups of borrowings in the fifth century, so as to fit in with his theory of two Patricks, but his arguments have not found acceptance. Jackson would assign the earlier Cothriche group, distinguished by such features as the substitution of *c* for *p* and the survival of some final syllables, to the mid-fifth century and the later Pádraig group to the sixth century. D. A. Binchy (1958) attempted to modify Jackson's presentation somewhat by insisting that many of the Pádraig words came into Irish through British and not directly from British Latin. Most of the borrowings carry the impress of the striking changes, such as lenition (q.v.), loss of final syllables and syncope (q.v.), which took place in Irish between the mid-fifth and mid-sixth centuries. The pattern of adaptation of individual sounds and morphological features, as evidenced in Old Irish sources, has been set out in some detail by Thurneysen (1946, 565–76). The Latin loanwords constitute the earliest substantial body of borrowings assimilated by Irish in historical times, and they have been subject to all the changes which have led to the emergence of the modern Goidelic languages.

In the Scottish Gaelic context MacBain (1896) lists some 250 words which he derives from Latin. Their ecclesiastical provenance is clearly reflected in their semantic concentration. There are biblical words such as *abstol* (L. *apostolus*), *aingeal* (L. *angelus*), *àirc* (L. *arca*), *altar* (L. *altāre*), *aoine* (L. *jejūnium*), *baist* (L. *babtizo*), *beannachd* (L. *benedictio*), *Càisg* (L. *pascha*), *ciombal* (L. *cymbalum*), *deamhan* (L. *daemon*), diabhal (L. *diabolus*), *eaglais* (L. *ecclēsia*), *easbaig* (L. *episcopus*), *iodhal* (L. *īdōlum*), *mallachd* (L. *maledictio*), *òraid* (L. *orātio*), *Sàbaid* (L. *sabbatum*), *spiorad* (L. *spiritus*), *teampall* (L. *templum*). There are words from the overlapping field of Church organization and liturgy: *aifreann* (L. *offerendum*), *bachall* (L. *baculum*) *Bìoball* (L. *biblia*), *cailis* (L. *calix*), *cailleach* (L. *pallium*), *cathair* (L. *cathēdra*), *creud* (L. *crēdo*), *mainisdir* (L. *monastērium*), *manach* (L. *monachus*), *nollaig* (L. *natalicia*), *purgadoir* (L. *purgatōrium*), *réilig* (L. *reliquiae*), *searmon* (L. *sermōnem*). The role of the Church in establishing literacy and book learning in Ireland is reflected in such words as *aibidil* (L. *abecedārium*), *caibideal* (L. *capitulum*), *leabhar* (L. *liber*), *leugh* (L. *lego*), *litir* (L. *lītera*), *peann* (L. *penna*), *sgoil* (L. *schola*), *sgrìobh* (L. *scrībo*), *ùghdair* (L. *auctor*). There are also words indicating the broader cultural influence of the Roman world: *airgead* (L. *argentum*), *càis* (L. *caseus*), *caisteal* (L. *castellum*), *Callainn* (L. *calendae*), *fìon* (L. *vīnum*), *iarmailt* (L. *firmamentum*), *innleachd* (L. *intellectus*), *mùr* (L. *mūrus*), *òr* (L. *aurum*), *sòrn* (L. *furnus*), *sùist* (L. *fustis*), *uair* (L. *hōra*).

A scatter of late, bookish borrowings appears in some late medieval and early modern works. Some examples from Gaelic medical writing are *buglosa* (L. *buglossa*), *maratrum* (L. *marathrum*), *scruball* (L. *scrupulus*), (H. C. Gillies 1911). Religious works, such as Carswell's translation of the Book of Common Order (R. L. Thomson 1970) and the Gaelic version of Calvin's Catechism (R. L. Thomson 1962) contain some examples like *ceremonia* (L. *ceremōnia*) and *diosmasaid* (L. *dispensātio*). KDMCD

loanwords, Norse Norse loanwords that are not names but appellative nouns, verbs, etc., are found in all Scottish Gaelic dialects but are less numerous than is usually assumed. (There are far more Latin and English loans in Scottish Gaelic than Norse ones.)

The following list (in which ON stands for Old Norse and ON nouns are cited in the accusative case rather than in the nominative), includes some of the commoner ones: *acair* (anchor), ON *akkeri*; *arsbag*, *farspach* (great black-backed gull), ON *suartbak*; *bac* ([sand]bank), ON *bakka*; *bacbòrd* (windward side [of vessel]), ON *bakborða*; *bìdeadh* (to bite), ON *bíta*; *bodha* (underwater rock), ON *boða*; *bogha* (bow), ON *boga*; *brùc*, *brùchd* (seaware cast ashore), ON *brúk*; *cleit* (rocky eminence), ON *klett*; *clobha* (tongs), ON *klofa*; *cnap* (lump), ON *knapp*; *cnébilt* (garter), ON

knébelti; *crùbadh* (to crouch), ON *kr(j)úpa* (to crawl); *dorgh* (fishing-line), ON *dorg*; *fadhail* (ford), ON *uaðil*; *gàrradh* (stone wall or fence), ON *garð*; *geàrraidh* (enclosure), ON *gerði*; *lagh* (law), ON *lǫg*; *langa* (ling), ON *langa* (nominative); *lobht* (loft), ON *lopt*; *lunn* (launching roller), ON *hlunn*; *mol* (beach), ON *mǫl*; *nàbaidh* (neighbour), ON *nábúa*; *rannsachadh* (to ransack), ON *rannsaka*; *rùghan* ([small] peat-stack), ON *hrúgu, hrúfu*; *saoidhean* (coalfish, saithe), ON *seið*; *sgarbh* (cormorant), ON *skarf*; *sgeir* (skerry), ON *sker*; *sgiobadh* (crew), ON *skipan*; *sìoman* (rope), ON *síma*; *sreang* (string), ON *streng*; *stiùir* (rudder), ON *stýri*; *stiùradh* (to steer), ON *stýra*; *tàbh* (hand-net), ON *háf* (landing-net); *taomadh* (to pour), ON *tóma* (to empty, later also to pour); *tòb* (bay, cove), ON *hóp*; *tobhta* (house site), ON *topt*; *tobhta* (oarsman's bench), ON *poptu*; *toirbhsgear* (peat-iron), ON *torfskera*; *trosg* (cod), ON *þorsk*.

Norse personal names are not numerous in the Gàidhealtachd. Among the names on the following list, some are used only as elements of clan or family names (the ON forms are still cited in the accusative): *Amhlaibh*, ON *Áleif, Ólaf*; *Asgall*, ON *Ásketil, Áskel*; *Goiridh*, *Goraidh* ON *Goð(f)røð*; *Ìomhar*, ON *Inguar, Íuar*; *Leòd*, ON *Liót*; *Mànus*, ON *Magnús*; *Raonailt*, ON *Ragnhildi*; *Raonull*, ON *Rǫgnuald*; *Ruairidh*, ON *Hrórek, Hróðrik*; *Somhairle*, ON *Sumarliða*; *Suain*, ON *Suein*; *Torcull*, ON *Þorketil, Þorkel*; *Tormod*, ON *Þormund*. MO

loanwords, Pictish, *see* loanwords, British and Pictish.

loanwords, Scots, *see* loanwords, English and Scots.

Loch, James (1780–1855) Commissioner of the Sutherland estates who master-minded the Clearances (q.v.) and published *An Account of the Improvements* on the Estates of the Marquess of Stafford (1820) and *A Memoir of George Granville, late Duke of Sutherland* (1834). (See Richards 1973.) IG

London, *see* Gaelic Society of London; Highland Society of London; London, Scots and Gaels in.

Lochaber bards, lesser-known Bards from the Lochaber and Laggan areas are discussed in McKellar (1886), in D. C. MacPherson (1868) and in Toal (1983). DST

London, Scots and Gaels in Scotland Yard recalls the Scottish Embassy that long stood in Whitehall. The Crown Court Church descends from the Embassy church. After 1603 the Scots community in London increased greatly. From 1613 a group of Scots, caring for their needy fellow countrymen, began to collect donations in their 'Scots Box', a brassbound chest that has survived to this day. In 1665 the still active Royal Scottish Corporation was incorporated as a 'charity to help needy Scots in London'. In 1690 Robert Kirk found in London a 'club of Scottish Presbyterian schoolmasters' that met regularly, spoke in Latin and cared for Scots incomers. In the eighteenth century Highlanders flooded into London and among them emerged first the Gaelic and Highland Societies and later Comunn nam Fior-Ghaidheal (the Club of True Highlanders), the Sons of Morven and several societies that still exist. Throughout the nineteenth century Gaelic services were held regularly in the Cross Street Gaelic Chapel, the Caledonian Church, the Regent Square Church and the Crown Court Church. In the last-named quarterly Gaelic services, arranged by a non-denominational committee, have continued since 1903, and Free Church and Free Presbyterian Churches also hold Gaelic services. (See K. M. Black 1906; G. C. Cameron 1979.) TMM

Lordship of the Isles Although the Lordship of the Isles is often taken to have emerged during the years around 1354, when John Macdonald of Islay assumed the style *Dominus Insularum*, its origins are to be looked for much earlier. The style *Dominus Insularum* reflects the Gaelic title *Rí Innse Gall* (King of the Foreigners' Isles), which had been in use since the tenth century.

After the centre of Gaelic power in Scotland moved from Dalriada to Pictland in the ninth century a new political entity took shape in the west, extending from the Butt of Lewis to the Calf of Man, and at first more Scandinavian than Gaelic in inspiration. By the end of the tenth century contemporary annals attest to the existence of a dynasty of Scandinavian sea kings. One of them, Godfrey (or Godred), son of Harald, is styled *Rí Innse Gall* in his *obit* of AD 989. Administrative arrangements for the island kingdom, traces of which still survive in the Manx Tynwald and House of Keys, may date from this period.

In the following century various rulers – the kings of Scotland and Norway, the earls of Orkney, the kings of Dublin and some Irish dynasts – vied for power in the Isles. About 1079 a second and more enduring Scandinavian dynasty was founded by Godfrey Crovan. Shortly after his death, the kings of Scotland and Norway agreed on their respective spheres of influence: the Isles were ceded to Norway and the mainland to Scotland. The rule of Godfrey's successors was challenged in the twelfth century by Somerled (q.v.), lord of Argyll, who had married Godfrey's granddaughter and who may himself have had an ancestral claim to the Isles. After a naval battle *c.*1156, Somerled forced a division of the Isles, taking rule in the southern Hebrides, including Islay and Mull. In 1164 Somerled *Rí Innse Gall* was killed when invading Scotland with an army drawn from Argyll, the Isles and Dublin.

For a hundred years authority in the Isles remained divided: Godfrey's line continued until 1265; from Somerled's son Dugald descended the Macdougall lords of Argyll and from his son, Ranald, the Macdonalds and the Macruaris. The island rulers were increasingly torn in their allegiance between the competing claims of Scotland and Norway. In 1249 the king of Scots died during an expedition against Ewen of Argyll. In 1263 the king of Norway died after the unsuccessful campaign of Largs. Finally, in 1266, Norway ceded sovereignty over the Hebrides to Scotland by the Treaty of Perth. Thereafter the island princes owed undivided though uneasy homage to the king of Scots.

During the Wars of Independence the Isle of Man was irretrievably lost to Scotland and detached from the rest of the islands. The Macdougalls opposed Robert Bruce and lost most of their possessions. Angus Óg Macdonald of Isla (q.v.), by contrast, benefited from his consistent support for Bruce. When Edward Bruce was killed in Ireland in 1318 those who fell with him included a Macdonald *Rí Airir Goidel* (Argyll) and a Macruari *Rí Innse Gall*.

By playing off Edward Balliol against David II, and by marrying first a Macruari heiress and second a daughter of Robert Stewart (later Robert II), John of Islay, son of Angus Óg, was able to establish himself in a position of greater dominance in the Hebrides than any of his ancestors had enjoyed for two hundred years. From 1354 onwards he used the style *Dominus Insularum*. When he died he controlled the entire Hebrides from Islay to Lewis, with the exception of Skye, as well as the mainland areas of Kintyre and Knapdale, Glencoe, Lochaber, Morvern, Ardnamurchan, Moydart, Knoydart, Arisaig and

Morar. The Irish Annals record his death as *Rí Innse Gall* in 1387.

Under John and his successors the Lordship became the focal point of Gaelic culture in Scotland, maintaining close links with Gaelic Ireland, renascent after the Bruce wars. Macdonald patronage of the arts is reflected alike in the poems in the Book of the Dean of Lismore (q.v.) and in the distinctive style of west Highland monumental sculpture (q.v.). Neither was the Church neglected. Responsibility for justice and administration lay with the Council of the Isles, which included Macdonald's chief kinsmen and vassals and had its headquarters at Loch Finlaggan on Islay. As ever, the power of the Lordship was based on control of the sea, a fact to which the sea gate at Dunvegan and the position of the castles of Dunchonnel and Cairnburg bear witness.

John's successors were drawn more and more into conflict with the Crown. At Harlaw in 1411 Donald of Islay fought to uphold his wife's claim to the earldom of Ross, including Skye. Although this claim was eventually conceded, and Donald's son Alexander was recognized as earl of Ross, it was a pyrrhic victory. The vassals of the earldom were restive; Macdonald power was over-extended; and the seeds of a bitter feud had been sown with the Crown. Alexander's son, John, aspired to be a sovereign prince. He assumed semi-regal powers, and by the Treaty of Westminster–Ardtornish, entered into in 1462 with Edward IV of England, he plotted the dismemberment of the kingdom of Scotland. In the event John destroyed the Lordship and fragmented his kindred. He was forfeited in 1475, restored in 1476 with the parliamentary title of Lord of the Isles but shorn of Ross, Kintyre and Knapdale. Later he was defeated by his son, Angus Óg, in civil conflict at Bloody Bay, off Mull. He was forfeited again in 1493 and died in 1503, a pensioner of the Crown, his son Angus already dead, his grandson Donald Dubh in prison.

Just as 1354 does not mark the beginning of the Lordship, neither does the forfeiture of John (II) mark its end. In 1499 John's cousin, John Mór Macdonald of Dunyveg, *Rí Innse Gall*, was hanged with his son John Cathanach and two grandsons on one gallows on the Boroughmuir of Edinburgh. In the sixteenth century various members of the Macdonald kindred sought to revive the Lordship – Donald Dubh, Donald Gallda of Lochalsh, Alexander of Dunyveg and Donald Gorm of Sleat. Donald Dubh's second attempt in 1544–5 might indeed have succeeded but for his sudden death in Ireland. He had no clear successor. As late as the Montrose wars the idea of the Lordship inspired the politics of the Earl of Antrim and Alasdair MacColla (q.v.) and the poetry of Iain Lom (q.v.). The hanging of Colla Ciotach from the mast of his own galley in 1647 may be seen as the symbolic end of 800 years of Hebridean sea power. (See Bannerman 1977c; Duncan and Brown 1956–7; I. F. Grant 1935; Gregory 1975; Kinvig 1978; R. W. Munro and J. M. Munro 1975; Sellar 1975b; Skene 1886–90.) WDHS

Lorn Ossianic Society Founded in Oban in about 1872 to cultivate Gaelic language, literature, traditions, and history and to collect books and manuscripts. The Society also organized lectures, games and competitions (Gaelic singing and reciting). From this coterie emerged the founders of An Comunn Gaidhealach (q.v.) in 1891. Some transactions were published. TMM

Lothian, Duncan (Donncha Loudainn/Loudaidh) (*c*.1730–*c*.1812). Born in Glen Lyon. Turner, associated with Dùghal Bochanan (q.v.) in Rannoch; lived latterly in Glen Fincastle. Author of 'Seanfhacail agus Comhadan', first published in 1797 (one can see mutual influence with Bochanan's work in this), a collection of poems (1780) and works on religious topics. (See P. Cameron 1894; D. Maclean 1915.) DST

Loudoun's Highlanders, *see* regiments, Highland.

Louisbourg, sieges of Louisbourg was a French fortress on the south-east coast of Cape Breton Island. Founded in 1713; completed in 1745. With a population of 5,000, Louisbourg became an important centre of the fishery and a key entrepôt of French trade in the North Atlantic.

Trade rivalry and the War of the Austrian Succession led to an attack on the fortress in 1745; after a seven-week siege, the fortress surrendered. It was returned to France in 1748, but the Seven Years War saw it captured again, by a largely British force of 15,000 soldiers, supported by over 150 ships. The French occupants were deported, and in 1760 Sir William Pitt ordered the fortress to be destroyed.

Reconstruction was begun by the Government of Canada in 1961 and will be completed in about 1990. (See J. S. McLennan 1918.) RJM

M

Mac a' Ghobhainn, Iain (Iain Phàdraig, or John Smith) (1848–81) Born Iarsiadar, Uig, Lewis. His father was a tacksman and a bard. Iain spent five years at the University of Edinburgh, studying medicine latterly, but he contracted tuberculosis and returned to Uig *c.*1774, the year of the Bernera Riot (q.v.). His surviving poetry is thought to belong mainly to his final seven years.

Like his contemporary Uilleam MacDhun-léibhe (q.v.), Mac a' Ghobhainn was keenly interested in history, wrote a poem on Bannockburn and showed some nationalist leanings; his interest in Ossianic balladry is evident in his heroic ballad on 'Coinneach Odhar'. He composed humorous and witty verse, a prime example being 'Oran an t-Seana Ghille' (The Bachelor's Song). But his best and most characteristic work is on the themes of landlordism, the oppression of the tenantry, the ethics of sporting estates, etc. On this, and on the theme of religious Pharisaism, he directs a sharply lucid intellectual scrutiny, which finds its finest flowering in 'Spiorad a' Charthannais' (The Spirit of Kindliness), which also contains the most savage comment on the petty tyrant, beginning ''N sin molaidh a' chnuimh shnàigeach thu' (The wriggling worm will praise you then). (See I. N. MacLeòid 1916, 67–131; D. S. Thomson 1974a, 237–45.)   DST

Mac a' Ghobhainn, Iain (Iain Chaluim Ruaidh) (late nineteenth century) From Bernera, Lewis. Bard and author of vivid and humorous song about a local whale hunt, 'Oran na Muice-mara'. (See I. N. MacLeòid 1916, 190.)   DST

Mac a' Ghobhainn, Iain (b. 1928), *see* Smith, Iain Crichton.

Mac a' Ghobhainn, Murchadh (Revd Murdo Smith) (1877–1936) Born Luerbost, Lewis. Taught in Ladies' Highland Association schools before becoming minister. Author of 'Tè bhàn, tè bhàn', 'Tha m'inntinn trom fo luasgan', etc. (See I. N. MacLeòid 1916, 133–50; *Gairm*, 93, 17–31.)   DST

MacAlister, Sir Donald (1854–1934) Of Tarbert. Principal, and later Chancellor, of the University of Glasgow. A distinguished scientist and noted linguist, he was President of An Comunn Gaidhealach (q.v.) in 1908 and showed a keen interest in Gaelic, the language of his infancy, although regretting that it had faded from his memory. (See E. F. B. MacAlister 1935.)   RAR

MacAlpine, Neil (1786–1867) Native of, and parochial schoolmaster in, Islay. Compiled Gaelic–English dictionary (1832 with many reissues and, from 1845, accompanied by John Mackenzie's English–Gaelic dictionary). (See N. Macalpine 1930; D. Maclean 1915, 173.)   TMM

MacAmhlaigh, Dòmhnall (Donald MacAulay) (b. 1930) Born Bernera, Lewis. Reader in Celtic, University of Aberdeen. The leading writer on Gaelic linguistics and editor of an anthology of new Gaelic verse (D. MacAulay 1976).

Dòmhnall MacAmhlaigh is a key figure in the modern renaissance of Gaelic poetry. His reputation is based on his one collection to date, *Seòbhrach as a' Chlaich* (1967) and on subsequent publications in periodicals. He is sometimes regarded as an 'intellectual' poet and is therefore not concerned, at least not primarily, with the patterns of auditory and visual sensuousness which have been developed to such perfection in Gaelic poetry. His poetry displays a fine intellectual control, which never allows his ideas to become gratuitously complex or perverse. His personality is generally kept in the background, so that one gets the impression of a moderate and unobtrusive quality pervading throughout. Even when the passion is strong the poems are quiet and subtle and charged with implosive energy. This means that they are sometimes deceptively transparent; MacAmhlaigh's work releases its total meaning only by slow degrees. There are occasional linguistic difficulties: previously unrecorded words from his own rich dialect of Bernera, Lewis, appear side by side with a mandarin kind of Gaelic.

MacAmhlaigh is one of the two leading exponents of *vers libre* in Gaelic, the other being Ruaraidh MacThómais (q.v.). This is a new departure of great interest in the development of Gaelic metrics. It has no immediate ancestry in Gaelic verse, but a parallel can be drawn between the *vers libre* of contemporary poetry and the metrical structure of certain traditional charms and incantations. This is of significance to criticism, particularly in view of some hostile reaction to such modern innovations. MacAmhlaigh's poetry exploits qualities which the language has already been shown to possess. The delicate, subtle rhythms which hold the poem together are an essential part of the statement it makes. He can also handle a wide variety of metres, including those with rhyme and other more or less traditional ornaments.

His native Bernera, its people, their attitudes and his own attitudes to all of these provide some of the themes of the poetry. When he writes as an émigré there is nostalgia in his poetry, but it is never the unexamined or extravagant nostalgia which tends to characterize such writing in all cultures. He is always unsentimental, aware of change, distance and ambivalence. 'Comharra Stiùiridh' (Landmark), (see MacAmhlaigh 1967, 35, 92), in which images of island and iceberg are compounded indicates his complex relationship to his background:

a primary landmark
dangerous, essential, demanding.

Themes come also from faraway places – Turkey, for example, where the poet spent his National Service. But the primary landmarks remain.

MacAmhlaigh's scope is suggested by a few titles: 'To Pasternak, for example . . .', 'Amasra, 1957', 'Re-armament . . . the reasoning', 'Nato 1960'. In his psychological exploration the range is wide in a different sense.

The unpretentiousness in this poetry is the more remarkable for being coupled with a hard, sceptical, uncompromising quality. (See D. MacAulay 1976; D. S. Thomson 1974b.) JMCI

Mac an Aba, Fionnlagh (d. 1525) Chief of Macnabs, Bovain, Glen Dochart. Addresses a poem to Dean MacGregor's father, proposing an anthology such as the Book of the Dean of Lismore (q.v.). (See W. J. Watson 1937, xvi, 2.) DST

Mac an Tòisich, Anndra (dates unknown) Author of two fragments in the Book of the Dean of Lismore (q.v.). (See Quiggin 1937, 97, 102.) DST

Mac an t-Saoir, am Bàrd, see Bàrd Mac an t-Saoir.

Mac an t-Saoir, Dòmhnall (Ruadh) (1889–1964) From Snaoiseabhal, South Uist. Stonemason, bricklayer. Settled in Paisley. Wrote much Gaelic verse (Macintyre, *Sporan Dhòmhnaill*) on political, sociological and other current affairs themes, using a copious vocabulary, fluent traditional metrics and an irreverent wit. He also made fine Burns translations. (See D. S. Thomson 1974a, 257.) DST

Mac-an-t-Saoir, Donnchadh Bàn (Duncan Bàn Macintyre) (1724–1812) Born Druim Liaghart, Glen Orchy. Served in Argyll Regiment of Militia, 1745–6; as forester in Glen Lochay, Ben Doran and Glen Etive, 1746–66; in Edinburgh City Guard, 1766–93; in Breadalbane Fencibles, 1793–c.99. He saw that the intensification of sheep farming was leading to severe depopulation and commented pungently on this in 'Oran nam balgairean', though he did not lay the blame at the right doors. He seems to have settled well in Edinburgh, playing up to his reputation as poet; being of a cheerful and convivial disposition, he was ready to compose occasional songs to suit any company. That he made six songs in praise of Gaelic and the bagpipes (1781–9) for the London Highland Society's competitions may suggest some lack of originality at this stage, and the truth is probably that his true inspiration, and perhaps his source of guidance, lay in the past, before he moved from the country in 1766. The first edition of his poems appeared in Edinburgh in 1768.

He composed a quota of competent praise songs and laments for Campbell chiefs and men of note, the earliest, 'Oran do Mhormhair Ghlinn Urchaidh', probably in 1746 and the latest, to the Earl of Breadalbane, in or after 1793. Though he had fought on the Hanoverian side in 1746, he shows a more Jacobite spirit in 'Oran don Bhriogais', occasioned by the Disclothing Act (1746). But his 'Oran don Rìgh' (ante-1768) is a sycophantic enough production. The core of his poetry is in the descriptive poems – not so much in 'Oran an t-Samhraidh', where he is probably too much a disciple of Alasdair Mac Mhaighstir Alasdair (q.v.), but in the hunting songs (e.g. 'Oran Seachran Seilge') and in 'Oran Coire a' Cheathaich' and 'Moladh Beinn Dòbhrain', all probably dating to the period 1751–66 and clearly influenced by Mac Mhaighstir Alasdair, whose poems were available in book form after 1751, and perhaps benefiting from critical help from the Stewarts of Killin Manse. It is likely that the form of 'Moladh Beinn Dòbhrain' was strongly influenced by the older poet's 'Moladh Mòraig' and that he adopted his habit of detailed natural description, using some of his formulations. Mac an t-Saoir, however, was an original also and stamped his own character and style firmly on the best of these descriptive poems, as is evident in the virtuosic deployment of diction in 'Oran Coire a' Cheathaich' or the delicate depicting of the sleeping fawn:

'S am minnean riabhach bu luime cliathach,
  Le chuinnean fiadhta, as fiadhaich ceann,
'Na chadal guamach an lagan uaigneach,
  Fo bhàrr 'na luachrach, 'na chuairteig chruinn.

And in his 'Praise of Ben Doran' (the *Moladh*) there are the additional factors of scale and weight (and possibly, though I am doubtful, a deeper conscious 'purpose'), making an impressive cumulative celebration of the mountain in terms of sense impressions and sound patterns. (See W. Gillies 1977; A. MacLeod 1952; I. C. Smith 1969; D. S. Thomson 1958c, 1974a.)   DST

Mac an t-Srònaich (Alexander Stronach) (fl. *c*.1830) Fugitive from justice in Lewis, *c*.1830–7, after murdering a female guest at his father's inn at Garve, Ross-shire. Said to have been apprehended and hanged. (See Urquhart 1962.)   WM

MacAoidh, Calum (Calum Ruairidh) (fl. ?1920) Author of 'Oran a' Mhargarine' etc. (See T. MacLeòid 1969, 63–5.)   DST

MacAonghais, Iain (dates unknown) Author of poem in the Book of the Dean of Lismore (q.v.). (See Quiggin 1937.)   DST

Macaskill, Alex John (b. 1922) From Back, Lewis. Headmaster, Portree, now Callander. Edited Murchadh MacPharlain's (q.v.) poems, *An Toinneamh Dìomhair* (1973) and *Rosg nan Eilean* (1966).   DST

MacAulay, Calum, *see* Calum Sgàire.

MacAulay, Donald, *see* MacAmhlaigh, Dòmhnall.

Macaulay, Fred (b. 1925) Born North Uist. BBC Gaelic producer; manager, BBC Highland, 1980–3. Presided over marked expansion of Gaelic radio broadcasting and beginnings of Gaelic TV (see **broadcasting, Gaelic**). Writes Gaelic verse under the pseudonym Eoin Gilios.   DST

MacAulay, Thomas Basset (1860–1942) Canadian of Lewis descent who held important positions in insurance. Made a significant contribution to the funding of Lewis Hospital, Stornoway Town Hall and Library, MacAulay Farm, etc.   DST

Macbain, Dr Alexander (1855–1907) From Badenoch. Eminent Celtic scholar and renowned headmaster of Raining's School, Inverness. Produced *Gaelic Etymological Dictionary* (1896; revised 1911). (For obituary, see W. J. Watson 1907, 381.)   TMM

Macbean, Francis (*c*.1794–1869) Native of Lochaber. Superintendent for Edinburgh Gaelic School Society, 1822–30. Preached under the auspices of the Original Secession Church in Highlands and Islands. Presided at the first *Coinneamh-cheist* (Question Meeting) in Western Isles, Stornoway, 1825–6. Joined Free Church. Minister at Fort Augustus. Influential in early days of Lewis Evangelicalism. (See J. MacLeod 1965.)   RMCL

Macbean, Lachlan (1853–1931) From Kiltarlity. Journalist and translator. His publications include the *Celtic Who's Who* and papers in the *Transactions of the Gaelic Society of Inverness*. He also wrote hymns and songs. (See Macbean 1921; M. Maclean 1925, 172; N. Macneill 1929, 511; *TGSI*, vol. 33, xv.)   TMM

MacBeth (d. 1057) Of the ruling family of the province of Moray, which derived its descent from the Cenél Loairn (q.v.) of Dalriada. Hence under the system of tanistry (q.v.) he had a legitimate claim to the kingship of the Scots, which he made good in 1040, when he killed Duncan I in battle. Unlike Shakespeare's portrayal of him, he was a successful king who reigned for seventeen years. So secure was he that he was able to make a pilgrimage to Rome in 1050, 'scattering money like seed'. He was killed in 1057 by Duncan's son, Malcolm III. (See Bannerman 1971, 77; Duncan 1975, 99–100.)   JW-MB

MacBethac, *see* Bethune, John.

Mac [an] Bhreatnaigh, Gilla Críost, *see* Gilla Críost Brúilingeach.

MacBrayne's shipping For over a hundred years from the mid-nineteenth century MacBrayne's was largely synonymous with west Highland sea transport. David MacBrayne (1814–1907) was born in Glasgow and became involved in shipping with the brothers David and Alexander Hutcheson. Their company took the name David MacBrayne's in 1879 and was involved in Clyde ferries and West Coast and Island sea transport. Their famous ship the *Columba* went into service in 1878; other notable names were the *Clansman* (1855), the *Claymore* (1881), the *Chieftain* (1907), the *Lochearn* and the *Lochmor* (both 1930), and the *Loch Seaforth* (1947).

DS

Mac Càba, Donnchadh Author of poem to Duncan, son of Allan, of Dunollie, in the Book of the Dean of Lismore (q.v.). DST

McCaig Trust (Catherine McCaig's Trust) Set up in 1933 to give effect to the testament of Catherine McCaig of Oban, last survivor of a local family which was responsible for building the McCaig Tower and had strong legal and property interests there. The Trust, administered by governors under successive schemes approved by the Scottish Education Department, provides bursaries and scholarships for students pursuing Gaelic/Celtic Studies at university, and grants for publication and other Gaelic purposes.

DST

MacCallum, Revd Dr Archibald Kelly (1816–93) Collected and translated Gaelic hymns. Left to the University of Glasgow his library and money with which to establish a Celtic lectureship. (See Whyte 1894.) TMM

MacCallum, Revd Donald (1849–1929) A native of Argyll and a Church of Scotland minister. The most prominent Presbyterian clergyman to support Highland crofters openly during the Land Agitation. His parishes 'coincided' with areas of strong anti-landlord resistance – Morvern, Waternish (Skye), Heylipol (Tiree) and Lochs (Lewis). His oratory contained an emotive blend of radical socialism and biblical illustration. Briefly imprisoned in Skye for 'inciting the lieges to violence and class hatred'; released without trial. (See Meek 1977a, 326; 1977c.)

DM

MacCallum, John (d. 1926) Born near Taynuilt. Learned many songs, including 'An Crònan Muileach', from Muckairn woodcutters and bark strippers. Made many airs and won Mod prizes for collections of unpublished airs. (See *An Gaidheal*, May 1926, 117.) DST

MacCodrum, John (1693–1779) Born in North Uist. Bard. Lived through the stirring times of the Jacobite risings (q.v.) and the far-reaching changes that took place consequently in Gaelic society. Much of his work survives, thanks to the diligence and enthusiasm of William Matheson, who collected from a still flourishing oral tradition in the 1930s and in 1938 published *The Songs of John MacCodrum*. (This is now out of print, but a new edition is in preparation.)

MacCodrum had an incisive wit and a keen eye, which may in part account for his exceptional popularity as a bard. Stories are still told of his irrepressible humour and his *bons mots* are still quoted. Certainly his poetry confirms his amused observation of the society in which he lived in North Uist and furthermore provides interesting and rewarding glimpses of customs and mores in the community. It also reveals a surprising awareness of national and international affairs of the period.

MacCodrum was an erudite *seanchaidh* (oral historian) and, according to his chief, could 'repeat for hours together' the poems and lays of Ossian. He was appointed bard to Sir James MacDonald of Sleat, Skye, in 1763 and was the last to be so honoured. (See W. Matheson 1938.) FM

MacCoinnich, Eòin (late seventeenth century) Author of two elegies (for his son and for Mackenzie of Applecross) in Fernaig Manuscript (q.v.). DST

MacColl, Donald (1905–77) Of Acharacle. Gamekeeper in Jura, Applecross and elsewhere. From an Ardnamurchan bardic family, he composed poems and songs notable for their accurate observation of nature and variety of tunes, some his own composition. AB

MacColla (or MacDonald), Alasdair (d. 1647) A son of Coll Ciotach MacDonald (q.v.), who became one of the greatest of Highland warriors, renowned in poem, song and legend. Though his greatest fame came when he commanded Irish and Highland forces under the Royalist Montrose (q.v.) in 1644–5, Alasdair fought primarily to recover the lands of his family (Colonsay) and of the Clan Ian Mór from the Campbells. As well as great personal skill and courage as a fighting man, he possessed considerable strategic and tactical ability and may have originated the 'Highland charge' (q.v.) in Ulster in 1642. He was killed in Ireland after being driven out of Scotland. (See D. Stevenson 1980.)   DST

MacColla, Eóghan (Bàrd Loch Fìne) (1808–98) Born Kenmore, Argyll. Emigrated to Canada, 1849. The first collection of his poetry, Gaelic and English, appeared in 1836; the definitive of *Clàrsach nam Beann* fourth edition (1937) includes still popular songs such as 'Ròsan an Leth-bhaile' and 'Mo Chaileag Shuaineartach'.   IMcD

MacCormick, Donald (b. 1837) Born in Kilphedir, South Uist. Crofter and school attendance officer. Made collections of waulking songs (q.v.) and proverbs (q.v.); composed hymns and an elegy to Fr. George Rigg; left in manuscript a long poem on the life of Our Lord. (See *An Gaidheal*, vol. 47; *Gairm*, no. 28; Duncan MacLean manuscripts; Rea 1964.)   JLC

MacCormick, John (*c.*1870–1947) From Mull but spent most of his life in Glasgow. He wrote Gaelic prolifically, especially short stories, usually stories of adventure strongly influenced in style by the *ceilidh*-house tradition of narration; examples are 'Am Bàillidh 's am Muilleir' and 'Spùinneadairean Shìne'. *Gun d'tug i spéis do'n Armunn* (?1907) is a long historical adventure story. His novel *Dun Aluinn* appeared in 1912 (see **novel, Gaelic**). Among his story collections are *Oiteagan o'n Iar* (1908) and *Seanchaidh na h-Airigh* (1911).   DST

MacCrimmons The development of piping in Scotland and the predominance today of the Highland bagpipe throughout the world are due very largely to the musical genius of one family, the MacCrimmons. They appeared in Skye some time in the sixteenth century and soon established themselves as the leading players, teachers and composers of bagpipe music. The head of the family was hereditary piper to the MacLeods of Dunvegan, and the family presided over a piping seminary for over 200 years.

We have to depend upon oral tradition for much of our Highland history, and the history of piping is no exception. However, once the obvious elaborations and exaggerations are removed, tradition can in some circumstances be as dependable as accounts written after the events. In addition the records in Dunvegan Castle contain references to the MacCrimmons stretching from 1595 to 1801, and so a fair history of this remarkable family can be compiled.

The origin of the MacCrimmons is obscure. The name is apparently unknown before the sixteenth century. All MacCrimmons in the world today are descended from this one family, which appeared suddenly in the parish of Glendale in Skye. It seems reasonable to assume therefore that they came from some other place and changed their name – or had their name changed – on arrival.

There are three principal theories regarding their origin – that they came from Harris, that they came from Ireland and that they came from Italy. The MacLeods owned land in Harris, and there was certainly some interchange of population between there and Skye. The Irish story is favoured by the Irish, but there is no real evidence to support it. The third suggestion, that the founder of the line was a Protestant musician from Cremona fleeing from the Inquisition, is fanciful but possible. Some at least of the later MacCrimmons believed it.

The earliest MacCrimmons we hear of are Finlay, Iain Odhar and Pàdraig Donn, all living in the sixteenth century. Their relationships to one another are not clear. It seems likely, however, that they were the men who set *pìobaireachd* on the road to what it is today – a highly developed art form capable of standing comparison with the classical music of any country. Before their time music for the bagpipe was almost certainly very simple and unsophisticated.

The next MacCrimmon was Donald Mòr, and from here on we know enough about the hereditary pipers to see them as separate characters. The family appears to have settled first at Galtrigall, about 6 miles across Loch Dunvegan from the Castle. Donald Mòr was born about 1570, although he did not succeed to the position of hereditary piper until 1620. In 1603, at the close of a long series of battles between the MacLeods and MacDonalds, he was called on to compose a special tune to play at the reconciliation banquet at Dunvegan Castle. In fact, he composed three tunes, 'The MacDonalds' Salute', 'The MacLeods' Salute' and 'MacLeods' Controversy'. These are important because they are all compositions of the highest merit, implying a previous long period of experiment and development. Better tunes have been composed since then, but no significant improvement in *ceòl mòr* (see **bagpipe**) has been achieved. The golden age of the MacCrimmons had reached the high plateau from which it was not to descend for 150 years.

About 1610 Donald Mòr's brother, Patrick Caogach, was murdered in Glenelg, and Donald Mòr's retaliation – the burning of houses in Kintail – resulted in the deaths of several people. To avoid further consequences, Donald Mòr fled to Sutherland, where he lived for several years before returning to Skye and succeeding as hereditary piper. He died in 1640. His other compositions include 'The Earl of Ross's March', 'Grain in Hides and Corn in Sacks', 'A Flame of Wrath for Squinting Patrick' and 'Too Long in this Condition'.

He was succeeded by his son, Patrick Mòr (1595–1670), who was the greatest composer of all the MacCrimmons. Tunes attributed to him include 'The Groat', 'MacLeod of MacLeod's Lament' (1626), 'Lament for Donald of Laggan' (1635), 'Lament for Donald Duaghal MacKay' (1649), 'Lament for the Children' (1650), 'I Got a Kiss of the King's Hand' (1651) and 'The Lament for MacSwan of Roag'.

Patrick Mòr was succeeded by his son, Patrick Óg (born 1645), perhaps the most famous of the line – the best player and the best teacher. Under his guidance the school reached the peak of its fame. Patrick Óg moved the establishment from Galtrigall to Boreraig, about a mile closer to Dunvegan. Boreraig became the magic name for pipers, as it remains today. Patrick Óg's compositions include 'The Lament for Iain Garve MacLeod of Raasay' (1688), 'The Pretty Dirk', 'The Half-Finished Piobaireachd' (with Iain Dall MacKay) and 'The Lament for Mary MacLeod' (1707). He died about 1730.

His successor was his son Malcolm (1690–1760), who continued the school until his death, but from 1746 it was an establishment in name only. The Act of Proscription of 1746 made it illegal to play bagpipes, although Malcolm continued to teach his sons and a few others. He composed one excellent tune, 'The Lament for Donald Bàn MacCrimmon' (his half brother killed at the Rout of Moy in 1746).

His sons, Iain Dubh and Donald Ruadh, both held the post of hereditary piper at different times. In 1770 a dispute regarding rents made Iain Dubh give up Boreraig. He died in Skye in 1822, and Donald Ruadh died in London in 1825, thus ending the long line of master pipers. (See Archibald Campbell 1948, 1962; F. T. MacLeod 1933; R. H. MacLeod 1973; A. MacKay 1838; S. MacNeill 1968; Pearston 1953; Poulter and Fisher 1936.)   SMCN

MacCulloch, Horatio (1805–67), *see* art, Gaelic, in modern times.

MacCulloch of Park, *see* Fear na Pàirce.

MacDhiarmaid, Donncha (*c.*1798–post-1850) Born Glendochart. Bard and singing teacher in Perthshire. (See P. Cameron 1894.)   DST

MacDhiarmada ('McKermont'), Donnchadh Author of poem on jealousy in the Book of the Dean of Lismore (q.v.). (See Quiggin 1937, 72.)   DST

MacDhòmhnaill, Fionnlagh Iain (b. 1926) Born Scarista, Harris. Gaelic broadcaster and short-story writer. Co-founder and co-editor (1952–64), with Ruaraidh MacThómais (q.v.), of *Gairm* (q.v.). Founder of the Glasgow Gaelic Drama Association. Editor of the Portree school magazine *An Cabairneach.*   DST

MacDhonnchaidh, an Tàillear, *see* MacPherson, Paul.

MacDhubhghaill, Féidhlim (dates unknown) Author of aphoristic verses in the Book of the Dean of Lismore (q.v.). (See W. J. Watson 1937, 240.)   DST

The MacCrimmon memorial cairn at Boreraig.

MacDhùghaill, Mgr Iain Mór, *see* MacDonald, Revd John (d. 1761).

MacDhùghaill, Rob (b. *c.*1797) Born Braes of Foss, Perthshire. Author of temperance verse. (See P. Cameron 1894.)   DST

MacDhun-léibhe, Donnchadh (1877–1964) From Tor-loisg, Mull. A mason by trade, he carved the lintel of the main door of St Columba's, Glasgow. He settled in South Africa *c.*1903, becoming a Clerk of Works in Pretoria. His Gaelic poetry and essays appeared late in his life, in *Gairm* (q.v.), *Teangadóir* and *Irisleabhar Ceilteach*. There are poems on African political themes and a fine lament, 'Cràdh', for his wife. (See D. S. Thomson 1974a, 255; 1982.)   DST

MacDhun-léibhe, Uilleam (William Livingstone) (1808–70) Born Kilarrow, Islay. A tailor by trade, he worked hard to educate himself in history, languages and literature, acquiring some Latin, Greek, Hebrew, French and Welsh. He lived latterly in Tradestown, Glasgow.

An ardent nationalist and Gaelic propagandist, Livingstone wrote verse concerned largely with heroic themes, reconstructing in imagination wars and battles, as in 'Na Lochlannaich an Ile' and 'Blàr Shunadail', as well as the specific battles of Bannock-burn, Tràigh Ghruineart and Alma. Heroic Gaels are always at the centre of the action. There is some stirring descriptive verse in these, but the long poems are formless and often bombastic; the epics may owe too much to Macpherson's Ossian, too little to Homer. Some of Livingstone's patriotic verse with an evictions background is much tauter, especially 'Fios thun a' Bhàird', with such fine lines as:

> Tha 'n nathair bhreac 'na lùban
> Air na h-ùrlair far an d'fhàs
> Na fir mhòra chunnaic mise . . . .

(The spotted adder's coiling on the floors whereon there grew the great men that I saw there . . . .)
(See MacDhun-léibhe 1882; Sorley Maclean 1963; D. S. Thomson 1974a.)   DST

MacDiarmid, Hugh (Eóghan) (d. 1801) From Perthshire. Minister of Gaelic Chapel of Ease, Glasgow, and at Arrochar, Comrie. Manuscript anthology of Gaelic verse (1770); *Searmona* (1804); manuscript account of Roman camp, Dalginross, in the keeping of the Perth Literary and Antiquarian Society.   DST

MacDonald, Alasdair, *see* MacColla, Alasdair.

East door of St Columba's church, Glasgow. Wooden lintel with Gaelic lettering, carved by MacDhun-léibhe.

MacDonald, Alexander (*c*.1695–*c*.1770), *see* Mac Mhaighstir Alasdair, Alasdair.

MacDonald, Alexander (Gleannach) (1860–1928) Author of *Còinneach 'us Coille* (songs, etc.) and of *Story and Song from Loch Ness-side* (1914, 1982). DST

MacDonald, Allan (Ailean an Ridge) (1794–1868) From Lochaber. Emigrated to Cape Breton, 1816; moved near to Antigonish, 1847. He composed songs and passed traditions, etc., to A. Maclean Sinclair. (See Sinclair 1890, 214ff.) DST

McDonald, Revd Fr Allan (1859–1905) Born Fort William. Related to D. C. MacPherson (q.v.). Educated at Blairs College and Scots College, Valladolid. Ordained Glasgow, 1882; with Bishop Angus Mac-Donald at Oban, 1882–4; parish priest, Daliburgh, South Uist, 1884–94; Eriskay, 1894–1905 Member of South Uist School Board and briefly county councillor. Collected local Gaelic folklore from 1887; published hymns in 1889 and 1893.

McDonald was frequently consulted by other folklorists and corresponded with Walter Blaikie, Alexander and Ella Carmichael (q.v.), Ada Goodrich Freer (q.v.), George Henderson (q.v.), William MacKenzie (q.v.), Neil Munro (q.v.), etc. He was involved in the investigation into second sight in the Highlands initiated by the Society for Psychical Research (*see* J. L. Campbell and Hall 1968) and collaborated with Amy Murray in collecting Gaelic folksongs on Eriskay in 1905. He was the original for 'Fr. MacCrimmon' in Frederic Breton's *Heroine in Homespun* (1893), and for 'Fr. Ludovic' in Neil Munro's *Children of the Tempest* (1903). His Gaelic poems were published in 1965. (See J. L. Campbell especially 1954; J. N. MacLeod, 1933; Rea 1964; surviving MSS in Glasgow and Edinburgh University Libraries.) JLC

MacDonald, Angus (Aonghas Mac Alasdair Ruaidh) (*c*.1665–1745) Of Glencoe. Author of poem on Killiecrankie and a 1745 Incitement. (See J. L. Campbell 1933.) DST

MacDonald, Angus (d. 1774) Of Borrodale. His tack was on the north shore of Loch nan Uamh, Arisaig. Prince Charlie stayed with him for some days after landing in 1745. (See I. R. Mackay 1963.) DST

MacDonald, Revd Angus (d. 1833) Born Eigg. Priest in Barra; Rector of Scots College, Rome, at time of his death. Author of 'Laoidh a' Phurgadair'. (See G. Henderson 1898.) DST

MacDonald, Angus (fl. 1860) From Glen Urquhart. The first Bard of the Gaelic Society of Inverness. DST

Macdonald, Revd Angus (1871–1934) Born Keose, Lewis. Soldiered in India and in the Boer War. Ordained missionary in Canada. Senior Chaplain to New Zealand forces in 1914–18 war. DST

MacDonald, Revd Dr Angus John Norman (1860–1932) From Benbecula. Minister at Killearnan. His manuscripts (the Killearnan Papers), concerned with Gaelic lore and history, are among the Carmichael Papers in Edinburgh University Library. (Collaborated in A. and A. MacDonald 1896–1904, 1911, 1924.) TMM

Duncan MacDonald of South Uist. Photographed at Callanish, Lewis during the International Conference on Celtic Folklore October 1953.

MacDonald, Angus Lewis (1890–1954) Born Dunvegan, Cape Breton. Great-grandson of Moidart emigrant. Gaelic speaker. Became leader of Nova Scotian Liberal Party in early 1920s. Prime Minister of Nova Scotia, 1933–40 and 1945–54. The Library in St Francis Xavier University is named after him.   DST

MacDonald, Archibald (Gilleasbaig Ruadh MacDhòmhnaill), *see* Ciaran Mabach.

MacDonald, Archibald (Gilleasbuig na Ceapaich) (d. 1682) 15th Chief of Keppoch; father of Sileas na Ceapaich. A number of poems attributed to him were published by D. C. MacPherson (1868) and A. and A. MacDonald (1911). (See also K. N. MacDonald 1900; 15.)   DAMCD

MacDonald, Archibald (Gille na Ciotaig: The Left-Handed Lad) (*c.*1750–*c.*1815) From North Uist. Bard, noted chiefly for his satirical and comic songs. Nicknamed because of a disabled hand and arm. Employed as clerk to the factor of the Clanranald estates in South Uist. (See A. MacDonald 1894, 142–72; A. and A. MacDonald 1911, xxii, 106–8; K. N. MacDonald 1900, 40–2.)   DAMCD

MacDonald, Revd Dr Archibald (1855–1948) Born in Harris, of Uist ancestry. Minister at Kiltarlity. Highland genealogist, translator and Gaelic prose writer. Collaborated in A. and A. MacDonald 1896–1904, 1911, 1924. (See D. Lamont 1948; T. M. Murchison 1948, 78; *TGSI*, vol. 37, xv.)   TMM

Macdonald, Callum (b. 1914) Born Bernera, Lewis. Founder of Macdonald Printers and Macdonald Publishers (Edinburgh).   DST

Macdonald, Colin (1882–1957) From near Strathpeffer. Gaelic-speaking member of Land Court in 1940s. Author of *Echoes of the Glen* (1936), *Croft and Ceilidh* (1947), etc.   DST

MacDonald, Coll Ciotach (*c.*1570–1647) One of the leading warriors of the Clan Ian Mór and father of Alasdair MacColla (q.v.). (See R. I. Black 1976, 201–43; D. Stevenson 1980.)   DS

MacDonald, Dan R. (1911–76) Born in Judique, Nova Scotia. Fifth-generation Gael of Eigg extraction. His legacy to the Gaelic world is a large repertoire of fiddle tunes, many of which have been heard,

through both his own rendition and that of others, over BBC and CBC radio and television.

SISTER MMCD

MacDonald, Dòmhnall, *see* Dòmhnall Donn.

MacDonald, Donald, of Corùna, *see* Dòmhnall Ruadh Chorùna.

MacDonald, Donald (fl. 1730) Son of Raghnall na Sgèithe (q.v.) from Glencoe. Author of poem on Sheriffmuir and of 'Bha claidheamh air Iain san t-searmoin'. Grandfather of Donald Campbell, author of *Language, Poetry and History of the Highland Clans.* (See K. N. MacDonald 1900, 22–4.)   DST

MacDonald, Donald (*c.*1780–1832), *see* Bàrd Conanach.

MacDonald, Donald (Bàrd Bharbhais) (1861–1916) Author of 'Eilean mo ghaoil', prose sketches, etc.

DST

Macdonald, Donald (Dolly Doctor) (1891–1961) Born Stornoway. Prime mover in project for a Lewis and Harris Folk Museum. Posthumous publication *Tales and Traditions of the Lewis* (1967).   DST

MacDonald, Duncan (d. 1938) Born Bernera, Lewis. Author of *Gnathasan Cainnte* (1927, enlarged edn 1932), plays, etc.   DST

MacDonald, Duncan (Donnchadh Clachair) (d. 1954) Notable South Uist storyteller. Some of his stories have been published for example, by Craig, in *Sgialachdan Dhunnchaidh.* (See *Gairm*, vol. 3, 170ff.)   DST

MacDonald, Flora (1722–90) Born Milton, in South Uist. She owes her fame to the ten days in 1746 during which she helped Prince Charles Edward to escape to the mainland from the Outer Hebrides. In 1774 she emigrated to North Carolina with her husband Allan MacDonald of Kingsburgh, to face tragedy when her family supported the losing side in the War of Independence. She returned to Scotland to die near Kingsburgh in Skye, where she was buried. (See Vining 1967.)   IG

Flora MacDonald. By Allan Ramsay. 1749. Ashmolean Museum Oxford. ▶

MacDonald, Sir Hector (1853–1903), *see* Fraser, Allan Henry Hector.

MacDonald, Hugh (Hudy) (1856–1940) Born Kirkwood, Lake Ainslie, of Ross-shire stock. Cape Breton athlete, 6ft 7in high and weighing 270lb. Won North American wrestling championship in Boston in 1881; reputed to have defeated John L. Sullivan in a fist-icuffs session. His support of the numerous Highland Games, which were becoming popular at the time, helped to assure their place in the culture of eastern Nova Scotia. (See biography file, Beaton Institute, Cape Breton.)   RJM

MacDonald, John (*c*.1625–post-1707), *see* Iain Lom.

MacDonald, John (Iain Dubh mac Iain mhic Ailein) (fl. 1700), *see* Aos-dàna.

MacDonald, John (Iain mac Dhùghaill mhic Lachlainn) (fl. 1715) The song 'Tha tighinn fodham', about the 1715 uprising, has been ascribed to him (MacDonald and Thomson, forthcoming).   DST

MacDonald, Revd John (Mgr Iain Mòr MacDhùghaill) (d. 1761) Lochaber priest. Author of 'Marbhrann do dh'Anna Dhòmhnallach'. (See K. N. MacDonald 1900, 17.)   DST

Macdonald, John (Footman) (b. 1741) Born Glen Urquhart. Footman to James (Ossian) MacPherson in 1774. Author of *Travels* (1790).   DST

MacDonald, John (1766–1865) From Lochbroom. Farmer at Scorraig, Lochbroom and Crobeag, Lewis. Author of the second set of words (the well-known one) of 'Màiri laghach'; Màiri was Mary MacIver of Stornoway (1786–1869). (See K. N. MacDonald 1900, 49–51.)   DST

MacDonald, Revd Dr John (1779–1849) 'Ministear Mòr na Tòisigheachd' (the 'Apostle of the North') was born in Reay and ministered at Berriedale, Edinburgh Gaelic Chapel and (from 1813 until his death) in Urquhart (Ferintosh), from 1843 as Free Church minister. In 1805 he collected heroic poetry in western Sutherland, Ross-shire and Inverness-shire (J. F. Campbell 1872, vii; for his elegies and spiritual poems, see Domhnallach 1912). His Gaelic version of the Shorter Catechism (1829) has been widely used. Probably the best-known Gaelic preacher of his own

or any time, his remarkable voice swayed thousands at great open-air services. (See J. Kennedy 1886; Maclauchlan, 1877, 17; K. D. MacDonald 1982.)   TMM

MacDonald, John (Iain Mac Dhòmhnaill 'ic Iain/ Iain Sealgair) (1795–1853) Born Lochaber; related to Bohuntin MacDonalds. Emigrated to Nova Scotia, 1834. Author of 'Oran do dh'America', etc. (See MacLean Sinclair 1901; article by Maureen Lonergan in *Dictionary of Canadian Biography*.)   DST

MacDonald, John (Iain Dòmhnallach an Dall) (*c*.1812–84) Born Mull; lived mainly in Oban. Hymnist. (See K. N. MacDonald 1900, 79.)   DST

MacDonald, John (1869–1953) A famous conductor of the Oban Gaelic Choir. Composer of melodies (e.g. for 'An Ataireachd Ard') and of melody and choral arrangement for 'Athchuinge'.   DST

MacDonald, John (b. 1883) Schoolmaster, Lairg. Editor *Leabhraichean Leughaidh IV* (1923), *Voices from the Hills* (1927).   DST

Macdonald, John (1886–1970) Born Milifiach, Inverness-shire. Graduate of Aberdeen and Cambridge Universities. Lecturer, then Reader in Celtic, University of Aberdeen, 1922–56. First editor, *Scottish Gaelic Studies*. Edited poems of Ewen MacLachlan (q.v.).   DST

MacDonald, Pipe-Major John (d. 1952) Of Inverness. Famous pipe teacher in MacCrimmon tradition. See **MacLeod, Donald** (1917–82).   DST

MacDonald, John A. (Jake) (1920–80) Born Skye. Head of Gaelic Department, Jordanhill College; retired 1978. Author of various Gaelic courses (e.g. *Gàidhlig Bheò*), broadcaster and popular compère.
                                                      DST

MacDonald, Joseph (1739–62) Son of Murdo MacDonald (q.v.), minister of Durness. Before leaving for India, where he died, he made the earliest analysis of *piobaireachd* in his *Compleat Theory of the Scots Highland Bagpipe* (1927) and compiled *A Collection of Highland Vocal Airs Never Hitherto Published*, which his brother Patrick, minister of Kilmore, published in 1784.   IG

MacDonald, Kenneth D. (b. 1937) Senior Lecturer in Celtic, University of Glasgow. Editor of the *Historical Dictionary of Scottish Gaelic* (see **dictionaries, Scottish Gaelic**) since its inception in 1966. DST

MacDonald, Marshal, *see* Tarentum, Duke of.

MacDonald, Mary (1817–*c*.1890) From Ardtun, Mull. Author of Gaelic carol 'Leanabh an Aigh', original of 'Child in the manger'. (See *An Gaidheal*, December 1944, 22.) DST

MacDonald, Murdo (1696–1763) Minister of Durness, 1726–63. A profound religious, literary and musical influence on Rob Donn (q.v.). Surviving portions of his diary were published in *Transactions of the Gaelic Society of Inverness*, vol. 11, and in Grimble (1979b). IG

Macdonald, Revd Dr Murdo Ewen (b. 1914) From Harris. Minister at Portree, Glasgow and Edinburgh; Professor of Practical Theology at the University of Glasgow since 1964. (For his publications, see the Bibliography.) TMM

Macdonald, Sir Murdoch (1866–1957) Received his early training as a civil engineer with the Highland Railway Company. In 1898 he joined the Egyptian Government. He was responsible for many important works, including the original Aswan Dam, the Gezira irrigation system and the Sennar Dam in the Sudan. He retired from the Egyptian Government in 1922, having been Under-Secretary of State for Public Works. He then founded his own consulting firm, which carried out works in Egypt, Jordan, Greece and the UK, where he designed the Loch Shin and Breadalbane Schemes for the North of Scotland Hydro-Electric Board (q.v.). From 1922 to 1950 he sat as National Liberal, and finally as Independent Liberal, Member of Parliament for Inverness-shire. HBS

MacDonald, Norman (Tormod Sona) (1853–1954) Native of Lewis. One of *Na Daoine* (the Men), laymen who attended services at Communion seasons in Gaelic congregations, and took a leading part in *Latha na Ceiste*, (Question Day) on Communion Friday. His sayings and religious experiences have passed into tradition. (See J. MacLeod 1948.) RMCL

MacDonald, Revd Patrick (1729–1824) Born Durness. Minister of Kilmore, Argyll. Published *Highland Vocal Airs* (1784). DST

MacDonald, Rachel (Raonaild Nighean Mhic Nèill) (fl. *c*.1800) From North Uist. Author of 'Oran Fir Heillsgeir'; certain other songs ascribed to her (e.g. D. A. Fergusson 1978, 42, 44) are more likely to be twentieth-century compositions. DST

MacDonald, Ranald (d. 1692), *see* Raghnall na Sgéithe.

MacDonald, Ranald (Raghnall Dubh) (*c*.1715–*c*.1805) Son of Alasdair Mac Mhaighstir Alasdair (q.v.). Substituted for him as school-master in Ardnamurchan in 1744. Published *Comhchruinneachidh Orannaigh Gaidhealach* (the Eigg Collection) in 1776, presumably based largely on collections made by his father but probably also drawing on Hector Maclean of Grulin's anthology (*c*.1768). A promised second volume never appeared. (See C. Ó Baoill, 1976c.) DST

MacDonald, Ranald (fl. 1821) Of Ard-nis, Arasaig. Published a collection of poems by himself and others in 1821. (See K. N. MacDonald 1900, 51–4.) DST

MacDonald, Robert (Rob Dòmhnallach) (b. 1795) Born near Loth, Sutherland. Gaelic schoolteacher. Author of hymns (R. MacDonald 1836) and translator of Bunyan's *Life and Death of Badman* (1824), *Sighs from Hell* (1829), etc. (See Beaton 1923, 43–4.) DST

Macdonald, Revd Roderick (b. 1920) From North Uist. Minister in Stornoway and, since 1967, at Insch, Aberdeenshire. Has published many Gaelic hymns, translated and original. Crowned Bard at Mod, 1977. (See Roderick Macdonald 1978.) TMM

MacDonald, Thomas Donald (1864–1937) Secretary of An Comunn Gaidhealach (q.v.), 1907–11. Author of some First World War verse (see Bibliography). DST

MacDonald's Highlanders, *see* regiments, Highland.

MacDonalds of Dalness This family had strong literary interests. Alasdair Mac Mhaighstir Alasdair (q.v.) married a daughter, Jane, in the early eighteenth century. Her father (?) was author of a verse dialogue between Queen Anne and Stewart of Appin (*TGSI*, 22, 173), and the fine song 'Tha mise seo 'm laighe' is attributed to a son of MacDonald of Dalness. (See *Gairm* 113, 79; Sinton, 1906, 42.)   DST

MacDonell, Alasdair Carrach (1st of Keppoch) (*c*.1380–*c*.1445) Fought at Harlaw (1411) and Inverlochy (1431).   DST

MacDonell, Farquhar D. (d. *c*.1897) From (?) Lochaber. Poet. Emigrated to New Zealand. (For his poems see, for example, *TGSI*, vols. 7 and 11.)   DST

MacDonnell, Angus Alex (1944–77) Born in Inverness, Nova Scotia, into a Gaelic-speaking family of Keppoch extractions. Ordained a priest in 1976. His major contribution to the Gaelic culture of eastern Nova Scotia was the establishment in Antigonish of a school of step-dancing, an art in which he was without peer.   SISTER MMCD

MacDonnell, Randal, 2nd Marquis of Antrim (1609–83) Organized the sending of an Irish expeditionary force to Scotland under Alasdair MacColla (q.v.) in 1644.   DS

MacDougall, Allan (Ailean Dall: Blind Allan) (*c*.1750–1828) Born Glencoe. Poet, who became family bard to Alasdair Ronaldson MacDonell of Glengarry. Composed numerous conventional panegyrics and amusing ribald songs, but his most important work is a bitter attack on the Lowland shepherds whose sheep symbolized the depopulation of the Highlands. His poems, edited by Ewen MacLachlan, were first published in 1798. (See J. MacDonald 1937; A. MacDougall 1798, 1829; A. MacKenzie 1881; J. MacKenzie 1865.)   JLC

MacDougall, Revd Donald (1854–1920) Born North Uist. Preached Gaelic in New York. Editor, *Caledonian Magazine*, 1901–20.   DST

MacDougall, Hector MacLean (1889–1954) From Coll. Served with Glasgow police. Wrote many Gaelic articles, stories, plays and poems, edited several books and broadcast frequently. Won many Mod literary prizes. Founded Glasgow Coll Association. (For obituary and bibliography, see MacCalmain 1954, 362.)   TMM

MacDougall, Revd James (1833–1906) Born Craignish. Minister of Duror from 1871. Collector of folktales and legends published in *Waifs and Strays* (Lord A. Campbell 1889, 1891a) and, posthumously, in *Folk Tales and Fairy Lore*. (See J. MacDougall 1910.)   AB

MacEachaig (?) Author of poem in the Book of the Dean of Lismore (q.v.) addressed to Iain Borb MacLeòid of Harlaw (1411). (See W. J. Watson 1937, 22.)   DST

Mac Eachainn Mhic Fhearchair Said in the Fernaig Manuscript (q.v.) to be the author of a set of 'counselling' verses to his Macintosh foster-son. (See MacPhàrlain 1923, 51, 328.)   DST

MacEacharn, Dòmhnall· (Donald MacKechnie) (1836–1908) Born Jura. Lived latterly in Edinburgh as part of the distinguished circle which included Donald Mackinnon, Alexander Carmichael and Sheriff Nicolson. A frequent prize winner at Mods at the turn of the century. His poetry is light, sometimes sentimental, and only a few pieces are remembered ('An Sruthan', 'Am Bothan Beag', 'Bean a' Chòtain Ruaidh'). He also translated from the *Rubaiyat*. His prose has worn better, his essays on various animals in particular illustrating his light, humorous touch, his use of incisive and idiomatic language and his unpretentious style; 'Am Fiadh' (The Deer) is the best-known of these.   DST

Macealair, Daibhidh (Mackellar, David) (fl. mid-eighteenth century) Native of Glendaruel. Author of a popular hymn on creation and redemption. (See D. Kennedy 1836, 123; MacKenzie 1877, 181.)   KDMCD

MacEwen poets We can reconstruct, with some confidence, the family tree of this line of late medieval and early modern classical Gaelic poets, but we have to be more speculative in identifying their surviving work. They are designated as a bardic family in 1558, when Colin Campbell of Glenorchy granted a charter to Eugenius McDuncane McCarne and to his son Arnaldus or Arnoldus and his heirs male after him who act as *Joculatores* ('wlgariter Rymouris'), giving them the two merklands of Barmullocht in the lordship of Lorne (Innes, 1855, 408). Over two centuries later (1779) Donald MacNicol (*Remarks*, 245) records the following tradition about the MacEwens:

The MacEwens had free lands in *Lorn* in Argyleshire, for acting as Bards to the family of *Argyle*, to that of *Breadalbane*, and likewise to Sir *John Macdougal of Dunolly*, in 1572. The two last of the race were *Airne* and his son *Neil*. The combined evidence of these two references suggests the succession (with some datings inserted): Eachthighearna (b. ?*c*.1380), Eóghan/Eóin, Athairne (fl. *c*.1475), Duncan, Eóghan (Eugenius of 1558 document), Athairne (cf. Arnaldus and [McC]arne, 1558), Neil (b. ?*c*.1570). The first name in the succession derives from the ascription, in the Book of the Dean of Lismore (q.v.), of a lament for Eóin Ciar MacDougall of Lorn (W. J. Watson 1937, 166) to Ane m̲ac Evin m̲hic Eaychirn̲n̲ (Quiggin's transcription). This ascription has been variously transliterated, the present suggestion being 'Athairne mac Eóghain mheic Eichthighearna'. The poem is a typical bardic elegy, with expanded and ingenious treatment of the pathetic fallacy motif.

A small group of seventeenth-century poems, addressed to the Campbells of Glenorchy and of Argyll, are likely to be by members of this family (W. J. Watson 1931), including the elegy on Sir Duncan (d. 1631) (W. J. Watson 1917). It may have been Neil MacEwen who translated Calvin's Catechism (1631; see R. L. Thomson 1962); this Neil also made a translation of the Shorter Catechism *c*. 1652. Two poems are ascribed to *Arne McKeuín* in the 1631 Catechism. (See D. S. Thomson 1974a; W. J. Watson 1922.)   DST

MacFadyen, John, *see* MacPhaidein, Iain.

MacFarlane, Walter Scott (1896–1979) Born Upper Margaree, Cape Breton. MacFarlane is considered one of the outstanding popular bards of Cape Breton. His Gaelic poetry is noted for its wit, his outstanding songs being 'Oran an "Telephone" anns an Eipheit' and 'Marbhrann do Phìobaire MacPhàrlain'.   RJM

MacFhionghuin, Alasdair (Alexander MacKinnon) (1770–1814) Son of Morar tacksman. Soldier in 92nd Regiment (Gordon Highlanders). Author of 'Blàr na h-Olaind (the battle fought on 2 October 1799), two poems on the Egyptian campaign, *c*. 1801, and 'An Dubh-ghleannach', a well wrought sea poem. (See J. Mackenzie 1877.)   DST

MacFhionnlaigh, Fearghas (MacKinlay, Fergus) Born Canada but brought up in Clydebank. Learned Gaelic. Author of a novel, *Có ghoid am Bogha-frois?* (*Who Stole the Rainbow?*) and of the long poem *A' Mheanbhchnileag* (*The Midge*), translated in *Cencrastus*, no. 10 (1982).   DST

MacGhilleMhoire, Murchadh (Murchadh Beag) (1898–1932) Born Habost Ness, Lewis. Author of 'An Ciaora'. (See T. MacLeòid 1969, 34–6.)   DST

MacGhilleMhoire, Uilleam M. (1866–1952) Born Lewis. Brother of Revd Roderick Morrison, minister of High Church, Stornoway. Pioneer translator of Shakespeare into Gaelic (*Iulius Ceasar* 1911).   DST

MacGill-Eain, Sómhairle (Sorley Maclean) (b. 1911) Born Raasay, Skye. Taught English in Mull, Skye and Edinburgh; latterly headmaster, Plockton High School. Has written on literary topics such as the verse of the Clearances, realism in Gaelic poetry and individual poets (S. Maclean 1946, 1962, 1963, 1966) and has contributed occasional prose items to *Gairm*, among other journals.

MacGill-Eain's main work has been poetry, especially the sequence of love poems *Dàin do Eimhir* (1943). His earliest publication was the pamphlet shared with Robert Garioch *17 Poems for 6d* (1939), and his third book was *Reothairt is Contraigh/Spring Tide and Neap Tide* (1977), which consists mainly of a selection from his 1943 book. His central poetic output dates from the 1930s and is concentrated largely in the years 1937–41. The precipitating agents of this poetry were his English studies, especially of the seventeenth-century metaphysicals and of 1930s poetry; his political beliefs, leaning strongly to communism but tempered by Scottish Nationalism; emotional involvements with two women (who coalesce to some extent as Eimhir); and the Spanish Civil War. Anti-landlord and anti-clerical views also feature strongly. The impetus for shaping poems on these themes into a sequence almost certainly owes much to the poet's admiration for Hugh MacDiarmid's *A Drunk Man Looks at the Thistle* (1926). The sequence is a rich blend of diverse preoccupations, emotion and intellect, free-thinking and conservatism. The love theme is constantly counterpointed by the others, and it is a matter for regret that the love sequence has been reshuffled and only partly reproduced in the 1977 volume. (For more detailed analysis, see D. S. Thomson 1977b, d.)

The 1943 collection also included the long poems 'Craobh nan Teud', on the theme of poetic inspiration (this theme is organically stated early in the poem, but the treatment later becomes more expository), and 'Coilltean Ratharsair', a symbolist poem which builds on Baudelaire's theory of *correspondances*. The 1977 volume includes the latest, and best, of these symbolist poems, 'Hallaig' (first published in *Gairm*, 1954).

MacGill-Eain's work in bringing cross-fertilizing influences to Gaelic verse is highly important: these relate both to theme and to poem structure, while in metrics he remains largely traditional (see D. S. Thomson 1974b). Donald MacAulay regards the 1943 volume as 'the vital and incomparable link between the old style and the new' (MacAulay 1976, 54). (See Ó Doibhlín 1973, and review in *TLS* 1977, 1087; I. C. Smith 1971a; D. S. Thomson 1974a.)

DST

Mac Gilleoin, Eóghan, *see* Maclean, Hugh.

Mac Giolla Fhionntóg an Fear-dána (fl. 1420) Author of eulogy of Maol Coluim MacGregor (chief, 1415–40) in the Book of the Dean of Lismore (q.v.); it has graceful stanzas describing his house and in compliment to his wife, a daughter of Lamont. (See W. J. Watson 1937, 26.)

DST

MacGregor, James (*c*.1480–1551) Vicar of Fortingall, Dean of Lismore, and notary public; probably principal compiler of Book of the Dean (q.v.).

DST

MacGregor, Revd Dr James (1759–1828) Born near Comrie, Perthshire. Emigrated to Nova Scotia in 1786, where he was the first Protestant Gaelic-speaking (Anabaptist) minister. Settled in Pictou county. Composed Calvinist hymns (1819) and translated the Confession of Faith, over a hundred of the Psalms and many paraphrases (unpublished). (See D. Maclean 1912, 39.)

DST

MacGregor, John (1848–post-1921) Born Lewis. Surgeon Lieut.-Col. in Indian Medical Service. Father of Alasdair Alpin MacGregor. Author of *Luinneagan Luaineach* (1897), which included anti-landlord verses; 'Fanndaigeadh na Gàidhlig', with its vivid personification of Gaelic's decline; and the stirring song 'Tìr nam beann àrd'.

DST

◄ *Somhairle MacGill-Eain (Sorley Maclean).*

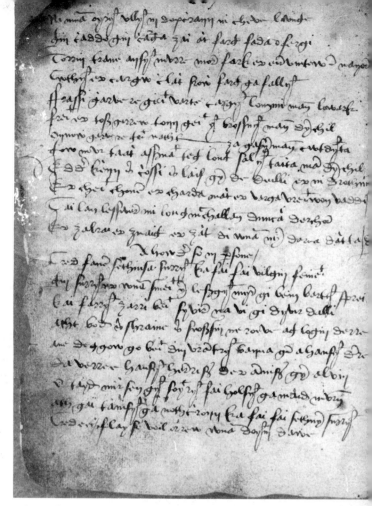

A page from the Book of the Dean of Lismore (q.v.), compiled by James MacGregor. National Library of Scotland Adv MS 72.1.37.

MacGregor, Rob Roy (1671–1734) Colourful Highland folk hero, renowned for his tireless feud against the Duke of Montrose, and his support for the poor and the oppressed. Some of his exploits may be wholly legendary, others have doubtless gained in retelling. Though a popular subject for nineteenth-century painters and illustrators, there is no contemporary portrait of him. Rob Roy is buried in Balquidder churchyard, Perthshire. (See next entry.)

MacGregors Iain, son of Malcolm of Glenorchy, chief of a clan claiming descent from the royal house of Alpín, was captured by the English in 1296. Subsequently Mariota, the heiress, married Iain Campbell, and his clan laid claim to Glenorchy, although the union was childless. Gregor of the Golden Bridles led the resistance movement and was succeeded by his son Iain MacGregor (who died in 1390); so the clan obtained its patronymic. In 1432 Mac Cailein Mór's second son, Sir Colin, received a charter to Glenorchy, and the Campbell campaign to dispossess the MacGregors culminated in 1603, when these were outlawed by statute and their name proscribed. The penal laws were repealed finally in 1774. The Book of the Dean of Lismore (q.v.), compiled by James Mac-Gregor (q.v.), illumines the clan's culture up to that period. Under the name of Gregory it contributed one of the most distinguished intellectual dynasties in Europe from the time of David of Kinairdie (1627–1720) and his brother James (1638–75), inventor of the reflecting telescope. By 1766 the descendants of David alone had provided fifteen university professors, and their eminence continued through the nineteenth century. In 1715 James Gregory, Professor of Medicine at Aberdeen was visited by his cousin Rob Roy (q.v.), leader of their proscribed clan. (See the Gregories in *DNB* and the *Encyclopaedia Britannica*, which list their most influential publications; see also W. H. Murray, which contains a comprehensive bibliography.)   IG

MacGriogóir, Domhnall Liath Author of broad poem in the Book of the Dean of Lismore (q.v.) about three girls of easy virtue. (See Quiggin 1937, 73.)   DST

MacGriogóir, Donnchadh mac Dhubhghaill Mhaoil (d. 1512) Brother of James MacGregor, Dean of Lismore (q.v.). He has four poems and a fragment in the Book of the Dean of Lismore, including one full of rhymed genealogy to John MacGregor (d. 1519), and 'Mairg bean nach bi ag aonshagart', broad sexual verses. (See W. J. Watson 1937, 212.)
                    DST

Mac Iain Deòrsa, *see* Hay, George Campbell.

MacIlleMhoire, Murchadh (Murdo Morrison) (b. 1884) Born Shader Barvas, Lewis. Emigrated to USA (Niagara Falls), 1911. Author of 'O seinnidh mise rann air an fhonn seo an dràsd'. (See MacIlleMhoire 1923; I. N. MacLeòid 1916, 151–60.)   DST

MacInnes, Revd Duncan (*c.*1820–1903) Of Oban. Minister of Cromdale, 1856–86. Author of a book of bilingual dialogues (D. MacInnes 1880) and collector of folktales for one volume of *Waifs and Strays* (Lord A. Campbell 1890).   AB

MacInnes, John (b. 1930) Born Baile na Cille, Lewis. On the staff of the School of Scottish Studies, University of Edinburgh, since 1958. Author of important articles on Gaelic song, poetry, etc. (see Bibliography).   DST

MacInnes, Revd Dr John (1893–1976) From Skye. Minister at Hopeman and elsewhere. An authority on Highland Church history and theology. Author of many books and articles, notably MacInnes (1951). (See Murchison 1977.)   TMM

MacInnes, Malcolm (1871–1951) Born Sleat, Skye. Secretary of Johannesburg School Board, 1907–26. Piping judge. Author of Gaelic operetta *Iseabail na h-Airigh* (1933); indexed new edition of *Gaelic Proverbs*, ed. Dr Alexander Nicolson (q.v.) (1951).   DST

Macintosh, Archbishop Donald (d. 1943) Born Morar. Roman Catholic Archbishop of Glasgow, 1921–43.   DST

Macintosh, Duncan (Donncha Gobha) (*c.*1806–*c.*1846) Named as author of 1831 Collection, but P. Cameron (1892) says that the songs in it were by his grandfather's (second) wife, Mairearad Ghobha, Atholl *bana-bhàrd* (poetess). According to Donald Maclean (D. Maclean 1915, 229–30) he was known as Am Bàrd Mùgach, and Maclean believed that Macintosh himself composed songs.   DST

McIntosh, Peter (*c.*1789–1876) Of Campbeltown. Teacher and Free Church catechist in Islay, Knapdale and Gigha. Author of *History of Kintyre* (1870), including legends from Gaelic oral tradition.   AB

Macintyre, Duncan Bàn, *see* Mac-an-t-Saoir, Donnchadh Bàn.

Macintyre, James (Fear Ghlinn Nodha) (fl. 1770) Fragments of his verse survive in the McLagan Manuscripts, including a sharp attack on Samuel Johnson (*TGSI*, 22, 177). He was involved in work on Gaelic dictionaries, etc.   DST

Macintyre, Revd Joseph (1735–1823) Minister of Glenorchy. His daughter Susan married John Stuart of Luss (q.v.).   DST

Macintyre, Malcolm, *see* Calum Dubh nam Protaigean.

MacIomhair, Dòmhnall (Donald Maciver) (1857–?1935) Born Uig, Lewis, son of a farmer (and Gaelic schoolmaster from 1869). Donald was headmaster of Bayble School, 1896–1922. Author of the fine song 'An ataireachd àrd' and a book of Lewis and Harris place names. (See Maciver 1934; I. N. MacLeòid 1916, 161–76.) DST

Maciver, Donald, *see* MacIomhair, Dòmhnall.

MacIver, Robert M. (1882–1970) Born Stornoway. Political scientist; author of *The Modern State* (1926), etc. DST

Mackay, Aeneas Thomas (1860–1922) Gaelic publisher, Stirling. DST

Mackay, Col. (fl. 1800) Son of James Mackay, tacksman of Skerray, Sutherland. Collector of some Ossianic ballads, now missing. (See Beaton 1923, 37.) DST

Mackay, Duncan, *see* Donnchadh Gobha.

Mackay, Revd George William (1863–1931) Minister of Killin. President An Comunn Gaidhealach (q.v.), 1919–22. DST

Mackay, J. G. (1869–1942) Translated many of the folktales collected by J. F. Campbell (q.v.), and edited *More West Highland Tales* (1940). DST

Mackay, John (1656–1754), *see* Pìobaire Dall, am.

Mackay, Revd John (1680–1753) Descended from Aodh Dubh, 12th chief of Strathnaver; grandfather of Donald Sage (q.v.). Educated at Edinburgh and Utrecht. Minister of Lairg, 1714–49. (His manuscript Gaelic sermons are reproduced in *SGS*, 9, 176ff.) DST

Mackay, John (fl. 1736–46) Of Mudale, Sutherland. A religious poet, whose work was published in *Dain Spioràdail* (1835) and in a volume edited by John Rose entitled *Baird na Gaidhealtachd* (1851). (See Grimble 1979b, 25–6, 69, 87–8, 155.) IG

Mackay, Revd Dr Mackintosh (1793–1873) From Sutherland. Edited the periodical *An Fhianuis*, 1845–50, and the Highland Society's Gaelic Dictionary (1828), and wrote a Gaelic history of the Church. (See J. Kennedy 1877, 79; H. Whyte 1908.) TMM

Mackay, William (1848–1928) Born Glen Urquhart. Inverness solicitor. President of An Comunn Gaidhealach (q.v.), 1909–12; a founder of the Gaelic Society of Inverness; author of *Urquhart and Glenmoriston* (1914), etc. DST

Mackay Country, *see* Dùthaich Mhic Aoidh.

Mackay's Regiment, *see* regiments, Highland.

Mackays of Gairloch The first of this line, Ruairidh, born in Sutherland in 1592, became piper to MacKenzie of Gairloch in 1609. He composed several *piobaireachd*, including 'Corrienessan's Salute'. His only son, Iain, born in 1656, became blind at the age of seven. Known thereafter as Iain Dall, he became famous as both a piper and a poet. He was taught by Patrick Óg MacCrimmon (*see* **MacCrimmons**) and became piper to MacKenzie in 1689 on the death of his father.

He is credited with thirty compositions, including 'The Unjust Incarceration', 'The Lament for Patrick Og MacCrimmon', 'Munro's Salute', 'Corrienessan's Lament', 'The Blind Piper's Obstinacy' and (with Patrick Óg MacCrimmon) 'The Half-Finished Tune'.

He had one son, Angus, born in 1725, and a daughter. Angus succeeded him as hereditary piper in 1754. His compositions include 'Mary's Praise', 'MacKenzie of Applecross's Salute', 'MacLeod of Raasay's Salute' and 'The Desperate Battle'.

Angus's son, John Roy, born 1753, followed in the family tradition but in about 1800 emigrated to Nova Scotia, where he died in 1835. SMCN

Mackays of Raasay John MacKay was born in Raasay in 1767. He had lessons from Iain Dubh MacCrimmon, Donald Ruadh MacCrimmon (see **MacCrimmons**) and Angus MacKay of Gairloch. In 1792 he won the Highland Society of London Prize Pipe at Edinburgh, and by the beginning of the nineteenth century he was recognized as the best player and teacher in Scotland. In 1823 he moved to Drummond Castle in Perthshire as piper, but about ten years later he returned to Skye, where he died at Kyleakin in 1848. He could play over two hundred *piobaireachds* from memory. He taught John Ban

MacKenzie (1796–1864), Angus Macpherson (1800–87), Donald Cameron (1810–68) and his own four sons. He composed a number of tunes, including 'MacLeod of Colbeck's Lament', 'The Battle of Waterloo', 'King George the Third's Lament', 'Davidson of Tulloch's Salute' and 'Lady Doyle's Salute'.

His sons Donald, Roderick, Angus and John were all notable pipers. Angus was the piping genius of the nineteenth century. He won the Prize Pipe in 1835, when he was already preparing for publication *A Collection of Ancient Pìobaireachd*, the first acceptable attempt to write *ceòl mòr* in staff notation.

He was piper to Campbell of Islay until 1843, when he was appointed piper to Queen Victoria. He edited *The Piper's Assistant*, a tutor for the bagpipe, and invented with Hugh MacKay (no relation) the competition-type march. His compositions include 'Glengarry Gathering', 'Balmoral Highlanders', 'Abercairney Highlanders', 'Blackmount Forest', 'Highland Wedding' and 'Bonnie Anne'. He developed a mental illness in 1854 and died in 1859.

SMCN

MacKechnie, Donald, *see* MacEacharn, Dòmhnall.

Mackechnie, Revd John (1897–1977) From Glasgow. Minister in Glasgow and Reader in Celtic at the University of Aberdeen. Produced *Catalogue of Gaelic Manuscripts* (1973) and other works. (See Murchison 1977b.)

TMM

Mackellar, David, *see* Macealair, Daibhidh.

Mackellar, Mrs Mary (1836–90) From Lochaber. Gaelic writer. (See *Celt. Mon.*, 1, 94, 117; Mackellar 1880; M. C. Macleod 1913, 58; *TGSI*.)

TMM

Mackenzie of Achilty, Alasdair (Alasdair mac Mhurchaidh) (d. 1642) Fourth chief of Achilty. Author of a few poems on the conflict between spirit and flesh and of 'Is tùrsach dhuinne ri port', in which he mourns the deaths of great men he has known (*c.*1600–43). His language has a light colouring of classical forms, and he uses both semi-bardic metres and the *ceangal*, or final binding stanza. (See S. Maclean 1953; D. S. Thomson 1974a.)

DST

Mackenzie of Achilty, Murdo (Murchadh Mór mac Mhic Mhurchaidh) (d. *c.* 1689) Fifth chief of

Achilty and Seaforth's factor in Lewis. A poet who, like his father, reverts to the spirit/flesh conflict. Two poems survive on the betrayal and exile of Charles II, a short poem on human vanity, an elegy on Donald of Sleat (1643), a love poem, a song for a grandson and a delightful poem about his boat, 'An Làir Dhonn'. His verse also has semi-bardic characteristics. (See W. Matheson 1969, 157–62, 178; D. S. Thomson 1974a, 113–15.)

DST

Mackenzie, Sir Alexander (1764–1820) Born Stornoway. Explorer of Mackenzie River (Canada), etc.

DST

Mackenzie, Alexander (1822–92) Born Logierait, Perthshire. First Liberal Prime Minister of Canada.

DST

Mackenzie, Alexander ('Clach') (1838–98) Clan historian. Editor of the periodical *Scottish Highlander*.

DST

MacKenzie, Archibald J. (Eairdsidh Sheumais) (1861–1939) Born in Rear Christmas Island, Cape Breton. Son of Seumas Dhomhnuill Ic Eachainn and Catriona Eachainn Ruaidh, of Barra, and father of Hugh F. MacKenzie. He was a schoolteacher but is best remembered as a Gaelic poet. His best-known works included 'Fàilt a Bhonnaich Choirc', 'An Tulach Bhòidheach' and 'Oran na h-aois', as well as numerous *sgeulachdan* (stories) noted for their humour and originality. His *History of Christmas Island Parish*, published in 1926, is a valuable source of information on Scottish settlement in central Cape Breton and is being updated for republication. (See *Canadian-American Gael*, vol. 2, 8.)

RJM

Mackenzie, Revd Colin N. (b. 1917) From Taransay, Harris. Bard at National Mod, 1952. Prolific author of short stories and tales of the supernatural (*Nach Neònach Sin* 1973), etc. Continues to publish poetry occasionally, including effective Burns translations. His first short-story collection, *Oirthir Tìm* (1969), takes subjects from the outer edges of consciousness; his short novel *A' Leth Eile* (1971) is a picaresque romance. The picaresque continues to be explored in his stories about tinkers (*Gairm*, late 1970s, continuing). His fine command of speech idioms sometimes leads to prolixity but is richly humorous. (See also D. Meek 1983.)

DST

Mackenzie, Donald Alexander (b. 1873) Contributor to *Celtic Review*, *Celtic Monthly*, etc., and author of numerous books on national myths. (See Macbean 1921.) DST

Mackenzie, Revd Donald William (1868–1943) Born Airigh-bhruthaich, Lewis. Taught in Ladies' Highland Association schools. Minister in Rothesay, Ulva, Kilmelford. Author of Burns translations, 'Puinneagan càil', etc. (See I. N. MacLeòid 1916, 39–57.) DST

Mackenzie, George (b. *c*.1655) 2nd of Gruineard. Author of 'An Obair Nodha', a poem on sexual licence to which Sìleas na Ceapaich (q.v.) replies. (See C. Ó Baoill 1972, 167.) DST

MacKenzie, Hugh F. (1895–1971) Born Christmas Island, Cape Breton. Piper, violinist, Gaelic instructor and radio broadcaster. One of the founders and *seanchaidh* (oral historian) of the Gaelic Society of Cape Breton. He worked closely with Sister Margaret Beaton (q.v.). He also broadcast a weekly Gaelic programme, *Mac Talla an Eilein*, on CBC and edited weekly Gaelic column in the *Cape Breton Highlander*. RJM

Mackenzie, John (1806–48) Born in parish of Gairloch. Edited first edition of Uilleam Ros, *Sàr Obair* (1841); author of *Eachdraidh a' Phrionnsa* (1844), *English-Gaelic Dictionary* (1845), etc. (See *An Gaidheal*, December 1934, August 1948.) DST

Mackenzie, Revd Lachlan (1754–1819) From Urray; schoolmaster and minister of Lochcarron (1782–1819). Venerated in folk-memory as a critic of landlord tyranny. (See Donald Maclean 1915, 252ff.; I. Murray 1979.) TMM

MacKenzie, Neil (1795–1879) Native of Arran. Influential minister in St Kilda, 1830–44; minister of Duror, 1844–5; Kilbrandon, 1845–52; Kilchrenan, 1852–79. At the centre of the St Kilda religious revival of 1842–4. Encouraged St Kildans 'to cultivate the art of reciting their ancient stories and of singing their pathetic Gaelic songs'. (See J. B. MacKenzie 1911, 3–4.) RMCL

Mackenzie regiments, *see* regiments, Highland.

Mackenzie, W. C. (1862–1952) Born Stornoway. Author of *History of the Outer Hebrides* (1903), *The Western Isles* (1932), etc. DST

Mackenzie, William (1748–1838) Born near Culduthel, Inverness-shire. His hymns and poems are to be found in J. Rose (ed.), *Metrical Reliques of 'the Men' in the Highlands* (1851). DST

Mackenzie, William (1857–1907) Born Lewis. Author of songs collected under the title *Cnoc Chùsbaig* (1936, 1982). DST

MacKenzies, rise to power The eponymous ancestor, Cainnech, is on record in 1264. He belonged to a family, originally from the Aird on the southern shore of the Beauly Firth, which held office as constables of Eilean Donan Castle, in Kintail, under the Earls of Ross. But they quarrelled with the Earl when he made his peace with Robert Bruce in 1307 and remained in alliance with the MacDougalls of Lorn. When Eilean Donan was successfully besieged in 1331 the ruin of the family was complete; surviving members took refuge in Lorn. Yet their cause never went wholly by default, as the confederate clans of Maclennan, MacIver and Macleay continued, on their behalf, to sustain a struggle that culminated in the battle of Bealach na Bròige in 1369. The Earl of Ross won the day, but he was last of his line, and his death three years later was a turning-point in the history of the MacKenzies – that, and the death in 1371 of David II, last of the house of Bruce. The exiled family was now able to return, though not to Kintail. It settled at Kinellan, near Strathpeffer, and the crannog in the loch was its place of defence. But the clan was divided, one faction adhering to the Lords of the Isles while the other, led by the Kinellan family, adopted as its motto 'Cuidich an Rìgh' (Help the King) and refused to take part in the Harlaw campaign. Thus was laid the foundation of the family's rise to power – a rise that was in inverse proportion to the decline and fall of the Lordship of the Isles. The earldom of Ross was detached from the Lordship and annexed to the Crown in 1476, and now the MacKenzies first appear in authentic records as recipients of land within its bounds. The process of aggrandizement had begun through which the clan became dominant in the northern Highlands until Jacobite times. (See W. MacKenzie 1894; W. Matheson 1963, 193–228; Warrand 1965.) WM

MacKinlay, Fergus, *see* MacFhionnlaigh, Fearghas.

MacKinnon, Alexander, *see* MacFhionghuin, Alasdair.

MacKinnon, Professor Donald (1839–1914) Born Colonsay. First holder of the Chair of Celtic, University of Edinburgh, 1882–1914. Author of *A Descriptive Catalogue of Gaelic Manuscripts* (1912); consultant editor for *Celtic Review;* author of essays on Gaelic proverbs, 'An seann sgoil', etc. (See L. Mackinnon 1956.)   DST

MacKinnon, Revd Dr Donald (1890–1966) From Applecross. Schoolmaster and then Free Church minister at Portree and Kennoway. Assiduous researcher into Highland genealogies, clan history and Church history; editor of *Clan Macleod Magazine.* (See Murchison 1966; A. H. Morrison 1967, 219.)   TMM

MacKinnon, Jonathan (1869–1944) Born in Whycocamagh, Cape Breton; of Skye descent. Founder and editor of *Mac Talla*, a Gaelic weekly (latterly fortnightly), 1892–1904, and of *Fear na Céilidh*, a monthly publication, 1928–30. Also translated and wrote local history. (See J. L. Campbell 1938b, 425–8; 1950, 3; 1952, 216–17; C. W. Dunn 1953, 83–8; D. Maclean Sinclair 1949, 254.)   JLC

MacKinnon, Lachlan, *see* Lachlann mac Theàrlaich Oig.

Mackintosh, Charles Rennie (1868–1928) Of Glasgow. Designer and architect. Principal figure of the Glasgow school of *art nouveau;* architect of both the Glasgow School of Art and its library and extensions (1897–1909) and of a number of houses near Glasgow (1899–1910); designer of the interior of four tearooms in Glasgow, together with all their furniture and equipment. The first British architect to acquire an international reputation since the eighteenth century. (See also **art, Gaelic, in modern times.**)   DST

Charles Rennie Macintosh's design for the Daily Record *building in Glasgow, 1901. Pencil, ink and watercolour. University of Glasgow, Mackintosh Collection.* ▶

MacLachlainn, Giolla Pàdraig (fl. ?1520) Author of poem in the Book of the Dean of Lismore (q.v.) addressed to James Campbell of Lawers. (See W. J. Watson 1937, 106.) DST

MacLachlainn, Uilleam (dates unknown) Author of poem in the Book of the Dean of Lismore (q.v.). (See Quiggin 1937, 72.) DST

MacLachlan, Ewen (1773–1822) From Lochaber. A notable classicist; Librarian of King's College, headmaster of Grammar School, Old Aberdeen. A proposal in about 1811 to appoint him to a professorship of Gaelic at Edinburgh University came to nothing (D. S. Thomson 1968, 212), but his work on Gaelic manuscripts and the Highland Society Dictionary shows why he was considered a likely candidate. Various letters by him survive, one of them a Gaelic letter, dated 1811, to his father (ibid., 210). He published *Metrical Effusions* in 1807 (enlarged edn 1816): these include Latin, Greek, Gaelic and English verse, with such items as a seventeen-page verse Valedictory Discourse and a lengthy metrical paraphrase of St John's Revelation.

MacLachlan had contributed Gaelic poems and translations to Allan MacDougall's *Orain Ghaidhealacha* (1798), but his main Gaelic work, a translation of Books 1–7 (8 incomplete) of the *Iliad*, remained unpublished until 1937 (John MacDonald 1937); it is a steady rather than an exciting performance, though there are touches of exuberance (e.g. *Ghoil an lionncuthaich m'a sgairt*, 1, 183). The 1937 collection includes four seasonal poems, which are more stylized than the earlier seasonal poems, various occasional pieces and the popular song 'Gur gile mo leannan'; not all his Gaelic verse is included here. (See P. J. Anderson 1918; D. MacKinnon 1912, e.g. p. 258; A. Maclean Sinclair 1890–6; D. S. Thomson 1968.) DST

MacLachlan, John (d. *c.*1750) Of the Kilbride family. Composed a poem on the birth of Prince Charles (who was regarded as a phoenix) in Rome. (See J. L. Campbell 1933.) DST

MacLachlan, John (1804–74) Of Rahoy. Physician and aristocrat. Representative of a group of nineteenth-century poets, of talent rather than genius, who are consummate craftsmen in the regularities of minor poetry. But MacLachlan's poetry of the Clearances, with its poignant realization of a devastated land, and in one poem bitter anger, rises above these limitations. JMCI

MacLachlans The MacLachlans of Craiginterve, Kilmartin, an hereditary medical family in the classical tradition of the Gaelic learned orders, were employed by the Campbells of Argyll at least from the second half of the fifteenth century to the beginning of the seventeenth. Perhaps by 1500 their more famous offshoot, the MacLachlans of Kilbride, Seil, had already made the transition from medicine to the Church, providing thereafter a long succession of clerics associated particularly with the parish church of Kilbrandon. Their continuing interest in Gaelic culture manifests itself in the Kilbride Collection of medieval Gaelic manuscripts, now in the National Library of Scotland. (See Bannerman 1977a, 1–34.) JWMB

McLagan, James (1728–1805) Born Ballechin, Perthshire. Minister at Amulree. Chaplain to 42nd (Black Watch) Regiment and served in N. Ireland, Isle of Man, America. Minister at Blair Atholl. Married Catherine, daughter of the Revd James Stuart of Killin. Made a large and valuable collection of songs and ballads and left various literary notes (see also **Gillies, John**). Supplied some Ossianic ballads to James Macpherson (q.v.) (D. S. Thomson 1952, 8 *et passim*). Manuscripts in Glasgow University Library. (For letter written 1771, urging compilation of Gaelic Dictionary, see *Edinburgh Monthly Magazine*, June 1817, 256–60. See also A. Cameron 1892–94, I, 295–370; R. L. Thomson 1961; D. S. Thomson 1958b.) DST

MacLaghmainn, Raibeart (dates unknown) Author of poem in the Book of the Dean of Lismore (q.v.). (See Quiggin 1937, 17.) DST

MacLaren, David and James (both d. 1953) Proprietors of Gaelic publishing firm of Alexander MacLaren and Sons, Glasgow. DST

MacLauchlan, Revd Dr Thomas (1815–86) From Moy, Inverness-shire. Minister in Edinburgh. Edited the Book of the Dean of Lismore (q.v.) and Carswell's (q.v.) Gaelic translation of Knox's Liturgy (1873). (See Leask 1905.) TMM

McLaurin, Alexander (1740–1820) From Cultybraggan, Comrie. SSPCK teacher, Strathbraan. Postmaster in Edinburgh, 1767–1809. An original promoter of Edinburgh Gaelic Schools Society and author of the Society's first Gaelic textbook (he paid for the printing of 3,000 copies). He also translated other religious texts. (See Harding 1980.)　　　DST

Maclaurin, Colin (1698–1746) Born in Glendaruel, Argyll. The youngest child of John Maclaurin, minister of the parish of Kilmodan, who was one of those responsible for the Gaelic metrical translation of the Psalms issued by the Synod of Argyll in 1694. Colin, who was a student at the University of Glasgow, became Professor of Mathematics at Marischal College, Aberdeen, and later at the University of Edinburgh and was, after Newton and Leibniz, perhaps the most distinguished mathematician of his time. He left Kilmodan at a very early age; it is not known whether he retained a knowledge of Gaelic in later life. (See *DNB*, 1893, 196; Mills 1982.)　　　RAR

MacLaurin, John (1658–98) From Inveraray. Minister of Kilmodan. Part-translator and editor of Gaelic Psalms published in 1694. (See *Fasti*; MacTabish 1934.)　　　IG

Maclean, Revd Calum (1895–1960) Born Scarp, Harris. Minister at Conon Bridge. Part-author, with I. M. Moffatt-Pender, of *Mo Nighean Donn Bhòidheach* (1924). Co-editor with T. M. Murchison, of *Alba* (1948). Maclean's daughter, Una, was married to John Macintosh MP.　　　DST

Maclean, Calum I. (1915–60) From Raasay (brother of Somhairle and John, q.v.). Worked with the Irish Folklore Commission collecting, recording and cataloguing Irish and Scottish Gaelic tales, songs, etc., then (from 1951) with the School of Scottish Studies. He made large collections from Seumas MacKinnon of Barra, Angus MacMillan of Benbecula, Duncan MacDonald of South Uist and John MacDonald of Lochaber. Published a highly individual book, *The Highlands* (1959). (See memoir by Seán Ó Súilleabháin in C. I. Maclean 1975.)　　　DST

Maclean, Dòmhnall Bàn (fl. ? early eighteenth century) One of the minor Maclean poets, to whom a poem of 1725 is ascribed, but nothing is known about him.　　　CÓB

Maclean, Revd Dr Donald (1869–1943) From Lochcarron. Free Church minister in Edinburgh; Professor of Church History in Free Church college there, 1920–43. Editor of *Evangelical Quarterly* and author of many books, notably *The Spiritual Songs of Dugald Buchanan* (1913), *Aspects of Scottish Church History* (1927) and *The Counter-Reformation in Scotland, 1560–1930* (1931). (See Macbean 1921, 102.)　　　TMM

Maclean, Duncan (1795–1871) Born Killin. Free Church minister, Glen Urquhart. Bard and contributor to *An Teachdaire Gaelach* under pen-name 'Fìor Ghael'. (See P. Cameron 1894.)　　　DST

Maclean, Hector (c.1490–c.1560), *see* Cléireach Beag, an.

Maclean, Hector (c.?1600–post-1651), *see* Eachann Bacach.

Maclean, Dr Hector (1703–84) Of Grulin. In the army in Flanders 1716–28. A medical doctor, he lived for many years in Glasgow, returning to Mull c.1767 (Maclean-Bristol 1980, 11–12, 15). He made an important manuscript collection of Gaelic poetry (C. Ó Baoill 1979, xxx) and probably wrote an extant genealogical account of the Macleans (W. Macfarlane 1900, I, 118).　　　CÓB

Maclean, Hector (d. 1893) From Islay. Editor of *Ultonian Hero Ballads* (1892).　　　DST

Maclean, Hugh (Eoghan Mac Gilleoin) (fl. late seventeenth century) schoolmaster at Kilchenzie, Kintyre, 1699. During the years 1690 to 1698 he wrote manuscripts containing 'Táin Bó Cuailnge' and other tales (NLS 72.1.36, 14873; TCD 1307, 1362). He met Edward Lhuyd (q.v.); and probably taught William MacMurchy (q.v.), whose Gaelic script resembles his. (See J. L. Campbell and D. S. Thomson 1963, 10.)　　　RIB

Maclean, John (Iain mac Ailein) (post-1650–ante-1745), *see* Aos-dàna.

Maclean, Revd John (c.1680–1756), *see* Maighstir Seathan.

MacLean, John (Bàrd Thighearna Cholla) (1787–1848) Born in Caolas, Tiree. A shoemaker by trade, he held the honorific position of bard to the Laird of Coll. His verse is mainly traditional eulogy, commemorating salient events in the laird's life (e.g. his purchase of the Island of Muck), although MacLean also composed some township verse and hymns. He emigrated to Nova Scotia in 1819, taking two important manuscript collections of Gaelic verse, one compiled by himself and the other by Dr Hector Maclean (q.v.) (originals in Public Archives, Halifax, Nova Scotia; copies in Aberdeen, Edinburgh and Glasgow University Libraries.) Best-known for his poem 'A' Choille Ghruamach' (The Gloomy Wood), reflecting his initial disillusionment with the New World. (See Cregeen and Mackenzie 1978, 7–10; J. MacLean 1835; A. MacLean Sinclair 1881; forthcoming article in *Dictionary of Canadian Biography* by Maureen Lonergan Williams.)   DEM

MacLean, John (Bàrd Bhaile Mhàrtainn) (1827–95) From Balemartin, Tiree. Versatile, witty composer of several popular love songs and humorous satires. Active in Land Agitation. (See H. Cameron 1932, 142–87; Cregeen and Mackenzie 1978, 19–22.)   DEM

Maclean, Lachlan (1798–1848) From Coll. A shopkeeper in Glasgow. A Gaelic enthusiast who acquired two nicknames, 'Lachlann na Gàidhlig' and 'Lachann nam Mogan'. He composed hymns and has been cited by Professor Donald MacKinnon as among the four best Gaelic prose writers. Contributed to Caraid nan Gaidheal's (q.v.) periodicals under the pennames 'Am Bùirdeiseach Bàn', 'An Gaidheal anns a' Bhaile', 'Eóghan Og' and 'MacTalla'. Edited *An Teachdaire Ur Gaidhealach*, 1835–6. Publications included a history of Iona and a book on etiquette, but notably *Adhamh agus Eubh* (1837), which put the case for Gaelic as the original language of mankind. (See E. MacDhughaill 1951, 31; D. J. Macleod 1977, 207.)   TMM

Maclean, Lachlann (late seventeenth – early eighteenth centuries) One of the minor Maclean poets. Two poems ascribed to him, dated 1687 and post-1715, may be by two different poets.   CÓB

Maclean, Dr Magnus (1858–1937) From Skye. Scientist and Gaelic scholar. Professor of Electrical Engineering at Glasgow Technical College; first lecturer in Celtic at the University of Glasgow. His lectures were published in *The Literature of the Celts* (1902) and *The Literature of the Highlands* (1903). (See *An Gaidheal*, vol. 33, 5; *Celtic Monthly*, vol. 20, 174.)   TMM

Maclean, Revd Norman (1869–1952) Born Skye. Minister of St Cuthbert's Edinburgh. Prolific English author. Zionist.   DST

Maclean, Sorley, *see* MacGill-Eain, Somhairle.

Maclean's Highlanders, *see* regiments, Highland.

Macleans, conflict with Campbells, *see* Campbells and Macleans, rise and conflict.

MacLellan, Angus (1869–1965) From South Uist. Author of autobiography, *Saoghal an Treobhaiche*, translated by J. L. Campbell as *The Furrow Behind Me* (1962), etc.   DST

MacLellan, Lauchie (b. 1910) Born Dunvegan, Inverness County, Nova Scotia. Gaelic singer, storyteller and folklore informant.   JS

Maclennan, Dolina Born Lewis. Appointed *Fèisire* (Festivals Officer) of An Comunn Gaidhealach (q.v.), 1980. Author of radio serial *Na Moireasdanaich*.   DST

Maclennan, Revd Dr Malcolm (1862–1931) From Lewis. Educated in Canada. Minister in Canada and Edinburgh. Edited *An Deò-gréine* (q.v.) and *An Fhianais Ghaidhealach*. Author of many publications, notably a Gaelic dictionary (1925). (See Macbean 1921, 103; Murchison 1951.)   TMM

MacLeod of Raasay, *see* Gille Caluim Garbh Mac Ghille Chaluim.

MacLeod, Alexander (1786–1869) Native of Sutherland. First of several Evangelical ministers introduced into Lewis by Mrs MacKenzie of Seaforth. Minister of Uig, 1824–43, Rogart, 1843–69. Joined Free Church in 1843. At centre of Uig revival of 1820s and 1830s. (See Beaton 1925.)   RMCL

MacLeod, Angus (1885–1960) Born Garrabost, Lewis. Rector of Oban High School, 1919–50. Meticulous editor of Gaelic texts, especially the work of Donnchadh Bàn (q.v.).   DST

MacLeod, Calum I. N. (d. 1977) Son of John N. MacLeod (Alasdair Mòr) (q.v.). Worked in Nova Scotia as Gaelic Adviser, then as Head of Celtic Studies Department, at St Francis Xavier University. Editor/author of *Gaelic Songs in Nova Scotia* (1964),

Sgeulachdan à Albainn Nuaidh (1969), *Bàrdachd à Albainn Nuaidh* (1970) and *Sgial is Eachdraidh* (1977), all of which gather together much Nova Scotian Gaelic writing. He also wrote original Gaelic poetry.   DST

MacLeod, Charles (1921–83) From Lewis. Headmaster, Shawbost. Author of '*S fheàirrde duine gàire* and *Devil in the Wind*, both containing much accurate observation of Lewis life.   DST

MacLeod, Mrs Christina (d. 1954) From Lewis. Author of songs and poems published in *Ceòlraidh Cridhe* (1943) and *An Sireadh* (1952).   DST

MacLeod, Donald (1677–1749) From Skye. Acted as Bonnie Prince Charlie's henchman and pilot for seven weeks after Culloden. (See N. MacDhomhnaill 1976, 343–50.)   DST

MacLeod, Donald (1787–1873), *see* Dòmhnall nan Oran.

MacLeod, Donald (fl. 1814–57) Born at Rossal in Strathnaver. Stonemason. He witnessed the Sutherland Clearances (q.v.) and described them in the *Edinburgh Weekly Chronicle*, 1840–1. Enlarged account in *Gloomy Memories*, published in 1857 in Toronto, where he settled.   IG

MacLeod, Donald (1917–82) From Stornoway. Seaforth Highlanders Pipe-Major 1941–62; pupil of Inverness piper John MacDonald in MacCrimmon (q.v.) tradition. Very notable player of *ceòl mór* and *ceòl beag* (see **bagpipe, Highland**).   DST

MacLeod, Donald James (1879–1955) Born Lewis. Chief Inspector of Schools, Highland Division. Awarded Rennes doctorate for translation of Donnchadh Bàn (q.v.) into French. (See D. J. MacLeod n.d.)   DST

MacLeod, Donald John (b. 1943) Born Harris. At one time lecturer in Celtic, University of Glasgow. Author/editor of *Bibliography of Twentieth Century Gaelic books* (1981), a short-story anthology entitled *Dorcha tro Ghlainne* (1970), *Can Seo* (1979), etc.   DST

MacLeod, Finlay (b. 1937) Born Adabroc, Lewis. Served in the Fire Service in London in the late 1950s and, on returning to Scotland, began to write and produce (with an Aberdeen University cast of fellow students) Pinteresque plays (e.g. *Ceann Cropaic*, which used witty, psychologically sophisticated dialogue, sometimes minimally). *Shoni* was also televised. This phase, unfortunately, did not very long outlast MacLeod's student days. After a period of research into aspects of bilingualism, he moved to become Primary Adviser, and later Deputy Director of Education of the Western Isles, with Comhairle nan Eilean (q.v.) and has produced a long series of children's books and school texts, some of the more notable being *O Tractar!*, *Tugainn Cuairt* and *Rònan agus Brianuilt*.   DST

'**MacLeod, Fiona**', *see* Sharp, William.

MacLeod, Frederick Thomas (b. 1872) Solicitor in Edinburgh. Author of articles and books on piping, MacLeods of Dunvegan, etc.   DST

MacLeod, Hector, *see* MacLeòid, Eachann.

MacLeod, Revd Hugh (1803–94) Born Tongue, Sutherland. Emigrated to Canada, 1845. Moderator of Presbyterian Church of Canada, 1877.   DST

MacLeod, John (*c*.1780–1832) Came to Lewis from Skye as Gaelic schoolteacher. Fell foul of Barvas parish minister. Lost official post but made impact during early period of Evangelicalism in Lewis as teacher and preacher, particularly in Uig.   RMCL

MacLeod, John (fl. 1875) Born Cul-cinn, Stoer, Assynt. Author of *Dàin agus Orain* (1900), including 'Airigh a' Chul-chinn'.   DST

Macleod, Revd John (b. 1918) From Lewis. Minister in Canada, Edinburgh and (since 1967) Oban. His 'Laoidh na Réite' ('Thoir dhomh do làmh') won first prize in a BBC competition and Killarney Celtic Festival. (See J. Macleod 1976.)   TMM

Macleod, Revd Dr Kenneth (1871–1955) From Eigg. Minister in Colonsay and Gigha. Bard and Gaelic prose writer steeped in the tradition of Clan Macleod and Clanranald. Collector of Gaelic folklore and folk song and author of 'The Road to the Isles' (song). Collaborated with Mrs Kennedy-Fraser (q.v.) in *The Songs of the Hebrides* (1909) (See Murchison forthcoming.)   TMM

MacLeod, Malcolm (1865–1943) Born Stornoway. Clerk to the Govan School Board, then first Depute Director of Education for Glasgow. Worked hard all his life for the Gaelic cause, especially for An Comunn Gaidhealach (q.v.). JAS

MacLeod, Revd Malcolm (1881–1946) From Lewis. Minister in Glasgow and Balquhidder, etc. President of An Comunn Gaidhealach (q.v.). Editor of *An Gaidheal* and of *An Laoidheadair* (1935); author of *An Iuchair Oir* (1950). (See Murchison 1950.) TMM

MacLeod, Malcolm Angus (1899–1978) Born Skir Dhu, Victoria County, Nova Scotia. Gaelic singer and song informant. JS

Macleod, Malcolm Chisholm (1872–1954) From Wester Ross. Postmaster and journalist in Dundee from *c.*1908 to *c.*1942. Edited Dundee Highland Society's *Yearbook*, 1910–11, *Celtic Annual* (1912–14). (See M. C. Macleod 1908.) TMM

MacLeod, Mary, *see* Màiri Nighean Alasdair Ruaidh.

MacLeod, Murdo (1811–98) Born Habost, Lewis. Free Church elder from 1843; catechist in Lochs, 1849–98. Father of Murchadh a' Cheisdeir (q.v.). DST

MacLeod, Murdo (1837–1914), *see* Murchadh a' Cheisdeir.

MacLeod, Sir Norman (d. 1705) of Bernera. Patron of Mary MacLeod. Fought at Worcester. Tomb in Rodel Churchyard. DST

MacLeod, Revd Dr Norman (1783–1862), *see* Caraid nan Gaidheal.

Macleod, Norman (d. 1931) From Lewis. Teacher in Glasgow; in 1923 appointed first lecturer in Gaelic at Jordanhill College. Edited and revised Duncan Reid's *Elementary Course of Gaelic* (1913). TMM

MacLeod, Norman (Bàrd Bochd) (d. 1970) Humorous verse writer. Editor of poetry authology entitled *Bàrdachd á Leódhas* (1969). (See D. S. Thomson 1974a, 262–4.) DST

MacLeod, Roderick (Maighstir Ruairidh) (1795–1868) From Skye. Most popular nineteenth-century Skye preacher. Minister at Bracadale, 1823–37, where he underwent a conversion experience, and at Snizort, 1837–68. Evangelical leader before and after Disruption. Free Church Moderator, 1863. Involved in three revival movements. Champion of crofters. (See D. Gillies n.d.; M. Mackay 1869.) RMCL

MacLeod, Rory Mór, *see* Ruairi Mór MacLeod.

Macleod's Highlanders, *see* regiments, Highland.

MacLeòid, Dòmhnall (Red) (fl. 1950) From Bayble, Lewis. Author of modern classics such as 'Bàs an eich' and 'Oran an A. I.' (See D. I. MacLeòid 1972.) DST

MacLeòid, Eachann (Hector MacLeod) (fl. 1750) A South Uist bard who lived in west Inverness-shire. His surviving verse is mostly descriptive (e.g. of Coille Chrois), but he has one poem akin to an *aisling* (dream prophecy) imagining a new post-Culloden rising. (See J. Mackenzie 1877.) DST

MacLeòid, Iain (b. 1934) Born Glasgow, of Skye parents. Gaelic Principal, Lochaber High School and Dingwall Academy. Author of a collection of short stories, *Sràidean is Sléibhtean* (1971). DST

MacLeòid, Iain Dubh (fl. 1880) From Skye. Brother of Niall MacLeòid (q.v.). He was a sailor and also wrote poetry, but his life was very different from his brother's, as was his poetry. He was a poet of 'strong, realistic, compassionate poetry' (J. MacInnes 1976, 62). He had the reputation of dabbling in the black arts, so he may have had powers of hypnosis. Nowadays he is remembered mainly for the song 'Tha gillean òga tapaidh an Gleanndail ag èirigh suas'. (See J. MacInnes 1976.) IMCL

MacLeòid, Iain N., *see* Alasdair Mór.

MacLeòid, Murchadh (Murchadh Chaluim Sheòrais) (b. *c.*1909) Born Crowlista, Lewis. Bard and contributor to the journal *Gairm*. (See T. MacLeòid 1969, 37–47.) DST

MacLeòid, Niall (1843–1924) Born Glendale. Son of the Skye poet Dòmhnall nan Oran (q.v.). At the age of twenty-two he went to Edinburgh and remained there for the rest of his life, employed in the tea business. His poetry was published in *Clàrsach an Doire* (1883, etc.). He was the most popular Gaelic poet of the nineteenth century. Though now regarded as rather facile and superficial, he was a competent craftsman with a strong musical quality. (See J. MacInnes 1976; D. S. Thomson 1974a.)   IMCL

MacLeòid, Seumas (1880–1947) Born Scalpay, Harris. Maternal uncle of poet Norman MacCaig. Shopkeeper in Glasgow and Scalpay. Author of the Gaelic novel *Cailin Sgiathanach* (1923) and the English one *Highland Waif* (1928). (See **novel, the Gaelic**; D. R. Moireasdan 1979.)   DST

Mac Mhaighstir Alasdair, Alasdair (Alexander MacDonald) (*c*.1695–*c*.1770) The most famous of the eighteenth-century Gaelic poets. He came of a notable Gaelic family; he was a great-grandson of Ranald MacDonald of Benbecula and of Mary, daughter of Angus MacDonald of Islay (so claiming descent from King Robert II). Flora MacDonald of the '45 was his first cousin. His father, Maighstir Alasdair, was minister of Eilean Fhìonain (graduated University of Glasgow, 1674). Alasdair is thought to have been a student there too, and he set some of his poems to airs played on the bells in the Tolbooth Steeple, not far from the Old College (Murchison 1952); he compares the sound of whisky being poured with such bells: *'S binne no cluig-chiùil ud Ghlascha/T'fhuaim le bastal dol sa' chorn* (*Ais-eiridh*, 80). It may be that an early marriage, to Jane Mac-Donald of Dalness, interfered with his studies.

We find mention of him in records from 1729 onwards, as SSPCK teacher and catechist, in Eilean Fhìonain first, later in Coire a' Mhuilinn in Ardna-murchan. In 1744 his son Ranald is acting as his substitute in Coire a' Mhuilinn, Alasdair having 'deserted' his post to help rally the Jacobite clans. He held a Captain's commission in Prince Charlie's army and is almost certainly the author of the *Journall and Memoirs of P – C – Expedition into Scotland etc. 1745–46* (Lockhart Papers, vol. II, 1817); from one or two references there it could be thought that he had taken part in the '15 also.

Mac Mhaighstir Alasdair's collection of poems, *Ais-eiridh na Sean Chánoin Albannaich* (*The Resurrection of the Ancient Scottish Tongue*), was the first secular printed work in Gaelic (apart from his *Vocabulary* of 1741). A good many of the poems can be dated or placed in sequence by internal references or stylistic analysis. In the earlier part of the sequence we can place such poems as 'Oran d'a chéile nuadh-phòsda', the song to the bride he got from 'the Rhymer' (i.e. MacDonald of Dalness) – his attraction to freshly minted compounds shows here; his elegy on a dove, influenced no doubt by Catullus's poem on the death of Lesbia's sparrow, (the hendeca-syllabic metre may have influenced the choice of Gaelic metre); the 'Guidhe no Urnaigh an Ughdair don Cheòlraidh', an address to the Muses in which he reflects ruefully on his own poetic powers; and his poem in praise of Gaelic (perhaps written after the publication of David Malcolme's letters, etc., in 1738). A little later may come the pure nature poems, describing summer and winter, in praise of Allt an t-Siùcair, etc., with their general thematic indebted-ness to James Thomson's *Seasons*, their exact and detailed observation and their restrained sensuous-ness. Then there are the poems of pre-'45 incitement, the campaign poems and the poems of post-'45 disil-lusionment, a heady amalgam at times of lyrical ardour and intellectual analysis, as where, addressing King George, he discusses the Act of Settlement of 1701:

> Ciod e do cheart-s' air crùn
> Ach adhaircean bhith sparradh ort?
> 'S co-sean ri d'chòir o thùs
> Brìos òir-cheard bha Renfriù;
> Ach bha ion-faileis ann
> Do thrustar do dh' act Pàrlamaid
> A dh'fhoil an crùn ma d'cheann;
> Ach tog seo leat nad sgèith:
> An t-Uilleam rinn an t-act-s' dhuit
> Gum b'eucoireach e fèin.

What right have you to a crown? You should have horns (a horned helmet?) thrust on you. An equally ancient entitlement was that of Bryce, the goldsmith from Renfrew; but there was a shady, miscreant Act of Parliament that hurriedly thrust the crown on your head; but take this thought with you: the William who made this Act for you was an unrightful heir himself.

His major poem, 'Birlinn Chlann Raghnaill' (The Galley of Clan Ranald), is probably to be dated close to 1750 and did not appear in the 1751 collection. This is a striking *tour-de-force* of dramatic descrip-tion, precisely constructed but accommodating elements of the fantastic and with echoes of 'runs' from the saga 'Cath Fionntràgha', a version of which is in the poet's hand (Nat. Lib. MS 72.2.11).

Another aspect of his verse is a concern with ribaldry and satire – a poem on an outbreak of sexual disease in Ardnamurchan, the 'Dispraise of Morag', a distasteful but linguistically vivid reversal of the 'Praise', 'An Airc' (The Ark), a Ragman's Roll of Campbells especially who were politically on the opposing side, satire of the Oban Poetess, etc.

He was a man of strong views and violent emotions but with a hard intellectual cast of mind also; he was learned in the Gaelic tradition and open to influence from his other reading; he was an innovator and a conservative; and his poetry is full of the stimulating contradictions that proceed from these diversities. (See for texts, biography, etc., J. L. Campbell 1935a, 1935b; A. and A. MacDonald 1924; W. Mackay 1885; A. MacLeod 1933; for criticism, D. S. Thomson 1961, 1974a.) DST

MacMhaoilein, Donnchadh Author of fragment in the Book of the Dean of Lismore (q.v.). (See Quiggin 1937.) DST

MacMharcuis family Possibly an offshoot of the Irish learned family of Mac Craith, among whom the Christian name Marcus is attested in the fifteenth century (O'Grady 1926, 342–3). This family is first recorded with John McMarkisch, holding lands in Kintyre in 1506, apparently as a professional poet of some kind: it is not clear how his function differed from that of his MacMhuirich neighbours. John's descendants can be sketchily traced for the next two centuries, carrying on a learned tradition down to the time of Dòmhnall, schoolmaster in Farr, Sutherland, in 1681 (A. Mackay 1906, 442) and catechist in Lochaber until after 1700 (Ó Baoill 1976a, 184). CÓB

Mac Mhathain, am Bàrd, see Aos-dàna.

MacMhuirich (?), Brian (fl. 1675), see Brian, am Bàrd Asainteach.

MacMhuirich, Brian (fl. ? seventeenth century) author of (?) seventeenth-century poem 'Oran mulaid a' phrìosanaich an Dun Raghnaill'. Said to be the illegitimate son of one of the MacMhuirich bards. (See A. and A. MacDonald 1911, lviii, 342; Carmichael-Watson Manuscript, Edinburgh University Library, 135, 131.) DST

MacMhuirich, Cathal (fl. 1625) Does not appear in the MacMhuirich pedigree of 1800 and may have come to the office of chief MacMhuirich poet through the failure of Niall Mór's son, Lachlann, to take up the succession. He appears as a witness to various Clanranald transactions in 1629, 1630 and 1634, in some cases described as Clanranald's servitor, or secretary. There is some evidence of a rift between him and Clanranald (Iain Mùideartach) (D. S. Thomson 1977a) and the transfer of his main allegiance to MacDonald of Sleat. Surviving datable poems range from a poem to Colla Ciotach, 'Saoth liom do chor, a Cholla' (c.1615) (D. Stevenson 1980, 56) to the elegy for John MacLeod of Dunvegan, 'Do ísligh onóir Ghaoidheal' (1649), and they include the eulogy for Domhnall Mac Ailín, 'Foraois éigeas Innse

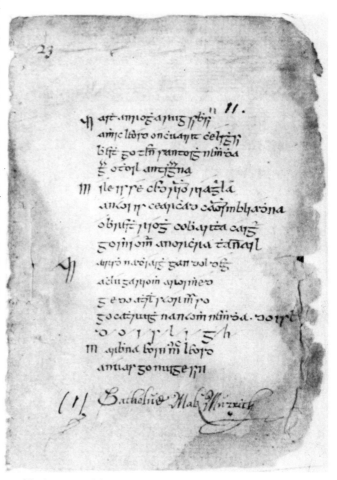

Final stanzas of Cathal Mac Mhuirich's poem 'Do ísligh onóir Ghaoidheal', 1649. Royal Irish Academy, MS E.i.3, p.23.

Gall' (pre-1618, and possibly the earliest surviving poem), a lament for four Clanranald gentlemen (c.1636), a poem on the death of Caitirfhíona, daughter of Dòmhnall Gorm of Sleat and wife of Mackenzie of Gairloch, 'Leasg linn gabháil go Gearrloch' (c.1635–40), a welcome to Dòmhnall MacEòin on his return from the Irish wars (c.1649), some short poems offering religious consolation to the bereaved, 'Sona do cheird, a Chalbhaigh', addressed to a bad poet, and 'Cionnas mhaireas mé am aonar', addressed to Eòin Mac Briain MacMhuirich (q.v.). Cathal MacMhuirich can be regarded as the finest poet of his line, combining technical skill with wit, intellectual strength and poetic originality. (See R. I. Black 1972, 1979a; Greene 1968; W. Matheson 1963; D. S. Thomson 1963, 1974a, 1977; W. J. Watson 1922.)

DST

MacMhuirich, Dòmhnall (fl. 1710) Son of Niall mac Dhòmhnaill Ghearr (see **MacMhuirich, Niall**). He taught his nephew, Niall (father of Lachlann of the 1800 pedigree) to read and write Gaelic history and poetry (Report, App. 276). Dòmhnall was granted the tack of half the bardic lands of Stadhlaigearraidh in 1707 and is on record as tenant of Drìomasdal in 1728 and as tacksman of Stadhlaigearraidh in 1732. He probably survived into the 1740s. Some rather dull poems by him survive, and his hand appears in the family manuscripts. He was the last practising MacMhuirich classical bard. (See D. S. Thomson 1963, and 1971, where he is wrongly referred to as the nephew of Niall.)

DST

MacMhuirich, Dòmhnall Geàrr (fl. 1650) Father of Niall MacMhuirich (q.v.), who signs a discharge to Clanranald in 1665 (SRO GD 201/1/84).

DST

MacMhuirich, Eòin (Mac Briain) (fl. ?1630) Cathal MacMhuirich has an elegy for him, 'Cionnas mhaireas mé am aonar', addressing him as mentor and fellow poet. He may be the person of that name who went to Ireland in 1647 and the Joannes McWirrich who was servitor to Ranald of Benbecula in 1625. (See Aitken, McDiarmid and Thomson 1977.)

DST

MacMhuirich, Giolla Coluim (Giolla Coluim Mac an Ollaimh) (fl. 1490) Identified, but with some reservations, as a MacMhuirich, possibly a son of Lachlann of 1485 (D. S. Thomson 1963, 18). Giolla Coluim has two, perhaps three poems in the Book of the Dean of Lismore (q.v.), one consisting both of

elegy for Angus Óg MacDonald (q.v.) and of attached analogue (W. J. Watson 1937, 82, and N. Ross 1939, 168), another being a more generalized lament for the Clan Donald, presumably relating to their final forfeiture in 1493 (W. J. Watson 1937, 90). The third poem, which Watson ascribed to Giolla Coluim and Quiggin to a Giolla Coimhdheadh Óg (Quiggin 1937, 100, 112), is a very amusing account of thiggers (beggars) who pester the poet (who refers to himself as the *ollamh* (doctor of poetry): W. J. Watson 1937, I. 697); the poet neatly turns the tables by asking John of the Isles to make good his losses (D. S. Thomson 1974a, 48–50).

DST

MacMhuirich, John (d. c.1510) Identified (D. S. Thomson 1963) as the Dean of Knoydart, who composed a poem to the head of Diarmad Ó Cairbre, murderer of Angus Óg of the Isles (q.v.) in 1490.

DST

MacMhuirich, John (fl. ?1520) Lands in south Kintyre and Glak in Kintyre were held by a poet of this name, according to various rentals from 1505 to 1541. The form 'Johannes McMurech Albany' is used in the Glak entry for 1541. Possibly the author of the Red Book (q.v.) poem 'Alba gan díon i ndiaidh Ailín' and of two poems in the Book of the Dean of Lismore (q.v.), 'Maith do chuid, a charbaid mhaoil' and 'Námha dhamh an dán', with the fragment 'Fir Alban 's ní hiad amháin'. (See D. S. Thomson 1963; W. Gillies 1977a.)

DST

MacMhuirich, Lachlann (fl. 1485) Witness to a charter of 1485 (given by Angus of the Isles to the monastery of St Columba on Iona). He appears as *Lacclannus mcmuredhaich archipoeta* and was presumably the chief MacMhuirich poet of his day.

DST

MacMhuirich, Lachlann Mór (fl. 1411) The *brosnachadh catha*, or battle incitement, known as the Harlaw Brosnachadh is ascribed to him; it is in an old unrhymed heptasyllabic metre and has an alphabetic structure. (See D. S. Thomson 1968.)

DST

MacMhuirich, Niall (c.1637–1726) Son of Dòmhnall Geàrr and successor of Cathal MacMhuirich (q.v.). His poems range in date from the early 1660s ('Dia bheatha ar ar los, a leinbh', on the birth of an heir to Dòmhnall mac Iain Mhùideartaich) to 1719 (Dá chúis ag milleadh ar meamna', in the year of the Glenshiel Rising), and they include an elegy for

Dòmhnall of Clanranald (1686), poems to Allan, the chief who succeeded him, poems on Allan's death after Sherrifmuir (1715) and two contributions to the dispute over the heraldic symbol of the Red Hand. A much less orthodox bard than Cathal (in terms of language and metrics), Niall shows an interest in metrics and has two poems in vernacular language and style. (See D. S. Thomson 1971, 1974a, 1977a.)

DST

MacMhuirich, Niall Mór (*c.*1550–post-1613). He was Niall MacLachlainn mhic Dhòmhnaill, his grandfather having probably held land in Kintyre in 1541; he may have been the first MacMhuirich poet to be firmly domiciled in Clanranald island territory. Of the few surviving poems ascribed to him, 'Sé hoidhche dhamhsa san Dún' probably dates to 1613; his fine lyric 'Soraidh slán don oidhche a-réir' is in the *dánta grádha* (literary, sometimes courtly) mode; and he probably composed the 'Seanchas na Píob o thús', a satirical and earthy piece on the bagpipes. (See D. S. Thomson 1977a.)

DST

Mac Mhurchaidh, Alasdair, *see* Mackenzie of Achilty, Alasdair.

MacMhurchaidh, Uilleam, *see* MacMurchy, William.

Macmillan, Angus (Aonghas Barrach) (1874–1954) From Benbecula. Notable storyteller. (See *Gairm*, vol. 3, 170ff.)

DST

MacMillan, Fr John (d. 1951) Priest in Barra. Poet and collector of traditional songs.

DST

Macmillan, Malcolm Kenneth (1913–78) From Lewis. Labour MP for Western Isles, 1935–70. Chairman of Highland Panel. Campaigner in 1960s for parliamentary democracy in Greece.

DST

MacMurchy, William (Uilleam MacMhurchaidh) (*c.*1700–78) Of Largie in Kintyre. Schoolmaster, tailor, weaver, piper, harper and poet as well as collector, writer and disseminator of manuscripts: he wrote NLS Adv. MSS. 72.2.12, 72.2.15, 73.2.2 (the Turner Manuscript) and the Inverneill Manuscript.

RIB

MacNaughton, John (fl. 1771) Preses (President) of the Gaelic Society, Edinburgh; the Revd James

MacLagan addressed a letter to him in 1771, urging the compilation of a Gaelic Dictionary (see *Edinburgh Monthly Magazine* June 1817, 256–60).

DST

MacNaughton, Peter (fl. 1880) From Baile-an-eas, Strathtay. Published translation of 'Ossian' (1887), turning the Gaelic translation of James MacPherson's work into unrhymed English verse.

DST

MacNeacail, Alasdair M. (Alexander Nicolson) (b. 1870) Born Lionel, Lewis. Author of 'An tèid thu leam a rìbhinn mhaiseach'. (See I. N. MacLeòid 1916, 177–84.)

DST

MacNeacail (? MacNeachdainn) an Tàillear (fl. ?1750) Perthshire author of heroic burlesque song. (See McLagan MS 60; also W. J. Watson 1918a.)

DST

MacNeacail, Aonghas (b. 1942) Born Uig, Skye. Poet in Gaelic (e.g. *Gairm*, 1969–76; *Words*, no. 8) and English (contribution to *A Poetry Quintet*, 1976;

Angus Macmillan.

imaginary wounds, 1980). *Sgrìobhadair* (writer in residence) at Sabhal Mór Ostaig (q.v.), 1977–79, and later with An Comunn Gaidhealach (q.v.) in Oban. Active publicist for Gaelic.   IMCD

MacNeacail, Calum (1792–1878) Born Skye. Free Church schoolmaster in Barvas, Lewis. Author of collection of hymns (1874). (See I. N. MacLeòid, 1916, 233–50.)   DST

MacNeil James A. (1869–1939) Native of Irish Vale, Cape Breton, Nova Scotia. Teacher and steel worker, who was committed to furthering the Gaelic cause in Canada. He worked to have Gaelic included in the Nova Scotia school curriculum and produced *Gaelic Lessons For Beginners* (1939). He also wrote a Gaelic column in *Sydney Post-Record*, 1934–9. In 1937 he hosted the first Gaelic programme (*Celtic Ceilidh*) on the CBC network. Publisher, between 1926 and 1930, of a monthly Gaelic magazine, *Teachdaire nan Gaidheal*.   RJM

MacNeil, Joe Neil (b. 1908) Born Reserve, Cape Breton County, Nova Scotia. Gaelic storyteller and folklore informant.   JS

Macneill, Revd Dr Nigel (1853–1910) From Islay. Congregational minister in England. (See N. Macneill 1872, 1886, 1892, 11ff.; Weir 1921, 117.)   TMM

MacNeill, Seumas (b. 1917) Born Glasgow. Senior Lecturer in Natural Philosophy, University of Glasgow, since 1955. Joint founder of the College of Piping, 1944. (See S. MacNeill 1953.)   DST

MacNicol, Revd Donald (1735–1802) From Glenorchy. Son of Nicol MacNicol, tacksman of Socach, and of Mary Stewart of the Invernahyle family. Minister of Saddell, then of Lismore. Married Lily Campbell in 1771; he had composed the song 'Ochòin a chailinn 's mo shùil ad dhéidh' for her. Wrote many of the songs of Donnchadh Bàn Macan-t-Saoir (q.v.) from the poet's dictation, *c.*1766. Collected heroic ballads (J. F. Campbell 1872) and other verse (G. Henderson 1910, 1915; see also **schools, bardic**). Author of *Remarks on Dr Samuel Johnson's Journey to the Hebrides* (1779), which contains some interesting information on questions of Gaelic literary history. Many of his manuscripts were apparently lost at sea; the balance reached the National Library of Scotland but have gone missing in recent years.   DST

MacNiven, Duncan (b. 1883) **and Charles** (b. *c.*1885) From Islay. The Kilchomain Bards. (See H. MacDougall 1936.)   DST

MacPhaidein, Iain (John MacFadyen) (1850–1935) Born Balevullin, Mull. Spent most of his life in Glasgow. His popular readings and poems were collected in *An t-Eileanach* (1890, 1921) and *Sgeulaiche nan Caol* (1902). His song 'Soraidh Leibh is Oidhche Mhath Leibh' is still sung at the close of Gaelic concerts.   IMCD

MacPhail, Donald (d. 1955) Born Dalmally, son of bard Calum Campbell MacPhail (author of *Am Filidh Latharnach*). Northern Organizer of An Comunn (q.v.), 1932–52.   DST

MacPhail, Dugald (1819–87) From Torosay, Mull. Author of Mull song 'An t-Eilean Muileach', etc.   DST

MacPhail, Revd Dr James Calder (1821–1908) From Moray. Minister at Pilrig, Edinburgh. For thirty years conducted scheme of grammar school competitive bursaries for Gaelic students.   TMM

MacPhails A little-known professional kindred in Lorn, clerics and physicians, found by the early seventeenth century in the service of the MacDougalls of Dunollie and the Campbells of Barbreck. Dubhghall Albannach mac mhic Pháil wrote religious texts (NLS Adv. MS 72.1.1, ff. 2–9) in Munster in 1467, later adding (f. 1) genealogies of the principal families in the sphere of influence of the Lords of the Isles (the '1467 MS'). The manuscript was embellished in the house of MacEgan, *brehon* (traditional judge) of Ormond. The surviving work of Eoghan mac Eoin mhic Eoghain (fl. 1603–38) includes a MacDougall genealogy and lease, medicine, tales and verse (see Adv. 72.1.9, 72.1.31, 72.1.34, 72.2.2, 72.2.10, TCD 1298).   RIB

MacPhàrlain, Calum (1853–1931) Born Dalavich. Brought up in Paisley. Active writer, translator and editor (see bibliography; see also M. C. MacLeod 1908). First editor of the Fernaig Manuscript (q.v.) and composer of many songs and tunes.   IMCD

MacPhàrlain, Murchadh (1901–82) Native of Lewis. Poet and song writer. Emigrated to Canada in the 1920s; returned to Lewis in 1932. Some of his songs were composed in Canada, including the widely known ''S fhada leam an Oidhche Gheamhraidh'. A talented composer of melodies (e.g. 'Mhòrag leat shiubhlainn', 'Naoi Ceud deug 's a Ceithir deug', etc.), first popularized by Na h-Oganaich, a group of singers and instrumentalists. He published a collection, *An Toinneamh Dìomhair*, in 1973.   JMCI

MacPhàrlain, Pàdraig (fl. 1800) Schoolmaster in Appin. Translator of religious texts (*see under* Guthrie, MacFarlane, etc., in D. Maclean 1915). Author of *New Vocabulary* (1815).   DST

Macphee, Hugh (1899–1980) Born Ballachulish. First BBC Gaelic producer and founder of Gaelic broadcasting. President of An Comunn Gaidhealach (q.v.), 1959–62.   FM

MacPherson, Donald (c.1787–post-1850) From Laggan, Badenoch. Sergeant in 75th Regiment; later bookseller in London. Author of *Melodies from the Gaelic* (1824). Papers in archives of Gaelic Society of London (now in National Library of Scotland). (See *Gairm*, vol. 99, 207.)   DST

MacPherson, Donald (Dòmhnall nan Cleas) (1905–81) Born Barra. Appointed by An Comunn Gaidhealach (q.v.) c.1938 to teach physical education through Gaelic. First recorded Nan Eachainn Fhionnlaigh of Vatersay (q.v.).   DST

MacPherson, Donald Campbell (1838–80) Born Bohuntin. Sub-Librarian of the Advocates' Library, Edinburgh. Published *An Duanaire* (1868), the seventh edition of the poems of Alexander MacDonald (q.v.) (1874) and, posthumously, *Practical Lessons in Gaelic* (1891). Contributed to J. F. Campbell's *Leabhar na Feinne* (1872), assisted with the 1885 edition of *Iùl a' Chrìosdaidh* and wrote for *An Gaidheal* and for the *Celtic Magazine* under the pen-name of 'Abrach'.   JLC

Macpherson, Ewan (d. 1801) Of Badenoch(?). Taught in Laggan; tutor to Sir John Macpherson, once Governor-General of India (who was a son of Dr John Macpherson of Sleat). Accompanied James Macpherson (q.v.) on his tour to the Outer Hebrides. (See A. Grant 1806, vol. 2, 133.)   DST

MacPherson, Ewen (1706–64), *see* Cluny of the '45.

MacPherson, Ian, *see* Strathcarron, Lord.

Macpherson, James (1736–96) Born Invertromie, Badenoch. Student at Aberdeen and Edinburgh Universities. Taught in Charity School, Ruthven (Badenoch); tutor in Edinburgh by 1758, when his epic poem *The Highlander* appeared. This anticipates the plot and some of the style of his later Ossianic epics. A meeting with John Home in 1759, followed by acquaintance with Dr Hugh Blair (Professor of Rhetoric and Belles Lettres at Edinburgh) and other literati, quickly brought his latent ambitions to flower. He had probably been stimulated by Jerome Stone's publication of a translation of the Fraoch ballad (*Scots Magazine*, 1756), and friendship with Blair led to the publication of his *Fragments* in 1760, to two Highland collecting tours and to the publication of *Fingal*, his main Ossianic epic, in December 1761. His third Ossianic work was *Temora* (1763).

James MacPherson (1736–1796). By an unknown artist, after Sir Joshua Reynolds. Scottish National Portrait Gallery.

It is clear that there was some close collaboration between Macpherson and Blair (Macpherson lodged for a time below Blair's rooms), especially regarding epic theory; the Introductions and footnotes to MacPherson's poems show this influence strongly; The *Fragments* and, later, the full-scale epics were presented as ancient (third century) works translated from Gaelic; the historical roles of Scotland and Ireland were largely reversed in the plot, and the Viking wars were pushed back into the period selected. This framework was supported by a mass of detailed and pseudo-scholarly argument in notes, etc., using sources such as Mallet's *Introduction à l'histoire de Dannemarc* (Copenhagen 1755–6) and O'Flaherty's *Ogygia*. The intention of this elaborate distortion was to demonstrate that an ancient Gaelic epic had been recovered and that Scotland was its locale, though there had been attempts to appropriate it in Ireland.

These assertions aroused controversy, which raged especially in the 1760s and 1770s, involving the philosopher Hume, the poet Gray, the lexicographer Johnson and many others. Scottish-English and Scottish-Irish literary hostilities arose. The epics were translated into Italian by Cesarotti (1763) and subsequently into German (1764) and French (1774), etc. (The process continues today – a Japanese translation appeared in 1971 and a Russian translation is due in 1983). The translations influenced many writers and other artists: Goethe (in *The Sorrows of Werther*), Herder, Schiller, Victor Hugo, Byron, Yeats, Alexander Runciman (in his etchings), Johannes Brahms, Mendelssohn. (For the 1974 Paris Ossian Exhibition, see *The Times Literary Supplement*, 12 April 1974 and *Le Monde*, 21 February 1974.) Sometimes the influence is vestigial (as Yeats's 'terrible beauty', perhaps coming from a footnote in *Temora*, 1763 edn, 69), sometimes pervasive, as in certain Celtic Twilight writers. There was a flood also of books and pamphlets arguing the authenticity or the reverse of the Ossianic poems, one of the saner landmarks in this flood being the Highland Society's *Report* of 1805.

MacPherson was neither as honest as he claimed nor as inventive as his opponents implied. In *Fingal*, his most elaborate work, we can identify at least twelve passages, some of them fairly lengthy, in which he used genuine Gaelic ballad sources, sometimes specific versions (see **McLagan, James**). He used, for example, ballads dealing with Garbh mac Stairn and Mànus for the groundwork of his plot, and three other ballads (Fingal's Visit to Norway,

'Duan na h-Inghinn' and 'Ossian's Courtship') for important episodes or sub-plots; other ballads were exploited in a more restricted way (see further, D. S. Thomson 1952). He used many names from the ballads, often distorting them violently (see D. S. Thomson 1979a), and he juggled historical data to suit his own ends. And he brought to bear his knowledge of the Classics, of Milton and of the Authorized Version of the Bible to produce his measured style. John J. Dunn thought that his achievement had been overshadowed by the fact that greater writers (e.g. Blake, Coleridge) 'developed the artistic direction that he was among the first to take' (J. J. Dunn 1966), and E. H. W. Meyerstein regarded him as one of the main originators of free verse (*English VII*, 1948, 96). He had a pernicious effect on later Gaelic writing (Thomson 1958) but also indirectly stimulated much Gaelic collection and research.

Macpherson moved from Scotland and from his Ossianic preoccupations in the early 1760s and later published a translation of the *Iliad* (1773), and his important *Original Papers, Containing the Secret History of Great Britain* (1775), but his interest in Ossian survived marginally, for he left a sum of money to be used for the publication of the Gaelic Ossian, which eventually appeared in 1807. (See G. F. Black 1926; Blair 1763; Saunders 1894; Smart 1905; A. Gillies 1933, 1969; D. S. Thomson 1952, 1963.)
DST

Macpherson, Sir John (1745–1821) From Sleat, Skye. Governor-General of India.
DST

MacPherson, John (the Glendale Martyr) (?1845–1924) Born Glendale, Skye. Popular crofter spokesman and campaigner in Land Agitation. Leader of group who organized defiance of Court of Session interdict forbidding grazing of cattle on Waterstein farm in 1883; five of its members (so-called 'Martyrs') were later arrested and served a two-month prison sentence in Calton Jail, Edinburgh. (See Hunter 1976, *passim*, esp. 147; I. M. M. MacPhail 1976a.)
DEM

MacPherson, John (1876–1955), *see* Coddy, the.

MacPherson, Lachlan (*c.*1723–*c.*1795) Of Strathmashie, Badenoch. Tacksman of Strathmashie, bard, musician, wit. Collaborator of James MacPherson (q.v.) and probably author of Gaelic version of seventh book of *Temora*. Over a dozen of his songs survive, including an honest elegy for Ewen Mac-Pherson of Cluny (q.v.), some serious but sprightly reflections on material wealth, two songs on the theme of hunting, a satire on the landlord of the Dunkeld stage-house and a number of very lively, humorous and sometimes broad songs, such as 'Comunn an uisge-bheatha', 'A' Bhanais bhàn' and 'Oran na briogais lachduinn,' with the characteristic verse:

Gur mise bh'anns an èisdeachd
'S na mnathan 'g ràdh ri chèile
Gum b'fheàrr leo orra fhèin i
Na bhith ceusadh an fhir chaim.

MacPherson is said to have sat in his porch, with fiddle and songs to hand, to entertain visitors. He has some of Rob Donn's (q.v.) type of wit and observation and a clear affinity with the village bards of later times. (Poems in E. Gillies 1786; Mac-an-tuairneir 1813; Sinton 1906; *TGSI*, 23 and 24; letter of Dr Hugh Blair, in Report, App., 8.)   DST

MacPherson, Mary (Màiri Mhór nan Oran) (1821–98) Born Skeabost, Skye. A nurse by profession, Mary MacPherson was distinguished by her physical weight, prolific poetry and political interests. Imprisoned in Inverness on a charge of theft, she began to protest her innocence in song. Her humiliation led her to support Highland crofters during the Land Agitation, which became a dominant theme in her verse. After retiring to Skye, she accompanied Charles Fraser-Mackintosh, the pro-crofter MP, on electioneering trips. Her most popular songs contain vivid portrayals of Skye, with references to her own and her people's suffering. (See MacLean 1961, 319: Meek 1977a, 1977b.)   DEM

MacPherson, Paul (an Tàillear MacDhonnchaidh) (fl. 1750) Author of praise song to Cluny of the '45 (q.v.), mentioning particularly the engagement at Penrith (*Pìorat*). (See Sinton 1906, 82.)   DST

Macphie, Donald (1852–1922) From Skye. For over forty years schoolmaster at Cumbernauld. Editor of *An Gaidheal* (q.v.), 1912–22, and of all except one of Blackie's *Gaelic Readers*. (See *Deò-Gréine*, vol. 17, 177; Macbean 1921, 108.)   TMM

MacQueen, Revd Donald (1740–85) Of Skye. Minister of Kilmuir. Dr Johnson was impressed by his learning (there are frequent references to it in Boswell's *Journal of a Tour*).   DST

MacRae, Donald (1756–1837) Born Petty, Inverness-shire. Author of hymns, of which a first edition was published in about 1827; they are reprinted in J. Rose, *Metrical Reliques* (1851).   DST

MacRae, Duncan, *see* Donnchadh nam Pìos.

MacRae, John (fl. 1774), *see* Iain mac Mhurchaidh.

MacRae, John (MacRath Mór) (1794–1876) Born Lochalsh. Schoolmaster in Lewis during formative years of Evangelicalism. Minister at Ness, Greenock, Lochs, Carloway. One of the most popular nineteenth-century Gaelic preachers. Joined the Free Church in 1843, his oratory being influential in the Disruption cause. (See Collins 1976; N. Nicolson 1939.)   RMCL

MacRae, Revd Kenneth (1883–1964) Born Dingwall. Free Church minister of Lochgilphead, Kilmuir, and of Stornoway, 1931–64; forthright preacher and Church leader. His diary was published posthumously. (See I. H. Murray 1980.)   DST

MacRaoiridh, Donnchadh (d. *c.*1630) Probably of hereditary bardic family that served MacDonald of Sleat. (The twentieth-century South Uist storyteller Duncan MacDonald, or Donnchadh Clachair, was descended from this family.) Author of four religious or elegiac poems in Fernaig Manuscript (q.v.), including the fine 'Beir mise leat', a death-bed poem. (See MacPhàrlain 1923.)   DST

MacRath Mór, *see* MacRae, John (1794–1876).

MacRitchie, David (1851–1925) Founder of the Gypsy Lore Society and founder member of St Andrew Society, Edinburgh. Author of books and numerous articles on ethnological and antiquarian subjects, drawing largely on traditional lore.   DAMCD

Mac Rùsgail Common name for trickster hero of folktales; provokes a farmer who insists on dire penalties for the breaking of a contract of employment into breaking it himself through the over-literal interpretation of his orders (Aarne and Thompson 1961, Nos. 1000ff.).   AB

Mac Shithich, Bàrd, *see* Aos-dàna.

William MacTaggart 'The Young Fishers' 1876. National Gallery of Scotland.

MacShithich, Seumas (d. *c*.1767) Of Glen Isla. Possibly the author of ''S mòr mo mhulad 's cha lugha m'èislean'. (See K. D. MacDonald and D. S. Thomson forthcoming; W. J. Watson 1918, etc.)
DST

MacTaggart, William (1835–1910) Born Machrie-hanish, Kintyre. Landscape painter and colourist. Among his paintings is *The Coming of St Columba*. (See also **art, Gaelic, in modern times**.)   DST

MacThòmais, Ruaraidh (D. S. Thomson) (b. 1921) Born Lewis. MacThòmais is the most productive of contemporary Gaelic poets and, to date, has published five collections, including *Collected Poems* (1982). He studied literature at Aberdeen and Cambridge Universities. Early poems appeared in *An Gaidheal* (February 1943, etc.). His poetry highlights the problems of bilingualism and bi-culturalism experienced by an intellectual displaced from his native environment (D. MacAulay 1976, 48) and, more broadly, the fate of Gaeldom in the advance of the English-speaking community. MacThòmais's is a markedly individualist poetry, expertly balancing intellect and emotions. Indeed, all aspects of his poetry exhibit a finely engineered counterpoise (I. MacDhùghaill 1976–7, 59). Coherence is maintained through the adoption of a progressive symbolist style and the resumption of previous themes, symbols and titles in later anthologies.

Love and nature are the main themes of *An Dealbh Briste* (1951). A smaller thematic grouping, however, explores the state of the Gaeltachd. He employs many regular rhymed verse structures and some irregular (Thomson 1974b, 292) but also experiments with free verse (of which he is the first major exponent in Gaelic).

In *Eadar Samhradh is Foghar* (1967), MacThòmais investigates different facets of his experience of Lewis, through a widening perspective (D. J. MacLeod 1969, 428). In 'Sgòthan' (p. 11) he comments, of Lewis landmarks:

ach chaidh mise bhuap air taod
cho fada 's a theid gaol bho fhuath . . .

but I have strayed from them on my rope
as far as love can go from hate . . . .

Increasingly, ironic (even absurdist) elements enter his poetry, lending it bitter potency and depth (D. MacAulay 1971, 5, 11). The language remains sensuously assonantal.

An Rathad Cian (1970) further examines the dilemma of MacThòmais's ethnic duality. The umbilical cord image, describing this condition, reappears in 'Bùrn is mòine 's coirc' (p. 6):

An cridhe ri bacan . . .
's an inntinn saor.
Is daor a cheannaich mi a saorsa.

The heart tied to a tethering post . . .
and the mind free.
I bought its freedom dearly.

The entire collection is in free verse.

In *Saorsa agus an Iolaire* (1977) a retrospective pessimism, previously evident, has been curtailed. MacThòmais has long seen the resolution of his problem in terms of nationalism (D. MacAulay 1976, 50), and here irony and subtle association are expertly manipulated to accentuate various aspects of the Gael's political conditioning and the propagandist support of the Presbyterian Church. This anthology marks the zenith of MacThòmais's poetic achievement. It entertains optimism, but only if the Gael assumes his cross and fights. (See M. Chapman 1978; Fulton 1974; Lindsay 1979; MacAulay 1966a; I. C. Smith 1961.)　　　　　　　　　　　　　　FAM

Maighstir Ruairidh, *see* MacLeod, Roderick.

Maighstir Seathan (Revd John Maclean) (*c*.1680–1756) From Mull. Poet and genealogist (Maclean-Bristol 1980, 11). Succeeded John Beaton (q.v.) as minister of Kilninian in Mull in 1702. Assisted Edward Lhuyd (q.v.) and began the work that led to Alasdair Mac Mhaighstir Alasdair's (q.v.) *Vocabulary* (1741). Four of his poems are extant and possibly a fifth.　　　　　　　　　　　　　　CÓB

Màire Nighean Néill (?) Author of quatrains in the Book of the Dean of Lismore (q.v.). (See Quiggin 1937.)　　　　　　　　　　　　　　DST

Mairearad Nighean Lachlainn (*c*.1660–1751) Of Mull. One of a group of women poets who flourished between the 1640s and the 1750s. She is conspicuously a panegyrist of the Macleans, whom she celebrates within the conventional frameworks but with great vividness of imagery, keen observation of contemporary events and an abundance of rhythmical vitality.　　　　　　　　　　　　　　JMCI

Màiri Mhór nan Oran, *see* MacPherson, Mary.

Màiri Nighean Alasdair Ruaidh (*c*.1615–*c*.1707) Born Rodel, Harris. Member of an aristocratic MacLeod family. She was the senior member of a group of women in different parts of the country whose poetry spans the period from the first half of the seventeenth century to beyond the middle of the eighteenth. This poetry uses a panegyric framework and deals both with personal themes and with social and political issues of Gaelic society. Màiri was closely associated with the household of MacLeod of Dunvegan but in oral tradition is connected more strongly with Berneray, Harris. The site of her house at Tobhta nan Craobh, given to her by Sir Norman MacLeod of Berneray, is still pointed out.

Màiri's songs present us with a model of the mandatory commonplaces of Gaelic praise poetry. Her manner of handling these could be said to represent the norm of vernacular high-style panegyric. It is essentially formal court poetry, almost wholly confined to the affairs and personages of Clan MacLeod, with an added dimension from the shifts of fortune in her own life. Regarded at one time as an absolute innovator, Màiri can now be seen as one of the most important mediators between classical and vernacular Gaelic. Her poetry is distinguished by its rhetorical assurance, the clarity of its imagery and its declamatory eloquence. (See W. Matheson 1953; J. C. Watson 1934.)　　　　　　　　　　　　　　JMCI

Malcolm II King of Scots (1005–34) Malcolm so thoroughly defeated a Northumbrian army at the Battle of Carham in 1018 that Lothian was finally secured for the Scots and the river Tweed became the southern boundary of Scotland to the east. One measure of his success as king was his long reign; another was the succession of his grandson, Duncan, the first in the direct line since the mid-ninth century. (See Duncan 1975, 97–9.)　　　　　　JWMB

Malcolm III Malcolm, king of Scots (1058–93), whose Gaelic epithet was 'Cennmor', invaded England no fewer than six times. The third invasion in 1070, and Malcolm's marriage shortly thereafter to Margaret – who with her brother Edgar, Anglo-Saxon heir to the English throne, had come to Scotland as a refugee from Norman persecution – provoked retaliation by William the Conqueror, and at Abernethy in 1071 Malcolm became his 'man'. On one occasion Malcolm is portrayed as translating into Gaelic Margaret's views on the Church for the benefit of the assembled Scottish churchmen. Three of their sons, Edgar, Alexander and David, became successive kings of Scots. (See Duncan 1975, 117–24; on Margaret see **monasticism**.)   JWMB

manuscripts, illuminated The origins of many of the manuscripts of the early Christian Church in the British Isles are contentious because of the wide diffusion of a common 'Hiberno-Saxon' art style, but some have plausibly been claimed as Scottish.

The Cathach (Battler) of St Columba (Royal Irish Academy, Dublin: *see* Henry 1965, 58–61; Lowe, 1972, no. 266; Nordenfalk, 1977, 12–14), a psalter bearing initials embellished with curvilinear ornament derived from Celtic metalwork, has been associated with the saint since at least the eleventh century and may well date from the half-century after his death in 597. Its later function, that of ensuring victory in battle to Ó Domhnaill, explains the name (Henry 1965, 58–61).

The influence of native metalwork and enamelling is evident in the Book of Durrow (Trinity College, Dublin, MS 57), which blends Celtic spiral art with Germanic animal ornament, Mediterranean interlace and evangelist symbols whose relationship to Pictish animal art, whether as copies or models, is disputed. Although Iona *c.*680 has been suggested as its place of manufacture (Nordenfalk 1977, 19–26, 34–47), a somewhat earlier origin in Northumbria is more likely (Lowe 1972, no. 273). The ornamental scheme of the Book of Durrow, with rich 'carpet pages' and elaborate decoration of certain significant texts, was amplified with arcaded canon tables and evangelist portraits in the Lindisfarne Gospels (British Library MS Cotton Nero D. IV) and other books of *c.*700, and reached its climax in the magnificent Book of Kells (Trinity College, Dublin, MS 58). This adds a series of religious scenes, and the words of the principal texts are almost submerged by abstract and animal ornament of fantastic complexity. It is possible that the Book (described in 1007 as 'the great Gospel of Colum Cille, the chief relic of the Western World') was begun at Iona *c.*800 and left partly unfinished when a few years later, following Viking attacks, the Columban monks moved to Kells, Co. Meath (Henry 1967, 6–7, 68–95; Henry 1974; Nor-

denfalk 1977, 108–25), but it has been suggested, because of its relationship with the Lindisfarne group of manuscripts and its links with Pictish art (I. Henderson 1982), that an origin in eastern Scotland in the middle of the eighth century is likely (T. J. Brown 1972). However, the stone crosses of Iona (*RCAHMS*, 1982) reveal a close relationship with the Book: in both, Northumbrian models are developed on an unprecedented scale and with a preponderance of Celtic ornament, and it is probable that both were created at Iona, perhaps to mark the enshrinement of Columba's remains in the middle of the eighth century.

The Book of Deer (Cambridge University Library MS Ii. 6.32), a tenth-century miniature Gospel book of Irish type, contains naive portraits of the Evangelists and of two seated ecclesiastics and other marginal ornament. Connections with eastern Scottish stone monuments and iconographical idiosyncracies show that it was produced in that area by a scribe who had had little contact with traditions of illumination (Hughes 1980), but it was valued highly enough for the Gaelic records of the monastery of Deer to be copied into it in the twelfth century (K. H. Jackson 1972; J. Stuart 1869).

The characteristic medieval Irish ornamental initial, an angular or geometrical ribbon-like animal, often interlaced with strands issuing from its tail or limbs, had developed by the tenth century (Henry 1967, 106–9; 1970, 46–73), and two books decorated in this style may have been made in Scotland. The Celtic Psalter in Edinburgh University Library, model for the initials in *Carmina Gadelica* (A. Carmichael 1900–71), was possibly at the Scottish court by the end of the eleventh century (Borland 1916, no. 56; Finlayson 1962), and the mid-twelfth-century psalter in Rome (Vatican Pal. Lat. 65) was at Coupar Angus Abbey in the following century but is related to manuscripts from eastern Ulster (Bannister 1910; Henry and Marsh-Micheli 1962, 157–9, pls. 33–4; Henry 1970, 69). Several late medieval Gaelic manuscripts of Scottish provenance have less brightly coloured initials of the same type, and although some (such as National Library of Scotland, Adv. 72.1.8: Bannerman, 1977a, pl. 1) were written in Ireland (*Éigse*, xvii, 584); others were probably Scottish, including Adv. 72.1.3 (Comrie 1932, vol. 1, frontispiece and p. 100) and Manchester University Library, John Rylands Irish MS 35 (see NLS MS 14,901). Zoomorphic initials and marginal animals are also found in Adv. 72.1. nos. 7, 19 and 40, while a

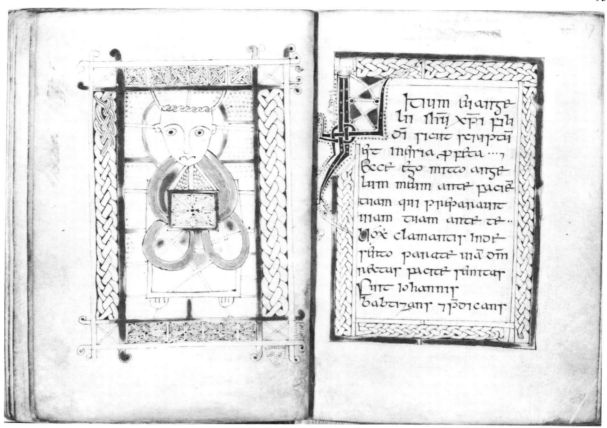

Manuscript illumination from the Book of Deer, Cambridge University Library, MS Ii.6.32. The evangelist is St Mark.

medical text (Adv. 72.1.2, fols. 1–3) adds signs of the zodiac in a style derived from Romanesque ornament. However, none of this late decoration shows the influence of good imported models, such as the fine early thirteenth-century Iona Psalter (NLS MS 10,000), produced probably in Oxford for a prioress of the Augustinian Nunnery of Iona.   IF

manuscripts, medical Twenty-nine of the eighty-three surviving Gaelic manuscripts of pre-1700 Scotland are medical. They were written by Beatons (q.v.), O'Conachers and others in Scotland and Ireland during the fifteenth to seventeenth centuries.

Reasons for the survival of medical material in such quantity have been put forward for sixteenth-century Ireland (Ó Cuív 1976, 518). These hold good for Scotland. They are the compilation of manuscripts by medical families for their own use and that of fellow doctors; the retention of such manuscripts within the family circle of the owner; the value known to have been placed on them; and the fact that medical men were persecuted less than members of other hereditary professions, possibly because their services were useful to all, possibly because of the cosmopolitan element in their training.

Gaelic medical texts represent four successive layers of medicine: Greek, Muslim, Continental and Gaelic.

The characteristic of Greek medicine is clinical observation; Hippocrates (*c*.460–370 BC) and Galen (AD 129–99) are constantly cited, and Hippocrates' *Aphorisms* are the most popular single text.

To this the Muslim world contributed pharmacology and astrology; the *Aphorisms* of Johannes Damascenus (AD 777–857) are second only in popularity to those of Hippocrates, and Avicenna (980–1037) is constantly cited. Prepositions occasionally reflect Arabic usage (O'Grady 1926, 233).

Continental medicine developed on these foundations initially at the school of Salerno, subsequently through the universities, notably Montpellier. Its contributions were its synthesizing of subject matter and its alignment with Christian doctrine (sin as the cause of disease) and, ultimately, surgery; scholastics, however, accepted Greek and Muslim practice as Holy Writ, discussing only details. The most popular Continental texts are a *materia medica* ascribed to Platearius of Salerno (fl. 1125) and the 'Lilium Medicinae' of Bernard of Gordon (fl. 1300), who taught at Montpellier. The *materia medica* begins, characteristically, *Aron, barba iarus, pes vituli .i. tri hanmanna in gheidhir* ('Aron, barba iarus, pes vituli, i.e. the three names of the cuckoo-pint') and ends with a colophon recording that it was compiled at Montpellier in 1415 by Tadhg Ó Cuinn, a Bachelor of Physic of that university (D. Mackinnon 1912, 21).

Gaelic authorities are seldom cited, unless we include the attribution of charms to Colum Cille (q.v.). Native material outwith main texts consists of charms and also of cures of a psychological or commonsense type: 'Write this on an apple divided into three. On the first piece, *Jesus Christus on leo on filius*. On the second, *on ovis on aries*. On the third, *on pater on glan on vermeis*. Then eat the pieces and it will help a fever' (National Library of Scotland Adv. MS. 72.1.2, f. 130r.). No overall assessment of the Gaelic contribution has yet been undertaken, but an indication of one kind is the insertion in Gordon's work of a passage on the warding off by faith of magic spells (*piseoga*). Renaissance medicine is hard to find, faith in the Hippocratic doctrine of the humours and in Galen's anatomy having survived to the end of our period. However, William Harvey (1578–1657), who discovered the circulation of the blood, is cited in a remarkable gynaecological treatise in NLS Adv. 18.2.11 by the Revd John Beaton (q.v.), the last physician to inherit the learned Gaelic tradition.

It has been suggested that the medical manuscripts were used merely to impress patients (F. Shaw 1961, 97). Indeed, their content is often arcane, and the pharmacopoeia is exotic. There is evidence, however, of Irish trade with the Near East from the sixth century, and traditional verse attests to the importation by Highland chiefs of Spanish swords, wine, wax and 'Galway silk'. Drugs and simples must have come in as well; and Galway being the entrepôt for Mediterranean trade, it need not surprise us that a branch of the Beatons was settled in Mayo. Ultima-

tely, the answer lies in the manuscripts themselves, however. The pages of NLS Adv. 72.1.13, which contain a treatise on medical theory, are of a virgin whiteness. 'It is not I who am responsible for the lies of this book,' remarks the copyist, 'but the beautiful, mendacious manuscript.' On the other hand, a page in Adv. 72.1.2 on the virtues of *aqua vitae* (*uisge beatha*) is almost illegible from rubbing and staining, while under a passage on betony in Adv. 72.1.3 James Beaton (fl. 1600–30) scribbles, 'Give a drink of this to Cathleen, daughter of Neil . . . .'

Some doctors tell us much about their activities. NLS Adv. 73.1.22 was written by MacDougall of Dunollie's physician, Duncan O'Conacher (1571–1647), and his fellow students at the O'Conacher school, near Kilkenny, Ireland, 1596–1600. NLS Adv. 72.2.10 was written in 1611–14 by the Skyeman Angus Beaton, on circuit in north Argyll, whither he had come to sit at Duncan's feet.

The manuscripts are in classical Gaelic; typically, only one vernacularism, *tacann* for *tachtann* (suffocates), occurs in Angus Beaton's 'Prognostics' of Hippocrates. Nevertheless, they would reward study as a model for the development of a modern technical vocabulary. Most are in the National Library of Scotland, with one each in the Edinburgh University Library, John Rylands University Library of Manchester, and the British Library. (Editions H. C. Gillies 1911; Ó Ceithearnaigh 1942–4; Wulff 1928.)   RIB

Manx, divergence from Scottish Gaelic, *see* Gaelic: divergence from Irish and Manx.

Maol Domhnaigh mac Mhànuis Mhuilich (dates unknown) Author of 'Ná léig mo mhealladh, a Mhuire', a Mary poem, in the Book of the Dean of Lismore (q.v.); possibly an Ó Muirgheasáin. (See Greene 1962; Quiggin 1937, 20.)   DST

Maol Rubha (642–722) Of Bangor. A monk, known also in Scottish tradition as Maruibhe, whose founding of a monastic community in Applecross, Rossshire, is noted in the Irish annals *sub anno* 673 (Reeves 1857–60). The sanctuary surrounding his church gave Applecross its Gaelic name, A' Chomraich, and the monastery became an important centre for the spread of Christianity and Gaelic culture among the northern Picts. Maol Rubha is widely commemorated in place-names, notably Loch Maree

(Reeves 1857–60; W. J. Watson 1926). Rituals associated with a debased memory of him appalled the Presbytery of Dingwall in the seventeenth century (W. Mackay 1896). KDMCD

Marjoribanks, George E. (d. 1940) Main inspiration for the founding and early years of Comunn na h-Oigridh, the Youth Movement run by An Comunn Gaidhealach (q.v.). (See *An Gaidheal*, September 1940.) DST

Martin, Bishop Donald (1873–1938) Born Ardnamurchan. Roman Catholic Bishop of Argyll, 1918–38. Worked to establish Oban Cathedral. DST

Martin, Martin (*c*.1660–1719) One of the Martins of Bealach, Skye. Graduated MA at the University of Edinburgh; MD at Leyden University, *c*.1712. Tutor in Sleat and in Dunvegan, *c*.1681–*c*.1692. Author of *A Late Voyage to St Kilda* (1697) and *A Description of the Western Islands of Scotland* (1703, written *c*.1695). (See *DNB*; D. J. MacLeod 1934.) DST

Matheson, Angus (1912–62) Reared in North Uist by Lewis parents. Head of the Celtic Department, University of Glasgow, 1938–62; Professor from 1956. A philologist and historian, Matheson made an important contribution to Gaelic scholarship in editing volumes 5 and 6 of *Carmina Gadelica* (q.v.) and the Gaelic text of J. F. Campbell's *More West Highland Tales*, volume 2. DST

Matheson, Donald (1719–82) From Kildonan, Sutherland. Religious poet published in J. Rose (ed.), *Baird na Gaidhealtachd mu Thuath* (1851). (See Grimble 1963, 139–41; 1979, 198–9.) IG

Matheson John (fl. 1843) Native of North Uist. Composed well-known song, 'Cailleach Mhór Stadhlaidh'. His biting satirical verses, such as 'Oran mu'n Eaglais', were used as anti-Established Church propaganda following the Disruption (q.v.). (See J. Matheson 1846.) RMCL

Matheson, Kay, *see* Stone of Destiny.

Matheson, William (b. 1910) Formerly Reader in Celtic, University of Edinburgh. Expert in Highland genealogy and has also produced fine editions of John MacCodrum (q.v.) and An Clàrsair Dall (q.v.). (See Bibliography.) DST

maxims, *see* proverbs, maxims and riddles.

Meek, Donald (b. 1949) Born Tiree. Assistant editor of Historical Dictionary of Scottish Gaelic (*see* **dictionaries, Scottish Gaelic**), 1973–9. Lecturer in Celtic, University of Edinburgh, since 1979. Has undertaken research into heroic poems in the Book of the Dean of Lismore (q.v.) and the literature of the Land Troubles. DST

Mendelssohn, Felix (1809–47) His Hebrides Overture (Fingal's Cave) was composed in 1830. DST

Fingal's cave, Staffa.

Menzies, Robert (fl. 1780) From Aberfeldy. Roman Catholic priest. Translator into Gaelic of Roman Catholic catechism, *Christian Doctrine* (1781) and of Thomas à Kempis's *Imitation of Christ* (1785).   DST

metalwork Highland metalworkers practised the same basic techniques as their brethren elsewhere in Europe. Scanty archaeological research in the area precludes detailed study, at this stage, of the more utilitarian wrought iron and copper objects of everyday use; it is the better-quality brooches and reliquaries that attract the most attention.

Goldsmiths and jewellers particularly favoured the use of filigree work and pearls, coral and crystals set in collets with teeth for greater security. Effective use was also made of niello (a black enamel-like substance) to bring out engraved designs. Most such work could be done with a very limited range of tools and equipment. The essential feature of this craftsmanship is its conservatism; once form and patterns were introduced, they tended to remain in vogue for a very long period. Inspiration was often sought from the work of earlier generations rather than from contemporary work elsewhere.

Very little metalwork of any quality survives in Scotland from the Middle Ages, but those few pieces that are the products of Highland craftsmen have been preserved not just because of their associations but because they are also fine pieces of work. One of the earliest and finest was found only accidentally, in about 1814, by workmen gathering stones for the construction of a dyke at Kilmichael Glassary in Argyll. It is a bell shrine, constructed of bronze plates in the shape of a truncated pyramid resting on four feet (two are missing) and with a handle at the top. This is the form of the hand bells associated with early saints of the Irish and Scotic Church, and it was to contain one of these precious relics that the shrine was designed – and indeed, it still contains it. It is thus related, in form and function, to Scoto-Irish work, though it has no very close parallels. Other features of its decoration seem to derive from this native source – the zoomorphic form given to the legs and the two sides of the handle and some panels of interlace work. But while it is in many ways a late manifestation of an earlier Irish or Scotic tradition of art, it stands, at the same time, on the threshold of a new flowering, a local twelfth-century interpretation of the Romanesque of the rest of Europe. The rest of its decoration, and in particular the crucifix with the hand of God above, give a Romanesque feeling to the whole work. The figure of Christ is a most accomplished and dignified piece of work, which far excels the contemporary run-of-the-mill Limousine figures which were so widely used in Europe, including Scotland.

Another bell shrine of West Highland origin was for long preserved at Guthrie Castle in Angus. It consists of the hand bell itself, to the front of which a decorated silver plate has been attached, and other ornaments as well. It is a work of many periods, but the plate itself and the silver figure of Christ date to the twelfth century. The latter has a strong Irish flavour – not surprisingly, considering the strong links that existed between the two countries – being a more accomplished version of the one on the Corp

The Guthrie Bell shrine. National Museum of Antiquities of Scotland.

Naomh in the National Museum, Dublin, but Romanesque all the same. The figure of St John (?) now attached to the side of the bell was probably originally placed at one side of the cross on the front with a now lost figure of the Virgin to balance it. The figures of God Almighty and the three bishops, on the other hand, appear to be fourteenth-century in character and may originally have belonged to another shrine, while the gilt settings for jewels and the panel, now attached upside-down, with *Iohannes alexan/dri me fieri fecit* in niello inlay, probably date to a reconstruction of the late fifteenth or early sixteenth century. This John was possibly John II, Lord of the Isles (q.v.).

The third surviving church reliquary from the Highland area is the *quigrich* or crozier of St Fillan, one of six relics of this saint that were entrusted to different hereditary Dewars, or Keepers, and in this case remained in the keeping of one family until late in the nineteenth century. The basic relic was the staff or crozier of the saint, which does not survive. Instead there is a silver crozier head, which was found to contain a bronze one of the late eleventh

The brooch of Lorne. National Museum of Antiquities of Scotland.

St Fillan's crozier. National Museum of Antiquities of Scotland.

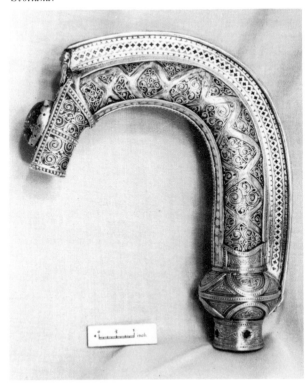

century. It has a characteristically Scoto-Irish shape, with a flattened fore-part to the crook, and is divided up into lozenge-shaped panels by raised bands containing niello. It appears that by the fourteenth century it had been decorated all over with silver plaques of filigree silver scroll work, and a rock crystal was mounted on the front of the crook with a small cast figure of the saint above. In a later development this head was stripped of all these ornaments, which were incorporated in the present silver crozier head together with a pierced ridge along its back and a knop at its base, decorated with interlace. The date of this last reconstruction is not certain, but it may have been at the end of the fifteenth century.

Unfortunately, practically nothing survives of the silver and bronze treasures of the Church in the Highlands other than a few crystals and settings which may have formed parts of book covers and reliquaries, but metalworking skills of an order similar to that used in the Guthrie bell shrine and St Fillan's crozier can be seen in a group of three reliquary brooches. The earliest seems to be the Brooch of Lorne, said to have been lost by Robert Bruce at the Battle of Dalry, when his cloak was torn from him by a dying assailant, and long preserved by the McDougalls of Dunollie. It is of silver and is an elaboration of the simple ring brooch popular from the thirteenth century onwards. The flat ring is decorated with silver filigree star designs alternating with eight tall collets containing pearls. The centre of the ring is infilled by a large capsule with scalloped outline surmounted by a hemispherical crystal, and the whole capsule screws off (presumably it was intended to contain a relic or memento of some sort). Despite the picturesque legend associated with it, it dates to some time after the era of Bruce, perhaps the later part of the fifteenth century. The Lochbuy and Ugadale brooches, also long preserved with West Highland families, are closely comparable but slightly later in date. The Lochbuy Brooch has an eighteenth-century inscription on its back that declares that it was made about 1500, and that is probably right. The Ugadale Brooch has a cast interlace pattern that is similar to one on the mid sixteenth-century Cadboll Cup, a composite work incorporating Highland decoration. This interlace on the Ugadale brooch, the Cadboll Cup and other things like St Fillan's crozier may be a conscious imitation of older patterns.

There are other brooches of simple ring form from the medieval period, like a very fine silver one of the fifteenth century from Mull. It has an octagonal outline and is decorated front and back with panels of foliage and flowers, animals and letters, all reserved in niello. The letters *anan* and *ihcn*, repeated in black letter, carry on the tradition of talismanic inscriptions prevalent on earlier brooches. The appearance of these decorative elements is of interest, since similar motifs were used again, together with interlace designs, on brooches in the seventeenth century. The reliquaries and brooches considered so far are exceptional in their quality and value; they are works commissioned and owned only by the rich. From the late sixteenth century onwards, however, there are many brooches and other objects in silver and bronze that belonged to all classes of people. The brooches, which were worn by the women, are typically formed as flat rings, sometimes over 6 inches in diameter, and are engraved all over with alternating roundels and panels containing interlace, foliage, spotted animals and, especially on the earlier brooches, a degenerate and incomprehensible form of black letter consisting merely of parallel lines. A fine early example of this style is the silver mount on Ruairi Mór's horn at Dunvegan Castle, which dates to *c.* 1600.

Although ring brooches have remained in use until the present day, the form of their decoration grad-

ually degenerated long before the seventeenth century was out. Basically, the engraving became simpler and more geometric, and many of the undecorated bronze brooches probably date to the later seventeenth and eighteenth centuries. A last manifestation of this Highland style can be seen in the attractive silver brooches produced by goldsmiths and jewellers in the Lowland towns in the eighteenth century. The earlier ones have recognizable animals, foliage and interlace, but in the later ones these have developed into geometric chequers with distinctive anchor patterns in niello.

St Fillan's crozier and the two bell shrines, now all in the National Museum of Antiquities of Scotland, are discussed at length in early volumes of the *Proceedings of the Society of Antiquaries of Scotland* (Eeles 1926; J. Stuart 1878; Wilson 1878, 1884). For the later brooches, see the booklet *Brooches in Scotland* (National Museum of Antiquities of Scotland, 1966), and for a general survey of Highland art, Caldwell 1980.   DHC

minerals The Highlands and Islands of Scotland have been described as a 'geologist's playground', and it is true that the old, hard rocks of this area contain practically every mineral substance known to man. Unfortunately from the economic point of view, few of these resources are commercially useful, either because the deposits are too small (or they have been worked out by previous extraction) or because the low value of the products does not justify the cost of extraction and transport to markets.

Materials for the construction industry are the most important economic contribution that local minerals make to the Highlands and Islands. The area is rich in deposits of sand, gravel and hardstone, and there are numerous quarries producing building sand, aggregate, and roadstone for local use. As supplies of aggregate and roadstone become increasingly scarce in south-east England and on the Continent, there is a possibility that a large coastal 'super-quarry' may be developed at a site where suitable rock is accessible to marine transport. South Harris has been identified as a promising location for such an undertaking, and there are other possible sites in Lochaber, Wester Ross and Shetland. In the past building stone was extensively quarried, and there were famous exports of flagstones from Caithness, granite from Mull and slate from Ballachulish and Easdale. Now only small quantities of Caithness flagstone and Easdale slate are produced, although

The rocky landscape of north-west Sutherland.

marble chips are sent from Torrin on Skye for pebble-dash and artificial stone manufacture.

The recent discovery of the Beatrice oilfield only twelve miles off the east coast of Sutherland has led at least one company to explore for oil on the adjacent shore, and the search may be extended elsewhere on the mainland. Coal was mined until comparatively recently at Brora and Machrihanish, but the most abundant source of fuel in the Highlands and Islands has always been peat (particularly in Caithness, Lewis and Yell). As peat is still used in many places for domestic heating and by distilleries, it is possible that as prices rise generally more commercial uses may be found for it, for power generation, as a coke for special smelting processes or for horticultural purposes. Uranium deposits have been found in Orkney and Caithness, but there are no plans to work them at present.

The only other minerals presently exported from the Highlands and Islands are glass sand from Lochaline and talc and chromite from Unst. However, a major development is now underway to reopen the famous old lead and zinc workings of Strontian (which gave its name to the element of strontium) to produce barytes, a mineral extensively used in drilling fluids in North Sea oilfield operations. In the past there were iron mines on Raasay and at Sandlodge in Shetland, where copper was also extracted, and diatomite was produced on Skye until fairly recently. Limestone is no longer extracted and kilned for local agricultural use as it once was all over the Highlands and Islands, but the potash deposits of north-west Sutherland may be utilized as a source of fertilizer.

The largest goldfield in Britain, located at Kildonan in Sutherland, was the scene of a hectic gold rush in the late 1860s. Nowadays goldpanning is promoted as a tourist activity.   DMH

Mod, the, *see* Comunn Gaidhealach, An.

Moffatt-Pender, Captain Iain MacAlister (1894–1961) From Perthshire. Founder of Clann an Fhraoich. (See *An Gaidheal*, 56, 89; *Gairm*, 5, 135; S. MacThomais 1961, 77; Murchison 1954, 1961.)

TMM

Moireach, Iain, *see* Murray, John

Moireach, Murchadh (Murdo Murray) (1890–1964) From Back, Lewis. Graduated from the University of Aberdeen, 1913. Teacher and Inspector of Schools. Author of vivid Gaelic war diary (1915–17), a few war poems, geographical essays and literary criticism, including essays on Mary MacPherson (q.v.) and John Munro (q.v.). (Collected writings in Moireach, 1970; see also D. S. Thomson 1974a, 252.)   DST

Moireasdan, Dòmhnall (Geinidh) (1911–64) Born Ness, Lewis. Author of ''N tèid thu leam, mo nighean donn', etc. (See D. I. MacLeòid 1972.)   DST

monastic orders, spread of (eleventh to fourteenth centuries) The Church throughout Scotland had been

Interior of abbey church, Iona, showing the north of the two-level thirteenth-century choir, with the fifteenth-century sacristy doorway and elaborate fifteenth century capitals in foreground.

permeated by Irish monastic ideals during the two centuries (*c*.850–1050) in which Scottish dominance had asserted itself over the non-Scottish regions of the Picts, Cumbrians and Angles. Some major churches, e.g. St Andrews and Abernethy, were either completely monastic communities of Irish type or were at least partly served by monastic clergy, especially by communities of *Céli Dé* (clients of God). Probably this was true of all the important churches, but their way of life did not find favour with the eleventh- and twelfth-century Church reformers who brought new varieties of Benedictine monachism to the British Isles from the 1090s onward. In Scotland the figure of Queen Margaret (d. 1093, canonized 1250) may be seen as pivotal. She revered the truly ascetic *Céli Dé* and other hermits and is said to have begun the restoration of Colum Cille's (q.v.) island monastery of Iona, but she also brought to Dunfermline the first Benedictine congregation to settle in Scotland, and in her debates with the Scottish clergy she clearly placed herself on the side of Continental and post-Conquest English movements of thought which were to prevail almost exclusively for the next four centuries. Most of the newer orders (dates refer to first settlement in Scotland) of Tiron (1113), Augustine (1115), Cîteaux (1136), Cluny (1163) and Val des Choux (*c*.1230) were first planted in the English-speaking south-east, but notable exceptions were Benedictine Dunfermline, promoted to an abbey under David I (1128), Augustinian Scone (1115), where the kings of Alba were wont to be inaugurated, and the cathedral priory at St Andrews, principal church of the realm (1144). But these orders were slow to penetrate the Highlands, most surprisingly in the case of the Cistercians, who had only one Highland abbey, Saddell (*c*.1207). Although the Benedictines were pioneers at Urquhart, near Elgin, it was the austere Valliscaulian order from Val des Choux in Burgundy that proved that reformed Benedictinism could adapt to Highland life at its three thirteenth-century foundations at Beauly, Pluscarden and Ardchattan. Meanwhile, despite mid-twelfth-century efforts at reform under Somerled of Argyll, the ancient Celtic abbey of Iona fell into decay before 1200 and, with the blessing of Pope Innocent III,

Queen Margaret, an Anglo-Saxon princess and the wife of Malcolm Canmore. She died in 1093 and was canonized in 1250. A manuscript illumination from a fifteenth-century Book of Hours (British Library Add. MS 39761 f.93v) in which she appears as St Margaret.

was converted into a Benedictine monastery. By 1421 it was impoverished and desolate, but must have been at least partially revived, for it was still functioning 150 years later. The island also had an Augustinian nunnery (c.1208), but in general the Highlands and Islands possessed very few religious houses of post-Celtic character; besides those already mentioned, there were only three small Augustinian houses (Inchmahome, Strathfillan and Oronsay) and the Premonstratensian abbey at (New) Fearn in Easter Ross (by 1238). (See I. B. Cowan 1981; I. B. Cowan and Easson 1976.) GWSB

Monro, Archdeacon Donald (fl. 1526–89) From Kiltearn. Became vicar of Snizort in Skye in 1526 and Archdeacon of the Isles in 1549. Published a useful description of the Isles. He conformed to the Reformation in 1560 and was appointed minister of Kiltearn. (See R. W. Munro 1961.) IG

Monro, Robert (d. c.1680) Covenanting general and author of the only regimental history of the Thirty Years' War in Germany, *Expedition with the worthy Scots Regiment called Mac-Keyes Regiment . . .* (1637). IG

Montgomerie's Highlanders, *see* regiments, Highland.

Montgomery, Catrìona (b. 1947) **and Mòrag** (1949) (NicGumaraid, Catrìona and Mòrag) Two sisters from Skye whose early poems were published as *A' Choille Chiar* (1974). DST

Montrose, 1st Marquis of (James Graham) (1612–50) Led Highland and Irish forces in a brilliant campaign against the Covenanters in 1644–5. (See E. J. Cowan 1977.) DS

Monymusk Reliquary, *see* Breccbennach, the.

Morison, Angus (d. c.1740) From Lewis. Brother of An Clàrsair Dall (q.v.), minister of Contin and author of some indelicate verses. (See W. Matheson 1970, 196, 223.) DST

Morison, Counnduillie Rankin (1856–1943) Of Dervaig, Mull. Authority on Mull traditions. Contributor to *MacLean Bards* (A. MacLean Sinclair 1898–1900). Manuscripts of songs, including waulk-ing songs (q.v.), collected locally by 'Counn' and other Morisons now deposited in the School of Scottish Studies (q.v.). AB

Morison, John (Iain mac Mhurch' 'c Ailein) (c.1630–1708) Tacksman of Bragar. Father of An Clàrsair Dall (q.v.). Author of 'Description of the Lewis' (c.1678–88) and of epigrammatic verses. (See W. Matheson 1970, esp. app. E.) DST

Morison, John (Gobha na Hearadh: the Blacksmith of Harris) (c.1796–1852) Native of Harris. Blacksmith, poet and Evangelical leader. Wrote Gaelic and English fluently. Appointed SSPCK catechist, 1828; closely associated with religious revival in Lewis and Harris, 1820s and 1830s; Free Church catechist after 1843 Disruption (q.v.) Strongly influenced by the Revd John MacDonald of Ferintosh (the 'Apostle of the North'), for whom he composed a 145-verse elegy. His hymn 'An Ionndrainn' (The Soul's Longing for God) has been described as 'one of the gems of the Gaelic language'. He was a leading nineteenth-century religious poet. Some compositions – for example, 'Còmhradh Eadar Soisgeulach agus Cuibheasach' (Dialogue between Evangelical and Moderate) – deal with the religious conflicts of the mid-nineteenth century. One of his best-known hymns, 'An Nuadh Bhreith' (The New Birth), is a graphic description of the battle between old and new nature in the soul of a convert. He also composed some vituperative satirical verse, e.g. 'An Sgiobaireachd' (Navigation). (See G. Henderson 1893.) RMCL

Morison, Roderick, *see* Clàrsair Dall, an.

Morisons of Ness, *see* (for their role as lawmen) law, Celtic survivals; institutions and orders, learned and professional.

morphology, Gaelic verbal, *see* Gaelic: morphology.

Morrison, Angus (1865–1942) From Loch Broom. Author of *Orain nam Beann* (1913) and *Duain agus Orain Ghaidhlig* (1929). DST

Morrison, Donald, *see* Moireasdan, Dòmhnall.

Morrison, George (the 'Breve') (b.1906) Born North Tolsta, Lewis. Glasgow headmaster. Author of

'Brevities' column in *Stornoway Gazette* (G. Morrison 1978) and of Gaelic poems. (See D. I. MacLeòid 1972; T. MacLeoid 1969). IG

Morrison, Hew (1849–1935) Born in Torrisdale, Sutherland. Headmaster in Brechin, 1875–87. Chief Librarian, Edinburgh Public Libraries, 1887–1922. LL.D., St Andrews University. Editor of *Rob Donn* (1899). IG

Morrison, John (1701–74), *see* Petty, Seer of.

Morrison, John (1787–1834) Born Harris. Collector of traditions and legends, especially of Lewis and Harris. Captain Thomas's papers in *Proceedings of the Society of Antiquaries of Scotland* for 1866 and 1878 are partly based on these, and W. C. Mackenzie published others in *The Western Isles* (1932). The legends were published privately, ed. N. MacDonald (1978). DST

Morrison, Murdo (1872–1975) From Tong, Lewis. Director of Education, Inverness-shire, 1919–37. DST

Morrison, Murdo (b. 1884), *see* MacIlleMhoire, Murchadh.

Morrison, Murdoch (1842–post-1929) Born Bernera, Harris; moved to Cape Breton Island *c*.1843. Author of *Orain Fuinn is Cladaich* (1931). DST

Mucanach, Bàrd, *see* Bàrd Mucanach.

Muireadhach Albanach Ó Dálaigh (fl. 1220) A member of the premier Irish bardic family, which originated in Westmeath. Known in Ireland as Muireadhach Lessa-an-doill. According to the Irish Annals (Four Masters, *sub* 1213; Latin Annals of Ulster, *sub* 1216), he fled to Scotland after killing Ó Domhnaill of Tír Chonaill's steward. He is the reputed ancestor of the MacMhuirich bards (q.v.) in Scotland, Lachlann of 1800 being eighteenth in descent from him. An intermediate poet, such as John of Kintyre (on record 1505–41), carries the suggestive title 'McMurech Albany'. There are two poems addressed by Muireadhach to persons in Scotland, one to Alún Earl of Lennox (d. 1217) and the other to Amhlaoíbh, probably Alún's son. A document of 1259, regarding a sale of land in Lennox, has a Kathil Macmurchy as witness; it is suggested that this may be a son of Muireadhach, and the first of the Scottish line that later moved to Kintyre and then to the Clanranald lands in the Hebrides. Muireadhach's finest poem is his elegy for his wife (Bergin 1970, 101). (See Ó Cuív 1968; D. S. Thomson 1974a.) DST

Mulroy, Battle of (1688) Last clan battle, between MacDonalds of Keppoch and MacIntoshes aided by Mackenzie of Suddie. (McLagan Manuscript 135 has two poems on it.) DST

Munro, Alexander, of Strathnaver (*c*.1605–*c*.1653) From Inverness. Became minister of Durness in 1634. He had a reputation as a versifier of Scripture (Wodrow 1842–3, i, 267–8); the Fernaig Manuscript (q.v.) contains two of his compositions, one a rehearsal of biblical deliverances, extending to the Apocrypha, and the other a contemplation of God as creator and judge. (See A. MacKenzie 1898; Scott, *Fasti*, vol. 7, 1928, 101.) KDMCD

Munro, an Dall, *see* Munro, Donald.

Munro, Dòmhnall (fl. 1860) Factor of Lewis, who because he held a key position in most local enterprises, was able to tyrannize the tenantry until his exposure at the trial of the 'Bernera Rioters' (q.v.) in 1874. DMCA

Munro, Donald (an Dall Munro: Blind Munro) (1773–1830) Native of Skye. Blinded by smallpox in youth, he combined the offices of fiddler and SSPCK catechist. He was converted by a visiting evangelist, John Farquharson, in 1805 and threw his fiddle away. A friend of the Revd Roderick MacLeod, Bracadale, and influential in the early days of Skye Evangelicalism. (See D. MacKinnon n.d.) RMCL

Munro, Finlay (fl. 1820) Native of Easter Ross. SSPCK teacher who became an itinerant evangelist, translating directly from the English Bible as he preached. One of those who paved the way for the coming of Evangelicalism to Lewis. (See Collins 1951.) RMCL

Munro, John, *see* Rothach, Iain.

Munro, Revd Malcolm Nicolson (1869–1934) Convener of the Mod and Music Committee of An Comunn (q.v.). (See Macbean 1921.) DST

Munro, Neil (1864–1930) Born Inveraray. Author of many Highland novels, stories, etc. – for example, *John Splendid*, *The New Road*, Para Handy stories. (See Wittig 1958, 270–3.) DST

Munro, Robert (later Lord Alness) (1868–1955) Son of the Revd A. R. Munro, Alness. Secretary of State for Scotland during post-1918 land raids and the controversy over Lord Leverhulme's plans for developing Lewis and Harris. DST

Murchadh a' Cheisdeir (Murdo MacLeod) (1837–1914) Born Luerbost, Lewis. Evangelist and agent for the Highland Temperance League. Author of the song 'Eilean an Fhraoich' and hymn writer. (See *Bàrdachd Mhurchaidh a' Cheisdeir*, 1962, and *Murchadh a' Cheisteir*, 1961.) DST

Murchadh Beag, *see* MacGhilleMhoire, Murchadh.

Murchadh Chaluim Sheòrais, *see* MacLeòid, Murchadh.

Murchadh Mór mac Mhic Mhurchaidh, *see* Mackenzie of Achilty, Murdo.

Murchison, Thomas Moffat (b. 1907) Born Glasgow; brought up in Skye. Minister in Glenelg, 1932–7; Glasgow, 1937–72. Joint editor of *Alba*, 1948. Edited *An Gaidheal*, 1946–58; Gaelic supplement of *Life and Work*, 1951–80; *Prose Writings of Donald Lamont* (1960). Vice-chairman of the Highland Development League. Contributed (1955–1983) weekly Gaelic column to *Stornoway Gazette*. Has published more Gaelic material than any other writer. RMCL

Murdoch, John (1818–1903) Born in Ardclach, Nairn; brought up in Islay. Inland Revenue officer serving in Dublin, where he was involved in Irish nationalist politics. Retired to Inverness and founded the *Highlander* newspaper (1873–81) to promote the crofters' cause during the Land Agitation (see **politics, Highland (nineteenth century)**). Tireless anti-landlord campaigner of major political signifi-

cance. (See Hunter 1976, 129, *passim*; I. M. M. MacPhail 1976b, 1977.) DEM

Murray, Amy (1865–1947) American musician and folksong collector. Visited Eriskay in 1905, where she is said to have collected 150 airs, of which twenty-six have been published and fourteen are known to survive in manuscript. (See J. L. Campbell 1954; Graves, 1913; A. Murray 1914, 1920, 1936.) JLC

Murray, John (Iain Moireach) (b. 1938) Born Barvas, Lewis. First received attention as a contributor to *Gairm* (poems, short stories); matured under that benign influence, publishing *An Aghaidh Choimheach* (1973), a collection of searching and humorous stories about the Gael in his home and city environments ('Am Pàrtaidh', Briseadh na Cloiche' and 'Feòil a' Gheamhraidh' are among the more outstanding of these). The stories combine accurate observation and well judged dialogue. Murray has also written plays. He was the first Editorial Officer of the Gaelic Books Council; later Director of Bilingual Project (see Murray, 1980); now an Assistant Director of Education with Comhairle nan Eilean (q.v.). DST

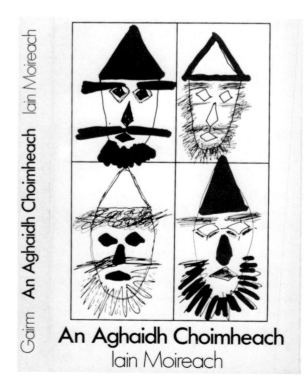

An Aghaidh Choimheach
Iain Moireach

David Allan, 'Highland Wedding' 1780. On loan to the National Gallery of Scotland. Niel Gow is accompanied by his brother Daniel on the cello. The piper in the background is ready to relieve them. There are several versions of this picture, which shows an occasion on the Athol Estate in the summer of 1780.

Murray, Murdo, *see* Moireach, Murchadh.

music, *see* bagpipe, Highland; fiddle music, Highland; folksong, early; folksong, later; MacCrimmons; music, choral; music, modal; music, of Gaelic Scotland; psalm tunes, Gaelic; psalms, metrical; song, Gaelic; songs, waulking.

music, choral In the mid-nineteenth century Joseph Mainzer's enthusiastic propagation of choral singing in Scotland combined with John Curwen's tonic sol-fa system to encourage the formation of choirs in Gaelic-speaking areas. Mainzer's impressive but anti-traditional setting of 'French', as sung at every National Mod, may have set the tone for the elementary and not always grammatical settings by some early conductors, who had not advanced beyond Stainer's *Harmony Primer* (1878).

It was natural that the first National Mod in 1892 should include choral classes, and from 1896 the test

pieces were published in collections under the title *Còisir a' Mhòid*. It is fascinating to follow over the years the advance in technique and imagination shown by the arrangers. An Comunn Gaidhealach's (q.v.) practice of inviting prominent musicians to make choral arrangements for specific competitions has produced some fine pieces of work, particularly since about 1950, as well as some monstrosities, such as the almost unsingable piece which has a few introductory bars intended to imitate the tuning-up of a bagpipe.

During the high period 1920–60 several choir trainers of exceptional talent emerged, among them Malcolm MacCallum and Norman McConochie. The subtlety of choral performances under their batons was sometimes little short of miraculous.   CTD

music, modal The basic modes of traditional Highland and Island song are the five pentatonic scales. These may be found on a piano by playing up the black notes only, the first starting on F sharp, the second on G sharp and so on. Such scales form the basis of folk music in many parts of the world and are possibly the consequence of the difficulty that unsophisticated singers have in pitching accurate semitones. However, in the days of oral transmission every singer was a law unto himself, and many versions of Scottish Gaelic folk tunes are on record in which the 'gaps' in the pentatonic scales are filled at certain melodic points by notes that must be at least approximately a semitone above or below one of the five principal degrees.

Some scholars have attempted to classify such versions as belonging to one or another of the so-called hexatonic scales; but grave difficulties of various kinds beset such systematists, who cannot agree on how many hexatonic scales theoretically exist. Even experts can become entangled in this web (as is shown in Collinson 1966, 10, 24, where the author discusses an air as hexatonic on one page and as pentatonic on another). However, it is beyond dispute that the most frequently found hexatonic scale is that containing the 'flat seventh', to be found by playing a black-note starting on C sharp and inserting a B natural between its fifth note and octave.

The printing and competitive singing of so-called definitive forms of Gaelic folk songs have in the last 150 years tended to obliterate the individual differences of utterance which at one time distinguished one singer from another in his personal use of semitones or near-semitones to extend the expressive possibilities of the pentatonic modes.

Certain beautiful modern tunes (e.g. 'An t-Eilean Muileach') have successfully captured the idiom of traditional Gaelic melody by deliberate use of the pentatonic and certain hexatonic modes, and the flattened seventh is a *sine qua non* of popular imitation Highland music. (See Collinson 1966; Grove 1954, 1981; Kennedy-Fraser 1909.)   CTD

music, of Gaelic Scotland According to the *Life* of Colum Cille (q.v.) written about 688–92 by Adamnán, ninth abbot of Iona, there existed in his time praise songs to the saint in the Irish language ('quaedam scoticae ling[u]ae laudum ipsius carmina'), whose singing effected a miraculous delivery from threatening enemies. The relation to musical practice (whether of Pictish-, Celtic- or Scandinavian-speaking peoples) of instruments depicted on *c.* ninth- to *c.* twelfth-century crosses and slabs is uncertain. These include a triangular harp as

David-symbol at Nigg and Aldbar, seated figures playing triangular harps (Monifieth, Dupplin), three cowled musician figures of Byzantine derivation (Ardchattan) and players of curved horn (Monifieth) and straight trumpets (Hilton of Cadboll).

No notated music for Gaelic texts existed before the eighteenth century, if we except the 'Gaelic Long Tunes' based on tunes of the English-language Scottish metrical psalter (initial publication, 1564), such as 'French', 'Martyrs', etc., which were presumably diffused by oral transmission during the seventeenth century (fifty psalms were printed in Gaelic in 1659, the whole psalter in 1690). The tunes, first 'lined out' by a precentor, were elongated in congregational singing with many decorative notes, a practice recorded by Dr Thorkild Knudsen in the 1960s in residual family worship in the home.

It can be speculated that the orally transmitted music of the Highlands and Western Islands in the Middle Ages included elements from both Gaelic and Scandinavian usages. Harp-playing among 'Irish'-speaking people of those regions was attested by John Major in 1521:

> For musical instruments and vocal music the Wild Scots use the harp, whose strings are of brass and not of animal gut; and on this they make the most pleasing melody.

Of two harps that survive, one is said to have belonged to the Lamont family of Argyll in 1464, while the so-called 'Queen Mary' harp must be dated earlier than the queen's lifetime. Though bagpipes are documented in Europe from the twelfth century, there is no firm evidence of them in Scotland or Ireland before the sixteenth century. Highland dances (?to bagpipe music) were performed at the reception of Anne of Denmark (queen of King James VI and I) at Edinburgh in 1590; in 1596 at Elgin three servants admitted to performing a dance 'callit gillatrype' while singing a 'foul Highland song'.

During the seventeenth century Gaelic-speaking society ceased to use harpers, whose instrument was perhaps unsuited to consorting with the new regularly stressed praise songs. Other musical activities recorded in the eighteenth century were no doubt well established in the seventeenth. Around 1730 Edward Burt observed the use of rhythmical work songs or bagpipe pieces at harvesting and waulking (i.e., fulling cloth), and of bagpiping for other kinds of strenuous joint labour (e.g. boat launching). He witnessed bagpipe playing under the clan chief's window in the morning, at meals and in the evening for the entertainment of guests. In Aberdeen he saw a funeral procession in Highland dress, preceded by a piper whose instrument was hung with crêpe.

By the eighteenth century dance tunes with Gaelic names were crossing the language border. 'Caper fei' and 'Tullochgorum' are in the section of Highland reels in David Young's manuscript collection of 1740; the latter tune and 'Shan Trowes' [sic] are among the reels in James Gillespie's manuscript of 1768. Nevertheless, Patrick Macdonald, compiler of the first printed collection of Highland vocal airs (Edinburgh, 1784), largely from the fieldwork of his younger brother Joseph (d. 1762), saw the distinctive character of Gaelic Scotland's music as an obstacle: 'Even those who wish to be pleased will find some difficulty.' To the present day the greater part of Highland and Western Island music is characterized by tune idioms that may loosely be called 'antique' (though this does not reflect on the actual date of individual pieces). A contemporary of Patrick Macdonald (in *The Caledonian Muse*, London, *c.*1790) noted the strangeness presented to an urban public by 'the affected omission of certain notes in the scale' (i.e. pentatonic tune structure), the use, in 'tunes apparently minor', of the unsharpened seventh, and the difficulties that adding an accompanying bass (then a requirement for all musics, whatever their original vocabulary) presented to an urban editor.

The distinctive tune frameworks of the Highland bagpipe repertory are determined by the fixed pitches of its nine-note scale – which is not the tempered scale of eighteenth- and nineteenth-century harmony. Its creative potentialities were first explained in print in Joseph Macdonald's *Compleat Theory of the Scots Highland Bagpipe* (written 1760, published in London in 1803). The impressive large-scale ground-and-variations form of *ceòl mòr* called *pìobaireachd* (pibroch) became, and has remained, the *champ-de-bataille* in which teaching lineages descending from earlier 'hereditary' piper successions have contended at the competition festivals of the Highland Society (from 1781). Some of the attached mythology has since been questioned. The chief documents are the early nineteenth-century manuscript called the *Campbell Canntaireachd* (a syllabic code), Donald MacDonald's *Collection* of 1822 and Angus Mackay's of 1838 and, in this century, the books published by Comunn na Pìobaireachd, Archibald Campbell's *Kilberry Book of Ceòl Mor* (1953) and Robert Ross's books called *Binneas is Boreraig* (1959).

A notable enterprise in documenting Gaelic songs was that of Frances Tolmie, begun in the 1870s. For their publication in 1911 these were disposed by text content in five groups: (1) songs of rest and recreation (cradle songs, nurses' songs, vocal dance music, i.e. *Puirt-a-Beul*, or mouth music); (2) songs of labour, many sung *sans* context (for waulking, reaping, rowing (*iorraim*), milking; (3) ancient heroic lays; (4) songs to chiefs and others; (5) laments, love lyrics, etc. (Marjorie Kennedy-Fraser and Kenneth MacLeod, in *Songs of the Hebrides*, 1909, altered and transmuted material from Tolmie and other sources for concert purposes.) Waulking songs, in their historical perspective and with translations and transcriptions of two significant collections of texts and electrical recordings respectively (including songs recorded in 1937 in Nova Scotia and some sung at an actual waulking in South Uist in 1951), have been admirably expounded in *Hebridean Folksongs* (J. L. Campbell and Collinson 1969). These songs' form elements are a refrain with meaningless text (e.g. 'Hó hao ri ri iù') and short texted stanzas, deployed in performance between soloist and chorus in various ways. The degree of antiquity attributed to Ossianic lays or ballads (Tolmie's Group 3) is customarily based on their mythological text content, originally common to Ireland and Scotland. These songs were still orally transmitted until recently, and some tunes contain elements of style that resemble the plainsong of the Latin Christian ritual. Gaelic songs recorded in Nova Scotia, mainly in Cape Breton Island, have been published with music and text translations into English in *Gaelic Songs in Nova Scotia* (Creighton and MacLeod 1964).

While Lowland song and fiddle repertories (and adaptations of them) have become widely known since the late eighteenth century and are used today both commercially and in 'folk revivals', the characteristic musics of the Gaelic-speaking regions have been less easily transferable to situations quite different from those in which they evolved.   FH

mutations, *see* Gaelic: mutations.

N

Na Doideagan Name given to Mull witches connected with Maclean of Duart, of whom one was credited with the sinking of the Armada ship *Florida* off Tobermory (1588). DST

names, Gaelic personal Name-giving serves both to differentiate and to connect an individual. These two aspects of identification are constant, and Gaelic names well exemplify the resulting tension between conservatism and innovation. (See, in general, G. F. Black 1946, xiii–lxviii; MacBain 1894–6.)

The oldest Gaelic personal names fall under three main headings: Class A, old simple names originating in adjectives and nouns with a descriptive force – e.g. Aodh (originally Fire), Fionn (Fair, Bright), Art (Bear); Class B, old close compounds functioning as simple names by historical times – e.g. *Dumnoualos (World-Strength) > Domhnall, *Moricatus (Sea-Battle) > Murchadh; Class C, a different type of 'double-barrelled' name, functioning as such – e.g. Donn-sléibhe (Brown [one] of [the] mountain).

New Class A names were still being coined in the Old Irish period, but they ceased to be productive thereafter, although many well established ones continued to be used. The same is true of Class B, of which a number have retained prestige and popularity to the present day, although the class as a whole has been in decline since prehistoric times. Class C, which may be pre-Celtic in origin, was revived in the Christian context, giving such names as Maol-Muire (Tonsured [one] of Mary), Gille-Crìosd (Servant of Christ). Some of these survive today in abbreviated form: e.g. Calum < Gille-Caluim (Servant of Columba). (See O'Brien 1973; cf. Woulfe 1923: 1–39.)

The generally declining vitality of these old formations was made good by innovations in various other respects, *inter alia* by the importation of foreign names at several different periods: e.g. Tormod < Old Norse Thormundr, Sìleas < Anglo-Norman Giles, Eairrdsidh < Modern Scots Archie (cf. MacBain 1896, App. B). Also to be viewed as an enlargement of the reservoir of available personal names is a new class of 'double-barrelled' names

found in the present-day Highlands: e.g. Domhnall Iain, Màiri Sìne.

Highland surnames owe their existence to the same principles and circumstances, for when the single name is insufficient for the purpose, the need arises for additional means of identification. In Gaelic Scotland this need has been met in various ways: by occupation, descriptive epithet or nickname, place of residence or origin, but principally by patronymic, e.g. Iain mac Dhomhnaill mhic Aonghuis, and nowadays Iain Dhomhnaill Aonghuis (John, son of Donald, son of Angus). That there is no reference to clan may cause surprise, but in fact, with so many clansmen occupying the same territory, clan affiliation would often fail to distinguish between individuals – that is, until the geographical context became wider than the traditional territorial bounds.

It is in that wider context that surnames came to be commonly used. This is not to assert that surnames were previously unknown, only that they were not the most practical means of denoting individual identity. However, in a kin-based society there was also the collective identity of the kindred, and surnames were available when the aim was to identify not only the individual but the kindred to which he belonged.

Surnames represent an extended usage whereby the additional means of identifying an individual were assumed by his descendants in order to identify themselves as a kindred or clan tracing their ancestry to him. Thus, for example, one Eoin mac Griogair (John, son of Gregor), who lived in the thirteenth century, was founder of a clan known as Clann Ghriogair whose individual members, in accord with this collective designation, adopted his patronymic Mac Griogair (MacGregor) as their surname, thereby making his father, Gregor, their eponymous ancestor. And other means of identifying individuals often became hereditary in the same fashion, especially at local level. Even when a man was a MacGregor by ancestry, he might be known locally as 'Calum Gobha', not necessarily because he was a blacksmith himself but because he was descended from one. He and his kin might come to be known in English as Gow or Smith and with the passing generations might even forget that they were MacGregors. This seldom happened where Gaelic was spoken and clan sentiment remained strong until relatively recent times; there the anglicized surnames officially used are mostly derived from patronymics. There are a few notable exceptions. The clan name Campbell dates back as far as the thirteenth century to one Dubhghall Caimbeul (Dougall Crooked-Mouth), and this epithet, descriptive of him, became the surname of his descendants. Surnames of this type are adjectival and provided a model when Norman French names were incorporated in the Gaelic system of nomenclature, as when Fresel became Friseal, anglicized as Fraser.

It will be seen from the foregoing that Gaelic surnames denoted identity in three dimensions: individual, collective and ancestral. How well do their anglicized derivatives do so today? Satisfactorily with regard to individual identity; but in other respects there are large reservations, and for various reasons. Collectively, the Highland clan was less homogeneous than is often supposed. Descendants of the eponymous ancestor held a dominant position, but associated with them were lineally unrelated families willing to give allegiance in return for favour and protection. Some were 'native men', representing the ancient inhabitants who occupied the land before the ruling family came into possession, a subject population with their own obscure surnames and largely unrecorded history. Others were descended from persons who for one reason or another had moved in from elsewhere. But however diverse of origin, many came to be known eventually by the surname of the clan with which they were so closely identified, especially in official documents, often drawn up by strangers unfamiliar with the variety of genealogical strands in the social fabric.

It is not so much that people changed their surnames, though there was a tendency for the obscure to be replaced by the more renowned; rather, changes occurred during transfer from oral tradition to the written record. The ignorance of strangers played its part. But even more damaging to the retention of collective and ancestral identities has been the practice of recording names in an alien orthography, whether of Latin, Scots or, latterly, English. This transformation from Gaelic has been attended by so much misunderstanding, ambiguity and error that the anglicized surnames in use today are unreliable, and often totally misleading, as evidence in respect of ancestry and clan affiliation.   WG/WM

Nan Eachainn Fhionnlaigh (MacKinnon) (b. 1903) Born Barra. Later associated with Vatersay. She recorded over 600 Gaelic traditional songs, especially in the 1950s.   DST

Napier Commission Set up as a result of Highland Land Agitation in the 1870s and early 1880s. Reported in 1884, recommending absolute security of tenure for crofters (*see* **crofting system**) and prompted the institution of the Crofters' Commission.   DST

nasalization, *see* Gaelic: mutations in.

Nasmyth, Alexander (1758–1840), *see* art, Gaelic, in modern times.

nature poetry The kind of poetry considered here is poetry which has as a main purpose, or includes as an intrinsic feature, the description of aspects of wild nature, including flora and fauna. Passages of descriptive verse of this kind often occur in poems whose main theme or purpose is of a different kind. Poems in praise of place (district, island, village etc.) normally include some such passages, as where Màiri Mhòr nan Oran (q.v.) describes the snow and the daisy kissing mouth to mouth in her 'Soraidh le Eilean a' Cheò' (Meek 1977b, 63). A love song may slip into the nature-descriptive mode, with praise that makes Mull surpass Egypt and Canaan, for example (Mac-na-Cèardadh 1876, 29). Poems on moral or religious themes sometimes have impressive passages of natural description, and it is with some surprise that we find this theme to be quite subsidiary to the other.

It is probably not too much of a generalization to say that poets in the Celtic languages in all ages have been powerfully drawn to the theme of nature, taking an intense delight in its variety, colour and changeableness and often finding in it release, escape, uplift or relaxation. Jackson drew attention to many aspects of this tradition, shared by early Welsh and Irish poetry, in his *Studies in Early Celtic Nature Poetry* (1935). Hermits were in close and peaceful communion with wild nature and helped to introduce the description and celebration of nature into early literature. From the early Irish Christian centuries we have sentiments such as the following (Greene and O'Connor 1967, 84):

A wall of woodland overlooks me; a blackbird's song sings to me – over my lined book the trilling of the birds sings to me.

A clear-voiced cuckoo sings to me in a green cloak of bush tops, a lovely utterance. The Lord be good to me on Judgement Day!

I write well under the woodland trees.

Alexander Nasmyth, design for a side wing, Glasgow theatre.

In a similar tradition there are tenth- or eleventh-century short poems on the seasons, vignettes of great tact and economy (ibid., 134ff.).

This tradition was inherited and shared by Gaelic Scotland, and we find it appearing at various literary levels and throughout the literary tradition. The religious poets who feature in the Fernaig Manuscript (q.v.) turn readily to nature to illustrate God's power or man's evanescence. Life is said to be like an October leaf, the foam on a wave, the pulse of the sea current on a rock (Murchadh Mòr Mackenzie of Achility). Joy is short-lived, according to John Stewart of Appin (late sixteenth century):

> The sweetest rose or lily,
> the plum or the red cherry
> are at their peak for a brief time:
> so indeed is mankind's mirth.

Màiri Nighean Alasdair Ruaidh (q.v.) often uses similes and metaphors drawn from nature, comparing Sir Norman MacLeod's eye in colour to the blaeberry, or describing a chief's death as the falling headlong of a great tree and the showering of seed to the ground. Some of these motifs come to her almost ready-made from the classical or bardic tradition, where the poets are often ready to make the idea of the pathetic fallacy, nature's sympathy with human catastrophes etc., the excuse for some detailed nature description, as where Cathal MacMhuirich writes of the deaths of four Clanranalds in the 1630s (Red Book of Clanranald, ff. 85ff., ll., 121–4):

> There is a sound of lamenting in the streams of the uplands, a weeping cry in the voices of birds, the net wins no profit from the pool, the rough weather has spoilt braird and grass . . . .

Poetry that has a stronger folk accent also has much nature reference: the author of 'Tàladh Dhòmhnaill Ghuirm' (MacDonald of Sleat's Lullaby, *c.*1600) asks for the strength of the storm and the tearing rumbling wind and the terrible thunderbolt to be 'between Donald Gorm and his shirt', and a MacGregor poet of the same era, warning MacGregor of Roro to be cautious, says; 'Though the squirrel is rare it can be caught; though the hawk is noble, it is often caught by guile.'

Such allusive references and descriptive inserts are almost a commonplace in praise poetry, though their intensity and elegance varies greatly with individual poets. When we come to the eighteenth century, however, we find a nature poetry in Gaelic that is essentially of a different kind. This new type is an end in itself, not a facet of poetry on other themes, and, unlike the very early poems on the seasons (in Irish) it has length, scale and detail that are new in the tradition.

There can be little doubt that we owe this change

of direction to one of these fruitful but half-arbitrary deflections that are a feature of literary development. The Lowland Scottish poet James Thomson published his four long poems collectively called *The Seasons* between 1726 and 1730, bringing a new dedication and direction to natural description in English poetry. We have no acknowledgement of indebtedness to this work on the part of any Gaelic poet of the time, but since scarcely any literary notes by these poets survive, this is not surprising. The chronological sequence, however, and some suggestive if inconclusive internal evidence, suggest that Alasdair Mac Mhaighstir Alasdair (q.v.) was stimulated by Thomson's work in such a way as to give fresh thought to descriptive nature writing. It is likely that he wrote his song 'Winter' in 1743 (Mays 1955); internal evidence of style and construction suggests that the poem on summer came earlier, and his 'Allt an t-Siùcair' (The Sugar Brook), with its description of that part of Ardnamurchan in which he lived for a few years up to 1744, is probably to be dated in the early 1740s also. It may have been some years after 1730 that he came to know *The Seasons*, and the seasonal theme may have occupied him off and on for a few years.

It seems likely that Mac Mhaighstir Alasdair took some sub-themes from Thomson's work but developed them in his own way (D. S. Thomson 1974a, 160–1). But it is in the overall approach that the two bodies of work make such different impressions. The Gaelic poet is almost clinical in his observation and reporting of the natural scene; he does not let any moral reflection intrude (as James Thomson does), and scarcely any emotion appears, overtly at least. But beneath the exact and carefully organized detail we can sense an exuberant and infectious pleasure in nature's richness and dynamism, and this pleasure must have sensuous and emotional springs. The result, especially in 'Oran an t-Samhraidh' (Song to Summer) and in 'Allt an t-Siùcair', is an extraordinarily vivid, detailed and kinetic kind of writing, involving close observation, a brilliant selection of descriptive vocabulary and a cunning and unobtrusive ordering of the detail that gives the impression of constant movement and development, which is of the essence of the world of nature, in its seen as well as its unseen aspects (ibid., 162–3). In his 'Galley of Clanranald' the same poet gives equally vivid, but more fantastic, descriptions of wild nature (the ocean).

It is clear that Mac Mhaighstir Alasdair's work is

the earliest in the sequence that includes Donnchadh Bàn's (q.v.) 'Praise of Ben Doran' and poems on the seasons by Donnchadh Bàn, Rob Donn (q.v.), Dùghall Bochanan (q.v.), Uilleam Ros (q.v.) and Ewen MacLachlan (q.v.). None of these others attains the polished finality of Mac Mhaighstir Alasdair's finest work, but they all develop certain aspects of description, as Donnchadh Bàn does of the vegetation and the hinds and stags, or express a more subjective and explicit emotional empathy, as in the case of Uilleam Ros.

After the remarkable concentration on nature poetry for its own sake in the eighteenth century, the theme reverts to a subsidiary though frequently recurring role, common in the homeland poetry, but occasionally more specific and ambitious examples occur, as Duncan Blair's (q.v.) poem on the Niagara Falls (in the metre of the 'Galley of Clanranald'), or Angus Robertson's (q.v.) 'Cnoc an Fhradhairc', a Gaelic eclogue written at the end of the 1930s, with a good deal of newly minted vocabulary. By this time we are on the threshold of a new era in Gaelic verse, and the theme of nature is reinterpreted by the new poets, often with close observation but generally without the adjectival exuberance of the eighteenth century (see especially **Hay, George Campbell, MacGhill-Eain, S.** and **MacThòmais, R.**), and nature is again used as a source of images, this time fresher and less conventional than earlier and often more organically related to the poems' structure.

DST

Nesbitt, Julian H. W. (b. 1877) Arranged many Gaelic songs. Author of Celtic suite, 'From Hebrid Seas' (1915), etc. DST

Niall mac Aoidh Bhig (dates unknown) Author of two pieces in the Book of the Dean of Lismore (q.v.). (See Quiggin 1937.) DST

Nic a' Bhriuthainn, Diorbhail (Dorothy Brown) (fl. 1645) Of Luing. Author of 'Oran do dh'Alasdair Mac Colla,' a fine blend of praise and love song. (See J. Mackenzie 1877.) DST

NicGillEathain, Catrìona (fl. 1680) Native of Coll. Poetess, probably related to Coll chiefs, who composed an elegy for Lachlan Maclean of Coll, (d. 1687) and poems addressed to other Maclean leaders. She used the eight-line stanza fluently, but her language lacks an inner life. (See A. Maclean Sinclair 1898.) DST

H*

NicGumaraid, Catrìona and Mòrag, *see* Montgomery, Catrìona and Mòrag.

NicMhuirich, Nighean Dhòmhnaill 'ic Cathail (dates unknown) Author of a South Uist song to Donnchadh MacCuilcein. (See *Carmina Gadelica* vol. V, 38.)   DST

Nicolson, Dr Alexander (1827–93) From Skye. Sheriff, writer in Gaelic and English and member of Argyll Education Commission, Napier Commission (q.v.) and revision committee for Gaelic Bible. (See A. Nicolson 1951; W. Smith 1893; H. Whyte 1908b.)
                                                      TMM

Nicolson, Alexander (b. 1870), *see* MacNeacail, Alasdair M.

Nicolson, Alexander Neil (1873–1960) Born Skye. Manager and co-editor of *Alba*, 1908–9; *An Sgeulaiche*, 1909. Secretary, Gaelic Society of Inverness, 1921–60. (See M. A. MacDonald 1971.)   DST

Nicolson, Alexander (1884–1966) From Skye. Teacher in Glasgow; lecturer in Gaelic at Jordanhill College, Glasgow; interim lecturer in Celtic at the University of Glasgow. (See *An Gaidheal*, vol. 62, 17; Murchison 1966; A. Nicolson 1930, 1936, 1938, 1939, etc.)   TMM

Nicholson, Rt Revd Patrick Joseph (1887–1965) Native of Cape Breton, Nova Scotia. Roman Catholic priest, educated at St Francis Xavier and Johns Hopkins. Professor of Physics, Dean and President (1944–54) of St Francis Xavier. Promoter of the literary and musical heritage of the Scottish Gael; longtime Gaelic columnist (Achadh nan Gaidheal) for the *Antigonish Casket;* compiler of a Nova Scotian Gaelic anthology, *Smeorach nan Cno's nan Gleann* (1939).
                                                      MMCD

Nighean Aonghais Oig (dates unknown) Lochaber Jacobite poetess. (See J. L. Campbell 1933.)   DST

Norse, influence on Scottish Gaelic, *see* Gaelic: Norse influence.

North Inch, Perth (1396) A judicial combat before Robert III, between two clans not yet securely identified. (See Nicholson 1974, 208.)   JWMB

North of Scotland Hydro-Electric Board In 1941 the late Mr Tom Johnston, then Secretary of State for Scotland, set up the Cooper Committee to examine the question of utilizing Highland water power for public use. The subsequent Hydro-Electric Development (Scotland) Act of 1943 embodied a clause enabling the new body

> so far as their powers and duties permit, [to] collaborate in carrying out any measures for the economic development and social improvement of the North of Scotland district, or any part thereof.

This 'social clause' makes the Hydro Board unique among British nationalized industries. No other has its reponsibilities spelt out with such precision.

Under the Act the Board was set the task of initiating and planning all large-scale developments of water power. Existing undertakings had to be reinforced to provide for existing consumers and also for new consumers outside the areas already supplied. The Board was also empowered to sell surplus electricity outside its area, using such revenue to finance the uneconomic distribution of electricity to remote mainland and island regions.

An extensive programme of construction resulted in the building of fifty-six major dams and fifty-four main power stations by the mid-1960s, and there has also been a substantial development in pumped storage through the schemes at Cruachan and Foyers. In terms of its social responsibilities, the Board now provides supply for about 99 per cent of its potential customers. It has also pioneered grass and grain drying, power development using peat, and fish conservation, in addition to attracting thirty-three new industries providing 16,000 new jobs.   HBS

Nova Scotia, Gaelic language in Like many of the Gaels observed by Samuel Johnson during his celebrated journey to western Scotland, thousands of Highland emigrants landed in Nova Scotia in the late eighteenth and early nineteenth centuries with little else but their language and their poverty. In time their poverty yielded to their industry and ingenuity, and their descendants came to enjoy a modest measure of prosperity. Their language is still the mother tongue of a large number of sixth- and even seventh-generation Gaels, most of whom are to be found in Cape Breton Island.

The oldest Gaelic work on record in Nova Scotia is the song ''*S àlainn an t-àite*' (Fair is the Place), com-

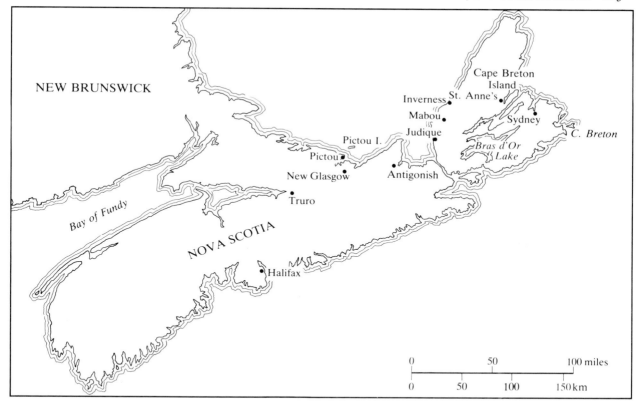

posed by Michael MacDonald at Judique, Inverness County, during the winter of 1775–6 (Mac-Talla 1895, 6). While Inverness County was destined to remain the most Gaelic of all counties, scores of Highland communities from Pictou to the eastern shores of Cape Breton retained their language in varying degrees until well into this century. At the turn of the century it could be stated authoritatively that parts of Cape Breton were as thoroughly Gaelic as any in the Highlands of Scotland: 'Tha cearnan dhe'n eilean anns a bheil an sluagh na'n cainnt cho Gaidhealach 's a gheibhear ann an cearn sam bith de Ghaidhealtachd na h-Alba' (Mac-Talla, 1902, 53). A few years later a Highland missionary made the same observation about the parish of Judique: 'Faodaidh mi ag ràdh, gun chunnart gu'n aichear e, gur i so sgìreachd cho Gaidhealach 'sa tha air aghaidh an t-saoghail' (G. C. I. Caimbeul 1908, 109).

Although Gaelic was not the language of commerce or education among Scots in Nova Scotia, it was the language of the home, the *cèilidh* and, to a marked degree, the Church. Its strength in all three institutions was enhanced by the impressive corpus of poetry and songs, printed works, periodicals and even newspapers, which emanated from several local communities. Every settlement had its *seanachaidhean*, (oral historians), literate and illiterate, tradition bearers who drew largely on the oral tradition but not infrequently on the printed page as well.

The extent to which both the Roman Catholic and the Protestant Churches contributed to the preservation of the language may be inferred from a brief account of their respective ministries as recorded in the Gaelic weekly newspaper *Mac-Talla* (1902, vol. 53):

The Gaels belong almost entirely to two Churches, the Presbyterian and the Catholic Church. The Presbyterians on the island (Cape Breton) have 39 churches and places of worship, and of these there are only 6 in which there is no Gaelic preaching. At the time of writing they have 35 ministers of whom 29 preach in Gaelic. Catholics have 37 parishes, only 6 of them without Gaelic. They have 40 priests, 31 of whom are Gaelic-speaking. (Translated from the Gaelic.)

Gaelic prayer books such as *Iùl a' Chrìostaidh*, catechisms and devotional tracts were widely known and used in Catholic homes and church services. Protestant Gaels were well supplied with Bibles and other reading matter in their native language; even homiletic treatises by John Bunyan (in translation) were to be found in remote farm houses in Cape Breton (C. W. Dunn 1953, 94–6).

The earliest Gaelic publication in Nova Scotia was a reprint of *Laoidhean Spioradail* by Donald Matheson, published at Tain in 1825. An original work, *Cuairtear Nan Og* (*The Youth's Companion*), by Alexander MacGillivray, was published at Pictou in 1836. These two works marked the beginning of a steady trickle of Gaelic publications down to the present day, the most innovative of which was the Gaelic weekly newspaper *Mac-Talla* (1892–1904), edited and largely financed by Jonathan MacKinnon. To MacKinnon, as to the Revd A. Maclean Sinclair, editor of many valuable collections of poetry and lore, the Gaelic world must be forever indebted. The *Casket*, originally *An Cuairtear Og Gaelach*, published at Antigonish since 1851, served the language for many years through its Gaelic column 'Achadh nan Gaidheal'. Journals such as *Am Mosgladh* (1922–33), anthologies of poetry such as *Fàilte Cheap Breatunn*, prose articles and Gaelic plays were among the twenty-one Gaelic publications printed in Nova Scotia from 1851 to 1942 (C. I. N. MacLeod 1958, 235). More recently *Cape Breton's Magazine* continues to publish Gaelic anecdotes, songs and variants of folktales extant in Cape Breton.

The first recorded appeal on behalf of the teaching of Gaelic in the schools was delivered in the old language in the Nova Scotia House of Assembly in 1879 by John D. Morrison, Member for Victoria County. Not until 1921 was it admitted as an optional subject in the curriculum. In 1950 the Department of Education established a Gaelic service under its Adult Education Division, and from 1950 to 1953 accredited Gaelic courses for teachers were offered during the regular summer school at Halifax. Under the direction of the late Major Calum I. N. MacLeod, these latter developments generated renewed interest in the language and culture. Nevertheless, formal instruction in Gaelic remained intermittent until it was redesignated a curriculum subject in 1969.

In 1972 the Department of Education provided funding to engage two Gaelic teachers on a circuit system in the schools of Inverness County. In Sep-

tember of that year the programme was launched with one teacher serving four schools and over 300 students. Two additional teachers were engaged in 1973 and the programme was extended to serve seven schools and approximately 900 students. In 1978 the programme was sharply reduced; financial cut-backs were cited as the reason. A satisfactory sequential programme of instruction in Gaelic is not yet in place, and further fiscal restraints may incur further cuts in the existing programme.

The record in post-secondary institutions has been better than that of the schools. Gaelic instruction has been offered from time to time at Dalhousie University in Halifax. At St Francis Xavier in Antigonish Gaelic has been taught as an accredited subject almost continuously since 1891, and since 1958 a full-time instructor has been engaged. For the past few years Gaelic has been taught at the College of Cape Breton in Sydney. The Gaelic College of Folk Arts and Home Crafts at St Ann's, Victoria County, though not an accredited college, has had an annual Gaelic summer school since its founding in 1939.

Census figures for Gaelic as the mother tongue were introduced in Canada only in 1931, at which time the total number was 32,008, of whom 24,303 were in Nova Scotia. Subsequent enumerations show curious fluctuations in the national number, with a very significant decline in the number in Nova Scotia:

	Persons in Canada with Gaelic as mother tongue	Persons in Nova Scotia with Gaelic as mother tongue
1931	32,008	24,303[1]
1941	32,708	12,065
1951	13,974	6,798[2]
1961	7,533	3,702
1971	21,200	1,420

1. 23,909 born in Nova Scotia.
2. 5,105 in rural areas.
Source: Census of Canada 1934–73, passim.

Notwithstanding the precarious state of the language reflected by these figures, there is still a solid core of Gaelic in Cape Breton Island. Even regional differences in dialect and patterns of speech linger to this day, as was noted by a Highland scholar a few years ago:

When the emigrants went across about 150 years ago, from the various regions of the Highlands, as much as possible they settled among their own relatives and friends. This is evident even today. Barra people live around Christmas Island, Boisdale, and Iona; Lewis and Harris people on the North Shore; North Uist and Bernaray people at Framboise; South Uist, Eigg, and Lochaber Gaels in Inverness County. (Translated from A. I. Mac a' Ghobhainn 1971, 71.)

The harvest of Gaelic material garnered in the three-year period 1977–80, under a federally funded project sponsored by St Francis Xavier University, has been remarkably large and varied. To date over 1,600 items – including over 800 songs, 96 folktales and an assortment of items pertaining to weather lore, religion, calendar customs, cures, and the like – have been collected, and much remains to be done yet.

Whether Gaelic in Nova Scotia can withstand the despotism of circumstance at this late stage remains to be seen. The obstacles to its survival are more formidable than ever, compounded in large measure by the steam-roller effect of the communications explosion and the ravages of urbanization. Yet, it is true today, as it was decades ago, that 'what to do with the Gaelic heritage in its modern survivals – language, dress, music, literature, customs, traditions – is a question that seems to be stirring in many minds' (M. MacLean 1907, 39). It is equally true that the fate of the language will be determined by the response to those 'stirrings'.　　　SISTER MMCD

Nova Scotia, Gaelic storytelling in Storytelling was a primary form of entertainment in the Gaelic-speaking areas of eastern Nova Scotia until shortly after 1900. Today the practice survives only among a small number of reciters on Cape Breton Island. Folktale materials collected in Cape Breton since the 1930s give some indication of the distribution of the various surviving types of Gaelic story.

Stories from the Fenian Cycle (mostly fragmentary) have been recorded in Cape Breton County and Inverness County from descendants of settlers from South Uist, Barra and the Inner Hebrides. Noteworthy tales recorded of this and related genres are 'Ceudach', 'Na Fiantaichean anns a' Bhruidhean Chaorthuinn', 'Sgeulachd Cois Céin' and 'Bàs Chu Chulainn'.

Lengthy, 'complex' tales are more widespread throughout the island and have been recorded recently in the South Uist and Barra settlements of Boisdale, Middle Cape and Christmas Island in Cape Breton County and Iona in Victoria County, from storytellers of Inner Hebridean extraction in Southern Inverness County and among Lochaber and Morar settlements between Mabou and Broadcove, Inverness County. An isolated Gearrloch settlement on the extreme northern border between Victoria and Inverness Counties has also preserved considerable parts of such stories. Very few complex tales have crossed over into English.

Shorter stories dealing with humour, local tradition and ghosts, along with simple anecdotes, are still common and can be found wherever Gaelic is spoken on the island.　　　JS

Nova Scotia, Roman Catholic Church in The façade of St Ninian's Cathedral bears the title Tigh Dhé (God's House), and fittingly, for the Roman Catholic Church in eastern Nova Scotia has since the early nineteenth century been distinctively Highland Scots.

The first five bishops of the diocese were Bishops Fraser, MacKinnon, Cameron, Morrison and Mac-Donald. Gaelic preaching, once very common, is still heard on special occasions.

The history of the Roman Catholic Church in eastern Nova Scotia is distinctive in three principal matters. First, well before the post-*Vatican II* age ecumenism was lived out in everyday life, more in practice than in preaching. Secondly, in 1853 the diocese founded St Francis Xavier University. Its early purpose, to provide priests and teachers, gradually enlarged until its scope today embraces all usual first-degree programmes and several at the post-graduate level. The Department of Celtic Studies has a lively record in teaching and scholarship. The partnership of diocese and university continues strong, although the university is now governed by an independent board and is operationally financed substantially by government. Thirdly, the interaction of the diocese and the university with the secular community and with other Churches has best been expressed in the Antigonish Movement, the university's outreach to help the people of the region improve their economic lot through adult education and organization, principally into co-operatives and credit unions.

This 'mastering of their own destiny' has attracted a flow (now of thousands) of community leaders from the Third World who wish to learn the Antigonish way of self-help and to apply its principles to the challenges of their own communities in Asia, Africa, Latin America and the Caribbean.

Thus 'Tigh Dhé' has striven not only to preach the Gospel to Catholics, but also to serve the educational and economic needs of all peoples both in its own region and, recently, in the wider world of the developing countries.   MMCD

novel, the Gaelic The art of novel writing was not practised in Gaelic until the twentieth century and the output of novels has been very small. There are probably sociological and economic explanations for this. The literate public has always been small, and when a nineteenth-century popular demand was created for Gaelic writings (through the Gaelic schools) it is likely that some prejudice existed against fiction ('untruth' as opposed to biblical 'truth'). There was a move towards fiction in the nineteenth-century periodical, but it was fiction tied to the apron strings of folktale and religious homily, and it did not embrace the dimensions of the novel. Economic factors reinforced this tardy development.

The earliest full-length Gaelic novel to be published was Iain MacCormaic's *Dùn-àluinn, no an t-Oighre 'na Dhìobarach* (*Dùn-àluinn, or the Heir an Exile*) (1912), though Angus Robertson's *An t-Ogha Mór* (*The Big Grandson*) (1913) had partly appeared in the periodical *An Sgeulaiche* (1909–10) and was itself an adaptation of his earlier story (see **Robertson, Angus**). A little earlier MacCormaic published a short novel *Gun d'thug i spéis do'n Armunn* (*She Gave her Love to the Hero*) (1908). Thus Robertson and MacCormaic stand side by side at the birth of the Gaelic novel.

Dùn-àluinn is a mixture of sentimentality, tub-thumping and the kind of anecdotage-with-repartee that is popular with Gaelic audiences. The hero, Dùn-àluinn, is the liberal-minded heir to a profligate and oppressive landlord, and the Ministear Mór (Big Minister) delivers some rousing diatribes against such oppression, leading to a riot. The plot has a love theme, some murders and scenes in New Zealand goldmines, and coincidences move the plot to its dénouement. The style, especially near the beginning, is reminiscent of MacPherson's Ossian, and to confirm this influence there are comparisons between Ossian and classical epic (pp. 43–4). *An t-Ogha Mór* is a historical novel, set in the period between the 1715 and 1745 Risings and located in Skye and London. It is a story of intrigue, with a love interest and with much detailed description, the most memorable being that of the Broadford Fair. A writer in the journal *Guth na Bliadhna* referred to its 'luxuriant crop of

beautiful verbiage', while the reviewer in the *Glasgow Evening News* wrote of Robertson's 'almost morbid Meredithian avoidance of the obvious in phrase'. The novel is most notable for its stylistic characteristics, the plot being crowded and not easy to follow.

Seumas MacLeòid's *Cailin Sgiathanach* (*Skye Maid*) (1923) suffers also from overloaded and pretentious language. The fundamental difficulty of finding appropriate registers has not been solved, and this is underlined by the relative felicity of some English letters quoted in the text (Mòrag's letter, pp. 202–3, has clarity and lucidity). The story is set in Skye in the second half of the eighteenth century and gives an opportunity for the airing of anti-landlord (and, even more, anti-clerical) sentiments. The plot is thin and conventional, and there is not much development of character, though a subsidiary character, MacGrùslaich, comes alive. There are some vivid episodes, such as Mòrag's opening of the grave (pp. 126ff.), and the unravelling of the plot is reasonably efficient.

Although much later, Cailein MacCoinnich's *A' Leth Eile* (*The Other Half*) (1971) has affinities with these early novels, having a picaresque element, a strong didactic purpose and a rich lexical and idiomatic texture; it is, however, less esoteric in its use of language than are the three early novels.

It was not until the 1970s that the Gaelic novel got its second wind, but it is still in doubt whether it will become a long-distance runner. Màiri NicGill-Eathain's *Gainmheach on Fhàsaich* (*Sand of the Desert*) (1971) is a romance set partly in the Islands, partly in South Africa. Cairistiona Dick's *Raonaid* (*Rachel*) (1981) is a love story for adolescents, carefully judged. Fearghas MacFhionnlaigh, in *Có ghoid am bogha-froise?* (*Who Stole the Rainbow?*) (1978), makes a political and religious allegory coalesce with an exciting space-and-adventure story. Tormod Caimbeul's first novel, *Deireadh an Fhoghair* (*End of Autumn*) (1979), has a carefully controlled tension and a precise observation that promise well. His novel has three characters, and the action is confined to twenty-four hours. The characters are old (survivors); appropriately enough, the stream-of-consciousness technique and radio-type fade-ins, etc., reveal some of their past history. There is a tendency towards catalogue (of birds, shellfish, place names, etc.), which can perhaps here be dramatically justified. The tone and register are uniform, and well judged.

The most impressive achievement in the Gaelic

novel to date is Iain Mac a' Ghobhainn's (q.v.). He has not written a long novel in Gaelic, but he has written three different kinds of novel and has shown a larger range of characters and situations than any of his Gaelic contemporaries in this form. His Gaelic work is, of course, related to his work in English (novels and short stories) and to his Gaelic short stories, so that we see the novels against this much larger background. His first Gaelic novel, *Iain am measg nan reultan* (*John among the Planets*) (1970), is space fiction drawing on stock characters such as Desperate Dan. His second, *An t-Aonaran* (*The Loner*) (1976), deals with the loner, in an assortment of personae, and is set in a claustrophobic, self-destructive small village. Although the plot has some melodrama, there is a controlled use of imagination and the underlying symbolism is rich and effective. The main theme of the book is concerned with art and communication and the vulnerability of the artistic temperament. (An English adaptation was published as the title story of *The Hermit*, 1977.) Mac a' Ghobhainn's *Murchadh* (*Murdo*) appeared in instalments in *Gairm* (nos. 106–9, 1979) and is again concerned with an artistic loner, this time more clearly on the brink of madness. The author has for long been strongly attracted to depicting psychotic states. There is some highly amusing description and incident in this novel.

All the Gaelic novels of recent years have been small-scale, but apart from the missing dimension of scale the form shows a healthy development in technique and tone that resembles, though it does not yet match, the development that has taken place in the short story. DST

novella, the Gaelic, *see* tales, romantic.

Nutt, Alfred (1856–1910) From London. Founder member and later President of the Folklore Society, particularly interested in Celtic and Arthurian literature. Publisher and *de facto* general editor of *Waifs and Strays*. (See Lord Archibald Campbell 1889–95.) AB

O'Boyle, Colm J. (b. 1938) From Northern Ireland. Lecturer in Celtic, University of Aberdeen. Editor of the poems of Sìleas na Ceapaich (q.v.), Eachann Bacach (q.v.) and others. Has done considerable work on Scottish Gaelic dialects. DST

Ó Brolchán family The most notable of the hereditary families of stonemasons who evolved the distinctive style of west Highland monumental sculpture (q.v.) centred on Iona from the mid-fourteenth century to *c.*1560. In the twelfth century they were associated mainly with the Columban monastery of Derry, and their threefold interest in the Church, learning and stoneworking was already evident. Neil Ó Brolchán, parson of Kilarrow, Islay, in 1382, is the first of his name on record in Scotland. Rogellus was a bachelor of decreets and secretary to Alexander, Lord of the Isles (d. 1449). A building inscription of about this date on the capital of a pier in the abbey Church of Iona reads *Donaldus O Brolchan fecit hoc opus* (Donald Ó Brolchán made this work). Finally, as the Latin inscription on it tells us, Eoghan MacDougall, prior of Ardchattan, 'caused this cross to be erected by John Ó Brolchán at Ardchattan in the year of Our Lord 1500'. (See Steer and Bannerman 1977, 106–9, 134–5.) JWMB

Ó Clumhain, an Caoch (dates unknown) Author of ballad 'Osnadh carad i gcluain Fraoich'. (See N. Ross 1939, 198.) DST

Ó Héanna (dates unknown) Poem on Eóin a h-Ìle (Cennas Ghaoidheal do Chlann Cholla) ascribed to him in Red Book of Clanranald (q.v.), 218–19. DST

Ó Muirgheasáin family One of the principal families of hereditary poet-historians in Gaelic Scotland: in Ireland the anglicized form of the name is Bryson, in Scotland Morison. A recurrent forename from the fifteenth century is Mac na h-Oidhche; Clann Mhic na h-Oidhche was to remain the Ó Muirgheasáins' byname in Skye.

Ó Muirgheasáins first appear as clerics in Inishowen, Donegal, in the fifteenth century. Until 1609 at least they held hereditary office there as keepers of the relics of Colum Cille (q.v.). Their shrine, the Míosach, now in Dublin, was made by Brian Ó Muirgheasáin in 1534.

The first known Ó Muirgheasáin in Scotland is Magnus of Mull, whose son, Maol Domhnaigh, composed an extravaganza of Marianism preserved in the Book of the Dean of Lismore (q.v.), which can be dated to 1512–42 (Greene 1962). Seventeenth- and eighteenth-century Ó Muirgheasáins are found in the service of the MacLeods. Toirdhealbhach wrote a Gaelic contract of fosterage (SRO RH 9/17/35) for Sir Ruairi Mór (1614) and took part in a raid on Lewis (1616). Eoin Óg composed Sir Ruairi's elegy (1626) (J. Macdonald 1955). Maol Domhnaigh mac Eoin praises Lewis and Harris. Donnchadh mac Maol Domhnaigh is the probable author of an elegy on Sir Ruairi's son, Sir Norman of Berneray (1705).

Maol Domhnaigh mac Eoin was 34 years in Ireland, where he was regarded as the last of the great bardic poets, but his surviving work is pedestrian by Eoin Óg's standards. He appears to have retired to Penmore in Mull as Duart's poet and to have died c.1662. Ó Muirgheasáins retained tack but not office for long after; their descendants remain in Mull. (See R. I. Black 1976–81; Bristol 1978; W. Matheson 1978.)   RIB

O'Rahilly, Thomas F. (1883–1953) Professor of Irish at Trinity College, Dublin. Discussion of Scottish Gaelic dialects in *Irish Dialects*, *Past and Present* (new edn 1972); etymological articles, etc., in *Scottish Gaelic Studies*.   DST

Ogam stones and early Christian Latin inscriptions The Ogam alphabet was an Irish invention of perhaps the fourth century AD, based on the Latin alphabet but with completely different 'letters' (Thurneysen 1946, 10), analogous to the Germanic runes. It comprised arrangements of grooves at an angle to a base line, suitable for easy engraving. The alphabet was used for epitaphs on gravestones in Ireland, chiefly in the fifth and sixth centuries before Latin gained universal currency, and was brought to Scotland by the Dalriadic (q.v.) colonists. However, there seem to be no certainly Gaelic Ogams in Scotland, not even the Gigha and Poltalloch examples. All the other Pictish Ogams, some twenty-seven at present known, date probably from the seventh to mid-ninth centuries and belong to the old Pictish Scotland north of the Forth and the Clyde; some are associated with 'Pictish symbols'. Of these, seven hail

from Shetland, three from Orkney, two from Caithness, one from Sutherland, eleven from the Pictish heartland between the Moray Firth and the Forth, and one each from Uist, Argyll (on the rock at Dunadd, beside the probably Pictish symbolic boar, unknown to most historians: K. H. Jackson 1965, 300), and Arran. All can be transcribed into Roman letters, except where the stone has been damaged or weathered, but the language they represent is completely unknown, two or three loanwords (q.v.) and Celtic names apart (see **Pictish languages**; Padel 1972).

The early Christian Latin inscriptions are in Roman letters with Latin and Celtic names, and are the product of the Celtic Church (q.v.) in Scotland between the fifth and the ninth century. Four belong to Pictland (Shetland, Ross-shire and two in Angus). The double inscription from Shetland on the 'chape' in the St Ninian's Isle treasure (q.v.), with two Pictish names, is well-known; and the ninth-century St Vigeans stone has two Pictish names, one Gaelic, and a probably Celtic-Pictish word, *ipe*, apparently meaning 'and'. There are also five on Iona.

In the 'British' country south of the Forth and the Clyde an interesting group of five inscriptions, dating to between the late fifth and the early seventh century, stretches in a line from Edinburgh southwards to near Newcastleton, with a sixth outlier in Northumberland, from Chesterholm, near Hadrian's Wall. The most remarkable of these are the 'Catstane' on Edinburgh airfield, dedicated to Vetta son (or daughter) of Victrus (probably a late form of Victor); the fine stone in Yarrow parish commemorating 'the most distinguished princes Nudus and Dumnogenus, sons of Liberalis'; and the inscription fairly recently discovered in Peebles, of the very late sixth century, in honour of 'Bishop Neitan'. There is another group of five at Whithorn, the site of St Ninian's original church, and at Kirkmadrine, near Stranraer, of the same period. One at Whithorn, from the very late fifth century, says:

> We praise thee, Lord. Latinus, aged 35, and his daughter, aged 4 years, made [this] sign here. [He was] grandson of Barrovadus. [British name, 'Mole-Head'.]

The 'sign' is the *chi-rho* Christian monogram on the top of the stone. At Kirkmadrine the early sixth-century inscription, 'Here lie the holy and eminent bishops i.e. Viventius and Mavorius', is also remarkable. All these British Latin inscriptions south of the Forth and the Clyde bear witness to post-Roman

The 'catstane', Kirkliston, Midlothian, east face.

P

influence from south of Hadrian's Wall and to the activities of the early Church of Ninian at Whithorn which stemmed from that influence. (See Macalister 1945, 184ff.)   KHJ

'Oisean an Déidh na Féinne' (Ossian after the Fenians) A strange folktale, well-known in Scotland but unknown in Ireland. The aged Ossian boasts to St Patrick that a blackbird's leg bone from his young days would be bigger than a stag's now, and he catches a blackbird to prove his point.   AB

Oran Mòr *see* song, Gaelic.

orders, learned, *see* institutions and orders, learned and professional.

orthography of Gaelic, *see* Gaelic: orthography.

paganism, survivals of There are many traces of the pagan past of Gaelic Scotland. Naturally, surviving beliefs are difficult to record, as people are reluctant to divulge them, but some practices are still evident vestigially or under another guise, and others can yet be culled from the folk memory.

There are many extant cult objects, archaic or more recent in origin. Examples are amulets in the form of stones, often holed or of a singular shape or colour. White quartz is widely used; the pebbles are known as 'fairy fire stones'. Sometimes venerated stones are blackened in the fire for purposes of a sinister nature. Others, such as those found at Killin, were until recently used for healing the sick. Figures for working woe, such as the *corp crèadha* (clay body), are used to the present day.

The magic apotropaic power of the horseshoe can be appreciated by the numbers of them nailed outside or inside house and byre alike; as in the past, belief in the power of iron and the semi-divine nature of the smith is strong, although here, as elsewhere, the old forces must eventually yield to the new magic of the media, and age-old tradition will bow down before the all-conquering god Television. But much yet lingers on. The rowan tree outside the house, or one of its branches hung within dwellings, are a reminder that belief in black witchcraft is not dead. Likewise, when modern medicine fails the powers of the healers (or 'charmers', as they are still called) are invoked. Wells believed to have special powers are still resorted to, and offerings are made to them in return for benefits received.

The cult of the severed head, which we may regard as the symbol of pagan Celtic religion, is attested in Gaelic Scotland, and there is evidence that here, as elsewhere in the once-Celtic world, it still lingers, although its origins are long forgotten. Two fine tricephaloi (three-faced heads), probably of pre-Roman date, come from Sutherland (A. Ross 1960, 10ff.) and Netherton (A. Ross 1974, 26ff.), the latter having been found at a source of the Clyde, named, as were so many Celtic rivers and streams, after a goddess, *Clōta* (She who washes) (W. J. Watson 1926, 44). The grim horned god from Muirton, Perth (A. Ross 1967, 81 and pl. 22a,b) is well matched by another, found in the Gogar Burn, now in the Scottish National Museum. Eight 'Celtic' heads adorn the so-called Druidic Stone on Craigmaddie Moor (Rock of the Dog); one, likewise horned (Alcock 1977), is to be found about 11 miles north of Glasgow; while several stone heads are set into a wall at Latheron, Caithness (*in situ*). Human skulls still play their ancient role as healing agents, while legends concerning the placing of severed heads in wells are still told (A. Ross 1967, 61ff.).

Traces of the old gods abound in place names – Taranus (the Thunderer) (W. J. Watson 1926, 431) and Lugos (Lothian) are suggested (Bromwich 1961, 421), while names for river goddesses are scattered over the whole area (W. J. Watson 1926, 425ff.). The names of the early tribes likewise indicate the divinities under whose aegis they placed themselves. The Lugi, near Loch Carron, would appear to have been worshippers of the god Lugos; the Smertae on the boundaries of Sutherland and Ross-shire may have venerated Rosmerta, (the Exceedingly Smeared One – smeared, no doubt, with the blood of sacrifices) or the god Smertullos. The river Oykel, which runs through their territory, may likewise have been sacred in pagan times to Uxellos (Gaelic *uasal*, 'high', E. Celtic *uxellos* having developed in Gaelic into ?*uckel* by Norse times) (A. Ross 1967, 431; W. J. Watson 1926, 209).

Among the surviving pagan rituals and ceremonies in Gaelic Scotland, some of the most elaborate and archaic are the calendar festivals. Many people can still recall practices, commonplace in their youth, of which the significance is now forgotten. A major festival was that of Imbolc (1 February) held in honour of the goddess (later saint) Brigit or Bride, the most popular of the Celtic female saints. She was much concerned with stock and with fertility. She was regarded as the midwife of the Virgin Mary (over whom she would, in fact, appear to have taken precedence in popularity), possibly because Candlemas (2 February), which so closely coincides with her feast day, was the date of the purification of Our Lord's mother.

Bride was also associated with the serpent, and there are clear hints of snake worship in Gaelic Scotland, as well as throughout the Celtic world down the ages (A. Carmichael 1900, vol. 1 (2nd edn 1928), 164ff.; A. Ross 1967, 406).

In all Celtic festivals fire played an important role. Bealltainn (1 May) was very much a fire festival for the purification of the stock and for its protection against evil forces while it was being taken to the summer grazings (*àirighean*). A special cake was baked, one portion of which was always found to be blackened. There are hints here, as with all the calendar festivals, of human sacrifice in propitiation of the gods. Within living memory an elaborate ceremony was performed in Glenlyon, in which the people gathered on a special plot that had been deturfed, and the one whose lot it was to receive the blackened piece of the bannock was ritually beaten out of the *temenos* (sacred area) as the scapegoat of the community. In earlier times his or her fate would no doubt have been more sinister. The festival to mark the summer solstice (21 June) was likewise celebrated by the lighting of great bonfires, the baking of a special cake, dancing and rejoicing.

One of the most important commemorative days in the Celtic calendar was that dedicated to the god Lugos, known as Lughnasa. This took place on 1 August and, like the other festivals, continues to be held in vestigial form. It was not a harvest thanksgiving but a feast to ensure that the god of prosperity would overcome the god of blight and secure a good harvest for his people (M. MacNeill 1962; A. Ross 1976, 138ff.). The end of the harvest was celebrated by the cutting of the last sheaf, and this is still done in some areas (A. Ross 1976, 142). The bundle of reaped grain was tied together and often fashioned into an elaborate female figure known as *a' Mhaighdean* (the 'Maiden'). In some areas, if the harvest was a bad one, she was known as *a' Chailleach* (the 'Hag').

Other important festivals include those of St Michael (Latha na Fèill Mìcheil) on 29 September (A. Carmichael 1900, vol. 1 (2nd edn 1928), 198), which had both agrarian and fertility associations and would likewise seem to be connected with the god Lugos (A. Ross 1976, 140). Elaborate ritual was traditionally associated with the Christmas festival (Nollaig), which coincides with the winter solstice. More important, and again with sinister undertones, was the Hogmanay celebration to welcome the New Year. The paganism of the old rites which took place on New Year's Eve (*Oidhche Challuinn*) is barely disguised (Carmichael 1928, 148ff.; A. Ross 1976, 119ff.). (For a fuller discussion of pagan survivals see A. Ross 1976, and its bibliography.)   AR

palatalization in Gaelic, *see* Gaelic: palatalization.

panegyric, *see* verse, panegyric.

Pearsan (Pearsún), an (the Parson) Author of poem in the Book of the Dean of Lismore (q.v.) in which he asks why he should avoid lovemaking. (See Quiggin 1937, 74.) DST

periodicals Periodicals in Gaelic are not very attractive propositions for commercial entrepreneurs, but in the days of cheap printing they could be run without much financial risk. Probably, however, they have almost always come into being in response to ideological or dogmatic needs: the need to supply suitable reading matter of an evangelical nature, the need to provide more Gaelic in print and so on.

The earliest periodical is *An Rosroine* (Glasgow, 1803, four numbers); the steady succession begins with Caraid nan Gaidheal's (q.v.) *An Teachdaire Gaelach* (Glasgow and Edinburgh, 1829–31), and continues with *An Teachdaire Ur Gaidhealach* (Glasgow, 1835–6), Caraid nan Gaidheal's *Cuairtear nan Gleann* (Glasgow, 1840–3), *Caraid nan Gaidheal* (Glasgow, 1844), *Teachdaire nan Gaidheal* (Glasgow, 1844–8) *An Fhianuis*, a Free Church periodical (Glasgow, 1845–50), *Fear-Tathaich nam Beann* (Glasgow, 1848–50). After a twenty-year hiatus a new wave begins with *An Gaidheal* (Glasgow and Edinburgh, 1871–7), *Bratach na Fìrinn* (Glasgow, 1873–4), the *Celtic Magazine*, mainly English (Inverness, 1876–88), *MacTalla* (Sydney and Cape Breton, 1892–1904) and *Am Bard*, Rory Erskine's (q.v.) early periodical (Edinburgh, 1901) (Maclean, Donald, 1915, 310–15). In addition there were a number of shorter-lived, or single-issue periodicals which failed, for one reason or another, to continue. There were also some short-lived overseas periodicals before the more resolute *Mac-Talla* – e.g. *An Teachdaire Gaidhealach* in Australia (1857), *Cuairtear na Coillte* in Ontario (1840–1), *An Cuairtear Og Gaidhealach* in Antigonish, Nova Scotia (1851). *The Celtic Monthly* (Glasgow, 1892–1917) included some Gaelic, as did such Church periodicals as *An Fhianuis* (Glasgow, 1893–1900), the *Monthly Record* (Glasgow and Edinburgh, 1900–), *An Fhianuis Ghaidhealach* (Glasgow/Edinburgh, 1904–29), *Life and Work* (Edinburgh, 1880–) and the *Magazine and Monthly Record* of the Free Presbyterian Church (Glasgow, 1895–).

In its first year (1829–30) *An Teachdaire Gaelach* featured such topics as the teaching of Gaelic in the Highlands, an account of a shinty match, legends, drinking at funerals, Culloden, and a fox-hunter's colloquy with a schoolmaster on smuggling, but also the management of bees, the Great Wall of China, the art of printing, Indian superstition, an account of the steam engine and the natural history of the silkworm. It also included articles on Ash Wednesday and baptism and moral reflections on various topics, together with poems and hymns. A minister describes his visit to the deathbed of a young child, sparing no detail, but the account of the Great Wall is quite crisp and economical. In this periodical we can see quite clearly the twin aims of evangelical instruction and the widening of the range of Gaelic writing, and probably these were not uncommon aims among Gaelic educationists and clergymen in the first half of the nineteenth century. The later periodicals veer away from the evangelical line (except for the Church periodicals), *An Gaidheal*, for example, showing a stronger preference for antiquarian, historical and literary topics but without neglecting current affairs or exotic topics.

Great credit is due to the nineteenth-century periodical writers, and to their editors, for their work in extending the range and registers of Gaelic writing, and the same might be said of twentieth-century periodicals. (Of course, this extension is one that has to be undertaken periodically and, ideally, continuously.)

The list of main Gaelic periodicals in the twentieth century runs as follows: *Guth na Bliadhna* (Perth, 1904–25), *An Deò-Gréine*, later *An Gaidheal* (Glasgow, 1905–67), *Alba*, a weekly newspaper (Perth, Greenock, 1908–09), *An Sgeulaiche* (Dumfries and Glasgow, 1909–11), *An Ròsarnach* (Glasgow, 1917, 1918, 1921, 1930), *Alba* (one issue only, Glasgow, 1948), *Gairm* (Glasgow, 1952–), *Sruth*, fortnightly, later monthly (Inverness and Stornoway, 1967–79), *Sradag*, a children's comic (Glasgow, 1960–2), *Crùisgean*, originally at three-weekly intervals (Berneray; Skye, 1977–9; 1980–) and *North 7* (Inverness, 1977–81). There were also Canadian periodicals: for example, *Mosgladh* (Sydney, 1922–33), *An Solus Iùil* (Sydney, 1925–7), *Teachdaire nan Gaidheal* (Sydney, 1925–34), *Fear na Ceilidh* (Sydney, 1928–30) and *Irisleabhar Ceilteach* (Toronto, 1952–4). University Highland student societies have published periodicals spasmodically (*Ossian* from Glasgow, 1933– ; *Crann* from Aberdeen, 1967–). Academic periodicals, including some Gaelic, are the *Celtic Review* (Edinburgh, 1904–16), *Scottish Gaelic Studies* (Aberdeen, 1926–), *Scottish Studies* (Edinburgh, 1957–) and *Tocher* (Edinburgh, 1971–). There are yearly publications, partly in Gaelic, such as *Eilean an Fhraoich Annual* (Stornoway, 1951–), and a number of Scottish literary periodicals include some Gaelic, especially poetry (e.g. *Akros, Lines Review, New Saltire, Scottish International, Chapman, Scotia, Cencrastus* and the *Scottish Review*).

No doubt the most sustained programme designed to extend the range of Gaelic writing in periodicals has been that of *Gairm*, currently the only surviving all-Gaelic periodical. This programme embraces different modes of the short story, serial novels and poetry, as well as writing on current affairs and exotic topics. It includes the freeing of prose styles from ecclesiastically dominated syntax and lexis and the partial adaptation of orthographical conventions, aimed at producing a closer fit between the written and the spoken form, while still preserving a standard written language. As to the range of subject matter, *Gairm* (followed later, with a more restricted range of topics, by *North 7*), for example has regularly fea-

tured articles on current affairs, life and travel in foreign countries, crofting topics, industry, politics, leisure pursuits, music, philosophy, cookery, fashion, philology, geography, biology, rheumatism, Japanese painting, etc. Often these articles are the occasion for the coining of new words and the trying out of unfamiliar registers, all this gradually forging a much stronger and more flexible Gaelic canon.

It is very evident that until now much periodical publication has been centred on Glasgow and Edinburgh, especially Glasgow, but there is at last some sign that the home Gaelic area is coming into the picture. A significant number of contributors to these periodicals have always had close or recent links with the Gaelic area, often reflecting the current location of language-maintenance enthusiasm (Perthshire, Argyll, Badenoch, Skye, Lewis, etc.). DST

Petty, Seer of (John Morrison) (1701–74) Nephew of Roderick Morrison (an Clàrsair Dall, q.v.). Minister of Petty, near Inverness, 1759–74. (See W. Matheson 1970, 197.) DST

phonemic structure of Gaelic, *see* Gaelic: phonemic structure.

phonetics, Gaelic, *see* Gaelic: phonetics, experimental and instrumental.

Pictish languages There were apparently two Pictish languages. One was P-Celtic, brought from Europe in the first millennium BC by Gallo-Brittonic settlers, ancestors of the historical aristocracy of Pictland. It is known from place-names and names of historical kings, etc. The other was not even Indo-European, being the language of the predecessors of the Celts in Scotland, who also introduced the non-Celtic customs of matrilinear succession and tattooing. It is preserved in the early inscriptions of Pictland (*see* **Ogam stones**); though unconnected with it, Basque is another such pre-Indo-European tongue preserved late in a remote corner of Europe. Its survival in inscriptions could be due to the Celts regarding it as a prestigious language of magic and using it for learned purposes, much as the Semitic Babylonians regarded and used pre-Semitic Sumerian. Examples of non-Celtic Pictish personal names are Bliesblituth, Canutulachama and, in the St Ninian's treasure (q.v.), Spusscio. Celtic Pictish was similar to the early ancestor of Welsh, etc., but perhaps not identical (see **place-names, British**

and Pictish). Early Celtic names of Pictish chiefs in Classical sources are Calgacus, Argentocoxos and Vepogenus. The Celticity of the aristocracy in the Dark Ages is established by names like Tarain, Onuist, Unuist, and Nechton/Naiton. (See **loanwords, British and Pictish**; K. H. Jackson 1955.)

KHJ

Pictland, *see* place-names, Gaelic, in Pictland.

Picts, pre-Union contact with the Scots Contemporary sources for the history of Roman Britain link the Scots from Ireland and the Picts from North Britain as raiders on the province from land and sea. But the Picts had also to defend their lands in the north, and it has rightly been said that the Pictish kingdom was a product of the Roman presence in Britain (Mann 1974, 41). Encounters between Picts and Scots, particularly in the Western Isles, must have been commonplace during the post-Roman period, and the permanent establishment of the Irish Dalriadic dynasty in Argyll around AD 500 takes its place as one event in a series of Irish settlements on the west coasts of Britain (C. Thomas 1972a, 251–74).

There is no record of conflict between the two peoples until 558, when, according to the Irish Annals, the Scots retreated before the forces of the Pictish king, Bridei, son of Maelchon (q.v.). The activities of Colum Cille (q.v.) after this period suggest that the Scots temporarily abandoned the idea of expansion into Pictish territory. From his monastic base on Iona, Colum Cille was closely involved with the affairs of the Dál Riata in Scotland, but he was also a life-long friend of Bridei (Brudei), who had allowed him to establish monasteries among the Picts in order to make a start on their conversion (A. O. and M. O. Anderson 1961, 81–7; I. Henderson 1975, 91–8). Bridei's fame as a 'most powerful king', mentioned by Bede in his account of Colum Cille's mission to the Picts (Bede, III, 4), may have been due as much to his capacity to maintain a politically unified kingdom as to his containment of the Scots.

An understanding of the relationship between the two peoples is limited by the scarcity and complexity of the written sources. The evidence in the Irish Annals collections is brief and irregular, and as the Scottish entries are based ultimately on an Iona record, it is written from a Dalriadic point of view. The material in the genealogies and king-lists has similar regional bias, and it also shows signs of having been constructed within antiquarian political theories which may be very far removed from historical reality (A. O. Anderson 1922; M. O. Anderson 1973; Bannerman 1974; M. Miller 1979a,b).

A few key figures emerge from the scattered references, but their very importance renders suspect the later material connected with them. All suggestions of early Dalriadic influence in the Pictish east must be treated with great caution, for this notion would obviously have been attractive to later medieval Scottish historians. The alleged Pictish campaigns of Aedán, son of Gabráin, king of Dál Riata in Ireland and Scotland (d. *c*.608) come into this category. Keeping to the earlier evidence alone, it is even possible to argue that Aedán and Bridei were allies. On the other hand, there is no doubt that Aedán was a powerful military leader who might well have revived the Scots ambitions to increase their territory at the expense of the Picts (A. O. and M. O. Anderson 1961, 45; M. O. Anderson 1973, 145–6; Bannerman 1974, 85–6).

During the first half of the seventh century the Dál Riata in Scotland lost control of their territory in Ireland, probably as a consequence of serious defeats suffered by their king Domnall Brecc (d. *c*.642) in Ireland and Scotland. Some of these may have been at the hands of the Picts, but this is not certain. Picts and Scots were fighting, however, according to the Irish Annals, in 649 and 654 (Bannerman 1974, 99–103). Not long after this the Scots, Britons and Picts came under the overlordship of the Northumbrians. Part of the Pictish kingdom was occupied by the English, and the Scots and Britons were 'made tributary' (Bede, II, 5). It is significant that when the Pictish king Bridei, son of Bili, defeated Ecgfrith of Northumbria at Nechtanesmere in Angus in 685 (Bede, IV, 26), his success released the Scots and the Britons from their obligations also (I. Henderson, 1967, 51–9). The good relations established between Picts and Scots at this point may have led to a redefining of the boundary between them, which, at the time when Adamnán was writing his *Life of Columba* (688–700), is given as the mountain range of Druim Alban (A. O. and M. O. Anderson 1961, 59).

The eighth century was a time of growing confidence and strength for the Picts. One aspect of this was the decision by the king Nechton, son of Derelei (d. *c*.732) to remove the Columban clergy from the churches in Pictland around 710 (Bede, V, 21). A short period of civil war produced in 729 an unambiguously aggressive Pictish king, Oengus, son of Fergus (d. 761). He had no success against the Britons but, taking advantage of the confused political situation in Dál Riata, he annexed the Scottish kingdom for a period (I. Henderson 1967, 60–6).

It has been suggested that the Pictish civil war may have disrupted the rules of Pictish inheritance (M. Miller 1979b, 53), and this and other factors may account for the intermingling of the Pictish and Dalriadic dynasties in the century which followed. This intermingling has been variously interpreted as Pictish domination of Dál Riata or Scottish infiltration of the Picts (M. O. Anderson 1973, 188–99; J. W. M. Bannerman 1971, 75–7; I. Henderson 1967, 91–103). Picts and Scots fought against each other in 768, but thereafter there is no record of fighting. A recent suggestion is that a measure of co-operation was instigated at this point (M. Miller 1979b, 46–8). Certainly after the disastrous defeat in 839, when both the Pictish and the Dalriadic kings were killed by the Vikings, co-operation might have seemed a necessity. Such an interpretation would account for the fact that while the later sources describe the defeat of the Scots by Kenneth, son of Alpín (d. 858), in the mid-ninth century in terms of genocide, no contemporary source records a significant victory at this point. The contemporary evidence can be most naturally interpreted as showing a gradual disappearance of Pictish institutions. The evidence of the most characteristic Pictish place names (those beginning with the prefix Pit-) bears this out.

Other features of Pictish social organization can also be traced in early medieval Scotland – for example, the office of *mormaer* and the concept of the thanage (K. H. Jackson 1972, 102–17). The migration of the Scots into the east need not of itself have swamped the Picts, but for some reason it was the Scottish dynasty which prevailed in the united kingdom, and thereafter Scottish writers of official history were at pains to play down the Pictish past.

IH

Picts, union with the Scots The development of North Britain during the eighth century, dominated by the successfully aggressive reign of Oengus, son of Fergus, who died in 761, must have seemed to point to the eventual triumph of the long-established and apparently well organized Pictish kingdom, despite unique succession rules militating against dynastic stability. (No son of a Pictish king might himself be king; only sons of women of the Pictish royal lineage

could succeed.) Yet by 843 Kenneth, son of Alpín (his father of obscure origin), king of the Scots of Dalriada, had made himself ruler of the Scottish mainland north of Clyde and Forth, save for the far north and north-west, already doubtless under Norse sway.

Certain facts may explain the Scots' surprising success. First, Viking attacks began towards the end of the eighth century, and permanent Norse settlement followed soon after 800, at first only in the Northern Isles but soon affecting the northern and western seaboard of the Scottish mainland. Secondly, intermarriage between the Pictish and Dalriadan royal families produced two successive kings (789–839) with valid title to be rulers of both Picts and Scots. A further factor may have been the collapse of Northumbrian Christianity under heathen Danish onslaught, allowing the post-Columban Church of the Scots to reassert its dominance. In any case, there must have been much Scottish (i.e. Gaelic) penetration of Pictish territory before 843; but while culturally victory lay with the Scots, whose name was given to the new country, politically and institutionally the older kingdom (Alba, Fortriu, Scotia) survived, with its centre of gravity on the lower Tay. (See M. O. Anderson 1973, 1980; Inverness Field Club 1972, 1975.)

GWSB

Pìobaire Dall, am (the Blind Piper: John Mackay) (1656–1754) Born Gairloch. Studied piping with Patrick Og MacCrimmon (see **MacCrimmons**); piper to Laird of Gairloch. His daughter was mother of Uilleam Ros (q.v.). (For a list of his pipe compositions, *see* J. Maclean 1953, 303.) Extant poems are 'Cumha Choire an Easain', detailed nature description dating from 1696, and poems addressed to Mackenzie and MacDonald chiefs, *c*.1730–5. (See J. Mackenzie 1877.)

DST

pìobaireachd (pibroch), *see* bagpipe, Highland.

place-names (**bibliographical note**) Scottish place-names have a fairly complex linguistic background. The earliest discernible linguistic layer, pre-Celtic but Indo-European, has been most intensively studied by W. F. H. Nicolaisen, in his doctoral thesis, in a series of articles in *Scottish Studies* (1957, etc.) and in later books such as *Scottish Place-Names* (1976). Celtic place-names, both British and Gaelic, have been definitively discussed by W. J. Watson in his *History of the Celtic Place-Names of Scotland*

(1926) and his *Place-Names of Ross and Cromarty* (1904, reissued 1976). Even this magisterial work is challenged on points of detail from time to time, but it has constituted the corner-stone of such studies for over fifty years and is likely to continue in that role. Invaluable insights into British names in Scotland have been given by Kenneth H. Jackson in his *Language and History in Early Britain* and in numerous papers discussing the interactions of Angles and Britons on both sides of the Scottish Border. Jackson has also set the question of Pictish and Pictish place-names in the clearest perspective yet achieved in his contributions to Wainwright, *The Problem of the Picts* (1955; rev. edn 1980). Anglian and English names in Scotland have not received definitive treatment as yet: we lack both the overall treatments of such place-name studies as Ekwall and Forster provided for England and the exhaustive county surveys also available for England. There are a few such county surveys which include Celtic names; for example, Angus Macdonald's *The Place-Names of West Lothian* (1941) and William M. Alexander's *The Place-Names of Aberdeenshire* (1952). John MacQueen has written on place-names in Galloway and south-west Scotland. There are various works of much more limited value, some of them however providing useful collections of names, such as H. Cameron Gillies's *The Place-Names of Argyll* (1906) and Donald Maciver's *Place-Names of Lewis and Harris*, and James B. Johnston's *Place-Names of Scotland* (1892 etc.), the latter to be used with extreme caution where Celtic origins are discussed. W. J. Watson had discussed Norse names in his book on Ross and Cromarty, as had Alexander MacBain (1893–4) and George Henderson (1910), but the most authoritative discussions of Norse names are those of Magne Oftedal, especially in his 'The Village Names of Lewis in the Outer Hebrides' (1954; *see also* Oftedal 1980); Nicolaisen (1969, 1976) has valuable chapters on Norse names; Bridget Gordon (1963) has written on Norse names (in Skye), as has Donald MacAulay in his paper on Bernera (Lewis) names, and chapters on Moray and Sutherland names in Omand (1976 and 1979); Ian A. Fraser has also written on Norse names (*see* I. A. Fraser 1979). (See also references in the entries below; bibliography in Nicolaisen 1976.)   DST

place-names, British and Pictish When the Gaels began settling in Argyll in about AD 500 Scotland was occupied by two Celtic peoples, the Britons south of Forth and Clyde and the Picts to the north. Both spoke P-Celtic languages, which were probably closely related – perhaps so closely as to be mere dialects, perhaps less closely, reflecting a difference in their European place of origin (K. H. Jackson 1955–80, 155ff.). The Celtic Pictish language of the north probably died out in the late ninth century, but the British (Welsh, more properly Cumbric) of the south may have lingered on until about 1100 in parts of the south-west; the former gave place to Gaelic, the latter to Gaelic and English. This P-Celticity is evident in many place-names in both regions. In the north a remarkable example is the fifty-odd names in *Aber* (river mouth), and these are significantly rare in the south, only some four or five, including Abercorn and Abermilk. Another, very characteristic of Pictland, is Pictish *pett* (parcel of land, agricultural unit; see **place-names, Gaelic in Pictland**) evident in hundreds of names in modern *Pit-*. This is scarcely found in the south, doubtless because the Welsh equivalent, *peth*, means 'thing'; the three in the Lothian littoral are obviously due to Pictish colonies south of Forth. Other P-Celtic elements in the north are *carden* (thicket) in several Kincardines and in Urquhart (*Urchardan*), Drumchardine, Pluscarden, etc.; *lanerc* ('glade': Lanrick, Lendrick); *pert* ('brake': Perth, Pert, Logiepert, etc.). Interesting river-names are Dee and Don, Pictish *Dewa* and *Dewona* respectively, both meaning Goddess; Esk, now thought to mean fishy [river] rather than water; and Tay, early Pictish *Tawia* (Silent One: maps, K. H. Jackson 1955/80, 147, 150).

It is in the British country that P-Celtic names are commonest, scattered now rather thinly but fairly evenly. British Strathclyde was *Strad Clud* (Strath of Clyde), and its capital Dumbarton was *Alt Clud* (Clyde rock); *Dumbarton* (fort of the Britons) is Gaelic. Melrose is *Melros* (bare moor); Leswalt is *Liswelt* (grassy courtyard). *Penn* (hill, end) is frequent, though it is significant that it is virtually unknown in Pictland, just as *pett* is in the south – hence Penpont (end of the bridge); Pencaitland (hill of the copse: Welsh *coedlann*); Penicuik (hill of the cuckoo: *cog*); Pennersax (the Englishman's hill) and Glensaxon (the Englishmen's glen), presumably both named when Anglian penetration into Dumfries-shire was not yet extensive (Sax(on) suggests not later than about 700). *Trev* (hamlet), common in Wales and Cornwall, is not rare in southern Scotland; so Tranent (twelfth-century Trevernent, 'hamlet of the brooks': Welsh *Tref y Neint*); and Terregles (fourteenth-century Trevereglys, 'hamlet with the church: Welsh *eglwys*). Other British names occur in the country occupied early by the Angles. Eddleston in Peebles-shire has a significant history. This had a hybrid Gaelic–English name, *Gillemorestun* (toun of Gillemoire), when it was granted about 1189 to an Anglian lord Eadwulf (hence *Eadwulfestun*), although the grant states it had formerly been *Penteiacob* (James's outhouses: Welsh *Pentai Iago*), a well preserved Cumbric name parallel to Pencaitland. This shows a British owner replaced by a Gaelic one after the region was absorbed by the Scots at about the end of the tenth century and passing to an Anglian lord some two centuries later. Names of witnesses to grants in Peebles-shire as late as the twelfth century are Cumbric often enough to suggest that the early Anglian and later Gaelic occupations had not entirely swamped the Cumbrian element there; the very name 'Peebles' is Cumbric (the tents: Welsh *pebyll*). There is a small group of Cumbric names in Stowe parish 12 miles east-north-east of Peebles which imply something similar. One of them not far from the parish boundary, Plenploth (sixteenth-century Plenploif) is probably Cumbric *Penn Ploev* (the bounds of the parish), a remarkable instance of what must have been a lateish Cumbric name surviving with its local demographic application to the present day. (See K. H. Jackson 1955/80, 146ff.; 1963, 60ff.; W. J. Watson 1926, 339ff.)   KHJ

place-names, ecclesiastical A separate account of Gaelic place names in this category is justified because of the extensive influence which the Church has had on the culture of Scottish Gaeldom since the first Irish missionaries set foot on Scottish soil in the wake of the establishment and gradual expansion of the Scottish Dalriada a millennium and a half ago. In many respects we have a fuller historical record of these names, as ecclesiastical ownership of land and any legal transactions concerning such property were not only recorded in secular registers but also regularly alluded to in the cartularies of monasteries, cathedrals, abbeys and other religious houses, institutions and divisions. In addition, oral tradition, in the form of legend, custom and belief, has preserved many minor names as part of a repertoire of narratives and traditions regarding the peregrinations, miraculous acts, commemorations and burial places of early saints, the beneficial properties of holy wells, important places of worship and pilgrimage and other similar matters. Naturally, the exact reference has often become obscured or totally obliterated over the

centuries, but the ecclesiastical connections of the names in question are nevertheless unmistakable.

The spectrum of surviving names in this category is understandably quite wide. There are, for example, names such as Rosneath (Dunbartonshire), Navitie (Fife), Nevay and Navar (Angus), Duneaves (Perthshire), Nevie (Banffshire), Dalnavie, Inchnavie, Nonakiln, Newmore, and Navity (Ross-shire), Navidale (Sutherland) and Finhaven (Angus) which, as their early spellings indicate (W. J. Watson 1926, 244–50), contain the Scottish Gaelic descendant of Old Irish *nemed* (sacred place, sanctuary), itself derived from an earlier *nemeton*, of similar meaning. Etymologically at least, these names preserve for us a reference to that early cultural seam that marked the point at which pagan concepts, and the places connected with them, were taken over by the Church. The notion of sanctuary is also implicit in such names as Comraich (Ross-shire) and Comraich na h-Eaglais (sanctuary of the church) and Comraich na Trianaid (sanctuary of the Trinity) (both in North Uist), as well as in *Termit* (Inverness-shire) and Tillytarmont (Banffshire), Gaelic *Tulach an Tearmaind* (sanctuary hill), both of which contain Gaelic *tearmann* (girth, sanctuary), from Latin *termo, termonis* (limit).

Places in some way set aside for the Church and its activities are also prominent in the place nomenclature found on Scottish maps: Inchaffray and Offerance (Perthshire) and Offers (Ross-shire) were probably places where mass (*aifreann, aifrionn* < Early Irish *oifrend* < Latin *offerendum*, 'an offering') was held. The idea of 'offering' or 'sacrifice' is also expressed by several places called Ibert in Perthshire and Stirlingshire (Gaelic *iobairt*), whereas Bendochy (Perthshire), Bannety (Fife) and others express the general notion of 'blessing' (Gaelic *beannachadh* or *beannachd*). Both the district of Appin in Argyllshire and Appin of Dull in Perthshire (Gaelic *Apuinn*) derive from Middle Irish *abdaine* (abbacy, abbey land: W. J. Watson 1926, 254–64).

Undoubtedly the most common ecclesiastical names are those associated with particular church dignitaries or individual saints. To the former class would belong Arnclerich, Arnvicar and Arnprior (Perthshire), all connected with the priory of Inchmahome in the Lake of Menteith. They are 'the churchman's portion' (Gaelic *earrann*), 'the vicar's portion' and 'the prior's portion', respectively. Pittentagart (Aberdeenshire) and Pithogarty (Ross-shire) are Pictish–Gaelic *peit an t-sagairt* (the priest's share), while Balvannich (Gaelic *Baile a' Mhanaich*) and Nuntown (Gaelic *Baile nan Cailleach*) in Benbecula are farmsteads or hamlets owned or inhabited by monks and nuns.

The names of saints are most commonly displayed as specifics in names with the element *cill*, the old dative-locative of Gaelic *ceall* (< Latin *cella*, cell, church, churchyard). Names like Kilbride, Kilmarnock, Kilmichael, Kilmacolm, Kilchenzie, Kilmaluag, Kilbrandon, Kilbarr, and Kilellan occur mostly in those areas of Scotaland which were settled by Gaelic-speaking Scots in the first four centuries after the establishment of a Scottish Dalriada. Their distribution and the datability of the saints in question make them excellent evidence for such an early layer within the Gaelic stratum. Most of the identifiable saints flourished particularly in the sixth and seventh centuries but also in the eighth century (Nicolaisen 1976, 142–4).

Not so datable are more impersonal names such as the several *Annats* (Gaelic *annaid*) which are said to refer to a 'patron saint's church' or 'a church that contains the relics of the founder' (Aidan MacDonald 1973, 135–46; W. J. Watson 1926, 250–4). The element also appears combined with other generics such as the frequent Achnahannet (Gaelic *Achadh na h-Annaide*, 'field of the *annat*'), Craigannet (Stirlingshire), Gaelic *Creag Annaide* (*annat* rock) or *Longannet* (Fife), probably Gaelic *Lann Annaide* (*annat* enclosure). Dysart in Fife and Angus, and the Gaelic name for Dalmally (Argyllshire), *Clachan an Dìseirt*, also commemorate anonymous ecclesiastics who went to such a *dìseart* (Middle Irish *dìsert* < Latin *desertum*, 'a desert') for solitary contemplation.

WFHN

place-names, English influence of the early burghs

The commercial revival of western Europe in the eleventh century affected Scotland strongly in the twelfth century, and urban privileges were given to a number of settlements on the fringe of the Gaelic area, notably Glasgow, Perth and Aberdeen, and Elgin and Inverness within it. These attracted significant numbers of English and Flemish settlers, who traded with the landward areas, buying cattle, wool hides and foodstuffs. Inverness had an important ship-construction yard. English was the language of these towns, hence increasingly the language of commerce, and at least in Lowland areas spread to the landward, where new settlements tend to have English names.

AAMD

place-names, Gaelic, in Galloway and Ayrshire

Although Gaelic was spoken in Galloway and Ayrshire for more than a thousand years, almost the only evidence for its existence is provided by place- and personal names. The language established itself at an early date and expanded in several stages. The earliest is indicated by non-settlement place-names in Slew- or Slae- (reflexes of *sliabh*, hill, rather than moor or mountain) and Carrick- (*carraig*, rock, fishing station); as similar names are found in Argyll but not, on the whole, in the remainder of Scotland, it seems likely that they indicate Gaelic settlement from Ireland roughly contemporary with that in Argyll during the fifth and early centuries AD. Examples are Slewcairn, Slewdonan, Slaewhullie, Carrickadown, Carrickafliou, Carrickahawkie. These names centre on the Rhinns, the extreme south-west peninsula of mainland Scotland, and indicate a settlement of hunters and fishermen, who were probably also small farmers (J. MacQueen 1953–4, 90–1: Nicolaisen 1976, 39–45).

This series of names overlaps with another, commemorating early Celtic (generally Irish) saints, and usually, but not invariably, prefixed by Kil- (*cill*, monastic cell, church). These are found in Dalriadic territory, in Galloway, Nithsdale and Carrick, but also in Cunninghame, Renfrewshire and Lanarkshire. They may well once have existed in Kyle, but, if so, all traces have been removed by the Anglian settlement of the middle and late eighth century. For the most part, they probably belong to the sixth, seventh and eighth centuries and indicate the spread of Irish monastic Christianity to the southern Scottish mainland. This spread may have been encouraged by the existence of important pre-Gaelic centres of Cumbric Christianity in what is now south-west Scotland. The earliest, and in many ways the most important, was Candida Casa, Whithorn in Wigtownshire, founded in the last days of Roman imperial power by Nynia or Ninian, a British monk consecrated probably in Roman Carlisle as bishop to Roman converts on the other side of the Solway Firth. He may well have had direct contacts with monastic Christianity as it had developed in Italy and Gaul. Throughout the Dark and Middle Ages Candida Casa seems to have attracted pilgrims and longer-term visitors from Ireland and elsewhere (J. MacQueen 1961; Thomas 1971, 75–82).

Examples of such early ecclesiastical place names are Kildonan (church of Donnan: cf. Slewdonan above), Kilfillan (of Faolán), Killasser (of Lassair),

Kilkerran (of Ciaran), Colmonell ([of] Colman Elo), Kilbarchan (of Berchan), Kilmacolm (of my Columba), Kilbride (of Brigid: see J. MacQueen 1973, 18–26: Nicolaisen 1976, 128–30; W. J. Watson 1926, 161–71, 187–97).

The third and probably most extensive stage is indicated by the name 'Galloway' (*Gall-ghàidhil*, foreign, Viking Gael). The *Gall-ghàidhil* probably constituted the bulk of settlement during the last quarter of the ninth century and first half of the tenth and embraced settlers from Ireland, the Hebrides and the northern mainland of Scotland. Their language was a Gaelic which included in its vocabulary some words either of Norse origin or mediated from Old English by way of Norse. The most familiar example is Norse *kirkja* (church), borrowed from Old English and ultimately from Greek; others are *gil* (ravine, narrow valley), *mosi* (bog, swamp, morass) and Old English *croft*. It seems likely that some at least of the leading settlers were Norse-speakers, although Norse never established itself in Galloway as it did in parts of the Hebrides.

Compound place-names – that is to say, names in which the first element is determined by the second, as is common in the Celtic languages, but in which the first element at least is Norse, sometimes English – are the chief sign of the *Gall-ghàidhil*. The 'Kirk-' compounds, which parallel and probably have sometimes replaced the earlier series in 'Kil-', are the most obvious. Examples are Kirkmaiden (of my-Etáin), Kirkinner (of Cainera), Kirkoswald (of [the Northumbrian king] Oswald, *c*.605–42, a martyred adherent to Columban Christianity), Kirkcudbright (of [the Celtic/Northumbrian] Cuthbert, d. 687). These names generally belong to places of some local importance (J. MacQueen 1956; Nicolaisen 1976, 108–11; W. J. Watson 1926, 161–71, 188).

The presence of the *Gall-ghàidhil* is also indicated by a number of place-names which contain a fiscal element. The most obvious are *peighinn* (pennyland) and its subdivisions *lethpheighinn* (halfpennyland) and *fairdean* (farthingland), examples of which include Pinmore, Pinminnoch, Leffin Donald, Leffnoll and Fardin. The 'penny' is the Old English silver penny, adopted by the Norse as a unit of land taxation and introduced under their influence into the territory of the *Gall-ghàidhil*. Settlement from the north and north-eastern mainland may be indicated by the non-monetary but still fiscal *dabhach* (davoch, vat [of payment in kind]), *ceathramh* (quarter [davoch]) and other subdivisions in such names as Doach, Docher-

neil, Kirriedarroch, Cog and Terraughty (J. MacQueen 1979; Megaw 1979; W. J. Watson 1926, 185, 191, 201).

The first recorded king of the *Gall-ghàidhil* belongs to the eleventh century. Suibne, son of Cinaeth, died in 1034. Nothing else is known about his reign, his predecessors or his immediate successors, but the place-name evidence suggests that his territory extended over modern Galloway, Carrick and Nithsdale, with a probable extension by way of Crawick Water and the Glespin Burn into upper Douglasdale and even the Nethan valley, but that the Gaelic-speakers of Cunninghame, Renfrewshire and Clydesdale lived under a different authority, presumably that of the kingdom of Strathclyde. Suibne's status probably corresponded to that of an Irish provincial king. In the twelfth and thirteenth centuries the kingship remained for four generations in a single family, with the legitimate male line of which it also disappeared. For the reigns of Fergus (d. 1161) and his sons, Uchtred (d. 1174) and Gilbert (d. 1185), reasonably authentic records have been preserved of the *Gall-ghàidhil* way of life during the campaigns which included the battles of Clitheroe and the Standard (1138) and during the visits of Ailred of Rievaux to Galloway in 1159 and 1164. Gilbert was succeeded by Roland (d. 1200), son of Uchtred, whom Gilbert had murdered, and Roland was succeeded by his son Alan (d. 1234), after whom the legitimate male issue failed. The Laws of Galloway, which presumably derived their authority originally from the kingship, remained in force until 1426 (Duncan 1975, index).

Like other Gaels the *Gall-ghàidhil* lived in groups, variously styled 'kindred' (*cenél*, *cineal*), 'clan' (*clann*) and 'household' (*muinntir*), represented by names such as Kenelman, Clenafren, Clan Connan, Clan-macgowin, Muntercasduff. In 1372 Robert II confirmed the office of kenkynol (*ceann-cineil*) of Carrick to Roland de Carrick and his heirs (Duncan 1975, 108–9; Kermack 1967, 65–8). The place names Balmaclellan and Balmaghie almost certainly indicate the site of chiefs' residences. The *Gall-ghàidhil* possessed a powerful fleet. The existence of a bardic class is indicated by such names as Dervaird (*doire a' bhaird*) and Loch Recar (*loch an reacaire*). Run-rig farming with outfield and manured infield is probably indicated by such names as Auchnotteroch (*achadh nan otrach*) and Talnotrie (*talamh an otraigh*), while names such as Airies, Airieolland and Airiequhillart indicate the practice of summer transhumance with the use of the shieling (*àiridh*: J. MacQueen 1973,

31; W. J. Watson 1926, index). A number of Gaelic family names – Hannay, Kennedy, MacClumpha, MacCulloch, MacDowall, MacGuffock, and Mac-Kitterick are familiar examples – belong primarily to the area.

Gaelic was still widely spoken during the sixteenth century but for no very obvious reasons seems to have declined during the next hundred years. In remote areas it may have survived into the eighteenth century (Lorimer 1949, 1953).   JMCQ

place-names, Gaelic, in Pictland Northern Scotland west of Druim Alban, occupied very early by the Gaels of Dalriada, was once Pictish country, but though Gaelic or part-Gaelic names are recorded there from the sixth century, they are not very numerous and many are of Pictish or unknown origin. Thus Coire Salcháin in Iona in Adamnán's *Life of Columba* (end of the seventh century) is purely Gaelic, but in Dunadd and Dunolly, first mentioned in the late seventh century, the second elements are obscure, and further east, in Dunkeld and Dumyat, they are the names of Pictish tribes. Of course, innumerable Gaelic names now exist throughout the Highlands, but there is little evidence that many are early. Pictland is taken here, then, to mean the country held by the Picts in the full historical period, seventh to mid-ninth centuries. Our first example of a genuine Gaelic name in this Pictland, representing deep Gaelic penetration east across Druim Alban, is Atholl, early Gaelic *Athfhódla* (New Ireland), obviously given by Gaelic newcomers. Since this name is recorded in the Irish Annals in 740, we know that they had reached northern Perthshire by then; but even after the annexation of all Pictland about 848 the same problems remain. Thus, St Andrews was *Rigmonad*, (King's moor), but this may be either Gaelic or Pictish. Further evidence is found in the names in Pictish *Pett-*, now *Pit-*, which are very common in Pictland. In some, their second element is clearly Pictish; hence Pitfour, Pictish Pett-Phor (*por*, pasture) or Pitcog, Pictish Pett-Cog (cuckoo). In others it is unclear from which language the name is derived, as Pitarrow, whose second element is either Pictish *tarw* or Gaelic *tarbh* (bull). But the great majority of *Pit-* names end in words certainly Gaelic, names given when Gaels were settling in Pictland and taking over the Pictish landholding system with its *pett*, some kind of agricultural unit. Examples are Pitcorthie, Pitcowden, Pittencrieff, Pittendamph, Pitkerrow, Pitmurchie, and Pittentagart, with a' Choir-

the, a' Challtuinn, na Craoibhe, an Daimh, a' Cheathraimh, Mhurchaidh, and an tSagairt (respectively 'of the pillar stone', 'the hazel', 'the tree', 'the ox', 'the quarterland', 'Murchadh' and 'the priest'). On the other hand Pitscottie (the *pett* of the Gaels) must have been named by local Picts at a time when Gaelic occupation was still rare enough in the neighbourhood to make the term distinctive. (See **loanwords, British and Pictish; place-names, British and Pictish;** W. J. Watson 1926.)   KHJ

place-names, Gaelic, in Scotland As for all languages spoken in Scotland – at one time or another, place-names serve primarily two functions in the elucidation of the role which Gaelic has played over the centuries: on the one hand, they help us to distinguish the Gaelic stratum from all other strata, both chronologically and geographically, and on the other they are valuable raw material in determining significant sub-strata within the Gaelic stratum itself. Naturally, very few place-names permit absolute dating, apart from the date at which they are first recorded in relevant documentary sources, but many of them are excellent source material for the establishment of relative chronologies. Similarly, their very nature as identifying markers for particular geographical features, both natural and man-made, makes them the best evidence available for the delineation of settlement areas of speakers of particular languages. They are, after all, names of places and therefore strongly anchored to the ground.

If one wishes to make visual the areas of Scotland in which Gaelic was at one time spoken (or is still spoken today), one can do no better than plot the distribution of names containing the two generics *baile* (village, hamlet, etc.) and *achadh* (field). Both make direct reference to the presence of human beings, either as residing in permanent settlements or as tilling the soil and tending the flocks. The fact that nowadays names containing *achadh* more often than not are also attached to settlements instead of, or in addition to, fields does not detract from their significance.

Examples of the several hundred place-names beginning with *baile* are: Balbeg, Balgown, Balmaclellan, Baltersan, Balbackie, Ballencrieff, Balerno, Balgreen, Ballageich, Balchalum, Baldinnie, Balfour, Balhagarty, Ballantrushal, etc.; and names containing the generic *achadh* are exemplified by Auchairn, Auchenree, Auchenfad, Auchentaggart, Auchingray, Auchindoon, Auchinhard, Auchentiber, Auchmore,

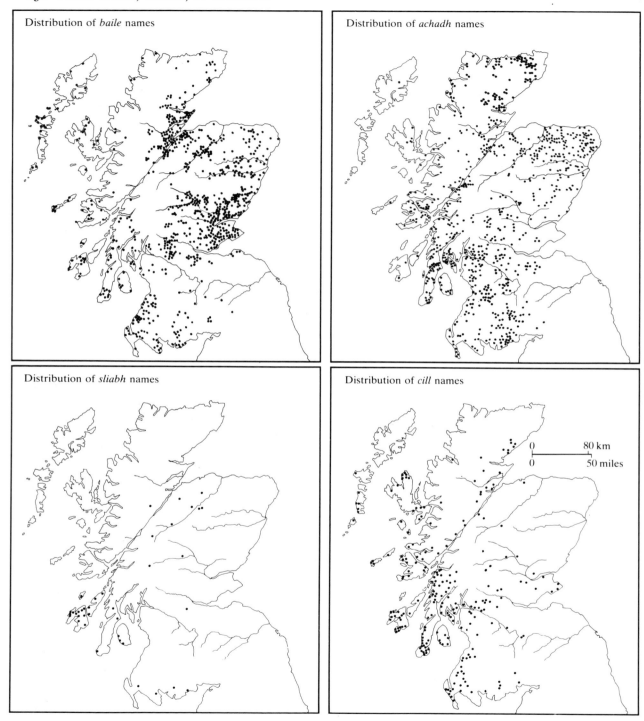

Distribution of *baile* names

Distribution of *achadh* names

Distribution of *sliabh* names

Distribution of *cill* names

Achnahannet, Auchintoul, etc. When mapped, singly and especially together, *baile* and *achadh* produce distribution patterns which are as instructive through the presence of names in which they occur as through their absence (Nicolaisen 1975, 4–5, 109; 1976, 123–8, 136–43). Their presence clearly confirms that Gaelic must have been at one time, perhaps in the eleventh or twelfth centuries or a little later, the language of most of Scotland, although its most extensive use may not have peaked in all the areas in question at exactly the same time. The place-name evidence makes it equally clear, however, that there has never been any time in Scottish history or prehistory when Gaelic was the everyday language of the whole of Scotland. In addition to the Northern Isles, important areas for which there is no indication of a notable and enduring presence of Gaelic at any time, are the border counties and the adjacent parts of the Lothians in the south-east of the country. It is also worth remembering that it is of course more than probable that names containing *baile* and *achadh* continued to be coined in the remaining strongholds of Gaelic even after English had begun to assert itself in a dominating role in parts of Scotland in which Gaelic used to be strong. Not every dot on maps 1 and 2 therefore implies Dark Age or even medieval origin. The overall pattern is nevertheless undoubtedly correct.

Whereas *baile* and *achadh* do not easily lend themselves to be exploited as indicators of stratified growth within the Gaelic stratum, the generics *sliabh* (hill) and *cill* (cell, church) can be felicitously used for that purpose. Since the latter element is more fully discussed under **place-names, ecclesiastical** it is sufficient to mention here that its geographical distribution points to its most creative period as having been before Gaelic settlers moved into Pictland in any great number and before Scandinavians occupied the north-eastern half of Caithness (i.e. before the middle of the ninth century). An even earlier settlement phase is indicated by *sliabh* whose distribution is practically limited to what are known to have been the earliest areas of 'Scots' settlement in the Scottish Dalriada and to the parts of Galloway closest to Ireland. Names such as Slewdonan, Slewfad, Slewcairn, Sliabh Mór, Sliabh na Moine, Sliabh Meadhonach, Sliabh Gaoil and Sliabh a' Chuir are consequently valuable survivals from the pre-Norse period of Gaelic in Scotland, a period otherwise so elusive to the investigator (Nicolaisen 1975, 5, 108; 1976, 39–45).

A sequence *sliabh – cill – baile – achadh*, if interpreted correctly, is a good illustration of the gradual advance of Gaelic and of speakers of Gaelic in Scotland after their arrival from Ireland. There are, of course, other name elements which are not to be found in the whole of the Gàidhealtachd. With few exceptions, their limited geographical scatter appears to signify dialectal differences, either in the topographical sector of the vocabulary or in naming practices, rather than chronological sequence. A circumscribed distribution pattern for a generic is by no means always also a pointer to chronologically limited productivity for that same generic.

Very few Gaelic place-names consist of a generic only, however; in other words they are complex or compound names rather than simple ones. It is in combination with their specifics that they acquire their precision as identifying markers of location, while at the same time affording us a glimpse of the world view of Gaelic namers and name users. Most of them are descriptive in the widest sense of that term, testifying to a keen sense of colour (Rubha Ruadh), shape (Coire Fada), and size (Beinn Mhór), as well as usability (Eilrig) or an awareness of the relationship between a named feature and its surroundings (Creag na h-Iolaire, Loch na h-Eaglaise, Beinn nan Dubh-Lochan, Aonach an Nid, Càrn an Fhuarain Duibh), or to other named features (Cruachan Beinn a' Chearcaill, Rubh' Arasaig, Monadh Gleann Uige, Ceann Caol Beinn na Lap). In this sense place names do not exist in isolation but depend upon one another. The identity of a location is not only limited by other identities but also made possible through them.
                                                                    WFHN

place-names, Norse In Scotland Norse place-names are found in three types of area: (a) where no Gaelic has been spoken since the period of Norse settlement, (b) where Norse was superseded by Gaelic and where Gaelic is still spoken, and (c) where Gaelic supplanted Norse but was later itself supplanted by English. Typical (a) areas are Orkney, Shetland and the larger part of Caithness; (b) areas are the Hebrides, large parts of the western and northern coasts of the Scottish mainland and a smaller section of the east coast. The classical (c) area is Galloway, where Gaelic died out in the seventeenth century, but other (c) areas are developing where the Gaelic/English frontier is receding, as on the North Sea coast of Sutherland and Ross and Cromarty. What follows deals mainly with areas of type (b),

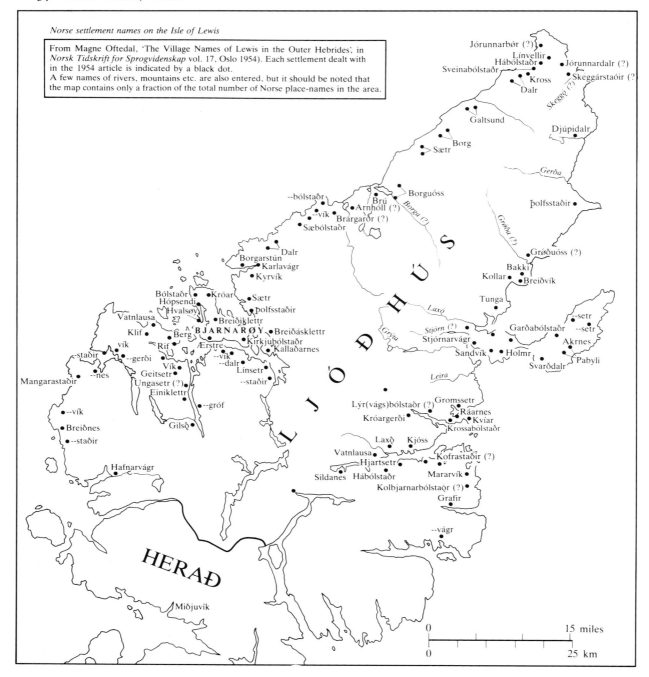

Norse settlement names on the Isle of Lewis

From Magne Oftedal, 'The Village Names of Lewis in the Outer Hebrides', in *Norsk Tidskrift for Sprogvidenskap* vol. 17, Oslo 1954). Each settlement dealt with in the 1954 article is indicated by a black dot.
A few names of rivers, mountains etc. are also entered, but it should be noted that the map contains only a fraction of the total number of Norse place-names in the area.

because these are more relevant for Gaelic studies than type (a) and because little, if any, adequate research has been carried out in (c) areas.

The term 'Norse place-names' is often used loosely to denote all names that contain Norse elements, but

this practice is not satisfactory. The name Sgeir nan Sgarbh, for instance, is not a Norse name in spite of its two Norse elements, *sgeir* and *sgarbh*. These elements were already parts of the Gaelic language when the name was created, and it was constructed after the rules of Gaelic grammar. It may be qualified as post-Norse Gaelic but it is decidedly a Gaelic name. On the other hand a name such as Sgarbha-sgeir would be a Norse name because it is structured according to Norse grammar and would have been adopted wholesale into Gaelic as a readymade place-name. This distinction is not merely hair-splitting: it is important because Sgarbha-sgeir (if it exists) is firmly linked with the place it denotes and is therefore unmistakable evidence of Norse settlement in the vicinity, whereas a name like Sgeir nan Sgarbh may have arisen anywhere in the Gàidhealtachd: the elements *sgeir* and *sgarbh* may have spread, as appellatives, to Gaelic dialects outside Norse-dominated territory before the compound name came into being. Thus a skerry anywhere in Gaelic Scotland, on the coast or in a freshwater loch, may have received such a name regardless of the presence or absence of a former Norse colony in the neighbourhood.

The density of Norse and post-Norse place-names varies considerably from one part of the Gàidhealtachd to another. It is impossible to give definite numbers or percentages, not only because of the impracticability of counting all the names in a given area but also because many names cannot be identified immediately as Norse or Gaelic. The proportion (80 per cent) sometimes given for the Isle of Lewis, as the area of greatest density, is definitely too high. Although it is a reasonably accurate estimate for names of settlements, it is not valid for names of minor entities, natural features, etc., among which the proportion of Gaelic names is a far larger percentage than 20. Nevertheless, the inventory of Norse place-names in the Gàidhealtachd is very rich, probably reaching a high four-digit number, and future research, if not postponed too long, will no doubt lead to many important discoveries. There would be little point in giving a list of examples in this brief introductory note: the material is too abundant and variegated to be presented equitably on this small scale. The reader can, for a first impression, study large-scale maps of the areas in question. If a name on a map is not evidently Gaelic or English, it is very likely to be Norse, although a number of names still remain unexplained and may be both pre-Gaelic and pre-Norse. Maps, however, must not be trusted beyond this point, as map spellings are often haphazard and sometimes very misleading.

The student in search of attempts to explain Norse names in Celtic Scotland is advised to consult W. J. Watson (1904), G. Henderson (1910), Nicolaisen

(1976) and Oftedal (1954). It will be seen from the work of these authors that the identification and interpretation of Norse names is not always an easy matter. The Old Norse names were of course adapted to the contemporary Gaelic sound system, so that the Gaels could pronounce them easily, and later developed phonetically, as did other Gaelic words. Accordingly, many names are difficult or impossible to explain from the forms they have today. Ancient written forms in rentals and other documents may be of some help, but they exist only for a small fraction of the names. In every case the researcher must record and study the local Gaelic pronunciation, without which any attempt at explanation is futile. One example: the village name Leurbost (Lewis) was explained by both Watson and Henderson as Old Norse *Leirbólstað* (accusative: clay stead), probably misled by the map spelling with *eu*, which suggests a long *é* (W. J. Watson 1904, 265; G. Henderson 1910, 355), although the former does mention a Gaelic spelling *Liurbost*. But the actual Gaelic pronunciation has a long *ù* (appropriate spelling (*Liùrbost*), which rules out any possibility of the presence of a Norse element *leir-* (Oftedal 1954, 399ff.). The use of linguistic data for the explanation of Norse place-names in Gaelic territory is a special branch of Gaelic and Scandinavian linguistics and demands a thorough knowledge of the dialectology and linguistic history of both languages (Oftedal 1972). On the systematization of the names, see Oftedal (1980), where many examples are given.   MO

place-names, pre-Celtic On Scottish maps today there are two kinds of place-name which may be ascribed to a pre-Celtic stratum: those which have an identifiable linguistic affiliation and those which cannot at present be placed convincingly in any linguistic framework. To the former category belong river names such as Adder (in Blackadder and Whiteadder), Ale, Allan, Ayr, Farrar, Nairn, Naver, Shiel, Shin and probably Ness, Tay, Teviot and Tyne. Not easily distinguishable from early Celtic names, most of these have exact counterparts or close relatives on the European continent in a fairly extensive network of western and northern European river names of Western Indo-European provenance, with Bronze Age connections (approximately 1500 BC) (Nicolaisen 1976, 179–91). In the category of unetymologized pre-Celtic names might be placed Hebridean island names such as Lewis, Uist, Skye,

Tiree, Mull and Islay (despite their later re-interpretations), or Unst and Yell in Shetland. To these and others have been variously attributed Phoenician, Basque, Berber, circumpolar and even more exotic origins, but none of these links has ever been established in any persuasive fashion. Naturally, there are many other Scottish place-names whose linguistic origins and derivations are unknown, mostly for lack of documentation. It would be erroneous, however, to assume that these are generally pre-Celtic. Opacity is not necessarily a sign of antiquity! It is also worth mentioning that although the presence of non-Celtic-speaking Picts, as distinct from Celtic-speaking ones, can be established on other grounds (K. H. Jackson 1955a, 152–60) we have no recognizable place-name evidence for them.   WFHN

place-names, pre-Gaelic Our chief source for the names of early peoples and tribes who inhabited Scotland before the arrival of the Gaels from Ireland, and for the names of their settlements, is the famous mathematician, astronomer and geographer Claudius Ptolemy of Alexandria (W. J. Watson 1926, 8; also 10–56). Flourishing in the first half of the second century AD, he is not the earliest recorder of Scottish names but incorporates in his *Introduction to Geography* contemporary as well as earlier knowledge.

Depending on how his name lists are read, he mentions and locates sixteen or eighteen tribal names in Scotland: the Caerēni, Cornavii, Lūgi, Smertae, Decantae, Carnonācae, Caledonii, Vacomagi, Taexali, Venicōnes, Creōnes (or Cerōnes), Epidii, Damnonii, Novantae, Selgovae, Otadini, and Gadeni (or Gadini). Although all are roughly locatable, only a few have echoes on the modern Scottish map. The Smertae are recalled by Carn Smeart in Strathcarron (Ross-shire); the Caledonians are well attested by the Perthshire cluster of Dunkeld (Gaelic *Dùn Chailleann*: fort of the Caledonians), Rohallion (Gaelic *Ràth Chailleann*: rath of the Caledonians), and Schiehallion (Gaelic *Sìdh Chailleann*: fairy hill of the Caledonians); and the *Novantae* are possibly connected with the river Nith (*Novios*) in Dumfriesshire. An implied tribal name is *Orcades* (or *Orcas* (boar people) for the inhabitants of the Orkney islands, which are still called *Arcaibh* (among the Orcs) in Gaelic, just as *Gallaibh* (among the strangers) is the Gaelic name for Caithness and *Cataibh* (among the Cats) the Gaelic name for Sutherland. The last of these is also reflected in

Norse *Katanes* (cat promontory), modern Caithness, and *Inse Catt*, the pre-Norse name of Shetland. Of Ptolemy's sixteen town names, *Dēvana*, a town of the Taexali, is clearly derived from the river name *Dēva*, i.e. the Aberdeenshire Dee, while *Loukopibia* and *Rerigonion*, both towns of the Novantae, are to be associated with Whithorn (Candida Casa) and Loch Ryan respectively.

Of tribal names recorded in other sources (W. J. Watson 1926, 56–69), those of the Maeatae (or Miathi), the Verturiones and the Picti are the most noteworthy. The name of the Maeatae is preserved in Dunmyat (fort of the Maeatae), a prominent hill in the Ochils not far from Stirling; and the Verturiones who, together with the Caledonians, formed the two great divisions of the Picts south of the Grampians, can be identified with *Fortrenn*, genitive of Fortriu, according to tradition one of the seven provinces of Alba, the others being *Cait*, *Cé*, *Círig*, *Fíb*, *Fidach* and *Fotla*. Fortriu, and therefore the region of the Verturiones, would be our modern Strathearn and Menteith in Perthshire.

The name of the Picts has given rise to much speculation (N. K. Chadwick 1958, 146–76), most prominently through pseudo-learned association of long standing with *pictus*, past participle of the Latin verb *pingo* (to paint, colour, inscribe). We do not know what the Picts called themselves, but it is obvious that a Roman soldiers' nickname would not give rise to the name for a whole people, especially since appropriate forms of the same name were also known to the Norsemen and the Angles (Nicolaisen 1976, 150–1). There can, however, be no doubt that the pre-Gaelic tribal names of Scotland were Celtic and were linguistically closely associated with the Celtic tribal names of southern Britain and with those of Gaul, sometimes even through identical equivalents. The pre-Gaelic Celts of Scotland were therefore speakers of P-Celtic, as were their English, Welsh, Cornish and Gaulish counterparts.   WFHN

poetry, *see* nature poetry; song; verse.

Pòl Crùbach (fl. 1650) Son of MacLeod of Lyndale in Skye. Known as author of a lament, 'Iorram na Truaighe' (W. J. Watson 1918a, 201), on the death of John, fourteenth chief of MacLeods of Harris and Skye, 1649. His name is still known in Skye tradition as a warrior of abnormal strength.   JMCI

Politician A ship that went aground off Eriskay in February 1941; she carried a large cargo of whisky. Subject of Gaelic songs and of Compton Mackenzie's novel *Whisky Galore*.   DST

politics, Highland (nineteenth century) Throughout the 130 years following the Battle of Culloden the mass of Gaelic-speaking Scots possessed no political influence. Even after the Reform Act of 1832 few Highlanders could participate in parliamentary politics, the franchise being limited to landlords, tenant farmers and other members of the Highlands' numerically small, and almost exclusively English-speaking, ruling class. For the greater part of the nineteenth century, therefore, northern Scotland was represented at Westminster by men who identified wholeheartedly with the region's landowning interests – men like James Loch (q.v.), who combined membership of the House of Commons with his organizing role in the Sutherland Clearances; Sir James Matheson and Donald Cameron of Lochiel, proprietors of extensive estates and, for lengthy periods, MPs for Ross and Cromarty and Inverness-shire respectively; the heirs to the dukedoms of Argyll and Sutherland.

Such individuals called themselves Whigs and Tories, Liberals and Conservatives. But so far as north-west Scotland's Gaelic-speaking majority was concerned these distinctions were of little account. The political differences of the Highlands' rulers did not extend to the realm of the estate management system in which they all participated, a system characterized by the pursuit of private profit at the expense of community wellbeing. The mass evictions and forced emigrations which were among nineteenth-century landlordism's more appalling consequences thus evoked no parliamentary concern, successive Governments confining themselves to subsidizing emigration, suppressing riots and generally supporting those forces which were effecting the social and cultural destruction of Scottish Gaeldom.

Demoralized, leaderless, poverty-stricken and without access to the centres of political power, Highlanders were unable to mount any effective challenge to their exploiters. However, in the autumn of 1881 the crofters of the Braes district of Skye initiated a rent strike with the aim of forcing their laird, Lord MacDonald, to return land lost to their settlements in the course of the Clearances. That protest, modelled on similar campaigns then being conducted by the equally oppressed Irish peasantry, was sym-

bolic of a new air of defiance, of a new conviction, encouraged by the writings of land reformers and Gaelic revivalists like John Murdoch (q.v.) and John Stuart Blackie, that Highlanders, if they acted in concert, could regain control of their own destiny.

Similar agitation soon spread to other parts of north-west Scotland. The Liberal Government of the day set up a Royal Commission, chaired by Lord Napier, to examine crofters' grievances. The Commission concluded that much was wrong with the Highlands' tenurial structure, but the Government took no action and, inevitably, unrest continued. Farmlands were seized and occupied; rents were universally withheld; there were violent clashes between crofters and the police; armed troops were deployed in Skye, Lewis, Tiree and elsewhere. Order, however, remained stubbornly unrestored.

A crofters' political party, the Highland Land Law Reform Association (subsequently renamed the Highland Land League), was established. And, crofters having been coincidentally enfranchised by the Third Reform Act of 1884, its candidates were returned in all but one of the Highland constituencies in the general election of 1885. In the parliamentary session following that election, Highland affairs took pride of place on the Westminster agenda for the first time since the demise of Jacobitism. And in 1886, arguing that such a concession was necessary to forestall further revolutionary upheaval in the Highlands, Gladstone's Liberal administration passed the first Crofters Act, which, by granting security of tenure to Highland smallholders, brought the era of the Clearances to an end.

Magnificent victory though it was, the 1886 Act did not altogether satisfy the crofting community, principally because it made scarcely any gesture in the direction of redistributing the land of which Gaelic-speaking tenants had been deprived during the early nineteenth century. In the Hebrides in particular there was consequently as much trouble after 1886 as there had been before, the source of discontent not being removed until a new round of land seizures in the years immediately following the First World War obliged the Lloyd-George Coalition Government to purchase scores of sheep farms, which were then resettled by crofters.

The land-settlement schemes of the 1920s, one more manifestation of an explicitly interventionist attitude dated from 1886 and took on a recognizably developmental guise after the setting up, in 1897, of the Congested Districts Board. Intended to increase employment opportunities in fishing, agriculture and industry, the Board was the remote ancestor of the present Highlands and Islands Development Board (q.v.). While such bodies have contributed substantially to the enhancement of Highland living standards, they have shown little inclination to tackle the fundamental causes of the Highlands' continuing problems.

Since the eighteenth century the Highlands' economic function has been that of a supplier of raw materials – cattle, kelp, wool, fish or oil – to southern industry. As has happened in other neo-colonial societies, therefore, Highland resources have been utilized in a manner which has ensured that the ensuing profits have not accrued to Highlanders, the wealth created having been largely invested elsewhere. This type of economic exploitation has been accompanied by repression of Highland culture and Highland language, Gaelic being at first persecuted and subsequently neglected by the state-sponsored, and consciously anglicizing, agencies in charge of matters such as education.

The late nineteenth-century democratization of the British political system somewhat mitigated these evils. But Highlanders, a rural minority on the periphery of one of the world's most highly urbanized states, have been able to persuade Governments to act forcefully on their behalf only when, as in the 1880s, they have obtained the requisite political muscle by acting unconstitutionally. The Highland Land League, heavily influenced by its contacts with Irish nationalists, eventually concluded that this particular obstacle to Highland progress could be circumvented only by recreating a parliament in Edinburgh. Hence the preponderance of Highlanders, Gaelic enthusiasts and Celticists of every hue in the Scottish national movement of the decades between 1880 and 1920, a period when Lowland Scots were generally happy with the working of the Union. For better or worse, however, the Scottish equivalent of the Sinn Fein vision of a Gaelic republic remained the prerogative of men like that quintessential romantic Ruaraidh Erskine of Mar (q.v.), men who were destined to make little permanent impact on the political development of modern Scotland.   JH

politics, Highland (twentieth century) The Highlands remain an important factor in British politics. The problems of the area are given much publicity,

and special measures are being taken to deal with them. Agencies of government such as the Crofters Commission, the Congested Districts Board and the Highlands and Islands Medical Services Board were in operation before the first world war. The Highland electorate had shown its independence at the time of the Crofters Party in the 1880s and continued to behave in a distinct way after 1900. This is hardly surprising in view of the problems of the area and its remoteness from the centre of government.

The political parties, based broadly on industrial or class divisions, find it difficult to relate to Highland problems, since these are largely rural and agricultural. Highlanders often prefer to judge the parties by their candidates rather than by their national policies, which are in any case adapted by the candidates themselves to local needs. Thus a Conservative, Liberal, Labour, Scottish Nationalist Party (SNP), or Social Democratic Party (SDP) label in a Highland constituency does not necessarily imply the same distinctions as in non-Highland seats. Yet Highland MPs have to work within their parties, and to use them to benefit their constituents. This frequently gives rise to tensions, as Highland interests do not easily translate into the terms of party battle. Most Highland MPs regard themselves as independents, despite the party labels, and Sir David Robertson (Caithness and Sutherland, 1950–64), actually resigned the Conservative Whip to stand as an Independent Unionist in 1959).

Parties without explicit class-based ideologies, such as the Liberals, the SDP and the SNP, have been popular in the Highlands and Islands, as the following summary of the political affiliation of Highlands and Islands constituencies since 1900 shows.

Argyll: Conservative, 1900–3; Liberal, 1903–24; Conservative, 1924–74; SNP, 1974–9; Conservative, 1979– . (After 1983, *Argyll and Bute.*)

Caithness and Sutherland: Caithness: Liberal, 1900–18. *Sutherland:* Liberal-Unionist, 1900–6; Liberal, 1906–18. *Caithness and Sutherland:* Liberal, 1918–45; Conservative, 1945–59; Independent Conservative, 1959–64; Liberal, 1964–6; Labour, 1966–81; SDP, 1981– .

Inverness Burghs: Liberal-Unionist, 1900–6; Liberal, 1906–18.

Inverness-shire: Liberal, 1900–31; National Liberal, 1931–45; Independent Liberal, 1945–50; Conservative, 1950–64; Liberal, 1964– . (After 1983, *Inverness, Nairn and Lochaber.*)

Orkney and Shetland: Liberal-Unionist, 1900–2; Independent Liberal, 1902–6; Liberal, 1906–35; Conservative, 1935–50; Liberal, 1950–   .

Ross and Cromarty: Liberal, 1900–31; National Liberal, 1931–6; National Labour, 1936–45; Independent Liberal, 1945–51; National Liberal, 1951–64; Liberal, 1964–70; Conservative, 1970–83; SDP, 1983–   . (After 1983, *Ross, Cromarty and Skye*.)

Western Isles: Liberal, 1918–31; National Liberal, 1931–5; Labour, 1935–70; SNP, 1970–   .

Wick Burghs: Liberal-Unionist, 1900–10; Liberal, 1910–18.

Highlands and Islands (European Assembly Election, 1979) SNP.

As can be seen, in the general election of 1983 Liberals were elected for Orkney and Shetland and Inverness-shire, the SNP retained the Western Isles, and the SDP won Caithness and Sutherland, and Ross, Cromarty and Skye. In the election for the European Assembly (1979), the Highlands and Islands seat was won by Mrs Winifred Ewing (SNP). Thus, 'third parties' won all the Highland seats except Argyll and Bute.

In local government party candidatures are infrequent, and local authorities are governed by groups of independents. Another feature of Highland local politics is the absence of contested elections. In 1980, for example, fifteen of the sixteen members of Caithness District Council were returned unopposed, and the remaining seat had no candidate. In 1978 only seven of the thirty seats on the Western Isles Islands Council, and under half of the seats in the Highland Region, were contested. At the same time, contests in parliamentary elections are keenly fought, and turnout is usually up to the national average.

The establishment of the Western Isles Islands Council in 1975 marked an important turning-point in Highland local government and in the political position of Gaelic. Until then the Western Isles had been split between predominantly English-speaking local authorities: Ross and Cromarty County Council (covering Lewis), governed from Dingwall, and Inverness-shire County Council (covering Harris, the Uists, and Barra), governed from Inverness. The new Western Isles authority, governed from Stornoway, united the Outer Hebrides and made Gaelic an official language (along with English), so that council business could be conducted in it. Officials were encouraged to use Gaelic, although it was not a con-

dition of appointment. Education in the Isles was now more geared to helping the Gaelic language, although it could not be made a medium of instruction for examinations, since that would require a change in the Scottish educational system as a whole.

Despite the general sympathy for Gaelic in Scotland, the language has not achieved the status of Welsh in Wales. The reason for this is that the Welsh language has become closely associated with Welsh national identity, and its promotion has been part of the Welsh national revival. The Scottish nation, on the other hand, does not identify with Gaelic (although it does not deny it either), and Scottish nationalism is based on political and economic demands rather than on cultural or linguistic ones. Moreover, a long-standing centralization in educational and cultural matters has prevailed in Scotland, with little time for local diversity. Thus Gaelic has been denied the status in secondary and further education which Welsh has in Wales.

Other important innovations in Highland government have been the Highlands and Islands Development Board (1965–   ) (q.v.), the North of Scotland Hydro-Electric Board (1943–   ) (q.v.), and the new Crofters Commission (1955–   ). The entry of Britain into the European Community in 1973 shifted to Brussels the focus of decision-making in such matters as fishing and aid to agriculture. Highlanders had to participate in new pressure groups such as the Scottish Fishermen's Federation in order to be represented in the Community. The large number of governmental activities relating to North Sea oil also involved Highland spokesmen, and some local authorities became closely involved in oil developments. Orkney and Shetland Islands councils achieved new powers over oil developments and a considerable income from them. Local authorities incurring oil-related expenditures receive a special grant from central government in compensation.

Highland MPs have played a notable part in the political life of the country. Mr Jo Grimond (Orkney and Shetland, 1950–83) was Leader of the Liberal Party from 1956 to 1967, and Mr Donald Stewart (Western Isles, 1970–   ) is Leader of the SNP. Mr Michael Noble (now Lord Glenkinglas) (Conservative, Argyllshire, 1958–74) was Secretary of State for Scotland from 1962 to 1964. Sir Archibald Sinclair (Liberal and National Liberal, Caithness and Sutherland, 1922–45) was Secretary of State for Scotland, 1931–2, and Secretary of State for Air, 1940–5. Mr Hamish Gray (Conservative, Ross and Crommarty, 1970–83) was Minister of State for Energy in the first Thatcher Government, and as Lord Gray, Minister of State at the Scottish Office in the second Thatcher Government. Several Highland MPs have been Gaelic-speakers, and Mr Donald Stewart in 1981 promoted a Private Member's Bill to make Gaelic an official language in Scotland and a medium of instruction in certain areas. This failed in February 1981.   JGK

Pope, Revd Alexander (fl. mid-eighteenth century) Minister of Reay, 1734–82. Began collecting Ossianic ballads c.1739. (See J. F. Campbell 1872.)   DST

Potato Blight By 1840 probably a majority of the people of the north-west Highlands and Islands were dependent for their food on the growing of potatoes on tiny holdings. The failure of the crop in 1846 threatened disaster. Government measures and the efforts of landlords, though tentative and much restricted by the non-interventionist dogmas of the time, were just sufficient to avert direct loss of life. The wound on the Highlands was deep, however, creating an abiding memory, a new impulse to emigrate and a fresh wave of land clearances by landlords more than ever convinced that a numerous tenantry was a burden on their estates. (See Flinn 1977, 431–8; Hunter 1976, 50–72.)   MG

preaspiration, *see* Gaelic: preaspiration.

press, Gaelic There is no Gaelic in the daily press in Scotland, but there is a relatively long tradition of using Gaelic in the weekly press, especially in Highland weeklies. This usually takes the form of a set piece or pieces. Thus John N. MacLeod's (Alasdair Mòr's) 'Litrichean a Beàrnaraigh' (Letters from Bernera) appeared in the *Stornoway Gazette* from 1917 to 1954, a selection, mainly from 1917 and 1925 appearing in book form in 1932 (I. N. MacLeòid 1932). MacLeòid was succeeded by the Revd T. M. Murchison, whose 'Còmhradh Cagailte' continued until 1983. These weekly columns can deal with contemporary events or literary or historical themes, or they can take the form of fiction, using stock characters often with real-life prototypes (Sìne, An Cat Ruadh). In addition, the *Gazette* spasmodically publishes Gaelic reviews of books and other articles, and one or two rural correspondents (most systematically the Scalpay, Harris correspondent) write their news items partly or wholly in Gaelic. The *Gazette* also includes frequently poems or songs (in recent years especially by Murchadh MacPhàrlain or Dòmhnall R. Moireasdan) and letters to the Editor. Some advertisers use Gaelic, and death notices frequently include Gaelic biblical quotations. When sheepmarks are referred to in advertisements they have to be in Gaelic also. The above represents the widest weekly coverage as yet achieved in the press. The *West Highland Free Press* also includes regular Gaelic articles.

The *Oban Times* for many years included a minimal amount of Gaelic but now prints regular, at present weekly, articles on current events of Gaelic interest, with an occasional Gaelic review. *The Scotsman* in the late 1970s, and again since 1982, printed occasional Gaelic articles in its Saturday magazine (sometimes, but not regularly, at fortnightly intervals). Other local weeklies or twice-weeklies (*Perthshire Advertiser*, etc.) may include occasional Gaelic features, and some national (Scottish) daily papers make an annual flourish with a Gaelic article at the time of the National Mod (see **Comunn Gaidhealach, An**). See also **periodicals**.   DST

professions (medieval), *see* institutions and orders, learned and professional.

prose, *see* novel, the Gaelic; prose, early Gaelic non-literary; prose, religious (post-1800); stories, short; tales, romantic.

prose, early Gaelic non-literary Excluding citations of proper names and personal names with descriptive labels or epithets (in, for example, Adamnán's *Life of Columba*, charters, public and ecclesiastical records), the earliest instance of continuous Gaelic prose in a Scottish manuscript is in the Book of Deer (q.v.). There is nothing further for some centuries, apart from genealogical notes and lists, although of course specific items from later manuscripts may have an original dating much earlier than that of the manuscript referred to above. It is thought that much information about Gaelic persons, and accounts of incidents involving them, had a Gaelic form which was perhaps often oral only and was translated or adapted to Latin or Scots for record purposes. There is only one Gaelic charter, dated 1408 (see **documents, Gaelic**). There are very few surviving non-literary documents in Gaelic prose from the sixteenth century (see **Argyll/An Calbhach Treaty** and the Gaelic letter under **documents,**

Gaelic) and from the early seventeenth century (see /contract of fosterage under **documents, Gaelic**), together with a note from Cathal MacMhuirich to Colla Ciotach (R. I. Black 1972). Indeed, examples of non-literary prose continue to be very infrequent even in the eighteenth and early nineteenth centuries (for a Gaelic letter by Ewen MacLachlan dated 1811, see D. S. Thomson 1968c, 210).   DST

prose, religious (eighteenth century) Gaelic religious prose of the eighteenth century reflects the aggressive thrust of Presbyterianism in the Highlands during that period and is dominated by translations of a confessional and catechetical nature. The first Gaelic translation of the Westminster Confession, *Admhail an Chreidimh*, produced by the Synod of Argyll, was published in 1725, bound with the first Gaelic printing of the Westminster Assembly's Larger Catechism, *An Cataichiosm Foirleathan*, and a reprint of the Shorter Catechism, *Foirceadul Aithghear Cheasnuighe*. An instructional digest of the Westminster documents was published in 1767 by the Society in Scotland for Propagating Christian Knowledge as *Suim an Eolais Shlainteil*. Catechetical works by individual authors also appeared in Gaelic translation as the century progressed. These included three works by the Revd John Willison of Dundee: his 'Mother's Catechism', *Leabhar Ceist na Mathair do'n leanabh Og* (1752), his *Eisempleir Shoilleir Ceasnuighe air Leabhar Aithghearr nan Ceist* (1773), a detailed application of the teaching of the Shorter Catechism running to 464 pages, and his catechism for young communicants, *Leabhar Ceist nan Og Luch-Communachaidh* (1798). Two of Isaac Watts's religious works for children appeared in Gaelic as *Da Leabhar Chestian agus Urnuighean* (1774) and *Tearmunn do'n Oigridh o Dhroch-Bheart agus Amaideachd* (1795). Thomas Shepherd's *The Christian Pocket Book* appeared in 1778 as *Leabhar Pochcaid a Chriosduidh*. A native work of anti-Romanist polemic was *Connsachadh eadar am Papa agus Reformation* (1797) by Duncan Lothian of Glenlyon.

The translation into Gaelic of popular Puritan works, which became a moderate flood in the nineteenth century, began with Richard Baxter's *Call to the Unconverted* (1750) and Joseph Alleine's *An Alarm to the Unconverted* (1781, 2nd edn 1782). The Revd Daniel Campbell's work on the sufferings of Christ appeared in Gaelic in 1786 as *Smuaintin Cudthromach mu Bhas agus Fhulangas ar Slanui'fhir*.

Surprisingly, few original Gaelic sermons of this period found their way into print, though it is possible that some fugitive publications of individual sermons may have disappeared without trace. The Revd D. Crawford, a native of Arran, had two of his sermons published at Fayetteville, North Carolina, in 1791, and his booklet, *Searmoin Do Mhnai'*, was published in Glasgow in 1795. A sermon for soldiers by the Revd Thomas Broughton appeared in Gaelic in 1797, with a special foreword from another hand for the Highland regiments. A volume of sermons by the Revd Hugh MacDiarmid, minister successively of Glasgow Gaelic Chapel, Arrochar and Comrie between 1772 and 1801, was published in 1804, and a manuscript volume of his sermons is in the possession of the Gaelic Society of Inverness. The manuscript sermons of the Revd John Mackay, minister of Lairg 1714–49, are of particular interest linguistically, as they present features of the Sutherland Gaelic of the period but little disguised by literary norms:

Na huibrichean moar & cumhachdach bha nar Tiarna Criosd a deanidh ann curs a mhinisdaracht, bha iad na nteisdanis go mbe Dia ans a neoil, & anois na huibribh moar a rinne e dar bha e fulig cha naid teisdanis ba lagh air firin a dhiaghacht. Do thuilligh reabigh bratroint an Teampuil le a chumhacht diaghie ha sinn a leabhidh nso san ransa & an ran adhe gon chrinich an talamh, gin scoilt na cragin, & gon duasgil na huaghichin & gon deirich moran do chuirp na naomh. Ach ha reabigh bratroint an teampuil air a chuir air hosach mar ni ans an rabh rudigin do headh diamhir & ighantach vuas cinn cumantis.

Four of his discourses have been published in *Scottish Gaelic Studies*, vol. 9, 1962.

The manuscript sermons of the Revd Archibald MacLea, minister of Rothesay, 1765–1824, of which some seventy are now lodged in the Department of Celtic, University of Glasgow, are couched in more literary language. The turgid style and weighty philosophizing of these discourses could scarcely have rendered them very gripping to the congregation to which each one was repeatedly preached at intervals of several years:

Uaidhe so, ge ata teagasg Chriosd air a chur ann ceil co'-soilear anns an tsoisgeal, as gu fead an ti a ritheas a leaghadh; agus ge do bha gach criosduidhe, anns gach am agus aite, air am baisteadh chum aidmheil an aon chreideamh, agus fa cheangal geil a thoirt do na haon aitheantaibh; gidheadh so uile, a bha an ni sin ris an abrar gu

coitcheann an crabhadh criosduidhe, ann amaibh
eidir-dhealaichte anns an aon duthaich, agus ata
e anois ann duthachannaibh eidir-dhealaichte,
coi'-eidir-dhealaichte uaidhe fein, as ata solus o
dhorchadas.

As a counter-thrust to the preponderance of
Reformed literature to come from the Gaelic presses
during this period, two works of Roman Catholic
instruction and devotion, both translated by the Revd
Robert Menzies of Aberfeldy, were published:
Aithghearradh na Teagaisg Chriosduidh (1781) and
Leanmhuin Chriosd (1785), a translation of Thomas à
Kempis's *Imitation of Christ*. Episcopalian literature
is represented by the translation of the Book of
Common Prayer, first published in Gaelic in 1794.

The religious works of the eighteenth century,
produced by a variety of translators from different
areas, played a significant part in establishing a literary prose style in Gaelic and in developing a flexible
theological vocabulary. The evidence they afford on
these matters has not yet been fully studied. (See
Durkacz 1983, esp. ch. 3; Donald Maclean 1915; D.
J. MacLeod 1977; Reid 1832.)   KDMcD

prose, religious (post-1800) Before 1800 there was
only a very small amount of Gaelic prose in print,
almost all of it religious: Carswell's (q.v.) Gaelic
translation of Knox's Liturgy, Calvin's Catechism,
the Westminster Confession of Faith and related
Catechisms (q.v.), the Bible (although not completed
until 1801), a Roman Catholic book, the Episcopal
Church's Prayer Book and translations of some
Puritan writers.

For generations school accommodation had been
scanty and attendance at school, even when available,
entirely voluntary. In 1800 almost the whole Highland populace was illiterate. There was therefore no
large reading public for which authors could write.
The intellectual appetite which, among English-
reading people, was being fed by essays, novels,
plays, etc., was in the Gaelic communities catered for
by traditional oral folktales and related oral material,
which was still abundant and widespread.

The pre-1800 Gaelic religious prose works referred
to above were published not so much in response to
what the people wanted but to provide what interested and concerned parties – Churches, institutions
and well-meaning individuals – thought they should
read, or should hear read to them, for the good of
their souls as well as for the nourishment of their

minds. The nineteenth century brought stronger
incentives to read and a great increase of aids to
acquiring reading skills. Gaelic reading was taught in
the pre-1872 parish schools, in the schools of the
Society in Scotland for the Propagation of Christian
Knowledge (SSPCK) after the 1760s, in the schools
of the various Gaelic school societies (q.v.) of the
Church of Scotland and of the Free Church, as well
as of the Ladies' Highland Association (q.v.). The
availability of the Gaelic Bible in handy, small, one-
volume form from 1807 onwards proved a great
incentive. The controversies associated with the Disruption (q.v.) of 1843 and the issues of Church
union, voluntaryism, and the disestablishment movement, etc., let loose a flood of books and pamphlets.
If ministers had not yet acquired the habit of publishing their sermons, loyal admirers sometimes
managed to take notes of sermons and put them into
print.

For detailed information about the different categories of Gaelic religious prose one may consult the
Revd Donald Maclean (Donald Maclean 1915) and
the Revd Professor Donald Maclean (Donald
Maclean 1912). Neither, however, includes the large
amount of material in the many periodicals and in
tracts, leaflets, and booklets issued by the Churches
and by various other bodies. Professor Maclean
arranges Gaelic religious prose in these categories:
biblical, theological, homiletical, devotional, catechetical and controversial, and educational. Most of
the material in these categories is translated from
English and, like translated non-religious prose (and
original Gaelic prose), varies greatly in quality.
However, if *blas na Beurla* (the flavour of English) is
sometimes present, much of the translation is thoroughly Gaelic in idiom and style.

The earlier translators should be acclaimed as
pioneers. With no models other than the Gaelic Bible
(q.v.), Confession and Catechisms, they laboured to
express abstruse theological concepts in Gaelic and
largely created the vocabulary and style of Gaelic
religious speech and writing. These translators were
mostly ministers and schoolmasters. Several schoolmasters employed by the SSPCK excelled in this
work. A competent judge (M. Maclennan 1920) wrote
thus:

These were some of the leading men who so
nobly served their day and generation in this
department of work, and to whom succeeding
generations were so deeply indebted. They were
men who made splendid use of their so limited

opportunities and whose mastery of their native language would do no small credit to the rank and file of ministers and men even of this generation. A careful proof-reading would polish off a few orthographical irregularities in their work, but they were masters of Gaelic idiom and of a plain Gaelic style. They drew on a rich store of current vocabulary, and they had not much to learn in the art of a vigorous and virile translation. There is a translation which is more concerned about the letter than about the spirit, whose movements are more mechanical than elegant, more like a jointed effigy than an athletic youth. Such a translation is a simple and an easy enough business, and, I am afraid, not altogether uncommon, but the translation which seizes on the thought and spirit and clothes them in plain but graceful homespun, without sacrificing much of the genius and the flavour of the original, is quite another matter. In that fine art some of the old masters succeeded in a degree that is highly commendable.

As 'shining examples' of that kind of translation Malcolm Maclennan cites Patrick Macfarlane's translation of Bunyan's *Pilgrim's Progress* (of which he himself made an excellent new translation in 1929) and John Rose's translation of Bunyan's *Holy War*. Patrick Macfarlane, schoolmaster in Appin, made many translations. His translation of MacGowan's *History of Joseph* was described as 'one of the best and most beautiful specimens of pure Gaelic prose at present extant' (Reid 1832, 131), and as 'the finest translation into Gaelic we have ever come across' (Donald Maclean 1915, 223).

Among the religious writers whose works proved widely and lastingly popular in Gaelic were John Bunyan, Richard Baxter, Thomas Boston, Robert Murray McCheyne, John Owen, and Charles H. Spurgeon. Apart from the Bible, the most often printed and most widely used Gaelic translation has been that of the Shorter Catechism, especially the translation by John Macdonald of Ferintosh. In the translating and revising of the Gaelic Bible itself of course many scholars participated, notably James Stewart of Killin and his son, John Stewart of Luss, John Smith of Campbeltown and Alexander Stewart of Dingwall, John Macdonald of Comrie, Thomas Maclauchlan, Archibald Clerk and Malcolm Maclennan. At the request of Prince Louis Lucien Bonaparte the Apocrypha was translated into Gaelic in 1860 by Alexander Macgregor; this is an excellent piece of Gaelic prose but, unfortunately, rarely obtainable.

Best known among writers of Gaelic religious prose, whether original or translated, are Norman Macleod of St Columba's, Archibald Clerk, Robert Blair, John Macrury, Donald Lamont, Mackintosh Mackay, John G. Macneill and Malcolm Maclennan. Good examples of religious prose in more recent times are: Donald J. Martin's *Teagasg nan Cosamhlachdan* (1914) and *Teagasg nam Mìorbhailean* (1916); Alexander Macdiarmid's *Urnaigh an Tighearna* (1921) and *Dòrlach Sìl* (Free Church sermons, 1931); Malcolm Macleod of Balquhidder's *Comasan na h-Urnaigh* (1913) and *An Iuchair Oir* (1950); and Donald Mackinnon's *An t-Ionad-fasgaidh* (1951). Older publications of special interest are the Gaelic sermons of Angus Macmillan (1853), John Macalister (1896) and Lachlan Mackenzie of Lochcarron (at various dates).

The Roman Catholic contribution to Gaelic prose includes the Gaelic translation of the New Testament (1875), several translations by the Revd Fr Ewen Maceachen (of dictionary fame), *An Cath Spioradail*, Thomas à Kempis's *Imitation of Christ* and other items. There is also *Iùl a' Chrìosdaidh* (1844) and *Lòchran an Anama* (1906).

Mention must also be made of the series of nineteen Gaelic booklets issued jointly by the Church of Scotland and the Free Church for HM Forces in the first world war and a similar series in the second. These contained old and new material and were all in Gaelic prose except for two excellent collections of hymns, *A' Chruit Oir* and *Mil nan Dàn*.   TMM

proverbs, maxims and riddles, collections of
Despite the great popularity and wealth of proverbial sayings in Gaelic there are no early systematic collections of them. Individual proverbs are often quoted in the margins of manuscripts, and poets may use them in their verses, as Mac Mhaighstir Alasdair (q.v.) does in his 'Oran a rinneadh a' bhliadhna 1746'. The earliest systematic collections may be those in Nat. Lib. Gaelic MSS LXII and LXV, both in Mac Mhaighstir Alasdair's hand (*see Reliquiae Celticae* vol. 1, 151–9 for MS LXII). Earlier, the Fernaig Manuscript (q.v.) includes a set of didactic verses, another variant of maxim lore (C. MacPhàrlain 1923, 51; cf. verses entitled 'Comhairlean Chormaic d'a Mhac' in Gillies Collection etc.).

Serious collection dates drom the latter part of the eighteenth century with Ewen MacDiarmid's collection, now partly lost or misplaced but used by Nicolson later (A. Nicolson 1881, xxxiii; D. Mackinnon 1912, 321) and Donald Macintosh's *Collection of Gaelic Proverbs* (1785, 1819), the first printed collection, partly obtained in Lochaber, partly in Macintosh's native east Perthshire. Duncan Lothian's *Proverbs in Verse* (1797, 1834, 1844) contain his famous 'Seanfhacail agus Comhadan'. Sheriff Alexander Nicolson, *A Collection of Gaelic Proverbs and Familiar Phrases* (1881), is based on Macintosh but expands it, adding some explanatory notes and parallels from other languages. This collection was reprinted with an index by Malcolm Macinnes (1951). Dr Alexander Cameron's collection is in *Reliquiae Celticae*, vol. 2 (1894), 475–507. *The [Alexander] Campbell Collection of Gaelic Proverbs and Proverbial Sayings* (1978) was edited by Donald E. Meek, with an introduction, glossary and Indexes.

There have been various short collections from particular places (for example, Angus Matheson's from Lewis) and collections published in periodicals and papers. Donald Mackinnon wrote a series of essays on proverbs (L. MacKinnon 1956), and J. L. Campbell's short pamphlet (1968) has a useful bibliography and a note on unpublished manuscript collections. Alexander Nicolson's *Gaelic Riddles and Enigmas* (1938) is the principal collection of such material.   DST

psalm tunes, Gaelic There are only a few Gaelic psalm tunes as such, but there are unique styles of singing a limited number of accepted Scottish psalter tunes in unison. These may be heard at the services of the various Protestant denominations in Gaelic-speaking parts of Scotland. The styles are traditional only in the loosest sense, contrary to widely held belief. They vary in detail from island to island and, indeed, within different parishes of the same island or region. Among those accustomed to orthodox Western music the first reaction is usually shock and distaste, the consequence of failure to understand the musical structure and the nasal (and harsh) tone quality.

After the Reformation and the subsequent translation of the psalms into Gaelic, congregations adopted fewer than a dozen tunes and evolved their own various methods of ornamentation, derived from ancient singing habits which in turn depended on geographic, climatic and social factors. The outcome was the 'long tune', in which the precentor gave out the psalm line by line, to be followed by the congre-

gation taking each note of the tune and applying to it grace notes and slurs individually. Some have likened this to the ornamentation in *pìobaireachd*, but the comparison is dubious except as between aspects of the same social expression.

The 'long tunes' disappeared towards the end of the nineteenth century because of the encroachment of more 'orthodox' musical habits, but the style and the tendency to ornament persist in their application to a wider range of more modern tunes. These may be heard in church in Gaelic-speaking communities and on radio in Sunday afternoon services in Gaelic. The subject has not yet been fully researched, but the School of Scottish Studies has a library of recordings, some of which are on sale to the public.

Non-Highland music lovers will usually find it rewarding to try to come to terms with this unique expression of communal culture. (See Collinson 1966; P. Millar 1949.)   CTD

psalms, metrical The Genevan order of service introduced into Scotland by the Reformation of 1560 required a metrical version of the psalms for congregational singing. Carswell (q.v.) translated the Book of Common Order in 1567 but did not attempt the psalms which accompanied it. The Synod of Argyll first moved to produce a translation in May 1653, but only after enforced steady work, begun in January 1658 by three minsters, Dugald Campbell of Knapdale, John Stewart of Kingarth and Alexander MacLaine of Strachur and Strathlachlan, were the first fifty psalms, the Caogad, completed. These were still metrically imperfect in places, the common metre required by the tunes being unfamiliar to the Gaelic ear in demanding, like classical Gaelic verse, a fixed number of syllables to the line, and, unlike it, a regular patterning of stresses. This version was approved by Synod in May 1658, subject to correction of the metre, and printed with the Shorter Catechism (q.v.) in 1659. The remainder of the work went on more rapidly, but the Restoration of 1660 also restored episcopacy and suspended the Synod's activities until after the Revolution of 1688. The text was recovered in 1690, and after some conservative revision of the Caogad was printed in 1694. (See also MacTavish 1934, 1943–4; R. L. Thomson 1976.)
                                                            RLT

publications, Gaelic *see* Comunn Gaidhealach, An; current affairs, coverage in Gaelic; Gaelic Books Council; press, Gaelic; publishing, Gaelic.

publishing, Gaelic The first Gaelic printed book in Scotland comes quite early, (1567): John Carswell's (q.v.) *Foirm na n-Urrnuidheadh*, in large part a Gaelic translation of the Book of Common Order (Edinburgh 1564) which was 'a revision of the Geneva Book, sometimes called John Knox's Liturgy, already printed in Edinburgh in 1562' (R. L. Thomson 1970, lix). This is the earliest printed book in Gaelic, whether in Scotland or in Ireland, and is written in a variety of Classical Common Gaelic. Yet there was a long gap between it and the next printed book, *Adtimchiol an Chreidimh*, the Gaelic version of Calvin's Catechism (*c.*1630) of which only one copy survives (R. L. Thomson 1962). Other Gaelic works of a religious or ecclesiastical kind were published at intervals over the next hundred years – for example, the Shorter Catechism, (?) 1651; the Catechism with the first fifty psalms, 1659; Charteris's Catechism, 1688; Kirk's metrical psalms, 1684; another version of the psalms, (?) 1694, Kirk's reissue of Bedell's Irish Bible, 1690; the Confession of Faith, 1725; other editions of the Catechism and Psalms. The first secular printed book in Gaelic was Mac Mhaighstir Alasdair's (q.v.) *Vocabulary* of 1741. It is abundantly clear that such initiative as there was in publishing Gaelic books lay with the Church, nor is this surprising, since the Church provided the bridge to the outside or European world, and the Gaelic literary establishment had to some extent retreated into a mental ghetto. When Niall MacMhuirich wrote his history of the Montrose Wars late in the seventeenth century specifically to correct the historical perspective as he saw it, it probably seemed totally adequate to him to have his account in manuscript, not in a printed book.

In the second half of the eighteenth century we can see a gradual weakening of the hegemony of the Church, and specifically of the hegemony of set forms, as more Evangelical views gained ground. A translation of Richard Baxter's *Call to the Unconverted* appeared in 1750, other translations and original sermons as the century continued, David Mackellar's *Hymn on Creation* in 1752 and (most decisively) Mac Mhaighstir Alasdair's *Ais-eiridh* (his secular poems) in 1751 and, after his son Ranald's publication of the *Eigg Collection* (1776), a fairly steady stream of collections of secular Gaelic poetry. It was to be much later, however, that secular prose became at all common in printed form; the Gaelic translation of the Bible (1767–1801) confirmed for a time the primacy of religious prose but also eventually helped to make possible the publication of a wider range of Gaelic prose.

The antiquarian interests that eighteenth-century Gaels shared with their European contemporaries, reinforced by the impetus of the Ossianic controversy, led to published dissertations on Highland history and antiquities and travellers' tales (q.v.), but also to printed dictionaries (q.v.), grammars (e.g. Shaw's, Stewart's), collections of proverbs (as Donald Macintosh's *A Collection of Gaelic Proverbs*), as well as collections of ballads and poems. A rough survey of Gaelic printed books (first editions only) in the eighteenth century gives the following decennial totals:

1700–10	1	1750–60	7
1710–20	0	1760–70	6
1720–30	1	1770–80	9
1730–40	0	1780–90	28
1740–50	1	1790–1800	17

This list shows the extremely modest level of publication and the relatively dramatic rise in the second half of the century, culminating in the last two decades. By this time we can see the effect of the Gaelic translation of the New Testament (1767), perhaps the effect of the schools of the Society in Scotland for the Propagation of Christian Knowledge, where Gaelic reading was taught with whatever reservations, and also the effect of the drift from the Highlands to towns and cities and the growth of urban colonies close to the printing presses.

Practically all the Gaelic publishing of the eighteenth century took place in Edinburgh and Glasgow, although Perth, London and Inverness each showed a few titles, along with such centres as Aberdeen, Falkirk, Greenock, Paisley, Dublin and Cork. Up to 1800 Edinburgh had published almost twice as many Gaelic books (including second and subsequent editions) as had Glasgow. Among publishers and printers whose names appear are Robert and Andrew Foulis, John Orr and Andrew Orr (all of Glasgow), D. Macphatraic, Balfour Auld and Smellie, Walter Ruddiman, John Moir, and C. Elliot (all of Edinburgh), John Gillies of Perth, and John Young of Inverness.

The nineteenth century saw an expanding pattern of publishing location, with the tally of titles (including second and subsequent editions in the statistics) as follows: Edinburgh (378), Glasgow (339), Inverness (146), London (37), Perth (14), Paisley (12), Greenock (9), Stirling (7), Aberdeen (6),

Elgin (5), Oban (4), Aberfeldy, Dingwall, Killin, Kirkaldy, Leith, Stornoway, Tain (2 each) and Campbeltown, Chelsea, Forres, Govan, Huntly, Invergordon, Kilmarnock, Leipzig, Liverpool, Montrose, Parkhill, Partick, Pultneytown, Sandbank and Wick (1 each). Glasgow was overtaking Edinburgh as the main centre of Gaelic publication and did so in the later decades of the century. Inverness moved decisively into third place; London remained fairly prominent; Perth did not maintain its impetus; Paisley and Greenock came into the picture, as did Stirling very late in the century; and the Gaelic diaspora is shown in the rest of the list. By the second half of the nineteenth century some modest Gaelic publishing was going on in America and Canada: Charlottetown (9 titles), Antigonish (8), Sydney and Pictou (5 each), Toronto (4), Halifax (3), Baddeck, Fayetteville, Kingston, Ottawa (1 each).

The new wave of Gaelic publishers was emerging: Alexander Gardner of Paisley by 1830, MacLauchlan and Stewart of Edinburgh by 1837, Archibald Sinclair of Glasgow by 1853 (Coventry 1983), Norman MacLeod and Alexander MacLaren towards the end of the century. The main output was shared by MacLauchlan and Stewart and Archibald Sinclair.

The rise of periodicals (q.v.) was broadening the range of prose writing, and the Gaelic school societies (q.v.) had created a reading public, while the Gaelic urban colonies threw up new writers, topics and trends (and, through their proximity to the presses, gave them more prominence than they would otherwise have achieved).

The first half of the twentieth century saw a much greater concentration of Gaelic publishing in Glasgow, with the development of An Comunn Gaidhealach (q.v.) and the location of its publication in Glasgow or Stirling, with the rise of Alexander MacLaren and Son and their taking over of other publishers (for example, Sinclair's Celtic Press). But Stirling had a notable share of this increased publishing activity, especially through Aeneas Mackay and Andrew Learmonth's work as printer to An Comunn. Meantime in Edinburgh Oliver and Boyd continued to publish a number of Gaelic books and acted as publishers for the Scottish Gaelic Texts Society (q.v.).

The 1939–45 war brought Gaelic publishing almost to a standstill, and by the time it was over MacLaren's were losing their drive (through lack of an involved family succession). An Comunn, despite an active phase of publishing Gaelic plays and some school textbooks in the post-war years, began to lose publishing drive also. Gradually, after the foundation of *Gairm*, the Gaelic quarterly, Gairm Publications also came into being, beginning book publication on a small scale in 1958, expanding publication in the second half of the 1960s and taking over MacLaren's list entirely in 1970. Gairm Publications currently have by far the largest backlist and have published a wide variety of titles, including manuals, dictionaries, school texts, children's books, novels, short stories, poetry, current affairs, religious books, music books and sheets (R. MacThómais 1977). Club Leabhar, Inverness, published for a number of years in the late 1960s and 1970s before being taken over. The company Acair, Stornoway, was launched in 1977 and publishes mainly for the Western Isles school market, many of its books being Gaelic versions of books published by other publishers (Longman, Oliver and Boyd etc.), though some are original. Its list includes children's books, short stories, Highland history, a dictionary and some English titles. Aberdeen University's Celtic Department began to publish Gaelic books in 1962, and this series was continued by Glasgow University's Celtic Department (with some fifteen titles), while Aberdeen restarted (1972) a Gaelic series there also. Other publishers (for example, Chambers and Macdonald's, and Canongate, all of Edinburgh) have included occasional Gaelic titles in their lists; the Academic Press publishes for the Scottish Gaelic Texts Society; and new small imprints have come into being – for example, Clò Beag (Glasgow), Buidheann-foillseachaidh nan Eilean an Iar (Stornoway), Crùisgean (North Uist) and Clò Chailleann (Aberfeldy). The current scene is not unhealthy, partly thanks to the work and grants of the Gaelic Books Council (q.v.). A very useful expansion of range and an improvement of design and presentation have been achieved for Gaelic books, though much remains to be done.

Gaelic book editions are often in the 1,000–2,000 range, normally 1,000 where a school take-up is not to be expected. Dictionary editions can run to 5,000, and one school text edition ran to 10,000 copies. Where there is neither school take-up nor strong learner involvement, however, it is not normally easy to sell in excess of 800–1,000 copies of a book. (For further comment on publication levels for the period 1930–75, and for a discussion and chart of the distribution of fourteen types of Gaelic book over these decades, with projection for the last one, see R. Mac-

Thómais 1976, 80–3, with summary, 86). (See also Donald Maclean 1912, esp. 27–32; D. S. Thomson, forthcoming.) DST

Puilean, am (Aonghas Caimbeul) (1903–82) Born in Ness, Lewis, at the age of fourteen Am Puilean moved from there to Bernera, Harris, where his father was a lay preacher. He spent most of the war in a prison camp in Poland. His youthful adventures and war experiences are documented in his funny, wise and always enthralling autobiography, *A' Suathadh ri Iomadh Rubha* (1973). Am Puilean is also a fine poet, whose work, basically in the village bard tradition, always extends that mode's perceptions and range with linguistic virtuosity, social analysis and wit. A collection, *Moll is Cruithneachd*, was published in 1972. DMCA

Pursell, Edward (1891–1964) Born Campbeltown, Argyll. Headmaster of Dalintober and Millknowe primary schools there. Painter and short-story writer. Devised first radio course for Gaelic learners (with best-selling booklet, *Learning Gaelic*), broadcast weekly by the BBC in 1949. Pursell put words to pipe and fiddle tunes (for example, 'Tuireadh Iain Ruaidh', based on a pibroch, and 'An Fhaidhir Mhuileach', based on a Strathspey). Wrote the popular song 'Fàgail Liosmòr'. CG

Q

Queen's Highlanders, *see* regiments, Highland.

Queen's Own Cameron Highlanders, *see* regiments, Highland.

Quiggin, Edmund C. (1875–1920) Lecturer in Celtic, University of Cambridge, from 1909. Undertook important work on classical Gaelic verse, including that in the Book of the Dean of Lismore (q.v.). DST

R

radio, *see* broadcasting, Gaelic.

Raeburn, Sir Henry (1756–1823) Born Stockbridge, Edinburgh. The leading portrait painter of his time in Scotland. His Highland subjects include chiefs in their finery, Neil Gow, James Macpherson (q.v.), etc. (See also **art, Gaelic, in modern times**.) DST

Raghnall Dubh, *see* MacDonald, Ranald (*c*.1715–*c*.1805).

Raghnall na Sgéithe (Ranald MacDonald) (d. 1692) From Glencoe (killed in the Massacre): Distinguished soldier under Montrose and Dundee; fought at Worcester. (See K. N. MacDonald 1900, 21, who wrongly attributes to him a poem on Killiecrankie.) DST

Raonaild Nighean Mhic Nèill, *see* MacDonald, Rachel.

'Red', *see* MacLeòid, Dòmhnall.

Red Book of Clanranald, *see* Clanranald, the Books of.

regiments, Highland Until the nineteenth century these had been raised on a largely tribal basis since the time when the chief of Mackay, the first Lord Reay, formed Mackay's Regiment in 1628 to fight in the Thirty Years' War. From this derived the Scots Brigade in Holland, which helped to achieve the Glorious Revolution of 1688 (Grimble, 1965). In 1725 companies of Highland militia were recruited, embodied in 1729 into a corps known as Am Freiceadan Dubh (the Black Watch), by contrast with redcoated troops. In 1749 it became the 42nd Regiment, and from 1758 it was designated the Royal Highland Regiment of Foot, but it has never lost its celebrated name of the Black Watch (Linklater and Linklater 1977). In 1745 this Hanoverian force was supplemented by another, raised just before the final Jacobite uprising and commanded by Campbells. It was

The 93rd Sutherland Highlanders, private, colour-sergeant and bandsman, 1852. By R. Poate.

named after its colonel, the Earl of Loudoun, while its lieutenant-colonel was the future Duke of Argyll. Loudoun's Highlanders served in Europe until peace was signed in 1748, when they were disbanded.

During the Seven Years' War (1756–63) William Pitt raised regiments from previously Jacobite as well as Hanoverian clans, telling Parliament, 'I sought for merit wherever it was to be found . . . and found it in the mountains of the north.' In 1757 were raised the 77th Regiment of Montgomerie's Highlanders, containing Frasers, MacDonalds, Camerons and Macleans, and the 78th Regiment of Fraser's Highlanders. The 87th and 88th Regiments of Keith's and Campbell's Highlanders and the 89th, consisting largely of Gordons, were added in 1759. In the following two years the 100th, commanded by Colonel Campbell of Kilberry, the 101st or Johnstone's

Surgeon Major Donald Macintyre. By Edward Dayes, c. 1770.

Highlanders, the 105th (or Queen's Highlanders) and Maclean's Highlanders joined the colours.

During the American War of Independence (1775–83) MacDonald's Highlanders were raised by the Chief of Sleat in 1777 and Argyll's Highlanders in 1778. While these served in America, two Mackenzie regiments were raised for India. In 1777 Lord MacLeod's Highlanders were formed by the Earl of Cromartie's son, and in 1778 the Mackenzie chief raised the Seaforth Highlanders. In that year the Murray chief raised the Athole Highlanders, who were among those sent to subjugate their fellow Gaels in Ireland.

The Napoleonic War gave rise to further massive recruitment. In 1793 Sir Allan Cameron of Erracht, subsequently a lieutenant-general, raised the regiment which was to become the Queen's Own Cameron Highlanders. In 1800 the 93rd Sutherland Highlanders were raised largely from the estates of the chieftainess of that name. In 1881 the Argyll and

Sutherland Highlanders were amalgamated, while the Cameron, Seaforth and Gordon Highlanders remained distinct, as did the Black Watch.

The numbers as well as the distinction of those who served before the population of the Highlands and Hebrides was decimated by the nineteenth-century Clearances (q.v.) are illustrated by the statistics of Skye. During the years 1797–1837 this island alone contributed 21 lieutenant- or major-generals, 45 colonels, 600 commissioned officers, 120 pipers and 10,000 other ranks, in addition to those who served in the Royal Navy (A. Nicolson 1930). The uglier aspects of the story are explored in Prebble 1975. Their gallant services are described in Adams 1952, Brander 1971, and Laffin 1974.　　IG

regnal succession, *see* tanistry.

Reid, Duncan (1849–1912) From Kintyre. First Gaelic teacher under the Glasgow School Board. Founded Glasgow High School Gaelic Class Ceilidh (1894), giving the word *céilidh* a broader significance. Published a Gaelic grammar and elementary course. (See *An Deò-gréine*, vol. 7, 1911, 85.)　　TMM

riddles, *see* proverbs, maxims and riddles, collections of.

Rob Dòmhnallach, *see* MacDonald, Robert.

Rob Donn (1714–78) Born in Strathmore beneath Ben Hope in Sutherland, Rob Donn was the son of a sub-tenant on the estate of the Mackay chief, the third Lord Reay. While he was still a child the chief's third cousin, Iain MacEachainn, became tacksman in Strathmore and, on hearing of the precocious rhyming herdboy, took Rob Donn into his household. Before his death in 1757 he was to declare in Gaelic: 'With every judge who has a knowledge of poetry, Rob Donn will be remembered forever' (Grimble 1979b, 85), while the bard delineated him and his family as no other tacksman is portrayed in Gaelic literature. Murdo MacDonald (q.v.), minister of Durness, exercised a strong religious, musical and literary influence upon him, while the fourth Lord Reay, who remained in Durness throughout his adult life, provided the admired model of a resident and conscientious chief.

To all three men Rob Donn paid his debt of gratitude in outstanding elegies. He also composed dia-logues in verse that revealed a dramatic gift, incisive satire and humorous songs. A moralist who exposed hypocrisy and cant, his judgements were penetrating and his expression of them fearless. Although an illiterate monoglot, he provides a portrait of traditional Gaelic society on the eve of its dissolution that is unique in its range.

The preservation of his poetry in such a complete form is due largely to John Thomson, MacDonald's broad-minded successor as minister of Durness, who permitted his daughter to write it down at the bard's dictation without censoring its bawdier passages. Rob Donn's first editor, however, not only attempted to render his Strathnaver dialect in standard Gaelic but also deleted lines which he considered to be of 'immoral tendency'. Hew Morrison, a later editor, altered the text without improving it and also attempted to prove that the bard was not a Mackay. But in the same year Gunn and MacFarlane made amends by publishing an edition which contained many of the airs to Rob Donn's songs. A newly edited, definitive text of this incomparable peasant poet is much needed.　　IG

Robertson, Angus (1873–1948) Born in Skye; came to Glasgow *c.*1890. Novelist, poet, publicist (see also **novel, the Gaelic**). By 1907 Robertson had founded the weekly illustrated paper *St Mungo*. Probably at Ruaraidh Erskine of Mar's suggestion, he adapted the story 'Black Alpin' which had appeared in *St Mungo*; thus three instalments of his novel *An t-Ogha Mór* appeared in the periodical *An Sgeulaiche* (1909–10). The complete novel appeared in 1913. While President of An Comunn Gaidhealach (q.v.), in 1924 he went to America to promote, unsuccessfully, a Gaelic university in Iona. While in London on business (1927–45), he published *Children of the Fore-World*, essays on Celtic notabilities, (1933), *Orain na Céilidh* and *Cnoc an Fhradhairc* (1940), including the long title poem, a philosophical pastoral.　　DST

Robertson, Revd Charles Moncrieff (1885–1927) From Strathtay. Minister in Port Charlotte, Islay. Author of important early papers on Scottish Gaelic dialects.　　DST

Robertson, Ewen (1842–95) Famous for the evidence he gave before the Napier Commission (q.v.), and for his Gaelic poems concerning the Sutherland Clearances (q.v.). (See *Gairm* 1962, 31; Grimble 1963; Menzies 1976, 62, 66.)　　IG

Robertson, John L. (1854–1927) Born Stornoway. Spent his professional life in Her Majesty's Inspectorate of Schools and exercised a long, profound and beneficial influence on Highland education at crucial stages of its development (particularly in relation to the Islands school boards and the 1908 and 1918 Education Acts). JAS

Roman Catholic Church In certain small areas of Gaelic Scotland the indigenous people have been Roman Catholic without interruption throughout the centuries. It is true that in the first hundred years after the Reformation memory of the ancient religion grew dim and distorted; as the pre-Reformation clergy died off, they were not immediately replaced by ministers or missionaries of the Kirk, and the people suffered from lack of Church discipline and authoritative teaching. But when missionaries eventually came they found that the main truths of the Christian faith were still known, for they had been passed on by oral tradition.

In the first half of the seventeenth century the plight of these people was of serious concern to Rome, and the Sacred Congregation for the Propagation of the Faith (commonly known as Propaganda) made an effort to establish a mission to the Scottish Highlands. But it was very difficult to recruit suitable missionaries, men who could preach to the people in their own language and who were prepared to endure the physical hardships of Highland life. The obvious place to look for such recruits was in the north of Ireland, whose people had such close kinship with the Scottish Gaels, and a mission was established under the charge of the Franciscans from County Antrim. They and men of other religious orders worked well for many years, but they were few in number, and their influence was restricted to those areas in which they were welcomed by friendly chiefs. Had they been more numerous and less dependent in trivial matters on the authority of Propaganda in far-off Rome, where the needs of the Highland Church were quite unknown, the religious history of Gaeldom would have been different. It is precisely in the areas in which these seventeenth-century missionaries laboured that the Catholic faith survived for the next three hundred years (Giblin 1964).

In the comparative peace in Scotland of Cromwell's time the Scottish Mission was established in 1653 by Propaganda, a company of secular priests under the authority of a Scottish prefect, and from 1694, under the authority of a Scottish bishop. The Mission was charged with the organization of the Catholic Church in Scotland into missions, each in the care of a missionary priest. These missionaries were trained in Scots colleges on the continent – in Rome, Paris, Madrid and Ratisbon.

But the difficulty of educating Gaelic missionaries persisted, and it was in order to give elementary education to boys who were willing to go to the seminaries on the European Continent that a junior college was founded in Morar in 1712. It did not survive the Rising of 1715 and was transferred to the mountains of Glenlivet. In spite of the 1715 Rising, however, the future of the Roman Catholic Church in the Highlands seemed promising, and in 1727 Propaganda finally realized that for missionary purposes the Gàidhealtachd could not be treated as part of the Scottish Mission but required a separate mission to itself. By then there were twelve Scottish Gaelic missionaries, so the Highland District was established, with its own bishop – Hugh MacDonald of the Morar family. It contained about 85 per cent of the Scottish Roman Catholic population. The Glenlivet seminary was now in the Lowland district, so Bishop MacDonald started again to give elementary education to boys in his little seminary in Morar.

The Jacobite Rising of 1745 brought the progress of the Roman Catholic Church in the Highlands to an abrupt halt. The clans which supported the Government cause now closed their territories to the activities of Roman Catholic missionaries, and by now it was urgent government policy to establish throughout the Highlands schools in which Reformed religion would be taught and the English language would be compulsory. The Society in Scotland for Propagating Christian Knowledge had been founded in the reign of Queen Anne, and by the mid-eighteenth century, thanks to the dedication and sacrifices of its teachers and missionaries, the Kirk was at last strongly represented in every parish. Today those small areas of the Gàidhealtachd in which the indigenous people are predominantly Roman Catholic are the same areas in which the small band of missionaries laboured in the seventeenth century.

Even in those small areas the Roman Catholic Church took a very long time to recover from the catastrophe of 1745. In his report to Propaganda in 1764 Bishop MacDonald, who was still under sentence of exile but in fact living quietly in Glengarry, counted 13,166 Roman Catholics, including infants, in the Highland District, served by only six priests.

Efforts were made to revive the Highland seminary in the west, first at Glenfinnan, then at Buorblach in Morar, later at Samalaman in Moidart and at Kilkerran in Lismore. In 1829 the two seminaries were to be amalgamated in Blairs College, near Aberdeen.

Gradually as the years went by the Roman Catholics ceased to be identified with the Stuart cause. To encourage this change the Glengarry Fencibles regiment was raised, consisting almost entirely of Roman Catholics, to fight in the wars against Napoleon. The regiment later went to Canada and served the cause of Empire there. The emigrations of the nineteenth century reduced the population of the whole Highland area drastically, and many of the most active priests went with their people overseas or to the industrial south. For fifty years, from 1827 to 1878, the Highland Roman Catholics were governed by a bishop residing in Glasgow, to their great disadvantage. When the Scottish Roman Catholic hierarchy was restored in 1878 almost all the Gaelic Catholics in the Highlands were in the county of Inverness and the diocese of Argyll and the Isles. Now, a hundred years later, the Gaelic language is hardly used in church at all, except in the Western Isles. When the liturgy was performed in Latin, the Gaelic Bible was never used, except for the readings from the New Testament on Sunday. Catechism was taught in Gaelic in schools, recited from beginning to end by heart. There were a few books of piety, the best known being *Iùl a' Chrìostaidh*, first compiled by Revd Evan McEachen (1769–1849). The seventh edition had become somewhat rare, and in 1963 the eighth edition, completely revised by the late Mgr Duncan MacLean of Dunoon, appeared. Alas, its publication coincided with the complete renewal of liturgical worship, and it was no longer of practical value to Roman Catholics. Stocks of the prayer book remain unsold. Now that the liturgy is celebrated in the vernacular the Gaelic priests have had to face the mammoth task of translating into Gaelic, week by week, the prayers and Scripture readings for Sunday Mass, as well as the ritual ceremonies for the Sacraments and other religious occasions. It is questionable whether it is possible, or even necessary, to continue this work to cover the whole weekday missal – indeed, a question mark hangs over the survival of the Gaelic language and culture itself. RM

Ros, Uilleam (William Ross) (1762–?91) Born Sìthean, Skye. Educated Forres; lived in Gairloch as schoolmaster and catechist. Ros is justly regarded as the leading poet of love of the eighteenth century. His short-lived romance with Mòr Ros of Stornoway, whom he met probably about 1780, two years before her marriage, has become legendary, and his finest love poetry (Feasgar Luain, Oran Cumhaidh and Oran Eile) are concerned with her; their passionate subjectivity is quite unusual in Gaelic verse of the time.

Ros is said to have burned his own poems; they survive in part from early oral versions, appearing first in A. and D. Stewart's *Collection* (1804) and later edited by John Mackenzie (?1832, 1834) and by George Calder (1937). The surviving work shows a good acquaintance with earlier Gaelic verse (for some detail, *see* D. S. Thomson 1959) and the work of his contemporaries Mac Mhaighstir Alasdair (q.v.) and John MacCodrum (q.v.) and probably also with Burns, Macpherson's *Ossian*, and classical verse. He also composed in the village bardic mode and seems to have reworked existing songs (Bruthaichean Ghlinn Braoin, Cuachag nan Craobh, in manuscript *c.*1756, but *see* W. Matheson 1969, 168). His light and ribald love songs, which are presumably a reflection of an old European tradition, are often neglected or dismissed, but some of them, especially 'Oran eadar am Bàrd agus Cailleach-mhilleadh-nan-dàn', show us the other side of the poet's nature and art.

'Feasgar Luain' is an elaborately wrought love poem (internal evidence suggesting strongly that it was composed after Mòr Ros's marriage); it is formal and classical in structure despite its legend. Even in 'Oran Cumhaidh' the poet has time to introduce an analogue from Gaelic history/legend, though this song has some of the most subjective and passionate lines in Gaelic verse:

> Carson nach d'rugadh dall mi
> Gun chainnt no gun lèirsinn,
> Ma facas t'aghaidh bhaindidh
> Rinn aimhleus nan ceudan . . . .

The 'Oran Eile', however, is the finest distillation of the poet's love and despair, unsentimental, spare, with much realistic detail and with an underlying passion which shows in the imagery and word craft. (See also U. MacMhathain 1955, 339–42; D. S. Thomson 1974a, 209–16.) DST

Ross, James (1923–71) Native of Skye. Gaelic scholar and collector of oral tradition. Published *Whisky* (1970) and several articles (see *Scottish Studies*, index, vol. 10; and *Éigse*, vol. 7, 217–39; vol.

8, 1–17, 350–8. Collected, *inter alia*, over 450 songs and 1,000 proverbs from Nan Eachainn Fhionnlaigh (q.v.), Vatersay.

JMCI

Ross, Neil (1873–1943) Native of Skye. From 1923 parish minister of Laggan. Editor of *An Gaidheal* (q.v.), 1923–36. Published *Heroic Poetry from The Book of the Dean of Lismore* (1939), *Armageddon* (1950). (See **verse, political (twentieth century)**.)

JMCI

Ross, Revd Thomas (1768–1843) Born Creich, Sutherland. Minister at Rotterdam, then Lochbroom. Prepared the Gaelic text for Hugh and John McCallum's *Poems of Ossian* (1816).

DST

Ross, William (1762–?91), *see* Ros, Uilleam.

Ross, Revd William (1836–1904) From Caithness. Taught Gaelic class for divinity students in Glasgow; his library is now in Glasgow University. (See J. M. E. Ross 1905.)

TMM

Rothach, Iain (1889–1918) From Swordale, Lewis. MA (Aberdeen), 1914; enlisted Seaforths; MC, 1918; killed three days later. Only a handful of his poems survive. Two of them, 'Ar Tìr 's ar Gaisgich a thuit sa' Bhlàr' and 'Air sgàth nan Sonn', show remarkable rhythmical mastery and mark Munro as the first strong voice in the new Gaelic verse of the twentieth century. (See M. Moireach 1970, 81; D. S. Thomson 1974a, 252.)

DST

Royal Highland and Agricultural Society of Scotland, *see* Highland Society of Scotland.

Royal Highland Regiment of Foot, *see* regiments, Highland.

Ruairidh, Calum, *see* MacAoidh, Calum.

Ruairi Mór MacLeod Chief of the MacLeods of Dunvegan and Harris from 1595, and led an expedition to Ireland in that year against the English authorities. A political figure of note in Scotland, he was knighted in 1613 and made a burgess of Edinburgh in 1623. Complying with the Statutes of Iona (q.v.), of which he was a signatory in 1609, he sent his sons to the University of Glasgow, but he himself was literate in Gaelic and a notable patron of the classical culture embodied in the elegy composed on his death in 1626 by Eoin Óg Ó Muirgheasáin. (See Grant 1959, 173–254; J. MacDonald 1958, 25–52.)

JWMB

Runciman, Alexander (1736–85) Native of Edinburgh. Artist trained in that city and in Rome. His 'Ossian' cycle of paintings at Penicuik House constituted his most important work, but, having been destroyed, they are represented only by surviving sketches. (See also **art, Gaelic, in modern times**.)

DST

Alexander Runciman, The Finding of Corban Carglas, etching c. 1773. One of several versions of this subject from Ossian which Runciman had painted as part of the decoration of Ossian's Hall at Penicuik House.

S

Sabhal Mór Ostaig A 'Gaelic college' founded in Skye in the mid-1970s. To date it has run short summer courses for Gaelic learners and occasional weekend conferences; it plans to start a full-time course in 1983–4.   DST

Sage, Revd Alexander (1753–1824) Minister of Kildonan, Sutherland, 1787–1824. Collected heroic ballads from reciters in Strathnaver and Strathmore in 1802. (See A. Cameron 1892–4; D. Sage 1889).
                                                              DST

Sage, Donald (1789–1869) Born Kildonan, Sutherland. Minister at Achness in Strathnaver, 1815–18, and thus an eyewitness of the Clearances (q.v.), which he described in the invaluable journal published in 1889 as *Memorabilia Domestica*.   IG

St Ninian's Isle treasure This collection of silver-work represents the treasured possessions of an eighth-century Pictish noble or ecclesiastic (Small *et al.*, 1973). It had been buried in a larchwood casket beneath the floor of the church on St Ninian's Isle off the south-west mainland of Shetland, no doubt in

Silver hanging bowl from St Ninian's Isle treasure, National Museum of Antiquities of Scotland.

order to conceal it from Viking plunderers, around AD 800. The treasure included a hanging bowl, six other bowls, twelve penannular brooches and a group of objects whose interpretation in secular or ecclesiastical terms remains in dispute (McRoberts 1960–1) See also illustration on p. 255. The hanging bowl is considered to be of Northumbrian origin and reflects Anglian influences on Pictish art, mediated through the Church from the early eighth century on. The other items, and especially the brooches (illustrated on p. 29, are characteristically Pictish and demonstrate the distinctive Pictish contribution to Insular zoomorphic art.   LA

St Veronica, Sister (1888–1973) Native of Broad Cove, Nova Scotia. Professor of history at St Francis Xavier University, Antigonish, 1938–71; an authority on Highland history and culture; linguistic director of the Mount St Bernard Gaelic Choir.

                                                   SISTER MMCD

saints of Gaelic Scotland In addition to the commanding figures of Colum Cille (q.v.) and Maol Rubha (q.v.), a large number of lesser personalities from the period of early Celtic Christianity have left shadowy traces of their presence or influence in Gaelic Scotland. In most cases their names survive in place-names, typically as the specific element following the generic *cill* (church). The distribution of *cill* names has been analysed and discussed by Nicolaisen (1976), and the names of saints occurring in Scottish toponymy have been fully surveyed by W. J. Watson (1926). There is room to mention only some of them.

Adamnán (q.v.) is commemorated in such names as Killeonan, near Campbeltown and Ardeonaig on Loch Tay. Blaan, an early seventh-century ecclesiastic, whose principal centre was Kingarth in Butè, has left his name at Kilblane, Southend, and in the east at Dunblane. Among saints bearing the name Brénaind were two prominent sixth-century Irish figures. The name is enshrined in the several Kilbrandons of Scotland, in Lorne, Mull and Islay. Similarly the name Brigid, borne by a number of notable women in addition to the celebrated early sixth-century Brigid of Kildare, has left the name Kilbride in a number of Scottish islands – Islay, Coll, Tiree, Bute, Arran, North Uist, Skye – as well as on the mainland. Brigid of Kildare's festival, 1 Feburary, is still known in Gaelic Scotland as Là Féill Brighde.

There were numerous saints bearing the name Colmán (Little Dove), at least one of whom is com-

Silver bowl, chape, spoon and ornamental mounts, all with animal ornament, from St Ninian's Isle treasure. National Museum of Antiquities of Scotland.

memorated in the names Portmahomack (Port mo-Cholmáig), in Easter Ross, and Kilmachalmaig (Cill mo-Chalmáig), in Sutherland. Watson alludes to a St Colm's Fair in Badenoch on 15 January, and a Féill Choluim in Dingwall on the second last Tuesday of July. Also associated principally with Easter Ross was Dubhthach of Tain, (Gaelic Baile Dhubhthaich), who is also remembered in the name Loch Dubhthaich (Loch Duich) in the west. Donnán of Eigg, who died in 617, was clearly a figure of some influence – the name Kildonan survives in Kintyre, Eigg, Skye, Arran, Uist, Loch Broom and Sutherland. There is also Eilean Donnáin (Donnán's Island), in Lochalsh.

Faolán (Little Wolf) was a fairly popular name among early ecclesiastics; it remains enshrined in such place names as Strathfillan in Perthshire and Kilillan, in Kintail.

Mo-Luóc of Lismore was a contemporary of Colum Cille, and the name Kilmaluag occurs in Lismore itself, in Tiree, in Mull, Raasay and in Skye. There was an early seventh-century saint called Mo-Laise, from a reduced form of Laisrén, who gave his name to Eilean Mo-Laise, whence Lamlash in Arran.

For such saints as can be traced in Irish sources the best guides to the literature are Kenney (1929) and Hughes (1972).   KDMcD

sanctuaries, temples, shrines Religion has always been a potent factor throughout the Celtic world (A. Ross 1967). Today many traces of the old beliefs and practices can be identified in Scotland (A. Ross 1976). As with Christianity, a focal point for communal worship was essential, whether a built structure or a natural feature sanctified by age-old custom and placed under the aegis of a guardian, sometimes later replaced by a saint. *Nemeton* is the old Celtic word for a sacred place (compare Scottish Gaelic *nèamh*, (heaven)), and names derived from *nemeton* abound in Scotland (W. J. Watson 1926, 244ff.). The Ravenna Cosmography (Richmond and Crawford 1949, p. 19) refers to *Medionemeton* (Central Sanctuary), in Dumbartonshire between the Roman forts of Barhill and Croy Hill (Feachem 1969). A ritual well at Barhill is suggestive of pre-Roman sanctity (A. Ross and Feachem, 1976, 237). An important group of names containing this element occurs in Perthshire, Duneaves in Fortingall parish being of particular interest (W. J. Watson 1926, 247). Situated at the entrance to Glenlyon, Fortingall boasts an ancient yew tree (cf. *Ioua insula*, 'Yew Island', modern Gaelic *Hi*), a Bronze Age barrow and other early monuments, and traces of many archaic superstitions and practices. At the upper end of this wild glen is one of the most remarkable survivals of an ancient cult (A. Ross 1967). The date of the associated structure is unknown, but local toponomy would support the hypothesis that the traditions are extremely archaic. This conclusion is also supported by another shrine, probably Iron Age, discovered at Ballachulish, some 24 miles distant as the crow flies. In both instances the 'guardian' of the shrine was a *cailleach* (hag, goddess). In Glenlyon the 'goddess' is accompanied by her mate and offspring. These are represented by anthropomorphically shaped river stones, the *cailleach* having a crude 'face' traced on her upturned head, perhaps improved upon by human hands.

Until the upper glen became depopulated when Loch Lyon was extended for hydro-electric purposes, the inhabitants gathered twice yearly at the small stone house on 1 May in order to thatch it for the summer months and to bring out the idols which had remained indoors during the winter. These were then washed in the nearby *Allt na Cailliche*, (the Hag's Stream) and placed at the door of their 'home'. If propitiated in the correct manner they were believed to bless the stock and the pasturage and to ensure good weather – a prerogative of the Celtic mother goddesses. On 1 November they were carefully replaced in their shrine, which was unthatched and covered with a turf and stone roof. The entrance was then blocked up. The memory of the ritual continues, but now it is faithfully carried out only by the shepherd of the upper glen. The wooden figure of the Ballachulish goddess with her inlaid pebble eyes (now in the National Museum of Scotland) seemingly occupied some kind of wickerwork shrine, and evidence suggests that practices similar to these were once widespread in Gaelic Scotland.

Wooden goddess from Ballachulish. National Museum of Antiquities of Scotland. ▶

Of even greater interest, perhaps, a cult legend is extant telling of the arrival of a divine couple in Gleann na Cailliche in the snows of midwinter, the woman near to labour. Because the glen provided them and their infant with shelter they remained there and are commemorated by these simple but significant stones, the largest being the Cailleach herself, the next in size the Bodach (husband, old Man) and the third the Nighean (girl, daughter).

There is a tradition that St Columba (see **Colum Cille**) found a colony of Druids on Hí (Yew Island) (Skene 1886–90), and this would accord well with what the Greek grammarian, Demetrius of Tarsus (first century BC) had to say about the sacred islands around Britain and their priestly inhabitants (Ogilvie and Richmond 1967).

A series of 'ritual' shafts, very similar to those which formed sanctuaries in the wider Celtic world, was discovered by Thomas Pennant in the eighteenth century (R. Stuart 1852, 205) on the banks of the Almond at *Bertha*, two miles north of Perth (A. Ross 1968, 260). We may compare these with the vast complex of shafts, pits and wells found at *Trimontium*, Newstead, Roxburghshire, the *oppidum* of the Selgovae ('Hunters', Gaelic *sealgairean*) (A. Ross 1968, 268ff.). The stone shrine to the local nymphs of the River Carron (Gaelic *carr*, 'rock shelf'; W. J. Watson 1926, 433), Stirlingshire, known as Arthur's O'on, is another example of Celtic water worship (M. J. T. Lewis 1965, 78), as are the well at Burghead, Morayshire, associated with the Dark Age vitrified fort, and stone slabs incised with Pictish symbols, among which are several representing bulls (Feachem 1977, 138). Another sanctuary of putative pagan origin and associated with a bull *cultus* is that on Eilean Ma-Ruibhe, a small island in Loch Maree (M. MacNeill 1962, 364ff.).

All the evidence indicates that Gaelic Scotland venerated – and in some instances continues to do so albeit in disguised form – its age-old gods and their loci much as did the other Celtic peoples, and copious comparanda are available.   AR

satire, *see* humour (post-1600); verse, courtly and satiric.

Scandinavia, contact with Although it is unlikely that there was no contact between Scotland and Scandinavia in earlier times, the first permanent, large-scale settlement of people from Norway in the Northern Isles of Shetland and Orkney is usually held to date from *c*.800, while comparable settlement on the northern Scottish mainland and in the Western Isles (especially Lewis) would have begun some fifty years later. In Lewis and northern Skye the majority of older settlement names are Scandinavian in origin, and in the northern Hebrides generally a high proportion of the names of the chief natural features are also Norse. The place-name evidence for the Western Isles as a whole points to fairly full-scale Viking settlement in the ninth and tenth centuries, appreciably less intensive than in the Northern Isles but dense enough to leave permanent traces in the ethnic constitution of today's population and to have affected its ancestral language, Gaelic. Scandinavianization seems to have been more thoroughgoing in the lands bordering the North Minch – Lewis and Harris, Skye, Raasay and the mainland seaboard from Loch Broom northward to Cape Wrath – than it was in the southern Hebrides and the Firth of Clyde. Further south still, however, the Isle of Man was colonized relatively thoroughly, and this colony in turn must have had close relations with the small but important Norse settlements established from 841 onwards along the eastern shores of Ireland, from Dublin to Waterford. It has been suggested that Olaf the White, Norse king of Dublin in the mid-ninth century, was of Hebridean origin. Certainly, Dublin and other Irish coastal towns were founded and used by the Norwegians as bases from which to plunder the rich and largely defenceless Irish monasteries and the wealthy English lowlands, not the Hebrides. The inference must be that the Scottish islands and West Highland littoral were areas attracting not plunder (at least not after Iona had been ransacked so completely that there was nothing left) but permanent settlement by comparatively humble west Norwegian families which, for the first two or three generations, gladly participated in Viking summer raids on Ireland, England and the north-west coastal territories of the continent. Norse Hebrideans, many of them Christian, also played a considerable part in the colonization of Iceland (late ninth century) and evidently took a hand in the 'Norwegian' settlement of English Cumbria.

For the later history of Scotland two consequences of the utmost importance stemmed from the Scandinavian occupation of the Western Isles and the West Highland seaboard. At the height of the Norse invasions the residual Celtic realms of Picts and Scots seem to have been compelled to merge, almost in self-defence. As a result of the merger the political centre of gravity of the Scots was shifted from Dalriada (q.v.) to the east, especially the Tay valley, and this would have intensified the displacement of Pictish (P Celtic) by Gaelic (Q Celtic) in Scotland north of the Forth. Secondly, and connected with this process, the links between Scottish Dalriada and its mother country in northern Ireland were broken to such an extent that the Western Isles acquired the name Innse Gall (Isles of the Foreigners); the mixed Scandinavian–Gaelic peoples who overran south-west Scotland in the ninth and tenth centuries were known as Gallghàidhil (Foreign Gael), whence the name Galloway; while the young warriors from Argyll and the Hebrides, who in medieval times made a living by fighting in Irish wars, were known to the Irish as gallóglaig (foreign youth).

The Scoto–Pictish kingdom was unable to reassert a hegemony over the west, where Norwegian overlordship was asserted by King Magnus Barelegs at the end of the eleventh century. His expedition of 1098 led to a treaty with Edgar, king of Scotland, which is said to have conceded to Norway rule over all the isles from Man to Lewis, together with Kintyre. One important consequence was that the church of the isles, the diocese of Sodor (i.e. suðreyjar, southern isles) and Man, was formally subordinated to the Norwegian metropolitan archbishop of Trondheim. The ecclesiastical link with Norway was to last for a century and more beyond the date at which secular sovereignty was transferred from the Norwegian to the Scottish Crown. By the treaty of Perth (1266) the Western Isles and Man were finally ceded to Scotland, although in fact the kings of Norway between Magnus Barelegs and Haakon IV Haakonsson (d. 1263) had been able to assert effective lordship only occasionally and for short periods. Geographically and historically the isles belonged to Scotland. Their acquisition by King Alexander III made it easier for the Scottish kingdom after his death (1286) and that of his heir Margaret (1290), herself the daughter of the king of Norway, to face the onslaught of Edward I of England and survive intact, albeit after much tribulation. Of the two national heroes, William Wallace and Robert Bruce, who led their country to victory and saved its independence for future generations, the latter at least had reason to appreciate the vital importance of the Highlands and Islands, a region in which he took refuge in 1306–7 and from which he received not only succour then but also substantial military support in the years of armed struggle culminating in Bannockburn (1314).

(See Kinvig 1978; Sawyer 1971; Smyth 1975, 1979; Wainwright 1962.) GWSB

School of Scottish Studies Founded within the University of Edinburgh in 1951 to collect and study traditional material relating to Scotland (tales, songs, music, folklore, oral history in Gaelic, Scots and English). A large tape archive has been built up, and selected material has been published on discs and tapes and in the house journal *Tocher*. DST

school societies, Gaelic The parent body, and the first of these societies to be established – the Edinburgh Society for the Support of Gaelic Schools – was set up in 1811, its 'sole object being to teach the inhabitants of the Highlands and Islands to read the Sacred Scriptures in their native tongue'. It undertook, for the accomplishment of this object, to 'maintain Circulating Schools in which the Gaelic language only shall be taught'.

The establishment of this new society attracted much initial interest and support. Auxiliary societies were soon being formed in Glasgow and Inverness. By 1828 the Edinburgh Society had no fewer than eighty-five schools functioning in the Highlands and Islands, and the other societies were doing correspondingly well. Unfortunately, after this period of rapid early growth the societies began to run into difficulties, and after a further period of relative stability they all went into steady decline around 1830. The main problem was finance, and it is probably fair to say also that they were not well administered. Shortly after 1850 the auxiliary societies had actually disappeared. The parent body, now strongly supported by the Edinburgh Ladies Association, kept going for many years more, and it was not finally wound up until 1892. JAS

schools, bardic The classical description of a bardic school is to be found in the memoirs of the Marquis of Clanricarde, a seventeenth-century Lord Deputy General of Ireland, who describes the building as: 'A snug, low hut, and beds in it at convenient distances, each within a small apartment . . . . No windows to let in the day, nor any light at all us'd but that of candles, and these brought in at a proper season only.' The students were given appropriate subjects, and went to their cubicles to work at them, 'each by himself upon his own bed, the whole next day in the dark, till at a certain hour in the night, lights being brought in, they committed it to writing'; this work was afterwards discussed and corrected, and fresh tasks were allocated for next day. The session lasted from Michaelmas to 25 March (Clanricarde, 1744, cviii–cix).

This description is of an Irish bardic school, but the outlines of it seem to be confirmed by Martin Martin, writing of the Western Isles in about 1695: 'they shut their doors and windows for a day's time, and lie on their backs, with a stone upon their belly, and plaids about their heads, and their eyes being covered, they pump their brains for rhetorical encomium or panegyric; and indeed they furnish such a style from this dark cell, as is understood by very few (D. J. MacLeod 1934, 176–7).

In the papers of the Revd Donald MacNicol there are several examples of bardic themes which are said to have been set in the bardic school at Inverness. These are described as *Thaesis or Sochdair Dhain* and lean towards flippancy and *doubles entendres*; one is *Muc, Sgia, Sagairt, Iom & Piob Thombachda*, which suggests a late burlesque on an old practice. The resulting exercise (surely a culpably brief one) is *Na'm bigh Muc aguin mar bhiagh/Agus Sgia aguin mar bhord, 'Sagart nach ithigh an Tìom/Sparragh mid a Phiob na thoin.*

It is highly probable that there were bardic schools connected with the main bardic dynasties in Scotland, but detailed evidence is lacking. (See also **verse bardic**, and references there, especially McKenna (1944), for 'textbooks' used in bardic schools.)   DST

schools broadcasting, *see* broadcasting, Gaelic.

schools, Gaelic Gaelic schools, (see also **school societies, Gaelic**) were exceptionally popular in their day, at least to begin with, and were often regarded with great affection. This was especially so in the Islands, where about half of them were located and which formed their last stronghold. In their immediate object the schools were generally successful; indeed, it would be difficult to find a more favourable educational situation. They enjoyed many advantages for such a time – free education, the involvement of all ages, the highest motivation, emotional excitement, religious fervour, communal support, dedicated teachers, constant catechizing and monitoring and so forth. Nevertheless, these schools seem to represent to us now not so much an educational achievement as an educational opportunity lost. The fact that they had a limited objective, even if it was a worthy one, and that no opportunity was pro-

vided for a fuller education in Gaelic, and in other subjects through Gaelic, was bound ultimately to cause dissatisfaction. Such a policy must have strengthened the existing pressure for literacy in English, which was already regarded by most people as the key to education and personal advancement. Indeed, although these schools were called Gaelic schools, it is probably quite unfair to judge them from this point of view. They were not really concerned with literacy or even with the Gaelic language as such. Their sole purpose was evangelistic and missionary. When these Gaelic schools and societies have to be judged historically, therefore, it must be for their contribution to the Disruption (q.v.) and the evangelical movement in the Highlands, and here their importance was quite significant. (See Gaelic Society School Records, *passim*, New College Library, Edinburgh; Harding, 1980; J. MacInnes 1951; Rederick MacLeod 1977.)   JAS

schools, Gaelic teaching in The first official reference to Gaelic in schools to follow the 1872 Act is to be found in the Schools (Scotland) Code of 1873, presumably the first code to be issued by the Scottish Education Department. This particular entry was not so much a new entry as the restoration of one of a number of entries from earlier codes of the nineteenth century that had disappeared about 1860. These entries, which gave teachers some freedom to use Gaelic in the classroom, had disappeared for a number of reasons but principally because they were not being used. Most of them were back in the Scottish Code again by 1878, and generally they give much more freedom than seems to be realized to school boards to finance the use of Gaelic as a teaching medium and as a specific subject. The issue was primarily one of faith in the language and willingness to allocate finance for that purpose.

This restoration of entries to the Code had been the result of internal debate within the Department (sometimes conducted in public) and of mounting pressure from outside bodies. In contrast to the deafening silence on the subject of Gaelic in schools at the time of the debate on the 1872 Bill, there was now considerable public interest in the position of Gaelic in schools. A survey forced on the Department in 1876 had revealed that a distinct majority of Highland school boards were in favour of including Gaelic in the curriculum. It had also revealed, perhaps more significantly, that some of those in Gaelic-speaking areas were not. It was one thing, of course, for the school boards to profess an interest in encouraging the use of Gaelic in schools but quite another matter to persuade them to do anything about it. This required some finance, and here the Gaelic problem became entangled with the greater problem of financing the Education Act locally.

While there may remain some doubts as to whether lack of finance was the main reason for the manifest reluctance of the boards in general to take advantage of the provisions of the Code, there is certainly none about the serious financial position of these boards in the Highlands and especially the Islands. So serious and pressing did these difficulties become that they had to be specially investigated, and simultaneously the Gaelic 'problem' was studied quite sympathetically. The result was the so-called 'Highland Minute' of 1887. Its principal purpose was to introduce special arrangements to help certain designated boards financially, and this in itself was helpful to Gaelic. It also recognized Gaelic as a specific subject in the higher classes of elementary schools and in secondary schools. It instituted grants to help the supply of Gaelic-speaking teachers and Gaelic pupil teachers, and it designated certain named localities as new secondary-school centres.

At this time, with the exception of Campbeltown Grammar School (which was an earlier foundation anyway of anglicized origin), there were no secondary schools whatsoever on the western seaboard of the Highlands, and these measures for the encouragement of secondary education in general were, doubtless, well intentioned. From the Gaelic point of view, they were also fraught with danger. The 1872 Act had already, (but not intentionally) cut off the main supply of Gaelic-speaking pupil teachers, from Raining's School, Inverness. These new measures were going to intensify the demand for well qualified teachers at a time when few Gaelic-speaking teachers of this kind were available. This meant that such teachers were going to come in from other areas who were not Gaelic-speaking and were apathetic, possibly hostile, to the language. It was a well-known problem, known long before 1872, and now it was to be intensified. Inevitably such a development would strengthen the forces of anglicization and the lack of faith among Gaelic speakers in their own language. The greatest mistake of all, however, was to make Gaelic a specific subject in the elementary school. At a time when the language was still healthy the emphasis should have been placed on the establishment, first of all, of Gaelic literacy in the primary

school and the use of Gaelic as a teaching medium. Instead Gaelic education went off in the wrong direction for many generations as primarily the study of a separate academic subject for fewer and fewer pupils.

By the last decade of the century, although the general building programme was still in progress, the state elementary educational system was firmly established, and the secondary school system was well under way. Together they were, of course, helping Gaelic to the extent that an increasing number of pupils were studying it specifically, but in other respects they constituted in combination the most potentially dangerous anglicizing force which the Gaelic language had yet faced. In the early twentieth century the emphasis moved very much to secondary, and some way to higher, education. A Leaving Certificate in Gaelic at the intermediate stage had been introduced in 1904, to be followed by a Higher in 1915. The time gap is significantly long. Education was beginning to boom in the Highlands and Islands, but it was essentially education for export, and the passport for material advancement had to be in English.

At no time in the period from 1872 to 1918 does one have the feeling that anything approaching a coherent policy for the use of Gaelic in schools had been worked out anywhere. The impression is rather of a series of makeshift arrangements to contain the problem until it disappeared. The story is very much one of opportunities missed or not even seen; the most illuminating comment to make on it is to point out what happened to Welsh in the same period. (In 1888 a Welsh deputation came to London to plead successfully for similar privileges to be extended to Welsh in the English Code as had already been conceded to Gaelic in the Scottish Code. By 1918 in most of the Welsh-speaking areas of Wales the establishment of literacy in Welsh was one of the chief purposes of the elementary schools. The country of Wales as a whole was committed in principle to a bilingual education policy.)

The main administrative change effected by the 1918 Education Act was to replace the school boards with large, ad hoc county authorities. In view of the historical record of the boards in relation to Gaelic since 1872, that change in itself should have been helpful to Gaelic in schools. The new Act also contained for the first time a clause relating to Gaelic which has remained in the Act ever since. It requires an education authority to make 'adequate provision' for the teaching of Gaelic 'in Gaelic-speaking areas'.

Although the Act came at a difficult time, in due course some encouraging results followed. The supply of specialist teachers rose noticeably. Quite a few Gaelic departments, long overdue in certain secondary schools, were opened and have largely remained open ever since. There was an increasing supply also of capable, well trained Gaelic teachers available to the primary school and even a certain amount of experimentation in Gaelic teaching at that stage.

As it happened, these ad hoc authorities lasted only for ten years or so, when they were replaced by all-purpose county authorities which carried much more executive and fiscal power. The change-over took place in 1929, and for the next few years all educational services everywhere were severely cut. By the middle 1930s, stimulated by the developments in bilingual education which had taken place in Wales and Eire but particularly in Wales, An Comunn Gaidhealach (q.v.) had set up a strong investigating committee, under Lord Strathcarron, to report on the operation of that 1918 clause. Their report gives a reliable picture of the Gaelic provision in Scotland in the period between the wars. It shows, particularly in its recommendations, how far Scotland had fallen behind Wales again since 1918.

At the end of the Second World War, as in 1918, there was another important Education Act. Indeed, in its influence on Gaelic in schools the Education Act of 1945, which is still our governing Act, has undoubtedly been the most relevant and the most beneficial of all the Acts, because it is based on a philosophy of education which is essentially 'child-centred'. The general educational climate created by this Act and our growing knowledge of the nature of bilingual situations have strengthened quite considerably the possibilities of real bilingual education for Gaelic-speaking children. In the decade following the Act, and possibly inspired by it to some extent, there also came a series of notable reports on primary and secondary education from the Scottish Advisory Council on Education and from the Scottish Education Department, which are similarly progressive and open-minded, although distinct. Their references to Gaelic in schools reveal a sympathy with, and understanding for, children in a bilingual situation which are far in advance of those of previous official sources.

In the same period there have also been some encouraging developments in the field. For example, although the Gaelic-speaking homeland area had receded by the end of the war more or less to the Hebrides, for various reasons more interest was taken in the language both within and without the area. As early as 1946 some city schools in Glasgow and elsewhere introduced Gaelic into the school curriculum for the first time. A new category of pupil emerged, the 'learner' (as distinct from the 'native speaker'), who can be from within or outside the language area. This new category of pupil was formally recognized in 1962 with the introduction of special Scottish Leaving Certificate papers for such pupils, and these new recruits are compensating to some extent for the continuing decline of native speakers. Again, the Scottish Council for Research in Education, which had been conducting various research studies into the nature of bilingualism during the war, resumed these studies after the war and made two surveys of the Gaelic situation in schools. Associated with this work was the first appointment by an education authority of a full-time Gaelic organizer in 1959, and the Inverness-shire Gaelic Education Scheme came into being as a result of that appointment. Its main interest is, at long last, a genuine bilingual approach to the Gaelic problem, with renewed emphasis on the position of the primary school and the creation of teaching materials in Gaelic.

Over the last twenty years those responsible for the provision of Gaelic in schools have had to cope with many problems, the majority of them probably inherited from the past, some of them quite new. The main problem is still lack of faith. With the new problems, however, fresh opportunities have arisen. Possibly the most significant developments in the history of Gaelic in schools are those taking place now in the Western Isles, where a newly appointed Regional Council has already committed itself to the implementation of a full bilingual policy. At the same time, financed jointly by the Council and the Scottish Education Department, there is a Bilingual Education Project in operation in all the primary schools in the Western Isles. This project represents the most ambitious advance to date in the use of Gaelic as the main educational medium in schools. If such a project can be carried over into the educational system in some permanent form, it could establish a Gaelic/English bilingual educational curriculum for the first time. The educational reasons for doing so, for educating Gaelic-speaking children in their own language as well as in English, are theoretically as sound now as ever they were, and the project has shown that the proposition is quite practicable. What has been done for some time now in Wales, only two or three hours from London by train, can surely be done still in the Western Isles. (See An Comunn Gaidhealach, 1907, 1936; J. L. Campbell 1950b; Durkacz 1977; Grimble and Thomson 1968; K. Mackinnon 1977; M. MacLeod 1966; MacNamara 1966; A. Nicholson 1866; Scottish Education Department 1946, 1947, 1950, 1955; Scottish Record Office 1884–7; J. A. Smith 1981; Welsh Office of Education 1927, 1948, 1953.)   JAS

schools, SSPCK The Society in Scotland for Propagating Christian Knowledge (SSPCK) was established by Royal Charter in Edinburgh in 1709. Its purpose, as stated in the proclamation, was 'to erect and maintain schools to teach to read, especially the Holy Scriptures and other good and pious books: as also to teach writing, arithmetic and such like degrees of knowledge in the Highlands, Islands, and remote corners of Scotland'. There was no doubt about the initial purpose: it was primarily missionary and evangelistic. Similarly, there was no doubt about the need for such a development at this particular time. The existing parish school system was obviously failing to make adequate educational provision in these areas and, furthermore, failing so badly that a large-scale expansion of schools on some viable basis had become a necessity.

The great strength of the SSPCK system and one of its outstanding features was its efficient central organization, a shrewd combination of missionary zeal and business expertise. By 1711 its first five schools had been established (including one in St Kilda), and thereafter expansion was rapid and continuous until the end of the century. In 1738 successful application was made for a second Royal Charter. This time it was for a patent or licence to provide 'working' schools for suitable children 'in husbandry and housewifery, or in trades and manufactures, or in such like applications'. Thus, but only after several failures in various directions, the Society settled down to conducting not only a large number of ordinary elementary schools, but also a large number of spinning schools and sewing schools, particularly for young females. By 1795 there were actually 323 SSPCK schools in Scotland, consisting of 229 ordinary schools and 96 'working' schools.

Early in the nineteenth century this process of expansion ceased; there was even a slight decline in the number of schools for a time, and then for the remainder of its history the number of Society schools remained fairly stationary. This state of affairs was probably due mainly to the entry into the educational field of several other agencies which were also of a religious or evangelical nature. The spinning schools disappeared altogether during the industrial revolution, but this was for economic reasons outwith the control of the Society. As late as 1872 there were still no fewer than 270 SSPCK schools in Scotland, comprising 194 ordinary schools and 76 sewing schools. With the coming of the state system, of course, the days of the SSPCK school system were numbered, and it was finally wound up in 1890.

The nature of these schools has to some extent been misrepresented by the undue emphasis given to certain prejudices or animus which inspired the Society originally. It has been said, for example, that these schools set out to do away with the Gaelic language, and certainly in their earliest regulations the language, like Latin, was expressly forbidden. It was an injunction, incidentally, which from the beginning was honoured more in the breach than in the observance, and in 1767 it was officially and completely reversed.

Again, the generalization that these schools were proselytizing and anti-Catholic, or that they were the favoured instruments of Hanoverian imperialism, can be shown to be similarly exaggerated. These charges relate obviously to attitudes or expressions of attitudes which, however unattractive they seem to us nowadays, represent views honestly held by many at that time among both the English- and the Gaelic-speaking populations. Despite their different management the SSPCK schools were not set up in competition with any other system. They came in originally to support the parish school system, and while at first they were more religious in character and not as concerned with educational standards, in practice they became more and more like the parish schools over the years. From the beginning they were also remarkably accessible to all and helpful to other schools.

In trying to judge the educational asset that the schools represented in the life of Scotland, and in particular of the areas which they served, it is comparatively easy to identify a number of specific contributions. There is, for example, the contribution that these schools made to the spiritual life of the areas, notably to the evangelical movement and to historic events such as the Disruption (q.v.). That is the kind of contribution which the founders had uppermost in mind and of which they would have approved. Then there is the contribution which these schools made to the training of pupil teachers. They always had their own training arrangements, their local managers and their inspectors, but in the nineteenth century they also pioneered the pupil-teacher system and recruited often from their own ranks. Again, their sewing schools were unique in that they included a distinct educational content, unlike their English counterparts, and so they were able to offer a type of female education which was unusual in its day and very influential in the community. Finally, far from being an enemy to Gaelic, if that was ever really the case, the SSPCK system early became one of its greatest benefactors, encouraging and subsidizing Gaelic publication on an extensive scale and, latterly, developing in Raining's School, Inverness, a training ground for a succession of notable Gaelic scholars like Alexander MacBain (q.v.) who taught there, George Henderson (q.v.), and for more Gaelic-speaking pupil-teachers than all the other schools put together.

It is an impressive list of specific contributions by any standards, yet it touches only the fringes of the main contribution which this school system made over two centuries. In that time the SSPCK developed and maintained a complete self-supporting system of education in certain areas, which constituted a credible alternative to the parish school system and which actually cost the nation nothing. The influence of these schools, in generation after generation, must have penetrated every aspect and corner of individual and communal life in the areas served. It was an influence that was carried to other parts of Scotland and often, by emigrants, to other lands and communities. The beneficial influence of this voluntary system of education, whatever its minor shortcomings, has been incalculable. It was one of the greatest educational forces in the Highlands and Islands and the remote areas of Scotland during the eighteenth and nineteenth centuries, and it has placed Scotland for ever in its debt. (See J. MacInnes 1951; Rederick MacLeod 1977; SSPCK records (Scottish Record Office), *passim*; SPCK, *A Summary Account . . . 1783*.) JAS

Scots Brigade, *see* regiments, Highland.

Scott, Revd Archibald Black (1864–1947) Born Turriff. Minister in Helmsdale. Prolific but now outdated writer on Picts, etc. DST

Scott, Walter, and the Highlands Walter Scott (1771–1832) was born and brought up the son of an Edinburgh solicitor, and in due course became an advocate in the capital himself. His parents were of Border extraction so quite naturally the first region of Scotland which he came to know well after Edinburgh and its environs was the east-central Border country, especially Roxburghshire and Selkirkshire. However, from an early age he was also intensely interested in Highland Scots, their history and traditions. In his teens he paid the first of many visits to Perthshire. He had an astonishingly retentive memory, which throve alike on the visual stimulus of fine landscape and historic scenes and on the stories he heard of Rob Roy, the '45 (still recalled with passion and vivid detail by many in his youth) and varied traditional customs north of the Highland Line.

In his creative writings he put to use all of his knowledge and impressions of the Highlands. It was a serious drawback that his Gaelic was severely limited, but more often than not he made up for this by sheer enthusiasm and by the range of reference at his command. As a result, Scott did more than any other single individual to stimulate curiosity about Scotland's heritage, both Highland and Lowland; he drew tourists in their thousands to the Trossachs and elsewhere; and he contributed to a growing awareness of the need for cross-cultural tolerance.

The works which proved most influential in communicating his own zest for the Highlands were *The Lady of the Lake* (1810), the third of his long verse tales, and two of his anonymously published novels, *Waverley* (1814), and *Rob Roy* (1817). *Waverley* explores the tensions and loyalties which divided Scotland in 1745. Its clear-sighted yet sympathetic portrayal of the chief landmark in Jacobite affairs is matched by the rich incidentals of Scott's storytelling. Scott came back to the Jacobite theme in what is possibly his best novel, *Redgauntlet* (1824). He also offered glimpses of Highland character and culture in stories such as 'The Two Drovers' and 'The Highland Widow'.

One view of Scott is that he 'spread a romantic patina' over the reality of the Highlands, producing a 'synthetic myth' (H. Trevor-Roper, *The Listener*, 3 March 1977). Whatever the truth of this assertion, it is clear that Scott's journeys and contacts in Highland Scotland directly inspired a significant part of his work (a further example is his poem 'The Lord of the Isles', drawing on travels in the summer of 1814) and that, but for Scott, ignorance of Gaelic Scotland would have remained even more pronounced. His efforts to persuade assorted lairds to wear the kilt when welcoming George IV to Scotland in 1822 may have been a little over-zealous, but Scott valued both Celt and Saxon. His breadth of outlook removes him beyond any man's scorn. DAL

Scottish Gaelic Texts Society, *see* societies, learned.

sculpture, monumental The craft that surpasses all others in terms of material remains in the Highlands is that of the stonemason. More than 600 richly carved crosses, grave slabs, effigies and tomb chests are still in existence. Those which can be dated, mainly from inscriptions in Latin, of which more than 100 are still legible in whole or in part, range from the mid-fourteenth century to *c*.1560. With three exceptions, all these monuments are or were situated within the area that coincided with the sphere of influence of the Lords of the Isles throughout this period. The largest single concentration, amounting to over eighty monuments, is on Iona, and there are important groups at the other three monastic centres of Oronsay, Ardchattan and Saddell, and at Lochaline in Morvern, at Kilmartin and at Keills and Kilmory in Knapdale.

There were four principal schools of carving: at Iona; in Kintyre, probably at the abbey of Saddell; at Oronsay Priory; and finally the 'Loch Awe School', possibly based at Kilmartin. Iona was the ecclesiastical capital of the Lordship and the widespread distribution of the carvings of the Iona school reinforces the conclusion, suggested by the analysis of the designs, that Iona was the original centre of medieval sculpture in the area. The general level of excellence attained by its products is another indication of its paramount position. It is no accident that with one exception the only West Highland stone masons of the medieval period who can be identified are associated directly with Iona or with monuments of the Iona school. They belong to two families whose surnames were Ó Brolchán and Ó Cuinn and who were clearly practising their craft on an hereditary basis, as was normal in the contemporary kin-based society.

The principal characteristic of their art is the profusion and variety of the decoration. The dominant

Oronsay cross, Argyll. West face. ►

single element is foliage, natural or stylized, often accompanied by interlacing. Figures, both divine and human, are portrayed, as are such animals as horses, deer, hounds, otters and the mythical griffins and manticoras. Illustrations drawn from contemporary life include those of ships, weapons, caskets, tools and implements of trade. The style of carving is firmly rooted in the common past of Scotland and Ireland and owes much to Romanesque art.

The people commemorated on these monuments are those who commissioned them, the heads of kindreds and their immediate families (women as well as men,) and members of the professions and crafts. One of the finest products of the Iona school is the great cross standing in its original socket-stone on a stepped pedestal near the priory church of Oronsay. The inscription on the shaft of the cross reads *Hec est crux Colini filii Cristini MeicDufaci* (This is the cross of Gille Coluim, son of Gille Criósd MacDuffie). A second inscription on the upper surface of the pedestal reveals the name of the craftsman whom Gille Coluim, chief of the MacDuffies of Colonsay (d. *c.*1509), had commissioned: *Malseachlaind saer Ó Cuinn fecit istam crucem* (Mael-Sechlainn Ó Cuinn, mason, made this cross) (Steer and Bannerman 1977).

JWMB

Seaforth Highlanders, *see* regiments, Highland.

Seceders When the Revolution Settlement established the Presbyterian Church of Scotland in 1690, the Cameronians remained aloof, reorganizing themselves as the Reformed Presbytery in 1743. Following the reintroduction of lay patronage in 1712, the Original Seceders formed their Associate Presbytery in 1733. These split into Burghers and Anti-burghers in 1747, over the oath which burgesses gave to uphold the Protestant religion. In 1782 the Anti-burgher synod was split by the Lifter controversy over whether the elements should be lifted before or after the prayer of consecration. Then New Light Burghers divided from Old Light Burghers: the Anti-burghers created a similar schism in 1806. Most of the Original Associate synod of the Old Light Burghers rejoined the Church of Scotland in 1839, in sympathy with the movement that caused the Disruption (q.v.) of 1843 and the creation of the Free Church (q.v.). In 1900 this combined with the United Presbyterians to form the United Free Church, from which a conservative element held aloof, as did another when the United Free Church

rejoined the national Church in 1929. (See Burleigh 1960; Fleming 1927–33.)

IG

Sellar, Patrick (1780–1851) From Moray. A lawyer who became a factor of the Sutherland estates and subsequently a sheep farmer there and in Morvern. He was tried and acquitted of various oppressions, but he remains an ogre of Gaelic folklore and a subject of academic controversy. (See R. J. Adams 1972; Grimble 1963; D. MacLeod 1857; Richards 1973; Sage 1889.)

IG

Senchus Fer nAlban (History of the Men of Scotland) Originally compiled in the mid-seventh century. Names the three chief peoples of Dalriada (q.v.) and gives the genealogies of their ruling families. Also records the number of houses belonging to each people, the number of armed men each could muster and the method of recruiting oarsmen for their naval forces. (See Bannerman 1974, 27–156.)

JWMB

Sgallach, Bàrd, *see* Bàrd Sgallach.

'Sgeulachd an Dìthreabhaich', *see* 'Fear na h-Eabaide'.

Shairp, Dr James Campbell (1819–85) From West Lothian. Principal at the University of St Andrews. Professor of Poetry at the University of Oxford, where he lectured on Gaelic poetry. (See Knight 1888; Shairp 1881.)

TMM

Sharp, William (Fiona MacLeod) (1856–1905) The author most closely associated with 'Celtic Twilight' writing. He seems to have been influenced by MacPherson's 'Ossian' as well as by the Pre-Raphaelites and the *fin-de-siècle* 'decadent' writers. The 'Celtic Twilight' style derived from a false idea of Gaelic literature, which is objective, concrete and free from mysticism. In place of the robust heroes of Gaelic mythology and tales, 'Celtic Twilight' writing gives us the rather wan and ethereal young men and women who appear in Pre-Raphaelite paintings. Nevertheless, Sharp is capable, at times, of fine, impressionistic writing. (See Wittig 1958, 270.)

IMCL

Shaw, Neil (1881–1961) Born Duntroon; brought up in Jura. Gaelic orator, writer, bard and piper. General Secretary and Organizer of An Comunn

Gaidhealach (q.v.), 1911–54; President, 1954–6. (See *An Gaidheal*, vol. 49, 11; vol. 56, 41–2; Murchison 1961a.)

TMM

Shaw, Revd William (1749–1831) Native of Arran. Graduate of Glasgow University. Published *An Analysis of the Galic Language* (1778), *A Galic and English Dictionary* (1780), *An Enquiry into the Authenticity of the Poems ascribed to Ossian* (1781) and the anonymous *Memoirs of the Life and Writings of Dr Samuel Johnson* (1785). (See K. D. MacDonald 1979.)

KDMCD

Sheumais, Murdo, *see* Dòmhnullach, Murchadh.

shinty Amateur team game demanding stamina and co-ordination of foot, eye and hand, referred to in the original Gaelic terminology as *iomain* or *camanachd*; the name derived from *sìnteag* (leap). The game is played with a stick (caman), usually made of hickory, ash or birch, and a seamed leather ball, scoring through goals, formerly hails (see diagrams). The history of the game is said to span a period of some 1,000 years or more and to have been considered the best exercise for battle among the Celtic warriors of old. Shinty has common origins with the Irish game of hurling, though there are now significant differences between the two codes. Similarly, there are fundamental differences between shinty and hockey, although both are played with stick and ball. The most obvious difference is that there is no restriction on the swing of the caman, the head of which is triangular in section, facilitating the striking of the ball on both sides. In this latter respect there is a close similarity between ice hockey and shinty.

Little mention of the game is to be found in Scotland, though, until the eighteenth century, the era of the Grand Tour and the somewhat romantic accounts of travellers such as Thomas Pennant. The organized history of shinty is relatively short; the rules (e.g. the twelve players per side restriction, though a six-a-side version of the game is played indoors and during the summer), referees, etc., appeared less than a century ago. The sport is played over a large area covering mainly the west and central Highlands, though there are strong pockets in the industrial belt and in Aberdeen and the West Coast. A geographical division is drawn between North and South, the areas administered by separate Committees. (Interestingly, shinty was also played virtually every Saturday in the winter season on Wimbledon Common in London

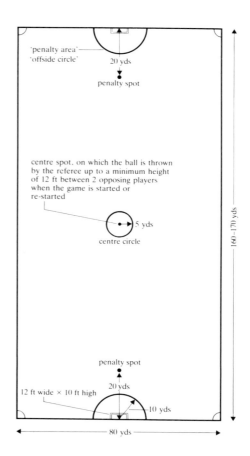

'penalty area'
'offside circle'   20 yds
penalty spot

centre spot, on which the ball is thrown by the referee up to a minimum height of 12 ft between 2 opposing players when the game is started or re-started

5 yds
centre circle

160–170 yds

penalty spot
20 yds
12 ft wide × 10 ft high
10 yds
80 yds

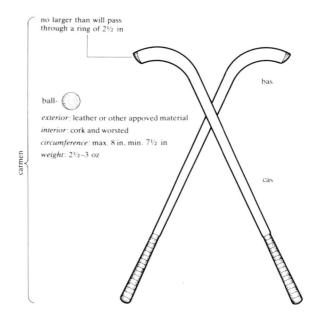

no larger than will pass through a ring of 2½ in

bas

ball-

exterior: leather or other appoved material
interior: cork and worsted
circumference: max. 8 in, min. 7½ in
weight: 2½–3 oz

cas

carmen

A mid-nineteenth-century shinty player.
Grant of Glenmoriston. (From R.R. McIan and J. Logan,
The Clans of the Scottish Highlands vol. vii, London 1847.)

between members of the London Camanachd Club in the 1920s, *Shinty Year Book* 1977–8, 38).

The sport was, until recently, administered by some six separate Associations (for example, the Schools' Camanachd Association, the Referees' Association, Glasgow Celtic Society, which is the sport's oldest established body, formed in 1879), but these are now fully integrated under the umbrella of the ruling body, the Camanachd Association. The playing season is traditionally and historically winter time, with special matches at Christmas or New Year. The modern season extends from August/September to June or July, depending on weather conditions, and culminates in the Camanachd Cup Final, which carries with it the Scottish Championship. The Final was first played for in 1896 and was won by Kingussie, whose near neighbours and rivals Newtonmore

are the record holders of the trophy. The clubs themselves, which often have a strong territorial allegiance, vary in playing strength, some having as many as five or six teams playing at different levels.

Shinty is justly known for the spirit and comradeship with which it is played. (See M. A. N. Caimbeul 1970; A. MacDonald 1924; J. N. MacDonald 1932; M. C. Macqueen *et al* 1939; O Maolfabhail 1973; H. D. MacLennan 1983.)   HDMCL

shrines, *see* sanctuaries, temples, shrines.

Sìleas na Ceapaich (Sìlis Nighean Mhic Raghnaill) (*c.*1660–*c.*1729) This MacDonald poet belongs to the period of transition between the seventeenth and eighteenth centuries. Daughter of Gilleasbuig na Ceapaich (q.v.), she married Alexander Gordon of Camdell, near Tomintoul, about 1685. Her poetry 'shows a good variety of interests and styles' (D. S. Thomson 1974a, 135–36), her best-known themes being the 1715 Rising (S. Maclean 1969, 100) and religion (W. Gillies 1974, 145). Her most famous poems, however, are laments for Alasdair Dubh of Glengarry, who died in 1721 (Atholl 1908, II, 334), and for Lachlann Dall, a harper who probably died in the 1720s (C. Ó Baoill 1972b, 70, 108).   CÓB

Sìlis Nighean Mhic Raghnaill, *see* Sìleas na Ceapaich.

silverwork, *see* arms and armour; metalwork; St Ninian's Isle treasure.

Sinclair, Alexander Maclean (1840–1923) Born Glenbard, Nova Scotia. His mother was a daughter of John Maclean (Bàrd Tighearna Cholla, q.v.). Minister in Pictou, Prince Edward Island, etc. Published book of Maclean history and genealogy and a long succession of anthologies of Gaelic verse – for example *Clàrsach na Coille* (1881), *Glenbard Collection* (1890) *The Gaelic Bards* (1890–6) etc. He frequently altered his sources, but brought much valuable Nova Scotian tradition to bear on his texts.   DST

Sinclair, Revd Allan (1821–88) Free Church minister, Kenmore. Author of book on Dugald Buchanan (A. Sinclair 1875). Ornate gravestone, with zoomorphic and interlace patterns, in Kenmore Churchyard.   DST

Sinclair, Dr Colin (1879–1957) Born Glasgow. Architect, artist and bard. Designed the Highland Clachans for the Glasgow Exhibitions of 1911 and 1938. (See C. Sinclair 1911, 1953; *An Gaidheal*, vol. 52, 121; Murchison 1957.)   TMM

Sinclair, Donald (fl. 1930) From Barra. Playwright and poet; contributor to the literary journal *Guth na Bliadhna*, etc.   DST

Sinclair, Sir John (1754–1835) Of Ulbster Organizer of First Statistical Account of Scotland.   DST

Sinclair, John (fl. 1812) Living in Glasgow at the time, he wrote in 1812–13, in the Gaelic hand, a manuscript which included the Gaelic 'Ossian' with many additional lines of his own. (See D. Mackinnon 1912, 261.)   DST

Sinton, Revd Dr Thomas (1855–1923) From Laggan, Inverness-shire: Minister at Glengarry and Dores. Published *The Poetry of Badenoch* (1906) and papers in *Transactions of the Gaelic Society of Inverness*.   TMM

Skene, William Forbes (1809–92) Born Knoydart. Edinburgh lawyer; Secretary of Relief Committee after the Potato Blight (q.v.). Historiographer Royal, 1881–92. Author of *The Highlanders of Scotland* (1902) and *Celtic Scotland* (1886–90).   DST

Smith, Dr Donald (d. 1805) From Glenorchy, brother of Revd Dr John Smith of Campbeltown (q.v.); surgeon in the Black Watch. Author of the 'Account of the principal manuscripts now in the possession of the Highland Society', *Report* (1805), App. XIX. (See also D. Mackinnon 1912; D. S. Thomson 1958a.)   DST

Smith, Iain Crichton (Mac a' Ghobhainn) (b. 1928) Born and brought up in the island of Lewis. An English Honours graduate of the University of Aberdeen, he was a schoolteacher for many years in Oban, Argyll, where he still lives, now writing full-time. A well-known and prolific writer in English as well as Gaelic, he was awarded the OBE in 1980.

Burn is Aran (*Bread and Water*, 1960) was the first collection of his poems and stories; together with the

Iain Crichton Smith. ▶

short-story collection *An Dubh is an Gorm* (*The Black and the Blue*, 1963) and the collection of poems *Bìobuill is Sanasan-Reice* (*Bibles and Advertisements*, 1963), it helped to establish him as one of the most important Gaelic writers of the post-war period. The distinctive voice which these volumes revealed has remained typical of his work, though there has been considerable development and innovation also.

His prose style is unadorned and straightforward. Its effects are achieved by terseness rather than by richness of texture. The stories are usually designed to reveal the inward world of their characters by establishing the protagonists in stressful situations which they proceed to work out, or by confronting one character with another and letting the confrontation impinge on each of them to reveal his nature and his predicament to us – and sometimes to himself. In these stories problems of communication between the protagonists is an important element. There is little overt plot in the traditional sense, and the movement usually involves progression from one state of realization to another. In addition to these collections two others, *Maighstirean is Ministeirean* (*Masters and Ministers* 1970) and *An t-Adhar Ameireaganach* (*The American Sky*, 1973), have appeared, as well as three short novels *Iain am measg nan Reultan* (*Iain among the Planets*, 1970), *An t-Aonaran* (*The Loner*, 1979) and *Am Bruadraiche* (*The Dreamer*, 1980). Of these *An t-Aonaran* is particularly good.

Smith's poetry has many of the stylistic virtues of his prose: it is neither fussy nor obscure. General philosophical themes and personal psychological ones are explored with insight and enlightenment, as are social themes; the theme of exile, for example, recurs to reveal both its many-sidedness and the narrow vision of it that the Gaelic community often holds. The poet also deals with the 'individual in the middle of his days' with sensitivity and compassion. His latest published poems are *Eadar Fealla-dhà is Glaschu* (*Fun and Glasgow*, 1974). In addition, Smith has written a number of Gaelic plays and has translated Gaelic verse into English – for example, *Poems to Eimhir* (1971). (See I. C. Smith 1979.)　　DMCA

Smith, Revd John (1747–1807) From Glenorchy. Minister in Campbeltown. Author of *Galic Antiquities* (1780), which includes a dissertation on the authenticity of the poems of Ossian and translations of Ossianic poems, and of *Sean Dàna* (1787), a collection of Gaelic Ossianic poems of which he is probably part-author (see D. S. Thomson 1958b, 180 ff.).

Published posthumously *Urnaighean arson Theaghlaichean* (1808), containing also some hymns; he is thought to have seen Duncan MacFadyen's *Spiritual Hymns* (1770) through the press as a Glasgow student. Translator of the fourth volume of the Old Testament (1786). (See *Fasti*, vol. 4, 50; Donald Maclean 1915, 15, 215.)　　DST

Smith, John (1848–81), *see* Mac a' Ghobhainn, Iain.

Smith, Revd Murdo, *see* Mac a' Ghobhainn, Murchadh.

Smith, Revd Dr Roderick (b. 1906) From Lewis. Minister at Lochcarron, Urray, and Edinburgh. Chairman of governors of Highlands and Islands Education Trust. (See R. Smith 1960.)　　TMM

societies, *see* Comunn Gaidhealach, An; Gaelic: language organizations; Gaelic Society of London; Highland Society of Glasgow; Highland Society of London; Highland Society of Scotland; Ladies' Highland Association; Lorn Ossianic Society; Royal Highland and Agricultural Society of Scotland; school societies, Gaelic; societies, learned; societies, territorial.

societies, learned The learned society, in the form in which it is familiar in the UK generally, to a large extent bypassed Gaelic society and Gaelic interests. Organizations such as the British Academy might occasionally feature a lecture on a Gaelic topic, but the field was hardly productive enough to sustain a society. Although the Highland and Agricultural Society began in 1784 with some idea of paying attention to cultural topics, farming interests soon took over. Nor did the Royal Society of Edinburgh, despite its early recognition of the humanities, enter into the Gaelic field.

The first sustained attempt to fill this gap was made by the Gaelic Society of Inverness, which still continues to serve some of the purposes of a learned society. It was founded in 1871, the original movers being William MacKay of Glenurquhart and William Mackenzie (later of the Crofters' Commission), and in its early years the Society had influential support from Charles Fraser Mackintosh, Professor Blackie and many others (Mairi A. MacDonald 1971). The work of the Society included regular meetings at which papers were read on historical, linguistic, literary, and antiquarian topics; the gradual acquisition of a Society library; the holding of annual dinners at which reviews of Highland topics were given in toasts; the restoration of Culloden memorials and, above all, the publication of *Transactions*.

The *Transactions* first appeared in 1872; it was not practical to publish an annual volume, but by the time that volume 50 appeared in 1979 the *Transactions* had seen the first publication of a large number of important contributions to learning – for example, papers by Alexander MacBain on the Norse element in Highland place names, by William MacKay on the history of Urquhart and Glenmoriston, by W. J. Watson on Classic Gaelic poetry of panegyric in Scotland. Watson served for long as Honorary Secretary, writing valuable annual reviews. The *Transactions* still attract a high proportion of important and original contributions to Gaelic scholarship. Meetings are not largely attended now, but the worldwide membership of the Society is maintained through the publication. (For details of chiefs, etc., *see* Màiri A. MacDonald 1971; for an index of volumes 1 to 34, *see* A. N. Nicolson 1935).

The achievement of the Gaelic Society of Glasgow is much more modest. It was founded in 1887; among those present at the inaugural meeting were Magnus Maclean, Malcolm MacFarlane, Archibald Sinclair and Henry Whyte. It published five volumes of *Transactions* between 1891 and 1958.

Perhaps fitting most closely the title of learned society is the Scottish Gaelic Texts Society, founded in 1934, the instigators of the Society being W. J. Watson and Fred T. Macleod. Successive Presidents have been Watson, Angus MacLeod, Angus Matheson and D. S. Thomson. Including the first publication in 1937 (Watson's *Scottish Verse from the Book of the Dean*), fifteen volumes have been published to date, providing in most cases definitive editions of the work of a range of Gaelic writers: John MacCodrum, the authors of heroic ballads in the Book of the Dean of Lismore, Donnchadh Bàn, Donald Mackinnon, Donald Lamont, Sìleas na Ceapaich, Mary MacLeod, Iain Lom, Dòmhnall Mac an t-Saoir, An Clàrsair Dall, and Eachann Bacach and other Maclean poets, together with editions of Carswell's Liturgy and the Gaelic version of Calvin's Catechism. Further works are in preparation.   DST

societies, territorial The Scottish Gael has long been noted for his clannishness. Wherever two or three Gaels foregather among aliens, there a society is formed – Highland, Gaelic, Caledonian, clan (the name is of little account; the aim is fellowship and the binding force a common loyalty). Of a special kind, crossing the divisions of clan and creed, are the territorial societies, long active in Glasgow, but also to some extent in Edinburgh, London and elsewhere. The city Gael finds himself living in two worlds – on the one hand, the world of his home, and Gaelic Church, and whatever Highland or Gaelic or clan or district Society he joins; on the other hand, the workaday world among neighbours and fellow workers whose native tongue is not Gaelic.

With the growth of industry in the nineteenth century, when economic deprivation was forcing thousands to quit their native districts for the south, Glasgow and Clydeside came to have a very large population of Gaels. Gaelic churches were provided, and they themselves, for mutual aid and fellowship, set about founding their territorial associations – 'The natives of – resident in Glasgow'.

The Scots Year Book, founded in 1905 by T. Atholl Robertson and edited by him until his death in 1955, lists many kinds of society throughout the world (Robertson 1905–55), and Neil Shaw listed many societies in Glasgow and its neighbourhood in 1920–1 (N. Shaw 1920). The following list (not necessarily complete) indicates the number and range of these societies in Glasgow, many of them still active: Glasgow Kintyre Society (founded 1825), Caithness (1836), Perthshire (1836), Arran (1843), Argyllshire (1851), Sutherland (1857). In the 1860s and after began the Islay, Cowal, Skye, Inverness-shire, Mull and Iona, Lochaber, Nairnshire, Ross and Cromarty, Lewis and Harris, Uist and Barra, Oban and Lorn, Jura, Tiree, Gairloch and Lochbroom, Wester Ross, North Uist and Bernera, Coll, Morvern, Mid-Argyll and others.

The great event for each was the Annual Gathering, at first called a 'Soiree' (pronounced 'Soo-ar-ee'), later to become more sophisticated, with a Grand Concert, and a Grand Dance opening with a Grand March. The year's programme included *céilidhs*, lectures and outings. The Glasgow Gaels supported each other's societies and especially the Annual Gatherings. They gave aid to their people in need and took an interest in the welfare of their home area. During the nineteenth century and again in the twentieth they joined together in a Federation of Highland Societies in support of common interests and for the benefit of the Highlands and Islands. They were usually affiliated to An Comunn

Gaidhealach (q.v.) and helped greatly with its money-raising schemes. Some had literary societies attached to them, and some supported shinty clubs – Glasgow Cowal, Glasgow Skye, Glasgow Mid-Argyll, etc. For many years their chief meeting-place was the Highlanders Institute (opened in 1925 but now defunct), but the great Annual Gatherings of the larger associations could be housed only in the city's largest public halls.   TMM

soldiers, Highland The seventeenth-century description of Highlanders as 'a people much given to fightinge and quareling and sudden murders' (James, 1953, 51) is justified by traditional song and story and by the evidence of official records. We know relatively little, save the results, of the clan battles, but it can be surmised that it was in those that the fighting men developed their supreme qualities – their devastating charge and their ability to create carnage at close quarters.

The Highlander is less often thought of as a soldier in an organized fighting force. Before Bannockburn, however, there had begun what was to be the way of life for many Islesmen for three centuries, service as mercenaries in Ireland, where they were known as 'gallowglasses' or 'foreign young warriors'; their successors, as the 'new Scots', opposed the English in Elizabeth's Irish wars (Hayes McCoy 1937). In the same way central and eastern Highlanders distinguished themselves in the European wars of the sixteenth and seventeenth centuries. Men from the Highlands were called upon by the Scottish state to do duty in the army at Bannockburn and Flodden; Huntly's Highlanders and Scots-Irish under Colkitto were Montrose's shock troops in his wonderful year (1645), and in 1678 the Government used Highland levies in a very different way, as the 'Highland Host' which overawed the Covenanters of the south-west (Elder 1914). Killiecrankie (1689), Sheriffmuir (1715) and the last battles fought by Charles's army showed Highland troops at their best and at their worst, much depending on the quality of their leadership. (See also **regiments, Highland**.)   SM

Effigy of Bricius (Gilbride, Gille-Brigde) MacKinnon, ▶
Iona abbey museum. The inscription on the pillow commemorates Bricius (who may have fought at Bannockburn) and his two sons. The type of armour and sword suggest that the effigy was carved during the mid or late fourteenth century, some time after Bricius's death. It belongs to the high period of Scottish momumental sculpture (see pp. 264–5).

Somerled Gaelic tradition is unanimous in ascribing the creation of the political entity later known as the Lordship of the Isles to Somerled (d. 1164). He was apparently descended from Gofraid, son of Fergus, supporter of Kenneth mac Alpín (d. 858) and leader of the Northern Uí Mace Uais settled in the Hebrides at least as early as the seventh century. Somerled began his successful offensive against Norse overlordship in Argyll, and he was probably leader of a contingent from there in the army of David I that invaded England in 1138. He supported an unsuccessful rebellion by his nephews, the sons of Malcolm MacHeth, immediately following the accession of Malcolm IV in 1153 as a minor and contrary to the rules of tanistry. He then turned to the recovery of the Hebrides ruled by the king of Man under Norse suzerainty which he probably regarded as his ancestral homeland. In 1156 and again in 1158 he defeated the king of Man, who fled to Norway. From his Gaelic title, *Rí Innse Gall* (King of the Hebrides), borne also by his successors, derives the Latin *Dominus Insularum* (Lord of the Isles), first recorded in 1354. Somerled was killed near Renfrew in 1164, having led another rebellion against Malcolm IV (Duncan 1975, 116–17; Sellar 1966, 123–42; Steer and Bannerman 1977, 201–2.)   JWMB

song, Gaelic As with any other national body of song, there can be two fairly distinct approaches to the study of Gaelic songs, the folk-orientated and that of the professional singer.

Folk-orientated study concentrates on getting its material 'live'. In its purest form that entails going right back to performers who were untouched by other outside traditions and the influences of musical development. Ideally, one would tap that tradition as it was (preferably pre-gramophone era) and try to assimilate, and then to continue, the wonderful honing that centuries of singers must have contributed to Gaelic songs, especially in a work context. Today such study can best be undertaken by making extensive use of the purest recordings available, both commercially and from archives (for example, those of the School of Scottish Studies and BBC Gaelic Department).

This approach has positive advantages. It is useful for comparative purposes; it also presents any song as a live entity and helps to cut corners in the learning process. Again, Gaelic folk groups such as Run Rig and the earlier notable Na h-Oganaich have made successful use particularly of some of the waulking-song material to try to generate a modern folk idiom which yet has native roots. One positive disadvantage is that this approach can lead to a more or less passive acceptance of a tradition and to a tendency to place too strong a reliance on recordings as being 'definitive'. Preservation of songs by recordings for study purposes by scholars, musicologists, students and singers is, of course, essential; but the conscious propagation of such material, as if both words and music were sacrosanct, in effect freezes any song unnaturally. This aspect is of particular concern to dedicated singers and others interested in the quality of Gaelic song performance and development. It has been highlighted for some years now by the growing shoals of singers performing the same 'stereotaped' *authentic traditional version* of certain songs.

The second approach, via the concentrated study of words and music and of every conceivable piece of information connected with both, does not preclude listening to recordings. A singer will then fuse this study with his or her own vocal technique to project an individual performance – an active process which can be enriching. This active approach is ideal for the study of the intricate and difficult songs which have come to be called *òrain mhòra* (literally 'great songs'). There is dubiety and disagreement about the name as a title for this class of songs, and it may have arisen almost accidentally from the titling of the harpist poet An Clàrsair Dall's (q.v.) 'Oran Mòr MhicLeòid' (*see*, e.g., W. Matheson 1970, 131). Some of the songs too may have had musical links with one side of the clàrsach (q.v.) tradition, and although the tune of An Clàrsair Dall's own 'Oran Mòr MhicLeòid' limits itself to a one-octave range, most of the tunes, whether in major or minor key, tend to range over one and a half octaves. They also have varying degrees of grace-note embellishment. In modern usage, too, the name does not simply define a metrical type, although as a form it does have affiliations with an older historical song form, the one known as *òran*. To some extent too the usage *òran mòr* has been imposed by the National Mod, usually on songs composed of eight-line stanzas, many of them by seventeenth- and eighteenth-century bards in praise of chiefs or clans. The following list is a representative selection to add to 'Oran Mòr MhicLeòid': 'Alasdair a Gleanna Garadh', 'Iain Caimbeul a' Bhanca', 'Murt na Ceapaich', 'Cumha Alasdair Dhuinn', 'Se mo bheachd ort a bhàis', 'Murt Ghlinne Comhann'. The authors of all these songs, and of many others which have been prescribed for the Mod *òran mòr* competition, are known, and most of the tunes have been recovered from traditional sources.

In addition there are other songs that fit into the classification but are anonymous, like 'An Gille Dubh Ciar Dubh' and 'Iain Ghlinn Cuaich'. The song 'Dòmhnall nan Dòmhnall' is something of a special case, as it is known only from the Kennedy Fraser (q.v.) song collection: it was recorded from Kirsty MacKinnon of Eigg. Donnchadh Ban's 'Moladh Beinn Dobhrain' and Rob Donn's 'Iseabail Nic Aoidh' are generally regarded as belonging to this category, although they do not have the metrical structure normally associated with it. One song which does, but has a modern tune composed by John Mac-Donald of Oban, is Donald Maciver's popular *'An Ataireachd Ard'*, which won a poetry prize at the National Mod in 1905 and seems to be becoming assimilated into this category.

For almost a century too this distinction in song-types has been recognized in the practice of their art by singers such as Roderick MacLeod and Margaret Duncan and, nearer our own time, most of all by James C. M. Campbell, a dedicated singer whose conscious learning of operatic and other demanding songs contributed to his masterly performance in this type of song.

The distinction was also certainly recognized by the setting up of special *òran mòr* competitions at the National Mod. (These are compulsory preliminary competitions of prescribed songs for the Men's and Women's Mod Gold Medals.) This was a visionary early innovation which has not only helped to bestow this title, and thus helps to define the genre, but has also had the interesting side-effect of developing the tradition of a class of Gaelic songs which invites technical and interpretative skills more often associated with *lieder* or *chansons*. Above all, these *òran mòr*

'Wool Waulking' by Keith Henderson. c. 1927–8.

competitions have helped to preserve the songs, since folklore enthusiasts have always tended to concentrate on other types of Gaelic song.

Whatever might have been the case in the long-distant past, the name *òran mòr*, which exists now and has done for most of this century, has long been recognized by singers as referring to a song of a particular type belonging to the class *òrain mhòra*. This is in a sense also a modern art form, with a defined persona of its own, which is worth developing and has a small but reasonably sophisticated following.

CG

songs, waulking, metres of The prosody of waulking-song metres is exceedingly complicated, involving as it does a variety of relationships between textual statement and refrain. The following note gives only an outline of some distinctive forms; for detailed discussion with examples, the reader is referred to the bibliography.

There are two approaches to the problem of analysing the metres. The first takes the song as it is actually sung at a waulking and accepts that the metrical unit is as given during the performance. The alternative approach seeks to reconstruct an original metrical form which has been altered for the purposes of accompanying communal labour. These approaches converge when exponents of both speak of the 'half-lines' in which certain types of waulking song are sung. This involves a reconstruction which gives a different pattern from that of the song as actually performed.

All waulking songs are characterized by refrains, which are composed of meaningless vocables, or a mixture of vocables and words, or of words alone. The last category does not appear to be old: most examples are no earlier than the eighteenth century. In one subdivision refrains precede the text as well as following it. This, however, is not to be confused with the singing of a refrain in order to begin the performance. Thus:

> *Hó na fileabhaig*   *bha mi latha*
> or: *Héman dubh*   *is truagh nach digeadh*

Usually another refrain is introduced after each section of four such textual units. In this particular class the units are clearly half-lines: often the refrain interrupts the sense, which becomes clear only when the two half-lines are combined. Even a name or patronymic may be interrupted in this manner. Half-lines are also found in other subdivisions of the waulking-song corpus.

The majority of the surviving body of waulking-songs are sung in single lines or couplets. The line may be followed by a refrain, and this pattern is sustained throughout the song; or the line is followed by a refrain, then repeated to a different melody followed by a second refrain.

Songs sung in couplets are also followed by a refrain. These fall into two groups: those in which the couplet is self-contained and is not repeated, and those in which the second line of the couplet is repeated to form the first line of the following couplet.

Certain songs which are sung in single lines, or in couplets in which a line is repeated to form the following couplet, can be reconstructed on the basis of rhyme to show a different metrical structure. The stanzaic units then become verse paragraphs of variable length – for example, a sequence of seven, three and five lines. This has given rise to a theory that posits the existence of such a poetic form in Gaelic literature in the past. It is true that songs from other metrical traditions have been assimilated to waulking-song metres and modified accordingly; these include heroic ballads. It is significant, however, that outside the waulking-song tradition no trace remains in Gaelic poetry of the paragraphic type described above. Further analysis is necessary before such problems are resolved. (See J. L. Campbell 1956b, 1958c; J. L. Campbell and Collinson 1969, 1977; J. Ross 1955/6, 1957a.)

JMcI

Souterrains Stone-built underground chambers, constructed in a variety of forms and for different (and often disputed) purposes, in Ireland, parts of western and northern Britain and Brittany throughout the last few centuries BC and much of the first millennium AD (Thomas 1972b).

A highly distinctive group of massive souterrains was built in Angus by the immediate ancestors of the historical Picts (Wainwright 1963). Some of these were demolished in Pictish times, but others remained in use (not, as Wainwright suggested, as cattle byres, but as cold stores). They formed, in fact, capacious cellars to normal peasant houses of stone or timber (Alcock 1980, 68–9).

In Ireland souterrains are frequently found in forts. They have defensive features, such as narrow entrances, and internal traps and undoubtedly served as places of refuge (Ó Ríordáin 1942; 1977, 65–73).

Ardestie souterrain, Tayside, showing the corbelling of the side walls, the central drain and the complex entrance.

The little-known souterrains of Caithness appear closer to the Irish than to the Angus examples.   LA

Stewart, Revd Alexander (1764–1821) Born Blair Atholl; minister at Moulin, Dingwall, Canongate. Revised Gaelic translation of Bible for the Society in Scotland for the Propagation of Christian Knowledge. Author of *Elements of Gaelic Grammar* (1801; revised and enlarged edn 1812).   DST

Stewart, Alexander (fl. 1804) From North Uist. Schoolmaster and compiler, with his brother, Donald, of a collection of poetry (1804) which, though in itself a primary source, is related to earlier collections (e.g. Stone, Eigg). Composed for Maria, daughter of the Revd Allan MacQueen, a song entitled 'A Mhàiri ghaolach'.   JMCI

Stewart, Revd Dr Alexander (1829–1901) Born Benbecula. Used 'Nether Lochaber' as pen-name; author of antiquarian essays and translations of poetry. (See M. C. MacLeod 1913.)   DST

Stewart, Alexander (1853–1941) From Glenlyon. Author of *A Highland Parish* (i.e. Fortingall) (1928).   DST

Stewart, Daniel (1741–1814) From Strathtay. Founded 'Free School' in Strathtay and Daniel Stewart's College, Edinburgh.   DST

Stewart, Donald (fl. 1804) From North Uist. Brother of Alexander (q.v.), with whom he compiled a collection of poetry.   JMCI

Stewart, Revd James (1700–89) Born Glenfinlas; graduate of University of St Andrews; minister of Killin, 1737–89. Translated the New Testament from Greek into Gaelic, published by the Society in Scotland for the Propagation of Christian Knowledge in 1767. His own corrections, taken from his interleaved copy, were incorporated in the revision undertaken by his son, Revd John Stuart (q.v.) of Luss. (See Donald MacKinnon 1930, 54–9.)   DST

Stewart, Sir John (late sixteenth century) Of Appin. Has two poems in the Fernaig Manuscript (q.v.) on religious themes, one embellished with nature imagery.   DST

Stewart, John Roy, *see* Stiùbhard, Iain Ruadh.

Stewart-Murray, Lady Evelyn (1868–1940) Third daughter of the seventh Duke of Atholl. In 1891 she recorded an important collection of 240 Gaelic folktales, legends and songs from many parts of west Perthshire; the mainly unpublished manuscripts are now in the School of Scottish Studies (q.v.). (See *Scottish Studies*, vol. 9, 1965, 153.)   AB

Stiùbhard, Iain Ruadh (John Roy Stewart) (1700–1752) Born Badenoch. Quartermaster, Scots Greys; arrested as spy; escaped to France; fought against British at Fontenoy; commanded Edinburgh regiment for Prince Charles; returned to France with Prince. Only a few poems of his survive, including a rueful song about a brandy spree, and two versions of John Roy's Psalm (English). He is remembered mainly for three post-Culloden poems, 'Latha Chuillodair' expressing vividly his pride and chagrin. (See J. L. Campbell 1933; Sinton 1906; E. E. Mackechnie 1947.)   DST

Stock-rearing Stock-rearing is a vital and characteristic component of Highland agriculture. Livestock and livestock products account for some nine-tenths of the value of total output in the region, and 'store' cattle and sheep sold to farmers outwith the region for fattening and finishing account for just under half of all livestock and livestock product output. Towards the geographical periphery of the region, and in the least environmentally favoured areas, the proportion of output from stock-rearing increases. Stock-rearing is therefore a key component in the survival, not to say progress, of these remoter and more difficult areas. Technological and policy changes which affect the system and viability of stock-rearing in the Highlands are thus of great economic, social and political significance.

In the period up to the eighteenth century stock-rearing in the area was affected by the predominantly small-scale and subsistence nature of agriculture and by the physical and other difficulties of trade. Goats were common as domestic animals; sheep were fewer in number and probably had more in common with the Soay, Shetland or North Ronaldsay breeds than with either the Blackface or the Cheviot. Cattle were small and slow-maturing, although apparently relatively numerous. Trade – legal or illegal – there certainly was, particularly in cattle which could be moved on foot over the drove roads, and evidence of trade in animals, hides and goat skins goes back to at least the twelfth century (Haldane 1952).

Great changes occurred during the eighteenth and nineteenth centuries, when land and people were 'cleared' to make way for the Cheviot and Blackface sheep and the technology associated with them. At the same time changes were occurring in cattle-breeding, originating from the selective in-breeding practised by Robert Bakewell (1726–95) (A. H. H. Fraser 1953; Symon 1959) and leading to increased specialization in cattle-breeding. Although of less social and economic significance initially than the changes in sheep-breeding and husbandry, the development of the Shorthorn and Aberdeen Angus breeds in particular were to have important effects on commercial cattle breeding in the region.

The nineteenth-century expansion of sheep and, to a lesser extent, cattle farming in the Highlands had stopped by the end of the century. Technological changes had by then enabled frozen meat and, of course, wool to be imported at rapidly declining cost from abroad. Free-trade policies were in Britain's interest, and while this favoured rapid industrial development, the livestock industry suffered. For economic and, some would say, ecological reasons, the twentieth century has seen a decline in sheep and cattle numbers in the Highlands and Islands, and although productivity is difficult to measure from available statistics, there is little sign of marked improvements in physical productivity of stock, and some evidence of deterioration over this period (Bryden and Houston 1976; Darling 1955). No doubt

A reconstructed Highland cattle drove between 'Bridge of Balgie' and Killin, Perthshire, 1982.

the situation would be even worse were it not for the introduction of the Hill Farming Acts in 1946, and the subsequent extension of various schemes of support for hill farming and for crofting (q.v.).

The pattern of sheep husbandry introduced during the nineteenth century has changed little to the present day. It is based on pure bred flocks, predominantly of Blackface south of Sutherland and Cheviot in Sutherland, Caithness and, to a lesser extent, Orkney. Only Shetland has remained to any degree impervious, with its large – if now somewhat diluted – native Shetland flock. The surplus ewe lambs from these flocks were sold to farmers in more fertile areas for cross-breeding with heavier breeds such as the Border Leicester or Suffolks, while surplus ram lambs were castrated and sold for feeding and finishing elsewhere.

Cattle present a more complex picture, partly because of the varying influence of increasingly specialized dairy herds (mainly in the Moray Firth, Caithness, Orkney, and the peninsula of Kintyre) and partly because of environmental and geographical differences. In the west, Highland cattle, originating from the native cattle, formed a vital part of the breeding chain, with their ability to survive in harsh environmental and feeding regimes. Cross-breeding, particularly with the Shorthorn, provided female breeding stock of earlier maturity, good mothering ability and the capacity to cross well with the finer beef breeds, such as the Aberdeen Angus and Hereford, in more fertile areas. Many believe that this particular chain represented the apogee of the West Highland cattle trade, and attempts have been made both to 'fix' the advantages of the Highland–Shorthorn cross by in-breeding (most recently by the Cadzow brothers with their Luing breed) and to reintroduce milkier strains of Shorthorn into the breeding herds of the Uists and Mull (through the Heifer Production Scheme introduced by the Highlands and Islands Development Board in 1977). In the more favoured areas of the north and east, from Speyside to Orkney, where in-wintering of stock is common, the Aberdeen Angus, Galloway and Hereford provide the mainstay of the beef breeding stock. Such generalizations, however, are increasingly hard to make; the widespread introduction of artificial insemination has led to considerable heterogeneity in the cattle-rearing scene in the Highlands, as elsewhere, and the so-called exotic breeds, particularly the Charolais and Simmental, are in increasing evidence in a complex cross-breeding picture that seems to fly in the face of the earlier revolution in selective in-breeding, and will doubtless have equally profound effects.

With both cattle and sheep there has been a healthy realization that 'half the breeding goes in through the mouth' and that there are breeds and strains of breeds that suit particular environments and systems. The work of the Hill Farming Research Organization (HFRO 1979) and the three Scottish Colleges of Agriculture has been particularly important in this regard, although much remains to be done both to implement research and to provide the climate of confidence among producers which will enable the necessary improvements to be made. JMB

stone circles Circles of standing stones are common throughout the upland regions of Britain and Ireland, including many areas of Scotland (a comprehensive survey, with full references is in Burl 1976). They are the visible remains of cults and ceremonials involving circles of stones and of wooden posts, circular embanked areas and round cairns and barrows that were widespread during the later third and much of the second millennia BC. The several elements may be variously combined: thus on Orkney, at Broggar and at Stenness, a ring of stones is enclosed by a circular bank and ditch; while east of Inverness, in the Clava group, rings of stone enclose circular tombs. Burials are frequently found within or beside the stone circles, perhaps as part of a dedicatory ritual. In other cases the whole monument appears to be dedicated to funerary purposes.

Outstanding among Scottish circles is that at Callanish on the west coast of Lewis (Ponting 1977). Indeed, it was first made widely known by Martin's plan and description in 1695. The central feature is an exceptionally tall, slender stone, set at the rear of a small circular tomb, which itself is eccentric to the main circle of thirteen tall stones. Leading off from the circle are four stone rows, aligned roughly north, south, east and west. That leading north is certainly a double row or avenue, and the other three may originally have been double.

As is the case at all other stone circles except for Stonehenge, the Callanish stones have not been dressed to shape. It is evident, none the less, that natural pillars of Lewissean gneiss have been very carefully selected for their banded colours and sinuous profiles. The visual impact of the monument is greatly enhanced by its siting on a ridge, visible from many of the neighbouring headlands and inlets. There are other important stone rows and circles in

The stone circle and alignments at Callanish, Lewis.

the vicinity, though none is as elaborate or spectacular as Callanish itself (University of Glasgow, Department of Geography 1978). Evidently the area was one of great ritual significance around 2000 BC.

It has been claimed that stone circles were laid out, with elaborate geometric constructions, in terms of a specific unit, the megalithic yard. The major and minor axes of these constructions were aligned on heavenly phenomena, including minor long-term variations in the setting of the moon. More detailed statistical analysis, however, now regards the megalithic yard as unproven and considers that a more likely unit was the human pace. Moreover, recent fieldwork has further undermined the credibility of most of the alleged astronomical alignments. Despite this, it is reasonable to claim that a minority of circles are laid out in relation to a major heavenly event, notably sunrise or sunset at the midsummer or midwinter solstice. The purpose of such solar orientations may not have been simple sun worship, but the need, in early agricultural communities, to establish a fixed calendar for the regulation of the farming year.

LA

Stone of Destiny, recovery of The Stone, at one time used in the coronation ceremony of the kings of Scotland, and removed to England by Edward I in 1296, was recovered from Westminster Abbey on Christmas Day 1950. Several weeks later a stone (often said to be a replica) was returned to the authorities. One of the party involved was Kay Matheson of Inverasdale, Wester Ross. Hilarious songs on the incident were made by John MacDonald of Highbridge, Lochaber, and Donald Macintyre (q.v.) of Paisley.

DST

stories, short The short story, in the broadest sense of the term, has long had a secure place in Gaelic literature. The sagas of medieval Gaelic bear testimony to this at a high cultural level. These sagas – the best of which, even when they are anonymous, are clearly the compositions of authors of great literary skill – circulated in manuscript and were transliterated from classical Gaelic into the vernacular in which they flourished orally, in some areas until quite recently. Much commoner, and of purely oral origin, are the short fictional narratives based on historical events. Gaelic writers have frequently modelled their stories on these and other realistic tales.

In the more limited sense the short story is a modern phenomenon with origins that go back little more than a hundred years. It has been greatly developed in that time and is now probably the most

Callanish, Lewis, the tall central stones.

popular literary form in Gaelic. This is due in large measure to the opportunities afforded by the literary journal *Gairm*, Gaelic radio producers and, to a lesser degree, literary prizes offered by An Comunn Gaidhealach (q.v.).

As the product of a bilingual community and bicultural sensibility, the short story is to some extent a borrowed form, influenced by English writing, to some extent a native growth. Individual Gaelic writers vary a good deal in this respect. Those who tend to be labelled traditional writers are regarded as favouring the techniques of oral storytelling while those who make use of techniques developed in English writing are regarded as innovators. In reality the situation is much more complex. What is traditional in Gaelic prose, not only in the short story, derives from the *written* tradition of the nineteenth century, which established a formal register of the language as a standard for expository and didactic purposes. This style had a profound and, on the whole, deleterious influence on creative writing. Oral narrative has its own formalities and variety of styles but Gaelic storytelling is invariably vivid: a dull storyteller soon loses his audience.

It has been argued that in those areas in which the *sgeulachd* (traditional story) has flourished best the modern short story is correspondingly weakest. There is some truth in this, but it is doubtful whether there is any direct causal connection. Modern Gaelic literature has its origins in parts of the Gàidhealtachd (including urban communities, especially in Glasgow) in which relatively high literacy was combined with traditions of radical, nonconformist and secular dissent. In such parts medieval romances and the like did not thrive. Their survival in more conservative areas is generally symptomatic of underlying social and cultural factors. This means that from the modern writer's point of view there is no evidence that the mere existence, or even popularity, of storytelling has inhibited the growth of the short story. In any event, every native speaking writer comes from a community in which the art of storytelling is developed to a very high degree. Nowadays the stories are not 'folktales' as that term is generally understood but naturalistic tales based on recent or contemporary characters or events. There are tragic stories of loss at sea, for example; tales of the supernatural; comic tales; anecdotes of wit, repartee, bawdiness; and vivid impressionistic description. Some of the styles are, of course, implicit in the structure of Gaelic itself, but beyond that few writers have drawn boldly upon this heritage and fewer still have succeeded in transferring its liveliness to the written page.

This is very marked in the first phase of the short story, which extends from about 1880 to 1938. Writers such as John MaFadyen, Neil MacLeod, K. W. Grant, John MacCormick, John Whyte and their immediate successors were concerned, as they looked back, usually from city residences, to their native townships, to project an image of propriety. This was natural at a time when there was still a great deal of anti-Gaelic prejudice in the country, but the defensive attitude had a reductive effect on their art. All these writers used oral tales or modelled original stories upon them, but retellings and originals alike all tend to divert creative exhuberance into more formal channels. (A useful contrast can be drawn between any of these tales and Derick Thomson's 'Bean a' Mhinisteir' (1970), which is based on a local story but recreated with conspicuous success in the written tradition.) At the same time, plots are usually well constructed and the language often colloquial. The popularity of this kind of literature is evident from the fact that some of the stories made their way back into the oral repertoire.

A rather unexpected influence, that of contemporary music-hall, is also recorded. This is clear in the work of MacFadyen and, in the Hebrides, where especially in Lewis a sort of local music-hall tradition developed, in the stories of Donald MacDonald, the bard of Barvas. It was precisely to rid Gaelic of this influence and the pernicious effects of 'peasant origins' that the Hon. Ruaraidh Erskine of Mar (q.v.) founded, edited or was otherwise associated with a succession of periodicals from 1901 to 1930. Erskine wanted to raise Gaelic to a metropolitan level. In the field of the short story he encouraged writers such as John MacCormick, Hector MacDougall, John N. MacLeod, Donald Sinclair and others, while he himself broke new ground with his series of detective stories. Of these the most important, and certainly the most prolific, was MacCormick, who published four collections. He was a careful craftsman with an elegant, highly polished style, and his adventure stories still make enjoyable reading. Nevertheless, most of the writers who contributed to Erskine's periodicals remained 'traditional' in the sense defined above; although Donald Sinclair's finely written 'Lughain Lir' is unique because of its use of religious symbolism.

From 1930, when the periodical *An Ròsarnach* came to an end, there are largely blank years until

1944, when the first issue of Portree High School's Gaelic magazine *An Cabairneach* appeared. The presiding genius of this venture was the Gaelic master, John Steele. Finlay J. MacDonald, Winnie Young, Paul MacInnes *et al.* introduced, as adolescents, an easy colloquial style and a vital, irreverent tone which have never deserted the genre. In 1952 Derick Thomson and Finlay J. MacDonald founded *Gairm*, thereby providing the single most important outlet for the short story since 1930, with BBC radio in a complementary role. The growth of cultural nationalism and the spread of Gaelic literacy had prepared potential writers; in the early 1950s stories such as John MacArthur's 'Mo Cheud Ghràdh', written in flexible colloquial Gaelic of an idiomatic simplicity, prefigured the main stylistic trend. By 1971 the editor of *Gairm* reported that a corpus of stories now existed which were 'humorous, satirical, sentimental, whimsical, psychological, atmospheric and off-beat' (D. S. Thomson 1971, 87). These exhibit the full range of techniques that characterize the form elsewhere. Some writers have tended to specialize: for instance, Eilidh Watt has published collections for children and young people, and D. J. MacIver's stories explore the paranormal. A number of anthologies have appeared – D. J. MacLeod (ed.), *Dorcha tro Ghlainne* (1970); K. MacDonald (ed.), *Briseadh na Cloiche* (1970); D. MacQuarrie (ed.), *Mun Cuairt an Cagailte* (1972); and *Amannan* (1979). Mary Maclean, Iain MacLeod and John Murray have each published one collection; Colin MacKenzie and Iain Crichton Smith three and four respectively. Smith and MacKenzie are usually cast in antithetical roles, MacKenzie in the part of traditional writer, Smith in that of the cosmopolitan. This is not an unfair assessment, although in fact both writers experiment and range widely for their themes. MacKenzie is an inventive author who has written space fiction, tales of mystery and detective stories as well as 'traditional' stories. The vitality of Smith's dialogue is often reminiscent of the dialogue in oral tales; it is properly traditional but in the sense that the inert formalities of nineteenth-century and later prose have been completely bypassed. Smith has brought to Gaelic prose a simplicity, almost an innocence, of style: it is one of the marks of his subtle craftsmanship. He has also assimilated with great skill a range of sophisticated techniques borrowed from other literatures. John Murray's world is outwardly more confined, almost all of his stories being specifically about Gaels, some in an urban setting, others in the Hebrides. Murray uses various techniques of modern writing to produce stories of great delicateness and perception. He is very much aware of the resources of his heritage of storytelling and in command of it: without any paradox he is able to be traditional (in the full sense) and avant-garde at the same time.

The short story is still developing in Gaelic and writers who have learned the language, such as Gordon Donald, Robert Shirley, and Duncan MacLaren are contributing to that development.

JMCI

storytelling Gaelic society in both Scotland and Ireland continued to provide a fertile environment for oral tradition right down to modern times. This is nowhere more evident than in their shared heritage of storytelling, widely acknowledged as being among the most remarkable in the world for its quality and diversity. For centuries the classical literature of the learned orders of bards and seanchaidhs (oral historians) – itself very much orally and traditionally orientated – had coexisted with a rich stream of popular lore, each of them constantly informing and enriching the other. The collapse of the old aristocratic social order in the seventeenth and eighteenth centuries meant that the educated élite, which had depended for its existence on the patronage of the Gaelic-speaking nobility, now became reduced to the ranks of the ordinary people. This resulted in a further enrichment and stimulation of the oral literature. The remnants and descendants of the scholarly classes brought with them, to their new and less exalted audiences, some of their learning and, indeed, some of their manuscript compendia of tales, history and poetry. Leaving aside the Irish evidence, the MacMhuirichs (q.v.) provide an interesting case in point in Scotland. (For a fascinating account of Irish storytelling and further references, see Delargy 1945, *passim*.) In short, it is probably due to the influence of the old scholars that examples of romances such as 'Fear na h-Eabaide', 'Conall Gulbann', 'An Ceatharnach Caol Riabhach' (q.v. all) survived to be collected from oral tradition in the 1950s, 1960s and 1970s.

The problem of relationships between written and oral materials is one of considerable complexity. Questions such as these, and other related matters, are admirably dealt with by Alan Bruford in his *Gaelic Folk Tales and Mediaeval Romances* (1969).

The fact that romantic hero tales found in manuscripts were composed or dressed up for the entertainment of noble patrons does not mean that oral versions of these same stories, which have reached the present day, are necessarily inferior to the written ones: the talents and artistry of generations of 'illiterate' seanchaidhs have sometimes resulted in versions that are demonstrably better than their manuscript exemplars.

As to actual performance, it is difficult for anyone who has experienced real storytelling to imagine how a tale read aloud from a manuscript could be as effective as some of the tellings we have heard in our own day. Storytelling at its best is very much a visual and dramatic art: one is tempted to wonder whether the 'readings' given by the professionals of former times may not often have been basically oral tellings, relying on the seanchaidh's memory of the text and using the manuscript or book rather as an *aide-mémoire* or even as a dramatic prop – to be flourished, glanced at, used as an object of prestige to stress his literacy and authority.

Whatever may be the ultimate facts in such matters, it is certainly indisputable that romantic hero tales of medieval and post-medieval origin, such as the three mentioned above, along with the earlier heroic tradition of the Ulster and Fenian cycles (see **tales, heroic**) and some of the great international tales (q.v.), supplied the most highly prized aspects of the Gaelic storyteller's stock-in-trade. It was on these prestigious categories that the best performers concentrated their memories and lavished the best of their remarkable skills. It is here that one is most likely to find the 'curious, impassioned and sentimental language' referred to by J. F. Campbell (q.v.) (1890, 22; see also Introduction, *passim*) and the ornate archaistic runs that were so much a feature of both oral and manuscript texts. (For some further points on typical repertoires, see **legends, historical; legends, supernatural; novel, the Gaelic; tales, heroic; tales, international; tales, romantic**.)

One constantly hears of astonishing feats of memory: it was not unusual for a practised seanchaidh, even in recent times; to be able to memorize long and complex tales at one hearing. The importance of telling a tale oneself, as soon as possible after first hearing it, has sometimes been stressed. Visual imagery would also seem to have played a vital role (D. A. MacDonald 1978, *passim*), and sheer verbal memory has clearly been a factor, for instance in

some tales told by the late Duncan MacDonald (q.v.) (Bruford 1978, *passim*).

By the second half of the nineteenth century the tradition was already in decay over most of the mainland Highlands. In the Hebrides, however, particularly in the Uists and Barra, it was still flourishing. Most storytellers were men – rather than women – 'with clear heads and wonderful memories . . . speaking only Gaelic' (Campbell 1890, xxiii). In every township there was at least one house noted as a '*céilidh* house'. These popular meeting places provided the main focus for the social and intellectual life of the surrounding areas. Storytellers, singers and musicians catered for the needs that later came to be supplied by books, newspapers, films, radio and television. At these informal gatherings the normal work of the household would often continue for most of the evening, but when serious storytelling began close attention and a respectful silence were expected, apart from exclamations prompted by some incident in the story or the discussion and comment that preceded or followed the telling of a tale. Such evenings of communal entertainment are well within living memory.

Despite natural and induced disasters, clerical disapproval and the advent in the 1870s of an alien system of education totally based on English, storytelling continued, in some areas, to hold its own reasonably well even into the twentieth century. The First World War is often mentioned as an important watershed. Constant news of deaths and woundings cast a gloom over whole communities. Though house-to-house visiting still went on, the old style of céilidhing began to decline sharply. After the war many ex-servicemen sought employment and homes on the mainland. Accelerating processes of economic, social and educational change contributed to the decay of the old system. As the demand for the services of storytellers decreased, so did their number and their prestige. Today there are few left who can tell any of the major tales, and those with an extensive repertoire and a practised style are very few indeed. Some are more or less 'passive' tradition-bearers who, through an early interest and the excellence of their memories, are able to recall some of what they heard in their youth.

Most of the stories one hears now are of the shorter, more anecdotal and legend types. Telling tends to be restricted to interested individuals who swap yarns or to the family circle. In instances such as these storytelling does continue to have at least some social function, and this is probably particularly true among certain Gaelic-speaking tinker families in their summer travelling camps.

A new access of interest and prestige has undoubtedly stemmed from the activities of collectors, both private and institutional, as well as from a developing awareness of the importance of tradition among the better informed and more intelligent element of the younger generation. Finally, it must be a matter for some satisfaction that even today it is possible, if only occasionally, to hear Gaelic stories told with artistry and conviction. (See: Campbell 1961b; K. H. Jackson 1952, 1961, chs. 1, 2; C. I. Maclean 1959.)   DAMCD

Strathcarron, Lord (formerly Ian MacPherson) (1880–1937) Gaelic-speaking MP and member of British Cabinet. Advocate of Gaelic Clause in 1918 Education Act.   DST

Strathnaver Museum Folk museum of the province, now part of Sutherland, defined in maps of Mercator (1595) and Pont (1662) on display there. Housed in former church of Farr parish, Bettyhill, feued in 1962 to seven native-born resident trustees, and opened in 1976.   IG

Stronach, Alexander, *see* Mac an t-Srònaich.

Stuart, Revd John (1743–1821) Son of the Revd James Stewart of Killin; minister of Arrochar, Weem and finally Luss. Identified many rare Alpine plants on Perthshire mountains (see Lightfoot's *Flora Scotica*). Superintended second (revised) edition of Gaelic New Testament (1796); involved in preparation of first three parts of Gaelic Old Testament, translating the third part (issued 1801). As a young man he helped to see the poems of Donnchadh Bàn (q.v.) through the press (1768).   DST

supernatural, *see* legends, supernatural.

Sutherland Highlanders, *see* regiments, Highland.

svarabhakti, *see* Gaelic, word tones and svarabhakti.

Swanson, John (1804–74) Born Gravesend, Kent; brought up in Cromarty. Schoolmate of Hugh Miller (Miller 1870, 114). Minister of Small Isles, 1839–47, and of Nigg, 1847–74. Learned to speak and write Gaelic with great fluency. Published religious pamphlets in Gaelic and English. (*see* Swanson 1841, 1844.)   RMCL

switching, *see* Gaelic: switching.

syncope, *see* Gaelic: syncope.

syntax, *see* Gaelic: syntax.

T

tacksmen Within the clan system, tacksmen (*Daoine uaisle* or *Fir-baile*) were gentry immediately subordinate to the clan chief and often his blood kin. They held large areas of land on 'tack' or lease and further sublet to tenant farmers. The tacksman's administrative unit was the 'baile' (township), comprising a few individual holdings and several joint farms or clachans, in which subtenants held a share and farmed according to the run-rig system (Gray 1957, 20).

According to status, tacksmen held one or more townships, and in an agrarian society largely dependent on trade they fulfilled the various roles of a mercantile middle class. They acted as entrepreneurs and bankers and were providers of 'steelbow', that is, basic tenant capital such as stock or seed. Some tacksmen had, further, the power to convene courts and garrison castles (Cregeen 1971, 97).

From the seventeenth century, however, chiefs spent more and more time 'riot[ing] in all the luxuries of South Britain' (Pennant 1774, 307), accruing expenses which forced them to look beyond the exploitation of black cattle (their one marketable cash product) for extra revenue. The Campbells thus initiated a new, commercial, individualist policy in the Highlands between 1710 and 1737. They induced subtenants to outbid tacksmen when leases lapsed, so that revenue came directly to the chiefs. Now that clan land was regarded as a capitalizable asset, severe hardship resulted. Competitive bidding greatly augmented rents, a defaulting tenant losing both lease and stock. Waste land previously cultivated by the tacksmen was left unproductive; there was no provision of steelbow; while many tacksmen emigrated together with large numbers of the peasantry. 'To banish the Tacksman is easy, to make a country plentiful by diminishing the people is an expeditious mode of husbandry; but that abundance which there is nobody to enjoy, contributes little to human happiness' (Johnson 1775, 79). (See Carter 1971; Cregeen 1970; Gailey 1962; Geddes 1948; I. MacKay 1964; McKerral 1947.) FMCD

Tàillear MacDhonnchaidh, an, *see* MacPherson, Paul.

tales, *see* Highlands and Islands, travellers' accounts of; legends, supernatural; Nova Scotia, Gaelic storytelling in; novel, the Gaelic; stories, short; storytelling; tales, heroic; tales, international; tales, romantic.

tales, heroic The longer heroic tales in Scottish Gaelic oral tradition are strongly influenced by early Irish literature. Thus easily the commonest name for the hero of such tales, which may follow well-known international plot types, is Mac Rìgh Éireann ('the king of Ireland's son'); he may otherwise be a prince of Greece, France, Spain or Lochlann (Norway) but rarely of Scotland. In other cases hero and story derive wholly from the Common Gaelic literary tradition. There is little evidence that anything has been passed down solely in oral tradition since the Old Irish period; though versions of the Deirdre story and parts of the *Táin* (the longest tale of the Ulster Cycle) have been recorded in Barra and South Uist, these can be found in manuscripts written by Scottish scribes, among others, up to the seventeenth century, along with late medieval romances such as 'A' Bhruidhean Chaorthuinn', 'Conall Gulbann' or 'Leigheas Coise Céin' (q.v. all), which became more widely known as folktales. These written romances were meant to be read aloud from manuscripts, and though by 1750 such readings must generally have died out, along with knowledge of the Irish hand and its many contractions, the stories were by then well established in oral tradition (see Bruford 1969, *passim*).

Some of these tales belonged to the prose portion of the Fenian Cycle, supplementing the 'Ossianic' ballads, and tell of the elopement of Diarmaid with Fionn's wife Gràinne, of the finding of Fionn's dog Bran, of battles with supernatural enemies in an underground *bruidhean* (other-world hall) or with mortal invaders on the seashore. The name of a typical Viking invader from the ballads, Mànus (perhaps based on the historical Magnus Barelegs), is used for the hero of several prose tales whose written originals cannot now be traced. Some popular Fenian tales, including the story of Fionn's own youth, and 'Gille nan Cochull Chraiceann' (q.v.), also cannot be traced directly to a written original, but as with 'An Tuairisgeul Mór' (q.v.), borrowings and cross-references suggest that they once circulated, if not in manuscript, certainly among professional storytellers. The case of 'Fear na h-Eabaide' (q.v.), well-known to Scottish storytellers even though the greater part of the story is missing from the one surviving manuscript, suggests that in other cases oral tradition may have preserved stories whose written exemplars have vanished entirely.

Literary hero tales supplied not only plots, sometimes compacted by oral transmission into a neater, more logically constructed and so more memorable form, but also a stock of names of characters and places, stereotyped descriptions and whole episodes or motifs which could be used in any suitable tale. Thus Conall Gulbann (or Conall Crò-bhi) reappears as the 'old robber' of AT 953, an international tale type akin to some of the adventures of Sinbad; his opponent Macaomh (Macan) Mór figures as an ogre in many tales; and the latter's mythical kingdom of Sorcha (originally Syria, identified by later antiquaries with Portugal, China or Ardnamurchan) appears in others. The same alliterative 'run', with passages of sonorous nonsense in which the archaisms of the literary original have been garbled, may be used to describe the hero going to sea or preparing for battle, whether his name be Conall or Fionn or Iain the widow's son. (Several typical phrases from sea runs are incorporated in Mac Mhaighstir Alasdair's (q.v.) 'Birlinn'.) The many borrowings of the episode in which Conall Gulbann lays out a whole barracks full of *amhuis* (mercenaries) by using one of them as a club are reflected in the development of the word *tamhasg* (which replaces *amhus* in most Scottish versions) to mean 'bonehead', 'poltroon' 'dwarf', as well as 'spectre' (which may be the original meaning).

Such names, runs and episodes are regularly borrowed to add to similar hero tales based on international folktale plots (see **tales, international**):

among these AT 300, 'The Dragon-Slayer' (sometimes with giants in place of dragons, or with a sequel, as AT 303, 'The Twins'), and AT 302, 'The Ogre's Heart in the Egg', are very popular in Gaelic; the latter is often combined with the native motif of the quest for the Sword of Light. Such quests are often set in motion by the convention that the loser of a game (be it cards, dice or shinty) can be placed by the winner under *geasan* (spells) forcing him to seek something without rest – sometimes answered by a counter-spell forcing the winner to wait for the loser's return in some uncomfortable position. Another international type, AT 301, in which a princess is rescued from an underground kingdom, was used as the basis of a literary romance, 'Eachtra Iollainn Airmdheirg' (The Adventures of Iollann of the Reddened Weapons), and most folk versions combine elements of the usual international pattern with features of the romance, such as the quest of the sons for their father's teeth, knocked out by a stranger. Other international types usually include less heroic elements, such as a helpful animal or supernatural being, but still allow giant killings or other feats of strength and valour to match the individual flavour of this class of storytelling, traditionally considered the highest form of the art in Scotland as in Ireland, where it had a special name, *fianaíocht*, and where women were normally forbidden to tell it.   AB

tales, international Tales spanning a broad spectrum of the international types listed in the Aarne–Thompson Classification (S. Thompson 1961) are well represented in the Gaelic storytelling tradition. A typical repertoire might be expected – at least until very recently – to include a fair number of specimens. The four main divisions of the AT Classification are: (1) animal tales; (2) ordinary folktales; (3) jokes and anecdotes; (4) formula tales. Not all international tales, however, were equally prestigious. Storytellers of any reputation – almost always men – would not normally be expected to concern themselves with animal tales or formula tales. Most of these would be regarded as children's stories, to be told within the family circle and not suitable for the more public forum of the *céilidh* house (see **storytelling**). Campbell of Islay (q.v.) notes, for instance, of 'A' Ghobhar Ghlas' (AT 123) that 'though everybody knows it, no one will tell it' (J. F. Campbell 1890). Much the same would apply to other animal tales, well known but not often recorded, for instance wolf and fox tales such as 'The Tail

Fisher' (AT 2) or 'The Theft of Butter by playing Godfather' (AT 15). The same general rule would apply to formula tales such as 'Am Bonnach Beag' (AT 2025) and 'Biorachan Beag agus Biorachan Mor' (cf. AT 2030).

Section 3, jokes and anecdotes, also contains much that would be regarded as scarcely worthy of the notice of a good storyteller. There are, however, stories in this class which might well form part of his repertoire. Random examples are 'The Master Thief' (AT 1525), 'The Fool as Murderer' (AT 1600), the 'Whittington's Cat' type (AT 1651).

Section 2, ordinary folk tales, is divided into four main subsections: (a) tales of magic; (b) religious tales; (c) novellas (romantic tales); (d) tales of the Stupid Ogre.

Subsection (a), tales of magic (often called wonder tales), includes the most highly regarded of the great international tales or *Märchen*. Some of these, along with the native tradition of Gaelic hero tales (q.v.) supplied the most prized aspects of the Gaelic storyteller's stock-in-trade. Some notable examples among many are 'The Dragon Slayer' (AT 300), 'The Twins' (AT 303), 'The Magic Flight' (AT 313, 314), 'The Maiden who seeks her Brothers' (AT 451), 'Cinderella' (AT 510), 'The Helpers' ('The Land and Water Ship', AT 513, 514).

In subsection (b) two well-known examples of religious tales are 'Christ and the Smith' (AT 753) and 'The Devil's Contract' (AT 756B).

For romantic tales/novellas (subsection (c)), see **tales, romantic**; for a typical Stupid Ogre sequence (sub-section (d)), see **Mac Rùsgail**; for some further points on international tales in relation to the native Gaelic tradition, see **tales, heroic**.   DAMCD

tales, romantic (novellas) International folktales classified as novellas or romantic tales are those which involve little or no magic and are not basically comic. Popular types in Gaelic include tales of luck such as the 'Whittington's Cat' type (AT 1651 – in Gaelic versions the rare commodity sold in Turkey for its weight in gold is usually coal or herring rather than a cat); tales of fate such as AT 930, in which a king or rich man vainly tries to get rid of the poor child whose marriage to his daughter (or son) has been prophesied; and tales of cleverness such as AT 875 ('The Clever Peasant Girl'), AT 901 ('The Taming of the Shrew'), or AT 922 ('The King and the Abbot'). As told in South Uist this last, much studied international type resembles a local legend: a landowner wants to impose Protestantism on his tenants and threatens to expel the priest unless he can answer three questions, but the priest's simple brother takes his place and confounds the landowner, finally answering the question 'What am I thinking?' with 'That I am the priest!' (Bruford 1973, 147–9).

Indeed these more realistic tales often begin at least in a local setting, with perhaps a widow's son from Barra becoming a wealthy merchant (J. F. Campbell 1890, vol. 2, 121ff.). Many such tales, revolving round the winning of a fortune (usually by foreign trade with the help of a wealthy merchant) and/or the eventual union of parted lovers, are told which cannot be assigned to known international types. Some may derive from novels, such as Elizabeth Helme's *St Clair of the Isles*, which were read aloud or retold in Gaelic (J. L. Campbell 1961b, 232–3), or from English ballads, chapbooks or popular translations of works such as the *Arabian Nights*. Others may well be the invention of storytellers, some of whom specialized in such romances. A notable example was the late Angus MacMillan (q.v.) from Benbecula, whose nine-hour-long 'Alasdair mac a' Cheird' (Alasdair the Tinker's Son) has been claimed as the longest story ever recorded in Europe (cf. MacGillEathain 1954, 173): the detailed recapitulation of the characters' generally pedestrian conversations accounts for much of the length.   AB

tales, travellers', *see* Highlands and Islands, travellers' accounts of.

tanistry Kin-based regnal succession. Any male descendant of a king, provided that he was of age and sound in mind and body, was eligible to succeed to the kingship. In practice the royal dynasty normally consisted of two or more segments, which shared the office. The head of each segment might expect to succeed in turn, producing a pattern of cousin succeeding cousin, each of whom was often the son of a previous king. The further removed he was from an ancestor who had been king, the more difficult it was for him to succeed, and segments constantly dropped out of the succession stakes, the heads of the more important sometimes being compensated by becoming enkinging or inaugural officials. During a king's reign, perhaps at its inception, the head of the most powerful segment of the kingship might be entitled *rígdomna* (material of a king) or *tánaise* (the expected one), that is, heir-designate (D. Ó Corráin 1971, 7–38). From *tánaise* derive *tanist* and *tanistry*, the

English terms for the system which operated at the level of the kings of Scots without interruption into the twelfth century. In the Lordship of the Isles particularly it remained a factor in determining succession to the chiefship of a kindred into the sixteenth century (Steer and Bannerman 1977, 100, 132–3, 148).   JWMB

Tarentum, Duke of (Marshall MacDonald) (fl. 1800), whom Napoleon created Duke of Taranto in 1809, was a son of Neil MacDonald from Howbeg, South Uist.   DST

tartan(s), *see* clan tartans.

Teàrlach a' Phosta (fl. 1930) From Braes, Skye. Witty village bard.   DST

television, *see* broadcasting, Gaelic.

Telford, Thomas (1757–1834) From Dumfriesshire. Son of a shepherd, he became Europe's outstanding civil engineer and built not only the Caledonian Canal but also many churches, roads, bridges and harbours in the Highlands. (See Pratt 1922; Telford 1838.)   IG

temples, *see* sanctuaries, temples, shrines.

textbooks, Gaelic, for schools Probably Mac Mhaighstir Alasdair's (q.v.) *Vocabulary* of 1741 is the first in the series of Gaelic school textbooks, and just as his work was intended for use in the SSPCK schools (q.v.), so the main early series was that prepared for use in the various circulating schools – for example, Alexander MacLaren's *First Book for Children in the Gaelic Language* (1811) and Christopher Anderson's *First Book for Class II* (1816). The hiatus between 1811 and 1816 is of a kind familiar in this field. Francis Macbean produced further titles in 1823 and 1824. The SSPCK produced a *Gaelic Spelling-book* in 1815, and the General Assembly schools had their own series of texts, four books published in 1826, with subsequent reprints. A book of Gaelic Scripture extracts, which appeared in 1825, may remind us of the strongly evangelical motivation of these Gaelic schools.

Professor Donald Mackinnon (q.v.) complains ('Seann Sgoil', Mackinnon 1956, 267) of the limited equipment of the Gaelic school of the 1840s (slate, cheap paper, oak sap ink, quill pen, Gray's *Arith-*

metic, the Shorter Catechism, Gaelic Bible and shinty stick), and probably there was very marginal improvement on this until the turn of the century. Mackinnon himself produced a Gaelic reading book for his own students at Edinburgh (1889), and Donald Maciver (q.v.) a bilingual textbook (1900). There had, of course, been a number of books of Gaelic grammar, some of which were used in schools. A considerable advance is associated with Professor W. J. Watson, who edited anthologies of prose (*Rosg Gàidhlig*, 1915) and verse (Bàrdachd Ghàidhlig, 1918), and was general editor for the series *Leabhraichean Sgoile Gàidhlig* (*c*.1920–3), with two individual editors Donald MacPhie and John MacDonald. James Thomson's (q.v.) *An Dìleab*, verse for Advanced Divisions (1932), and Lachlan Mackinnon's *Cascheum nam Bard* (1939) and his new series of *Leabhraichean Leughaidh* (*c*.1948) continued to add some variety to the scene, An Comunn Gaidhealach (q.v.) being the main publisher.

A fresh wave of publication began in the late 1950s and 1960s, with texts issued by Gairm Publications – for example, *Crìochan Ura* (1958), *Seumas Beag* (1968), twelve books in the *Alasdair agus Màiri* series (1969–71) – and by the Celtic Department at Aberdeen University (later at Glasgow University), e.g. *Làithean Geala* (1962) and *Bun-chùrsa Gàidhlig* (1978). These publishers have been joined since 1977 by An Comunn Gaidhealach and Acair, sometimes in conjunction with English publishers such as Longman's, as in the series of twelve Spàgan texts; while Finlay MacLeod, former Primary Adviser for the Western Isles, has written many books for use in the schools there, e.g. *Rònan agus Brianuilt* (1978) and *O Tractar!* (1979). Iain C. Smith's *Na h-Ainmhidhean* (illustrated bird rhymes, etc.) appeared from Clò Chailleann in 1979, gaining the top design award for books published in 1978–9. Various workbooks and aids have appeared but not in sufficient range. And textbooks for the secondary school, apart from texts of prose and poetry and a Gaelic biology are in thin supply. (See *Leabhraichean Gàidhlig*, 1983.)   DST

textile manufacture Over the centuries the conversion in the Highlands of fibre to yarn, of yarn to cloth, and of cloth to garments developed. In the Middle Ages the *lèine chròich* (protective shirt) of Celtic warriors was linen, but in addition woollen plaiding and blanketing were produced, as well as *drògaid* (drugget cloth), which was made with a linen warp and woollen weft. During the greater part of the eighteenth century the manufacture of linen cloth was the most important Scottish industry. At that time it required three or four hand spinners to keep a weaver occupied (I. F. Grant 1961, 220). For a full account of Highland fabrics, see Bain (1977, 25–31) and Grant (1961, 119ff.); for the manufacture of English and Scottish woollen cloth, see Gulven (1973).

If a tuft of fibres is held in one hand and a small number of the fibres is carefully drawn from the tuft with the thumb and forefinger of the other hand, the fibres thus attenuated being simultaneously twisted, a yarn can be formed. The next logical step in the development of spinning was the substitution of a *dealgan, fearsaid* (spindle) for the insertion of twist. The earliest spindles were possibly lengths of wood about 12 inches long, weighted at their lower ends with whorls (other terms are 'wharf' or 'wharve') to give both stability and momentum. To hold the untwisted tuft of fibres a *cuigeal* (distaff) was frequently used with the spindle. The distaff was a longer piece of wood, which was tucked into the left oxter and crook of the spinner's arm. It had the fibres held loosely at its upper end, and these were drawn and controlled by hand towards the spindle. This method of spinning is still widely practised in many parts of the world, notably in some South American countries, where it allows the spinner to move about freely while herding sheep, llamas and alpacas on the higher slopes of the Andes (Morton and Wray 1962, 135).

Spinning by hand is a time-consuming process, and when spinning for markets was developed the process was speeded up by a *cuibhle shnìomh* (spinning wheel). By the end of the eighteenth century spinning wheels were in general use in the eastern Highlands. It was much later, however, before wheels were used in the remoter parts of Scotland, and even as late as 1850 most Hebridean women were still using the spindle (I. F. Grant 1961, 222; H. Miller 1854, 284).

Two kinds of spinning wheel were introduced to the Highlands – the 'muckle wheel' and the Saxony wheel (I. F. Grant 1961, 223), both suitable for the spinning of flax or wool. The latter wheel is an ingenious device (Leonardo da Vinci is credited with its invention), although the first was made by a Brunswick wood-carver, Johan Jürgen, in 1530 (Morton and Wray 1962, 149).

The earliest looms used in the Highlands and Islands were upright, being used for woollen as well as for linen cloths (I. F. Grant 1961, 226). These were later superseded by the horizontal loom, an early version of the narrow *beart bheag* (hand loom). These latter looms were in use in the Hebrides until about the turn of the present century; their wooden shuttles, which were hand-thrown through the warp threads, were boat-shaped and carried spindles, round which the shin bone of a sheep revolved, carrying the weft thread.

It would be impossible to establish an exact date for the beginning of the making of woollen cloth in the Outer Hebrides, but it must have been made in these islands for several centuries. During the expansion of Stornoway airport at the beginning of the second world war a number of whorls and a weaver's comb were unearthed. These implements have been dated late Stone Age, but it cannot be stated that they were used for a wool cloth or by Hebrideans. In the year 1630 Captain Dymes, who visited Lewis and wrote a report, listed among the exports from Stornoway plaiding and tartan (W. C. MacKenzie 1903, App. F). 'Tartan' weaving is referred to by Martin Martin, one of the first Hebridean historians (Martin 1934).

Harris tweed became a marketable commodity during the nineteenth century, when the Dunmores, proprietors of south Harris, adopted the coarse *clò mòr* for their own use. Their example was emulated by sporting visitors to the Islands who favoured the cloth for its durability, its waterproofing and the subdued colouring produced by the vegetable dyes used in its manufacture. Later the Duchess of Sutherland, a promoter of home industries, did much to popularize the cloth for the sportsman's wardrobe. The word 'Harris' is appended to the name of the cloth because it was first promoted and marketed from Harris, although it was also woven in various parts of Lewis. The word 'tweed' is considered to be derived from the error of a London clerk who misread the Scots word 'tweel' (twill) for tweed, inadvertently relating a cloth from a Border town to the River Tweed; 'tweed' is now a term used to describe a 'homespun' cloth made from yarn produced on the woollen system of yarn processing. As a result of a Scottish High Court decision in 1964, Harris tweed is now established as tweed 'made from pure, Scottish, virgin wool, spun, dyed, and finished in the Outer Hebrides, and hand-woven by the islanders at their own homes'.

Blackfaced sheep were introduced to the Hebrides in about 1762 (Moisley, 1961, 354). Before that time the breed of sheep to be found in the islands was the small indigenous, tan-faced animal, which yielded about a pound of short, fine wool. Despite interbreeding between the two types of sheep, Hebridean wool was finer than its mainland-of-Scotland counterpart, so that when the demand for cloth grew to such an extent that the islands' clip became insufficient to meet it, mainland Blackfaced wool had to be blended, as it still is, with finer, softer fibres from Cheviot, Half-bred and Cross-bred wools. At present most of the wool used in the trade is purchased from mainland wool brokers and is already blended to the required specification.

Because of the promotion of Harris tweed, the demand for the cloth grew and, after the first world war, developed into a boom, so that the time-consuming stages in its traditional manufacture had to be considerably speeded up. Hand-carding, oiling and teasing gave way to machine processes, hand-spinning to mule and frame-spinning and vegetable dyeing to chemical dyeing, so that today the only hand-operated processes left are those of warping (arranging the longitudinal set of threads for the loom) and weaving. (A small amount of yarn is still hand-spun.)

The *beart bheag* was replaced by wider looms, supplied by southern loom-makers, including, *c.* 1914, Thomas Kennedy of Galashiels and Robert Scott. On these looms the *beart mheadhoin* (going part) carried boxes at either end of the sley board and the shuttles were hand-thrown, by means of cords and pickers, from side to side, carrying the weft thread, as in John Kay's invention of 1733. A few of these looms are still used in parts of Harris.

The type of hand loom used in the industry today is the Hattersley Domestic. The first thirty Domestics were sent to the islands in 1919. These were of 36-inch reed space and had single shuttle boxes. In 1924 the first six-shuttle, 40-inch reed space Hattersley looms arrived in Stornoway, and these looms, each of which is the property of the individual weaver, are the type that is used almost exclusively nowadays. Prepared warps are dispatched to weavers from the spinning mills, together with the requisite amount of weft yarn; the woven webs of tweed are collected and then subjected to various finishing processes, including scouring and milling (shrinking), which have replaced the rough washing, drying and waulking of an earlier age.

At the beginning of the century a danger was foreseen in the indiscriminate use of mill-spun yarn for the making of Harris tweed, and in 1911 the Harris Tweed Association was registered with the Board of Trade, which granted the 'Orb' certification mark that is applied to the finished cloth, every 3 yards, by Association inspectors. The Association is the custodian of this mark and has over the years protected the cloth against imitation by outside interests and against the lowering of standards from within.

YARDAGE OF HARRIS TWEED STAMPED
1911–79

	Yards		Yards		Yards
1911	12,381	1934*	95,241	1957	6,328,043
1912	132,936	1935	1,485,246	1958	4,348,533
1913	101,708	1936	2,331,740	1959	6,166,888
1914	67,814	1937	3,672,775	1960	5,410,714
1915	35,133	1938	2,897,104	1961	4,954,459
1916	31,826	1939	3,987,676	1962	5,081,407
1917	44,490	1940	4,188,822	1963	5,563,426
1918	25,847	1941	3,201,137	1964	5,901,800
1919	40,497	1942	2,212,816	1965	6,537,555
1920	19,563	1943	1,722,307	1966	7,627,397
1921	25,764	1944	1,923,396	1967	5,452,202
1922	33,201	1945	2,195,423	1968	6,698,069
1923	38,454	1946	3,049,680	1969	6,506,528
1924	30,300	1947	3,967,920	1970	5,102,533
1925	27,658	1948	4,463,713	1971	4,712,067
1926	25,640	1949	4,101,029	1972	4,070,855
1927	29,745	1950	3,779,570	1973	3,967,825
1928	30,283	1951	2,799,570	1974	3,403,824
1929	31,158	1952	4,034,351	1975	2,622,021
1930	31,004	1953	4,939,898	1976	2,999,901
1931	42,190	1954	5,150,355	1977	3,499,201
1932	47,294	1955	5,840,158	1978	4,089,572
1933	22,018	1956	6,623,529	1979	4,246,496

* The Certification Trade Mark was amended in November 1934.
Source: The Harris Tweed Association.

Harris Tweed enjoys period booms (*see* table of stamped yardages), although the number of weavers has declined from about 1,500 in the 1960s to approximately 600 today. AMMCL

Thighearna Cholla, Bàrd, *see* Maclean, John (1747–1848).

Thomson, Derick Smith (b. 1921) Born Stornoway. Son of James Thomson (q.v.), Lecturer in Welsh, Glasgow; Reader in Celtic, Aberdeen; Professor of Celtic, Glasgow, since 1964; co-founder and

A Hatterfley domestic loom.

Editor of the literary journal *Gairm;* Chairman, Gaelic Books Council; first recipient of Ossian Prize (1974). Author of numerous books and articles on Gaelic topics – for example, James Macpherson's 'Ossian', the MacMhuirichs, medieval professional classes, twentieth-century verse, including *An Introduction to Gaelic Poetry* (1974). For his poetry, see **MacThòmais, Ruaraidh**. JMCI

Thomson, Donald (1907–80) Born Ness, Lewis. Twice Provost of Oban; President of An Comunn Gaidhealach (q.v.), 1962–5; Convener of the Mod and Music Committee, 1965–79. A colourful champion of Gaelic, he was the chief campaigner for the Gaelic Learners' examinations introduced in 1962 (Ordinary) and 1967 (Higher). DST

Thomson, James (fl. 1740) From Speyside; settled in Lewis as SSPCK teacher in 1737. Progenitor of rural Thomsons in Lewis. DST

Thomson, James (1888–1971) Born Tong, Lewis. Gaelic master at Nicolson Institute, Stornoway, then headmaster of Bayble School, Lewis, 1922–53. Gaelic prose writer and bard. First Crowned Bard of National Mod, 1923. Pioneered development of Gaelic teaching in secondary schools. Edited *An Dìleab* (Gaelic poems for schools); co-edited *Eilean Fraoich*, a collection of Lewis songs; contributed articles to *An Rosarnach*, *Gairm*, etc. Editor of *An Gaidheal*, 1958–62. His collected poems, many of them on philosophical and religious themes, are published in *Fasgnadh* (1953); three Gaelic hymns by him are to be found in R. Macleod (1938). (See also under **verse, religious**; *An Gaidheal*, vol. 23, 98; Murchison 1971.)   TMM

Thomson, Revd John (1778–1840), *see* art, Gaelic, in modern times.

Thomson, Robert Leith (b. 1924) Reader in Celtic, University of Leeds. Editor of medieval Welsh texts; foremost authority on Manx; editor of early religious Scottish Gaelic texts (e.g. Gaelic versions of Carswell's Liturgy and Calvin's Catechism). (See R. L. Thomson 1961, 1962, 1963, 1970, 1971, 1976, 1977.)
                                                              DST

Thùrnaig, Bàrd, *see* Cameron, Alasdair.

Tochradh Nighean a' Chathanaich, *see* Angus Óg, Lord of the Isles.

Tolmie, Frances (1840–1926) Born Uiginish, Isle of Skye. Discriminating collector of folksongs and folklore. The issue of the *Journal of the Folksong Society* of December 1911 includes 105 songs of occupation that she collected in the Western Isles. (See Bassin 1977.)   CG

Tormod Sona, *see* MacDonald, Norman.

Torran Dubh, Rogart (*c.*1517) A defeat for the Mackays of Strathnaver in the continuing strife between them and the men of Sutherland. (See Gunn 1969, 68–71.)   JWMB

towers, round A distinctive feature of monasteries in Ireland and Scotland from the tenth century onwards; they are built of stone and normally stand near the western wall of the church. They are about 120 feet high and 16 feet 6 inches in diameter. The

Round tower at Abernethy, Perthshire. ▶

thickness of the walls at ground level is from 3 to 4 feet, but this decreases as the tower tapers to its conical stone roof. They functioned partly as bell towers and watch towers but also for defence, particularly for the protection of the precious relics of the monastery (Henry 1967, 49–57). The best-preserved examples in Scotland are at Abernethy and Brechin.

JWMB

Traprain Law A massive whale-back hill dominating the rich farmlands of Haddingtonshire, which was fortified as an *oppidum* (defended town) by the British tribe of the Votadini (Feachem 1963, 1977, 120–1; MacKie 1975, 95–7). Poor-quality excavations have revealed that it was inhabited throughout much of the first millennium BC and the succeeding Roman period (Jobey 1976, 190–204). The famous silver treasure was a Roman bribe to keep the Votadini quiet in the late 4th century, but there is no evidence that occupation continued beyond *c.*AD 450 (Alcock 1979, 135–6). The association with Taniu, mother of St Kentigern (Jackson 1958b, 289) has, therefore, no historical basis.

LA

Traquhair, Phoebe (1852–1936), *see* art, Gaelic, in modern times.

'Tuairisgeul Mór, An' Folktale with literary affinities. A prince, sent by giant Tuairisgeul's son to discover how his father was killed, forces the aged king to recount how he was turned into a wolf and caught the child-stealing giant. (See J. G. McKay 1935, 1–112; Bruford 1969, 158–9.)

AB

tweed, Harris, *see* textile manufacture.

U

Uilleam Ruighe 'n Uidhe (William Gow) (? early nineteenth century) From Badenoch. Author of 'Allt an Lochain Uaine'. (See Sinton 1906, 172–6, etc.)

DST

universities and colleges, Gaelic studies in When Johnson and Boswell came to Scotland in 1773 they were hard-pressed to find anyone in the Scottish universities who was knowledgeable about Gaelic manuscripts or culture; no doubt similar observations could have been made at any time from the founding of the earliest Scottish university (1411) to the last decade of the eighteenth century. Some Gaels, often of chiefly (or, later, of tacksman) families, went to university, as John Carswell (q.v.) to St Andrews and Dean James MacGregor (q.v.), presumably, also. Roderick MacLeod, brother of MacLeod of Talisker, was Principal of King's College, Aberdeen, in Boswell's times, but there is no evidence that Gaelic language or literature found any recognition in a Scottish university before the time of Ewen MacLachlan (q.v.), Librarian of King's College, Aberdeen, who copied and commented on Gaelic manuscripts and worked on the compilation of a Gaelic dictionary; the first Principal of the united University of Aberdeen (1860) was Peter Colin Campbell, a Gael who had been Professor of Greek.

University graduates became very prominent in Gaelic matters as collectors, editors, translators, grammarians, etc., in the second half of the eighteenth century, however, and the Ossianic controversy ensured the long continuance of an interest or curiosity in Gaelic history and traditions.

Moves to introduce university teaching in Gaelic/ Celtic at Aberdeen in the 1840s came to nothing, and the first Scottish university appointment in the subject was that of Donald Mackinnon to the newly founded Edinburgh Chair in 1882. This was followed by the introduction of lectures on Celtic literature at Glasgow in 1900 (Magnus Maclean, the Professor of Electrical Engineering, being the pioneer), although Gaelic classes were conducted in the university buildings (but under the auspices of the Free Church College) from 1876. Celtic at Glasgow was put on a more regular footing with Kuno Meyer's appointment (1903–6) and that of George Henderson (1906–12). Henderson was succeeded by George Calder in 1912 and Mackinnon of Edinburgh by W. J. Watson in 1914; Calder and Watson reigned until the mid-1930s, engendering many anecdotes about their idiosyncrasies and antipathies. Meantime John Fraser had been appointed to the recently instituted lectureship (1916) at Aberdeen and, on moving to Oxford, was succeeded by John Macdonald (1922). Calder was succeeded in 1935 by James Carmichael Watson, who succeeded his father in Edinburgh in 1938, being succeeded at Glasgow by Angus Matheson, who later became the first holder of the Glasgow Chair (1956). Matheson died in office and was succeeded by D. S. Thomson in 1963. J. C. Watson of Edinburgh, who was killed on active service, was succeeded in the Chair by Myles Dillon (1947), Dillon by K. H. Jackson (1950) and Jackson by William Gillies (1979). Meantime in Aberdeen John Macdonald was succeeded by D. S. Thomson (1956), Thomson by John Mackechnie (1964) and Mackechnie by Donald MacAulay (1967).

The three Celtic Departments were one-teacher Departments until 1939, when David Greene served briefly along with Matheson at Glasgow. In 1948 D. S. Thomson was appointed assistant to Dillon at Edinburgh and in 1949 Annie Mackenzie to Macdonald at Aberdeen. In 1949 Glasgow introduced the post of Lecturer in Welsh, and in the last thirty years all three Departments experienced some modest expansion of staff (Glasgow in 1981 had five, Aberdeen and Edinburgh three on the lecturing staff).

The content and emphasis of the courses have changed greatly over the last hundred years. To begin with, and basically until after the Second War, the emphasis was strongly on textual studies, including much older Irish; place-names and a little literary history and criticism also featured in the work, together with the study of grammar and comparative philology and the writing of Scottish Gaelic. There was almost an assumption that students would be fluent and literate in Gaelic and should explore other matters at university. That assumption has since been both challenged from within the universities and undermined in the everyday Gaelic world, and this has led to an expansion of purely Scottish Gaelic studies (for example, in the range of work read, the extent of critical discussion, the fields of study, including work on dialects, socio-linguistics, language development, etc.). And as the emphasis in Ordinary degree courses shifted from Middle and Old Irish, some Modern Irish Studies came in (Glasgow making a special appointment, James Gleasure's, for this purpose in 1966, and Aberdeen finding itself with two Irishmen, Colm Ó Baoil and Cathair Ó Dochartaigh, in the late 1960s and 1970s). Glasgow had a native Welsh lecturer from 1956 to 1981 and offers an Ordinary Welsh course. All three Celtic Departments offer a range of Welsh courses for the Honours degree.

The Honours courses have been radically restructured in the period since 1949, at different paces and in differing directions at the three universities. It is normal now to require an element of Welsh study in the Honours course, and this can be considerable if the relevant options are chosen. In some cases the Honours course can be weighted decisively in favour of Scottish Gaelic, Irish or Welsh by the individual student, but without sacrificing breadth. This is especially so in Celtic Studies (Honours). Numerous combined Honours courses are also available – for example, Celtic with Latin, English, German, Spanish, linguistics, medieval history, Scottish history, archaeology, geography. It is hoped that combinations with geography, and presumably other social sciences, will prove useful in a practical sense and will fit students for work in local government and development agencies.

The research interests of staff are wide, and there are good opportunities for postgraduate research on textual, linguistic, literary, philological, historical and socio-linguistic topics. The large and important research projects embraced by the School of Scottish Studies (q.v.), the Linguistic Survey (q.v.), the place-names survey and the Historical Dictionary of Scottish Gaelic (see **dictionaries**) have added greatly to the potential of the Celtic field of study in Scotland and have helped to build up communities of scholars, with important cross-fertilizing benefits.

The outlets for qualified students have, of course, changed in the period, as the Church and teaching have lost some of their supremacy and have made room for the media (press, radio, TV), publishing, library work, and work in the public sector.

In more recent times all three Celtic Departments have introduced parallel courses for non-native speakers, variously called Celtic B, Gaelic Studies, etc. These have attracted fairly good recruitment and will probably grow further.

The situation with regard to Gaelic in the Colleges of Education is less satisfactory. Jordanhill (following on Stow College) has throughout the century provided Gaelic courses for Gaelic graduates under the successive guidance of Norman MacLeod, Alex Nicolson, Donald Grant, John A. MacDonald, Ian Polson and now Boyd Robertson, and Jordanhill has also developed Celtic Studies courses, including these in the B.Ed. Aberdeen College of Education opted out of this kind of provision in the 1950s and has not restored a satisfactory course. The other Colleges of Education have not provided courses of this kind. Jordanhill has co-operated with the teaching authorities throughout, running important teachers' conferences and in-service courses especially under the direction of John A. Smith, and is also involved in the Western Isles Bilingual Project, Mr Smith having been the Chairman of the Committee since its inception.

Some of the Further Education Colleges offer Gaelic courses leading to O-level, Higher and, at one time, A-level Gaelic. Notable in this work are Langside (under Roderick MacNeil) and also Aberdeen Commercial College (Bill Blacklaw) and Napier College, Edinburgh (Anthony Dilworth), and Lewis Castle College also provides Gaelic courses.   DST

Urquhart, Mrs Ann (b. 1901) Born Keose, Lewis. The first woman to be Provost of Stornoway (1965–8); Vice-Convener Ross-shire County Council, 1967–70.   DST

Urquhart, David (b. 1875) Schoolmaster, Kyle of Lochalsh. Wrote on geographical topics (*Deò Gréine*, 1919–20); he and his wife Catherine collaborated with Gordon Bottomley in his play *Deirdire* (1944).   DST

V

verse, bardic Verse in Classical Common Gaelic, or in variously vernacularized versions of it, was quite widely practised in Scotland. Although our detailed knowledge of the genre is based on Irish sources, we can probably assume that similar, but perhaps often less stringent, regulations governed its production in Scotland. Its practitioners were periodically reinforced from Ireland and seem to have returned there for instruction, so we find that the MacMhuirichs are an off-shoot of the Ó Dálaighs; the Ó Muirgheasáins appear relatively late and retain the Irish Ó for a time; and there are strong traditions of poets spending time 'at the schools' in Ireland (see members of the **MacMhuirich** family; **Ó Muirgheasáin family**; **MacMharcuis family**; **MacEwen poets**).

Professional poets from Scotland visited Irish patrons and vice versa (see **Giolla Críost Brúilingeach**, etc.).

Such verse, in both countries, basically served the needs of the native ruling classes and the professional literati that came to be associated with them. Thus an important part of its stock-in-trade was eulogy and elegy, which incorporated history and legend and could be used for purposes of propaganda and aggrandizement. But these basic purposes did not preclude the development of historical and archival interests and also allowed for the burgeoning of individual interests, whether these were of a religious, a satirical or a more purely literary kind. Bardic families, and the patrons they served, frequently compiled anthologies (*duanaire* being the usual term for this), which might be more or less eclectic in their choice of poems. The leading poets often ran schools to train other poets, and some details of courses and methods survive (see **schools, bardic**). (For accounts of the early organization of the bardic order and descriptions of the general body of work, the metrics, etc., see Carney 1966; Clanricarde 1744; Greene 1961; Knott 1957; MacAirt 1958; McKenna 1944; Quiggin 1913.)

In Scotland we have datable examples of verse of this kind ranging from about 1250 to the 1730s (see D. S. Thomson 1974a), and the system in a sense lasted in Scotland for close on a century after its collapse in Ireland, coming to an end in the person of Donald MacMhuirich (q.v.). An analysis of the work of three seventeenth-century MacMhuirich poets (see D. S. Thomson 1977) shows how much of the range of subject-matter and mannerism survived at that relatively late period in Scotland: the preponderance of eulogies, salutations and elegies, with the admixture of satire, political verse, love poetry and religious poetry; the deployment of history and legend; the harping on patronage and its mutual obligations; the description of chiefly mien and character; internal dialogue about the poet's art. A short series of translated quotations will help to establish the profile:

. . . apple-blossom from the Islay soil, salmon from a nook in Kintyre.

The sons of Mílidh themselves survive no longer, the race of Conn and of Colla are both lost, Clan Donald follows after them . . . .

The gentle, noble Conchobhar, because of jealousy which caused instability, killed at drinking the sons of Uisneach: it was a matter for tears, a story from which Ireland brought forth her sorrows.

Their garments were not concealed from the poets, nor their steeds, nor their golden goblets.

Clearly, it is a loss to your family, when it comes to enumerating their battles or their original rights, that they should lack gracious knowledge . . . .

Should it come about that Clanranald, who never turned their backs on good learning, were not clear at all about other people's rights, it would be a great mark of change.

The bardic order encouraged the growth of poetic dynasties, of which several can be distinguished in Scotland, such as those of the MacMhuirichs (q.v.), the Ó Muirgheasáins (q.v.), the MacEwens (q.v.) and the MacMarcases (q.v.). There were undoubtedly others: we can see signs of those connected with the MacGregors and with the MacDonalds of Sleat, and probably some of the individual poets (e.g. MacLachlans, Mac[a'] Bhreatnaighs) in the Book of the Dean of Lismore (q.v.) belonged to such dynasties. Unsettled social conditions and the incidence of civil strife have destroyed much of the evidence, and accounts by travellers and observers come too late to record much of this evidence.

Mention should be made, however, of a late Scottish account, in a letter from Professor Garden of King's College, Aberdeen, to the English antiquary John Aubrey in 1692. Garden passes on information that he has from a Speyside student: this seems to describe a loose bardic association (within the Cliar Sheanchain or strolling bards) which distinguishes between the grades of the *phili* (poet), the *sheanachin* (historian) and another grade probably to be equated with that of *reacaire* (reciter) (C. A. Gordon 1955).

The main repository of such bardic verse is the Book of the Dean of Lismore. Other important sources are the manuscripts associated with the MacMhuirichs (not always written by them) – for example, the Red Book of Clanranald (National Museum of Antiquities of Scotland, MCR 39), MSS 72.1.36 (Gaelic MS XXXVI), 72.1.48 (Gaelic MS XLVIII and 72.2.2 (Gaelic MS LII) of the National Library of Scotland, Trinity Coll. Dublin MS 1337/2 (H.3.18), and MSS A v Z and E i 3 of the Royal Irish Academy. Occasional items occur in other manuscripts, etc.: for example, RIA. MS A iv 3, the address to Aonghus of Islay, c.1250 (ed. Bergin, 1934) and a 16th-century poem (ed. Bergin 1970); RIA.

23.N.12, which includes the Ó Muirgheasáin elegy for Ruaidhri Mór (d. 1626) (John MacDonald 1955); NLS 72.1.36 (Gaelic MS XXXVI) which has two Campbell praise poems, probably by MacEwens (W. J. Watson 1931); the Scottish Register House MS Nat. MSS Part III, no. XCVI, which has the elegy for Donnchadh Dubh (W. J. Watson 1917); the Turner MS (*Rel. Celt.*, II, 310–420); the MacLagan MSS; and Leabhar na Féinne.   DST

verse, courtly and satiric Gaelic manuscript sources show fairly widespread evidence of occasional poetry composed by members of the learned orders and sometimes by their patrons. This verse, which covers a wide range of subject-matter, includes love poetry and also compositions which may be termed satirical in the usual English sense – distinct, that is, from the malevolent incantations of *aoir* (satire).

The Early Modern love poetry clearly owes something to the *amour courtois* of Provence, whose influence was felt throughout Western Europe from the twelfth century onwards (Ó Tuama 1960, 149–73). The channels by which the exotic ingredient was introduced are obscure; but it is perhaps significant that the earliest name associated with this sort of poetry is that of the Norman-Irish Gerald fitz-Maurice, third Earl of Desmond (d. 1398). The normal vehicle for such compositions is informal syllabic verse. They present love as a sickness or derangement, from which only the (unattainable) desired one's kiss can liberate the sufferer. The poets revel in the paradoxes implicit in this fatal yet life-giving condition, and tantalize with anagrams and acrostics concealing the lady's name. Bardic techniques are employed to depict her, and native literature provides the mythological framework (Flower 1947, 142–64). The earliest Scottish examples, those in the Book of the Dean of Lismore (q.v.), are ascribed both to professional poets (e.g. Eòin MacMhuirich) and to members of the aristocracy (e.g. the 'Earl of Argyll'); the same source also contains several poems ascribed to Earl Gerald (W. Gillies 1977a). Later examples include 'Soraidh slán don oidhche a-réir', attributed to Niall Mór MacMhuirich in the Red Book of Clanranald (q.v.). In the post-bardic era amatory odes composed by members of the Highland gentry, and surviving in the early printed collections of Gaelic verse, preserve an echo of the genre and its aristocratic milieu (cf. C. Ó Baoill 1979, 248–9).

These lyrics exist beside poems *about* women, of a

sort which again reflects modes and preoccupations ubiquitous in the literature of late medieval Europe. These too are well represented in the Dean's Book. They may present the case for the prosecution against women or (more rarely) their defence. They appear as character-revealing dialogues, as epigrams or as renunciations of women. The implication of a debate about women is often explicit, always to be understood. These poems are often closely paralleled in English or Scots literature; in the Gaelic context they form part of a wider group which also contains erotic, humorous and burlesque verse and combinations of these types (W. Gillies 1977a). WG

verse, heroic Heroic verse forms a substantial part of the literary heritage of Ireland and Gaelic Scotland from the Middle Ages. This term embraces narrative 'ballads', elegiac poems, dialogues, metrical catalogues and naturalistic vignettes, usually composed in loose forms of bardic metres. Such poems were generally known to Gaelic speakers as *laoidhean* (lays) and were intended for singing or recitation. The adjective 'heroic' reflects their main interest – the exploits of Fionn mac Cumhaill and his band of warrior-hunters, the Fian. Fionn enjoyed great popularity in Ireland (where he was originally localized) and in Gaelic Scotland until recently. Occasionally lays feature warriors from the early province of Ulaidh (Ulster), whose chief hero was Cú Chulainn.

The earliest selection of heroic verse in Scotland is found in the Book of the Dean of Lismore (q.v.) (Nat. Lib. Scot. MS 72.1.37). The inclusion of twenty-seven lays in the manuscript indicates their importance in Gaelic Scotland *c*.1500. The vigour of the tradition was such that at least two versions of several lays were known to the scribe(s). This is evidenced by alternative line readings, additional quatrains placed after the end of poems and scribal directions for the reordering of quatrains. Such detailed editing strongly suggests access to written, rather than oral, sources.

Most of the lays in the manuscript concern Fionn mac Cumhaill; only two relate to Ulaidh warriors. Of the total, less than a quarter are peculiar to the manuscript; the majority occur, in part or in whole, in later Scottish Gaelic and Irish tradition (sometimes in both).

A few lays clearly originated in Ireland. One contains a catalogue of over eighty Irish places where pairs of wild animals were collected as a ransom to free Fionn. Another possible example tells of the killing of the Connacht warrior, Fraoch, by a water monster. Oral versions of the latter (with tunes) were current in Scotland this century.

The similarity of the tradition in Ireland and Gaelic Scotland makes the provenance of some lays less certain, and poems of Scottish origin are difficult to detect. A Scottish example may be the Lay of Diarmaid, describing Diarmaid's fatal encounter with a venomous boar. The hero enjoyed prestige as the legendary ancestor of the Campbells.

Only five lays in the manuscript are ascribed to real authors – two to Ailein mac Ruaidhri (q.v.) and one each to Giolla Coluim mac an Ollaimh (q.v.), An Caoch ó Chluain and a certain O Floinn. Of these, four describe the deaths of warriors, and this may indicate that the elegy had greater status than other heroic verse types, which are usually anonymous in the manuscript or attributed to legendary figures like Oisean, son of Fionn. (See Meek 1982; Murphy 1953; N. Ross 1939; D. S. Thomson 1974a, 99–105.)

Comparatively few specimens of heroic verse survive in manuscripts compiled in Scotland between 1550 and 1700. The genre remained popular, nevertheless, and considerable manuscript evidence has probably been lost. After 1700 a wave of important collecting began, deriving much material from oral transmission. Collectors were stimulated initially by a growing appreciation of the literary value of heroic verse and also by the threat to its survival in marginal areas. It is noticeable that collecting moved gradually from east to west during the eighteenth and nineteenth centuries. James Macpherson's (q.v.) 'epics' provided a powerful incentive after 1760, although they also encouraged the unfortunate practice of 'improving' versions.

Prominent among the eighteenth-century collectors were ministers and schoolmasters. These included the Revd Alexander Pope (q.v.) of Reay, the Revd James McLagan (q.v.) of Amulrie and Blair Atholl, the Revd Donald MacNicol (q.v.) of Lismore and Jerome Stone, schoolmaster in Dunkeld. All had assembled valuable material before 1760, Pope's collection being the earliest (*c*.1739) and McLagan's the largest, extending to approximately 9,670 lines (D. S. Thomson 1958b). Two other important collectors, active before 1760, were the peripatetic Peter Turner and Archibald Fletcher, a non-literate farmer from Glenorchy. After 1760 material was assembled by the Revd Ewen MacDiarmid of Weem, Duncan Kennedy, schoolmaster at Kilbrandon (two collections), Thomas Ford Hill, and Bishop Matthew

Young of Clonfert (from a Mull source). Kennedy's collections (especially the second) require careful handling, since they are influenced by Macpherson. In 1786 John Gillies of Perth published *A Collection of Ancient and Modern Gaelic Poems*, containing *inter alia* twenty-four lays, mainly from earlier manuscript sources.

Some eighteenth-century collectors preserve vivid glimpses of their informants. The collections of Mac-Nicol and Hill correspond closely in parts, the common source being a blacksmith from Dalmally called MacNab, who, says Hill, 'had made it his business to collect and copy many of the songs attributed to Ossian'. MacNab's main source was the Mac-Nicol family from Glenorchy, evidently known also to McLagan. The MacNicols possessed manuscripts, but many informants were non-literate. Popular esteem for the tradition is captured by Pope of Reay, who obtained a version of the Lay of Diarmaid from 'an old fellow in this parish that very gravely takes off his bonnet as often as he sings *Duan Dearmot* . . . . he told me it was out of regard to the memory of that Hero.'

Collecting continued into the nineteenth century, doubtless stimulated by the activity surrounding the Highland Society's Report on Macpherson's 'Ossian' (1805). Significant collections were made by Revd Alexander Irvine of Little Dunkeld (1801), MacDonald of Staffa (1802), the Revd Alexander Campbell of Portree (1803), A. and D. Stewart (1804), the Revd John MacDonald of Ferintosh (1805) and Hugh and John MacCallum (1816). Although these preserve much genuine material, Macpherson casts his shadow over several collectors. From 1860 material was gathered in Argyll and the Hebrides from men 'with clear heads and wonderful memories' by Alexander Carmichael, John Dewar, the Revd John Gregorson Campbell of Tiree and John Francis Campbell (q.v.). J. F. Campbell's labours included extensive field trips to the Hebrides and the systematic collation of his own and earlier versions in *Leabhar na Féinne*, vol. I (1872), a work of immense usefulness.

Heroic verse survived into the twentieth century, and further versions of lays have been recorded by the School of Scottish Studies (q.v.). (See A. Cameron 1892–4; J. F. Campbell 1872; Christiansen 1931; Hill 1782; Nutt 1910; Stern 1900; Stone 1889; D. S. Thomson 1958b.)   DEM

verse, Jacobite Jacobite sentiments and verse have their origin in the late seventeenth century, in the Revolution of 1688 which led to the usurpation of James VII's (and II's) crown by William of Orange. Gaelic poets were soon commenting on these events and their consequences – for example, Iain Lom (or his son?) in his Song to the Army of King James (1689) (A. M. Mackenzie 1964, 184) or Iain Lom in 'Oran air Rìgh Uilleam agus Bànrigh Màiri (*c*.1692) (ibid., 202) with such sentiments as 'see now the Prince of Orange turning justice upside down'. Duncan MacRae of Inverinate wrote poems on this theme also (C. MacPhàrlain 1923, 170ff.), commenting wryly on change of allegiance ('Caochlaidh sinn mar chaochlas struth/Seumas an dé, am Prionns an diugh') and concerned equally about dynastic and religious questions. A poem with some Jacobite references (*c*.1693) is attributed to An Clàrsair Dall (q.v.) (W. Matheson 1970, 20).

There is some continuity between these poems and Iain Lom's poem on the Union of the Parliaments (1707), for example; also with the poetry that harks back to the Act of Settlement (1701). And there is some general pro-Jacobite sentiment in some poems by Iain Mac Ailein (q.v.). But the majority of Jacobite poems are linked to the Risings of 1715 and 1745 (the 1719 Rising also featured but less prominently.) Sìleas na Ceapaich (q.v.) composed a poem to the Old Pretender in 1714 (C. Ó Baoill 1972b, 16), a battle incitement for Mar's army in 1715 inviting various chiefs to join and three poems on the Battle of Sheriffmuir (1715), one celebrating notabilities who died there, another those who fled and a third beginning with a detailed description of preparations for the battle but disintegrating in a series of disjointed reflections (ibid., 38). Niall MacMhuirich has three poems on Sheriffmuir and Alan of Clanranald's mortal wounding there, two being in strophic vernacular verse, one in syllabic metre and classical Gaelic (D. S. Thomson 1971); his main concern is panegyric and lament. Iain Dubh Mac Iain 'ic Ailein (q.v.) also has a lament for Allan, and he composed a fairly elaborate battle incitement in 1715, urging some twenty-five clans to join the standard, giving a full stanza to the more important or newsworthy clans and cramming as many as five less important ones into one stanza (J. Mackenzie 1877, 72).

Niall MacMhuirich has a poem on the 1719 Glenshiel Rising; this has denser political content than the 1715 poems, being more reminiscent in this respect of Iain Lom's work (D. S. Thomson 1971).

The largest group of surviving Jacobite poems is that associated with the '45 Rising. J. L. Campbell

(1933) located about seventy poems 'which could be called Jacobite, that is to say, which were concerned with some aspect of the dynastic struggle and its consequences, apart from those which only gave it passing reference'. Campbell notes that only six of these were composed before the Rising took place; the total includes eight songs to the tartan, three songs and an elegy on Prince Charlie and songs and elegies on other chiefs (J. L. Campbell 1933, xx). John Mackenzie, in the first edition of his *Bliadhna Theàrlaich* (1844), had included seventeen songs in an appendix. Nearly half of Campbell's seventy poems were by Alasdair Mac Mhaighstir Alasdair (q.v.). The next most prominent Jacobite poet was Iain Ruadh Stiùbhart (q.v.); Donnchadh Bàn (q.v.) is sometimes a Jacobite, sometimes a Hanoverian; Rob Donn (q.v.) composed in 1745 a rather formal poem to the Prince and a more characteristically subtle poem on the Black Coats (after the Proscription of Arms and Highland Dress), in which he anticipates some rough treatment for the Gaels (*searsaigeadh mionaich* perhaps being better interpreted as 'a charge in the midriff'), and sees the Gaelic falcons chained to (English) kites (J. L. Campbell 1933, 240); Uilleam Ros (q.v.) was born well after the '45 but has a poem on hearing news of Prince Charlie's death (1688). Undoubtedly Mac Mhaighstir Alasdair's (q.v.) contribution to this theme is by far the most wide-ranging and interesting, drawing on much first-hand experience and a variety of moods and purposes and clearly bringing a knowledge of history to bear. Though there are hints of sentimentalism and romanticism in a few items of Jacobite verse, these are very subdued; it is immediate and usually practical in a way that Lady Nairn's Scots songs, for example, could hardly be.   DST

verse, panegyric Panegyric is not so much a form as a pervasive style in Gaelic poetry. Formally, however, it has a special connection with strophic metre, which in the Middle Ages was evidently the *métier* of the praise singers, the relatively low-grade poets who were called bards. Panegyric imagery was brought to a high pitch of refinement and elegance in Classical Gaelic poetry: vernacular poets drew upon this stock and developed it. From such origins the style spread so far that its influence is traceable even in choral work songs. The rhetoric of praise is employed with certain variations in different metrical contexts. In addition to limitations and opportunities imposed or offered by each metrical category, there are differences in the treatment of panegyric themes: Gaelic poets observe the conventions appropriate to the form.

In general panegyric enshrines the customary expectations of Gaelic society. In effect this means that it lays great stress on the survival of the group of aristocratic warrior-hunters at the top of society. The diction is codified in sets of conventional images, most densely concentrated in the heroic elegy composed at the point of crisis brought about by the death of a leader – in other words, when it was most necessary to reaffirm the traditional values of the community. One of the stock conventions is to rehearse the allies – real or ideal – of a clan. This reaches its height in 'Oran na Fineachan Gàidhealach' (The Song of the Gaelic Clans), composed at the time of the Jacobite Rising of 1715. A similar poem is associated with 1745. Such compositions are bardic propaganda for Gaelic nationalism – the 1715 poem opens with a reference to a prophecy that the Gaels will come into their own again in Scotland. Through such uses of the panegyric code Gaelic poets preserved at least a notional unity of the Gaelic nation, even when the policies of Crown and Parliament had reduced that nation to a multiplicity of warring units. (See J. MacInnes 1979.)   JMcI

verse, political (seventeenth century) The public nature of the poet's role in late medieval Gaelic society, and the fact that so much of the bardic craft was expended on the eulogy of chiefs, means that glancing references to major political events in which these personalities were involved are not uncommon. Sometimes a political trend can be the main theme of a poem, as in the case of Giolla Coluim Mac an Ollaimh's 'Ní h-éibhneas gan Chlainn Domhnaill', reflecting the eclipse of MacDonald power at the end of the fifteenth century (W. J. Watson 1937, 90–4). For a survey of the dominant themes in the corpus of three MacMhuirich bards, see Derick Thomson's paper in the volume *Bards and Makars* (Aitken *et al.*, 1977).

It is with the turbulent years of struggle between king and Parliament in the 1640s, and the eventual deposition of the Stuart dynasty towards the end of the seventeenth century, that national events, in the widest sense, become a preoccupation of Gaelic poets, though they may often be concerned more with local and incidental aspects of these events than with the major issues themselves. Thus the Civil War as fought in the Highlands is often seen and celebrated as an inter-clan conflict. For a recent and detailed historical analysis of this period in the Highlands, see Stevenson's work on Alasdair MacColla (D. Stevenson 1980).

The most trenchant and wide-ranging political commentator among all the Gaelic poets of the seventeenth century is Iain Lom (q.v.). His handling of the events of the 1640s is sometimes quite narrowly focused, the Battle of Inverlochy in 1645 becoming the occasion for a fierce song of exultation at the discomfiture and slaughter of the Campbells, and the Battle of Auldearn producing a eulogy of the Mac-Donald champion, Alasdair Mac Cholla (A. M. MacKenzie 1964). The emphasis on the *dramatis personae* is sustained with songs on the death of Alasdair Mac Cholla (1647), the imprisonment of Maclean of Duart (1647), the capture (1647) and death (1649) of the Marquis of Huntly and the execution of Montrose (1650). Curiously enough, there is no extant song by Iain Lom on the execution of Charles I. The lament for Montrose sees the submission of Scotland to the Protectorate as an instance of English tyranny comparable with the oppression of the Israelites in Egypt. The thudding monosyllabic endings of the stanzas make this one of Iain Lom's most powerful pieces. The aftermath of the Battle of Inverkeithing (1651), which brought royalist aspirations in Scotland effectively to an end at this time, is reflected in the 'Iorram do Mhac Gille Eathain', and moves Iain Lom to long for another Clan Donald invasion from Ireland. With the Restoration the poet's mood changes to one of elation and gleeful anticipation of the fate soon to befall the Marquis of Argyll.

Later in the century a number of Iain Lom's songs reflect aspects of the protracted struggle between the Campbells and the Macleans, and national events come to the forefront again only with the dynastic revolution of 1688–9. Of the two poems on the Battle of Killiecrankie ascribed to Iain Lom, one, a detailed account by a participant in the action, is probably not his; the other mingles lament for the fallen with contemptuous condemnation of King William's supporters. The song somewhat misleadingly entitled 'The Massacre of Glencoe', as it has only a passing reference to that event, longs for the distribution of Campbell territories among various septs of Clan Donald. Iain Lom's powerful and uncompromising voice survives into the early years of the eighteenth century, but his last political poem of the seventeenth century is a scurrilous attack on King William and Queen Mary, adducing the favourite biblical analogue of Absalom's rebellion against David.

Some of the authors represented in the Fernaig Manuscript (q.v.) have poems in support of the Royalist and Jacobite side of the seventeenth-century conflicts. Murchadh Mac Mhic Mhurchaidh has a poem on the betrayal of Charles I, which he sees as an illustration of the fickleness of the world, and another on the banishment of Charles II (M. Mac-Farlane 1923). Duncan MacRae, the compiler of the manuscript, reflects in similar vein on the deposition of James VII: 'Caochlaidh sinn mar chaochlas sruth/ Seumas an-dè, am Prionns an-diugh' (We change as a stream shifts – James yesterday, the Prince today). Two other poems, without ascriptions of authorship, deal with the same event. There is a poem on the Battle of Killiecrankie, translations of two contemporary English ballads, 'Jock Britain's Complaint' and 'The True Protestant's Complaint', and an exchange of verses on the vacillating conduct of some Highland officers after the Revolution between an Clàrsair Dall (q.v.) and Duncan MacRae (W. Matheson 1970).

The characteristically Celtic regard for kinship and heredity strongly underlies the royalist and Jacobite verse of the seventeenth century. A song on the Battle of Killiecrankie by the Glencoe bard Aonghus Mac Alasdair Ruaidh argues that even religion must take second place to the claims of the rightful heir (A. and A. MacDonald 1911, 80):

> Chan eil e ceadaicht' dhuinn claonadh
> No 'n rìgh saoghalta mhùchadh,
> 'S gur e 'n t-oighre fìor dhligheach
> On a ghineadh o thùs e.
> Chan fhaod deifir an creideamh
> No neo-chreideamh ar tàladh,
> 'S gun ùghdarras laghail
> Is gnìomh foilleil dhuinn àicheadh.   KDMCD

verse, political (twentieth century) Gaelic political attitudes, implicit or explicit, cannot be viewed apart from the growth of cultural nationalism. Most living poets are radicals or Home Rulers of one sort or another, or both. Poets of an older generation are more varied. At one distinct extreme Niall Ros's 'Armageddon' celebrates the 'well-knit Empire' and its 'beneficent sway' over 'distant colonies owned and wisely governed' and draws on memories of battle honours earned in the Imperial Service. Diametrically opposed is Donnchadh MacDhunlèibhe's comment on whites in Africa: 'Restless as the winds . . . ingenious as the Devil's son . . . pitiless . . . intolerant . . . loving sword's edge more than might . . . wealth and power their twin gods'. Some poets assert the continuity of Gaelic identity by looking back to the security of an older social order before policies of ethnocide were introduced. This is not to be mistaken for reaction: the same poets are usually committed to contemporary political radicalism. In such poetry patrician and proletarian attitudes exist side by side. Domhnall Ruadh Mac an t-Saoir honours his Gaelic inheritance; his politics, strongly influenced by 'Red Clydeside', are unequivocally left-wing and nationalist.

Nevertheless there are important differences in perspective and strategy between the older poets, who naturally view Gaelic and Scottish politics in a British imperial context, and the poets of the renaissance. Deorsa Caimbeul Hay's (q.v.) poem of the young soldier speaking from the grave or the verdict of the drowned sailor: 'Folk of the Isles, you have paid a high price for the greatness of Britain', stands in stark contrast to scores of poems of military glory. Hay's nationalism is always explicit: 'Men and women of Scotland, tempestuous race that I love . . . . Be we Lowland, my dear, or Gaels, it was she [Scotland] that nurtured us.' It is also optimistic, forward-looking and unparochial. Somhairle MacGillean's Marxism, and his concern with the Spanish Civil War as a paradigm of capitalist exploitation vindicated by religious interests, has its earliest roots in the events of the Highland Clearances. The idealism of the vision is evident even in the baffled disillusionment of 'Palach':

There was a time I thought
if the Red Army came across Europe
the tryst would not be bitter . . .
There is no text in my words . . . .

He brings the whole of history into a socialist perspective in his political writing, but it is the Scottish, and particularly the Gaelic, historical experience that gives the poetry its poignant intensity. Ruaraidh MacThómais's (q.v.) first explicitly political poem is dated 1942–3; like Hay's work of the same years, it expresses a buoyant nationalism. MacThómais's political concern has remained essentially constant over almost forty years, although the tone of the poetry has become progressively bleaker, more sceptical, more sophisticated.

The Land of the Ever-Young is in France
and when you reach the Promised Land
unless you are on your toes
a bland Englishman will meet you
and say to you that God, his uncle, has given him a
title to the land.

His latest work is charged with more political consciousness than is any other comparable collection of the last years. Highlands and Lowlands are conspicuously linked in this vision:

The Gael's exultant cry
coming from the chest of the Lowlands
if only the flame lasted
it would write 'Freedom' on Scotland's sky yet.

The twentieth century has seen a complementary growth of awareness of international issues, and Gaelic poets have responded with passion and concern to its terrible events. The expression of this, however, has been less overtly political.   JMCI

verse, religious Probably the oldest stratum of religious verse to survive in Scottish Gaelic is the body of anonymous charms, incantations and prayers represented, notably, by Alexander Carmichael's remarkable collection from the nineteenth century (A. Carmichael 1900–71), and the gleanings of other collectors such as Fr Allan McDonald (q.v.), Alexander MacBain (MacBain, 1892) and William MacKenzie (W. MacKenzie 1894). These prayers seek the aid of divine power and saintly intercession at various points in the daily or yearly round, at critical junctures in human life and as antidotes to physical calamities or malign powers. Many of them have doubtless evolved through the christianizing of the rituals and formulae of pagan magic. The simple directness and exuberance of their expression gives them an enduring freshness:

O Ios' gun lochd,
A Rìgh nam bochd,
A chìosadh goirt
Fo bhinn nan olc,
Dìon-s' a-nochd
Bho Iùdas mi.

O sinless Jesus, king of the poor, sorely subdued under sentence of the wicked, shield me this night from Judas.

Some of Carmichael's English versions have been separately published by Bittleston (Bittleston 1960) and in greater bulk, with some reworking, by MacLean (G. R. D. MacLean 1961).

The professional bardic poets frequently turned to religious themes for their occasional compositions, though the corpus of such verse that can with certainty be attributed to Scottish authors is not large, and most of what there is remains unedited. The principal manuscript sources are described in the 'Religious and Ecclesiastical' section of MacKinnon's *Catalogue* (D. MacKinnon 1912, 72–105); the religious compositions, many of them Irish, in the Book of the Dean of Lismore (q.v.) can be picked out from O'Rahilly's index (O'Rahilly, 1934); and Cameron's transcript of poems from Edinburgh MS XLVIII includes one or two religious pieces (Cameron 1892–4, vol. 1, 119–50). A good representative example is Giolla Coluim mac Illebhrìghde's poem, 'Mairg do ni uaill as óige', a *memento mori* reinforced by the analogue of an avaricious hedgehog. A mid-seventeenth century poem by Cathal Mac Muireadhaigh, castigating the body as the seat of sinful passions, has been edited by Angus Matheson (A. Matheson 1963). For the religious content in the poems of Niall Mór, Cathal and Niall MacMhuirich, see the survey by D. S. Thomson (1977c). A fuller appreciation of the typical themes and devices of bardic religious verse can be gained only from the study of the more copious Irish materials assembled and edited by Lambert McKenna (McKenna 1922).

The influence of bardic style is still very much present in the Fernaig Manuscript (q.v.), the principal seventeenth-century repository of Gaelic religious verse, though in this mainly Protestant company some of the distinctive medieval features, such as devotion to the Virgin and appeals for the intercession of saints, are absent. The major emphases of these poems are well represented in those ascribed to the compiler of the manuscript, Donnchadh nam Pìos (q.v.). The theme of disillusionment with the world, its pleasures and pretensions, is pointed by such first lines as 'A shaoghail, is diombuan do mhùirn' (O world, short-lived is your joy) and 'Is corrach do chor, a shaoghail (O world, precarious is your condition). There are poems on the biblical themes of the Fall and the Day of Judgement and a composition in praise of God as creator. The theme of penitence and yearning after grace and spiritual renewal is strongly present. One of these poems was triggered by the illness of MacRae's wife and recounts some biblical instances of healing and deliverance. Another of MacRae's reflections on personal sinfulness uses the medieval device of a conversation between the soul and the body and deals at length with the sinful misuse of the Lord's Day. The keynotes of these religious poems in the Fernaig Manuscript have been discussed by the Revd Dr John MacInnes (J. MacInnes 1971b).

Post-Reformation Roman Catholic hymn writing in Gaelic is of comparatively small bulk. There is a moving poem of resignation, wrung by the pains of his last illness from Archibald MacDonald, chief of Keppoch, who died in 1682 (A. and A. MacDonald 1911, 69). His daughter, Sìleas na Ceapaich (q.v.) was a hymn writer of some note, and though her surviving hymns probably date from her later years, they can more naturally be grouped along with compositions of the seventeenth century than with those of the eighteenth. They are interesting for their range of theme and imagery. Death occupies a prominent place in her thought, whether as the ravager who has deprived her of her husband and child, the stern claimant with whom she altercates or the macabre dissolver of her physical body. She has a morning hymn, in which spiritual discipline is presented in terms of household chores, and the seven deadly sins are seen as the heads of a monster, to be slain by the arrows of righteous living. One of her hymns portrays the Roman Catholic Church under the common medieval figure of an impregnable castle (C. Ó Baoill 1972b; J. L. Campbell 1956a).

The eighteenth century saw the beginnings of a fresh surge of Gaelic religious verse, going hand in hand with the advance of evangelical religion, with its emphasis on individual salvation nurtured by a thoroughgoing application of biblical doctrine. It gained considerable momentum in the nineteenth century, and has continued to the present, the number of separate publications whether of individual pieces or larger collections, being in the region of two hundred (D. Maclean 1915).

The eighteenth-century religious poets reflect the missionary phase of the evangelical movement (J. MacInnes 1951 and 1971b), the period when the Bible was either still untranslated into Scottish Gaelic or inaccessible to non-literate Gaelic speakers. There is a strong catechetical emphasis in their hymns, the presentation of versified and easily memorized summaries of biblical teaching. Dùghall Bochanan (q.v.) represents this thrust, though he stands apart by virtue of his intellectual freshness and artistic skill.

More typical are the northern poets represented in Rose's *Metrical Reliques* (Rose 1851). John Mackay of Mudale (q.v.) dwells mainly on the cardinal doctrines of the Fall and redemption through Christ. Donald Matheson of Kildonan (q.v.) has a more subjective cast to his mind, contemplating his inner corruption and spiritual struggles, but he too summarizes the story of the Exodus as the exemplar of spiritual liberation. Lachlan MacLachlan, with his elegy to the Revd Hector MacPhail, stands at the start of a long line of such compositions. William MacKenzie condenses some biblical passages but moves also into the area of polemic with a versified debate between Reformation and the Pope. Donald MacRae of Petty is mainly concerned with self-examination. A group of poets with a south-westerly ambience is represented in Duncan Kennedy's collection (D. Kennedy 1786). Iain Bàn Maor chooses themes such as the Incarnation, the Passion and the Judgement; Bean a' Bharra links the Exodus and the Atonement; and Iain Caimbeul Sgoilear summarizes the Gospel narrative. The versification of theological subjects is further developed in the work of the Revd James MacGregor (q.v.). In verses set to the tunes of popular Gaelic songs, he handles such themes as the Law, the Covenant of Works, the Covenant of Grace, Sin, the Gospel, Faith, the Work of the Holy Spirit, Death, the Resurrection, Heaven, and Hell (J. MacGregor 1819).

The religious verse of the nineteenth century reflects the more widespread settlement of evangelical ministries and, in general, the greater theological sophistication of the Highland audience. One of the most notable religious poets of the earlier part of the century was Dr John MacDonald of Ferintosh (q.v.). He substantially developed the tradition of religious elegies with his long poems on prominent ministers, highlighting the twin crises of conversion and death, as well as the general character of the intervening preaching and pastoral labours. His outstanding composition is his poem in memory of his own father, a kind of 'Pilgrim's Progress' remarkable for the neatness and precision with which theological subtleties are debated in smooth-flowing verse (J. MacDonald 1897). His contemporary, Iain Gobha na Hearadh (q.v.), used his very considerable resources of Gaelic vocabulary and idiom, sometimes in poems of undisciplined length, to reflect on his own religious experience as well as some of the principal personalities and disputes of the Disruption era (Henderson 1893). Another early nineteenth-century hymn writer of

similar *gravitas* was John Maclean, Bàrd Thighearna Cholla (q.v.), who in later life turned to religious compositions. These dwell on the main biblical themes, perhaps drawing some of their inspiration from Bunyan, for there are pieces entitled 'The Pilgrim's Progress' and 'The Holy War' (J. Maclean 1880).

A less heavily doctrinal style of religious verse with a higher emotional temperature is seen in the work of Pàdraig Grannd (q.v.). As the nineteenth century progressed there was an increasing tendency for Gaelic hymns to be composed to lighter, more jaunty Gaelic and even Lowland tunes. This is seen, for example, in the compositions of Archibald Farquharson of Tiree (Farquharson 1870), and Murdo Macleod (Murchadh a' Cheisdeir, q.v.) is in the same tradition (M. MacLeod 1962). The translation of popular English hymns into Gaelic became a considerable industry, as evidenced by the publication of MacCallum's collection (A. K. MacCallum 1894) the St Columba hymn book (St Columba Church 1906), and the hymns for Gaelic missions published by Duncan MacColl (MacColl, 1899); and translations from the hand of the Revd Roderick MacDonald still regularly appear in the Gaelic supplement to the Church of Scotland magazine, *Life and Work*.

There has been a much more limited output of Roman Catholic hymn writing in Gaelic. In 1893 Father Allan McDonald published a representative collection (Fr A. MacDonald 1893; J. L. Campbell 1956a), containing quite a number of translations. Father Allan's own poetry includes some pieces of warm devotion (J. L. Campbell 1965), and more recently Donald MacDonald of Eriskay included translations of six hymns in his published collection (MacDhòmhnaill 1981).

Of twentieth-century practitioners composing religious verse in the well-established evangelical tradition, two of the most prominent have been John Smith of Bernera, Lewis, a collection of whose hymns is shortly to be published (J. Smith forthcoming) and Hector Mackinnon (d. 1954) of Berneray, North Uist, whose hymns remain unpublished but enjoy a wide oral circulation.

A less affirmative, more questioning, note, combined with a more lyrical expression and more adventurous metrical forms, is characteristic of James Thomson's (q.v.) religious poems (J. Thomson 1953). An even more resolute attempt to transcend the familiar stereotypes is seen in the verse of Roderick MacDonald (Roderick MacDonald 1978). But the most innovative and exciting of contemporary religious poets in Gaelic is Fearghas MacFhionnlaigh (q.v.), who has published short poems in *Gairm* but whose most impressive production is the long poem, *A' Mheanbhchuileag* (MacFhionnlaigh 1980), portraying the invading grace of God in the bleak setting of contemporary existentialism and materialism. MacFhionnlaigh has shown an increasing mastery of Gaelic as a medium, and it is likely that the full flowering of his talent is yet to come.   KDMCD

verse, semi-bardic The label 'semi-bardic verse' has been applied to a range of work which shows the influence of classical bardic verse either in language or in metre, and frequently in both, though its language is predominantly vernacular Scottish Gaelic. The label could be used for vernacularized heroic ballads, some of which began their life as classical poems, while others must have been first composed in less strict metre and language. More generally, however, 'semi-bardic' is a term applied to the work of a succession of sixteenth- and seventeenth-century poets who composed poems on religious, panegyric, personal and occasional themes, using strict classical metres or more relaxed variants of these, and a vernacular Scottish Gaelic laced with morphological and occasionally lexical archaisms (e.g. verbal forms such as *atá*, *atáim*, *do bhí*, *do dhul*, *thugais*, *smuainmid*, *creidfeam*, *thigeas*, *fágbhail*, the negatives *ní* and *níor*, and lexical items such as *a sunn*, *oircheas*, *fa thrí*, *dairchruaidh*). The classical metres Rannaigheacht bheag mhór, Snéadhbhairdne and Deibhidhe are the ones most used; these and certain other classical metres continue to be used by vernacular poets well after the seventeenth century.

We can identify verse of the kind described dating from *c.*1520 to the mid-eighteenth century, taking 'An Duanag Ullamh', (W. J. Watson 1918a, 259), praise by a Mull bard of an Argyll chief, as the earliest non-ballad item in the style and ending with the Turner Manuscript, a mid-eighteenth-century Kintyre compilation which is virtually an anthology of semi-bardic verse, including aphoristic verses, heroic ballads, religious verse such as 'An Chreud' (The Creed), elegy, such as 'Marbhrainn Neill Oig Mhachraidh Shanais' (Elegy for Neil of Machriehanish), occasional verse e.g. 'Failte an Chait' (Welcome to the Cat), 'Caoi Mhic Ui Mhaoilchiarain' (Lament for the Son of Maol Ciarain), etc. (A. Cameron 1894, 310–420). In between these limits we have religious verse by MacCulloch of Park and John

Stewart of Appin, elegiac and nostalgic verses by Gille Caluim Garbh of Raasay and Donnchadh Mac-Raoiridh, and similar verse by the Mackenzies of Achilty, together with more spirited poems such as 'An Làir Dhonn' (see separate entries for all these poets).

Probably we should identify links between this body of verse and the occasionally surviving work of people of social rank such as Isabel of Argyll (q.v.), the Earl of Argyll (q.v.) whose work appears in the Book of the Dean of Lismore (q.v.), and John Carswell (q.v.), the latter of course using Classical Gaelic extensively in his prose. (For some brief discussion of sixteenth- and seventeenth-century chiefs' ability to write Gaelic, see Bannerman and Black 1978, 62–3.) We should see links also with the semi-classical verse of a MacMharcais poet or the authors of the dedicatory odes in Lhuyd's *Archaeologia* (1707), and the late survival of Gaelic interest and expertise in such chiefs as MacFarlane of Arrochar (a patron of Mac Mhaighstir Alasdair) and Macintyre of Glen Noe, and probably with other families such as the MacDonalds of Dalness and Mac Mhaighstir Alasdair's own family. Gaelic manuscripts, and the skill of writing the old hand, survived into the middle of the eighteenth century.

What seems to be suggested by all this is that the training facilities which were used by the classical bards, and/or by historians, scribes, archivists and medical men, provided some access also for persons of social rank and influence in the Gaelic world and may later have been mediated to the successors of these social and professional classes – for example, to the *aos-dàna* (q.v.), latter-day seanchaidhs (oral historians), scribes and scions of leading families. Such a transmission of training facilities in the use of Gaelic seems to have continued well into the eighteenth century, so that it made contact with a handful of the university-educated scions of the literate and ruling families involved. The topic is one which calls for closer investigation. (See D. S. Thomson 1955; 1974a.)   DST

verse, village Probably for many centuries the village or district poet has had an important role as the chronicler and critic of local contemporary events and attitudes. His poems are primarily addressed to a local audience and often depend on an intimate knowledge of characters and incidents. The poems may have a moral or didactic function, but usually a prime motivation is to provide amusement, and so

the genre is strongly marked by wit, linguistic dexter-
ity, situational humour, often a catchy rhythm and
perhaps unusual rhymes. The language is closer to
the current speech norm than that of many other
kinds of verse.

The strongly local aspect of such verse may restrict
its general appeal and generally confines the verse to
an oral circulation. This makes it difficult, probably
impossible, to identify anything like a starting-point
for verse of this kind. All that we can say is that at
various stages in the Gaelic verse tradition we can
recognize work that is similar to the local verse that is
so well attested in the last two centuries. Much of
Rob Donn's (q.v.) verse fits into this category,
though the circumstances of his life allowed him to
include tacksmen and ministers in his bardic parish,
and his particular genius enabled his best work to
transcend parish boundaries. Some of John MacCodrum's (q.v.) verse also is in this genre. Earlier Iain
Mac Ailein (q.v.) had satirized Fear nan Druimnean
in a style that belongs to this tradition also, and
perhaps we should see Duncan Campbell of Glenorchy's 'Cia don phléid as ceann uidhe' and Giolla
Coluim's 'Mor an feidhm freagairt na bhfaighdheach'
(W. J. Watson 1937, 14, 66) as in some senses,
sixteenth- and fifteenth-century examples. This takes
us close enough to the beginning of our well attested
verse tradition.

It was the nineteenth-century spread of popular
Gaelic literacy, and the growth of Gaelic publishing
to serve it, that made the verse of the *bàrd baile* more
generally accessible. A selection of this work would
include songs by Dòmhnall MacLeòid (q.v.) of Skye
(Oran Mhurchaidh Bhig, etc.) and his two sons Iain
Dubh (q.v.) and Niall (q.v.), though Niall
MacLeòid's parish was to become Edinburgh; by
Calum MacAoidh (q.v.) of Bragar; John Maclean of
Baile Mhàrtainn (q.v.); Iain MacPhaidein (q.v.) of
Mull but operating a Glasgow 'parish'; Donnchadh
MacNimhein of Islay (Oran ait); Uilleam Iain 'ic
Choinnich of Lewis (though humour is not a leading
characteristic of his work); Neil Morrison (Bàrd
Phabaigh), with his 'Oran a' Bhuntàta' on the Potato
Blight of 1846; and examples from virtually any com-
munity that was thoroughly Gaelic-speaking.

The genre continues to attract composers up to the
present, with, for example, recent songs such as
'Oran an A.I.' (on artificial insemination of cattle), a
song about the new Comhairle nan Eilean (q.v.), etc.
Fine examples can be found in *Bàrdachd á Leòdhas*
(ed. Tormod MacLeòid), *Na Bàird Thirisdeach* (ed.

Hector Cameron), 'Bàrdachd Uibhist-a-deas', collected by John MacMillan (*Gairm*, vol. 17 onwards),
and in individual collections – for example, Am
Puilean's 'A' Ialliùgo is Bàta Tòthan' (A. Caimbeul
1972, 20). Much work of this kind remains unpublished in print; some of it has been published on
record and tape and broadcast especially on radio. It
had a fair claim to be considered the popular culture
before the recent onset of Country and Western
pastiche.   DST

Wade, Field Marshal George (1673–1748) Born in
Ireland. Appointed after the 1715 uprising to disarm
the clans. In 1724 he recommended the recruitment
of Highlanders under Gaelic-speaking officers, thus
reviving the Black Watch (see **regiments, Highland**). He held the Highland command from 1726 to
1737, when he built roads and bridges from Dunkeld
to Inverness and down the Great Glen. (See Salmond
1934.)   IG

Walker, George (fl. late eighteenth century), *see* art,
Gaelic, in modern times.

Walker, Revd Dr John (1731–1803) Born in Edinburgh. Minister of Moffat, etc. Professor of Natural
History, University of Edinburgh. Author of reports
on Hebrides (1761–71) containing useful agricultural,
demographic and other information (M. M. McKay
1980).   DST

Wars of Independence Probably the dominant
Highland family in 1296 were the Comyns of Badenoch, with castles at Lochindorb and Inverlochy. On
the western seaboard the descendants of Somerled
(q.v.), the Macdonalds of Islay, the Macdougalls of
Argyll and the Macruairidhs of Garmoran, shared
power, again with notable castles (for example, Dun-

staffnage, Inchconnel, Mingarry and Caisteal Tioram). Already the Macdonalds had established a connection with the Bruces and were found with them in Edward I's army (1296), gaining authority in Kintyre. The Macdougalls were connected by marriage to the Comyns and hence supported the Balliol cause. All three families had a considerable following in galleys and were important because of this control of links with Ireland.

The revolts of 1297 included one in and near Inverness led by Sir Andrew Moray, and the control established by Edward I in 1296 in the north was soon broken. Highland lords undoubtedly sent contingents to the patriotic armies, though others, notably the Macruairidhs, played a self-interested game. In 1304–5 English control was re-established.

Bruce's murder of Comyn began a civil war in which he had little initial support – hence his defeat (19 June 1306) and flight through Athol and Lennox to Kintyre and thence by sea probably to Dunyveg (Dùn Naomhaig), where Angus Macdonald reluctantly submitted and then to Garmoran whence the Macruairidhs gave him a force to return to Carrick. His failure there turned to success when he went north (September 1307) by Loch Ness to Moray, Ross and Buchan. With a small but mobile force he neutralized or defeated his enemies singly, expelling the Comyns from Buchan and taking the key castles of Urquhart, Inverness and Elgin (1308). From this largely Highland base he seized control of Scotland to the Tay and in 1309 defeated the Macdougalls on the slope of Cruachan, took Dunstaffnage and expelled them. The islemen sent a contingent to the Scottish army at Bannockburn. The Campbells (a Lowland family connected with the earls of Carrick) and the Macdonalds, who seem to have joined Bruce with more enthusiasm at this time, were given Macdougall lands and c.1318 Argyll was made a sheriffdom, with a sheriff at Tarbert and constables at Dunoon and Dunstaffnage.

In the Highlands Comyn power was replaced by Thomas Randolph, the king's nephew, who in 1312 was given a new earldom of Moray, stretching from Ross to Banffshire and south to include Lochaber; in this vast territory he enjoyed unprecedented privileges.

When the war was renewed, in 1333 Edward III sought to restore the Balliols and the Macdougalls. In the Highlands the Strathbogie earls of Athol, expelled by Bruce in 1314 for desertion, returned and perhaps found some support. The patriotic leader, Andrew Moray (son of his 1297 namesake) also drew support

The Battle of Bannockburn, 1314. From John of Fordun's Scotichronicon, *Corpus Christi College Cambridge MS 171, f.265v.*

from the Highlands, and English and Balliol forces, which were never able to subdue the country completely, had effectively withdrawn by 1337. A Highland force joined David II in 1346 to invade England, but the earl of Ross murdered Ranald Macruairidh at Perth and withdrew his contingent – a sad symptom of the feuds which occasionally disturbed both Highland and Lowland society. The Macdonald–Macdougall feud, however, reached a settlement in 1354, which restored a small nucleus of the Macdougall lands, leaving the Macdonalds, under their long-lived chief John, to build up a hegemony, the lordship of the Isles. (See Barrow 1965, 1973; A. and A. Macdonald 1896–1904.)

AAMD

Watson, Professor James Carmichael (1910–42) Son of W. J. Watson (q.v.), whom he succeeded as Professor of Celtic at the University of Edinburgh in 1938. In the short years of his maturity he published editions of Mary MacLeod and the medieval Irish saga *Mesca Ulad* and edited volumes 4 and 5 of his grandfather's *Carmina Gadelica*.

DST

Watson, Professor William John (1865–1948) Born Easter Ross. Educated Aberdeen and Oxford. Rector, Inverness Royal Academy and Edinburgh's Royal High School. Professor of Celtic at the University of Edinburgh, 1914–38. His major work was *The History of the Celtic Place-Names of Scotland*

(1926). He also put the study of the Book of the Dean of Lismore (q.v.) on a scholarly basis, edited the fine anthologies *Rosg Gàidhlig* (1915) and *Bàrdachd Ghàidhlig* (1918), founded the Scottish Gaelic Texts Society (q.v.) and inspired much good scholarship.

DST

waulking songs, *see* songs, waulking, metres of.

weapons, *see* arms and armour; metalwork.

Western Isles Regional Council, *see* Comhairle nan Eilean.

'Whale Hunt, The', *see* Mac a' Ghobhainn, Iain (Iain Chaluim Ruaidh).

Whisky The word (spelled whiskey in the USA and in Ireland) comes from the Gaelic *uisge beatha* (water

'Highland whisky still'. Edwin Landseer, c. 1826. Victoria and Albert Museum. Whisky has been distilled in Scotland for hundreds of years — references to it become common during the seventeenth century. After 1707 English revenue officers mounted a lengthy and largely unsuccessful campaign to impose excise duties, resulting in widespread illicit distilling which prevailed until a Royal Commission culminated in an Act of 1823 setting more reasonable and easily applicable rates of taxation. This picture is one of a series painted by Landseer depicting scenes of Highland life in the early nineteenth century. The still itself, only partly visible in the interior of the shelter, appears to consist of a water barrel or tank linked by cisterns, one heated by a fire from underneath. The central shadowy figure of the distiller holds a conical funnel.

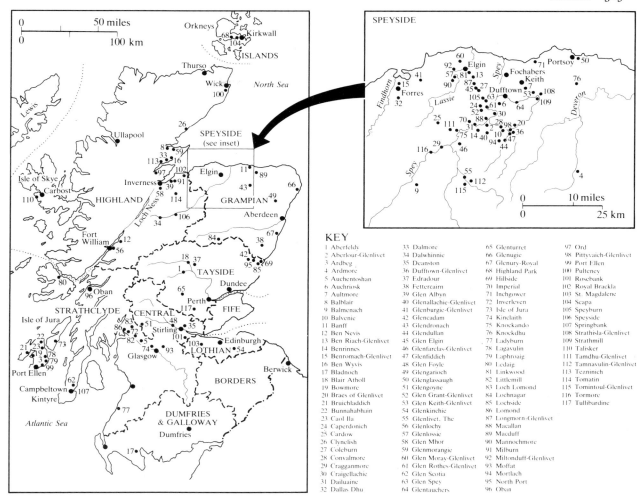

Distribution of malt whisky distilleries

Malt whiskies divide themselves into four distinct regional groups – Lowland, south of a line from Greenock to Dundee; Highland, north of the same line, with its subgroup Speyside; Islay; and Campbeltown. The regions have their own distinct characteristics, and so do the individual whiskies. Why this should be – to the extent that adjacent Speyside distilleries produce malts of entirely different qualities – has been attributed to, among other things, local climate and water, the soil in the barley fields, the shape of the still, the method and length of storage and the constituents of the peat fire over which the green malt is dried before grinding and malting. The consequence, at any rate, is a range of flavour and bouquet that no other distilled spirit comes near to matching – and an ability to meet every mood and occasion.

KEY

1 Aberfeldy	33 Dalmore	65 Glenturret	97 Ord
2 Aberlour-Glenlivet	34 Dalwhinnie	66 Glenugie	98 Pittyvaich-Glenlivet
3 Ardbeg	35 Deanston	67 Glenury-Royal	99 Port Ellen
4 Ardmore	36 Dufftown-Glenlivet	68 Highland Park	100 Pulteney
5 Auchentoshan	37 Edradour	69 Hillside	101 Rosebank
6 Auchriosk	38 Fettercairn	70 Imperial	102 Royal Brackla
7 Aultmore	39 Glen Albyn	71 Inchgower	103 St. Magdalene
8 Balblair	40 Glenallachie-Glenlivet	72 Inverleven	104 Scapa
9 Balmenach	41 Glenburgie-Glenlivet	73 Isle of Jura	105 Speyburn
10 Balvenie	42 Glencadam	74 Kinclaith	106 Speyside
11 Banff	43 Glendronach	75 Knockando	107 Springbank
12 Ben Nevis	44 Glendullan	76 Knockdhu	108 Strathisla-Glenlivet
13 Ben Riach-Glenlivet	45 Glen Elgin	77 Ladyburn	109 Strathmill
14 Benrinnes	46 Glenfarclas-Glenlivet	78 Lagavulin	110 Talisker
15 Benromach-Glenlivet	47 Glenfiddich	79 Laphroaig	111 Tamdhu-Glenlivet
16 Ben Wyvis	48 Glen Foyle	80 Ledaig	112 Tamnavulin-Glenlivet
17 Bladnoch	49 Glengarioch	81 Linkwood	113 Teaninich
18 Blair Atholl	50 Glenglassaugh	82 Littlemill	114 Tomatin
19 Bowmore	51 Glengoyne	83 Loch Lomond	115 Tomintoul-Glenlivet
20 Braes of Glenlivet	52 Glen Grant-Glenlivet	84 Lochnagar	116 Tormore
21 Bruichladdich	53 Glen Keith-Glenlivet	85 Lochside	117 Tullibardine
22 Bunnahabhain	54 Glenkinchie	86 Lomond	
23 Caol Ila	55 Glenlivet, The	87 Longmorn-Glenlivet	
24 Caperdonich	56 Glenlochy	88 Macallan	
25 Cardow	57 Glenlossie	89 Macduff	
26 Clynelish	58 Glen Mhor	90 Mannochmore	
27 Convalmore	59 Glenmorangie	91 Milburn	
28 Cragganmore	60 Glen Moray-Glenlivet	92 Miltonduff-Glenlivet	
29 Craigellachie	61 Glen Rothes-Glenlivet	93 Moffat	
30 Craigellachie	62 Glen Scotia	94 Mortlach	
31 Dailuaine	63 Glen Spey	95 North Port	
32 Dallas Dhu	64 Glentauchers	96 Oban	

of life, cf. *aqua vitae* and *eau-de-vie*). There are, in general, two main kinds of whisky, malt whisky and blended whisky. The former is made entirely from malted barley (for example, Glenlivet, Glenmorangie, Glenfiddich, Talisker, Laphroaig, etc.). Each has its own individual character. Blended whisky is made from grain (mainly maize), with up to 40 per cent of various malts added to give flavour and consistency. In the production of a blended whisky up to twenty different malts may be used to give such well-known brands as White Horse, Dewar's, Bell's, Crawford's, Johnnie Walker, etc.

In the manufacture of malt whisky the barley is soaked in water for between fifty and sixty hours and then transferred to a concrete floor, where it is spread to a depth of about 3 feet. The barley begins to germinate or sprout. This generates heat, and the malt-man has to keep reducing the depth by turning and spreading the grain with a wooden shovel (skip). This also prevents the rootlets from becoming entangled. In a large distillery the turning and spreading of the sprouting barley may be done mechanically. Some distilleries, on the other hand, no longer do their own 'malting' but buy the malt ready-made from maltsters.

After about twelve days the rootlets begin to wither and the grain becomes chalky. At this stage the barley is judged to be 'malted' and is spread on a wire-mesh floor in a kiln, where it is dried to stop germination. The heat is supplied by a peat/coke fire – the ratio of peat to coke is varied according to the brand of malt whisky being produced. Obviously, the peat smoke and other pyrogens give the characteristic peaty flavour to the finished product.

Germination of the barley produces an enzyme (organic catalyst), diastase, which converts the starch to a soluble sugar called maltose:

$$(C_6H_5O_{11})_n^- + \frac{n}{2}H_2O \xrightarrow{\text{diastase}} \frac{n}{2}(C_{12}H_{22}O_{11})$$

$$\text{starch} \qquad \text{water} \qquad\qquad \text{maltose}$$

The malt is then roughly ground and extracted four times with hot water to dissolve the maltose. This process is called mashing. The residue (draff), along with the rootlets, make a valuable cattle food.

The extract, containing the dissolved maltose (called wort) is cooled to about 80°F and put into a wooden 'wash-back' (5,000 gallons or more); a suitable strain of yeast added. The yeast contains two enzymes, maltase and zymase. The first converts the maltose to glucose, and the second converts the glucose to alcohol:

$$C_{12}H_{22}O_{11}^- + H_2O \xrightarrow{\text{diastase}} 2C_6H_{12}O_6$$

$$\text{maltose} \qquad \text{water} \qquad\qquad \text{glucose}$$

$$C_6H_{12}O_6 \xrightarrow{\text{zymase}} 2C_2H_5OH + 2CO_2$$

$$\text{glucose} \qquad\qquad \text{alcohol} \qquad \text{carbon dioxide}$$

When the fermentation is over, the liquor, now known as wash, is transferred to the first of the copper pot stills in which distillation takes place, yielding 'low wines'. The low wines then go to a second pot still – the spirit still – and are redistilled. The first runnings of the still, or 'foreshots', contain aldehydes and other unpleasant and toxic substances; these are collected separately, to be redistilled with the next batch. Collection of the whisky or spirit fraction which goes into the spirit receiver is started at about 26° over proof – indicated by the Sykes hydrometer – and is reduced down to a strength of 5° over proof. Beyond this point the distillate, called feints, goes back into the still along with the next batch.

The process of distillation serves to separate the alcohol (B. pt. 78·4°C) from the aqueous or watery material (B. pt. 100°C). The spirit so collected is 15°–20° over proof. This is reduced to 11° over proof with spring water and put in oak casks to mature.

Originally, proof meant a mixture of alcohol and water which, when poured onto gunpowder, would just prevent it from igniting when a light was applied. In 1816, however, the Sykes hydrometer was officially introduced and adopted by the Customs and

A malt distillery in the Speyside area.

Pot stills at Talisker, the only distillery on the Isle of Skye. Talisker has produced a distinctive malt whisky since 1830. It is one of over forty distilleries which produce malt whisky for the Scotch whisky blending houses of the Distillers Company Limited.

Excise officials. Proof spirit is now arbitrarily defined as 'a spirit which at 51°F weighs 12/13ths of an equal volume of distilled water at the same temperature'. In practice this means 57·1 per cent alcohol by volume at 60°F. In the USA proof means 50 per cent alcohol by volume at 60°F. Absolute or pure alcohol is 73·35° over proof.

Whisky, then, is matured at 11° over proof in sherry casks – if these are available – to give the whisky its traditional colour; if sherry casks are not available, caramel is used. Malt whisky, before it is marketed or used for blending, must mature by law for a minimum of three years. Many think that this period should be at least five years. On the other hand, whisky 'goes off' if left in casks for fifteen years. The ideal time for maturation would be between eight and twelve years. The chemical changes which take place during the maturing are very complex and are little understood, but the whisky is undoubtedly greatly improved in flavour, bouquet and palatability.

Blended whisky, as has been noted, is made mainly from maize. Maize contains no diastase, so some malted barley must be added to supply the deficiency. Fermentation of the starch to maltose, to glucose and finally to alcohol takes place as described above, but distillation is carried out in a patent, silent or Coffey still. This rectifying device delivers a very strong pure spirit – about 95 per cent alcohol – which requires little or no maturing.

Although many will maintain that pure malt whisky is the only 'real' whisky, blends are by no means to be despised, for great skill and experience goes into blending to give a product that is consistent in taste and bouquet. (See Daiches 1969; N. M. Gunn 1935; Lockhart 1951; Robb 1950.) MBW

Whyte, Annetta Campbell (b. 1889) Daughter of Henry Whyte (q.v.). Mod Gold Medallist, 1903. Co-editor, *Celtic Garland* (enlarged edn 1920). DST

Whyte, Henry (1852–1913) From Easdale. Pen-name 'Fionn'. A prolific Gaelic writer of stories, songs and essays, and a translator and editor. (See *Celtic Review*, vol. 9, 332; *Celtic Monthly*, vol. 1, 17; vol. 22, 14; *An Gaidheal*, vol. 9, 73.) TMM

Whyte, John (d. 1913) From Easdale. Brother of Henry Whyte (q.v.). Pen-names 'MacMharcuis' and 'IBO' (?'Iain Bàn Og'). Journalist, translator, librarian. Edited (old) *Gaidheal*. Collaborated in M. Macpherson (1891), A. Macbain (1906); edited MacCaluim (1894). TMM

word tones, Gaelic, *see* Gaelic: word tones and svarabhakti.

Chronology

Some of the Principal Milestones in the History of Gaelic Scotland
with a few comparative dates

55–54 BC	Julius Caesar's expeditions to Britain
80 AD	Agricola's invasion of North Britain
84	Battle of Mons Graupius
297	Picti and Hiberni referred to as enemies of the South Scottish Britons
360–65	Scotti and Picti operating as allies against the Romans
c.500	Foundation of kingdom of Dalriada
c.501	Death of Fergus Mór mac Eirc
563	Arrival of Columba (Colum Cille) in Iona
575	Convention of Druim Cett
602	Battle of Degsastan
c.608	Death of Aedán mac Gabráin
c.624	Birth of Adamnán
c.642	Battle of Strathcarron and death of Domnall Brecc
664	Synod of Whitby
c.680	Book of Durrow
685	Battle of Nectansmere
c.698–721	Lindisfarne Gospels
731	Completion of Bede's *Ecclesiastical History*
736	Capture of Dunadd by king of the Picts
750–800	Book of Kells
c.780–800	Norse settlement in Scottish Isles begins
c.843	Union of kingdoms of Picts and Scots
849	Administrative centre of Celtic Church in Scotland moves from Iona to Dunkeld
917	Battle of Brunanburh
1018	Battle of Carham
1057	Death of MacBeth, king of Scots
1069	Marriage of Malcom Canmore and Margaret
1131–53	Gaelic *notitiae* entered in Book of Deer
1164	Death of Somerled, founder of lordship of the Isles
1263	Battle of Largs
1266	Treaty of Perth
1314	Battle of Bannockburn
1408	Islay Gaelic Charter
1411	Foundation of University of St Andrews; Battle of Harlaw
1451	Foundation of University of Glasgow
1490	Murder of Angus Óg MacDonald
1491	Blàr na Pàirc (Battle)
1493	Forfeiture of lordship of the Isles
1494	Foundation of University of Aberdeen

1512–26	Main part of Book of Dean of Lismore compiled
1513	Battle of Flodden
1544	Blàr na Léine (Battle)
1560	The Reformation
1567	Publication of first printed Gaelic book, Carswell's *Liturgy*
1582	Foundation of University of Edinburgh
1588	Spanish Armada; sinking of Armada ship *Florida* off Tobermory
1603	Union of the crowns of Scotland and England
1609	Statutes of Iona
1618–48	Thirty Years War
1626	Death of Ruairi Mór MacLeod
1645	Battles of Inverlochy and Auldearn
1647	Massacre of Dunaverty; death of Alasdair Mac Colla
1650	Execution of Montrose
1658–59	Publication of first fifty Gaelic Psalms
1678	Highland Host quartered in Ayrshire etc.
1689	Battle of Killiecrankie
1690	Establishment of Church of Scotland as national church
1692	Massacre of Glencoe
1707	Union of the Parliaments of Scotland and England
1709	Foundation of the SSPCK
1715	First Jacobite Rising
1719	Minor Jacobite Rising (Glenshiel)
1745	Second Jacobite Rising
1746	Battles of Falkirk and Culloden
1749–75	Emigration of tacksmen and followers to America
1751	Publication of Alasdair Mac Mhaighstir Alasdair's poems, *Ais-eiridh*
1760–63	Publication of James Macpherson's Ossianic poems
1767	Publication of Gaelic New Testament
1769	Invention of Watt's steam-engine
1772	Runciman's Ossianic paintings at Penicuik House
1773	Tour of the Hebrides by Samuel Johnson and James Boswell
1776	Declaration of American Independence
1783	Foundation of Royal Society of Edinburgh
1784	Foundation of Highland Society of Scotland
1788	Death of Prince Charles Edward
1789	Start of French Revolution
1792	Bliadhna nan Caorach (Year of the Sheep)
1801	Publication of complete Gaelic Bible
1811	Foundation of Edinburgh Gaelic Schools Society
1815	Battle of Waterloo
1824	Completion of Caledonian Canal
1830	Composition of Mendelssohn's 'Hebrides Overture'
1843	The Disruption and the founding of the Free Church
1846	Potato Blight in Scotland
1854	Outbreak of Crimean War
1872	Education Act (Scotland)
1874	Bernera Riot
1881	First Gaelic Census
1882	Foundation of Celtic Chair, University of Edinburgh; Battle of the Braes

1884   Report of Napier Commission
1886   Setting up of Crofters Commission and Highland Land League
1891   Foundation of An Comann Gaidhealach
1900   Union of the Free and the United Presbyterian Churches of Scotland
1911   Setting up of Harris Tweed Association
1914–18   First World War
1917   Russian Revolution
1921   Creation of Irish Free State
1923   Date of first Gaelic radio broadcast
1939–45   Second World War
1943   Setting up of North of Scotland Hydro-electric Board
1951   Foundation of School of Scottish Studies
1952   Founding of quarterly *Gairm*
1956   Foundation of Celtic Chair, University of Glasgow
1965   Setting up of Highlands and Islands Development Board
1966   Work on *Historical Dictionary of Scottish Gaelic* begins
1968   Setting up of Gaelic Books Council
1970   Donald Stewart becomes Nationalist MP for Western Isles
1973   Entry of United Kingdom into the European Economic Community
1975   Reorganization of Local Government in Scotland

Bibliography

The following abbreviations are used:

Fasti	*Fasti Ecclesiae Scoticanae*, ed. H. Scott.
HIDB	Highlands and Islands Development Board
NLS	National Library of Scotland
NTS	*Norsk Tidsskrift for Sprogvidenskap*
PSAS	*Proceedings of the Society of Antiquaries of Scotland*
PSHS	Publications of the Scottish History Society
RCAHMS	Royal Commission on Ancient and Historical Monuments of Scotland
SGS	*Scottish Gaelic Studies*
SC	*Studia Celtica*
SHR	*Scottish Historical Review*
SS	*Scottish Studies*
TGSI	*Transactions of the Gaelic Society of Inverness*

Adamnán: *Vitae S. Columbae*, ed. W. F. Skene (1874). Edinburgh.

Adams, F. 1952: *The Clans, Septs and Regiments of the Scottish Highlands*. Edinburgh and London.

Adams, R.J. ed. 1960: *John Home's Survey of Assynt*. PSHS 3rd series vol. 52.

— ed. 1972: *Papers on the Sutherland Estate Management*. PSHS.

Aikman, J. 1827–9: *The History of Scotland*, translated from the Latin of George Buchanan. Glasgow.

Aitken, A.J., McDiarmid, M.P., and Thomson, D.S., eds. 1977: *Bards and Makars*. Glasgow.

Alburger, M.A. 1983: *Scottish Fiddlers and Their Music*. London.

Alcock, L. 1971: *Arthur's Britain*. London.

— 1975–6: 'A Multi-Disciplinary Chronology for Alt Clut, Castle Rock, Dumbarton', *PSAS* 107.

— 1977: 'The Auld Wives' Lifts', *Antiquity* 51.

— 1979: 'The North Britons, the Picts and the Scots'. In P.J. Casey, ed., *The End of Roman Britain*. Oxford.

— 1980: 'Populi Bestiales Pictorum Feroci Animo: A Survey of Pictish Settlement Archaeology'. In W.S. Hanson and L.J.F. Keppie, eds., *Roman Frontier Studies 1979*. Oxford.

— 1981: 'Early Historic Fortifications in Scotland'. In G. Guilbert, ed. *Hillfort Studies*. Leicester.

Allardyce, A. 1888: *Scotland and Scotsmen in the Eighteenth Century*, vol. ii. Edinburgh.

Allen, J.R. 1903: *The Early Christian Monuments of Scotland*, parts 2 and 3. Edinburgh.

An Account of the Depredations committed on The Clan Campbell, and their followers, during the years 1685 and 1686... (1816). Edinburgh.

An Comunn Gaidhealach 1907: *The Teaching of Gaelic in Highland Schools.*

— 1936: *Report on Gaelic in Schools and Colleges.*

An Gaidheal 1873–7: Paipeir-Naidheachd agus Leabhar-Sgeoil Gaidhealach. Edinburgh.

Andersen, J. 1977: *The Witch on the Wall*. Copenhagen and London.

Anderson, A.O. 1922: *Early Sources of Scottish History AD 500 to 1286*. 2 vols., London.

—, and Anderson, M.O. 1961: *Adomnan's Life of Columba*. London.

Anderson, G., and Anderson, P. n.d.: *Guide to the Highlands and Islands of Scotland.*

Anderson, M.L. 1967: *A History of Scottish Forestry*, ed. C.J. Taylor. 2 vols., Edinburgh.

Anderson, M.O. 1973: *Kings and Kingship in Early Scotland*. Edinburgh and London. 2nd edn 1980.

Anderson, P.J. 1918: 'Ewen Mac Lachlan, Librarian to University and King's College, Aberdeen 1800–1818', *Aberdeen University Library Bulletin* 18.

Andersson, O. 1952: 'On Gaelic Folk Music from the Isle of Lewis', in *Budklaven*, Åbo.

Armstrong, R.A. 1825: *A Gaelic Dictionary*. London.

Ashley, A. 1958: *The Church in the Isle of Man*. London.

Atholl, J., 7th Duke of, 1908: *Chronicles of the Atholl and Tullibardine Families*. 5 vols., Edinburgh.

Ayton, R. 1814–25: *A Voyage round Great Britain... with a series of views... drawn and engraved by W. Daniell*. 8 vols., London.

Bain, Robert 1977: *The Clans and Tartans of Scotland*. Glasgow and London.

Baines, A. 1960: *Bagpipes*. Oxford.

Balfour Melville, E.W.M. ed. 1954: *An Account of the*

Proceedings of the Estates in Scotland 1689–90. PSHS 3rd series vol. 46.

Bannerman, J.M. (Lord Bannerman of Kildonan) 1972: *Memoirs*, ed. J. Fowler. Aberdeen.

Bannerman, J.W.M. 1962: Appendix to K. Hughes, *The Church and the World*. In *IHS* vol. 12. Dublin.

— 1966: 'The Convention of Druim Cett', *SGS* 11.

— 1971: 'The Scots of Dalriada', In G. Menzies, ed., *Who Are the Scots?* London.

— 1972–4: 'Two Early Post-Reformation Inscriptions in Argyll', *PSAS* 105.

— 1974: *Studies in the History of Dalriada*. Edinburgh.

— 1975: 'The Scots of Dalriada'. In P. McNeill and R. Nicholson, eds., *An Historical Atlas of Scotland: c.400–c.1600*. St Andrews.

— 1977a: 'The MacLachlans of Kilbride and their Manuscripts', *SS* 21.

— 1977b: 'The Lordship of the Isles: Historical Background'. In K.A. Steer and J.W.M. Bannerman, eds., *Late Medieval Monumental Sculpture in the West Highlands*, Appendix II. London.

— 1977c: 'The Lordship of the Isles'. In J.M. Brown, ed., *Scottish Society in the Fifteenth Century*. London.

— 1983: 'Literacy in the Highlands'. In I.B. Cowan and D. Shaw, eds., *The Renaissance and Reformation in Scotland*. Edinburgh.

— forthcoming: 'The Beatons', *SGS*.

—, and Black, R. 1978: 'A Sixteenth Century Gaelic Letter', *SGS* 13.

Bannister, H.M. 1910: *Specimen Pages of Two Manuscripts of the Abbey of Coupar-Angus in Scotland*. Rome.

Barron, Evan M. 1934: *The Scottish War of Independence*. Inverness.

Barrow, G.W.S. 1965: *Robert Bruce and the Community of the Realm of Scotland*. London.

— 1966: 'The Scottish *judex* in the Twelfth and Thirteenth Centuries', *SHR* 45.

— 1973: *The Kingdom of the Scots*. London.

— 1980: *The Anglo–Norman Era in Scottish History*. Oxford.

Bassin, E. 1977: *The Old Songs of Skye: Frances Tolmie and her Circle*, ed. Derek Bowman. London.

Baynes, J. 1970: *The Jacobite Rising of 1715*. London.

Beaton, D. 1923: *Bibliography of Gaelic Books, Pamphlets and Magazine Articles for the Counties of Caithness and Sutherland*. Wick.

Beaton, D. 1925: *Diary and Sermons of the Rev. Alexander MacLeod*. Wick.

Bede: *Historia Ecclesiastica Gentis Anglorum*. In *Baedae Opera Historica*, ed. C. Plummer, 2 vols., Oxford. Also ed. and trans. B. Colgrave and R.A.B. Mynors (1969). Oxford.

Beith, Alexander 1874: *A Highland Tour with Dr Candlish* [in 1845].

Bell, R.F. 1916: 'Memorials of John Murray of Broughton Sometime Secretary to Prince Charles Edward 1740–1747'. PSHS 2nd series vol. 2.

Bergin, Osborn 1935: 'Address to Sémas mac Aonghais', *SGS* 4.

— 1970: *Irish Bardic Poetry*. Dublin.

Bickmore, D.P., and Shaw, M.A. eds. 1963: *Atlas of Great Britain and Northern Ireland*. Oxford.

Binchy, D.A. 1958: Review of K.H. Jackson *Language and History in Early Britain*, Celtica 4.

Bittleston, A. ed. 1960: *The Sun Dances*. Edinburgh.

Black, George F. 1926: 'Macpherson's Ossian and the Ossianic Controversy: Contribution towards a Bibliography', *Bulletin of the New York Public Library* 30, parts 1 and 2.

— 1946: *The Surnames of Scotland*. New York.

Black, Kenneth M. 1906: *The Scots Churches in England*.

Black, R.I. 1972: 'A Manuscript of Cathal MacMuireadhaigh', *Celtica* 10.

— 1976: 'Colla Ciotach', *TGSI* 48.

— 1976/81: 'Poems by Maol Domhnaigh Ó Muirgheasáin', *SGS* 12–13.

— 1979a: 'The Genius of Cathal MacMhuirich', *TGSI* 50.

— 1979b: 'In Search of the Red Book of Clanranald', *Clan Donald Magazine* 8.

— forthcoming: 'The Books of Clanranald', *SGS*.

— unpublished: 'The Cultural Contribution of the Highland Society of Scotland'.

Blackie, John Stuart 1876: *The Language and Literature of the Scottish Highlands*. Edinburgh.

— 1885: *The Scottish Highlanders and the Land Laws*. Edinburgh.

Blaikie, W.B. ed. 1916: *Origins of the '45 and Other Narratives*. PSHS.

Blair, Hugh 1763: *A Critical Dissertation on the Poems of Ossian, the Son of Fingal*. London.

Borgstrøm, C.Hj. 1937: 'The Dialect of Barra in the Outer Hebrides', *NTS* 8.

— 1938: 'Scottish Gaelic as a Source of Information about the Early History of Irish', *SGS* 5.

— 1940: *The Dialects of the Outer Hebrides*, NTS supplementary vol. 1.

— 1941a: *The Dialects of Skye and Ross-shire*, NTS supplementary vol. 2.

— 1941b: *The Dialects of the Outer Hebrides (A Linguistic Survey of the Gaelic Dialects of Scotland)*, NTS supplementary vol. 2.

— 1974: 'On the Influence of Norse on Scottish Gaelic', *NTS* supplementary vol. 11 (= *Lochlann*, vol. 6).

Borland, C.R. 1916: *A Descriptive Catalogue of the Western Medieval Manuscripts in Edinburgh University Library*. Edinburgh.

Brander, Michael 1971: *The Scottish Highlanders and their Regiments*. London.

Breathnach, R.B. 1940: 'A Note on the Voicing of Sibilants in the Irish of Cape Clear Island, Co. Cork', *Éigse* 2.

Bristol, N. 1978: 'The O'Muirgheasáin Bardic Family', *Notes and Queries of the Society of West Highland and Island Historical Research* 6.

Bromwich, R. 1961: *Trioedd Ynys Prydein*. Cardiff.
— 1963: 'Scotland and the Earliest Arthurian Tradition', *Bibliographical Bulletin of the International Arthurian Society* 5.
— 1975–6: 'Concepts of Arthur', *SC* 10–11.
Brooches in Scotland 1966: National Museum of Antiquities of Scotland.
Brown, P. Hume ed. 1891: *Early Travellers in Scotland*. Edinburgh.
Brown, T. 1890: *Annals of the Disruption*. Edinburgh.
Brown T.J. 1972: 'Northumbria and the Book of Kells', *Anglo-Saxon England* 1. Cambridge.
Bruford, Alan 1963: 'Eachtra Chonaill Gulban', *Béaloideas* 31.
— 1965: 'A Lost MacMhuirich Manuscript', *SGS* 10.
— 1968: 'Murchadh mac Briain agus an Díthreabhach', *Éigse* 12.
— 1969: *Gaelic Folk-Tales and Mediaeval Romances*. Dublin.
— 1973: 'The King's Questions (AT 922) in Scotland', *SS* 17.
— 1978: 'Recitation or Re-creation? Examples from South Uist Storytelling', *SS* 22.
Bryden, J., and Houston, G. 1976: *Agrarian Change in the Scottish Highlands*, Glasgow Social and Economic Research Studies vol. iv. Oxford.
Bryden, J. 1979: 'Land Use Policy', address to the Edinburgh Agricultural Economics Discussion Circle, 3 December; available from author.
Buchan, A. 1818: 'Description of St Kilda', *Miscellanea Scotica* 2.
Buchanan, George 1829: *History of Scotland...*, ed. James Aikman. 6 vols., Edinburgh.
Buchanan, R. 1852: *The Ten Years' Conflict*. Glasgow.
Budge, D. 1976: 'Beathag Mhor, Bana Bhard Sgiathanach', *TGSI* 48.
Bumsted, J.M. 1982: *The People's Clearance: Highland Emigration to British North America 1770–1815*. Edinburgh and Manitoba.
Burl, A. 1976: *The Stone Circles of the British Isles*. New Haven and London.
Burleigh, J.H.S. 1960: *A Church History of Scotland*. Oxford.
Caimbeul, Aonghas 1972: *Moll is Cruithneachd*. Glasgow.
Caimbeul, Aonghas 1978: *Bàrdachd a' Bhocsair*. Loanhead.
Caimbeul, Gilleasbuig, C.I. 1908: 'Dùthaich na Saorsa', *Guth na Bliadhna* 5.
Caimbeul, Iain 1884: *Poems*. Edinburgh.
Caimbeul, M.A.N. 1970: 'Scottish Camanachd: A Study of the Traditional, Historical and Cultural Background with an Outline of the Modern Organization'. Unpublished PhD thesis, Celtic Department, Aberdeen University (summary in *Shinty Yearbook*, 1971).
Caimbeul, Seonaidh 1936: *Orain Ghàidhlig le Seonaidh Caimbeul*. Dun Pharlain.
Caird, J. B. ed. 1958: 'Park: A Geographical Study of a Lewis Crofting District'. Geographical Field Group, Nottingham.
— 1972: 'Changes in the Highlands and Islands of Scotland, 1951–1971', *Geoforum* 12.
— 1979a: 'Land Use in the Uists since 1800', *Proceedings of the Royal Society of Edinburgh* 77b.
— 1979b: 'The Making of the Crofting Landscape', *Journal of the Scottish Association of Geography Teachers* 8.
—, and Diamond, D.R. eds. 1965: [Map of] *Scotland: Population Distribution on the Night of 23rd April 1961*. Glasgow.
—, and Moisley, H.A. 1961: 'Leadership and Innovation in the Crofting Communities...', *Sociological Review* 9.
Calder, George 1912: *The Gaelic Songs of Duncan MacIntyre*. Edinburgh.
— 1923: *A Gaelic Grammar*. Glasgow.
— 1937: *Gaelic Songs by William Ross*. Edinburgh and London.
Caldwell, David H. 1979: *The Scottish Armoury*. Edinburgh.
— 1980: *Highland Art*.
— 1981: *Scottish Weapons and Fortifications 1100–1800*. Edinburgh.
Cameron, A. 1892–4: *Reliquiae Celticae*, ed. A. MacBain and J. Kennedy. 2 vols., Inverness.
Cameron, George C. 1979: *The Scots Kirk in London*.
Cameron, H. ed. 1932: *Na Bàird Thirisdeach*. Glasgow.
Cameron, James 1912: *The Old and the New Highlands and Hebrides*.
Cameron, John 1883: *Gaelic Names of Plants*. Edinburgh and London.
Cameron, John 1936: *An Introductory Survey of the Sources and Literature of Scots Law*.
— 1937: *Celtic Law: The Senchus Mor and the Book of Aicill, and the Traces of an Early Gaelic System of Law in Scotland*. London, Edinburgh and Glasgow.
— 1938: 'Law in the Glens'. In D.N. Mackay, ed., *The Highlands and the Highlanders*.
— 1939: 'The Gaelic Notitiae in the Book of Deer', *Juridical Review* 51.
— 1941: Obituary of George Calder by 'J.C.' in *An Gaidheal* 36.
— ed. 1949: *The Justiciary Records of Argyll and the Isles* vol. i: *1664–1705*. Stair Society vol. xii, Edinburgh.
Cameron, Paul 1892–4: 'Perthshire Gaelic Songs and their Composers', *TGSI* 17, 18.
Campbell, Alexander 1816–18: *Albyn's Anthology*. Edinburgh.
Campbell, Archibald 1948: *The Kilberry Book of Ceol Mor*. Glasgow. 2nd edn 1953.
— 1950: 'The History and Art of Angus MacKay', *Piping Times* 2 nos. 5, 6, 7.
— 1962: 'The Highland Bagpipe', *Piping Times* 14 no. 10.
Campbell, Donald 1862: *A Treatise on the Language, Poetry and Music of the Highland Clans*, Edinburgh.
Campbell, D., and MacLean, R.A. 1974: *Beyond the Atlantic Roar: A Study of the Nova Scotia Scots*. Toronto.

Campbell, D.M.: *The Campbell Collection of Gaelic Proverbs and Proverbial Sayings*, ed. Donald E. Meek (1978). Inverness.

Campbell, J.F. 1872: *Leabhar na Féinne* 1. London. Reprinted with introduction by D.S. Thomson, Shannon 1972.

— 1880: *Canntaireachd: Articulate Music*. Glasgow.

— 1890: *Popular Tales of the West Highlands*. Paisley and London.

Campbell, John Gregorson 1891: *The Fians*. Waifs and Strays series No. 4. London.

— 1895: *Clan Traditions and Popular Tales*. Waifs and Strays series No. 5. London.

— 1900: *Superstitions of the Highlands and Islands of Scotland*. Glasgow.

— 1902: *Witchcraft and Second Sight in the Highlands and Islands of Scotland*. Glasgow.

Campbell, J.L. n.d.: *Gaelic Folksongs from the Isle of Barra*. London.

— 1933: *Highland Songs of the Forty-Five*. Edinburgh.

— 1935a: 'Gaelic MS 63 of the National Library', *SGS* 4.

— 1935b: 'Alexander MacDonald, Portrait of a Traditionalist', *Scots Magazine* October.

— 1937: 'The First Printed Gaelic Vocabulary', *Scots Magazine* October.

— 1938a: 'An Early Scottish Gaelic Vocabulary', *SGS* 5.

— 1938b: 'A Visit to Cape Breton', *Scots Magazine* September.

— 1939: *Sia Sgialachdan*. Edinburgh.

— 1950a: 'MacTalla', *An Gaidheal* January.

— 1950b: *Gaelic in Scottish Education and Life*. Edinburgh.

— 1952: 'Jonathan MacKinnon (Nécrologie)', *Études Celtiques* 6.

— 1954: *Fr Allan McDonald of Eriskay 1859–1905, Priest, Poet and Folklorist*. Edinburgh.

— 1956a: 'The Sources of the Gaelic Hymnal, 1893', *Innes Review* 7.

— 1956b: 'Some Notes on Scottish Gaelic Waulking Songs', *Éigse* 8.

— 1958a: *Gaelic Words and Expressions from South Uist and Eriskay Collected by Rev. Fr Allan MacDonald*. Dublin. 2nd edn with supplement, Oxford n.d.

— 1958b: 'The Late Fr Allan MacDonald, Miss Goodrich Freer and Hebridean Folklore', *SS* 2.

— 1958c: 'More Notes on Scottish Gaelic Waulking Songs', *Éigse* 9.

— 1960 *et seq.*: *Told by the Coddy*. Edinburgh.

— 1961a: 'Scottish Gaelic Translations of John Ray's Dictionariolum Trilingue', *SGS* 9.

— 1961b: *Stories from South Uist told by Angus MacLellan*. London.

— 1965: *Bàrdachd Mhgr Ailein*. Edinburgh.

— 1968: *Seanfhocail agus Comhadan*. Inverness.

— 1971: 'The Expurgating of Mac Mhaighstir Alasdair', *SGS* 12.

— ed. 1972: 'Saoghal an Treobhaiche', *Lochlann* 5.

— ed. 1975: *A Collection of Highland Rites and Customes, Copied by Edward Lhuyd from the Manuscript of the Rev. James Kirkwood (1650–1709) and Annotated by him with the Aid of the Rev. John Beaton*. Cambridge.

— 1976: 'Unpublished Letters by Edward Lhuyd in the National Library of Scotland', *Celtica* 11.

— 1978: 'Notes on Hamish Robertson's "Studies in Carmichael's *Carmina Gadelica*"', *SGS* 13.

—, and Collinson, F. 1969: *Hebridean Folksongs: A Collection of Waulking Songs Made by Donald MacCormick in Kilphedir in South Uist in the Year 1893* vol. i. Oxford. Vol. ii 1977; vol. iii 1981.

—, and Hall, T.H. 1968: *Strange Things: The Enquiry by the Society for Psychical Research into Second Sight in the Scottish Highlands*. London.

—, and Thomson, Derick 1963: *Edward Lhuyd in the Scottish Highlands 1699–1700*. Oxford (contains a comprehensive bibliography).

Campbell, John Macmaster 1927: 'An Comunn Gaidhealach, its Accomplishments and Aspirations', *Féill a' Chomuinn Ghaidhealaich*. Glasgow.

Campbell, Lord Archibald 1885: *Records of Argyll*. Edinburgh and London.

— 1889–95: *Waifs and Strays of Celtic Tradition*. 5 vols., London. Vol. i 1889: *Craignish Tales...*; vol. ii 1890: *Folk and Hero Tales*, collected, edited and translated by Duncan MacInnes; vol. iii 1891: *Folk and Hero Tales*, collected, edited, translated and annotated by James MacDougall; vol. iv 1891: *The Fians*, collected, edited and translated by John Gregorson Campbell; vol. v 1895: *Clan Traditions and Popular Tales*, collected, edited and translated by John Gregorson Campbell.

Campbell, L., and Sinclair, Colin n.d.: *Housing in the Highlands – A Plea for the Appropriate*, with introduction by Neil Munro. An Comunn Gaidhealach.

Camshron, Alasdair 1957: 'Gormshuil Mhór na Maighe', *An Gaidheal* March.

Cannon, R.D. 1980: *A Bibliography of Bagpipe Music*. Edinburgh.

Carlyle, H.J. 1978: 'Store Stock Marketing by Small Farms in the Crofting Counties', *Scottish Geographical Magazine* 94.

Carmichael, Alexander 1884: 'Grazing and Agrestic Customs in the Outer Hebrides', reprint from Napier Crofting Commission Report.

— 1900 *et seq.*: *Carmina Gadelica: Hymns and Incantations, etc..* 6 vols. (vols. 1 and 2 only edited by Carmichael), Edinburgh.

Carney, James ed. 1966: *Early Irish Literature*. London.

—, and Greene, D. eds. 1968: *Celtic Studies, Essays in Memory of Angus Matheson 1912–1962*. London.

Carter, I. 1971: 'Economic Models and Recent History of the Highlands', *SS* 15.

— 1972: 'The Highlands of Scotland as an Underdeveloped

Region'. In E. de Kadt and G. Williams, eds., *Sociology and Development*. London.

Centre for Agricultural Strategy 1980: *Strategy for the UK Forest Industry*. CAS Report no. 6, University of Reading.

Chadwick, H.M., and Chadwick, N.K. 1932: *The Growth of Literature*. 3 vols., Cambridge.

Chadwick, N.K. 1958: 'The Name Pict', *SGS* 8.

Chapman, M. 1978: *The Gaelic Vision in Scottish Culture*. London.

Chapman, R.W. ed. 1924: *Johnson and Boswell: A Journey to the Western Islands of Scotland; The Journal of a Tour to the Hebrides* (1773). London.

Charles, Stewart 1884: *The Killin Collection of Gaelic Songs with Music and Translations*. Edinburgh.

Christiansen, R. 1931: *The Vikings and the Viking Wars in Irish and Gaelic Tradition*. Oslo.

Clanricarde, Marquis of 1744: *Memoirs*. Dublin.

Clement, R.D. forthcoming: 'Preaspiration in Gaelic'.

Close-Brooks, J., and Stevenson, R.B.K. 1982: *Dark Age Sculpture*. Edinburgh.

Colgrave, B., and Mynors, R.A.B. 1969: *Bede's Ecclesiastical History of the English People*. Oxford.

Collier, A. 1953: *The Crofting Problem*. Cambridge.

Collins, G.N.M. 1951: *Principal John MacLeod* (chapter on Finlay Munro). Edinburgh.

— 1974: *The Heritage of Our Fathers*. Edinburgh.

— 1976: *Big Macrae*. Edinburgh.

Collinson, F. 1966: *The Traditional and National Music of Scotland*. London.

— 1975: *The Bagpipe: The History of a Musical Instrument*. London.

Comrie, J.D. 1932: *History of Scottish Medicine*, 2nd edn. London.

Cooke, P. 1972: 'Problems of Notating Pibroch: A Study of "Maol Donn"', *SS* 16.

— 1978: 'Changing Styles in Pibroch Playing: Cadence E's and Beates on A″', *International Piper* 1 nos. 2 and 3.

Cooper, Derek 1979: *Road to the Isles – Travellers in the Hebrides, 1770–1914*.

Coventry, Teàrlach 1983: 'An Clò-bheairt Ceilteach', *Gairm* 122.

Cowan, E.J. 1977: *Montrose: For Covenant and King*. London.

Cowan, I.B. 1981: 'The Medieval Church in the Highlands', in *The Highlands in the Middle Ages*. Inverness.

—, and Easson, D.E. 1976: *Medieval Religious Houses of Scotland*. London.

Cox, J.T. 1964: 'Constitution of the Church of Scotland', in *Practice and Procedure of the Church of Scotland*, 5th edn, revised by J.B. Longmuir. Edinburgh.

Craig, K.C. 1949: *Orain Luaidh*. Glasgow.

— 1950: *Leigheas Cas O Céin*. Stirling.

Cregeen, E.R. ed. 1964: *The Argyll Estate Instructions, Mull, Morven and Tiree, 1771–1805*. Edinburgh.

— 1970: 'The Changing Role of the House of Argyll in the Scottish Highlands'. In N.T. Phillipson and R. Mitchison, eds., *Scotland in the Age of Improvement*. Edinburgh.

— 1971: 'The Tacksmen and their Successors: A Study of Tenurial Reorganisation in Mull, Morvern and Tiree in the Eighteenth Century', *SS* 13.

— and Mackenzie, D.W. 1978: *Tiree Bards and their Bardachd*. Coll.

Creighton, H., and MacLeod, C.I.N. 1964: *Gaelic Songs in Nova Scotia*. Ottawa.

Crowley, D.W. 1956: 'The Crofters' Party, 1885–92', *SHR* 35.

Cruden, S. 1960: *The Scottish Castle*. Edinburgh.

— 1964: *Early Christian and Pictish Monuments of Scotland*. London.

Cruickshank, A.B., and Jowett, A.J. 1972: 'The Loch Linnhe District', *British Landscapes through Maps*. Sheffield.

Cruickshanks, Eveline, ed. 1982: *Ideology and Conspiracy: Aspects of Jacobitism 1689–1759*. Edinburgh.

Cunningham, A. 1919: 'The Revolution Government in the Highlands', *SHR* 16.

— 1932: *The Loyal Clans*. Cambridge.

Daiches, David 1969: *Scotch Whisky: Its Past and Present*. London.

Dalyell, J. G. 1849: *Musical Memoirs of Scotland*. Edinburgh.

Darling, F.F. 1955: *West Highland Survey – An Essay in Human Ecology*. Oxford.

— and Boyd, J. Morton 1969: *The Highlands and Islands*, 2nd edn. London.

Day, John P. 1918: *Public Administration in the Highlands and Islands of Scotland*. London.

de Blácam, Aodh 1929: *Gaelic Literature Surveyed*. Dublin. 2nd edn 1933; 3rd edn 1973.

Delargy, J.H. 1945: 'The Gaelic Storyteller', *Proceedings of the British Academy* 31.

Department of Agriculture and Fisheries for Scotland 1964: *Land Use in the Highlands and Islands*, Report of the Highlands and Islands Advisory Panel.

Dickie, M.A.M. 1961: *The Crofting Counties – Problems and Prospects*.

Dickinson, W.C. ed. 1928: *The Sheriff Court Book of Fife 1515–1522*. Edinburgh.

— 1941: 'The toschederach', *Juridical Review* 53.

— 1961: *Scotland from the Earliest Times to 1603*. London.

Dickson, W.K. 1895: *The Jacobite Attempt of 1719*. PSHS vol. 19.

Dieckhoff, H.C. 1932: *A Pronouncing Dictionary of Scottish Gaelic*. Edinburgh and London.

Dillon, M., and Chadwick, N. 1967: *The Celtic Realms*. London.

Dilworth, A. 1958: *Mainland Dialects of Scottish Gaelic*. Fort Augustus.

Dixon, G.A. 1981: 'The 1743 Lord Lovat/David Fraser Piping Indenture', *International Piper* 4.

Doherty, C. 1966: 'Some Aspects of Preaspiration in

Scottish Gaelic'. Unpublished class essay, University of Edinburgh.

Dòmhnallach, Dòmhnall 1969: *Dòmhnall Ruadh Chorùna.* Glasgow.

Domhnallach, I. 1912: *Marbhrainn a Rinneadh air Diadhairibh Urramach nach maireann agus Dana Spioradail.* Edinburgh.

Domhnallach, Tormod Calum 1978: *Call na h-Iolaire.* Stornoway.

Donaldson, G. 1965: *Scotland, James V – James VII,* Edinburgh History of Scotland, vol. iii. Edinburgh.

— 1974: *Scottish Historical Documents.* Edinburgh and London.

Donnelly, S. 1981: 'The Warpipe in Ireland', *Ceòl* 1.

Dorian, N.C. 1978: *East Sutherland Gaelic.* Dublin.

Dow, Daniel 1775: *A Collection of Ancient Scottish Music.* Edinburgh.

Drummond, A.L., and Bulloch, J. 1973: *The Scottish Church, 1688–1843.* Edinburgh.

— 1975: *The Church in Victorian Scotland, 1843–74.* Edinburgh.

— 1978: *The Church in Late Victorian Scotland, 1874–1900.* Edinburgh.

Drummond, J. 1842: *Memoirs of Sir Ewen Cameron of Locheill.* Edinburgh.

Dun, Finlay 1860: *Orain na h-Albam* [*recte* Alban]. Edinburgh.

Dunbar, J.G. 1978a: *The Architecture of Scotland,* rev. edn. London.

— 1978b: 'Kisimul Castle, Isle of Barra', *Glasgow Archaeological Journal* 5.

— 1981: 'The Medieval Architecture of the Scottish Highlands'. In L. Maclean, ed., *The Middle Ages in the Highlands.* Inverness.

Dunbar, J. Telfer 1962: *History of Highland Dress.* Edinburgh.

Duncan, A.A.M. 1975: *Scotland: The Making of the Kingdom.* Edinburgh.

— 1981: 'Bede, Iona and the Picts'. In R.H.C. Davis and J.M. Wallace-Hadrill, eds., *The Writing of History in the Middle Ages: Essays Presented to Richard William Southern.*

Duncan, A.A.M., and Brown, A.L. 1956–7: 'Argyll and the Isles in the Earlier Middle Ages', *PSAS* 90.

Dunlop, J. 1978: *The British Fisheries Society 1786–1896.* Edinburgh.

Dunn, C.W. 1953: *Highland Settler.* Toronto.

Dunn, John J. ed. 1966: *Fragments....* Los Angeles.

— 1971: 'Macpherson's Ossian and the Ossianic Controversy: A Supplementary Bibliography', *Bulletin of the New York Public Library* 75 no. 9.

Durkacz, V.E. 1977: 'Gaelic Education in the Nineteenth Century', *Scottish Educational Studies* 9.

— 1978: 'The Source of the Language Problem in Scottish Education, 1688–1709', *SHR* 57.

— 1983: *The Decline of the Celtic Languages.* Edinburgh.

Dwelly, Edward 1920: *The Illustrated Gaelic–English Dictionary,* 2nd edn. Glasgow. 9th edn 1977.

Eeles, F.C. 1926: 'The Guthrie Bell and its Shrine', *PSAS* 60.

— 1933–4: 'The Monymusk Reliquary or Breccbennach of St Columba', *PSAS* 68.

Elder, J.R. 1914: *The Highland Host of 1678.* Glasgow.

Emmerson, G. 1967: *Scotland through her Country Dances.*

Evidence Taken by Her Majesty's Commissioners of Enquiry into the Condition of Crofters and Cottars in the Highlands and Islands of Scotland (1884). Edinburgh.

Fairhurst, H. 1964: 'Surveys for the Sutherland Clearances', *SS* 8.

Farquharson, A. 1870: *Laoidhean Shioin.* Glasgow.

Feachem, R.W. de F. 1963: *A Guide to Prehistoric Scotland.* London. 2nd edn 1977.

— 1969: 'Medionemeton on the Limes of Antonius Pius, Scotland', *Collection Latomus* 103.

Fenton, A. 1976: *Scottish Country Life.* Edinburgh.

Ferguson, W. 1968: *Scotland 1689 to the Present.* Edinburgh and London.

— 1977: *Scotland's Relations with England: A Survey to 1707.* Edinburgh.

Fergusson, D.A. 1977: *Beyond the Hebrides.* London.

— 1978: *From the Farthest Hebrides.* Toronto.

Fergusson, J. 1951: *Argyll in the Forty-Five.* London.

Feuds and Conflicts, 1764: Glasgow.

Finlayson, C.P. 1962: *Celtic Psalter: Edinburgh University Library MS 56.* Amsterdam.

Fleming, J.R. 1927–33: *The Church in Scotland 1843–1929.* 2 vols., Edinburgh.

Flett, J.F., and Flett, T.M. 1964: *Traditional Dancing in Scotland.*

Flinn, M.W. ed. 1977: *Scottish Population History from the 17th Century to the 1930s.* Cambridge.

Flower, R. 1947: *The Irish Tradition.* Oxford.

Forbes, Alexander R. 1905: *Gaelic Names of Beasts (Mammalian), Birds, Fishes, Insects, Reptiles, etc.,* Edinburgh.

Fraser, Allan H.H. 1953: *Beef Cattle Husbandry.* Crosby Lockwood.

— 1972: *The Bull.* Reading.

— 1979: *Eachunn nan Cath.* Glasgow.

Fraser, Ian A. 1979: 'Gaelic and Norse Elements in Coastal Place Names in the Western Isles', *TGSI* 50.

Fraser, John 1912: 'The Present and Future Tenses of the Verb in Scottish Gaelic', *ZCP* 10.

— 1914: 'Remarks on the Fernaig Manuscript', *TGSI* 28.

— 1924: Review of Calum MacPhàrlain, *Làmh-Sgriobhainn Mhic Rath, Revue Celtique* 41.

— 1926: 'The Language of the Fernaig Manuscript', *SGS* 1.

— 1928: 'Some Terms of Old Scots Law', *SGS* 2.

— 1934: Review of T.F. O'Rahilly, *Irish Dialects Past and Present, SGS* 4.

— 1938: 'The Gaelic *Notitiae* in the Book of Deer', *SGS* 5.

Fraser, S. 1816: *The Airs and Melodies Peculiar to the Highlands of Scotland and the Isles*. Edinburgh. Reprinted Sydney, Nova Scotia, 1982.

Freer, Ada Goodrich 1899: *The Alleged Haunting of Ballechin House*. London.

— 1902: *Outer Isles*. London.

Fulton, Robin 1974: *Contemporary Scottish Poetry*. Loanhead.

Gaelic Books Council 1983: *Leabhraichean Gaidhlig: A Classified Catalogue of Gaelic Books in Print*, 3rd edn. Glasgow.

Gailey, R.A. 1960: 'Settlement and Population in Kintyre, 1750–1800', *Scottish Geographical Magazine* 76.

— 1962: 'The Evolution of Highland Rural Settlement with Particular Reference to Argyllshire', *SS* 6.

— 1963: 'Agrarian Improvement and the Development of Enclosure in the South-West Highlands of Scotland', *SHR* 42.

Gaskell, P. 1968: *Morvern Transformed: A Highland Parish in the Nineteenth Century*. London.

Geddes, E. 1948: 'Conjoint Tenants and Tacksmen in the Isle of Lewis, 1715–26', *Economic History Review* 1.

General Register Office, Scotland 1975: *Index of Scottish Place-Names from 1971 Census*. Edinburgh.

Giblin, Cathaldus 1964: *Irish Franciscan Mission to Scotland, 1619–1646*. Dublin.

Gibson, J.S. 1967: *Ships of the '45*. London.

Gillanders, F. 1968: 'The Economic Life of Gaelic Scotland Today'. In I. Grimble and D.S. Thomson, eds., *The Future of the Highlands*. London.

Gillespie, R. 1977–8: 'Camanachd gu bràth on Wimbledon Common', *Shinty Year Book*.

Gillies, Alexander 1933: *Herder und Ossian*. Berlin.

Gillies, Alexander 1969: *A Hebridean in Goethe's Weimar*. Oxford.

Gillies, D. n.d.: *The Life and Work of the Very Reverend Roderick MacLeod*.

Gillies, Eoin 1786: *Sean Dàin agus Orain Ghaidhealach*. Perth.

Gillies, H. Cameron 1898: *Gaelic Names of Diseases and of Diseased States*. Glasgow.

— 1906: *The Place-Names of Argyll*. London.

— ed. 1911: *Regimen Sanitatis*. Glasgow.

Gillies, W. A. 1938: *In Famed Breadalbane*, Perth; reprinted Ballechin, 1980.

Gillies, William 1974: 'Bàrdachd Shìlis na Ceapaich' (review), *SS* 18.

— 1977a: 'Courtly and Satiric Poems in the Book of the Dean of Lismore', *SS* 21.

— 1977b: 'The Poem in Praise of Ben Dobhrain', *Lines Review* 63.

— 1978–83: 'The Gaelic Poems of Sir Duncan Campbell of Glenorchy', *SGS* 13 and 14.

— forthcoming: *The Red and Black Books of Clanranald*.

Gleasure, J.W. 1968: Review of *Gàidhlig Uidhist a Deas*, *SGS* 9.

Goldie, F. 1961: *A Short History of the Episcopal Church in Scotland*. 2nd edn 1976.

Gordon, Bridget 1963: 'Some Norse Place-Names in Trotternish, Isle of Skye', *SGS* 10.

Gordon, C. A. 1955: 'Letter to John Aubrey from Professor James Garden', *SGS* 8.

— 1964–6: 'The Pictish Animals Observed', *PSAS* 98.

Gordon, R. 1813: *A Genealogical History of the Earldom of Sutherland*. Edinburgh.

Graham, A. 1946–7: 'Some Observations on the Brochs', *PSAS* 81.

Grannd, D. 1971: *Tìr an Aigh*. Glasgow.

Grant, Anne 1806: *Letters from the Mountains* [1773–1803]. London.

Grant, I.F. 1935: *The Lordship of the Isles*. Edinburgh and London.

— 1959: *The MacLeods*. London.

— 1961: *Highland Folk Ways*. London.

Grant, J.S. 1967: *Crofting*, pamphlet published by An Comunn Gaidhealach.

— 1981: 'Two Lewis Spinsters and a Mutineer', *Stornoway Gazette* 17 January.

Grant, K.W. 1911: *Aig Tigh na Beinne*. Oban.

Grassie, James 1983: *Highland Experiment: The Story of the Highlands and Islands Development Board*. Aberdeen. University Press.

Graves, A.P. 1913: *Irish Literary and Musical Studies*. London.

Gray, Malcolm 1951: 'The Kelp Industry in the Highlands and Islands', *Economic History Review* 2nd series vol. 4.

— 1957: *The Highland Economy 1750–1850*. Edinburgh.

— 1978: *The Fishing Industries of Scotland, 1790–1914*. Oxford.

Greene, David 1961: 'The Professional Poets', in *Seven Centuries of Irish Learning*. Dublin.

— 1962: 'Ná léig mo mhealladh, a Mhuire', *SGS* 9.

— 1966: 'The Making of Insular Celtic', *Proceedings of the Second International Congress of Celtic Studies*. Cardiff.

— 1968: 'A Satire by Cathal Mac Muireadhaigh'. In James Carney and David Greene, eds. *Celtic Studies: Essays in Memory of Angus Matheson 1912–1962*. London.

— forthcoming: 'Perfect and Passive in Eastern and Western Gaelic', *SC*.

— and O'Connor, F. 1967: *A Golden Treasury of Irish Poetry*. London.

Gregory, D. 1836: *The History of the Western Highlands and Isles of Scotland*. Edinburgh. Reprinted 1975.

Grieve, R. 1972: 'Problems and Objectives in the Highlands and Islands'. In J. Ashton and W.H. Long, eds., *The Remoter Rural Areas of Britain*. Edinburgh.

Grigor, I.F. 1979: *Mightier than a Lord: The Highland Crofters' Struggle for the Land*. Stornoway.

Grimble, Ian 1963a: 'Emigration in the Time of Rob Donn, 1714–1778', *SS* 7.

— 1963b: *The Trial of Patrick Sellar*. London.

— 1965: *Chief of Mackay*. London.

— 1979a: *Scottish Clans and Tartans*. Edinburgh.

— 1979b: *The World of Rob Donn*. Edinburgh.

— and Thomson, D.S. 1968: *The Future of the Highlands*. London.

Gulvin, Clifford 1973: *The Tweedmakers*. Newton Abbot.

Gunn, Adam, and Macfarlane, Malcolm 1899: *Songs and Poems by Rob Donn Mackay*. Glasgow.

Gunn, M.R. 1969: *History of the Clan Gunn*. Glasgow.

Gunn, Neil M. 1935: *Whisky and Scotland*. London.

Haddow, A.J. 1974: 'The MacKay Tunes', *Proc. of the Piobaireachd Soc.* 2.

— 1982: *The History and Structure of Ceol Mor*. Glasgow.

Haldane, A.R.B. 1952: *The Drove Roads of Scotland*. London.

— 1962: *New Ways Through the Glens*. Bath.

Hamilton, J.R.C. 1962: 'Brochs and Broch Builders'. In F.T. Wainwright, ed., *The Northern Isles*. Edinburgh and London.

— 1966: 'Forts, Brochs and Wheelhouses in Northern Scotland'. In A.L.F. Rivet, ed., *The Iron Age in Northern Britain*. Edinburgh.

Hamp, E.P. 1970: 'Systems of Lateral Sounds and Perception', *Proceedings of the Sixth International Congress of Phonetic Sciences* (1967). Prague.

Harding, A.W. 1980: 'Sgoilean Chrìosd 1811–1861: A Study of the Edinburgh Society for the Support of Gaelic Schools'. M. Litt. thesis, University of Glasgow.

Hay, George Campbell 1947: *Fuaran Slèibh*. Glasgow.

— 1948: *Wind on Loch Fyne*. Edinburgh.

— 1952: *O na Ceithir Airdean*. Edinburgh.

— 1982: *Mochtàr is Dùghall*. Glasgow.

Hay, John MacDougall 1914: *Gillespie*. Edinburgh. Reprinted London 1963.

Hayes-McCoy, Gerard H. 1937: *Scots Mercenary Forces in Ireland*. Dublin.

Henderson, George ed. 1893: *Dàin Iain Ghobha*. Glasgow and Edinburgh.

— 1898: *Leabhar nan Gleann*. Edinburgh.

— 1903: 'Sgeulachd Cois o' Cein', *TGSI* 25.

— 1910a: 'Aonghus nan Aoir or an Irish Bard in the Highlands', *TGSI* 26.

— 1910b: *The Norse Influence on Celtic Scotland*. Glasgow.

— 1915: 'Làmh-sgrìobhainnean Mhic-Neacail', *TGSI* 27.

Henderson, Isabel 1957–8: 'The Origin Centre of the Pictish Symbol Stones', *PSAS* 91.

— 1967: *The Picts*. London.

— 1971: 'The Meaning of the Pictish Symbol Stones', in *The Dark Ages in the Highlands*. Inverness.

— 1975: 'Inverness, a Pictish Capital', in *The Hub of the Highlands*. Edinburgh.

— 1978: 'Sculpture North of the Forth after the Takeover by the Scots'. In J. Lang, ed., *Anglo-Saxon and Viking Age Sculpture*, British Archaeological Reports, British Series vol. 49. Oxford.

— 1982: 'Pictish Art and the Book of Kells'. In R. McKitterick *et al.*, eds., *Ireland in Early Medieval Europe: Studies in Memory of Kathleen Hughes*. Cambridge.

Henry, F. 1965: *Irish Art in the Early Christian Period, to AD 800*. London.

— 1967: *Irish Art during the Viking Invasion, 800–1020 AD*. London.

— 1970: *Irish Art in the Romanesque Period (1020–1170 AD)*. London.

— 1974: *The Book of Kells*. London.

— and Marsh-Micheli, G.L. 1962: 'A Century of Irish Illumination (1070–1170', *Proceedings of the Royal Irish Academy* 62 sect. C.

Highet, John 1950: *The Churches in Scotland Today*.

Highlands and Islands Development Board 1968: *The Moray Firth: A Plan for Growth in a Sub-Region of the Scottish Highlands*, report prepared by the Jack Holmes Planning Group. London.

— 1970: *Strath of Kildonan: Proposals for Development*, Special Report no. 5. Inverness.

— 1972: *In Great Waters: A Study of the Social and Economic Impact of Investment in Fisheries in the Highlands and Islands*, Special Report no. 7. Inverness.

— 1973: *The Island of Mull: Survey and Proposals for Development*, Special Report no. 10. Inverness.

— 1976: *Highland Agriculture and Land Use: Past Activities and Future Policies of the Highlands and Islands Development Board*, Occasional Bulletin no. 7. Inverness.

— 1977: *The Highlands and Islands: A Contemporary Account*. Inverness.

Highland Society 1805: *Report on Ossian*. Edinburgh.

— 1828: *Dictionarium Scoto-Celticum: A Dictionary of the Gaelic Language*. Edinburgh and London.

Hill, T.F. 1782: 'Antient Erse Poems, Collected among the Scottish Highlands', *Gentleman's Magazine* December.

Hill Farming Research Organization 1979: *Science and Hill Farming*.

Hilleary, E.L. 1938: *The Highlands and Islands – Economic Conditions and Recommendation*.

History of the Free Presbyterian Church of Scotland, 1893–1933 1965.

History of the Feuds and Conflicts among the Clans (1780). Perth.

Hogg, James 1802–3: 'A Journey through the Highlands of Scotland in July and August 1802', *Scots Magazine* vols. 64 and 65.

— 1888: 'A Tour in the Highlands in 1803. A Series of Letters to Sir Walter Scott'. Reprinted from the *Scottish Review*.

Holloway, J., and Errington, L. 1978: *The Discovery of Scotland: The Appreciation of Scottish Scenery through Two Centuries of Painting*. Edinburgh.

Holmer, N.M. 1938: *Studies on Argyllshire Gaelic*. Uppsala and Leipzig.

— 1957: *The Gaelic of Arran*. Dublin.

— 1962: *The Gaelic of Kintyre*. Dublin.

Holmes, D.T. 1909: *Literary Tours in the Highlands and Islands of Scotland*.

Hughes, K. 1966: *The Church in Early Irish Society*. London.

— 1972: *Early Christian Ireland: Introduction to the Sources*. London.

— 1980: *Celtic Britain in the Early Middle Ages: Studies in Scottish and Welsh Sources*. Ipswich.

Hunter, J. 1974a: 'The Emergence of the Crofting Community...', *SS* 18.

— 1974b: 'The Politics of Highland Land Reform', *SHR* 53.

— 1975: 'The Gaelic Connection: the Highlands, Ireland and Nationalism', *SHR* 54.

— 1976: *The Making of the Crofting Community*. Edinburgh.

Imrie, J. ed. 1969: *The Justiciary Records of Argyll and the Isles* vol. ii: *1705–1742*. Stair Society vol. xxv, Edinburgh.

Innes, C. 1855: *Black Book of Taymouth*. Edinburgh.

Insh, G.P. 1952: *The Scottish Jacobite Movement*. Edinburgh.

Inverness Field Club 1972: *The Dark Ages in the Highlands*. Inverness.

— 1975: *The Hub of the Highlands*. Inverness.

Jackson, A. 1971: 'Pictish Social Structure and Symbol-Stones', *SS* 15.

Jackson, K.H. 1945: 'Once Again Arthur's Battles', *Modern Philology* 43.

— 1951a: *A Celtic Miscellany*. London.

— 1951b: *Common Gaelic: The Evolution of the Gaelic Languages, Sir John Rhys Memorial Lecture*. London. Also in *Proceedings of the British Academy* 37 (1951).

— 1952: 'The Folktale in Gaelic Scotland', *Proceedings of the Scottish Anthropological and Folklore Society*.

— 1953: *Language and History in Early Britain*. Edinburgh.

— 1955a: *Contributions to the Study of Manx Phonology*.

— 1955b: 'The Britons in Southern Scotland', *Antiquity* 29.

— 1955c: 'The Pictish Language'. In F.T. Wainwright, ed., *The Problems of the Picts*. Edinburgh and London. Reprinted with addenda and corrigenda Perth 1980.

— 1956: 'The Poem *A ēolcha Alban uile*', *Celtica* 3.

— 1957: 'The Duan Albanach', *SHR* 36.

— 1958a: 'The Situation of the Scottish Gaelic Language and the Work of the Linguistic Survey of Scotland', *Lochlann* 1.

— 1958b: 'The Sources for the Life of St Kentigern'. In N.K. Chadwick, ed., *Studies in the Early British Church*. Cambridge.

— 1958c: 'The Site of Mount Badon', *Journal of Celtic Studies* 2.

— 1959: 'The Arthur of History'. In R.S. Loomis, ed., *Arthurian Literature in the Middle Ages*. Oxford.

— 1961: *The International Popular Tale and Early Welsh Tradition*. Cardiff.

— 1962: 'The Celtic Languages during the Viking Period', *Proceedings of the International Congress of Celtic Studies*. Dublin.

— 1963: 'Angles and Britons in Northumbria and Cumbria'. In H. Lewis, ed., *Angles and Britons: O'Donnell Lectures*. Cardiff.

— 1965: 'The Ogam Inscription at Dunadd', *Antiquity* 39.

— 1967: 'Palatalization of Labials in the Gaelic Languages'. In W. Meid, ed., *Beitrage zur Indo-germaniatik und Keltologu*.

— 1968: 'The Breaking of Original Long e in Scottish Gaelic'. In James Carney and David Greene, eds., *Celtic Studies: Essays in Memory of Angus Matheson 1912–1962*. London.

— 1972: *The Gaelic Notes in the Book of Deer*. Cambridge.

James, Richard 1953: 'Description of Shetland, Orkney and the Highlands of Scotland', *Orkney Miscellany* 1.

Jobey, G. 1976: 'Traprain Law: a Summary'. In D.W. Harding, ed., *Hillforts: Later Prehistoric Earthworks in Britain and Ireland*. London.

Johnson, D. 1972: *Music and Society in Lowland Scotland in the Eighteenth Century*. London.

— 1983: *Scottish Fiddle Music in the Eighteenth Century*. Edinburgh.

Johnson, Samuel 1924: *A Journey to the Western Isles of Scotland* (1775). London.

Johnston, W., and Johnston, A.K. *Clan Histories*. Edinburgh and London.

Jones, G.H. 1954: *The Mainstream of Jacobitism*. Cambridge.

Jones, T. 1964: 'The Early Evolution of the Legend of Arthur', *Nottingham Medieval Studies* 8.

Keltie, J.S. 1877: *History of the Scottish Highland Clans and Highland Regiments*. London.

Kennedy, D. 1786: *An Laoidheadair Gaelic*. Glasgow. 2nd edn 1836.

Kennedy, J. n.d.: *Three Gaelic Poems by Mrs Clark of Torra-Dhamh, Badenoch*. Edinburgh.

Kennedy, John 1877: 'Rev. Mackintosh Mackay, LL.D.', in *Disruption Worthies of the Highlands*.

— 1886: *The Apostle of the North*. 2nd edn, edited by John Macleod, 1932.

— 1892–4: 'Memoir of Dr Cameron'. In A. Macbain and J. Kennedy, eds., *Reliquiae Celticae*. 2 vols., Inverness.

Kennedy-Fraser, Marjory 1909: *Songs of the Hebrides*. London.

— 1929: *A Life of Song*. London.

Kenney, J.F. 1929: *Tne Sources for the Early History of Ireland*, vol. i: *Ecclesiastical*. New York. Reprinted 1966.

Kermack, W.R. 1953: *The Clan MacGregor*. Edinburgh and London.

— 1957: *The Scottish Highlands*. Edinburgh and London.

— 1967: *The Scottish Borders (with Galloway) to 1603*. Edinburgh and London.

Kilbride-Jones, H. 1980: *Zoomorphic Penannular Brooches*. London.

Kinvig, R.H. 1978: *The Isle of Man*. 3rd edn. Liverpool.

Knight, William 1888: *Principal Shairp and His Friends*.

Knott, Eleanor 1957: *An Introduction to Irish Syllabic Poetry . . . 1200–1600*. 2nd edn. Dublin.

Kyd, J.G. ed. 1952: *Scottish Population Studies*. PSHS 44.

Laffin, John 1974: *Scotland the Brave*. London.

Lamont, Claire 1975: 'A Note on Gaelic Proverbs in *Waverley*', *Notes and Queries of the Society of Highland and Island Historical Research* vol. 22.

Lamont, Donald 1913: *Srath: In Isle of Skye*. Glasgow.

— 1948: Obituary of Dr Archibald Macdonald, *Life and Work*, Gaelic Supplement, March.

Lamont, W.D. 1960: 'The Islay Charter', *Proceedings of the Royal Irish Academy* 60 C4.

Lea, K. J. 1969: 'Hydro-Electric Power Generation in the Highlands of Scotland', *Transactions of the Institute of British Geographers* 46.

Leask, Keith 1905: *Thomas Maclauchlan*.

Leigh, Margaret M. 1929: 'The Crofting Problem, 1780–1883'.

Lenman, B. 1977: *An Economic History of Modern Scotland 1660–1976*. London.

— 1980: *The Jacobite Risings in Britain 1689–1746*. London.

Leverhulme, Am Morair 1919: *Oraid. . . .* Port Sunlight.

Lewis, H., and Pedersen, H. 1937: *A Concise Comparative Celtic Grammar*. Göttingen. Reprinted 1961.

Lewis, M.J.T. 1965: *Temples in Roman Britain*. Cambridge.

Lhuyd, Edward 1707: *Archaeologia Britannica*. Oxford.

Lindsay, Maurice 1979: *As I Remember*. London.

Linklater, Eric, and Linklater, Andro 1977: *The Black Watch*. London.

Lockhart, Robert Bruce 1951: *Scotch: The Whisky of Scotland in Fact and Story*. London.

Logan, James 1831a: *The Clans of the Scottish Highlands*.

— 1831b: *The Scottish Gael*. 2 vols., London.

— 1840: *Sketch of the Origins and Progress of Scottish Societies in London and Elsewhere*. London. Reprinted 1977.

Loomis, R.S. 1955–6: 'Scotland and the Arthurian Tradition', *PSAS* 89.

Lorimer, R.L.C. 1962: 'Studies in Pibroch', *SS* 6.

— 1964: 'Studies in Pibroch', *SS* 8.

Lorimer, W.L. 1949: 'The Persistence of Gaelic in Galloway and Carrick', *SGS* 6.

— 1953: 'The Persistence of Gaelic in Galloway and Carrick', *SGS* 7.

Lothian, Duncan 1797: *Connsachadh eadar am Papa agus Reformation maille ri Sean fhocail, etc.* Edinburgh.

— 1797: *Proverbs in Verse*. Edinburgh.

Lowe, E.A. 1972: *Codices Latini Antiquiores*, Part II, 2nd edn. Oxford.

Mac A' Ghobhainn, Aonghas Iain 1971: 'Gaidheil Cheap Breatunn', *Gairm* 77.

Mac a' Ghobhainn, S. 1972: 'Ruaraidh Arascain is Mhairr', *Stornoway Gazette* 19 February.

MacAirt, Seán 1958: 'Filidecht and Coingne', *Ériu* 18.

MacAlister, Edith F.B. 1935: *Sir Donald MacAlister of Tarbert*. London.

Macalister, R.A.S. 1945: *Corpus Inscriptionum Insularum Celticarum* 1. Dublin.

MacAlpine, Neil 1833: *A Pronouncing Gaelic Dictionary*. Edinburgh. Revised, with biography of Macalpine, 1930.

MacAmhlaigh, D. 1967: *Seòbhach as a' Chlaich*. Glasgow.

— 1981: *Oighreachd agus Gabhaltas*. Aberdeen.

Mac-an-tuairneir, Paruig 1813: *Comhchruinneacha do dh'orain taghta Ghaidhealach*. Edinburgh.

McArthur, M.M. ed. 1936: *Survey of Lochtayside 1769*. PSHS 3rd series vol. 37.

MacAulay, D. 1962: 'Notes on Some Noun-Initial Mutations in a Dialect of Scottish Gaelic', *SGS* 9.

— 1966a: 'On Some Aspects of the Appreciation of Modern Gaelic Poetry', *SGS* 11 and 12.

— 1966b: 'Palatalization of Labials in Scottish Gaelic and Some Related Problems in Phonology', *SGS* 11.

— 1971: Introduction to *The Far Road and Other Poems*, *Lines Review* 39.

— 1972: 'Studying the Place Names of Bernera, Lewis', *TGSI* 46.

— ed. 1976: *Nua Bhàrdachd Ghàidhlig*. Edinburgh.

— 1978: 'Intra-Dialectal Variation as an Area of Gaelic Linguistic Research', *SGS* 13 part 1.

— 1979: 'The State of Gaelic Language Studies'. In A.J. Aitken and T. McArthur, eds., *Languages of Scotland*.

— 1981: 'George Campbell Hay'. In D. Daiches, ed., *A Companion to Scottish Culture*. London.

— 1982a: 'Register Range and Choice in Scottish Gaelic', *International Journal of the Sociology of Language* 35.

— 1982b: 'Borrow, Calque and Switch: the Law of the English Frontier'. In John Anderson, ed., *Language Form and Linguistic Variation: Papers Dedicated to Angus McIntosh* (Current Issues in Linguistic Theory vol. 15). Amsterdam.

Macaulay, F.E.G. 1953: 'Some Aspects of Preaspiration of Plosives in Scottish Gaelic'. Unpublished class essay, University of Edinburgh.

MacBain, A. 1892: 'Gaelic Incantations', *TGSI* 17.

— 1894: 'The Dialect of Badenoch', *TGSI* 18.

— 1895: 'The Norse Element in the Topography of the Highlands and Isles', *TGSI* 19.

— 1897: 'The Old Gaelic System of Personal Names', *TGSI* 20.

— 1896: *An Etymological Dictionary of the Gaelic Language*. Inverness. New and revised edn Stirling 1911. Reprinted 1982.

— 1900: 'Early Highland Personal Names', *TGSI* 22.

— ed. 1902: *Skene's Highlanders of Scotland*.

— and Whyte, John 1906: *How to Learn Gaelic*. 4th edn. Inverness.

Macbean, Lachlan 1919: *Buchanan, the Sacred Bard of the Scottish Highlands*. London.

— 1921: *The Celtic Who's Who*. Kirkcaldy.

MacCallum, A.K. 1894: *Laoidhean agus Dàin Spioradail*. Glasgow.

MacCallum, D. ('Ajax') 1909: *Highland Patriots*.
— 1912: 'My Arrest'. In James Cameron, ed., *The Old and the New Highlands and Hebrides*. Kirkcaldy.
MacColla, Eóghan 1937: *Clàrsach nam Beann*. Glasgow.
MacCalmain, T.M. 1954: 'Eachann MacDhughaill', *Gairm* 2. Glasgow.
— 1958: 'An Eaglais anns a' Ghaidhealtachd anns an Ochdamh Linn Deug', *Transactions of the Gaelic Society of Glasgow* 5.
MacCaluim, Gilleasbaig K. 1894: *Laoidhean agus Dain Spioradail*. Glasgow.
Mac-Choinnich, Iain 1906: *Eachdraidh a' Phrionnsa*. Paisley.
McClintoch, H.F. 1950: *Old Irish and Highland Dress*. Dundalk.
MacCoinnich, Cailein T. 1969: *Oirthir Tìm*. Glasgow.
— 1971a: *A' Leth Eile*. Glasgow.
— 1971b: *Mar Sgeul a dh'innseas Neach*. Glasgow.
— 1973: *Nach Neònach Sin*. Glasgow.
MacCoinnich, John 1923: *The Island of Mull*. Stirling.
MacColl, D. 1899: *Leabhar Laoidh*. Glasgow.
McConechy, J. ed. 1845: *Papers Illustrative of the Political Condition of the Highlands of Scotland 1689 to 1696*. Maitland Club, Glasgow.
MacCuish, Donald J. 1966: 'The Origin and Development of Crofting Law', *TGSI* 43.
— 1971: 'The Case for Converting Crofting Tenure to Ownership', *TGSI* 46.
— 1976: 'Reform of Crofting Tenure', *TGSI* 48.
— 1979: 'Ninety Years of Crofting Legislation and Administration', *TGSI* 50.
MacDhòmhnaill, Dòmhnall 1981: *Rannan a Eilean na h-Oige*. Glasgow.
MacDhòmhnaill, Niall 1976: 'Dòmhnall MacLeòid: Fear-iùil a' Phrionnsa', *Gairm* 96.
MacDhùghaill, Eachann, 'Lachlann nam Mogan', *An Gaidheal* 46.
MacDhùghaill, I. 1976–7: 'An Dealbh Briste – Ath-sgrùdadh', *Gairm* 97.
MacDhunlèibhe, Uilleam 1882: *Duain agus Orain*. Glasgow.
MacDonald, Rev. A. 1894: *The Uist Collection*. Inverness.
MacDonald, A. 1924: 'Shinty: Historical and Traditional', *TGSI* 30.
MacDonald, Aidan 1973: 'Annat in Scotland: a Provisional Review', *SS* 17.
MacDonald, Alexander 1741: *Leabhar a Theagasc Ainminnin*. Edinburgh.
MacDonald, Alexander 1922: 'Some Rare Gaelic Words and Phrases', *TGSI* 29.
McDonald, Fr Allan 1893: *Comh-chruinneachadh de Laoidhean Spioradail*. Oban.
MacDonald, A., and Macdonald, A. 1896, 1900, 1904: *The Clan Donald*. 3 vols. Inverness.
— 1911: *The MacDonald Collection of Gaelic Poetry*. Inverness.
— 1924: *The Poems of Alexander MacDonald*. Inverness.
Macdonald, Colin 1955: *Crofts and Crofters*. Edinburgh.

MacDonald, D. 1822: *A Collection of Ancient Martial Music of Caledonia, Called Piobaireachd*. Edinburgh.
MacDonald, D.A. 1978: 'A Visual Memory', *SS* 22.
— and Bruford, Alan 1970: 'An Ceatharnach Caol Riabhach', *SS* 14.
Macdonald, D.G.F. 1878: *The Highland Crofters of Scotland*, 3rd edn. London.
MacDonald, D.J. 1965: *Slaughter under Trust*. London.
MacDonald, Duncan 1946: 'Some Rare Gaelic Words and Phrases', *TGSI* 37.
MacDonald, J. 1811: *General View of the Agriculture of the Hebrides*. Edinburgh.
MacDonald, J. 1897: *Marbhrainn agus Dàna Spioradail Eile*. Edinburgh.
Macdonald, John 1790: *Travels*. London.
Macdonald, John ed. 1927: *Voices from the Hills* (*Guthan o na Beanntaibh*). Glasgow.
Macdonald, John ed. 1937: *Ewen MacLachlan's Gaelic Verse*. Aberdeen. 2nd edn with Foreword 1980.
— 1955: 'An Elergy for Ruaidhrí Mór (Eóin Og O Muirgheasáin's *Creach Gaoidheal i réilig Rois*), *SGS* 8. Aberdeen.
MacDonald, John A. 1976–7: *Gàidhlig Bheò*. Cambridge.
— and Renton, R. 1979: *Abair* (Pocket Dictionary). Glasgow.
MacDonald, J. Ninian 1932: *Shinty: A Short History of the Ancient Game*. Inverness.
MacDonald, Kenneth D. ed. 1970: *Briseadh na Cloiche agus sgeulachdan eile*. Glasgow.
— 1979: 'The Rev. William Shaw – Pioneer Gaelic Lexicographer', *TGSI* 50.
— 1982: 'Dòmhnallach na Tòisidheachd', *Gairm* 121.
— and Thomson, D.S. forthcoming: *The MacDiarmid Anthology*.
Macdonald, K.N. 1895: *The Gesto Collection*. Leipzig.
— 1900: *Macdonald Bards from Mediaeval Times*. Glasgow.
MacDonald, Mairi A. 1971: 'History of the Gaelic Society of Inverness 1871–1971', *TGSI* 46.
MacDonald, M.E. 1955: *The Vitality of Faith*.
— 1959: *The Need to Believe*.
— 1963: *The Call to Obey*.
— 1971: *Crisis of Belief: Sermons for Today*.
— 1975: *The Call to Communicate*.
MacDonald, Norman 1966: 'Some Rare Hebridean Gaelic Words and Phrases', *SGS* 11.
McDonald, Patrick 1781: *A Collection of Highland Vocal Airs*. Edinburgh.
Macdonald, Ranald 1776: *Comh-chruinneachidh Orannaigh Gaidhealach* (Eigg Collection). Edinburgh.
Macdonald, R. Gordon 1928: *The Highlanders of Waipu*.
Macdonald, Robert 1836: *Oranan Nuadh....* Inverness.
MacDonald, Roderick 1978: *Leth-cheud Bliadhna (Contemporary Poems in Gaelic and English)*. Glasgow.
MacDonald, T.D. n.d., c. 1919: *Dàin agus Dealbhan-fhacail*. Glasgow.
MacDougall, Allan 1798: *Orain Ghaidhealach: Le Ailein Dughallach fear ciuil an Ionbhar Lochaidh, maille ri*

Co'-chruinneachadh oran is dhan le Ughdairibh eile.
Edinburgh.

MacDougall, Allan 1829: *Orain, Marbhrannan, agus Duanagan Ghaidhealach.* Inverness.

MacDougall, H. ed. 1926: *Spiritual Songs by Rev. Peter Grant.* Glasgow.

MacDougall, Hector 1936: *Bàird Chill-Chomain.* Glasgow.

MacDougall, James 1910: *Folk Tales and Fairy Lore*, ed. George Calder. Edinburgh.

MacDougall, Robert 1841: *Ceann-Iuil an Fhir-imrich do Dh-America mu thuath.* Glasgow.

MacEacharn, Dòmhnall 1904: *Am Fear-ciùil.* Glasgow. 2nd edn Edinburgh 1910; 3rd edn Glasgow 1940.

MacEachen, Ewen 1842: *Faclair Gailig us Beurla.* Perth.

MacFarlan, Robert 1795: *Nuadh Fhoclair Gaidhlig, agus Beurla.* Edinburgh.

MacFarlane, Malcolm 1889: *The Phonetics of the Gaelic Language.* Paisley.

— 1905: 'An Comunn Gaidhealach, its Inception and Development', *An Deò-Créine* 1.

— 1912: *The School Gaelic Dictionary.* Stirling.

— 1923: *Làmh-Sgriobhainn Mhic Rath.* Dundee.

— and Whitehead, Fr W. 1902: *Songs of the Highlands.* Inverness.

MacFarlane, Peter 1815: *A New and Copious English and Gaelic Vocabulary.* Edinburgh.

Macfarlane, W. 1900: *Genealogical Collections Concerning Families in Scotland.* 2 vols., Edinburgh.

MacFhionnlaigh, F. 1980: *A' Mheanbhchuileag.* Glasgow.

MacGibbon, D., and Ross, T. 1887–92: *The Castellated and Domestic Architecture of Scotland.* Edinburgh.

— 1896–7: *The Ecclesiastical Architecture of Scotland.* Edinburgh.

MacGill-Eain, Somhairle 1977: *Reothairt is Contraigh/ Spring Tide and Neap Tide.* Edinburgh.

— and Garioch, Robert 1939, 1940: *17 Poems for 6d.* Edinburgh.

MacGill-Eathain, Calum I. 1954: 'Aonghus agus Donnchadh', *Gairm* 10.

MacGill-Fhinnein, G. 1966: *Gàidhlig Uidhist a Deas.*

MacGilleMhoire, U.M. 1911: *Iulius Caesar.* Edinburgh.

McGlashan, A. 1778: *A Collection of Strathspey Reels....* Edinburgh.

MacGregor, James 1819a: *Dàin [a] Chomhnadh crabhuidh.* Glasgow.

— 1819b: *Spiritual Hymns.* Glasgow. 4th edn with biography Edinburgh 1847.

MacGregor, John 1897: *Luinneagan Luaineach.* London.

Macgregor, W.M. 1907: *Our Church in the Highlands.* Edinburgh and London.

MacIlleMhoire, Murchadh 1923: *Fear Siubhal nan Gleann.* Glasgow.

MacInnes, Duncan 1880: *Comhraidhean 'an Gaelig 's 'am Beurla.* Edinburgh.

MacInnes, John 1951: *The Evangelical Movement in the Highlands of Scotland, 1688 to 1800.* Aberdeen.

— 1971: 'Gaelic Spiritual Verse', *TGSI* 46.

MacInnes, John 1968: 'The Oral Tradition in Scottish Gaelic Poetry', *SS* 12.

— 1971: 'The Choral Tradition in Scottish Gaelic Songs', *TGSI* 46.

— 1976: 'The Gaelic Literary Tradition', in *Scottish Literature in the Secondary School.* Edinburgh.

— 1977: 'Some Gaelic Words and Usages', *TGSI* 49.

— 1979: 'The Panegyric Code in Gaelic Poetry and its Historical Background', *TGSI* 50.

Macinnes, Malcolm ed. 1951: *Gaelic Proverbs*, reprint of A. Nicolson's work with index. Glasgow.

McIntosh, Peter 1870: *History of Kintyre*, 3rd edn. Campbeltown.

Macintyre, Donald 1968: *Sporan Dhòmhnaill*, ed. Somerled MacMillan. Edinburgh.

MacIver, D. 1934: *Place-Names of Lewis and Harris.* Stornoway.

MacKay, Angus 1838: *A Collection of Ancient Piobaireachd.* Edinburgh.

Mackay, Angus 1906: *The Book of Mackay.* Edinburgh.

— 1912: Appreciation of George Calder, *Celtic Monthly* 20.

MacKay, I. 1964: 'Clanranald's Tacksmen of the Late Eighteenth Century', *TGSI* 44.

Mackay, I.R. 1963: 'Angus Macdonald of Borrodale', *An Gaidheal* May.

Mackay, John 1914: *The Church in the Highlands, 563–1843.* London.

McKay, J.G. 1935: 'An Tuairisgeal', *TGSI* 34.

Mackay, M. 1869: *Sermon Preached in the Free Church, Snizort, Skye, on the Occasion of the Decease of the Rev. Roderick MacLeod....* Edinburgh.

Mackay, Mackintosh 1829: *Songs and Poems in the Gaelic Language.* Inverness.

McKay, Margaret M. ed. 1980: [John Walker's] *Report on the Hebrides of 1764 and 1771.* Edinburgh.

Mackay, Robert 1829: *The House and Clan of Mackay.* Edinburgh.

Mackay, William 1885: 'Presbyterian Notices of Mac Mhaighstir Alastair, and Some of his Contemporaries in Ardnamurchan and Morven', *TGSI* 11.

— 1893: *Urquhart and Glenmoriston.* Inverness.

— ed. 1896: *Records of the Presbyteries of Inverness and Dingwall 1643–1688.* PSHS vol. 24.

— 1905: *Chronicles of the Frasers* (the Wardlaw MS). Edinburgh.

MacKay, W.R. 1980: 'More Highland Rites and Customs', *Notes and Queries of the Society of West Highland and Island Historical Research* 12.

Mackechnie, Elizabeth E. 1947: *The Poems of John Roy Stewart.* Glasgow.

Mackechnie, John 1951: 'Treaty between Argyll and O'Donnell', *SGS* 7.

Mackellar, Mary 1880: *Poems and Songs, Gaelic and English.* Edinburgh.

— 1886: 'Unknown Lochaber Bards', *TGSI* 12.

McKenna, Lambert ed. 1922: *Dán Dé*. Dublin.
— 1938: *Dioghluim Dána*. Dublin.
— 1939: *Aithdioghluim Dána*. Dublin.
— 1944: *Bardic Syntactical Tracts*. Dublin.
Mackenzie, Alexander 1877: *The Prophecies of the Brahan Seer* (Coinneach Odhar Fiosaiche). Inverness.
— 1881: *History of the MacDonalds and Lords of the Isles*. Inverness.
— 1883a: *The Highland Clearances*. Inverness.
— 1883b: *The Isle of Skye in 1882–83*.
— 1894: *History of the Mackenzies*, 2nd edn. Inverness.
— 1898: *History of the Munros of Fowlis*. Inverness.
Mackenzie, Annie M. 1963: 'Lochaber Bards', *SGS* 10.
— ed. 1964: *Orain Iain Luim*. Edinburgh.
MacKenzie, J.B. 1911: *Episode in the Life of the Rev. Neil MacKenzie at St Kilda from 1829 to 1843*. Printed privately.
Mackenzie, James 1971: 'The Odyssey of John MacRae', *State* (North Carolina) December.
Mackenzie, John ed. 1830: *Orain Ghae'lach, le Uilleam Ros*. Inverness.
— 1844: *Eachdraidh a' Phrionnsa no Bliadhna Thearlaich*. Edinburgh.
—: *Sar-Obair nam Bard Gaelach, or the Beauties of Gaelic Poetry*, 4th edn. Edinburgh.
MacKenzie, W. 1894: 'Gaelic Incantations', *TGSI* 18.
Mackenzie, W.C. 1903: *History of the Outer Hebrides*. Paisley.
—: *Lovat of the Forty-Five*. Edinburgh and London.
McKerral, A. 1947: 'The Tacksman and his Holding in the South-West Highlands', *SHR* 26.
MacKie, E.W. 1965: 'Brochs and the Hebridean Iron Age', *Antiquity* 39.
— 1975: *Scotland: An Archaeological Guide*. London.
MacKinnon, D. n.d.: *Domhnull 'Munro' an Dall*. Portree.
— 1930: *The Gaelic Bible and Psalter*. Dingwall.
MacKinnon, Donald 1885: 'The Fernaig Manuscript', *TGSI* 11.
— 1912: *A Descriptive Catalogue of Gaelic Manuscripts in the Advocates' Library, Edinburgh, and Elsewhere in Scotland*. Edinburgh.
MacKinnon, J.G. (Eoin Mac Fhionghuin) n.d.: *The Highland Scots*.
— 1919a: *Old Sydney*. Sydney, Cape Breton.
— 1919b: *Am Piobaire Breac agus da Sgeul Eile*. Sydney, Cape Breton.
— 1924: *Far am bi Gradh, bidh Dia*. Sydney, Cape Breton.
— 1938: *Sgeul an Draoidh Eile*. Dunfermline.
— 1944: *An Triuir Choigreach*. Edinburgh.
MacKinnon, Kenneth 1974: *The Lion's Tongue*. Inverness.
— 1977: *Language, Education and Society and Society Processes*. London.
— 1978: *Gaelic in Scotland 1971*. Hatfield.
— and MacDonald, M. 1980: *Ethnic Communities: The Transmission of Language and Culture*. London and Hatfield.

Mackinnon, Lachlan 1956: *Prose Writings of Donald MacKinnon*. Edinburgh.
Mackintosh, Donald 1785: *Collection of Gaelic Proverbs and Familiar Phrases*. Edinburgh. Reprinted 1819.
Mackintosh, Donald T. 1947: 'James Macpherson and the Book of the Dean of Lismore', *SGS* 6.
MacLachlan, John (of Rahoy) 1869: *Dàin agus Orain*. Glasgow.
Maclauchlan, Thomas 1877: 'Rev. John Macdonald, DD, of Ferintosh', in *Disruption Worthies of the Highlands*.
McLaurin, Alexander 1806: Gaelic translation of R. Dodsley's *Economy of Life*. Edinburgh.
— 1811: *The First Book for Children in the Gaelic Language*. Edinburgh.
Maclean, Calum I. 1959: *The Highlands*. London. Reprinted with Memoir, etc., Inverness 1975.
Maclean, Donald 1912: *The Literature of the Scottish Gael*. Reprinted from *Celtic Review* 7 and 8. Edinburgh and London.
— 1915: *Typographia Scoto-Gadelica*. Edinburgh. 2nd edn Dublin 1972.
Maclean, Donald ed. 1913: *The Spiritual Songs of Dugald Buchanan*. Edinburgh.
— 1927a: 'The Life and Literary Labours of the Rev. Robert Kirk, of Aberfoyle', *TGSI* 31.
— 1927b: *Aspects of Scottish Church History*.
— 1931: *The Counter-Reformation in Scotland 1560–1930*.
Maclean, G.R.D. 1961: *Poems of the Western Highlanders*. London.
MacLean, J. 1835: *Spiritual Hymns*. Glasgow.
Maclean, J. 1880: *Laoidhean Spioradail*. Edinburgh.
Maclean, John 1953: 'Am Piobaire Dall', *TGSI* 41.
MacLean, L. 1975: *The Hub of the Highlands: The Book of the Inverness District*. Edinburgh.
MacLean, Magnus 1902: *The Literature of the Celts*. Revised edn 1926.
— 1904: *The Literature of the Highlands*. Glasgow. 2nd edn 1925.
— 1907: 'The Gaelic Outlook', in *Am Bolg Solair*. Glasgow.
Maclean, Norman 1911: *The Burnt Offering*.
Maclean, S. 1946: 'Realism in Gaelic Poetry', *TGSI* 37.
— 1953: 'Alasdair Mac Mhurchaidh', *TGSI* 41.
— 1962: 'The Poetry of the Clearances', *TGSI* 38.
— 1963: 'The Poetry of William Livingstone', *TGSI* 39–40.
— 1966: 'Notes on Sea Imagery in 17th Century Gaelic Poetry', *TGSI* 43.
Maclean, A. 1969: 'Silis of Keppoch', *TGSI* 45.
Maclean-Bristol, N. 1980: 'Maclean Family Manuscripts (Part 2)', *Notes and Queries of the Society of West Highland and Island Historical Research* 11.
MacLennan, H.D. 1983: *Shinty: Coaching Manual and Rules of Play*. Inverness.
McLennan, John S. 1918: *Louisbourg from its Foundation to its Fall, 1713–1758*. London.
MacLennan, Malcolm 1920: 'Modern Gaelic Prose', *Celtic Congress Report*.

— 1925: *A Pronouncing and Etymological Dictionary of the Gaelic Language*. Edinburgh. 3rd impression Stornoway and Aberdeen 1979.

MacLeod, Angus 1933: *Sàr Orain*. Glasgow.

— ed. 1952: *The Songs of Duncan Ban Macintyre*. Edinburgh.

MacLeod, Calum I.N. 1958: 'The Gaelic Tradition in Nova Scotia', *Lochlann* 1.

MacLeod, Donald 1811: *Orain Nuadh Ghaeleach*. Inverness.

MacLeod, Donald 1857: *Gloomy Memories of the Highlands of Scotland*. Toronto.

— 1871: *Dàin agus Orain*. Glasgow.

MacLeod, Donald James n.d.: *Donnchadh Bàn Mac an t-Saoir....* Inverness.

— 1918: Essay on Donnchadh Bàn and Mac Mhaighstir Alasdair, in *An Solaraiche*. Glasgow.

— ed. 1934: *Martin's Description of the Western Isles* [published 1703]; *Martin's Voyage to St Kilda* [1698]; *Monro's Description of the Western Isles in 1549*. Stirling.

MacLeod, Donald John 1969: 'Twentiety-Century Gaelic Literature: A Description Comprising Critical Study and a Comprehensive Bibliography'. PhD thesis, Glasgow University.

— 1977: 'Gaelic Prose', *TGSI* 49.

— 1980: *Twentieth Century Publications in Scottish Gaelic*. Edinburgh.

MacLeod, Finlay 1970: 'Experimental Investigation into Some Problems of Bilingualism'. PhD thesis, University of Aberdeen.

MacLeod, Frederick T. 1933: *The MacCrimmons of Skye*. Edinburgh.

MacLeod, J. 1948: *Am Measg nan Lili*. Inverness.

— 1965: *By-Paths of Highland Church History*. Edinburgh.

Macleod, J.N. 1933: Articles in *Stornoway Gazette* 27 October; 3, 10 and 17 November.

Macleod, John 1976: 'Laoidh na Rèite', *Life and Work*, Gaelic Supplement, June.

Macleod, Joseph 1917: *Highland Heroes of the Land Reform Movement*. Inverness.

MacLeod, M. 1962: *Bàrdachd Mhurchaidh a' Cheisdeir*. Edinburgh.

— 1966: 'Gaelic in Highland Education', *TGSI* 43.

Macleod, Malcolm C. ed. 1908: *Modern Gaelic Bards*. Stirling. 2nd series part 1 Dundee 1913; part 2 in preparation.

— 1921: 'The Gaelic Mod', *Celtic Congress Report*.

MacLeod, N. 1828: *A Collection of Piobaireachd of Pipe Tunes ... as Taken from John McCrummen*. Edinburgh. Full modern edition in preparation.

Macleod, Norman ed. 1913: Duncan Reid's *Elementary Course of Gaelic*, enlarged edn. Glasgow.

MacLeod, Norman, and Dewar, Daniel 1831: *A Dictionary of the Gaelic Language*. Glasgow.

MacLeod, R.H. 1973: 'Sir Rory Mor's Influence on Piobaireachd', *Piping Times* 26 no. 3.

— 1977a: 'Early MacCrimmon Records', *Piping Times* 29 no. 5.

— 1977b: 'The MacCrimmons and the '45', *Piping Times* 29 no. 6.

— 1977c: 'The End of the MacCrimmon College', *Piping Times* 29 no. 8.

MacLeod, Rederick 1977: 'The Progress of Evangelicalism in the Western Isles'. PhD thesis, University of Edinburgh.

Macleod, Robert ed. 1935: *An Laoidheadair*. Edinburgh.

MacLeòid, Dòmhnall Iain ed. 1972: *An t-Eilean a Tuath*. Glasgow.

MacLeòid, Iain 1900: *Dàin agus Orain*. Edinburgh.

MacLeòid, Iain 1971: *Sràidean is Sléibhtean*. Glasgow.

MacLeòid, Iain N. 1916: *Bàrdachd Leódhais*. Glasgow.

MacLeòid, Iain N. 1932: *Litrichean Alasdair Mhóir*. Stornoway.

MacLeòid, Niall 1883: *Clàrsach an Doire*. Edinburgh. Latest edn Glasgow 1975.

MacLeòid, R. 1976: *Bith-eòlas*, translated by Ruaraidh MacThòmais. Glasgow.

MacLeòid, Tormod 1969: *Bàrdachd á Leódhas*. Glasgow.

McLynn, F.J. 1983: *The Jacobite Army in England 1745: The Final Campaign*. Edinburgh.

MacMhathain, Aonghas 1954–5: 'Aos Dàna', *Gairm* 2 and 3.

MacMhathain, Uilleam 1955: 'Mòr Ross', *Gairm* 3.

MacMillan, Somerled ed. 1968: Donald Macintyre's *Sporan Dhòmhnaill*. Edinburgh.

Mac-na-Ceàrdadh, Gilleasbuig 1876–79: *An t-Oranaiche*. Glasgow.

McNab, P.A. 1971: *The Isle of Mull*. Newton Abbot.

MacNamara, John 1966: *Bilingualism and Primary Education*. Edinburgh.

MacNeacail, Calum 1874: *Dàin Spioradail*. Glasgow.

MacNeill, E. 1931: 'Beginnings of Latin Culture in Ireland', *Studies* 20.

MacNeill, M. 1962: *The Festival of Lughnasa*. Oxford.

Macneill, Nigel 1872: *Cian Dhain, le Dànaibh Eile*. Edinburgh.

— 1886: *Clàrsair Shioin: The Highland Hymnal*. Glasgow.

— 1892: *The Literature of the Highlanders*. Stirling. Reissued with additional chapter, Stirling 1929.

McNeill, P.G.B., and Nicholson, R. 1975: *An Historical Atlas of Scotland c.400–c.1600*. St Andrews. 2nd edn 1980.

MacNeill, Seumas (with Lenihan, J.M.A.) 1953: 'An Acoustical Study of the Highland Bagpipe', *Acustica* 3.

— 1968: *Piobaireachd*. Edinburgh.

MacNicol, Donald 1779: *Remarks on Dr Samuel Johnson's Journey to the Hebrides*. London.

MacPhaidein, Iain 1902: *Sgeulaiche nan Caol*. Glasgow.

— 1912: *Companach na Cloinne*, ed. Calum MacPhàrlain. Stirling.

— 1921: *An t-Eileanach*. Glasgow.

MacPhail, I.M.M. 1976a: 'The Napier Commission', *TGSI* 48.

— 1976b: 'The Skye Military Expeditions of 1884–85', *TGSI* 48.

— 1977: 'Prelude to the Crofters' War, 1870–80', *TGSI* 49.

— 1979a: *Dumbarton Castle*. Edinburgh.

— 1979b: 'The Highland Elections of 1884–86', *TGSI* 50.

MacPhail, J.R.N. ed. 1914–34: *Highland Papers*. 4 vols., Edinburgh.

MacPhàrlain, Calum 1903–12: *An Treòraiche*, Stirling 1903; *Dàin Thaghte*, Stirling 1906; *Binneas nam Bàrd*, Stirling 1908; *An Lòn-Dubh*, Paisley 1908; *An Smeòrach*, Stirling 1908; *Am Brù-Dhearg*, Stirling 1909; *An Comh-Threòraiche*, Stirling 1911; *Uirsgeulan Gaidhealach* Stirling 1912.

— 1912: *Am Briathrachan Beag/The School Gaelic Dictionary*. Stirling.

— ed. 1923: *Dòrlach Laoidhean* ... (edition of Làmh-Sgrìobhainn MhicRath, or the Fernaig Manuscript). Dundee.

— ed. 1925: Gaelic edition of Seònaid Given, *Clàrsach a' Ghlinne*. Glasgow.

— 1926: *Am Mosgladh Mór*. Glasgow.

— and MacGille-Bhàin, Eanraig eds. 1894: *An Uiseag*. Glasgow.

MacPherson, Donald C. 1868: *An Duanaire*. Edinburgh.

— 1879: 'The Clandonald of Keppoch', *Celtic Magazine* 4.

— 1891: *Practical Lessons in Gaelic for the Use of English-Speaking Students*. Edinburgh.

MacPherson, J. 1870: *Cunntas Aithghearr mu Bheatha 'n Urramaich Raibeart Fiunlason*. Edinburgh.

Macpherson, James 1760: *Fragments of Ancient Poetry*. Edinburgh.

— 1761, 1762: *Fingal*. London.

— 1763: *Temora*. London.

Macpherson, Mary 1891: *Gaelic Poems and Songs*. Inverness.

MacQueen, John 1953–4: 'Welsh and Gaelic in Galloway', *Transactions of the Dumfries-shire and Galloway Natural History and Antiquarian Society* 32.

— 1956: 'Kirk- and Kil- in Galloway Place-Names', *Archivum Linguisticum* 8.

— 1961: *St Nynia*. Edinburgh and London.

— 1973: 'The Gaelic Speakers of Galloway and Carrick', *SS* 17.

— 1979: 'Pennyland and Davoch in South-Western Scotland: a Preliminary Note', *SS* 23.

Macqueen, M.C. MacDonald, A., MacKintosh, C., and Stuart, E. 1939: *The Game of Shinty and Rules of Play*. Camanachd Association/Schools' Camanachd Association.

MacRae, A. ed. n.d.: *Mary MacPherson, Bean Torra Dhamh, her Poems and Life*. Glasgow.

MacRae, A. 1899: *History of the Clan MacRae*. Dingwall.

McRoberts, D. 1960–1: 'The Ecclesiastical Significance of the St Ninian's Isle Treasure', *PSAS* 94.

MacTavish, D.C. 1934: *The Gaelic Psalms 1694*. Lochgilphead.

— 1943–4: *Minutes of the Synod of Argyll*: vol. i *1639–51*; vol. ii *1652–61*. Edinburgh.

MacThòmais, Ruaraidh 1951: *An Dealbh Briste*. Edinburgh.

— 1967: *Eadar Samhradh is Foghar*. Glasgow.

— 1970: *An Rathad Cian*. Glasgow.

— 1976: 'Leabhraichean, Litreachas, Foillseachadh', in *Gàidhlig ann an Albainn/Gaelic in Scotland*. Glasgow.

— 1977a: 'Gairm – 1952–1977', *Gairm* 100.

— 1977b: *Saorsa agus an Iolaire*. Glasgow.

— 1982: *Creachadh na Clàrsaich*. Edinburgh.

MacThomais, S. 1961: 'Iain M. Moffatt-Pender', *An Gaidheal* 56.

Maidment, J. 1834/7: *Analecta Scotica*. 2 vols., Edinburgh.

Malcolme, David 1738: *Essay on the Antiquities of Britain and Ireland*. Edinburgh.

Mallet, Paul Henri 1755–6: *Introduction à l'histoire de Dannemarc*. Copenhagen.

— 1756: *Monuments de la mythologie et de la poésie des Celtes*. Copenhagen.

Mann, J.C. 1974: 'The Northern Frontier after AD 369', *Glasgow Archaeology Journal* 3.

Marshall, R.K. 1973: *The Days of Duchess Anne*. London.

Martin, Martin 1703: *A Description of the Western Islands of Scotland*. London. Rptd 1934, Stirling. Ed. D.J. Macleod.

Martinet, A. 1952: 'Celtic Lenition and Western Romance Consonants', *Language* 28.

Mason, J. 1947: 'Conditions in the Highlands after the Forty-Five', *Scottish Review* 26.

Masson, D. ed. 1889: *Register of the Privy Council of Scotland*: vol. ix *1610–1613*. Edinburgh.

— ed. 1891: *Register of the Privy Council of Scotland*: vol. x *1613–1616*. Edinburgh.

Mather, A.S. 1971: 'Problems of Afforestation in North Scotland', *Transactions of the Institute of British Geographers* 54.

— 1979: 'Land Use Changes in the Highlands and Islands, 1946–75: a Statistical Review', *Scottish Geographic Magazine* 95.

— and Ritchie, W. 1976: *The Beaches of the Highlands and Islands of Scotland*. Aberdeen.

Matheson, Angus 1949: 'Some Proverbs and Proverbial Expressions from Lewis', *Journal of Celtic Studies* 1.

— ed. 1954: Alexander Carmichael's *Carmina Gadelica* 5. Edinburgh and London.

— 1958: 'Traditions of Alasdair MacColla', *Transactions of the Gaelic Society of Glasgow* 5.

— 1960: *More West Highland Tales*, Gaelic edn, vol. ii. Edinburgh and London.

— 1963: 'Poems from a Manuscript of Cathal Mac Muireadhaigh', *Éigse* 10.

— 1964: 'Poems from a Manuscript of Cathal Mac Muireadhaigh', *Éigse* 11.

— 1971: Alexander Carmichael's *Carmina Gadelica* 6. Edinburgh and London.

— and Thomson, Derick S. eds. 1953: *Fear na h-Eabaid*, transcription and translation of Duncan MacDonald's version, printed privately.

Matheson, J. 1846: *Oran mu'n Eaglais*. Edinburgh.

Matheson, W. 1938: *The Songs of John MacCodrum.* Edinburgh.

Matheson, W. 1953: 'Notes on Mary MacLeod', *TGSI* 41.

Matheson, W. 1962: 'Co-chruinneachadh de shaothair nam bard Uibhisteach', *TGSI* 38.

— 1963: 'Traditions of the Mackenzies', *TGSI* 39–40.

— 1965: 'Traditions of the Mathesons', *TGSI* 42.

— 1969: 'Further Gleanings from the Dornie Manuscript', *TGSI* 45.

— 1970: *The Blind Harper: An Clarsair Dall.* Edinburgh.

— 1971: 'The historical Coinneach Odhar and some Prophecies attributed to him', *TGSI* 46.

— 1972: 'Genealogies of the Mathesons', *TGSI* 47.

— 1977a: 'Aonghus nan Aoir: a Case of Mistaken Identity', *SS* 21.

— 1977b: 'Co-chruinneachadh eile de shaothair nam bard Uibhisteach', *TGSI* 49.

— 1978: 'The O'Muirgheasáin Bardic Family', *Notes and Queries of the Society of West Highland and Island Historical Research* 7.

— 1979: 'The Morisons of Ness', *TGSI* 50.

Mays, W.J. 1955: 'Note Concerning the Date of Composition of Mac-Mhaighstir Alasdair's Òran a Gheamhraidh', *SGS* 8.

Meehan, D. ed. 1958: *Adamnan's De Locis Sanctis.* Scriptores Latini Hiberniae vol. iii. Dublin.

Meek, Donald 1977a: 'Gaelic Poets of the Land Agitation', *TGSI* 49.

— 1977b: *Màiri Mhór nan Oran.* Glasgow.

— 1977c: 'The Prophet of Waternish', *West Highland Free Press* 271, 8 July.

— 1977d: *An t-Aiseag an Iar.* Glasgow.

— ed. 1978: *The Campbell Collection of Gaelic Proverbs. . . .* Inverness.

— and Kirk, James 1975: 'John Carswell, Superintendent of Argyll: a Reassessment', *Records of the Scottish Church History Society* 19.

— 1982: 'The Corpus of Heroic Verse in the Book of the Dean of Lismore'. Unpublished doctoral dissertation, University of Glasgow.

— 1983: 'Ath-sgrùdadh: Cailein T. MacCoinnich', *Gairm* 123.

Megaw, B.R.S. 1979: 'Note on "Pennyland and Davoch in South-Western Scotland"', *SS* 23.

Menzies G. ed. 1976: *History is My Witness.* London.

Mewett, P.G. 1977: 'Occupational Pluralism in Crofting. . .', *Scottish Journal of Sociology* 2.

Meyer, K. ed. 1905: *Cáin Adamnáin, Anecdota Oxoniensia.* Medieval and Modern Series, Part 12. Oxford.

Millar, Patrick 1949: *Four Centuries of Scottish Psalmody.* London.

Miller, A.H. ed. 1909: *A Selection of the Forfeited Estates Papers.* PSHS vol. 57.

Miller, H. 1870: *The Cruise of the Betsey.* 6th edn. Edinburgh.

Miller, H. 1905: *My Schools and Schoolmasters.* Edinburgh.

Miller, M. 1979a: 'The Disputed Historical Horizon of the Pictish Kinglists', *SHR* 58.

— 1979b: 'The Last Century of Pictish Succession', *SS* 23.

Millman, R. N. 1969: 'The Marches of Highland Estates', *Scottish Geographic Magazine* 85.

— 1970: 'The Landed Properties of Northern Scotland', *Scottish Geographic Magazine* 86.

Mitchell, Arthur 1902: *Travels and Tours in Scotland, 1296–1900.*

— and Toshach, J. eds. 1906–8: *Macfarlane's Geographical Collections.* 3 vols., Edinburgh.

Mitchell, D. 1900: *History of the Highlands and Gaelic Scotland.* Paisley.

Mills, Stella 1982: *The Collected Letters of Colin Maclaurin.* Nantwich.

Mitchell, J.B. 1962: *Great Britain: Geographical Essays.* London.

Mitchison, R. 1970: 'The Government and the Highlands 1707–45'. In N.T. Phillipson and R. Mitchison, eds., *Scotland in the Age of Improvement.* Edinburgh.

Moffatt-Pender, I.M. 1926: *Am Bàrd.* Edinburgh.

Moireach, Iain 1973: *An Aghaidh Choimheach.* Glasgow.

Moireach, Murchadh 1970a: *Luach na Saorsa.* Glasgow.

— 1970b: 'Màiri Nighean Iain Bhàin (Mary MacPherson)' *Luach na Saorsa.* Glasgow.

Moireasdan, D.R. 1979: 'Seumas MacLeòid', *Gairm* 108.

Moisley, H.A. 1961: *Harris Tweed – a Growing Highland Industry,* reprint from *Economic Geography* 37 no. 4.

— 1962a: 'The Highlands and Islands: a Crofting Region?', *Transactions of the Institute of British Geographers* 31.

Moisley, H.A. ed. n.d., ?1962b: *Uig: A Hebridean Crofting Parish.* Nottingham.

— 1966: 'The Deserted Hebrides', *SS* 10.

Moncreiffe, Sir Iain 1967: *The Highland Clans.* London.

Monro, Donald 1961: *Monro's Western Isles of Scotland.* Edinburgh.

Morrison, A. 1967: 'The Contullich Papers, 1706–1720', *TGSI* 44.

Morrison, Alick H. 1967: 'Rev. Dr Donald Mackinnon', *Clan Macleod Magazine* 5 no. 32.

Morrison, George 1978: *One Man's Lewis.* Stornoway.

Morrison, Hew 1899: *Songs and Poems in the Gaelic Language.* Edinburgh.

Morton, N., and Wray, N. 1962: *An Introduction to the Study of Spinning.* London.

Munro, M.N. 1907: 'An Comunn Gaidhealach, its Origins and Aims', in *Feill a' Chomuinn Ghaidhealaich.* Glasgow.

Munro, R.W. ed. 1961: *Monro's Western Isles of Scotland.* Edinburgh.

— 1977: *Highland Clans and Tartans.* Edinburgh.

— and Munro, J.M. 1975: 'The Lordship of the Isles'. In P.G.B. McNeill and R. Nicholson, eds., *An Historical Atlas of Scotland c. 400–c.1600.* St Andrews.

Murchison, T.M. 1935: *The Plight of the Smallholders: Petition and Memorandum to the Secretary of State for Scotland.* Edinburgh.

— 1948: Obituary of Dr Archibald Macdonald, *An Gaidheal* 43.

— 1950: Obituary of Dr John Cameron, *An Gaidheal* 45.

— 1951: Biography of Malcolm Maclennan, in Maclennan's Gaelic translation of Bunyan's *Pilgrim's Progress*. London.

— 1952: 'Alasdair Mac Mhaighstir Alasdair', *An Gaidheal* 47.

— 1953: Jubilee Mod Souvenir Programme. Glasgow.

— 1954: 'A Generous and Enduring Gift', *Perthshire Advertiser* 24 November.

— 1955a: 'Story of An Comunn (up to 1912)', *An Gaidheal* 50.

— 1955b: 'A Century of Hebridean Missions: Centenary of West Coast Mission', *Glasgow Herald* 16 December.

— 1957: 'Scholar and Architect', obituary of Colin Sinclair, *Perthshire Advertiser* 6 November.

— ed. 1960: *Prose Writings of Donald Lamont 1874–1958*. Edinburgh.

— 1961a: 'Grand Old Man of Gaelic [Neil Shaw]', *Perthshire Advertiser* 21 June.

— 1961b: 'Gaelic Enthusiast', *Perthshire Advertiser* 25 October.

— 1962: 'The Synod of Glenelg, 1725–1851: Notes from the Records', *TGSI* 38.

— 1966a: 'Historian of Skye', obituary of Alexander Nicolson, *Perthshire Advertiser* 11 December.

— 1966b: 'Clan Historian', obituary of Donald Mackinnon, *Perthshire Advertiser* 13 July.

— 1967: 'The Presbytery of Gairloch, 1724–50', *TGSI* 44.

— 1971: 'Schoolmaster and Bard [James Thomson]', *Perthshire Advertiser* 6 October.

— 1972: 'The Presbytery of Gairloch (or Lochcarron), 1751–1827', *TGSI* 47.

— 1977a: Obituary of Dr John MacInnes, *Life and Work*, Gaelic Supplement.

— 1977b: 'Passing of a Gaelic Scholar', *Perthshire Advertiser* 23 February.

— forthcoming: *The Gaelic Prose Writings of Kenneth Macleod*, including Memoir.

Murphy, G. 1953: *Duanaire Finn*, Part iii. Dublin.

Murray, Amy 1914/20: *Fr Allan's Island*. New York. Edinburgh 1936.

— 1936: 'An Fhideag Airgid' (with music) and 'Child-Songs in the Island of Youth' (with music), *Celtic Review* 2.

Murray, Iain 1979: *The Happy Mac: The Abiding Influence of Lachlan Mackenzie*.

— 1980: *Diary of Kenneth MacRae*. Edinburgh.

Murray, J.A.H. 1870–2: 'The Dialect of the Southern Counties of Scotland', *Transactions of the Philological Society*.

Murray, John 1981: *The Report of the Bilingual Education Project*. Stornoway.

Murray, W.H. 1982: *Rob Roy MacGregor*. Glasgow.

Necker de Saussure, L.A. 1821: *Voyage en Écosse et aux Isle Hébrides*. 3 vols. Geneva.

New Statistical Account of Scotland 1834–45: Edinburgh.

NicGumaraid, Catriona, and NicGumaraid, Mòrag 1974: *A' Choille Chiar*. Glasgow.

Nicholson, R. 1974: *Scotland: The Later Middle Ages*. Edinburgh.

Nicolaisen, W.F.H. 1957: 'The Semantic Structure of Scottish Hydronymy', *SS* 2.

— 1958 *et seq.*: 'Notes on Scottish Place Names', *SS* 2 no. 1 and succeeding numbers.

— 1969: 'Norse Settlement in the Northern and Western Isles: Some Place-Name Evidence', *SHR* 48.

— 1975: 'Gaelic Place Names'. In P.G.B. McNeill and R. Nicholson, eds., *An Historical Atlas of Scotland c.400–c.1600*. St Andrews.

— 1976: *Scottish Place Names: Their Study and Significance*. London.

Nicholson, A. 1866: *Report on the State of Education in the Hebrides*. Third Report of the Argyll Commission. Edinburgh.

Nicolson, Alex 1936: *Modern Gaelic: A Basic Grammar*. Glasgow.

— 1938: *Gaelic Riddles and Enigmas (Toumhseachain agus Dubh-fhacail)*. Glasgow.

— 1939: *Am Breacadh: A Basic Gaelic Reader*. Glasgow.

Nicolson, Alex N. 1935: 'Index of Papers, etc., from 1871 to 1928, with Names of Contributors, etc.', *TGSI* 35.

Nicolson, Alexander 1881: *A Collection of Gaelic Proverbs, etc.* Edinburgh.

Nicolson, Alexander 1951: *Gaelic Proverbs*. Reprinted with index and biographical note by Malcolm MacInnes. Glasgow.

Nicolson, Alexander 1930: *History of Skye*. Glasgow.

Nicolson, N. 1939: *An t-Urramach Iain MacRath*. 4th edn. Glasgow.

Nisbet, H.C., and Gailey, R.A. 1960: 'A Survey of the Antiquities of North Rona', *Archaeological Journal* 117.

Nordenfalk, C. 1977: *Celtic and Anglo–Saxon Painting*. London.

Nutt, A. 1910: *Ossian and the Ossianic Literature*. London.

Ó Baoill, C. 1972a: 'Some Irish Harpers in Scotland', *TGSI* 47.

— 1972b: *Bàrdachd Shìlis na Ceapaich c.1660–c.1729*. Edinburgh.

— 1976a: 'Domhnall Mac Mharcuis', *SGS* 12.

— 1976b: 'Inis Moccu Chéin', *SGS* 12.

— 1976c: 'Raghnall Dubh and Hector Maclean', *SGS* 12.

— 1978a: *Contributions to a Comparative Study of Ulster Irish and Scottish Gaelic*. Belfast.

— 1978b: 'Some Notes on "An Aigeannach"', *SGS* 13.

— 1979: *Eachann Bacach and Other Maclean Poets*. Edinburgh.

— and Wagner, H. 1969: *Linguistic Atlas and Survey of Irish Dialects* 4. Dublin.

Ó Baoill, D.P. 1980: 'Pre-aspiration, Epenthesis and Vowel Lengthening...', *Celtica* 13.

O'Boyle, Colm J.: see Ó Baoill, C.

O'Brien, M.A. 1973: 'Notes on Early Irish Personal Names', *Celtica* 10.

Ó Ceithearnaigh, S. 1942–4: *Regimen na Sláinte*. 3 vols., Dublin.

Ó Concheannáin, Tomás 1975: 'The Scribe of John Beaton's "Broad Book"', *Eriu* 26.

Ó Corráin, D. 1971: 'Irish Regnal Succession: a Reappraisal', *Studia Hibernica* 11.

Ó Cuív, Brian 1968: 'A Poem Attributed to Muireadhach Ó Dálaigh'. In J. Carney and D. Greene, eds., *Celtic Studies*. London.

— 1976: 'The Irish Language in the Early Modern Period'. In Moody, Martin and Byrne, eds., *A New History of Ireland* vol. iii. Oxford.

O'Dell, A.C. 1966: 'Highlands and Islands Developments', *Scottish Geographic Magazine* 82.

— and Walton, K. 1962: *The Highlands and Islands of Scotland*. London.

Ó Doibhlín, Breandan 1973: 'Mórfhile Ghael Alban', in *Irisleabhar Mhá Nuad*. Maynooth.

O'Flaherty, Roderic 1685: *Ogygia*. London.

O'Grady, S.H. 1926: *Catalogue of Irish Manuscripts in the British Museum* 1. London.

O Maolfabhail, A. 1973: *Caman: 2,000 Years of Hurling in Ireland*. Dundalk.

O'Meara, J.J. trans. 1951: *The First Version of the Topography of Ireland by Giraldus Cambrensis*. Dundalk.

Ó Murchú, M. 1976: 'The Article in a Variety of Perthshire Gaelic', *Celtica* 11.

O'Rahilly, T.F. 1932: *Irish Dialects Past and Present*. Dublin. With additional indexing 1972.

— 1934: 'Indexes to the Book of the Dean of Lismore', *SGS* 4.

— 1942: *The Two Patricks*. Dublin.

Ó Ríordáin, S.P. 1942: *Antiquities of the Irish Countryside*. Cork. 5th edn, revised by R. de Valera, London and New York 1979.

Ó Tuama, S. 1960: *An Grá in Amhráin na ndaoine*. Dublin.

Ó Tuathail, É. 1939: 'On the Irish Sibilants', *Éigse* 1.

Oftedal, Magne 1954: 'The Village Names of Lewis in the Outer Hebrides', *NTS* 17.

— 1956: *The Gaelic of Leurbost, Isle of Lewis (A Linguistic Survey of the Gaelic Dialects of Scotland* vol. iii), *NTS* supplementary 4.

— 1962: 'On the Frequency of Norse Loanwords in Scottish Gaelic', *SGS* 9 part 2.

— 1963: 'On "Palatalized" Labials in Scottish Gaelic', *SGS* 10.

— 1968: 'The Scottish Gaelic Dialect Survey', *Lochlann* 4.

— 1972: 'Ardroil', in H. Pilch and J. Thurow (eds.), *Indo-Celtica: Gedachtnisschrift für Alf Sommerfelt*. Munich.

— 1975: Review of E. Ternes, *The Phonemic Analysis of Scottish Gaelic*, Hamburg, 1973. In *Phonetica* 32, pp. 130–140.

— 1978: 'Nordic Accent Patterns in Scottish Gaelic'. Unpublished paper read at the Symposium on Nordic Prosody, Lund, 14–16 June.

— 1980: 'Scandinavian Place-Names in Celtic Territory: an Attempt at a Linguistic Classification'. In T. Andersson, E. Brylla and A. Rostvik, eds., *Ortnamn och sprakkontakt*. Göteborg.

Ogilvie, R.M., and Richmond, I.A. eds. 1967: *Cornelii Taciti de Vita Agricolae*. Oxford.

Omand, D. 1973: *The Caithness Book*, revised edn. Inverness.

— 1976: *The Moray Book*. Edinburgh.

— 1979: *The Sutherland Book*. Golspie.

Owen, T.M. 1956: 'The Communion Season and Presbyterianism in a Hebridean Community', *Gwerin* 1.

— 1958: 'The Role of the Township in a Hebridean Crofting Economy', *Gwerin* 2.

Padel, O. 1972: 'The Inscriptions of Pictland'. M. Litt. thesis, University of Edinburgh.

Parman, S. 1972: 'Sociological Change in a Scottish Crofting Township'. PhD thesis, Rice University, Houston, Texas.

Paton, H. ed. 1895–6: *The Lyon in Mourning, 1746–75*. 3 vols. PSHS vols. 20–2.

Pattison, Thomas 1866: *The Gaelic Bards*. Glasgow.

Pearston, Thomas 1963: 'Cremona and the MacCrimmons', *Piping Times* 5.

Pennant, T. 1774: *Tour in Scotland and Voyage to the Hebrides*. Chester.

Petrie, Charles 1959: *The Jacobite Movement*. London.

Phemister, J. 1960: *The Northern Highlands*, 3rd edn. Edinburgh.

Piggott, Stuart 1982: *Scotland before History*. Edinburgh.

Piobaireachd Society 1925–80: *Piobaireachd* bks 1–13. Edinburgh.

Ponting, G., and Ponting, M. 1977: *The Standing Stones of Callanish*. Stornoway.

Pottle, F.A., and Bennett, C.H. eds. 1936: *Boswell's Journal of a Tour to the Hebrides with Samuel Johnson*. London.

Poulter, G.C.B. 1938–9: *A History of the Clan MacCrimmon*, parts 1 and 2. London.

— and Fisher, C.P. 1936: *The MacCrimmon Family, 1500–1936*. Camberley.

Pratt, E.A. 1922: *Scottish Canals and Waterways*. London.

Prebble, John 1961: *Culloden*. London.

— 1963: *The Highland Clearances*. London.

— 1966: *Glencoe*. London.

— 1968: *The Darien Disaster*. London.

— 1975: *Mutiny: Highland Regiments in Revolt 1743–1804*. London.

Price, G. 1979: 'Gaelic in Scotland at the End of the Eighteenth Century', *Bulletin, Board of Celtic Studies* 27.

Price, R.J. 1976: *Highland Landforms*. Inverness.

Quiggin, E.C. 1913: 'Prolegomena to the Study of the Later Irish Bards (1200–1500)', *Proceedings of the British Academy* 5.

— 1937: *Poems from the Book of the Dean of Lismore*, ed. John Fraser. Cambridge.

Ramsay, A. 1879: *History of the Highland and Agricultural Society of Scotland*. Edinburgh and London.

Rankin, R.A. 1958: 'Oran na Comhachaig', *Transactions of the Gaelic Society of Glasgow* 5.

Ravenstein, E.G. 1879: 'On the Celtic Languages in the British Isles: a Statistical Survey', *Journal of the Royal Statistical Society*.

RCAHMS: see Royal Commission on the Ancient and Historical Monuments of Scotland.

Rea, Frederick 1964: *A School in South Uist*, ed. J.L. Campbell. London.

Reeves, W. ed. 1857: *The Life of St Columba*. Dublin.

— 1857–60: 'St Maelrubha: his History and Churches', *PSAS* 3.

— 1864: *The Culdees of the British Islands*. Dublin.

Reid, John 1832: *Bibliotheca Scoto-Celtica*. Glasgow.

Report of Her Majesty's Commissioners of Inquiry into the Condition of the Crofters and Cottars in the Highlands and Islands of Scotland 1884. Edinburgh.

Report of the Trial of the So-Called Bernera Rioters at Stornoway on the 17th and 18th July 1874 1874. Edinburgh.

Richards, Eric 1973: *The Leviathan of Wealth*. London.

— 1982: *A History of the Highland Clearances: Agrarian Transformation and the Evictions 1746–1886*. London.

Richmond, I.A. ed. 1958: *Roman and Native in North Britain*. Edinburgh.

— and Crawford, O.G.S. 1949: 'The British Section of the Ravenna Cosmography', *Archaeologia* 93.

Risk, H. 1974: 'French Loan-words in Irish', *Études Celtiques* 14, esp. pp. 72–91.

Ritchie, G., and Ritchie, A. 1981: *Scotland: Archaeology and Early History*. London.

Robb, J.M. 1950: *Scotch Whisky: An Illustrated Guide*. London and Edinburgh.

Robertson, C.M. 1897–8: 'Gaelic Dialect of Arran', *TGSI* 21; 'Sutherland Gaelic', *TGSI* 25.

— 1900: 'The Peculiarities of Gaelic as Spoken in the Writer's District', *TGSI* 22.

Robertson, Hamish 1976: 'Studies in Carmichael's *Carmina Gadelica*', *SGS* 12.

Robertson, T. Atholl ed. 1905–55: *Scots Year-Book*.

Rose, J. ed. 1851: *Metrical Reliques of 'the Men' in the Highlands*. Inverness.

Ross, A. 1960: 'The Human Head in Insular Pagan Celtic Religion', *PSAS* 91.

— 1967: *Pagan Celtic Britain*. London and New York.

— 1968: 'Shafts, Pits, Wells – Sanctuaries of the Belgic Britons?'. In J.M. Coles and D.D.A. Simpson, eds., *Studies in Ancient Europe*. Leicester.

— 1974: 'A Pagan Celtic Tricephalos from Netherton, Lanarkshire', *Glasgow Archaeological Journal* 3.

— 1976: *The Folklore of the Scottish Highlands*. London.

— and Feachem, R.W. 1976: 'Ritual Rubbish – the Newstead

Pits'. In J.V.S. Megaw, ed., *To Illustrate the Monuments*. London.

Ross, J.M.E. 1905: *William Ross of Cowcaddens*. Glasgow.

Ross, James 1955–6: 'The Sub-Literary Tradition in Scottish Gaelic Song-Poetry', pts 1 and 2, *Éigse* 7 and 8.

— 1957a: 'The Classification of Gaelic Folksong', *SS* 1.

— 1957b: 'Further Remarks on Gaelic Song Metre', *Éigse* 8.

— 1958: 'A Rhampsinitus Story from Skye – Goban Saor agus a Mhac', *SS* 2.

— 1959: 'Formulaic Composition in Gaelic Oral Literature', *Modern Philology* 57 no. 1.

Ross, N. ed. 1939: *Heroic Poetry from the Book of the Dean of Lismore*. Edinburgh.

Ross, Robert 1959–?: *Binneas is Boreraig* 1–5. Edinburgh.

Royal Commission on the Ancient and Historical Monuments of Scotland 1928: *Inventory of Monuments… in the Outer Hebrides, Skye and the Small Isles*. Edinburgh.

— 1971–82. *Argyll: An Inventory of the Monuments:* vol. i, *Kintyre*, Edinburgh, 1971; vol. ii, *Lorn*, 1975; vol. iii, *Mull, Tiree, Coll and Northern Argyll*, 1980; vol. iv, *Iona*, 1982; vol. v, *Islay, Jura and Colonsay*, forthcoming.

Royal Scottish Geographical Society 1973: *The Early Maps of Scotland to 1850* vol. i. Edinburgh.

Sage, Donald 1889: *Memorabilia Domestica*. Wick.

St Columba Church 1906: *Leabhar Laoidhean Eaglais Chaluim Chille an Glaschu*. Glasgow.

Salmond, James B. 1934: *Wade in Scotland*.

Sandvik, O.M. 1940: *Norsk Musikkgransking Aarbok*. Oslo.

Sanger, K. 1979: 'Murdoch Macdonald the Harper', *Notes and Queries of the Society of West Highland and Island Historical Research* 10.

Sarauw, Chr. 1900: *Irske Studier*. Copenhagen.

Saunders, Bailey 1894: *Life and Letters of James Macpherson*. London.

Sawyer, P.H. 1971: *The Age of the Vikings*, 2nd edn. London.

School of Scottish Studies 1960: *Gaelic and Scots Folk Tales. Gaelic and Scots Folk Songs. Scottish Instrumental Music*, with three long-playing discs. Edinburgh.

— 1972: *Waulking Songs from Barra*. London.

Scobie, H. MacKay, *et al.* 1971: 'Notices of Pipers', *Piping Times* 24 nos. 2, 3.

Scott, H. 1915–50: *Fasti Ecclesiae Scoticanae*. Edinburgh.

Scottish Council for Research in Education 1961: *Gaelic-Speaking Children in Highland Schools*. London.

Scottish Education Department 1946: *Primary Education* (Advisory Council), Cmd 6973. Edinburgh and London.

— 1947: *Secondary Education* (Advisory Council), Cmd 7005. Edinburgh and London.

— 1955: *Junior Secondary Education*. Edinburgh and London.

Scottish Record Office, various reports, especially under ED7 (e.g. Report on Highland Schools by Sir H. Craik, 1884–7).

Scottish Weapons 1963: Special Number of the *Scottish Art Review* 9.

Selkirk, 5th Earl of 1806: *Observations on the Present State of the Highlands of Scotland, with a View of the Causes and Probable Consequences of Emigration*, 2nd edn. London.

Sellar, W.D.H. 1966: 'The Origins and Ancestry of Somerled', *SHR* 45.

— 1971: 'Family Origins in Cowal and Knapdale', *SS* 15.

— 1973: 'The Earliest Campbell – Norman, Briton or Gael?', *SS* 17.

— 1975a: 'The Western Isles c.800–1095'. In P.G.B. McNeill and R. Nicholson, eds., *An Historical Atlas of Scotland c.400–c.1600*. St Andrews.

— 1975b: 'The Western Isles c.1095–1286'. In P.G.B. McNeill and R. Nicholson, eds., *An Historical Atlas of Scotland c.400–c.1600*. St Andrews.

Serjeantson, Mary S. 1935: *A History of Foreign Words in English*. London.

Seton, B., and Arnot, J.G. eds. 1928: *The Prisoners of the '45*. PSHS vols. 13–15.

Shairp, James Campbell 1881: *Aspects of Poetry*. Oxford.

Sharp, L.W. 1937: *Early Letters of Robert Wodrow*. PSHS 3rd series vol. 24.

Shaw, F. 1961: 'Irish Medical Men and Philosophers'. In B.Ó. Cuív, ed., *Seven Centuries of Irish Learning*. Dublin.

Shaw, Margaret Fay 1955: *Folksongs and Folklore of South Uist*. London. Reprinted Oxford 1977.

Shaw, Neil 1920: *Glasgow Highland and Clan Association Directory, 1920–21*. Glasgow.

Shaw, William 1773: *An Analysis of the Galic Language*. London. Reprinted Menston 1972.

— 1780: *A Galic and English Dictionary*. London.

Shuken, C.R. 1977a: 'Perception of Syllables and Diphthongs in Some Scottish Gaelic Vowels', *Work in Progress* (Linguistics Department, University of Edinburgh) 10.

— 1977b: 'Some Physiological and Acoustic Characteristics of Stop Consonants in Scottish Gaelic', *Proceedings of the Celtic Phonology Conference*, Coleraine, 23 June – 1 July.

— 1979: 'Aspiration in Scottish Gaelic Stop Consonants', *Current Issues in Linguistic Theory* 9.

— 1980: 'An Instrumental Investigation of Some Scottish Gaelic Consonants'. PhD thesis, University of Edinburgh.

Simpson, P.C. 1909: *The Life of Principal Rainy*, 2 vols., see esp. vol. 1 pp. 429ff.

Simpson, W.D. 1963: 'The Early Romanesque Tower at Restenneth Priory, Angus', *Antiquaries Journal* 43.

Sinclair, Allan 1875: *Reminiscences of the Life and Labours of Dugald Buchanan*. Edinburgh.

Sinclair, Archibald 1876–9: *An t-Oranaiche*. Glasgow.

Sinclair, A. MacLean ed. 1881: *Clarsach na Coille*. Glasgow.

— 1890–6: *The Gaelic Bards (1411–1825)*. 3 vols., Charlottetown, Nova Scotia.

— 1890: *The Glenbard Collection*. Charlottetown, Nova Scotia.

— 1898/1900: *Na Baird Leathanaich/The MacLean Bards*. 2 vols., Charlottetown, Nova Scotia.

— 1899: *The Clan Gillean*. Charlottetown, Nova Scotia.

Sinclair, Colin 1911: 'Buildings and Dress in the Old Highlands'. In D.N. Mackay, ed., *Home Life of the Highlanders, 1400–1746*.

Sinclair, Colin 1953: *The Thatched Houses of the Old Highlands*.

Sinclair, D. Maclean 1949: 'Gaelic in Nova Scotia', article read at a meeting of the Humanities Conference at Halifax, Nova Scotia, 10 June.

Sinclair, Sir J. ed. 1791–9: *The Statistical Account of Scotland* vols. i–xxi. London.

Sinclair, John 1891: 'Some Letters from the Pen of Ewen MacLachlan, Old Aberdeen', *TGSI* 16.

Sinton, Thomas 1906: *The Poetry of Badenoch*. Inverness.

Skene, W.F. 1902: *The Highlanders of Scotland*. Edinburgh.

— 1886–90: *Celtic Scotland*. 3 vols., 2nd edn, Edinburgh.

Small, A., and Cottam, M.B. 1972: *Craig Phadrig*. Dundee.

Small, A., and Smith, J.S. 1971: 'The Strathpeffer and Inverness Area', *British Landscapes through Maps*. Sheffield.

Small, A., Thomas, C., and Wilson, D.M. 1973: *St Ninian's Isle and its Treasure*. 2 vols., Oxford.

Smart, J.S. 1905: *James Macpherson: An Episode in Literature*. London.

Smith, F.T. 1939: *The Land of Britain: Sutherland*. London.

Smith, Iain Crichton 1961: 'The Future of Gaelic Literature', *TGSI* 43.

— 1969: *Ben Dorain*, English translation. Preston.

Smith, Iain Crichton (1970), *Four points of a Saltire: The Poetry of Sorley Maclean, George Campbell Hay, William Neill and Stuart Macgregor*. Edinburgh.

— 1971b: *Poems to Eimhir*, English translation. London.

— 1979: 'Between Sea and Moor'. In M. Lindsay, ed., *As I Remember*. London.

— 1981 (recte 1982): *Selected Poems 1955–1980*. Edinburgh.

Smith, J. 1983: *A' Chulaidh as Feàrr*. Stornoway.

Smith, James (Seumas Mac a' Ghobhainn) 1973: 'The 2nd Highland Land League', *Stornoway Gazette* 16 June.

Smith, John A. 1981: 'The 1872 Education (Scotland) Act and Gaelic Education', *TGSI* 51.

Smith, Roderick 1960: 'Norman Macleod, 1812–72'. In R. Selby Wright, ed., *Fathers of the Kirk*. Edinburgh.

Smith, Walter ed. 1893: *Verses by Alexander Nicolson, with Memoir*.

Smout, T.C. 1963: *Scottish Trade on the Eve of Union, 1660–1707*. Edinburgh.

Smyth, A.P. 1972: 'The Earliest Irish Annals', *Proceedings of the Royal Irish Academy* 72.

— 1975/9: *Scandinavian York and Dublin*. 2 vols., Dublin.

Society in Scotland for the Propagation of Christian Knowledge 1783: *A Summary Account of the Rise and*

Progress of the Society in Scotland. Edinburgh.

Stamp, L.D. 1948: *The Land of Britain: Its Use and Misuse*. London.

— ed. 1964: 'Land Use in the Highlands and Islands', *British Association for the Advancement of Science* 21.

Starmore, Graham 1980: 'The Knoydart Alternative', *North* 7 July/August.

Stell, G. 1973: 'Highland Garrisons 1717–23. Bernera Barracks', *Post-Medieval Archaeology* 7.

Steer, K.A., and Bannerman, J.W.M. 1977: *Late Medieval Monumental Sculpture in the West Highlands*. Edinburgh.

Stern, L. 1899: 'Crosanachd Illebhrìghde', *Zeitschrift für Celtische Philologie* 2.

— 1900: 'Ossianic Heroic Poetry', trans. J.L. Robertson, *TGSI* 22.

Stevenson, D. 1975: 'The Massacre at Dunaverty, 1647', *SS* 19.

— 1979: 'The Irish Franciscan Mission to Scotland and the Irish Rebellion of 1641', *Innes Review* 30.

— 1980: *Alasdair MacColla and the Highland Problem in the Seventeenth Century*. Edinburgh.

Stevenson, R.B.K. 1955: 'Pictish Art', in F.T. Wainwright ed., *The Problem of the Picts*. Edinburgh.

— 1956–7: 'The Chronology and Relationships of Some Irish and Scottish Crosses', *Journal of the Royal Society of Antiquaries of Ireland* 86–7.

— 1958–9: 'The Inchyra Stone and Other Unpublished Early Christian Monuments', *PSAS* 92.

— 1971: 'Sculpture in Scotland in the 6th–9th Centuries AD', *Kolloquium über spätantike und frümitteralterliche Skulptur* (Heidelberg, 1970). Mainz.

— 1974: 'The Hunterston Brooch and its Significance', *Medieval Archaeology* 18.

— 1976: 'The Earlier Metalwork of Pictland'. In J.V.S. Megaw, ed., *To Illustrate the Monuments*. London.

Stewart, A., and Cameron, J.K. n.d.: *The Free Church of Scotland*. Edinburgh and Glasgow.

Stewart, A., and Stewart, D. 1804: *Cochruinneacha Taoghta. . . .* Edinburgh.

Stewart, Alexander 1801: *Elements of Gaelic Grammar*. Edinburgh.

Stewart, Alexander 1883: *Nether Lochaber*.

— 1885: *Twixt Ben Nevis and Glencoe*.

Stewart, C. 1884: *The Killin Collection of Gaelic Songs*. Edinburgh.

Stewart, D. 1822: *Sketches of the Characters, Institutions and Customs of the Highlanders of Scotland*. 2 vols., Edinburgh.

Stewart, Donald Calder 1974: *Setts of the Scottish Tartans*.

Stewart, Mrs Norman 1966: *A Brief History of the Gaelic Society of London*.

Stirling, H. Austin 1932: *Duncan MacColl: An Apostle to Highlanders*.

Stone, J. ed. 1889: 'A Collection of Ossianic Ballads by Jerome Stone', *TGSI* 14.

Storrie, M.C. 1961: 'Islay, a Hebridean Exception', *Geographical Review* 57.

Strang, John 1864: *Glasgow and its Clubs*. Glasgow.

Struthers, A.M. ed. n.d.: *Scotland's Changing Population*, Scottish Council of Social Service.

Stuart, J. 1869: *The Book of Deer*. Edinburgh.

— 1878: 'Historical Notes of St Fillan's Crozier and of the Devotion of King Robert Bruce to St Fillan', *PSAS* 12.

Stuart, John, and Stuart, Charles Edward 1842: *Vestiarium Scoticum*. Edinburgh.

Stuart, R. 1852: *Caledonia Romana*. Edinburgh.

Sutherland, A.C. 1875: 'The Poetry of Dugald Buchanan, the Rannach Bard', *TGSI* 3–4.

Swanson, J. 1841: *Aideachadh a Chreidimh Chatholaich agus diultadh Teagasg a Phapa*. Inverness.

— 1844: *A Leisure Hour in the Floating Manse*. Edinburgh.

Symon, J.A. 1959: *Scottish Farming Past and Present*. Edinburgh.

Tayler, A.N., and Tayler, H. 1936: *1715: The Story of the Rising*. London.

— 1938: *1745 and After*. London.

— 1939: *John Grahame of Claverhouse*. London.

— eds. 1980: *Jacobite Letters to Lord Pitsligo 1745–1746*. Aberdeen.

Tayler, H. ed. 1938: *The Jacobite Court at Rome in 1719*. PSHS 3rd series vol. 31.

Telford, Thomas 1838: *Life of Thomas Telford*. London.

Ternes, E. 1973: *The Phonemic Analysis of Scottish Gaelic*. Hamburg.

— 1980: 'Scottish Gaelic Phonemics Viewed in a Typological Perspective', *Lingua* 52.

Terry, C.S. 1905: *John Grahame of Claverhouse, Viscount of Dundee, 1648–1689*. London.

Thomas, C. 1961: 'The Animal Art of the Scottish Iron Age and its Origins', *Archaeological Journal* 118.

— 1963: 'The Interpretation of the Pictish Symbols', *Archaeological Journal* 120.

— 1971: *Britain and Ireland in Early Christian Times AD 400–800*. London.

— 1972a: 'The Irish Settlements in post-Roman Western Britain: a Survey of the Evidence', *Journal of the Royal Institute of Cornwall* 6.

— 1972b: 'Souterrains in the Irish Sea Province: a Note'. In C. Thomas, ed., *The Iron Age in the Irish Sea Province*. London.

Thompson, F. 1974: *The Uists and Barra*. Newton Abbot.

— 1979: *The National Mod*. Stornoway.

Thompson, S. 1961: *The Types of the Folktale*. Helsinki.

Thomson, D.S. 1952: *The Gaelic Sources of Macpherson's Ossian*. Edinburgh and London.

— 1954: 'The Gaelic Oral Tradition', *Proceedings of the Scottish Anthropological and Folklore Society* 5.

— 1955: 'Scottish Gaelic Folk-Poetry ante 1650', *SGS* 8.

— 1958a: 'Bogus Gaelic Literature c.1750–c.1820', *Transactions of the Gaelic Society of Glasgow* 5.

— 1958b: 'A Catalogue and Indexes of the Ossianic Ballads in the McLagan MSS', *SGS* 8.

— 1958c: 'Donnchadh Bàn mac-an-t-Saoir', *An Gaidheal* 53.

— 1958d: 'Dùghall Bochanan', *An Gaidheal* 53.

— 1959: 'William Ross', *An Gaidheal* 54.

— 1961: 'Alasdair Mac Mhaighstir Alasdair', *An Gaidheal* 56.

— 1963a: '"Ossian", Macpherson and the Gaelic World of the Eighteenth Century', *Aberdeen University Review* 40.

— 1963b: 'The MacMhuirich Bardic Family', *TGSI* 43.

— 1968a: 'The Harlaw Brosnachadh: an Early Fifteenth-Century Literary Curio'. In J. Carney and D. Greene, eds., *Celtic Studies: Essays in Memory of Angus Matheson 1912–1962*. London.

— 1968b: 'Gaelic Learned Orders and Literati in Medieval Scotland', *SS* 12.

— 1968c: 'Unpublished Letters by the Poet Ewen MacLachlan', *SGS* 11.

— 1970: 'The Poetry of Niall MacMhuirich', *TGSI* 46.

— 1971: 'Scottish Gaelic Literature: the Contemporary Situation'. In J.E.C. Williams, ed., *Literature in Celtic Countries*. Cardiff.

— 1974a: *An Introduction to Gaelic Poetry*. London.

— 1974b: *The New Verse in Scottish Gaelic: A Structural Analysis*. Dublin.

— 1976a: 'An Anthology of Recent Gaelic Verse', *Akros* 31.

— 1976b: *Gaidhlig ann an Albainn*. Glasgow.

— 1977a: 'Niall Mór MacMhuirich', *TGSI* 49.

— 1977b: Review of S. Maclean *Reothairt is Contraigh*, *Scottish Review* 8.

— 1977c: 'Three Seventeenth-Century Bardic Poets: Niall Mór, Cathal and Niall MacMhuirich'. In A.J. Aitken, M.P. McDiarmid and D.S. Thomson, eds., *Bards and Makars*. Glasgow.

— 1979a: Foreword to reprint of James Macpherson *Fragments*, 2nd edn. Dundee.

— 1979b: 'Gaelic: its Range of Uses'. In A.J. Aitken and T. McArthur, eds., *Languages of Scotland*. Edinburgh.

— 1979c: 'Words and Expressions from Lewis', *TGSI* 50.

— 1981: 'Gaelic in Scotland: Assessment and Prognosis'. In E. Haugen, J.D. McClure and D.S. Thomson, eds., *Minority Languages Today*. Edinburgh.

— 1982: 'Donnchadh MacDhun-léibhe', *Gairm* 119.

— forthcoming: 'Publishing in Scottish Gaelic', a paper given to the Second Conference on Minority Languages, Turkn, Finland, June 1983.

— forthcoming: 'The Poetic Tradition in Gaelic Scotland'. *Proceedings of the Seventh International Congress of Celtic Studies* (Oxford July 1983).

Thomson, J. 1953: *Fasgnadh*. Stirling.

Thomson, James 1932/4: *An Dileab*. Glasgow.

Thomson, R.L. 1961: 'McLagan Manuscript 180', *SGS* 9.

— 1962: *Adtimchiol an Chreidimh: The Gaelic Version of John Calvin's Catechismus Ecclesiae Genevensis*. Edinburgh.

— 1963: 'The Celtic Element in the English Vocabulary', *University of Leeds Review* 8.

— 1970: *Foirm na n-Urrnuidheadh: John Carswell's Gaelic Translation of the Book of Common Order*. Edinburgh.

— 1971: 'The Language of the Shorter Catechism', *SGS* 12.

— 1976: 'The Language of the Caogad', *SGS* 12.

— 1977: 'The Emergence of Scottish Gaelic'. In A.J. Aitken, M.P. McDiarmid and D.S. Thomson, eds., *Bards and Makars*. Glasgow.

Thurneysen, R. 1946: *A Grammar of Old Irish*. Dublin.

Tivy, J. 1959: 'The Geography of the Garth Area – the Central Highlands in Miniature', Scottish Field Studies Association *Annual Report*.

— 1965: 'Easter Ross, a Residual Crofting Area', *SS* 9.

— 1973: *The Organic Resources of Scotland: Their Nature and Evaluation*. Edinburgh.

Toal, John 1983: 'A Survey of the Poetry and Songs of Brae Lochaber'. Celtic Honours dissertation, University of Glasgow.

Tocher 1971: Tales, songs and traditions selected from the archives of the School of Scottish Studies. Edinburgh.

Tolmie, Frances 1911: Collection of Gaelic songs in *Journal of the Folk-Song Society*. London.

Tomasson, K. 1958: *The Jacobite General*. Edinburgh.

Tourism Recreation Research Unit 1978: *Tourism in the Highlands and Islands*, Research Report no. 27.

Turnock, D. 1970: *Patterns of Highland Development*. London.

— 1974: *Scotland's Highlands and Islands*. London.

— ed. 1977: *The Lochaber Area: a Case Study of Changing Rural Land Use in the West Highlands of Scotland*, Geographical Field Group Regional Studies no. 20. Nottingham.

— 1979: 'Highland Transport', *Town and Country Planning* 46.

University of Glasgow, Dept of Geography 1978: *Callanish: A Map of the Standing Stones*. Glasgow.

Urquhart, A. 1962: 'Mac an t-Srònaich', *TGSI* 38.

Vallee, F.G. 1954: 'Social Structure and Organisation in a Hebridean Community'. Unpublished PhD thesis, University of London.

Vince, S.W.E. 1944a: *The Land of Britain: Caithness*. London.

— 1944b: *The Land of Britain: The Highlands* (Ross and Cromarty, Inverness, Argyll and Perthshire). London.

Vining, Elizabeth Gray 1967: *Flora MacDonald: Her Life in the Highlands and America*. London.

Wagner, H. 1958: *Linguistic Atlas and Survey of Irish Dialects* 1. Dublin.

— 1959: *Das Verbum in den Sprachen der britischen Inseln*. Tübingen.

— and Ó Baoill, C. 1969: *Linguistic Atlas and Survey of Irish Dialects* 4. Dublin.

Wainwright, F.T. 1959: *The Inchyra Ogam*. Dundee.

— ed. 1962: *The Northern Isles*. Edinburgh.

— 1963: *The Souterrains of Southern Pictland*. London.

Walker, J. 1808: *An Economical History of the Hebrides and Highlands*. Edinburgh.

Walker, N.L. 1896: *Chapters from the History of the Free Church*.

Warrand, Duncan 1965: *Some Mackenzie Pedigrees*. Inverness.

Watson, J. 1974: 'A Gaelic Dialect of NE Ross-shire: the Vowel System and General Remarks', *Lochlann* 6.

Watson, J.C. 1934: *Gaelic Songs of Mary MacLeod*. London and Glasgow.

— ed. 1940/1: Alexander Carmichael's *Carmina Gadelica* 3 and 4. Edinburgh and London.

— 1942: *Mesca Ulad*. Dublin.

Watson, J.T.S. 1954: *Pathmakers in the Isles, 1850–1949*, with Postcript by T.M. Murchison.

Watson, W.J. 1904: *Place-Names of Ross and Cromarty*. Inverness. Reissued by the Ross and Cromarty Heritage Society, Inverness 1976.

— 1907: 'Alexander Macbain, LL.D.', *Celtic Review* 3.

— 1915: *Rosg Gàidhlig: Specimens of Gaelic Prose*. Glasgow. 2nd edn 1929.

— ed. 1917a: 'Mór am bróinsgél bás í Dhuibhne', *An Deò-Gréine*.

— 1917b: *Marbhnadh Dhonnchaidh Duibh*, reprinted from *An Deò-Gréine*. Glasgow.

— 1918a: *Bàrdachd Ghàidhlig*. Glasgow. 2nd edn Stirling 1932; 3rd edn Glasgow 1959; 4th edn Inverness 1976.

— 1918b: 'From the Fernaig Manuscript', *An Deò-Gréine* 13.

— 1921: 'From the Fernaig Manuscript', *An Deò-Gréine* 16.

— 1922: 'Classic Gaelic Poetry of Panegyric in Scotland', *TGSI* 29.

— 1926: *History of the Celtic Place-Names of Scotland*. Edinburgh and London.

— 1929: 'Còir-fhearainn Bhriain Mhic Aoidh', in *Rosg Gàidhlig*, 2nd edn. Glasgow.

— 1931: 'Unpublished Gaelic Poetry', *SGS* 3.

— 1937: *Scottish Verse from the Book of the Dean of Lismore*. Edinburgh.

— *et al.* 1940: *More West Highland Tales* 1. Edinburgh.

'Webster's Population of Scotland, 1755' 1952. In J.G. Kyd, ed., *Scottish Population Statistics*, PSHS 44.

Webster, David 1973: *Scottish Highland Games*. Edinburgh.

Weir, L. Macneil 1921: *Guide to Islay*.

Welsh Office of Education 1948: *Welsh in Education and Life*. Cardiff.

— 1953: *The Place of Welsh and English in the Schools of Wales* (Advisory Council). Cardiff.

Whiteford, D.M. 1966–8: 'Jacobitism as a Factor in Presbyterian–Episcopalian Relationships in Scotland: 1689–1714' Parts 1 and 2. *Records of the Scottish Church History Society* 16.

Whyte, A. 1972: 'Scottish Gaelic Folksong 1500–1800'. M. Litt. thesis, University of Glasgow.

Whyte, Henry ('Fionn') 1908a: 'Rev. Mackintosh Mackay, LL.D.', *Celtic Monthly* 16.

— 1908b: 'Sheriff Nicolson', *Celtic Monthly* 16.

Whyte, Iain 1894: *Laoidhean agus Dàin Spioradail*.

Willcock, J. 1903: *The Great Marquess*. Edinburgh and London.

— 1907: *A Scots Earl of Covenanting Times*. Edinburgh and London.

Williams, J.E.C. 1971: *Literature in Celtic Countries*. Cardiff.

Wilson, D. 1878: 'Notices of the Quigrich or Crozier of St Fillan and of its Hereditary Keepers', *PSAS* 12.

— 1884: 'The Kilmichael–Glassrie Bell-Shrine', *PSAS* 18.

Withers, C.W.J. 1980: 'The Highland Parishes in 1698: An Examination of Sources for the Definition of the Gaidhealtachd', *SS* 24.

Wittig, Kurt 1958: *The Scottish Tradition in Literature*. Edinburgh and London.

Wodrow, R. 1842–3: *Analecta*. Maitland Club, Edinburgh.

Woolley, J.S. 1954: *Bibliography for Scottish Linguistic Studies*. Edinburgh.

Woulfe, Fr P. 1923: *Sloinnte Gaedheal is Gall*. Dublin.

Wulff, W. 1928: *Rosa Anglica*. Irish Texts Society, London.

Youngson, A.J. 1973: *After the Forty-Five: The Economic Impact on the Scottish Highlands*. Edinburgh.

— 1974: *Beyond the Highland Line*. London.

Index

The index contains references to people, places and subjects mentioned in the text. Page references in bold type (e.g. **123–4**) indicate that the topic is the subject of an article in its own right on those pages, or is dealt with substantially in an article on a germane topic. Where this is so the significant page reference is given first, the others following in numerical sequence. 'p' following a page reference indicates either an illustration or a map, or material in a caption.

Purely bibliographical references are not indexed in view of the extensive bibliography on pages 313–35. The titles of poems, books, plays, songs, or other pieces of literature or music are indexed only if seminal, or discussed significantly in the text. Readers will find access to material of this kind by consulting and using the index either under the name of the author or composer, or through the general references under literature, verse, music, etc.